Outer Space

Problems of Law and Policy

SECOND EDITION

Outer Space

Problems of Law and Policy

Glenn H. Reynolds

University of Tennessee

Robert P. Merges

University of California at Berkeley

Routledge
Taylor & Francis Group
LONDON AND NEW YORK

First published 1989, 1997 by Westview Press

Published 2019 by Routledge
52 Vanderbilt Avenue, New York, NY 10017
2 Park Square, Milton Park, Abingdon, Oxon OX14 4RN

Routledge is an imprint of the Taylor & Francis Group, an informa business

Library of Congress Cataloging-in-Publication Data
Reynolds, Glenn H.
Outer space : problems of law and policy / Glenn H. Reynolds and Robert P. Merges. — 2nd ed.
p. cm.
Includes bibliographical references and index.
ISBN 0-8133-1802-5 (hc) — ISBN 0-8133-6680-1 (pbk.)
1. Space law—Cases. I. Merges, Robert P.
JX5810.R49 1997
341.4′7—dc21 **96-48451**
CIP

ISBN 13: 978-0-367-28207-3 (hbk)
ISBN 13: 978-0-367-29753-4 (pbk)

Contents

Preface to the Second Edition

Almost eight years have passed since the first edition of this book went to the publisher. In writing it, we attempted to produce a work that would be useful in the sometimes contradictory roles of classroom text and self-teaching tool for interested lawyers, academics, and laypersons. Judging from the many gratifying reviews that the first edition received, we were generally successful. However, the passage of time changes many things, and we considered it important to keep this book up to date. Although some aspects of space law remain largely unaltered, others—particularly in the fast-growing field of commercial space activity (both in terms of its regulation, and of the international trade friction that it creates) and the contentious area of control over space resources—have changed a great deal. Our updating efforts have thus been greatest in those departments. We have also given additional attention to the burgeoning topic of space environmental issues. When the first edition of this book appeared, that subject had received little attention, and some thought our brief treatment somewhat daring for its mere existence. That has changed now, with topics like orbital debris and planetary protection receiving considerable attention in the literature, an expansion that has been matched in our treatment as well. And, naturally, the entire book has been brought up to date with reference to changes in the literature, the statutory background, and the general climate.

Of course, the greatest change that has occurred since the publication of the first edition is the apparent end of the Cold War, along with the breakup of the former Soviet Union into its various constituent states. Formally, this is of relatively little importance to the field of space law, as those constituent states, particularly the Russian Federation, remain adherents to all of the important international agreements. Realistically, however, the shift from a bipolar Cold War world to a multipolar post–Cold War world is of enormous importance for outer space policy, as the field is itself virtually a creation of the Cold War. The exact consequences of this change continue to be played out, and we do not pretend to be able to predict them all. However, we have done our best to anticipate and point out those features of space law that are most dependent on Cold War assumptions or politics, and suggest how those might change in the post–Cold War era. The rest, as the old mathematics textbooks used to say, is left as an exercise for the reader.

A number of individuals and organizations have provided assistance in the revision of this book. First and foremost are the reviewers of the first edition: Edward Gordon in *Science*, Carl Christol in the *American Journal of International Law*, Edward Binkowski in the *Fordham International Law Journal*, Wayne Dillingham in *Jurimetrics*, Stephanie Lessard in *Annals of Air and Space Law*, Robert O'Connell in *The Air and Space Lawyer*, and various student reviewers in the *Harvard Law Review*, the *Harvard International Law Journal*, the *George Washington Journal of International Law and Economics*, and the *Harvard Journal of Law and Technology*. We have not always followed the advice contained in those reviews, but we have considered, and appreciated, all of it.

In addition, we would like to thank our students and colleagues at the University of Tennessee and Boston University, and at the University of Virginia where one of us (Reynolds) taught space law to a startlingly large class of interested and interesting students in the spring of 1993 as this revision was underway. In addition, many other individuals have taken the time to correspond or speak with us regarding various issues; they include James Bennett, Barry Beringer, Linda Billings, former Justice William Brennan, Jr., Arthur C. Clarke, David Brandt, Dan Burk, Carl Christol, Richard DalBello, Hamilton DeSaussure, Eric Drexler, Lori Garver, Steven Gorove, Mark Hopkins, Beth Inadomi, Margaret Jordan, John Logsdon, Charles Miller, Nick McCall, Gerald Musarra, Scott Pace, John Pike, John Ragosta, Jim Schoettler, Courtney Stadd, Linda Strine, Charles Walker, and Alan Wasser. We have also received valuable feedback from groups to whom we made presentations or talks on topics covered in this book: Those groups include the U.S. Air Force Academy, the Harvard Law and Technology Society, the National Space Society, the University of New Mexico School of Law, the Princeton Planetary Society, the University of Tennessee Space Institute, and attendees at several American Bar Association and National Space Society convention programs.

Highly valuable research assistance was provided by Patricia Crotwell-Bentley, William Coffey, Jennifer Ashley, Elizabeth Bailey, Micaela Burnham, Brannon Denning, and the semi-bionic Brian Piperno. And last—but certainly not least—secretarial support above and beyond the call of duty was provided by Jackie Bonvin.

As we conclude this revision, we have one regret: The book is still too short. In the first edition we made a conscious decision to sacrifice comprehensiveness for clarity. We have thus limited our coverage of the trees in order to provide a clear picture of the forest. Nonetheless, there are aspects that we wish could have received more attention. We encourage readers to go about filling in the gaps themselves, with articles and student Notes on topics that we have left untreated or merely hinted at. The growth of space law is a project for many minds. This is our contribution; it is up to you to make yours.

We hope that readers will take up this challenge. We have devoted considerable time and attention to this subject in spite of the fact that other aspects of our work are more professionally (and even financially) remunerative. We have done so because we believe that this field will not remain a quiet backwater for academics and a cozy niche for practitioners: We expect it to become far more important in the next several decades, and throughout the coming century. If that is true, then this subject will demand the best thinking available from all concerned, and we believe that it is time to start the conversation in earnest. This is,

of course, something of an act of faith on our part. To take space law seriously as a subject, one must believe in a future in which humanity flourishes, and one in which law can make a difference for good. To us, that is part of the appeal. We hope that it is for others as well.

Glenn H. Reynolds
Robert P. Merges

Introduction

To many, "space law" still belongs to the realm of science fiction. Yet many real-life lawyers work in the field already, and their numbers are growing rapidly. Their work cuts across the boundaries of traditional legal disciplines—from commercial law and contracts to international law and even torts—but is unified, like that of Admiralty lawyers, by the demands of an industry with unique problems. That industry is growing steadily and is placing new demands on its legal counsel (and on government officials responsible for regulating the area) every day. Furthermore, study of the problems faced (and created) by space industries and other uses of space helps to shed light on issues growing from high technology areas in general and is thus a useful part of an overall legal education.

In response, many law schools have begun teaching courses in space law, and many practitioners have had to educate themselves in an *ad hoc* manner. What has been lacking, though, is a comprehensive introduction to the subject. That is the purpose of this book.

The book is organized around the needs of the space industry and those who deal with it. As private companies become involved in providing launch services and in conducting research and manufacturing in outer space, and as governments band together for multinational space stations and other ventures, legal questions are raised that touch on virtually every subject in the law school curriculum, but in new settings. As a consequence, it is not enough for a lawyer in this industry to know just the traditional legal subjects; she must also know how to apply that knowledge to the special needs of the industry—although space contracts are still contracts, to be useful they must anticipate the kinds of problems that are likely to arise only in this industry. Those in the industry, meanwhile, will find it useful to familiarize themselves with the legal issues that are likely to be important to them.

In addition, it helps immeasurably to know something about the technical and scientific basis for the industry. One need not know how to design a rocket engine, or how to service a satellite. Nor does one need an exhaustive knowledge of the history behind the industry and the legal regime that has grown up around it. But to understand the problems the industry is likely to present, it will help to know something about the basics. For this reason, we provide a brief introduction to the history and technology behind the industry, as well as extensive references to the literature on those subjects.

Because government has traditionally played a major role in the shaping of the industry, lawyers and clients alike are likely to have to persuade policymakers to pay attention to their particular problems for some time. For that matter, law schools (both in the United States and, increasingly, in other countries) are key training grounds for future policymakers, meaning that those taking courses in this area may well be the space decision-makers of the future. For these reasons, we pay considerable attention to the policy issues involved, both in the context of individual areas of the law and more general discussions of various policy issues.

We also discuss a wide variety of international law issues. Many, like the jurisdictional provisions of the Outer Space Treaty, touch directly on the space industry. Others, like the ABM Treaty, do not. All, however, are an important part of space law and form part of the background against which events take place. And, of course, international law issues are of considerable importance to government lawyers and to policymakers.

Most legal texts are casebooks. That presents a problem in the aerospace field because there are so few cases. But the casebook format has many advantages, providing a variety of viewpoints and a sense of how legal rules are applied in courts. In addition, it presents the subject matter in discrete units, allowing the teacher more flexibility in organizing a course. With this in mind, we have emulated the casebook format by including excerpts from leading publications and from key legal sources such as treaties and statutes. However, in order to provide context and background, and to remedy gaps in the published literature, we provide a much greater than usual amount of original commentary and notes. Discussion points and study questions, along with references to additional reading, are also included. The result, we hope, is a book that will be useful both as a text in law school classes and as a tool for self-education by practitioners and interested people both within and outside the legal profession.

If the space industry is to develop as it should, there must be a body of law that supports its growth. That law is developing now, through the efforts of scholars and practitioners. It is our sincere hope, reflected in the pages of this book, that we can contribute to this process.

G.H.R.
R.P.M.

1

Some History and Background

This is a book about space law, not the history and technology of space exploration. But just as lawyers in other fields must know something (often a great deal) about their clients, lawyers serving the space industry must know something about the context in which they work. This brief introductory chapter provides an overview of how spaceflight (and space law) came to be a reality, of the key technical concepts needed to understand many important issues, and of the industry's directions in the future, along with a number of references for further reading. Readers are strongly encouraged to pursue those references, as what is set out here is the briefest synopsis (a "capsule version," if you will) of a rich and interesting literature.

SPACE HISTORY—*THE BRICK MOON* AND ALL THAT

The idea of space travel is not new—trips to the Moon and beyond have been the subject of fanciful tales for thousands of years. But not until the last century or so did people begin seriously examining the methods and implications of going into space. It is amazing, in retrospect, how much of the work of early pioneers has remained useful—even essential—to carrying out operations in space, and how clearly some of those early figures foresaw the problems and opportunities that would arise as human beings moved into outer space.

One of the first to do so, and in many ways the undisputed pioneer of space studies, was a Russian, Konstantin Tsiolkovsky. Tsiolkovsky's work, which started over a century ago, laid the foundation for many technological developments that followed, and anticipated much that still seems futuristic today. In 1883 he wrote of the problems likely to be encountered in zero gravity; in 1903 he published an essay entitled *Exploration of Cosmic Space with Reactive Devices* that outlined the principles of navigation in space. Throughout the rest of his life, he wrote and pondered not only the practical, but the philosophical aspects of outer space development.

Tsiolkovsky envisioned an era in which space exploration would lead to cities in space and, ultimately, to utopian societies throughout the solar system—a vision shared by many space supporters today. Because these societies would have access to unlimited solar energy and to all the resources of the solar system's planets and asteroids, Tsiolkovsky reasoned, they would be free from the scarcities that plague earthbound economies and hence free from social problems stemming from unequal distribution of wealth. When the Bolsheviks came to power in 1917, they found Tsiolkovsky's theories well-suited to their own professed belief that social injustices stemmed from unequal distribution of wealth—and found research into rockets a promising part of efforts (first by Lenin, then by Stalin) to build up the Soviet Union's technological base and armaments industry. Tsiolkovsky, previously an obscure schoolteacher, received a seat on the Soviet Academy, and his disciples (such as Sergei Korolev, F. A. Tsander, and Valentin Glushko) began serious work on rocketry, work that was to lead to a succession of firsts by the Soviet Union in the late 1950s and early 1960s.

Although Tsiolkovsky was the first to conduct serious study into problems of space flight, many others were soon doing the same—indeed, the American Edward Everett Hale had published a science fiction story about an artificial satellite used for navigation, entitled *The Brick Moon,* in the *Atlantic Monthly* as early as 1869. Serious work on the subject in the United States, however, began with Robert Goddard. Goddard published a paper in 1919 entitled *A Method of Reaching Extreme Altitudes* that described the prospects for reaching outer space using rockets. Although many skeptics (including the editors of the *New York Times*) subjected Goddard to ridicule for what were then thought of as far-fetched ideas (such as sending a probe to the Moon), he devoted his life to the perfection of liquid-fueled rockets and provided considerable inspiration and information to the German rocket pioneers who began organizing in the early 1920s. Goddard was the first to successfully launch a liquid-fueled rocket, and the first to demonstrate a working guidance system. Aside from Goddard, various groups of enthusiasts in the United States such as the American Rocket Society, the Cleveland Rocket Society, and the Yale Rocket Club did significant initial work in the development of rocket technology and in laying other important groundwork for later space exploration efforts.

In Britain, meanwhile, the Explosives Act of 1875 (which banned all private research in ordnance) proved a near-absolute barrier to actual experimentation, providing a concrete example of how bad or shortsighted law can frustrate space development. This did not stop British enthusiasts from contributing, however—it simply forced the British Interplanetary Society, including individuals like Phil Cleator and Arthur C. Clarke, to devote energies to long range studies, such as a famous 1939 plan for a Moon mission that served as the foundation for the actual Moon landing thirty years later.

Germany, too, had its pioneer in Hermann Oberth, who in 1923 published *Die Rakete zu den Planetenaumen* (The Rocket into Planetary Space). Oberth's book was far more ambitious than Goddard's work, discussing ways of putting human beings into space in the (relatively) near term and the problems (such as the need for space suits, the composition of space food, and the minutiae of operating space stations) that would have to be overcome. Oberth's book was followed in short order by a number of works by other German enthusiasts, most notably Walter Hohmann, whose 1925 work on celestial mechanics set out principles still relied on today and for whom the economical "Hohmann transfer orbit" used by interplanetary space probes is named.

The next twenty years were to see a flowering of German rocket science (unhampered by Explosives Laws) that began with small groups of dedicated individuals and culminated with the immense government-financed effort that produced the V-2 missile (designated the A-4 by its inventors). The V-2 was of dubious value as a weapon of war—each missile cost as much to build as a bomber, delivered a smaller load of explosives, and was destroyed at the end of a single mission—but it was the first really viable space booster.

W. McDougall, ... the Heavens and the Earth: A Political History of the Space Age 43 (1985)

The A-4

In 1929 the Ordnance Ballistic Section of the German army assigned Walter Dornberger to develop a liquid fuel rocket of longer range than any existing gun, a sobering assignment, given that the Big Berthas of World War I fired projectiles sixty-five miles. Dornberger visited the "rocketport" of the amateur Verein fur Raumschiffahrt in Berlin, set young Wernher von Braun to work completing his doctorate, and together they recruited the Rocket Team. Just as in the Soviet Union, the rocketeers did not find state support—the state found them, and at a propitious moment. "The more time I have to think about it," wrote Willy Ley, "the more I have arrived at the conclusion that the VfR progressed as far as any club can progress. ... Experimentation had reached a state where continuation would have been too expensive for any organization except a millionaires' club."

Von Braun and Dornberger chose for their lonely, spacious test site a sweep of sandy coast on the Usedom Peninsula beyond the mouth of the Peene River. But by the time Peenemunde opened in the fall of 1939, the Wehrmacht was rolling over Poland, and Hitler decided the big rockets would not be needed. Von Braun and Dornberger pressed on, with reduced budgets, toward a prototype of their majestic A-4, the first medium-range ballistic missile, standing 46.1 feet high. It was a single-stage rocket powered by LOX [liquid oxygen] and alcohol, developing a thrust of 56,000 pounds, a payload of 2,200 pounds, and a velocity of 3,500 miles per hour while inertially guided by gyroscopes and leveling pendulums to its target 200 miles distant. The first A-4 flight test finally took place in June 1942. It failed, and so did the next. But the third bird, in October, rose from the Baltic dunes in a stable and gentle arc fifty miles high until it passed out of sight en route to the impact area 119 miles downrange. Dornberger's team watched in exultation—like the Alamogordo physicists three years later, they attended in the delivery room as a new Power was born. But where the elemental blast of the atomic bomb rendered its makers diminished, apprehensive, in a sense imprisoned, the elegant, finned cylinder of the A-4 was a metaphor of liberation, defying gravity as it soared aloft with little hint—after the first moments—of the brute force it contained. An aspiring and creative thing, it had brushed the sleeves of space.

Although their work was financed by the military and led to the V-2, von Braun's team secretly dreamed of building rockets that would carry human beings into outer space. Unbeknownst to their superiors, the German rocket teams designed larger and more powerful rockets, winged spacecraft, and atmosphere-skipping rocket/ramjet space planes. With the end of World War II, von Braun and virtually all of his key staff signed on to work for the United States, bringing their designs and the remaining stock of V-2s with them.

The immediate postwar period saw a brief flurry of interest in space activity. The exploits of the German rocket scientists were still fresh in everyone's mind, which lent credibility to plans that would have been thought outlandish in the prewar era. Arthur C. Clarke published a paper proposing the use of satellites placed in geosynchronous orbits (where they would remain in position above the same point on earth) as a means of relaying communications; shortly thereafter the RAND Corporation issued a prophetic report on the feasibility of using earth satellites for military purposes such as intelligence collection and weather observations.

But the postwar era was not fertile ground for rapid progress in the space field. America was occupied with satisfying the pent-up demand of its consumers, with helping Europe rebuild, and with countering the gradually unfolding Soviet threat, while the European powers that had played an important role in prewar years were in no position to undertake any projects beyond recovering from devastation. The Soviet Union *was* working on development of large boosters as a counter to American air superiority, but results were not to come for some time and no one outside a select group of Soviet leaders and engineers knew what was going on.

Still, work on space boosters continued to progress slowly in the United States, and some American scholars, politicians, and diplomats began to take an interest in issues of space law. As the Soviet Union acquired the status of America's key adversary, interest in using satellites for reconnaissance grew. There were, however, serious concerns about the international law ramifications of satellite overflights, concerns that were sharpened considerably after the Soviet Union launched the world's first satellite, Sputnik. Some argued that such overflights would constitute violations of the sovereignty of the nations overflown, with injury being added to insult where the flights were for reconnaissance purposes. Much of U.S. strategy was influenced by these debates.

W. McDougall, ... the Heavens and the Earth: A Political History of the Space Age 185–189 (1985)

Few diplomatic issues seemed as urgent and loaded with implications for world peace as the law of outer space. Here were a new complex of frightening technologies *and* a virtually limitless medium, opened up simultaneously for human exploitation. And just as the voyages of the Age of Discovery stimulated inquiry into the law of the sea that advanced international law generally through the work of Hugo Grotius and others, so the launching of the Space Age inspired a burst of inquiry on the fundamental principles that ought to guide *all* the deeds of nation-states. The most beguiling legal problems were those tied to sovereignty: could nations claim space; divide it into zones according to some scientific, political, or technical principle; make it off-limits to weaponry; extend the cooperative framework of the IGY [International Geophysical Year]? What legislative and enforcement mechanisms were preferable for space law? What arrangements could be made for advance notice of launches, exchange of data, assessment of liability for damage caused by space vehicles? Who owned the moon or the electromagnetic spectrum? How could space boosters be distinguished from military missiles? Was space development best served by an international effort or by national programs operating under ground rules? A handful of visionaries tackled such puzzles even before Sputnik. John Cobb Cooper, air law expert and fellow of Princeton's Institute for Advanced Study, took up the question of sovereignty in a 1951 article, reviewing the history of air law from the Romans (who said land ownership extended "*usque and coelum*") to the great jurisprudential theorists of the seventeenth and eighteenth centuries (Samuel von Pufendorf limited sovereignty in the air to the ability for "effective control"), to the Chicago Convention of 1944 (which recognized complete and exclusive national sovereignty over air space). But how far up did air extend? Sounding rockets revealed that the atmosphere did not just stop, but gradually dissipated. Cooper opted for "effective control" (also the formula chosen by the 1885 Berlin Conference, which set rules for the colonization of Africa). "The territory of each state extends upward into space as far as the scientific progress of any state ... permits such state to control it."

After Sputnik, numerous proposals were advanced for defining outer space. The so-called von Karman line set the boundary at the point at which a vehicle traveling seven kilometers a second loses aerodynamic lift and becomes a "spacecraft." Such an event would occur about fifty-three miles up. Cooper and common law (post–October 4, 1957) indicated that space simply stopped at that point below which an orbit could not be sustained. But such "lines" were a function of velocity and therefore of technology, and were in no way innate. Everyone knew where land ended and the ocean began, but now man had entered a realm that, in a real sense, did not exist except as a function of man's own tools. Any definition of outer space was a solipsism.

The critical variable in the definition of space was perceived military interest. The higher the boundary of national sovereignty, the greater the protection against unfriendly overflight, but the lesser the ability to ply the lower reaches of space for any purpose. It was guesswork in 1958 as to which would best suit American or Soviet interests. Similarly, whether a low limit was good or bad depended on the international regime that would obtain in space. If a rigid system of international control was instituted, then national freedom was best served by a high boundary. If a laissez-faire regime arose in space, then national freedom would be greatest by lowering "outer space" as close to the earth as possible: "Open Skies."

These ambiguities gave spacefaring nations no incentive to solve the riddle. State Department counsel Becker explained that the United States, while not recognizing any top limit to its airspace, conferred the right to ply space wherever it was. In short, the United States believed in "freedom of space," but reserved its position on what that freedom entailed or where it took effect. "Moreover," he continued, "there are very great risks in attempting to transmute a body of law based on one determined set of facts (e.g., air or sea law) into a body of law with respect to which the basic facts have not been determined." The State Department was "inclined to view with great reserve any such suggestions as that the principles of the law of space should be codified. ..."

The principal concern of American policy was always the protection of spy satellites. But the right to launch satellites over the territory of other states was already established during the IGY. In this connection, George J. Feldman, counsel to the Senate Space Committee, declared that security considerations alone would preserve the principle of sovereign air space and work just as powerfully against a definition of where that air space ended. Satellites had already been launched without protest, implying that formal consent to satellite overflight was either unnecessary or implicitly given. "It is tempting to accept the first explanation—which would mean, for example, that President Eisenhower's Open Skies proposal is an accomplished fact. However, any such assumption would be premature and unjustified." Limited agreements on space might be made, but none should be sought "which are more comprehensive or explicit than our present knowledge warrants."

The same caution obtained in debate over sovereignty on heavenly bodies. As early as 1952 a UN lawyer, Oscar Schachter, asked "Who owns the universe?" and worried that we might someday read of colonial rivalries in space, of "lunar Washingtons and New Yorks, perhaps of King George mountains and Stalin craters." He suggested that space and celestial bodies belong, like the high seas, to all mankind. States should be allowed to develop settlements and mineral deposits, but in such a way as not to cause waste and destruction "against the general interest of mankind." The fear of a "scramble for colonies" in space, more rapacious even than the nineteenth century's scramble in Africa, also motivated space law theorists after Sputnik. But if space was not subject to sovereignty, what was its legal status? Was it *res nullius*—space as belonging to no one, but presumably subject to claims? Or *res communis omnium*—space as "the heritage of all mankind" with an implied right for all powers to regulate and reap the benefits of spaceflight? Or *res extra commercium*—with sovereignty and jurisdiction vested in the UN? The first threatened to stampede the powers, but the others implied an international control over national technology that the US and USSR alike were unlikely to accept.

Early discussion of such problems fell roughly into two categories, a fact acknowledged by leaders of the schools themselves, Andrew Haley and Myres McDougal. The former, an amateur rocketeer turned lawyer, counsel to the ARS [American Rocket Society] and president of the International Astronautical Federation, was the major exponent of the "natural law school." According to Haley, law rested on universal moral principles derived from the nature of man: moral precepts such as the Golden Rule that found expression in all great religions. Codified natural law theory arose, significantly, in response to problems posed by European discovery of the New World. But the law of nations, as the moral law of individuals writ large, did not constrain the states of early modern Europe, with unfortunate results. Now the world's governments again faced virgin territory. This time states must join in advance of the conquest of space to set standards and principles of conduct, and so avoid the old pattern of abuse and competition.

The "positivist school" of space law, associated with McDougal of Yale, argued that law emerged from patterns of common usage and could not be invented in advance of knowledge of the facts and emerging national interest. The difficulty in separating military and civilian activities rendered prohibition of the latter all but impossible, and space law in any case would always be a function, not a determinant, of international politics. High-blown principles and futile attempts to shackle the space powers would only make the principles appear ridiculous. Instead, the patterns of usage of space must be allowed to establish themselves before codification.

The two schools could aptly be termed the idealist and the realist. The most striking vindication of the realistic positivists was the fact that the secret NSC decisions had already rendered the space law debate academic. The reasons for the Superpowers' aloofness included the one offered in disparagement by the natural law idealists—that nations were obsessed by power and flouted the ethical imperatives embedded in every human being—*and* the one offered in sweet reason by the positivists—that it would be folly to make artificial rules for a vast area of human activity before the facts were known. Hence the USSR boycotted the Ad Hoc COPUOS [Committee On the Peaceful Uses of Outer Space] entirely, while the United States sharply circumscribed its agenda. The upshot was that discussion would proceed on such things as spacecraft registration and liability, sharing the radio spectrum and scientific data, but not on restrictions on the development and use of space technology by competing national states. Many space law theorists expressed their disgust with this narrow nationalism and hypocrisy, but the cries of "space for peace" and "space for all mankind" carried no further than if they had been shouted in the vacuum of space itself. The irony is that those enthusiastic about the human adventure in space should have been rejoicing. Competition was the engine of spaceflight. Had space exploration been truly internationalized or demilitarized, the Superpowers would have had little incentive to make huge investments for its realization. Space programs would have been stunted with malnutrition.

As the above passage demonstrates, the space law debate of the 1950s was of more than academic significance. Indeed, many believe that some elements of the United States government favored allowing the Soviet Union to launch the first satellite, as it did with Sputnik, on the ground that that would estop the Soviets from complaining about overflights by United States satellites. Whether or not that was the intention, it was certainly the effect—although there were a few *pro forma* complaints about intelligence satellites, the Soviet Union never seriously challenged the right of the United States to gather information that way.

That constituted a substantial victory for the American government: As an open society locked in cold-war struggle with a closed one, the United States found itself heavily dependent on the ability to gather information via technical means, of which aerial photography was the most significant. Originally, such information was gathered largely by high-altitude aircraft such as Canberra bombers and the U-2, but increasing Soviet proficiency at fighter interception and antiaircraft missile design made that risky. As a result, U.S. political and diplomatic strategy in the space arena throughout the ten years following the Sputnik launch centered around protecting the legality of satellite intelligence-gathering.

Through vigorous efforts in the UN's Committee on the Peaceful Uses of Outer Space (COPUOS), in the General Assembly and the Security Council, and in the negotiations and public posturing that led to the Outer Space Treaty, the United States championed a view of space as reserved for "peaceful" activities but open to military presences that did not violate this principle—i.e., reconnaissance satellites.

The Soviet Union, surprisingly to some, wound up going along. Perhaps this was because some farsighted Soviet officials realized that in the long run space surveillance was in their interest as well, or perhaps it was because the formulation that was chosen also did not outlaw ballistic missiles (which pass through space in flight), a technology in which the Soviets had invested much and demonstrated considerable competence.

Whatever the reason, this view was accepted and made part of the Outer Space Treaty; in fact, a few years later the Soviet Union wound up formally recognizing the legitimacy of satellite observation as part of the SALT I Treaty, which bound the U.S. and the Soviet Union to refrain from interfering with each other's "national technical means of verification," a term that encompassed reconnaissance satellites. Other agreements in the post–Outer Space Treaty period, such as the ABM Treaty, the Accident Measures Agreement, etc. (see Chapters 4 and 5, *infra,* for more on these and other space agreements), followed this pattern, establishing outer space as a place in which military presences were permitted, but in which aggressive acts were not. This formulation, however, in large part reflected the technical capabilities of the two countries and their political and military needs; it remains to be seen whether it will survive coming changes in those factors.

Although the centerpiece of U.S. policy, however, issues of space militarization were not the only ones addressed in the negotiations leading up to the Outer Space Treaty (see Chapter 3). There was also a struggle over what limits existed to national sovereignty over outer space, the circumstances under which resources in space might be exploited, etc. This struggle was reflected in the Outer Space Treaty's statement that space should be used for the "common benefit of mankind," and "on the basis of equality," terms which were ultimately to prove insufficient to satisfy many "Third World" countries who feared that more developed nations would gain hegemony over outer space resources—or that exploitation of resources in outer space (such as metals and energy) would drive down market prices for their own exports. This led to an attempt to renegotiate matters in the form of the Moon Treaty (discussed in Chapter 4), which declared space resources part of the "Common Heritage of Mankind" and proposed an international regime for dividing up the profits from extracting them. U.S. ratification of that treaty was blocked by a coalition of industry and space activists, putting a damper (for some years at least) on international efforts at redistribution.

The aftermath of the Outer Space Treaty and related agreements saw a series of dramatic achievements in outer space. Unmanned probes visited most of the planets in the solar system (only tiny, distant Pluto being excepted). Manned missions first explored orbit (in American Mercury and Gemini missions and Soviet Vostok, Voskhod, and Soyuz missions), Americans landed on the Moon, the United States orbited Skylab, U.S. and Soviet spacecraft docked in orbit, the United States space shuttle flew, and the Soviets established first one, then a second, permanently manned space station in orbit.

Commercial activities in space had begun even before the Treaty, in the communications satellite field, and began spreading to include space manufacturing and research ventures, private launch services, and other efforts. Meanwhile, even more grandiose plans appeared on the drawing boards, plans for asteroid mining, solar power satellites, and space colonies. By the 1990s the movement of people into space seemed unstoppable except by nuclear war or some similar calamity—for although individual nations might decide not to participate, the high level of overall involvement ensured that others would forge on regardless.

SOME OBSERVATIONS

It would be presumptuous to attempt to draw lessons, in the context of a space law text, regarding the future of humankind's expansion into outer space. However, the history of that expansion to date does hold some lessons for the space lawyer and for government and industry officials concerned with issues of space law.

One is that space technologies seem to grow faster than anyone, even among space enthusiasts, generally expects. When Arthur Clarke proposed the communications satellite it was openly pooh-poohed as science fiction—and even much later when INTELSAT, the international communications satellite consortium, was formed many wondered why such systems would ever be necessary given the dozens of telephone circuits supported by existing transatlantic cables. Today, however, the communications satellite industry has revenues in the billions of dollars per year, and circuits are measured in the thousands and tens of thousands per satellite. And even Tsiolkovsky, who was so prophetic in many ways, did not see humanity venturing into space until the twenty-first century, an estimate that proved wildly pessimistic. Thus, in giving advice concerning larger issues it is important to keep an eye on the future, with the realization that the future may become the present more rapidly than anyone expects.

Another is that matters of national interest and security are more important in the space context than in many other areas, and that the law of outer space (in both the international and domestic contexts) tends to be driven by those interests rather than the other way around. Advice to clients—and plans by those clients and by governments—must take into account not only the "black letter" law where that is present, but the political circumstances involved. Prior to the late 1950s the "black letter" answer to the overflight question was that national sovereignty extended infinitely upward, but that answer was rapidly rendered obsolete by the changed circumstances of the Cold War and the Soviet Sputnik launch.

Lastly, it should be noted that the history of outer space is to a surprising degree the history of dedicated individuals and small groups manipulating larger powers in order to pursue their own goals, with Wernher von Braun's programs the paradigmatic (but far from the only) example. As outer space enterprises are integrated into everyday life, and as the entire field of space endeavors becomes larger and hence possessed of greater inertia, this may cease to be the case. However, it probably has not done so yet—the battle to block U.S. ratification of the Moon Treaty, for example, was spearheaded by what was then a small and new organization, the L5 Society (now the National Space Society), with great effect. The possibility that something like it may happen again should be kept in mind, and ways of dealing with such groups in crucial circumstances (for example, budget battles and future treaty negotiations and ratifications) should be explored. Otherwise space lawyers and their clients may find that someone else is making the rules by which they play.

FURTHER READING

W. Bainbridge, The Spaceflight Revolution: A Sociological Study (1976)
W. Burrows, Deep Black: Space Espionage and National Security (1986)
M. Collins, Liftoff (1988)
N. Daniloff, The Kremlin and the Cosmos (1972)
Dembling & Arons, The Evolution of the Outer Space Treaty, 33 Journal of Air Law & Commerce 419 (1967)
The Illustrated Encyclopedia of Space Technology (K. Gatland ed. 1984)
Goldman, The Moon Treaty: Reflections on the Proposed Moon Treaty, Space Law, and the Future, in People In Space (J. Katz ed. 1985)
T. McDonough, Space: The Next Twenty-Five Years (1987)
W. McDougall,... the Heavens and the Earth: A Political History of the Space Age (1985)
National Commission on Space, Pioneering the Space Frontier (1986)
Office of Technology Assessment, International Cooperation and Competition in Civilian Space Activities (1985)
Reynolds & Merges, The Role of Commercial Development in Preventing War in Outer Space, 25 Jurimetrics: Journal of Law, Science & Technology 130 (1985)
F. Winter, Prelude to the Space Age: The Rocket Societies: 1924–1940 (1983)

THE SPACE ENVIRONMENT

Space has changed in the years since the Second World War. Or, to be more precise, our understanding of space has changed. As Walter McDougall puts it, space is no longer the realm of dreams; it is now the realm of *Homo faber*, man (or, more properly, humanity) the tool-maker.

Since the peculiarities of space activity, including space commerce and space law, stem in large part from the special features of the space environment, it is important to understand something about that environment. Without such an understanding, it is simply impossible to appreciate the challenges that the space industry faces.

WHERE DOES SPACE BEGIN?

To a surprising extent, the answer to this question depends on who is asking it. As the excerpt from McDougall's book earlier in this chapter demonstrates, the question of where outer space begins is one of human definition, not practical delimitation. Below an altitude of approximately 69 miles, sustained orbit is practically impossible. Above an altitude of approximately 53–62 miles (the so-called von Karman line) aerodynamic lift is largely nonexistent. Yet X-15 aircraft flew higher than 62 miles, and satellites and other spacecraft pass through orbits lower than 69 miles—and, once experiments with tethered satellites have borne fruit, may stay there for some time.

As you can see, there is no clear answer to the question of where space begins. But equally clearly, at some point above the earth, there exists an environment completely different from the one we have here. A sort of customary law has developed, discussed in following chapters, to the effect that any object in orbit is in space, and that seems enough to satisfy everyone for the time being. Whether that will remain so is unclear. *See generally* McDougal, The Emerging Customary Law of Space, 58 Northwestern University Law Review 618 (1963).

WHAT'S IT LIKE UP THERE?

Photos and movies taken in space give it a peaceful, serene appearance. It looks like a place where the give and take of the atmosphere is replaced by a sort of perpetual stillness. But the appearance is deceptive.

In fact our atmosphere protects us from much of what is dangerous in space. First, there is a great deal of radiation. Visible light, X rays, infrared, radio and other forms of energy—collectively called electromagnetic radiation—are everywhere. This presents a danger, in terms of wear and tear on machinery and possible health effects on astronauts. (It also presents an opportunity, since many spacecraft are powered by these forces, both by generating electricity from sunlight using solar panels and—in the future—using light pressure from sunlight to propel spacecraft using "solar sails"). One of the primary problems caused by radiation is simple heat buildup: since the temperature of an unprotected object will rise rapidly on its sunlit side, special reflective and insulating materials have been developed to keep equipment (and people!) operational in space. In addition, this electromagnetic energy (when at frequencies other than those of infrared and visible light) can produce interference with communication, guidance and navigation equipment.

Second, subatomic particles from various sources shoot through space quite frequently. Many come from the sun; in fact, the flow of such particles from the sun is so steady it is referred to as the "solar wind." Fortunately for space travel, due to the small amount of mass and energy in these particles they do not normally pose a serious threat to activities in space.

A third source of potential trouble is radiation trapped in the earth's magnetic field—the Van Allen Radiation Belts. These are two bands of charged particles, one beginning at 250–750 miles up and ending at about 6,200 miles, and the other beginning at about 6,200 miles and extending to 37,000 to 52,000 miles. The composition of the two belts differs slightly, but flight trajectories for manned spacecraft must be designed carefully to avoid spending too much time within them. Unmanned craft, such as communications satellites, can and do operate within the belts, however; they can be designed to withstand the effects of the radiation for many years.

The high-speed solar protons emitted by a solar flare on the surface of the sun are probably the most dangerous of the radiation hazards to space flight. Flares themselves are the most spectacular disturbances seen on the sun. They appear as a sudden, large increase in light and radiation from a portion of the sun's atmosphere. Even on the earth, they can cause substantial problems—such as radio noise storms that interfere with communications. But from the point of view of the space traveller, the real danger caused by solar flares is the large number of high-energy solar protons they release into space. They can carry extremely high energies. As a consequence, they can cause the release of lethal doses of secondary radiation, such as gamma rays, when they collide with spacecraft. Until now this has never happened, largely because spacecraft can be shielded to protect against much of the radiation in this form. Nevertheless, solar flare radiation remains a real threat to human health in space.

METEOROIDS AND MICROMETEOROIDS

Space is also populated by larger particles, some with masses as large as several tons, called meteoroids. Most, however, are quite small, and are known as micrometeoroids. When a meteoroid enters the earth's atmosphere, it is called a meteor; remnants of meteors are often found on earth.

In space, micrometeoroids regularly strike satellites and other space vehicles. (In fact, some space scientists believe they are responsible for several otherwise inexplicable satellite malfunctions.) Over time, micrometeoroid impact can be expected to wear down the surface of satellites or space stations. This is especially important where sensitive materials, such as optical lenses or reflective coatings, must be exposed for the satellite or space station to do its job.

But even though micrometeoroid impact can be expected, the probability of impact with a devastatingly large meteoroid is quite low. Not all dangerous objects in space are of natural origin, however: as a result of accidental explosions and military antisatellite tests some orbits contain considerable quantities of artificial debris, a problem that is growing and may soon pose a real threat to many space activities. This issue is discussed further in Chapter 5.

VACUUM AND MICROGRAVITY

Two other features of the space environment are the relative absence of gases and other matter and the relative absence of gravitational pull—vacuum and microgravity, respectively.

Space is, by the standards of earth dwellers, quite empty. Yet space contains gases, albeit at concentrations that are tiny compared to the earth's atmosphere.

This relative absence of gases is one of the features of the space environment that makes it attractive for manufacturing purposes. It is thought, for instance, that the space atmosphere will permit greater purity by reducing unwanted gases that are introduced in certain manufacturing processes on earth even when sophisticated vacuum pumps are used.

The other, more important, aspect of space for purposes of potential manufacturing applications is minimal gravity. The term "microgravity" is usually used to describe this characteristic of space. As this term implies, objects in space are affected by gravitational forces, which exist everywhere in the universe. The point is simply that these forces are less apparent within the frame of reference of an object in space than on the surface of a planet.

Space consequently is thought by some to hold great potential as a manufacturing site for the future. Advanced materials, for example, are often mentioned as possible products. On earth, alloys and other materials are susceptible to imperfections caused by tiny currents. These "convection currents," as materials scientists call them, result from the action of gravity during the cooling of alloys and other materials. Manufacturing in the microgravity environment of space can eliminate these imperfections.

Moreover, space may provide a more hospitable environment for growing intricate crystals, such as those used in semiconductor manufacture. It also allows the use of methods of separation (such as those used in McDonnell Douglas's Continuous Flow Electrophoresis experiment flown on board the Space Shuttle) that rely on forces too weak to be of much use under gravity. These are just a few examples of how scientists on earth plan to make use of the special environment of space; other ideas will no doubt appear as we gain more experience.

GETTING THERE AND STAYING THERE

The essential mathematics of rocket launches and earth orbits were worked out by astronomers in the seventeenth century, especially Johannes Kepler and Sir Isaac Newton. Of course, they probably had no expectation that their laws of celestial mechanics would have any application to practical engineering problems. But as it turns out the problems of determining how to get an object into space and how to keep it there are just two special cases of more general astronomical problems.

The key is that for the purpose of calculating orbits and trajectories a space vehicle is just another celestial body, whose motion is governed by the same laws that dictate the movement of the planets. To be sure, it is a tiny body relative to the earth. But the beauty of the astronomical laws of motion is that they apply regardless of the size of the object. (Until you reach sub-atomic sizes, anyway; much different forces operate at that level.)

Although many people believe the reason for weightlessness in space is that a spacecraft in orbit is "beyond gravity," that is not the case—in fact, the pull of gravity at the altitude of most orbiting spacecraft is not much less than it is on the surface of the earth. Nor is that a bad thing, since orbits themselves would not be possible if it were not for the pull of gravity. A spacecraft orbits not because it is beyond the influence of gravity but because the product of its forward velocity and the pull of gravity is such that it neither falls to earth nor goes sailing off into the void. Because of its forward velocity, a spacecraft in orbit is in a sort of never ending circular fall, in which the surface of the earth curves away as fast as the spacecraft approaches it. The greater the altitude, the smaller the forward velocity required to keep an object in orbit, and the more time required to complete an orbit. Thus, satellites at low orbits complete a circuit of the earth in ninety minutes, while those higher up may take twenty-four hours or longer.

Orbits taking exactly twenty-four hours for a circuit (which requires an altitude of approximately 22,400 miles) are called *geosynchronous* orbits, because the satellite completes a circuit in exactly the same time that the earth takes to revolve once; if the satellite's orbit is directly above the equator with no inclination (tilt), it will appear to remain precisely above the same spot at all times. That has many advantages, especially for communications satellites, as it means that antennas need not swivel to track the satellite but may remain pointed in the same direction constantly since the satellite appears motionless relative to the ground. Geosynchronous orbits are often called *Clarke* orbits after Arthur C. Clarke, who first proposed their use for communications satellites; they are also sometimes abbreviated as GEO, standing for GEosynchronous Orbit. Orbits of lower altitude than geosynchronous are often called Low Earth or Near Earth Orbits, and abbreviated LEO or NEO.

Orbits inclined at 90 degrees to the equator are known as *polar* orbits because they pass over both poles. They are useful for reconnaissance and resource sensing, since they ensure that the satellite will pass over the entire earth as it turns; such orbits can be timed so that every pass of the satellite over a particular point will occur at the same time of day, in which case they are known as *sun synchronous* orbits. These orbits are typically used by military photoreconnaissance satellites.

In addition, there are a number of locations in the earth-Moon system that have special qualities because of the interactions between the earth's and the Moon's gravitational fields. The best known of these are the Lagrangian points, named for Pierre Lagrange, the French mathematician who first calculated their existence. These are points of unusual orbital stability, so that if a satellite or other object is placed in them it will not tend to drift away under the perturbing gravitational influence of other planets. Because of this, these points have been proposed as ideal locations for space colonies—indeed, one space activist group, the L5 Society (now merged into the National Space Society), took its name from one of the points. On the other hand, the unique gravitational characteristics of these points have considerable military significance, which could make them unlikely candidates for peaceful colonies.

ROCKETS AND PROPULSION

To get a spacecraft into orbit in the first place requires a phenomenal amount of thrust. Enough force must be applied to overcome the craft's inertia, i.e., to get it moving, and then to overcome enough of the pull of gravity to place it in one of the orbits described above.

Rocket engines operate on the principle of Newton's Third Law, popularly stated as "For every action, there is an equal and opposite reaction." A highly combustible material is ignited in a small chamber; the explosive thrust generated by the combustion is directed out of a narrow exhaust nozzle. The unbalanced force within the rocket's thrust chamber resulting from the exhaust's exiting the nozzle causes an equal and opposite reaction—the rocket is hurled in the direction opposite the nozzle. Unlike other types of combustion engines (e.g., aircraft jet engines) rockets do not depend on atmospheric oxygen for combustion; instead, they carry their own source of oxygen, called the oxidizer, to support combustion. This is what allows them to burn in the vacuum of space.

There are two common types of rocket engines: solid and liquid fueled; the solid/liquid hybrid combines features of the two but is just beginning to enter common use. Liquid fueled engines have several advantages, most notably controllable thrust and restart capability, not present in solid fueled engines. Liquid fueled engines typically use liquid oxygen or nitric acid as an oxidizer, with kerosene or liquid hydrogen as the fuel. Solid propellants, on the other hand, are more stable, and easier to manufacture and store. They are also cheaper. Solid rockets contain powdered fuel and oxidizer cast in a plastic or glue-like compound. A third type of engine is a cross between the other two: the so-called solid/liquid hybrid engine, which uses solid fuel, but a liquid oxidizer. It combines an advantage of some liquid propellants, the ability to stop and restart combustion, with several of the functional advantages of solid propellants. A number of other experimental engines have been proposed, but they have not yet been made operational.

There are a variety of other types of rocket engines that are not in general use but that may appear soon. One is the ion drive, in which electrical forces are used to expel small quantities of propellant at extremely high speeds; these engines produce low thrusts but can operate for long periods with low fuel consumption, making them suitable for interplanetary probes or other long distance applications. Another is the so-called ORION drive (named for the secret military project that developed it), which uses atomic explosives for propulsion. Although the idea struck many as absurd, a (non-nuclear) working model was tested in the late 1950s with excellent results. Because the Limited Test Ban Treaty (see discussion *infra* in Chapter 3) prohibits the detonation of nuclear explosives in the atmosphere or in outer space, partly for environmental reasons, ORION type drives are unlikely to be put to use any time soon. However, the concept has been validated, and the fact that such drives allow the acceleration of large payloads at low expense using proven technology may encourage some nation to explore the possibility of using ORION drives in the future.

Besides ORION drives, a number of other proposed launch systems are close enough to feasibility to warrant a brief mention. First is the Solar Sail, a simple concept that takes advantage of the small but measurable force exerted by photons emitted from the sun—or, in some conceptions, by giant lasers. These very large sails would be useful for moving cargoes around the solar system at low cost, or for cheaply and efficiently powering deep space probes. Second are laser launch systems, which work by directing a ground-based energy beam at a combustion chamber on the bottom of a rocket; the energy ignites the air in the combustion chamber and powers the rocket into orbit. The third launch system is the most unusual one: beanstalks. These would be essentially very long tethers, anchored on the earth and extending out into space beyond the geosynchronous orbit. The tethers would be launched using a conventional rocket; once in place, however, centrifugal or inertial force would keep them from falling back to earth. Solar power cells in space could then be used to supply the energy to lift objects up along the beanstalk and into orbit. While only at the conceptual stage of development, beanstalks offer an intriguing possibility for routine, cheap launches in the future. Other possibilities include "ram cannons," in which a projectile is fired through a barrel filled with gaseous propellant mixture, igniting the mixture like the centerbody of a ramjet engine. At this writing, experimental ram cannons have already reached 20 percent of the velocity needed to achieve orbit and could easily be scaled up to reach orbital velocities, although the enormous accelerations involved would limit them to cargo launches. In addition, the Air Force has been exploring the possibility of using anti-hydrogen as a propellant; antimatter hydrogen would be combined with ordinary hydrogen to produce highly efficient propulsion throughout the solar system. Only 35 milligrams of antimatter could propel a 120-ton aerospace plane carrying 30 tons of cargo to LEO at shuttle-like accelerations. Antimatter is being produced and stored at the time of this writing in very small quantities, and according to the Office of Technology Assessment could be produced and stored in the relatively near-term at costs of approximately $10 million per milligram. For more on these and other launch technologies see U.S. Congress Office of Technology Assessment, Launch Options for the Future (1988).

While these technologies are not yet operational, one or more of them will probably be developed in the future. This would likely have important political and economic consequences. The physics of beanstalks, for example, put a premium on equatorial launch bases. A number of equatorial nations have already declared sovereignty over the geosynchronous orbital slots above the equator (see the discussion of the Bogota Declaration in Chapter 4, *infra*), but these claims have been widely condemned and consistently ignored by spacefaring nations. Beanstalk technology would transform this conflict from a paper battle at the U.N. into a very real clash.

Likewise, cheaper launch capabilities would put space within reach of many more countries. This would in turn escalate the competition for scarce orbital slots, such as prime geosynchronous orbits for satellites. Moreover, since space capability has long been associated with military as well as civilian missions, cheap launches could make space a part of the military strategy of even small nations. Antimatter propulsion offers other possibilities: antimatter could conceivably be used in bombs of capacity equivalent to thermonuclear weapons. Such use is unlikely, though, as existing nuclear devices are cheaper and more reliable than antimatter devices are ever likely to be, and destructive enough to satisfy anyone.

WHEN YOU ARE THERE: WHAT PEOPLE DO IN SPACE

Satellites

Today, space is useful primarily because of the perspective it provides. Orbiting satellites, for example, make communication between distant points on earth much easier. Because of this, the satellite industry is the largest sector of commercial space activities today, as described in the following excerpt.

Byerly, The Commercial/Industrial Uses of Space, in Beyond Spaceship Earth: Environmental Ethics and the Solar System (E. Hargrove ed., 1986)

Communications satellites ... are now big business. Their use began with NASA experiments using the satellite Echo I in 1960. NASA conducted ten successful development flights between then and 1974. ...

[NASA's work spawned] a healthy industry. For example, the most recent figures show that about $2 billion worth of U.S.-produced satellite-communications ground systems were shipped in 1984, and service revenues for the seven U.S. common carriers were $555 million in 1984. In addition, the Communications Satellite Corporation (COMSAT) earned about $291 million in operating revenues in 1983 from communications to and from the United States. Currently, COMSAT has a monopoly on this international service, but there are efforts by other companies to [launch satellites and] enter this field. Some 109 nations are members of the International Tele-communications Satellite Organization and seven nations have their own domestic communications satellites.

A significant issue facing the communications satellite industry is the emerging congestion of the geostationary arc. [See this section, *supra*, for description.] ... This arc is becoming crowded, not because the satellites are near to bumping into one another but because of radio interference between adjacent satellites.

There needs to be about a 2-degree angular spacing between satellites in order to avoid such radio interference.

*   *   *

Two additional large operational activities in space are ... weather satellites and navigation satellites. Weather satellites—called metsats—have been operational since 1964. The United States normally has two of these in polar orbit and two in geostationary orbit. Those in polar orbit are [sun-synchronous, as defined above]. These satellites look down at the Earth to generate data on cloud cover, temperature, and water-vapor density and make a significant contribution to our ability to forecast the weather. The data that U.S. satellites generate is broadcast directly to the ground and anyone with the proper equipment can receive it. ...

Navigation satellites can be used with relatively simple equipment to find one's position on the Earth to within about 100 meters horizontally and about 1,000 meters vertically (that is, in altitude). The first Navstar satellite—the name of the U.S. satellites—was launched in 1978, and several more will be launched until the government constellation is complete in [the late 1980s]. The total system ... is called the Global Positioning System.

*   *   *

A [space technology] that has not really become fully operational [, but that has already given rise to a $10 million per year industry] is civilian remote sensing of the surface of the Earth. This technology can be used to generate data about the the Earth's surface, which in turn is used for mineral prospecting, for agricultural surveys and crop monitoring, for planning major construction projects such as pipelines, and for environmental monitoring and research. It has recently been used for fire-fighting purposes: the infrared sensors on a U.S. satellite were used to locate hot-spots despite a very thick blanket of smoke that was preventing firefighters from knowing where to attack the fire. There is currently in planning a large research program called the International Geosphere/Biosphere Program, which will attempt to study the Earth as a system in order to understand how our fundamental life-support system changes due both to natural and man-made causes. This program, when it gets underway, will undoubtedly use much data generated by remote sensing of the Earth from space.

Solar Power

The unending stream of energy from the Sun already serves as the power source for many spacecraft, especially space probes and satellites. But in an era of perceived energy scarcity on Earth, some have proposed tapping this vast resource for use here as well.

Power Stations in the Sky, in The Illustrated Encyclopedia of Space Technology 226–231 (K. Gatland ed., 1984)

Can space technology help to solve the energy crisis? Specifically, is it really practicable to think of tapping the "inexhaustible" energy of sunlight in space and beaming it back to Earth?

* * *

In 1968 Dr. Peter E. Glaser of the Arthur D. Little Company proposed the concept of satellite solar power stations [SSPS]. The idea depended on the establishment of a huge array of solar cells to concentrate the maximum amount of sunlight for the purpose of generating electricity by the process known as photovoltaic conversion.

The energy thus generated would be transmitted to Earth in the form of microwaves where it would be transformed back into electricity for use in the national grid.

* * *

One of the major United States companies looking into the future of solar energy is Boeing Aerospace, whose aim is to bring the concept closer to engineering reality. They envisage a structure the size of a small city producing twice the usable power generated by Grand Coulee, America's largest hydroelectric dam. They calculate that it would take 45 of these gigantic satellites to match the present total electrical generating power of the United States.

* * *

Critics of the SSPS wish to know more about possible environmental effects of the microwave beams. Is it really true that there will be no adverse [effects] on flora and fauna from a satellite power station that is not so restricted in output as to be wholly uneconomic? Then again, would not the microwave beams adversely affect the environment by heating up the atmosphere?

* * *

All the same, the detailed studies so far carried out have shown that, given the political will, [SSPS systems] could be developed in the foreseeable future, certainly by the end of the century. There is obviously still much work to do on such aspects as [transmission] frequencies least affected by the weather, on minimizing spillover, on waste of the beam, on efficient conversion techniques, and on proving beyond question that exposure of living things to the beam is without risk.

Research and Development

To date, much of what has taken place in space must be characterized as basic research. Beginning with the early space probes, past the Apollo moon landings, and into the era of the Space Shuttle, space scientists collected data on the features of the space environment. Even now, a major initiative in space research is the Hubble Space Telescope.

Microgravity experiments on the Apollo, Skylab, and Space Shuttle missions produced the first results that suggested a more practical side to the space environment. These experiments showed some intriguing possibilities for manufacturing materials in space. As a result of these experiments, some observers believe that certain pharmaceuticals and composite materials will one day be made routinely in space. For today, however, it is only safe to say that the true potential of space as a manufacturing environment is as yet unknown. One of the primary reasons the U.S. Space Station is being built is to provide an environment to explore these possibilities.

Since research and development are critical to corporate survival, and since space has been identified as a likely site for these activities in the future, commercial concerns in the mid-1980s began to express some anxiety about the applicability of U.S. patent law to space activities. Since patents are one of the primary means of securing a return on R&D investment in the U.S., firms wanted to make sure they would be available for the fruits of research endeavors undertaken in space. Legislation which would deal with some of these problems by extending U.S. jurisdiction for patent purposes into space was introduced in several Congresses and has now passed. It is described *infra* in Chapter 8.

Space Colonies

To some, space is nothing less than the Final Frontier, or even the next logical step in human evolution. The idea of space colonies is not a new one—such colonies were proposed by the seminal Russian space writer Konstantin Tsiolkovsky in the early part of this century. More recently, however, the idea has begun to be treated seriously by a number of scholars.

In 1969, Princeton physicist Gerard K. O'Neill asked his students a question inspired by the Apollo moon landings of the same year: "Is a planetary surface the right place for an expanding technological civilization?" After considerable research and debate, the answer that he was given was "No." Instead, humanity would be better off in a number of self-supporting habitats, making use of solar energy and lunar and asteroidal materials. Further research, and consultation with such leading scientists as physicist Freeman Dyson, led to a design based on large cylinders of up to several miles in length, rotating to produce artificial gravity. The design called for the colonies to be located at Lagrangian points, where they would remain stable as a result of Earth-Moon-Sun gravitational interactions without additional station-keeping assistance. One space activist group, the L5 society, took its name from one of the Lagrangian points as a statement of its support for the O'Neill concept and lobbied actively (and successfully, in the case of its effort to block ratification of the Moon Treaty) prior to merging with another group to become the National Space Society.

These initial designs have been refined a number of times, and will likely go through many changes before there is any substantial chance of their being implemented. In this, they may resemble the early British Interplanetary Society moon mission plans—better at anticipating the general nature of the problems encountered and their solutions than at diagramming the precise nature of future craft.

Yet such colonies are a distinct possibility over the long run, and would raise a variety of interesting legal questions. For example, the Outer Space Treaty and the Registration Convention provide for national jurisdiction and control over all space objects (*see* Chapters 3 and 5, *infra*), but the inhabitants of a space colony, sooner or later, are likely to object to a regime in which only earthside sovereignty is recognized. And, in the case of a U.S. colony, there would be interesting questions raised as to whether the Constitution would "follow the flag" in that context. Under the auspices of the Smithsonian Institution, a conference of leading academics and lawyers, including one Supreme Court Justice, has looked into these issues and drafted a "Declaration of First Principles" for the governance of space societies. Such issues are likely to receive further discussion in the future. *See* Chapter 9, *infra,* for a discussion of these questions.

Military Activities

Since before Sputnik, military use of outer space has been a major topic. In the first thirty years of the space age, the primary military use of space has been for communications and reconnaissance, one that most experts agree has exerted a stabilizing and beneficial effect on world affairs. Although there have been some efforts at developing techniques for denying enemies the ability to use space in this fashion—beginning with U.S. projects (named Bold Orion and SAINT) in the late 1950s and operational (or so it was claimed) systems on the part of both the United States and the Soviet Union in the 1960s and 1970s—it was not until the 1980s that serious prospects for more active military uses of outer space began to develop.

In principle, outer space may be used militarily in the same way that land, sea, and air are used: As a base for attacking the enemy, as a source of materials, as a vantage for observation, and as a means of rapid movement. Most proposals for future military uses of outer space, however, focus on antisatellite (ASAT) and ballistic missile defense (BMD) systems. Some of these pose legal problems—BMD systems based on nuclear weapons, for example, would violate the Outer Space Treaty (not to mention the more specific ABM Treaty), while the use of an antisatellite weapon to disable a satellite would undoubtedly constitute an aggressive act in contravention of the United Nations Charter. These topics are discussed *infra,* along with other topics growing out of the international law of outer space. For more on these topics see P. Stares, Space and National Security (1987); Reynolds, National Security on the High Frontier, 2 High Technology Law Journal 281 (1988).

Current military uses of space involve the use of three kinds of satellites: intelligence, communications, and early warning. Intelligence satellites are capable of taking photographs of dramatic resolution (reportedly, as good as a few inches), of monitoring communications (as activity known to the intelligence community as electronic intelligence or ELINT), and of producing all sorts of less dramatic but often important information concerning things like crop yields, rainfall, etc. Communications satellites allow central commanders to exercise control over far-flung forces to a degree that was not possible previously, and to receive real-time information about the progress of campaigns or about possible enemy action. Early warning satellites monitor enemy territory for missile launches, providing additional minutes of warning time that could prove crucial in a war—or, more importantly, deter a first strike to begin with.

In addition, meteorological satellites (metsats, in military jargon) provide data important for military operations and ICBM targeting adjustments. All of these, however, are what are known as "force multiplier" applications, meaning that their military role is one of amplifying the effect of other, more conventional, forces, not one of taking action on their own. Satellites capable of attacking targets on the ground are some time away, although eventually they could revolutionize land warfare, probably putting a premium on speed and concealment to a greater degree than any other type of weapon. For the coming decades, though, the key issues are likely to involve various objects in space and their relations with one another: ASAT weapons, and weapons capable of knocking out ICBMs during the spaceflight phase of their trajectory. Those are likely to prove challenging enough.

FURTHER READING

The New Solar System (J. Beatty, B. O'Leary & A. Chaikin eds. 1982).

W. Burrows, Deep Black: Space Espionage and National Security (1986).

K. Gatland, The Illustrated Encyclopedia of Space Technology (1984).

Goldman, The Moon Treaty: Reflections on the Proposed Moon Treaty, Space Law, and the Future, in J. Katz, People In Space (1985).

T. McDonough, Space: The Next Twenty-Five Years (1987).

W. McDougall, ... the Heavens and the Earth: A Political History of the Space Age (1985).
National Commission on Space, Pioneering the Space Frontier (1986).
Office of Technology Assessment, International Cooperation and Competition in Civilian Space Activities (1985).
Reynolds & Merges, The Role of Commercial Development in Preventing War in Outer Space, 25 Jurimetrics: Journal of Law, Science & Technology 130 (1985).
U.S. Air Force, Space Handbook (C. Cochran, D. Gorman, & J. Dumoulin eds. 1985).
F. Winter, Prelude to the Space Age: The Rocket Societies: 1924–1940 (1983).

2

The International Law of Outer Space: Basic Principles

INTRODUCTION

The activities of nations in outer space are governed by public international law. Although this is not a text in international law, it may be worthwhile to review some basic principles before going on to the specific rules applying to outer space. For more on these topics see Restatement (Third) of Foreign Relations Law, ss 101–103 (1987).

International law may stem from several sources. *Treaties* are the most obvious—relevant treaties may be directly concerned with outer space (for example, the Outer Space Treaty of 1967) or may address outer space activity as part of more general subject matter (for example, the Limited Test Ban Treaty of 1963). But although treaties seem satisfyingly legalistic because they are signed, formal documents, they are not the only source of international law. *Custom* (the first, and still an important, source of international law) is another; by custom international law commentators mean general principles of international law not embodied in any treaty but observed, and considered binding, by civilized nations.

These are the authoritative sources of international law. In applying international law, courts, legal advisors, and other decision-makers and counselors often rely on other sources as well. Frequently, writings by respected commentators are given great weight. And resolutions of the United Nations General Assembly, although not legally binding themselves, are often regarded as expressing a consensus view on the extent or nature of a rule.

One problem that many people, lawyers and non-lawyers alike, have with international law is that to them it does not seem like law at all because it lacks the sort of well-established enforcement mechanisms that domestic legal systems have. Violate the domestic law of a nation (say, by refusing to pay your taxes) and you will find yourself subject to all sorts of clearly defined penalties (like jail) meted out by officials and organizations whose responsibility it is to punish lawbreakers. The consequences of violating international law, on the other hand, are far less clear—especially as the violators are likely to be sovereign nations, equipped with armies, air forces, etc., and hence hard to arrest. What punishments can be inflicted—via opinions of the World Court, resolutions of the United Nations General Assembly, or economic sanctions inflicted by the world community—are often of largely symbolic importance.

The enforcement problem has led some people to argue that there is no such thing as international law, and others to avoid the issue entirely by focusing on "black letter" legal issues while asserting that enforcement is a different problem altogether. Neither approach is helpful—nations in fact obey international law far more often than they violate it, and it is important to understand why they do so. On the other hand, nations will violate even well-established rules of international law when the stakes are high enough, and it is important to understand why they do that as well. For more on this topic *see* Reisman, Sanctions and Enforcement, in International Law Essays 381 (M. McDougal & W. M. Reisman eds. 1981). The discussion of those two issues could easily make up a book of its own, but following are a few observations that may be helpful in understanding why international law exists even in the absence of effective enforcement, and why and how problems will arise and nations will violate it from time to time.

1. *A system of international law is in the general interest of all nations.* While nations may (and inevitably do) disagree over specific rules, the global nature of modern business, the frequency of travel, and the tendency of problems of all kinds to extend across borders all require that governments deal with one another constantly. Without some framework for such dealings, enormous amounts of time would be wasted, and important problems would go unaddressed. Thus, it is in their interest for nations to agree on a set of rules that make cooperation easier and prevent the need for repetitive bargaining over ground rules and expected behavior. In some areas, such as public health, the framework for international cooperation has been quite successful. In other areas—where the benefits of cooperation are not as visible, or where the stakes or the incentives to cheat are higher—it has been less so. For a discussion of how mutual interests can lead to cooperation even in the absence of external enforcement mechanisms, or among adversaries, *see* R. Axelrod, The Evolution of Cooperation (1984). *See also* Kronman, Contract Law and the State of Nature, 1 Journal of Law Economics & Organization 5 (1985).

2. *Cooperation among nations is imperfect.* While it may be in the interest of nations to cooperate on many matters, the process for doing so involves human beings, who tend to make mistakes and act irrationally. Even where parties are acting rationally and in good faith, it is possible for both parties to an agreement to have different ideas about what was meant; in addition, no agreement can clearly address all possible situations that may arise. What is more, parties may find that it is necessary to address some topics ambiguously in order to accomplish an agreement on others.

The treaty mechanism attempts to deal with these problems by memorializing an agreement in concrete form in order to minimize confusion about what was agreed to; various rules of interpretation, etc. exist in order to deal (with varying degrees of success) with ambiguities and unforeseen situations in a way that is consistent with the intent of the parties. This set of rules, and the agreements to which they are applied, constitutes the most "legalistic" part of international law. The same sorts of problems arise with regard to customary law when it is confronted with new or unforeseen problems. In both contexts, the community of international legal scholars plays an unusually important role—because very few international legal disputes are ever decided by authoritative bodies, the consensus among scholars is often the closest thing to a judicial opinion that can be achieved. For an example of the interpretive process at work, *see* the Memorandum of the Department of State's Legal Adviser reproduced in Chapter 6.

Not all international legal problems stem from good faith disagreements, of course: there are also problems resulting from bad faith and dishonesty. With regard to these, matters of power and interest are of more importance than questions of law. However, nations that violate international law too often or too blatantly do pay a price in terms of isolation from the world community, reduced foreign trade and investment, etc. To avoid these consequences, nations that violate international law will almost always attempt to argue that their actions are in fact lawful; criticism of such arguments is an important role for international scholars, and (since such criticism can affect the way other nations respond to the violation) may in fact be regarded as part of the enforcement system of international law.

Generally, the guidelines on interpreting treaties resemble those used to interpret contracts, statutes, and other legal documents. Interpreters look to the language, the intent of the parties, and general rules of construction in interpreting international agreements. Naturally there is often room for dispute, and sometimes dispute where little room exists, as the discussion in Chapter 4 concerning the ABM Treaty demonstrates. *See generally* Restatement (Third) of Foreign Relations Law, §§ 111–113 (1987) (discussing treaty interpretation and related issues).

3. *Nations guard their own interests*. Any nation will violate the norms of international law when the stakes are high enough. How high the stakes have to be depends on the nation, the likely consequences of violation, etc. What is more, the absence of any authoritative decision-making body means that nations who wish to challenge a norm not embodied in a treaty must often violate it in order to do so. *See* Reisman, International Incidents: Introduction to a New Genre in the Study of International Law, 10 Yale Journal of International Law 1 (1984).

THE ROOTS OF SPACE LAW

The international law of outer space springs from several sources, most notably maritime law (represented in the fact that a nation's jurisdiction extends to any spacecraft under its flag), air law (which provides perspective on overflight issues and other related problems), and the legal aspirations embodied in the

United Nations, which was still quite new when the Space Age began. To provide some of the flavor of those issues, a few excerpts from writings on each of these subjects follow. As you read them, you might keep these questions in mind: (1) How reasonable are analogies between the laws governing other fields, like aviation and shipping, and outer space law; and (2) What are some other ways of developing law that will respond to the practical needs of space industries and activities in a way that serves global needs?

AIR AND SEA LAW: RULES GOVERNING OVERFLIGHT AND TERRITORIAL WATERS

The principal sources of air and sea law are custom, embodied in the practice of nations over time; the 1944 Chicago Convention (governing air law); and the 1958 Convention on the High Seas (governing sea law). In addition, the Law of the Sea Treaty sets out a number of rules but cannot at this point be regarded as an authoritative source of sea law as many major sea powers, including the United States, have refused to ratify it. The Chicago Convention sets out rules on safety, training, certification and registration and declares the existence of national sovereignty over air space. The High Seas Convention does the same for the oceans, providing that national jurisdiction follows a vessel wherever it goes, delimiting the extent of territorial waters, and setting rules as to safety, etc. These topics are discussed further in Chapter 8.

DeSaussure, Maritime and Space Law, Comparisons and Contrasts (An Oceanic View of Space Transport), 9 Journal of Space Law 93 (1981)

Few realized, when the first Echo satellites were launched in the early sixties, the dramatic way in which communications satellites would fill the skies. Nor did they realize how crowded the geostationary orbit would become and how great the need would be for international regulation. The first satellite to operate in geostationary orbit was Syncom 2, which was launched in 1963. Between one hundred and ten and one hundred and twenty satellites now occupy that orbit. From one-quarter to one-half of them are functioning. A recent NASA study concluded that by the year 2000 there would be a tenfold increase in the international demand for communications satellite circuits.

The emergence of a transportation system in space, particularly a reusable system, will promote the same exponential growth in the carriage of cargo, and in human activity. How will it grow? Will it be by each nation regulating its own transport systems independently, by commonly agreed upon standards and practices, or by a new international agreement regulating space transportation?

The answer lies partially in the degree to which the most technologically advanced states believe it to their advantage to work out internationally accepted practices for their space operations. The U.S. will have the Space Shuttle, the USSR their Salyut-Soyuz-Progress system, and France has Ariane. The Soviets are reported to be planning a reusable spacecraft. China and Japan are trying to develop more sophisticated launch systems. The answer also lies in how much priority the U.N. Committee on Peaceful Uses of Outer Space (COPUOS) assigns to the formulation of an international regime for space transportation.

* * *

Whether a space transport regime takes shape through unilateral practice, concordant national rules, or multilateral treaty, the maritime and aviation regimes for international carriage are important references. Commerce at sea and in the air space has flourished by virtue of stable, internationally accepted rules, which regulate navigation. The purpose of this paper is to examine a few of the more important aspects of the maritime analogy for their applicability to space transport.

* * *

There has always been a need accurately to define aircraft and ships and to distinguish them from other objects which transit or occupy their respective spheres. A similar need will emerge to define those spacecraft used for transport and to distinguish them from other space objects.

The International Regulations for Preventing Collisions at Sea define vessels to include, "every description of water craft, including non-displacement craft and seaplanes, used or capable of being used *as a means of transportation* on water" (emphasis added). The INMARSAT Agreement defines the term *ship* as meaning "a vessel of any type operating in the marine environment (including *inter alia*) hydrofoil boats, air-cushion vehicles, submersibles, floating craft and platforms not permanently moored."

It seems that as space travel grows, we will need to establish a common definition of transport spacecraft or space vehicles. That is, spacecraft used primarily to carry goods or personnel from one place to another. It will also be necessary to distinguish them legally from other varieties of space objects. The key to defining the spacecraft for transport is navigability. Does it have the *primary* function of transportation? Is is designed basically for space flight rather than parking in a particular orbit? The fact that many satellites have internal rocket propulsion enabling ground controllers to reposition them in space does not endow them with navigability. Communications, remote sensing, weather, and reconnaissance satellites are not designed or intended for navigation in space. They carry only sufficient fuel to reach the desired orbit and perform their mission. INTELSAT satellites have been recently supplied just enough extra fuel to kick them out of the geostationary orbit at the end of their useful life. A true navigable craft however has enough fuel to traverse space and return to a particular place or orbit.

Navigate has been defined as steering or directing a ship or aircraft. Of all the space objects, it will be the spacecraft for the transport [of people and goods] that most nearly resembles ships and aircraft. How should they be described to differentiate them from other space objects? Webster's dictionary defines *spaceship* as "a rocket propelled vehicle for 'travel' in outer space." One might have preferred a definition which substituted the word *transport* for the word *travel*. It is broader. Transport clearly embraces cargo as well as human beings. If one adopts the test of navigability as described above, then a spaceship could be manned or unmanned. The U.S. Space Shuttle clearly qualifies as a spaceship. So, I submit, do the unmanned transport orbiters being developed by the Soviet Union, Japan, and the European Space Agency.

Once having defined the spacecraft for transport as a spaceship, its classification according to ownership and use becomes important. At sea, different rights and responsibilities flow from a ship's legal characterization. There are warships, other governmental vessels (with a subclassification depending on commercial or public use) and private merchant vessels. At the highest end of the scale is the warship. It enjoys complete sovereign immunity from foreign jurisdiction and has certain extraordinary rights on the high seas. Other governmental ships used for public purposes also have sovereign immunity, but not the special rights of warships. In most states, governmental ships used for private purposes no longer have immunity and, of course, neither do private merchant vessels. It has been necessary to classify vessels in order that all who use the high seas, or participate in maritime activity, understand the respective rights and duties of each type of vessel.

* * *

Should spaceships from the very outset be separately classified according to mission? In my view the answer is yes. Unlike other space objects, spaceships are instrumentalities of navigation. Those ships operated by the military for military purposes, like their counterparts at sea and in the airspace, need particular identification. Following along the lines of the Law of the Sea draft, military spaceships should be defined as those which are under military control and whose ground controller or space crew are subject to military discipline.

* * *

Without delving into the subject of maritime liens, it is apparent that to vest spaceships with the same quality of responsibility attributed to vessels could have dramatic implications. A spaceship, part of whose payload is carried under contract with a private corporation, which lands on foreign soil through intent or accident, might find itself the subject of an *in rem* proceeding brought by a foreign claimant. Nothing in the Liability Convention prevents judicial recourse by private claimants even where that Convention might apply.

As spaceship operations become routine and the options they afford for commercial venture more advanced, their legal status becomes a matter of great importance and so will the analogy to public and private vessels.

The Right of Passage

Defining and classifying spaceships is only the start. Greater activity in space means more launches, which could mean more launch sites, or, as they will certainly come to be known, spaceports. There are probably fewer than a dozen separate launch facilities in the world today. ... Eight nations have expressed interest in establishing new international launch facilities. Five of these are equatorial states. Will there be, before the end of the century, an explosion in space transport to equal that generated by air transport in the last quarter of a century? It is certainly a distinct possibility.

The rapid proliferation of communications satellites may prove an interesting precedent. Technological advances and economies of increased spacecraft production will provide direct access to space for more and more states. This will require the greater traverse of foreign airspace.

Many writers have addressed the problem of innocent passage through airspace to the [realm of] outer space and have suggested the development of a rule comparable to the right of innocent passage for ships through territorial waters. I prefer the analogy to the landlocked state. That state has no access to the unique environment of the oceans except through the territory of another. It has no sea coast. In the same manner, states who develop the capability to launch vehicles in space may not be geographically positioned to do so without transiting foreign airspace. They too are landlocked. The Geneva Convention on the High Seas provides that landlocked states shall enjoy the right of free access to the sea and equal treatment in ports. A similar right is needed in space. It is at the outset of an active transport era that the greatest opportunity lies for the establishment of the principle of free transit to and from space. This right is less likely to emerge from the practice of states than by bilateral or multilateral agreement. Free transit through foreign air space would reduce the urgency to set forth a geometric border between air and outer space.

The Exercise of Exceptional Jurisdiction

The maneuverability of the spaceship will make it possible to approach and inspect alien satellites which are suspected of being a threat to the earth environment. It will be possible to remove the satellite to a high energy orbit, neutralize it, or control its return to earth. The Outer Space Treaty makes it clear, however, that the registry state retains jurisdiction and control over its space objects and undoubtedly this is meant to be exclusive. Any exercise of control over a foreign satellite would have to be on exceptional grounds.

The corollary to the principle of the freedom of the high seas is that all states normally have a duty not to interfere with foreign ships outside territorial waters. In a famous admiralty case a British Judge declared,

> In places where no local authority exists, where the subjects of all States meet upon a footing of entire equality and independence, no one State, or any of its subjects, has a right to assume or exercise authority over the subjects of another.

However, there is an exception to this principle of freedom of navigation. This exception involves the high seas right of approach. It is the right of any warship to approach a suspicious merchant vessel and verify her nationality and ensure she is not violating international law relating to fishing, submarine cable, and piracy, as well as misuse of the national flag. If the crew of the warship decides to board the suspect vessel, there is a heavy burden to substantiate the suspicion. Failure to do so makes the flag state liable for the loss, damage or delay to the merchant ship. Whether a similar exceptional right of approach will develop in space rests on the good will of spacefaring states. Both the fall to earth of the Soviet Cosmos 954, breaking up over an area of northwest Canada about the size of Austria, and the uncontrolled return to earth of parts of the eighty-five ton Skylab, illustrate the risks involved in deteriorating satellites.

* * *

Safety of Navigation

It might appear at present that space voyages will not require the type of uniform rules for navigation that govern at sea. Space is limitless, the public oceans are not. Sea transit will far exceed space transit for decades to come. The risk of actual collision between two manned craft in space is minimal when compared to shipwreck and collision. However, the near earth and geostationary orbits will be the most frequented areas of space and as noted above there is already overcrowding in the latter orbit. As fully reusable launch systems transport large payloads from earth to low orbit and return them, and as reusable space-based orbital vehicles develop to transfer men and equipment from low to high orbit and to land on celestial bodies, uniform rules will be required to govern landing, docking, staging and inter-orbital transfers. It is an inexorable certainty that a navigation code will become as necessary for space safety as it became for traffic safety in the air space and at sea.

International rules of navigation applicable to high seas navigation have been enacted by virtually all maritime states, and amendments are usually made simultaneously by international agreement. The International Regulations for Preventing Collisions at Sea of 1972 are a part of these rules. They set forth measures to avoid collision, for maneuvering, towing, warning and distress signals. There have been a number of conferences between maritime states called for the purpose of standardizing rules for structural safety, fire and life saving equipment, and the use of radio and other navigational aids.

Whether an international space traffic code emerges through the concordant national legislation and regulation of the principal spacefaring nations, or through formal international agreement, it will become imperative to achieve uniform standards and practices. The Scientific and Technical Subcommittee working group on the use of nuclear power sources should be invited to consider the larger question of spaceship safety and to set forth suggested rules for uniform practices.

Status of Crew and Others

The Outer Space Treaty provides that all parties should regard astronauts as envoys of mankind. What special protection this affords, apart from providing all possible assistance in the event of accidents, distress, or emergency, is not clear. It is true they will not be treated as diplomatic envoys with governmental immunity. If they are forced down in foreign territory or on the high seas they will have a temporary diplomatic immunity until they are returned to their own country. To what further protection are they entitled?

Seamen have long been regarded as wards of the admiralty. They are endowed special protection not accorded fellow workers on land, except by statute. Two ancient rights which they have acquired through practice and usage are the rights to maintenance and cure, and to a seaworthy vessel. Whenever a seaman becomes disabled during a sea voyage through sickness or accident, he is entitled to the continuance of his wages until restored to health, and to all medical expenses. ... The seaworthiness of the vessel is also an absolute requirement, and due diligence and care by the shipowner provides no exoneration for him if the court finds the vessel was not fit for whatever reason or cause. The concordant practice of maritime states has shaped a very strong maritime law in this regard.

Will states whose nationals sojourn into space develop a similar set of protective rules for all spacefarers? I think it likely. Land-based rules for employer liability are shaped around work done "in the course of employment" and "within the scope of authority." On-duty and off-duty status and whether the aggrieved employee was deviating from his normal route or performance become important considerations. In space, as at sea, the spacefarer should be comprehensively protected without regard to any of the legal considerations. Whether his travel into space is for only a few days, or for weeks or months, he has a high risk occupation and his duty period, like that of the sailor, is for twenty-four hours each day. Consider how appropriate to the future spaceman is the language used by Justice Rutledge in describing the sailor's life. He wrote:

> ... Unlike men employed in service on land, the seaman, when he finishes his day's work, is neither relieved of obligations to his employer nor wholly free to dispose of his leisure as he sees fit. Of necessity, during the voyage he must eat, drink, lodge and divert himself within the confines of the ship. In short, during the period of his

> tenure the vessel is not merely his place of employment; it is the framework of his existence. For that reason, among others, his employer's responsibility for maintenance and cure extends beyond injuries sustained because of, or while engaged in activities required by his employment.

Federated States such as the U.S. should exercise legislative and judicial jurisdiction only at the national level. In the United States, a Federal Wrongful Death statute for outer space is needed which would preempt state law. It might be useful to extend the Death on the High Seas Act to activities in space. The Federal Tort Claims Act should be amended to specifically cover acts in space and further revised to include claims based on strict liability for governmental conduct. As long duration voyages and habitation in space become a reality, the relatively short statute of limitations for judicial recourse needs to be extended. In admiralty, by constitutional grant, Federal jurisdiction is exclusive (with certain exceptions not relevant here). A uniform national space law is preferable to the hodgepodge of tort law applicable to aviation mishaps where state as well as Federal law is relevant. The working conditions of space crews and other personnel, minimum health standards for space flight, the provision for medical care and the extent of disciplinary authority of the mission and flight commanders must be defined only at the national and international levels.

On March 7, 1980, NASA promulgated rules on the authority of the shuttle commander in flight. Shuttle commanders have been given authority similar to that held by sea captains and aircraft commanders including the power to arrest and to use force if necessary to maintain law and order in orbit. The rules also establish a chain of command on board the shuttle in the event the commander or his copilot are incapacitated. The new rules recognize that the shuttle will carry non-NASA scientists, engineers and foreign researchers.

* * *

Salvage

Some years ago, Mr. Page, the President of the General Electric Missiles and Space Division, predicted there would be a million satellites in earth orbit in the 1990s. As time slips by, this prediction seems much too optimistic. There are approximately 4,500 space objects orbiting earth at the present, about one fourth of which are functioning. Although he may have miscalculated, the problems implicit in his prediction will be generated. The U.N. Secretariat's Report states it will "almost certainly" be necessary in time to sweep non-geostationary orbits planned for extremely large structures, such as those planned for in space construction of solar power satellites. It is also true that much of the artifacts brought into space will be salvageable. The Astronaut Agreement does not address the question of salvage. It does provide that, upon request, objects launched into space found outside the launching state shall be returned or held at that state's disposal. It also provides for the recoupment of expenses.

At sea, every recovery of lost or abandoned property, or property at peril, is subject to a salvage claim. Though limited to the value of the property saved, the award can be far in excess of expenses. This depends on the hazards involved, the value of the property at risk, the value of the property saved, and other considerations.

* * *

It is not too early for an appropriate body such as COPUOS to consider whether a salvage law for space will require an international agreement comparable, perhaps, to the Brussels Salvage Convention of 1910, or whether it can best develop through national law and practice.

Protection of the Environment

Already mentioned in connection with the need to control earth-threatening satellites such as unstable nuclear powered satellites is the need for a safety regime in space. However, the question of back and forward contamination in space is much broader than just the exercise of any right of removal of deleterious space objects. A special set of safety standards, uniformly adopted throughout the community of spacefaring states, is extremely desirable.

The Geneva High Seas Convention provides that every state shall draw up regulations to prevent pollution of the seas by the discharge of oil from ships and shall take measures to prevent pollution from the dumping of radio-active waste. ... While it should be superficially attractive to transfer concepts being developed in this most vital area from the sea to space, it probably is not a useful analogy. First, because the law of the sea is itself in a state of confusion on this subject, and second, because the distinctive characteristics of the two environments call for entirely different approaches to the problem. Nevertheless, there must be a uniformity of approach, common standards and an international repository for the communication and exchange of all information on space contamination.

Conclusion

While the law of the sea does not represent an infallible guide to the developing law of space, space lawyers need some appreciation of maritime law. They need to become conversant with basic admiralty rules to vessel identification, navigation, management of ships, rights of seamen, the law of salvage, limitations of liability and governmental activity in sea commerce. It is with this perspective that they can compare the two environments, consider the relevance of maritime law, and select for adoption for space transport those legal principles which have proved beneficial to commerce on the oceans.

I. White, Decision-Making for Space: Law and Politics in Air, Sea and Outer Space 179 *et seq.* (1971)

Are Air, Sea and Outer Space Legal Problems Comparable?

In Part II, selected international air and sea law rules were determined. The question now posed is this: Are the selected air and sea legal problems or problem areas and certain outer space legal problems comparable and are similar interests or preconditions perceived by national decision-makers in the three environments?

* * *

Access and Passage

Freedom of the high seas is a universally recognized general principle of international law. Coastal and landlocked states alike have a right of freedom of access and use. Subject to certain limitations, there is also a right of innocent passage through territorial seas.

The aircraft of all states may fly freely over the high seas. However, innocent passage through territorial airspace is not a general right in international air law. Passage through territorial airspace must be authorized either by a contractual arrangement or by special permission. ... National decision-makers seem to accept the principle of the freedom of the high seas primarily to protect or enhance an economic interest. Sharing the high seas for such uses as, for example, communications, transportation, or fishing is functional to both primarily exclusive and inclusive interests of a majority of states. Apparently the same finding applies in general to the airspace above the high seas.

It is clear, on the basis of the discussions of sovereignty and delimitation and resources in this chapter, that national decision-makers perceive an inclusive interest in outer space similar to that perceived in the high seas and the airspace over the high seas. A number of statements have been cited in which outer space, at least by implication, is characterized as a *res communis*. In fact, the [1967 Outer Space Treaty], and several of the General Assembly resolutions which it in effect supersedes, provide for free access and joint usage of outer space and celestial bodies.

* * *

Recognition of an inclusive interest in the right of access and usage came almost with the orbiting of the first satellites. ... In 1958, Antonio Ambrosini, an Italian delegate in the First Committee, stated that in his opinion the lack of protest by overflown states amounted to a "tacit and unanimous agreement." The Yugoslavian delegate, Dobrivoje Vidic, in discussing freedom of movement in outer space, observed that:

> [B]y virtue of its very nature, and of the fact that penetration into it has been brought about by the common efforts and progress of the whole of mankind, no less so than by virtue of the fact that its abuse could be fatal to the whole world, outer space can only be regarded as *res communis*.

* * *

Costa Rica's Gonzalo Ortiz Martin stated the claim from the viewpoint of the small states: "If our small country had the economic and scientific means to shoot off satellites that might be placed in orbit, no one would dare to deny us the right to do so, as no one has denied the right to do so to those who have led the scientific race."

* * *

Apparently, the two fundamental reasons for insisting that ships and planes have a nationality and/or be registered are to assign responsibility and to afford protection. ... [I]t was found that the state of nationality and registration is held responsible for enforcing, for example, safety standards and crew licensing requirements. Claims made concerning liability, nationality and registration, and safety are obviously interrelated. As there is no general enforcement agency, assigning responsibility to the flag state is likely to be the most effective means of enforcing what are essentially the protective rules concerning liability and safety. This same observation seems to apply to spacecraft.

* * *

The most important point, however, is that the types of injuries, damages, and losses being protected against are identically the same surface damages concerning which states have made claims and counterclaims in international air law. The only change seems to be the specific vehicle which is being protected against. That is, at its present state of development the spacecraft may warrant treatment as extrahazardous as, for example, did aircraft in the early days of aviation and so do nuclear ships now.

* * *

Safety is, of course, also a concern in spacecraft. Currently this is mainly a concern for surface damages which might result from spacecraft. However, there must increasingly be concern for personnel safety in manned vehicles, a point emphasized by the unfortunate tragedy in January 1967, involving the flight crew for the first Apollo flight.

Control over spacecraft is a primary concern in connection with surface damages. For example, the use of destruct devices gives launching states a degree of control over the hazards associated with launching a spacecraft. Another type of control is associated with both safety and interference, the ability to recover or destroy spacecraft which have completed their mission and simply clutter space. A more limited kind of control is the ability to free frequencies by "turning off" spacecraft when their mission is completed.

Concern for the safety of personnel in spacecraft has been limited since only highly specialized and well qualified crews have been permitted to man spacecraft. When and if spacecraft come to be used as common carriers, the concern will, of course, become more general and it might be expected that comprehensive rules comparable to those for air and sea common carriers will be agreed upon.

The problems of liability, nationality and registration, and safety, then, are quite comparable to the same problems in the air and sea environments. A smaller number of vehicles is currently involved in space and the hazards are generally greater. Otherwise the interests are basically if not identically the same and even the preliminary and tentative steps toward solution are comparable to those which have proved functional in the other two environments.

*   *   *

The problems of sovereignty and delimitation in air, sea, and outer space, while not identical, are reasonably comparable. And the fundamental interests which decision-makers perceive in relation to these problems appear to be identical. While particular air and sea rules are not directly applicable, the problems are comparable enough that knowing what the preconditions of rule acceptance are in air and sea law will be helpful in formulating acceptable rules for the space environment.

*   *   *

Of all problems or problem areas, liability, nationality and registration, and safety are most comparable in the three environments. Solutions to these kinds of problems are necessary and functional to peaceful and routine interaction in all environments. And while there are now far fewer spacecraft than ships and planes, and while the hazards from spacecraft are generally greater, the fundamental interests which decision-makers seek to protect and/or enhance are identical. In fact, the preliminary and tentative steps taken toward solving these problems are comparable to those which have proved successful in the air and sea environments.

Center for Research of Air and Space Law, Space Activities and Emerging International Law 161 *et seq.* (N. Matte, Ed. 1984)

1. Early Aeronautical Law

a. The "Freedom of the Air" Doctrine

During the period from the time of the first manned aircraft to the conclusion of the Paris Convention of 1919, a number of differing opinions have been advanced as to the principles governing the status of the airspace. Theories range from the "freedom of the air," as advanced by the French jurist Fauchille, to the theory of "absolute sovereignty," which later became the generally accepted doctrine. Interposed was the notion of limited freedom of the air (above a territorial air zone) and a variety of compromise theories.

Of particular interest is the freedom theory advanced by Fauchille who argued that there were no presupposed sovereign rights over the air-space above a state.

* * *

Although this approach was widely accepted, state practice evolved towards the theory of sovereignty over air-space. The main reason for this was one of security. World War I and the growing use of aircraft for belligerent purposes showed that such a need did in fact exist. As a consequence, the theory of exclusive and complete sovereignty of the subjacent state over its air-space gained general acceptance.

b. The Legal Status of Air-space

In practice, a number of European states had implicitly recognized the theory of sovereignty over air-space before the First World War.

* * *

Various European states, such as France, the United Kingdom, Austria-Hungary and Germany passed national laws or regulations for the control of overflight over their territory.

* * *

In practice, therefore, the theory of freedom of the air had already been rejected before the First World War, not only for reasons of security, but also for reasons of safety, practicability, and doubtless also with a view to economic aspects of aviation.

c. The Regulation of Commercial Activities

States soon realized that the theory of sovereignty over air-space was of greater economic and commercial advantage than the theory of absolute freedom. In particular the granting of rights for landing could be made on a reciprocal basis or dependent on the grant of other favourable economic concessions. As a consequence, the Paris Convention of 1919 provided in Article XV that "every contracting State may make conditional on its prior authorization the establishment of international airways and the creation and operation of regular international air navigation routes with or without landing on its territory." Similarly, articles XXXVI and XXVIII of the Conventions provided that air commerce could only be carried out with the special permission of each state overflown. Thus, commercial freedom was excluded from the Paris Convention of 1919 and, at that early state of aviation, left to regulation by bilateral agreements between states. This approach for the carrying out of air commerce was confirmed in the Chicago Convention of 1944 and continues to apply today. The legal regime of air commerce is therefore predicated on the general acceptance of the theory of absolute and exclusive sovereignty over air-space.

2. The Air-Space over the High Seas

a. The Chicago Convention and the Law of the Sea

According to Article 12 of the Chicago Convention, the rules applicable to flight over the high seas shall be those established according to the Convention. This provision refers to the rule-making power of the Council of the International Civil Aviation Organization (which is established by the Convention), with respect to the enactment of annexes to the Convention. The powers of the ICAO Council with respect to rule-making for the High Seas have been called "real international legislative powers."

*   *   *

b. The Legal Status of the Air-space Above the High Seas

It is generally recognized that the legal status of the air-space above the high seas is analogous to that of the high seas itself. The basic principle is that of *res omnium communis*. No state may exercise sovereign rights over any portion either of the high seas or of the air-space above. Furthermore, all states enjoy the freedom of use and navigation on and above the high seas.

*   *   *

c. The Regulation of Commercial Activities

The rule of freedom of air navigation above the high seas is applicable to both commercial and non-commercial services. As a consequence, the ICAO Council is empowered to make rules for the operation of both above the high seas.

* * *

3. The Relevance for the International Regulation of Space Activities

a. The Relevance of Analogies in General

The relevance of analogies taken from general international law in relation to the notions and concepts of space law has been the subject of much discussion. While it may be argued that such analogies have insufficient common ground to permit valid conclusions, it appears more meritorious to consider analogous notions and concepts as an auxiliary means of interpreting the legal status of outer space. The Outer Space Treaty has, after all, been drafted in the context of international legal instruments as well as general public international law. It must therefore be presumed that there is, in certain respects, a catena of notions which justifies a comparison between the concepts applicable to outer space with those of other environments.

b. Relevance for the Legal Status of Outer Space, the Moon and other Celestial Bodies

A number of notions and concepts of laws applicable to Antarctica, as contained in the Treaty of 1959, are of immediate relevance to the law of outer space. First, the freedom of scientific investigation provided for Antarctica served to inspire the negotiators and drafters of the Outer Space Treaty. By examining state conduct with regard to Antarctica in view of the Treaty and how it had been interpreted, this may assist in clarifying the exact meaning of the principle of freedom of use and exploration of outer space as established in the Outer Space Treaty. The freedom of exploration and use can be regarded as an extension of the earlier freedom established under the Antarctic Treaty. Similarly, the demilitarized status of Antarctica as provided under the Antarctic Treaty has clearly been the basis for the partly demilitarized status of outer space under the Outer Space Treaty and also for the totally demilitarized status of the moon and other celestial bodies under the Moon Treaty. Nevertheless, issues relating to claims of sovereignty regarding Antarctica have received quite different consideration and treatment as compared with outer space.

The concept developed in early aeronautical law regarding freedom of use has the greatest similarity with existing space law. However, if one considers the factors leading to the decline of the freedom of the air doctrine, the present status of outer space, the moon and other celestial bodies, may change when economic, military or other advantages induce states to lay claim on certain parts of outer space. A similar conclusion may be drawn from the evolution of freedoms in the law of the sea. As to the status of the air-space above the high seas, the freedom of use and of navigation may be compared with that prevailing presently in outer space. However, there is no single body responsible for regulating the freedom of use and navigation of outer space, as the International Civil Aviation Organization does for the air-space above the high seas. This may change, particularly if space transportation activities increase in the future to such an extent that regulation by an international body would become a necessity.

* * *

c. The Regulation of Commercial Activities

A comparison with the Antarctic Treaty and the legal status of Antarctica lends support to the conclusion that commercial activities in outer space are fully consistent with its legal status. This finding is corroborated by Article VI of the Outer Space Treaty which countenances space activities in outer space under the supervision of state authorities. Commercial activities in outer space can thus be considered fully consistent with the freedom of use and exploration of outer space. A similar analogy can be drawn with the legal status of the air-space above the high seas, as well as with the status of air-space under the doctrine of the freedom of the air in early aeronautical law. The conduct of commercial activities was considered legal, whether carried out by commercial enterprises or by state bodies or other non-commercial entities. However, a major difference is that the Outer Space Treaty, as well as the Moon Treaty, contains express safeguards to ensure that commercial activities carried out by non-governmental entities are supervised to ensure that they act in accordance with both treaties.

NOTES

1. Nations on the high seas have in the past established temporary exclusion zones, barring vessels of other countries from particular areas of the ocean during military maneuvers. They have also established permanent zones of limited access on and over the high seas—for example, Air Defense Identification Zones stretching hundreds of miles beyond U.S. territorial waters, or exclusion zones around U.S. offshore radar installations (the so-called Texas towers facilities). *See, e.g.*, 14 C.F.R. §§ 99.1 *et seq.* (1988) (Air Defense Identification Zones). Might nations establish similar "keep out zones" around space facilities? Some have made such proposals: *see* Schwetje, Protecting Space Assets: A Legal

Analysis of "Keep Out Zones," 15 Journal of Space Law 131 (1987). As you read the following chapters, with their discussion of treaty restrictions on military activity and treaty guarantees of equal access to space, you might consider whether such zones would be legal under international law, as well as whether they would contribute to stability or suspicion.

2. Spacecraft must expend considerable energy to make significant alterations in course—so much so that their ability to change path is very limited once they are in flight. In this respect they are very different from ships and aircraft. How might this affect notions of freedom of space, or the ability of nations to deny other nations access to some areas of space?

3. How much do astronauts really resemble seamen? While it is true that they must spend extended periods confined in their vessels, astronauts (unlike most seamen) are highly educated professionals who have chosen their careers in preference to many (often more lucrative) alternatives in order to have the opportunity to fly in space. This may change with time, of course, but until it does, proposals to model law governing the treatment of astronauts on that relating to seamen may be inappropriate in many respects. Seamen have traditionally received great protection from Admiralty courts because they have been presumed to be lacking in formal education (and hence easily bilked) while specialized in occupation (and hence unable to change jobs readily). *See* G. Gilmore & C. Black, The Law of Admiralty (2d ed. 1975) at 272 *et seq.*

4. While many specifics of the space environment differ from those of the air and sea environments, there are many similarities as well. One is that all three have very important potential for both military and economic uses; another is that many of their resources are not consumed by use—for example, ships do not "use up" the ocean by passing over it, and satellites do not "use up" outer space by passing through it. Of course, some unusual locations depart from this statement: some narrow straits impose limits on the ability of traffic to pass through them, while some orbits (chiefly the geosynchronous orbit) have limited capacity and no satisfactory substitutes. For a discussion of how rules regarding ocean navigation and fishing might provide models for an international regime governing space activity, *see* Reynolds & Merges, The Role of Commercial Development in Preventing War in Outer Space, 25 Jurimetrics: Journal of Law, Science, & Technology 130 (1985).

UN EFFORTS AND ASPIRATIONS

The 1967 Outer Space Treaty discussed in the next chapter did not appear all at once, but was the result of an evolutionary process in which the United Nations General Assembly, various scholars, and special negotiating committees took part. The following excerpt from an article by Myres McDougal and Leon Lipson, two Yale professors who were leading figures in the early evolution of space law, provides some perspective on the way in which that happened.

McDougal & Lipson, Perspectives for a Law of Outer Space, 52 American Journal of International Law 407 (1958)

The patterns of use of outer space will of course unfold in a context of conditions which even now, we suggest, can be identified as being certain to affect the law of space as it develops over the years. Some of these conditions are common to many areas of human conduct and interest; some are, in a measure, peculiar to the use of outer space. Those that are noted below are intended to be illustrative only.

One condition of first importance is the extraordinary interdependence of scientific, military, commercial, and other objectives that may be advanced by the same activities in space. Scientific observations on cosmic radiation may some day serve as a basis for the development of radiological warfare. A television relay station may be capable of use to interfere with communications instead of facilitating them. A reconnaissance satellite may be made to yield important economic benefits from services to meteorology. Geodetic observations made by celestial mechanicians may improve the accuracy of intercontinental ballistic missiles by making international maps more precise. For an orbiting satellite carrying a nuclear warhead, it is perhaps not easy to imagine an immediate commercial or scientific use that would not be served more efficiently by some other device, but it would be rash to say that no such use is possible.

By reason of this interdependence, it may be difficult to apply some well-known legal techniques—prohibition, conditional permission, allocation of responsibility for damage, regulation, and so on—on the basis of a supposed predominant category of use. If we want certain benefits we may have to accept certain risks. Especially in the preliminary exploratory stage (which may last for generations), we may have to stress those aspects of legal control that permit and encourage development, while doing our best to measure the size of the risk to which we are being exposed. This does not mean that we ought to reject the possibility of reaching, or at least talking about, an agreement to outlaw certain uses of outer space, for the marginal gains to be expected from those uses may not be worth their price; but it does imply that it will not be easy to define "peaceful purposes" or "scientific purposes" without risk of hampering activities that have multiple uses.

* * *

It is characteristic of the loose and primitive structure of the contemporary earth arena that many of the nation-state officials who will make the decisions are the same who will be making the claims. The difference in role may make a significant difference in self-image, in the length of the time range for the calculation of interest, and in recognition of need for reciprocity; but the objectives of their action as decision-makers will of course in measure overlap the objectives of their action as claimants. They will be, and they will take care to appear to be, concerned for the attainment of some modicum of security: the indefinite postponement of unacceptably destructive violence, the achievement of some stability of expectation as to modes of exercising effective power, the maintenance of public order against hostile or reckless or capricious threats. They will wish to conserve the potentially vast resources of space for the production of the largest net gain in all values, though their respective preferences for the distribution of the gain may be mutually incompatible. They will probably concur in demanding that as many of the uses of outer space as are capable of being shared without serious inconvenience be kept available for sharing. They will seek in various ways to adapt to their existing power objectives the potentialities opened up by the access to the new resource environment; the brave new worlds will not for some time suffice to redress or greatly distort the balance of the old.

* * *

A durable agreement by explicit international convention on anything like a code of law for outer space is not, in our opinion, something now to be expected or desired. One may indeed expect with rather more confidence a series of agreements, gradually arrived at, on particular subjects, such as the continuation of the International Geophysical Year; the exchange of certain types of information, such as tracking data and some signaling codes, beyond present levels; the use or abstention from use of certain radio frequencies; and the coordination of launching schedules. Particular projects, like the establishment of television or radio relay satellites, might (in addition to whatever economic or scientific merits they possess) serve to test the possibilities of broad international cooperation more fruitfully than conferences on "the law of space." Agreement might be reached—not necessarily by the execution of formal documents—to abstain from the pollution of space by shrapnel or other "junk," which might otherwise be thrown up in an attempt to impede the flight of hostile satellites or hostile communications; such agreement would probably depend on the assurance either that other means of averting the danger from the hostile activities were adequate or that the activities did not present a danger sufficiently great to justify the pollution.

The modes of reaching such agreements cannot now be charted with any precision. Some agreements may be explicit and formal; some may be simply a consensus achieved by the gradual accretion of custom from repeated instances of mutual toleration. Some may be bilateral, others trilateral or multilateral; some may be within the framework of the United Nations, others within some other existing organization or some machinery yet to be set up. Their details and sequence must, like much else in an indeterminate universe, depend on the order of experience in space as well as on the changing political context.

We recognize, however, that the order of that experience will in turn be affected by expectations which decision-making officials in the nation states possessing space capabilities entertain as to the space plans of others and by the reactions and attitudes of the earth community. In order to help allay anxieties about the possible weapons uses of space satellites and to help lay a foundation for closer cooperation in peaceful activities in space for common benefit—a cooperation from which an adequate and effective customary or conventional law might eventually emerge—the following suggestions might even now be considered by responsible officials:

(1) It was suggested in this JOURNAL early in 1957 that each state about to launch a satellite could register its intent to do so with an international agency, filing a flight plan and a description of certain characteristics of the satellite, such as load, weight, and size. This could be combined with willingness to submit to international inspection, to assure that the payload conforms to the description filed. This suggestion could be put into practice by any state, regardless of the agreement of any other state; but the decision to do so might well be affected by the communicated willingness of other launching states to agree to corresponding measures.

(2) Agreement might be reached to abstain from the launching of satellites fitted with nuclear or other explosive warheads. Such an agreement probably would have to be contingent on the availability of effective prelaunching inspection of the type that is illustrated by the first proposal above. Whether it should or could be coupled with an agreement on the prohibition of the use of intercontinental ballistic missiles, and whether it should or could be considered as part of a possible general agreement on nuclear or universal disarmament, are matters of strategy, community and national, dependent upon the course of many variables.

(3) States possessing the capability of launching satellites might offer to launch certain types of satellites on behalf of, or even as trustee for, the United Nations. The launching state could retain responsibility for the launching operation, preserving control over the security of its rocketry; the United Nations would decide upon the purpose of the flight, determine the payload, design the instrumentation, and finance the construction of the satellite and its contents. The necessary United Nations decisions could be made by an arm of the United Nations, or authority to make them could be delegated to the launching state or conceivably to some other agent. The existence of such "trust satellites" would not necessarily preclude national satellites with similar or identical functions.

NOTES

1. Many of the suggestions made in this early article were ultimately embodied in later treaties—registration of spacecraft, for example, was provided for in the Outer Space Treaty and the Registration Convention, both discussed *infra*, while the Outer Space Treaty also bars the orbiting of nuclear weapons. The "trust satellite" concept never really came off (although the use of international organizations, such as INTELSAT, to administer some satellite functions bears

some resemblance to the scheme envisioned by McDougal and Lipson); it survives, however, via repeated suggestions that the United Nations orbit its own reconnaissance satellites for the purpose of assisting in arms control verification and keeping an eye on potential trouble spots. So far the superpowers, who retain a monopoly on sophisticated satellite reconnaissance facilities, have resisted such efforts. That monopoly is eroding, however, and as the technology becomes cheaper and more readily available we are likely to see other nations, as well as private entities such as news networks and possibly even arms control groups, orbiting their own reconnaissance satellites. Perhaps once such enterprises are obviously imminent, the superpowers will be more friendly to the acquisition of such capabilities by the United Nations. Other potential concerns mentioned by McDougal and Lipson, such as pollution of the space environment by orbital debris, are of growing importance but have not yet been addressed. For more on these topics, see Chapter 5.

2. Shortly after the publication of the above article, the United Nations organized COPUOS, the Committee on the Peaceful Uses of Outer Space. That committee was until the mid-1970s the most important single source of international law relating to space activities. Since the mid-1970s, however, COPUOS has fallen victim to the increased factionalism of the United Nations, and its effectiveness has been diminished. For a discussion of the origins of COPUOS, see Jessup & Taubenfeld, The United Nations Ad Hoc Committee on the Peaceful Uses of Outer Space, 53 American Journal of International Law 877 (1959). One interesting question is whether the traditional technique of arriving at multilateral treaties through COPUOS, which is based on consensus, is still an effective method. *See generally* Gennady Danilenko, Outer Space and the Multilateral Treaty-Making Process, 4 High Technology Law Journal 217 (1990); Eilene Galloway, Consensus Decisionmaking by the United Nations Committee on the Peaceful Uses of Outer Space, 7 Journal of Space Law 3 (1979). Does the end of the Cold War help or hurt the prospects for reaching consensus in large multinational bodies?

3

Early Treaties Governing Activity in Outer Space

The previous chapter outlined the basic principles of general international law governing activities in outer space. With this chapter we will begin to discuss the important early treaties providing more specific legal norms for nations' space activities: the Limited Test Ban Treaty of 1963 and the Outer Space Treaty of 1967. The process by which these were developed was a gradual one: the Limited Test Ban Treaty, which among other things prohibits nuclear explosions in outer space, was the result of discussions begun in the early 1950s, and of international pressure orchestrated by Nobel laureate Linus Pauling, who created worldwide concern regarding the hazards of nuclear fallout from atmospheric tests; the Outer Space Treaty developed as the result of a lengthy process of negotiation and refinement of language in the UN's Committee on the Peaceful Uses of Outer Space (COPUOS), the creation of which is described in the article by Jessup & Taubenfeld, *infra*. The negotiations leading up to the Outer Space Treaty are discussed at considerable length in Dembling & Arons, also *infra;* what becomes apparent from even a superficial reading of that piece is that one reason for the lengthy negotiation was that many of the nations involved lacked a clear sense of their interests—both future and contemporaneous—in any particular space regime. Most of the participants had only hazy ideas of what would come to pass in the space field, and how it would affect their own destinies, and even the United States and the Soviet Union seemed far more willing than usual to be persuaded by one another on most issues.

Paradoxically, this comparative lack of specifically self-serving goals may be one reason why the Outer Space Treaty is viewed with such respect—approaching reverence at times—by so many. Having been arrived at by nations operating behind an almost Rawlsian veil of ignorance, the Treaty can be said to represent a more general view of the interests of humanity instead of being merely a compromise among interested parties, shaped primarily by the balance of power. How close this perception is to the facts is another matter: the United States, at least, was quite concerned about maintaining its ability to operate intelligence-gathering satellites and hence was not unclear about its interests in that regard.

Still, excepting such relatively narrow issues, it probably *is* the case that the participants in the processes leading up to the Outer Space Treaty took a broader and longer view than is typical in international negotiations, and that the Outer Space Treaty does gain in legitimacy as a result. Whether this circumstance can be duplicated in the future is unclear, but worth bearing in mind as a goal. This climate of reasonably objective, if not actually altruistic, debate can be contrasted with the much more self-interested debate over the Moon Treaty, described in the next chapter; the dismal results of the latter process speak for themselves.

The following excerpt from an article by Jessup & Taubenfeld describes the formation of the Committee on the Peaceful Uses of Outer Space. The COPUOS continues to be the United Nations' primary space-related body, although its influence has diminished along with that of the UN in general in recent years. As the article demonstrates, however, the key issues later dealt with in the Outer Space Treaty were identified early on.

Jessup & Taubenfeld, The United Nations *Ad Hoc* Committee on the Peaceful Uses of Outer Space, 53 American Journal of International Law 877 (1959)

After formal inaugural meetings, the *Ad Hoc* Committee formed a Technical and a Legal Committee. By mid-June these two Committees had completed their reports and the Secretariat had also prepared a Report on "the activities and resources of the United Nations, of its specialized agencies and of other international bodies related to the peaceful uses of outer space."

The members of the Technical Committee took as a basis working papers circulated by the United States and Italy on the scientific possibilities of use of outer space and on the activities and resources of the United Nations and the specialized agencies in the field of outer space. The Technical Committee also received oral comments from persons connected with such organizations as UNESCO, the World Meteorological Organization (WMO), the International Telecommunications Union (ITU) and the International Civil Aviation Organization (ICAO). There was general agreement that the exploration of space was "a task vast enough to enlist the talents of scientists of all nations." Just as there was no way to limit the definition of "atmosphere" for WMO's weather purposes, there was general agreement that outer space was scientifically indivisible. The usefulness of participation in space efforts by nations lacking launching capabilities, particularly through such voluntary cooperative scientific arrangements as the IGY's successor in this field, COSPAR (Committee on Space Research), was emphasized and the United States was complimented several times on its offers to permit scientists from other nations to design experiments to be carried out by U.S.-launched satellites. The stress was on cooperative efforts of the COSPAR type, though it was generally agreed that, when the research stage was passed, functioning intergovernmental arrangements of the WMO, ITU type were probably essential. The possibility of international launching sites was also raised.

The Technical Committee's report was approved by the *Ad Hoc* Committee on June 18, and became part of the report to the General Assembly. This report stressed that to make best use of all available talent and, in some cases, due to the costs involved, "space activities, scientific and technological ... even more than ... astronomy ... inherently ignore national boundaries. Space activities must to a large extent be an effort of Planet Earth as a whole." The connection between military activities and space research with its hampering effect on exchange of information was also noted, but it was concluded that the development of space vehicles has reached the point in several countries where it was a question of engineering only, not of science.

* * *

The Legal Committee proceeded with the aid of working papers and drafts submitted by the United States and Mexico. Its report was also approved by the *Ad Hoc* Committee on June 18. The Committee observed that the provisions of the United Nations Charter and of the Statute of the International Court of Justice are, as a matter of principle, not limited in their operation to the confines of the Earth. It was agreed that not enough was now known about the actual and prospective uses of outer space to make a comprehensive code practicable or desirable, but that it was necessary to take "timely, constructive action and to make the law of space responsive to the facts of space."

> It was unanimously recognized that the principles and procedures developed ... to govern the use of such areas as the air space and the sea deserved attentive study for possible fruitful analogies ... [though] outer space activities were distinguished by many specific factual conditions ... that would render many of its legal problems unique.

Among legal problems susceptible of priority treatment, it was suggested, is the broad one of freedom of outer space for exploration and use. Here, the Legal Committee, in mentioning the flight of space vehicles "over" countries during the IGY, suggested that

> with this practice, there may have been initiated the recognition or establishment of a generally accepted rule to the effect that, in principle, outer space is, on conditions of equality, freely available for exploration and use by all in accordance with existing or future international law or agreements.

Other priority problems included by the Committee were liability for injury or damage caused by space vehicles, including the need for machinery to determine liability and ensure payment of compensation. Here, the Committee suggested the compulsory submission to the International Court of Justice of disputes between states as to liability, and considered relevant ICAO experience with respect to the 1952 Convention on Damage Caused by Foreign Aircraft to Third Parties on the Surface. Allocation of radio frequencies, termination of transmissions, avoidance of interference between space vehicles and aircraft, identification and registration of vehicles through markings, call signs and orbit and transit characteristics, registration and co-ordination of launchings, and re-entry and landing problems were also considered of current importance.

Problems which may be ignored for the present, as either too remote from the point of view of technological development or because activities can be conducted without their resolution, were thought to include the determination of precise limits between airspace and outer space, the provision of regulations against contamination of outer space or from outer space, the promulgation of rules covering sovereignty, exploration, settlement and exploration of celestial bodies and rules for the avoidance of interference among space vehicles. As is obvious, the report avoids commitments on several problems which many feel are more imminent than the Committee is cautiously willing to acknowledge.

Thus, the Committee stressed at most a role of co-ordination or the promotion of co-operation for the United Nations, though the Swedish representative expressed fears that there might be an increasing gap between the great forward surge of space activities and the efforts of the United Nations to promote the use of space for the benefit of all mankind, unless immediate action was taken within the United Nations. Others, however, insisted on "modest proposals" to meet only the most pressing needs. The *Ad Hoc* Committee's caution is quite understandable in the political circumstances, since in any actual program for promoting the peaceful uses of outer space, the non-participation of the Soviet Union would rob the effort of much of its value. It was the obvious hope that if Soviet nonparticipation were due to any misunderstanding of the Committee's functions, that difficulty would be overcome. Of course, if, as a matter of national policy, the Soviet Union does not wish to co-operate in this effort, it will find pretexts for further refusals.

The Committee finished its work and approved its Report to the General Assembly on June 25, 1959.

THE LIMITED TEST BAN TREATY

Although a number of Resolutions by the United Nations General Assembly had previously called upon the space powers to refrain from military uses of outer space, the first legally binding document renouncing any such uses was the Limited Test Ban Treaty of 1963. That treaty, signed by the United States, the Soviet Union, and Great Britain (other nuclear powers, such as France and

China, have not signed the treaty), forbids the explosion of nuclear devices in the oceans, the atmosphere, or in outer space. The text of the treaty itself follows; we will then discuss some of the issues raised by the treaty.

Multilateral Treaty Banning Nuclear Weapon Tests in the Atmosphere, in Outer Space and Under Water, *entered into force* Oct. 10, 1963, 14 U.S.T. 1313, 480 U.N.T.S. 43

Done at Moscow August 5, 1963;

Ratification advised by the Senate of the United States of America September 24, 1963;

Ratified by the President of the United States of America October 7, 1963;

Ratifications of the Governments of the United States of America, the United Kingdom of Great Britain and Northern Ireland, and the Union of Soviet Socialist Republics deposited with the same Governments at Washington, London, and Moscow October 10, 1963;

Proclaimed by the President of the United States of America October 10, 1963;

Entered into force October 10, 1963.

The Governments of the United States of America, the United Kingdom of Great Britain and Northern Ireland, and the Union of Soviet Socialist Republics, hereinafter referred to as the "Original Parties,"

Proclaiming as their principal aim the speediest possible achievement of an agreement on general and complete disarmament under strict international control in accordance with the objectives of the United Nations which would put an end to the armaments race and eliminate the incentive to the production and testing of all kinds of weapons, including nuclear weapons.

Seeking to achieve the discontinuance of all test explosions of nuclear weapons for all time, determined to continue negotiations to this end, and desiring to put an end to the contamination of man's environment by radioactive substances,

Have agreed as follows:

Article I

1. Each of the Parties to this Treaty undertakes to prohibit, to prevent, and not to carry out any nuclear weapon test explosion, or any other nuclear explosion, at any place under its jurisdiction or control:

(a) in the atmosphere; beyond its limits, including outer space; or underwater, including territorial waters or high seas; or

(b) in any other environment if such explosion causes radioactive debris to be present outside the territorial limits of the State under whose jurisdiction or control such explosion is conducted. It is understood in this connection that the provisions of this subparagraph are without prejudice to the conclusion of a treaty resulting in the permanent banning of all nuclear test explosions, including all such explosions underground, the conclusion of which, as the Parties have stated in the Preamble to this Treaty, they seek to achieve.

2. Each of the Parties to this Treaty undertakes furthermore to refrain from causing, encouraging, or in any way participating in, the carrying out of any nuclear weapon test explosion, or any other nuclear explosion, anywhere which would take place in any of the environments described, or have the effect referred to, in paragraph 1 of this Article.

Article II

1. Any Party may propose amendments to this Treaty. The text of any proposed amendment shall be submitted to the Depositary Governments which shall circulate it to all Parties to this Treaty. Thereafter, if requested to do so by one-third or more of the Parties, the Depositary Governments shall convene a conference, to which they shall invite all the Parties, to consider such amendment.

2. Any amendment to this Treaty must be approved by a majority of the votes of all the Parties to this Treaty, including the votes of all of the Original Parties. The amendment shall enter into force for all Parties upon the deposit of instruments of ratification by a majority of all the Parties, including the instruments of ratification of all of the Original Parties.

Article III

1. This Treaty shall be open to all States for signature. Any State which does not sign this Treaty before its entry into force in accordance with paragraph 3 of this Article may accede to it at any time.

2. This Treaty shall be subject to ratification by signatory States, instruments of ratification and instruments of access shall be deposited with the Governments of the Original Parties—the United States of America, the United Kingdom of Great Britain and Northern Ireland, and the Union of Soviet Socialist Republics—which are hereby designated the Depositary Governments.

3. This Treaty shall enter into force after its ratification by all the Original Parties and the deposit of their instruments of ratification.

4. For States whose instruments of ratification or accession are deposited subsequent to the entry into force of this Treaty, it shall enter into force on the date of the deposit of their instruments of ratification or accession.

5. The Depositary Governments shall promptly inform all signatory and acceding States of the date of each signature, the date of deposit of each instrument of ratification of and accession to this Treaty, the date of its entry into force, and the date of receipt of any requests for conferences or other notices.

6. This Treaty shall be registered by the Depositary Governments pursuant to Article 102 of the Charter of the United Nations.

Article IV

This Treaty shall be of unlimited duration.

Each Party shall in exercising its national sovereignty have the right to withdraw from the Treaty if it decides that extraordinary events, related to the subject matter of this Treaty, have jeopardized the supreme interests of its country. It shall give notice of such withdrawal to all other Parties to the Treaty three months in advance.

Article V

This Treaty, of which the English and Russian texts are equally authentic, shall be deposited in the archives of the Depositary Governments. Duly certified copies of this Treaty shall be transmitted by the Depositary Governments to the Governments of the signatory and acceding States.

DONE in triplicate at the city of Moscow the fifth day of August, one thousand nine hundred and sixty-three.

NOTE

The primary goal of the Limited Test Ban Treaty was not arms control, but the prevention of global nuclear contamination; even the provisions barring nuclear explosions in outer space were designed to protect against problems stemming from radiation and electromagnetic pulse—experiments with high-altitude nuclear explosions having caused damage to orbiting satellites and to electronic devices on the surface at great distances, as well as having created an artificial radiation belt that persisted for some years. The Test Ban Treaty can thus be viewed primarily as an environmental agreement rather than a military one, though it was, of course, of military importance.

Matte, The Treaty Banning Nuclear Weapons Tests in the Atmosphere, in Outer Space and Under Water (10 October 1963) and the Peaceful Uses of Outer Space, 9 Annals of Air & Space Law 391 (1984)

The atomic bombs which were dropped on two Japanese cities in 1945 may have ended the Second World War, but they left behind an awesome legacy which continues to haunt the "peace" that subsequently ensued. Two politically antagonistic powers, the U.S.A. and the U.S.S.R., which joined together to fight a common enemy (Hitler) for a limited purpose and short duration, continued their rivalry and mistrust of each other once the war had ended. The Soviet Union having gained veto power in, and permanent membership of, the U.N. Security Council, secured its long desired political parity with the West. However, American mastery over nuclear technology resulted in vast resources being invested by the U.S.S.R. in order to catch up. The intensity of its competition with the West was the cause of the U.S.S.R.'s rejection of the Baruch Plan of 1946 with respect to the prohibition of the manufacture of nuclear weapons and the internationalism of control of this new technology. There was undoubtedly a lack of mutual trust between the super powers and the plan, while it "seemed to be in conformity with the requirements of technical reality, ... did not adequately reflect the conditions of political reality."

On August 29, 1949, the U.S.S.R. tested its first atomic bomb and thus entered the nuclear race. However, its efforts were not totally devoted to the development of nuclear technology but also to long-range rockets and jet propulsion in order to perfect the delivery system for its nuclear weapons. It was a refined version of the German V-2 rockets which helped the U.S.S.R. to launch Sputnik I on October 4, 1957. Every opportunity was taken to publicize, both at home and abroad, the U.S.S.R.'s superiority in the field of science and technology and in military capability. Up until the launch of Sputnik I, the U.S. had been the unrivaled world leader in technological achievements and military capabilities and, although assured that Sputnik I was of limited military significance, the U.S. President felt that something had to be done to follow the Soviet success. Civilian and military technological capabilities were thus geared to catch up with the Russians, especially after the launch failure of the Vanguard I satellite on December 6, 1957. Von Braun, with his army ballistic missile team, was given only three months by the then Secretary of Defense to convert a Redstone missile into a Jupiter C launcher, which finally brought the U.S. into the space age on January 31, 1958 when its first satellite, Explorer I, was launched.

*   *   *

Having acquired the necessary technology to build their first nuclear weapons, the U.S. and the U.S.S.R. continued the further development and testing of their nuclear arsenals. Between 1945 and 1958, the U.S. conducted 139 nuclear tests in the atmosphere and 18 under ground. The U.S.S.R. on the other hand conducted 55 similar tests, during the period between 1949 and 1958, all in the atmosphere. The extent of these tests caused serious concern not only with respect to the continued stockpiling of nuclear weapons but also about the adverse effects of radiation fall-out on the environment, as well as living beings. Already on December 3, 1955, the U.N. General Assembly had established the Scientific Committee on the Effects of Atomic Radiation, and at the London meeting of the Subcommittee on Disarmament the issue of banning nuclear tests dominated the discussions. However, while "the West argued that the establishment of a control system and the cessation of the production of fissionable materials for military purposes should precede any agreement to limit nuclear testing, the Soviets argued that a test ban was of such importance that it should be implemented immediately independent of any other disarmament measure and without control." France, which had not yet tested its nuclear weapons, did not share the views of the Western or Socialist powers and started to remove itself from the negotiations on disarmament, especially on the test ban issue. In 1958, the three nuclear powers—the U.S., the U.S.S.R., and the U.K.—convened a tripartite "Conference on the Discontinuation of Nuclear Weapons Tests" in Geneva. In 1962, the functions of the tripartite Conference were taken over by the U.N. Eighteen Nation Disarmament Committee's (ENDC's) "Subcommittee on a Treaty for the Discontinuation of Nuclear Weapons Tests." The U.N. Scientific Committee on the Effects of Atomic Radiation conducted studies and prepared two reports for submission to the General Assembly in 1958 and 1962. It concluded that nuclear tests might have serious adverse effects on the health of people exposed to nuclear radiation. In its 1962 report, the Committee emphasized that

> As there are no effective measures to prevent the occurrence of harmful effects of global radioactive contamination from nuclear explosions, the achievement of a final cessation of nuclear tests would benefit present and future generations of mankind.

However, the political realities of 1962 were such that "final cessation of nuclear tests" was not acceptable to the super powers. "Relations between the United States and the Soviet Union" as described by Barton and Weiler, "had been so dominated by cold war attitudes early in the era that comprehensive agreements would have been almost unthinkable."

President Kennedy was convinced that the space program should continue on the basis of strict competition with the U.S.S.R. since "he considered it essential to the national interest that the U.S. continue to develop the capabilities necessary for a full mastery of space and not pull back at a time when the U.S.S.R. was in the lead." The Cuban missile crisis obliged a more conciliatory attitude. The President was convinced that the only way to diffuse Cold War tensions was to develop areas of common interest with the U.S.S.R., "in a manner and scale that would involve meaningful movement towards a genuine rapprochement between the two countries." Specific areas of bilateral cooperation which were singled out under this policy of rapprochement and intensive negotiations with the U.S.S.R. resulted in

1. the 1962 Dryden Blagonravov agreement regarding scientific and research cooperation,
2. the 1963 "Hot Line" Agreement with respect to the establishment of a direct communications link between Moscow and Washington,
3. the 1963 bilateral understanding to support the U.N. General Assembly resolution on banning the placement of nuclear weapons in orbit around the Earth, and
4. the tripartite 1963 Treaty Banning Nuclear Weapons Tests in the Atmosphere, in Outer Space, and under water.

It was the policy of selective rapprochement which contributed to U.S. acceptance of the partial nuclear test ban when, at the 1963 Moscow trilateral talks, all the "efforts to agree on a comprehensive treaty foundered on the inspection issue. The American negotiators knew that the Senate would not consent to a comprehensive test ban treaty that did not provide more on-site inspections on Soviet soil than the Soviets would accept."

The Soviet Union's willingness to conclude a treaty on nuclear test bans doubtlessly stemmed from its ability to monitor compliance with such a treaty; it had already developed surveillance satellites of such a degree of precision that it could match the U.S.A.'s technology in this field. There was also a desire to develop cordial relations with the West, in the pursuit of a policy of peaceful coexistence, given that relations with its communist ally, China, were rapidly deteriorating.

3. The Provisions of the 1963 Treaty

(a) Aim

The principal aim of the three original parties to the Treaty, i.e. the U.S.A., the U.S.S.R. and the U.K., in negotiating this Treaty was the speediest possible achievement of an agreement on general and complete disarmament which would put an end to the armament race and eliminate the incentive to the production and testing of all kinds of weapons, including nuclear weapons, at all times. To achieve this aim, they declared their determination to continue negotiations in this regard and expressed their desire to put an end to the contamination of man's environment by radioactive substances. To what extent this determination and desire have been executed shall be assessed later in this paper.

(b) Application

The Treaty has only five articles. Article I, which contains the main prohibition against nuclear tests, provides that

> Each of the Parties to this Treaty undertakes to prohibit, to prevent, and not to carry out any nuclear weapon test explosion or any other nuclear explosion, at any place under its jurisdiction or control:
>
> (a) in the atmosphere; beyond its limits, including outer space; or under water, including territorial waters or high seas; or
>
> (b) in any other environment if such explosion causes radioactive debris to be present outside the territorial limits of the state under whose jurisdiction or control such explosion is conducted.

A careful reading of this provision shows that nuclear explosions are prohibited in all environments except underground tests carried out within the territorial limits of the parties to the Treaty. Moreover, underground tests which could cause radioactive debris to be present outside the territorial limits of the concerned state party are also prohibited.

It is interesting to note that the drafters of the Treaty "avoided the doctrinal question where outer space begins since the prohibition runs within the atmosphere and beyond its limits." In other words, the 1963 Treaty considers both air and outer space as a single medium for the purposes of prohibition of nuclear tests. This view has long been advocated by the writer who considers it only logical to speak of an aerospace continuum governed by the norms and the rules of aerospace law, than to draw artificial boundaries between the air space, on the one hand, and outer space on the other. The 1963 Treaty is very clear on the areas to which it applies, in contrast to the 1967 Outer Space Treaty which is silent in this respect.

The prohibition contained in the 1963 Treaty seems to apply to all nuclear tests carried out in outer space, irrespective of the distance of their test sites from the Earth, since there is no outer limit of outer space. Similarly, such prohibition would apply to nuclear tests conducted on celestial bodies, since they form part of outer space and testing could result in contamination. This interpretation seems to be in line with the description given in article I of the Treaty of all environments in which nuclear tests are prohibited.

During the Treaty negotiations, prohibition of nuclear tests in the atmosphere and in outer space was readily accepted by the U.S.S.R. as well as the U.S. and the U.K. because monitoring was considered to be relatively easy and feasible. No provision was included with respect to verification of compliance with the Treaty. It was generally understood that each party could monitor the nuclear tests of the other parties by national means of verification.

During the U.S. Senate hearings on the 1963 Treaty, various senators expressed concern about the possibility of conducting nuclear tests in deep space and thus avoiding detection by monitoring devices. Robert S. McNamara, the then U.S. Secretary of Defense, in response to these concerns, stated that:

> Multimegaton weapons development tests would have to be conducted more than 20 million miles from the earth—80 times as far away as the moon—if they were to have a good chance of escaping detection by a ground-based system. ...
>
> The United States on its own can deploy earth and solar satellite systems for detection of deep space nuclear explosions; ...
>
> While tests at extreme ranges are a technological possibility, they would involve years of preparation plus several months to a year of actual execution, and they could cost hundreds of millions of dollars per successful experiment.

He concluded that although "as a practical matter, illegal clandestine testing in deep space is not a reasonable proposition" one can properly protect against such testing.

The prohibition of explosions in the specified environments relates to "any ... nuclear explosion." This phrase was inserted in article I to cover "peace-time nuclear explosions that are not weapons tests." Hence, nuclear explosions for peaceful purposes are also prohibited under the terms of article I. However, it is important to note that the prohibition applies to "nuclear" tests and not to those of a conventional, chemical or biological nature, or to high energy laser beam weapons etc. States parties must not only prohibit, prevent and not carry out nuclear tests but must also refrain from causing, encouraging, or in any way participating in, the carrying out of any of the prohibited tests. It was because of the broad nature of this undertaking that the U.S. refused to transport French personnel to the French Polynesian islands at a time when France was planning to conduct nuclear tests there. This would have been to encourage and participate in an indirect way in the conduct of the prohibited nuclear tests, and thus a violation of U.S. Treaty obligations.

* * *

4. Analysis and Assessment

The major advantage of the 1963 Treaty is the establishment of essentially favorable conditions for the peaceful use of outer space relatively free from the adverse effects of electromagnetic pulse (EMP) which can be created by a nuclear explosion in the atmosphere or in outer space. In space, the pulse is not dissipated by the atmosphere and the effect of a single two-megaton bomb exploded 50 km or higher above the earth could affect circuits in nearly all satellites in geostationary orbit, 36,000 km above the earth. New military satellites are being protected against EMP but commercial satellites are still very much threatened. Although commercial satellite systems can be reinforced against EMP, it may not be possible to keep them within cost-effective limits. Similarly, the Treaty has contributed to the world's relative freedom from radioactive contamination, since the major nuclear powers (the U.S.A., the U.S.S.R. and the U.K.) stopped high altitude nuclear testing after signature of the 1963 Treaty. Since it has been widely accepted and its provisions consistently respected, there is every reason to believe that this situation will continue to prevail in the future.

Nonetheless, it should not be forgotten that the Treaty was merely the outcome of selective rapprochement between the super powers, which alienated at least two other major powers, i.e. France and the Peoples Republic of China. They never became parties to the Treaty. While France considered it to be of only "limited practical importance," China "called the Treaty a 'big fraud to fool the people of the world' and accused the Soviets of 'selling out the communist camp.' The Treaty thus intensified the Sino-Soviet split." Both countries continued their altitude nuclear tests; between 1963 and 1982, France conducted 41 and China 22 such tests, and thus diminished the significance of the Treaty's prohibitions.

While the desire of the original parties "to put an end to the contamination of man's environment by radioactive substances" seems, to a limited extent, to have been fulfilled, their objective to "put an end to the armaments race" continues to be elusive. After signature of the 1963 Treaty, the U.S.S.R., the U.S.A. and the U.K. stopped nuclear tests in the atmosphere, but intensified and accelerated underground explosions. The nuclear stock-pile (not counting the increased destructive power) of the three original parties, according to the most conservative estimates, increased from 26,439 nuclear warheads in 1965 to 42,310 in 1982. According to Hussain, who undertook a thorough study of the impact of weapons test restrictions on arms control and disarmament,

> the hopes for the Partial Test Ban Treaty (PTBT) were that it should slow the technological progress and innovation of nuclear weapons by making tests more difficult and more costly to conduct. ... It has not been particularly effective. Certainly, the PTBT has not slowed the rate of innovation of systems; on the contrary, most current technology has been derived from experimental underground nuclear test explosions following the Treaty's implementation.

Concern about the proliferation of nuclear weapons and the danger of nuclear war, resulted in adoption of the Treaty on the Non-Proliferation of Nuclear Weapons in 1968 (hereinafter referred to as the Non Proliferation Treaty). However, both Treaties have been ineffective in this respect. India, for example—a party to the 1963 Treaty—exploded underground its nuclear device in 1974 and other countries such as Israel, Pakistan, South Africa, South Korea, Brazil, Argentina, Taiwan, etc., in addition to France and China, have developed, and are developing their nuclear weapons' capability.

In retrospect, therefore, the expressed aims of the Treaty seem to have been nothing more than a political exercise to enhance and improve the image of the super powers. While the American President declared that the 1963 Treaty was "The first concrete result of 18 years of efforts by United States to impose limits on the nuclear arms race," it was clearly understood by the American government that the Treaty would "not reduce weapons in being or prevent their production" and moreover that "this Treaty is not in that direction—this treaty is not itself dealing with that problem."

NOTE

Aside from its obvious bars to nuclear explosions in outer space, the Test Ban Treaty would impose (among its signatories) a ban on nuclear fission as a means of space propulsion. As was mentioned in Chapter 1, the late 1950s and early 1960s saw considerable experimentation with ORION propulsion systems (so named because of the code name of the military project under which the experiments were conducted) that would use small atomic bombs as fuel. Those experiments were abandoned after the ratification of the Test Ban Treaty, whose plain ban on "any nuclear weapon test explosion *or any other nuclear explosion*" (emphasis added) in outer space does not admit of any loophole that would support nuclear explosive propulsion. For a short, clear history of the ORION project and how it was ended by the Treaty, *see* F. Dyson, Saturn by 1970, in Disturbing the Universe 107 (1979).

However, many nations with nuclear and space capabilities are not signatories to the Test Ban Treaty and would face no such impediment. As discussed *infra*, the Outer Space Treaty (to which many more nations are signatories) is not a bar to the use of nuclear explosives for propulsion so long as appropriate precautions against harm to other nations are observed. Although ORION technology is in some ways rather crude, its crudity may well be offset by its ability to deliver extremely powerful propulsion with relatively few new technical demands, allowing a new space power (such as a third world country not bound by the Test Ban Treaty) to perform impressive feats without developing the sophisticated technologies possessed by more experienced space powers.

Such uses by countries not signatories to the Test Ban Treaty might well lead to an amendment of the treaty to allow its signatories to do the same—or to pressure on nonsignatories to conform to its limits. This is a lesson worth bearing in mind with regard to arms control treaties in general: given the rapid spread of space technology, treaties binding only existing space powers—or worse yet, treaties binding only the United States and the Soviet Union—are likely to become obsolete, and may even become sources of conflict themselves. *See* the discussion regarding the ABM Treaty in Chapter 4, *infra*, for other examples of how overly narrow treaties may become subject to obsolescence.

THE OUTER SPACE TREATY OF 1967

Among all of the treaties relating to activity in outer space, the Outer Space Treaty of 1967 enjoys the broadest subscription and the highest regard. Although some of the regard for the Treaty may stem as much from sentiment as from any concrete benefits it provides—the Outer Space Treaty having been a triumph of consensus and forward-looking thought at a time when Cold War tensions and narrow nationalism were the norm—the Outer Space Treaty does accomplish a great deal. It provides limits on military activities beyond earth, prevents the extension of terrestrial sovereignty to space or celestial bodies, and establishes a framework for the further development of law governing activity in outer space, serving as a precursor and underpinning to such essential documents as the Liability Convention, the Rescue and Return Agreement, and so on. On the other hand, the Treaty leaves many important questions unanswered.

Multilateral Treaty on Principles Governing the Activities of States in the Exploration and Use of Outer Space, Including the Moon and Other Celestial Bodies, *entered into force* Oct. 10, 1967, 18 U.S.T. 2,410, 610 U.N.T.S. 205

Done at Washington, London, and Moscow January 27, 1967;

Ratification advised by the Senate of the United States of America April 25, 1967;

Ratified by the President of the United States of America May 24, 1967;

Ratification of the United States of America deposited at Washington, London, and Moscow October 10, 1967;

Proclaimed by the President of the United States of America October 10, 1967;

Entered into force October 10, 1967.

The States Parties to this Treaty,

Inspired by the greater prospects opening up before mankind as a result of man's entry into outer space,

Recognizing the common interest of all mankind in the progress of the exploration and use of outer space for peaceful purposes,

Believing that the exploration and use of outer space should be carried on for the benefit of all peoples irrespective of the degree of their economic or scientific development,

Desiring to contribute to broad international cooperation in the scientific as well as the legal aspects of the exploration and use of outer space for peaceful purposes,

Believing that such cooperation will contribute to the development of mutual understanding and to the strengthening of friendly relations between States and peoples,

Recalling resolution 1962 (XVIII), entitled "Declaration of Legal Principles Governing the Activities of States in the Exploration and Use of Outer Space," which was adopted unanimously by the United Nations General Assembly on 13 December 1963.

Recalling resolution 1884 (XVIII), calling upon States to refrain from placing in orbit around the Earth any objects carrying nuclear weapons or any other kinds of weapons of mass destruction or from installing such weapons on celestial bodies, which was adopted unanimously by the United Nations General Assembly on 17 October 1963,

Taking account of United Nations General Assembly resolution 110(II) of 3 November 1947, which condemned propaganda designed or likely to provoke or encourage any threat to the peace, breach of the peace or act of aggression, and considering that the aforementioned resolution is applicable to outer space,

Convinced that a Treaty on Principles Governing the Activities of States in the Exploration and Use of Outer Space, including the Moon and Other Celestial Bodies, will further the Purposes and Principles of the Charter of the United Nations,

Have agreed on the following:

Article I

The exploration and use of outer space, including the moon and other celestial bodies, shall be carried out for the benefit and in the interests of all countries, irrespective of their degree of economic or scientific development, and shall be the province of all mankind.

Outer space, including the moon and other celestial bodies, shall be free for exploration and use by all States without discrimination of any kind, on a basis of equality and in accordance with International law, and there shall be free access to all areas of celestial bodies.

There shall be freedom of scientific investigation in outer space, including the moon and other celestial bodies, and States shall facilitate and encourage international co-operation in such investigation.

Article II

Outer space, including the moon and other celestial bodies, is not subject to national appropriation by claim of sovereignty, by means of use or occupation, or by any other means.

Article III

States Parties to the Treaty shall carry on activities in the exploration and use of outer space, including the moon and other celestial bodies, in accordance with international law, including the Charter of the United Nations, in the interest of maintaining international peace and security and promoting international cooperation and understanding.

Article IV

States Parties to the Treaty undertake not to place in orbit around the Earth any objects carrying nuclear weapons or any other kinds of weapons of mass destruction, install such weapons on celestial bodies, or station such weapons in outer space in any other manner.

The moon and other celestial bodies shall be used by the States Parties to the Treaty exclusively for peaceful purposes. The establishment of military bases, installations and fortifications, the testing of any type of weapons and the conduct of military maneuvers on celestial bodies shall be forbidden. The use of military personnel for scientific research or for any other peaceful purposes shall not be prohibited. The use of any equipment or facility necessary for peaceful exploration of the moon and other celestial bodies shall also not be prohibited.

Article V

States Parties to the Treaty shall regard astronauts as envoys of mankind in outer space and shall render to them all possible assistance in the event of accident, distress, or emergency landing on the territory of another State Party or on the high seas. When astronauts make such a landing, they shall be safely and promptly returned to the State of registry of their space vehicle.

In carrying on activities in outer space and on celestial bodies, the astronauts of one State Party shall render all possible assistance to the astronauts of other States Parties.

States Parties to the Treaty shall immediately inform the other States Parties to the Treaty or the Secretary-General of the United Nations of any phenomena they discover in outer space, including the moon and other celestial bodies, which could constitute a danger to the life or health of astronauts.

Article VI

States Parties to the Treaty shall bear international responsibility for national activities in outer space, including the moon and other celestial bodies, whether such activities are carried on by governmental agencies or by non-governmental entities, and for assuring that national activities are carried out in conformity with the provisions set forth in the present Treaty. The activities of non-governmental entities in outer space, including the moon and other celestial bodies, shall require authorization and continuing supervision by the appropriate State Party to the Treaty. When activities are carried on in outer space, including the moon and other celestial bodies, by an international organization, responsibility for compliance with this Treaty shall be borne both by the International organization and by the States Parties to the Treaty participating in such organization.

Article VII

Each State Party to the Treaty that launches or procures the launching of an object into outer space, including the moon and other celestial bodies, and each State Party from whose territory or facility an object is launched, is internationally liable for damage to another State Party to the Treaty or to its natural or juridical persons by such object or its component parts on the Earth, in air space or in outer space, including the moon and other celestial bodies.

Article VIII

A State Party to the Treaty on whose registry an object launched into outer space is carried shall retain jurisdiction and control over such object, and over any personnel thereof, while in outer space or on a celestial body. Ownership of objects launched into outer space, including objects landed or constructed on a celestial body, and of their component parts, is not affected by their presence in outer space or on a celestial body or by their return to the Earth. Such objects or component parts found beyond the limits of the State Party to the Treaty on whose registry they are carried shall be returned to that State Party, which shall, upon request, furnish identifying data prior to their return.

Article IX

In the exploration and use of outer space, including the moon and other celestial bodies, States Parties to the Treaty shall be guided by the principle of cooperation and mutual assistance and shall conduct all their activities in outer space, including the moon and other celestial bodies, with due regard to the corresponding interests of all other States Parties to the Treaty. States Parties to the Treaty shall pursue studies of outer space, including the moon and other celestial bodies, and conduct exploration of them so as to avoid their harmful contamination and also adverse changes in the environment of the Earth resulting from the introduction of extraterrestrial matter and, where necessary, shall adopt appropriate measures for this purpose. If a State Party to the Treaty has reason to believe that an activity or experiment planned by it or its nationals in outer space, including the moon and other celestial bodies, would cause potentially harmful interference with activities of other States Parties in the peaceful exploration and use of outer space, including the moon and other celestial bodies, it shall undertake appropriate international consultations before proceeding with any such activity or experiment. A State Party to the Treaty which has reason to believe that an activity or experiment planned by another State Party in outer space, including the moon and other celestial bodies, would cause potentially harmful interference with activities in the peaceful exploration and use of outer space, including the moon and other celestial bodies, may request consultation concerning the activity or experiment.

Article X

In order to promote international co-operation in the exploration and use of outer space, including the moon and other celestial bodies, in conformity with the purposes of this Treaty, the States Parties to the Treaty shall consider on a basis of equality any requests by other States Parties to the Treaty to be afforded an opportunity to observe the flight of space objects launched by those States.

The nature of such an opportunity for observation and the conditions under which it could be afforded shall be determined by agreement between the States concerned.

Article XI

In order to promote international co-operation in the peaceful exploration and use of outer space, States Parties to the Treaty conducting activities in outer space, including the moon and other celestial bodies, agree to inform the Secretary-General of the United Nations as well as the public and the international scientific community, to the greatest extent feasible and practicable, of the nature, conduct, locations and results of such activities. On receiving the said information, the Secretary-General of the United Nations should be prepared to disseminate it immediately and effectively.

Article XII

All stations, installations, equipment and space vehicles on the moon and other celestial bodies shall be open to representatives of other States Parties to the Treaty on a basis of reciprocity. Such representatives shall give reasonable advance notice of a projected visit, in order that appropriate consultations may be held and that maximum precautions may be taken to assure safety and to avoid interference with normal operations in the facility to be visited.

Article XIII

The provisions of this Treaty shall apply to the activities of States Parties to the Treaty in the exploration and use of outer space, including the moon and other celestial bodies, whether such activities are carried on by a single State Party to the Treaty or jointly with other States, including cases where they are carried on within the framework of international inter-governmental organizations.

Any practical questions arising in connection with activities carried on by international inter-governmental organizations in the exploration and use of outer space, including the moon and other celestial bodies, shall be resolved by the States Parties to the Treaty either with the appropriate international organization or with one or more States members of that international organization, which are Parties to the Treaty.

Article XIV

1. This Treaty shall be open to all States for signature. Any State which does not sign this Treaty before its entry into force in accordance with paragraph 3 of this article may accede to it at any time.

2. This Treaty shall be subject to ratification by signatory States. Instruments of ratification and instruments of accession shall be deposited with the Governments of the United States of America, the United Kingdom of Great Britain and Northern Ireland and the Union of Soviet Socialist Republics, which are hereby designated the Depositary Governments.

3. This Treaty shall enter into force upon the deposit of instruments of ratification by the five Governments including the Governments designated as Depositary Governments under this Treaty.

4. For States whose instruments of ratification of accession are deposited subsequent to the entry into force of this Treaty, it shall enter into force on the date of the deposit of their instruments of ratification.

5. The Depositary Governments shall promptly inform all signatory and acceding States of the date of each signature, the date of deposit of each instrument of ratification of and accession to this Treaty, the date of its entry into force and other notices.

6. This Treaty shall be registered by the Depositary Government pursuant to Article 102 of the Charter of the United Nations.

Article XV

Any State Party to the Treaty may propose amendments to this Treaty. Amendments shall enter into force for each State Party to the Treaty accepting the amendments upon their acceptance by a majority of the States Parties to the Treaty and thereafter for each remaining State Party to the Treaty on the date of acceptance by it.

Article XVI

Any State Party to the Treaty may give notice of its withdrawal from the Treaty one year after its entry into force by written notification to the Depositary

Governments. Such withdrawal shall take effect one year from the date of receipt of this notification.

Article XVII

This Treaty, of which the English, Russian, French, Spanish and Chinese texts are equally authentic, shall be deposited in the archives of the Depositary Governments. Duly certified copies of this Treaty shall be transmitted by the Depositary Governments to the Governments of the signatory and acceding States.

NOTE

In order to understand the Outer Space Treaty's provisions, and the high regard in which it is held, it is important to know something of the process by which it was developed. The Treaty grew gradually out of a series of conferences on outer space law and a number of General Assembly declarations stating general principles for international activity in outer space. This process is chronicled in the article by Dembling & Arons from which the following, rather lengthy, excerpt comes. The excerpt sets out some of the history prior to the negotiations of the Fifth Legal Subcommittee that led to the Treaty's final form, as well as the key happenings at the Legal Subcommittee during those negotiations. Together, these pieces of history provide considerable information regarding the positions of different parties and the contemporaneous understanding of drafters regarding the Outer Space Treaty's key provisions. Paul Dembling was General Counsel for NASA when the article was written; he is now a partner at the Washington, D.C., office of Schnader, Harrison, Segal & Lewis.

Dembling & Arons, The Evolution of the Outer Space Treaty, 33 Journal of Air Law & Commerce 419 (1967)

An announcement was made on 8 December 1966, that agreement had been achieved among the members of the twenty-eight nation United Nations Outer Space Committee on the text of a treaty governing the activities of states in the exploration and use of outer space, the moon, and other celestial bodies. Approval of the Treaty was recommended unanimously by the Political Committee of the General Assembly on 17 December 1966. Two days later, the Treaty was endorsed by a unanimous vote of the General Assembly. Regardless of the total number of States which may sign and ratify the Treaty, a remarkable endeavor of great significance to international law and politics has reached fruition. Nations often in conflict with one another and adhering to widely divergent political philosophies have agreed on the first Treaty of general applicability governing activity in outer space.

The principles set forth in the Treaty had been advanced previously in the form of General Assembly resolutions, analogous international agreements, domestic legislation, statements by government officials, articles by scholars in the field and other expressions of views. However, agreement on the Treaty was primarily the product of the labors of the twenty-eight member Legal Subcommittee of the United Nations General Assembly's Committee on the Peaceful Uses of Outer Space during the Subcommittee's Fifth Session held in Geneva from 12 July to 4 August 1966, and in New York from 12 to 16 September 1966. The few issues requiring resolution subsequent to the conclusion of the Fifth Session were the subject of various bilateral negotiations and other discussions held during the Twenty-First Session of the General Assembly. Agreement was obtained on those issues shortly before the 8 December announcement that agreement on the Treaty as a whole had been reached.

* * *

Although the scope of the Treaty as eventually agreed upon includes both outer space and celestial bodies, an important aspect of the deliberations leading to agreement on the Treaty is the extent to which the nations and individuals involved were concerned, for the first time, with the formulation of realistic principles which might govern activity on celestial bodies in addition to, but as distinct from, outer space. This consideration of celestial bodies was based upon a body of thought and action that preceded the Fifth Session of the Legal Subcommittee. Even prior to 1960, a considerable amount of commentary existed on the question of "whether it is possible for a terrestrial nation-state to acquire sovereignty over all or part of a natural celestial body, and what would be required under existing law to make such a claim legally valid." Analogies were drawn to the manner in which nations had previously sought to exert legal claims to sovereignty over portions of the earth's surface, *e.g.*, through discovery, occupation, annexation and contiguity. Considerable discussion arose over the legal effect of the reported striking of the moon by an early Soviet satellite carrying the Soviet flag. However, the Soviet Union did not seek to exert any claim of sovereignty based upon this occurrence.

Although writers regarded the legal principles derived from exploration of the earth's surface as potentially applicable to exploration of celestial bodies, they did not consider such applicability to be desirable. The suggestion was made that "both public and private groups ... work towards formulating standards and procedures that will guarantee access by all to these resources on equitable terms and prevent interference by one state with scientific programs of another. As early as 1959, the American Bar Association passed a resolution declaring that in the common interest of mankind ... celestial bodies should not be subject to exclusive appropriation." A similar concern was evidenced at the official level. The

United Nations Ad Hoc Committee on the Peaceful Uses of Outer Space, created by the General Assembly in 1959, took the position in its report that "some form of international administration over celestial bodies might be adopted." In an address before the General Assembly in September 1960, President Eisenhower proposed that:

1. We agree that celestial bodies are not subject to national appropriation by any claims of sovereignty.
2. We agree that the nations of the world shall not engage in warlike activities on these bodies.
3. We agree, subject to verification, that no nation will put into orbit or station in outer space weapons of mass destruction. All launchings of spacecraft shall be verified by the United Nations.

* * *

That a sense of urgency had developed concerning the need for an international agreement on the exploration of the moon and other celestial bodies was made clear in a statement by President Lyndon B. Johnson in May 1966. He emphasized the need to "take action now ... to insure that explorations of the moon and other celestial bodies will be for peaceful purposes only" and "to be sure that our astronauts and those of other nations can freely conduct scientific investigations of the moon." The President suggested a treaty containing the following elements:

1. The moon and other celestial bodies should be free for exploration and use by all countries. No country should be permitted to advance a claim of sovereignty.
2. There should be freedom of scientific investigation, and all countries should cooperate in scientific activities relating to celestial bodies.
3. Studies should be made to avoid harmful contamination.
4. Astronauts of one country should give any necessary help to astronauts of another country.
5. No country should be permitted to station weapons of mass destruction on a celestial body. Weapons tests and military maneuvers should be forbidden.

Two days after the president made his statement, United States Ambassador to the United Nations Arthur J. Goldberg addressed a letter to Dr. Kurt Waldheim of Austria, the Chairman of the Committee on the Peaceful Uses of Outer Space, requesting an early convening of the Legal Subcommittee to consider the treaty proposed by President Johnson. ...

C. No Weapons of Mass Destruction Shall Be Placed in Orbit or on Celestial Bodies, or Stationed in Outer Space in any Other Manner; Celestial Bodies Shall Be Used Exclusively for Peaceful Purposes.

Article IV of the Treaty constitutes, as President Johnson stated, "the most important arms control development since the 1963 treaty banning nuclear testing in the atmosphere, in space and under water." Ambassador Goldberg explained to the Political Committee of the General Assembly that:

> This article restricts military activities in two ways:
>
> First, it contains an undertaking not to place in orbit around the earth, install on the moon or any other celestial body, or otherwise station in outer space nuclear or any other weapons of mass destruction.
>
> Second, it limits the use of the moon and other celestial bodies exclusively to peaceful purposes and expressly prohibits their use for establishing military bases, installations or fortifications, testing weapons of any kind, or conducting military maneuvers.

Article IV is taken from Articles 8 and 9 of the United States draft. Both the United States and Soviet drafts reflect principles previously agreed upon in the Nuclear Test Ban Treaty, and the United Nations Resolution 1884 (XVIII), adopted by the General Assembly by acclamation on 17 October 1963. In addition, the last sentence of Article 9 of the United States draft, which provided for the use of military personnel, facilities, or equipment for peaceful purposes, is quite similar to Article I, Paragraph 2, of the Antarctic Treaty. Ambassador Goldberg explained to the Legal Subcommittee that:

> As in the exploration of the Antarctic, man could not have penetrated outer space and survived in that hostile environment unless he had been able to draw upon the benefits of all research, civilian or military, involving both personnel and equipment. For any country engaging in space activity, military personnel, facilities and equipment played an indispensable role and would continue to be an essential part of future space programs.

Except for two differences of opinion, to be discussed below, agreement on the final text of Article IV was reached towards the conclusion of the Geneva portion of the Session on the basis of acceptance by the United States delegation of the language of the first sentence of Article IV of the Soviet draft, and acceptance by the Soviet delegation of the United States desire to include provision for the use of military personnel for peaceful purposes.

It is noteworthy that the prohibition contained in the first paragraph of Article IV applies to both outer space and celestial bodies, while the prohibition contained in the second paragraph of the article applies to celestial bodies only. Several of the delegations questioned the propriety of excluding outer space from the coverage of the second paragraph, the implication being that outer space may be used for nonpeaceful purposes. However, it is a well-known fact that both the United States and the Soviet Union have already launched satellites into outer space for military purposes, and examination of a ban on such satellites would have raised controversial issues presently within the purview of disarmament negotiations. The text of Article IV as agreed upon was conceded to be the most practical solution from the standpoint of expeditious conclusion of a treaty on outer space. As the Soviet delegate stated, "A number of questions would, of course, remain to be dealt with after the elaboration of the Treaty, particularly the use of outer space for exclusively peaceful purposes." In the interim, one might conclude that any military use of outer space must be restricted to nonaggressive purposes in view of Article III, which makes applicable international law including the Charter of the United Nations.

At the conclusion of the Geneva portion of the Session, two matters had not been resolved with respect to Article IV. The United States had previously revised and consolidated Articles 8 and 9 of its draft and tabled a single, two-paragraph article quite similar to Article IV of the Soviet draft. The second paragraph of the revised United States article read as follows:

> The moon and other celestial bodies shall be used exclusively for peaceful purposes. Establishment of military bases and fortifications, the testing of any type of weapons, and the conduct of military maneuvers shall be forbidden. The present Treaty does not prohibit the use of any types of personnel or equipment for scientific research or any other peaceful purpose.

The Soviet Union desired, however, to include the word "installations" between "military bases" and "fortifications," and to ban the use of "military equipment" on celestial bodies.

Concerning the use of the term "installations," the Soviet delegate did not articulate any reason for his delegation's insistence on the inclusion of that word, except for the possibility that the words "bases" and "fortifications," in Russian translation, do not adequately describe all of the possible structures that might be erected for military use on celestial bodies. The United States delegate argued that the term "installation" is too vague, possibly viewing "bases" and "fortifications" as terms connoting use of a facility for military purposes, while "installations" might be constructed to apply to a facility used for peaceful purposes but constructed or inhabited by military personnel.

A more important point of disagreement was whether military equipment may be used on celestial bodies. Notwithstanding the analogy in Article I, Paragraph

2, of the Antarctic Treaty, the Soviet delegate argued that "if the use of military equipment in outer space was allowed, the essence of the treaty would be distorted and a loophole would be created for evading one of its most fundamental provisions." The United States position was that "Equipment used in outer space had, in many cases, been developed through military research; that was the case, in particular, with respect to the rockets carrying astronauts; that could not, however, be said to constitute a violation of the principle of the peaceful uses of outer space." The British delegate added that "The fact that a piece of equipment owed its origin to military development should not preclude its use for peaceful purposes foreseen by the Treaty and apparent to all as peaceful purposes."

As a reading of the second paragraph of Article IV indicates, the United States and its supporters eventually agreed to accept the use of the term "installations," while the Soviet Union and its supporters agreed to the inclusion of a provision which would not ban the use of military equipment on celestial bodies. Emphasis on the purpose for which a piece of military equipment is to be used on a celestial body, as stressed by the United States delegate, is reflected in the last sentence of Article IV. Thus, aside from the first paragraph of Article IV, the placement of a weapon or other item of military equipment of any description on a celestial body would appear to be prohibited unless it can be demonstrated that the item of military equipment will be devoted solely to the peaceful exploration or use of the celestial body. Agreement of the final text of Article IV was not reached until after the close of the New York portion of the Session in the course of compromising the few outstanding differences which stood at that time as a barrier to announcement of the agreement on the treaty.

D. Assistance and Return of Astronauts and Space Vehicles; Notification of Dangerous Phenomena in Outer Space or on Celestial Bodies.

Article V of the Treaty contains two distinct though related principles. The first two paragraphs set forth the principle of assistance to and return of astronauts, a subject which had been discussed in considerable detail during previous sessions of the Legal Subcommittee. The text of the first two paragraphs of the Article was taken almost verbatim from Article IX of the Soviet draft which restated Paragraph 9 of the *Declaration of Legal Principles*. Although the principles of assistance and return are contained in Article 5 of the United States draft, the United States delegate acceded to the Soviet version subject to minor drafting changes. The third paragraph of Article V is derived from a proposal made by the United States during the Geneva portion of the Session as follows:

> A State conducting activities in outer space, including the moon and other celestial bodies, shall promptly notify the Secretary-General of the United Nations of any information relating to the physical safety of astronauts.

In the Working Group, this proposal was revised to require notification of either the other parties to the Treaty or the Secretary-General. It is noteworthy that the third paragraph of Article V constitutes a mandatory reporting obligation which the Soviet Union accepted. As discussed in connection with Article XI, the Soviet delegation rigorously adhered to its position that the reporting of activities in outer space and on celestial bodies generally should be only on a voluntary basis. As a result of the Soviet view, Article XI is ambiguous, as distinguished from the comparatively unequivocal obligation imposed on parties to the Treaty by the third paragraph of Article V.

The principles of assistance to astronauts in distress and their return to the launching State or other State of registry were already accepted by the members of the Legal Subcommittee as constituting humanitarian obligations.

*   *   *

E. Parties Shall Bear International Responsibility for National Activities in Outer Space.

Article VI of the Treaty assures that the parties cannot escape their international obligations under the treaty by virtue of the fact that activity in outer space or on celestial bodies is conducted through the medium of nongovernmental entities or international organizations. Perhaps the most important of the three sentences from the standpoint of domestic concern is the second, which states that the activities of nongovernmental entities in outer space and on celestial bodies shall require authorization and continuing supervision by the State concerned. The obvious example of activity covered by the second sentence is that of the Communications Satellite Corporation, a nongovernmental entity whose activities are authorized and regulated by United States federal agencies pursuant to federal statutes and regulations. However, while no one would doubt the need for governmental control over space activity at its present stage, the second sentence of Article VI would prohibit, as a matter of treaty obligation, strictly private, unregulated activity in outer space or on celestial bodies even at a time when such private activity becomes most common-place. Although the terms "authorization" and "continuing supervision" are open to different interpretations, it would appear that Article VI requires a certain minimum of licensing and enforced adherence to government-imposed regulations.

*   *   *

F. Parties to the Treaty That Launch or Procure the Launching of Objects into Outer Space Shall Be Liable for Damages.

Article VII concerning liability was also taken almost verbatim from an article of the Soviet draft, in this case Article VII. The Soviet draft was based on Paragraph 8 of the Declaration of Legal Principles. Although the United States draft contained no similar provision, the United States delegate readily agreed to the inclusion of Article VII of the Soviet draft, subject to minor drafting changes. The United States delegate, along with others, recognized that the Legal Subcommittee was in the process of drafting a detailed treaty on liability, but no objection was raised to the mere inclusion of an article stating the general principle in the present Treaty on outer space and celestial bodies. As the French delegate stated:

> The questions of liability and assistance were extremely complicated, and if any reference to them was included in the treaty under discussion, it should be very brief and simple and should merely establish the principle concerned. Any additional details might deal too rapidly with problems which had not yet been settled.

On this basis, agreement was reached shortly before the close of the Geneva portion of the Session on the inclusion of Article VII of the Soviet draft with minor modifications.

The subject of international liability for damage caused by space vehicles is indeed one involving a multitude of problems, discussed elsewhere by the authors in connection with the work of the Legal Subcommittee on the draft conventions on liability. Since Article VII of the Treaty is essentially a repetition of Paragraph 8 of the *Declaration of Legal Principles*, these problems were hardly touched upon during the Fifth Session in the course of discussion on liability. However, the Indian delegate questioned the meaning of the word "internationally," as used to modify "liable," and stated that the article would only be acceptable if "internationally" meant "absolutely." But other delegations noted that the concept of "absolute liability" was still being refined in discussions of the detailed draft treaties on liability and doubted the feasibility of embodying the concept of absolute liability in the text of Article VII. As the Australian delegate noted, "At earlier sessions the Subcommittee had found that absolute liability was necessarily subject to limitations and qualifications if justice was to be achieved."

* * *

G. Jurisdiction and Control over Personnel and Objects Are Not Affected by Their Presence in Outer Space or on Celestial Bodies.

Article VIII of the Treaty consists of three sentences, two of which state general rules concerning control and ownership of personnel and objects while in outer space and on celestial bodies. The third sentence imposes an obligation upon parties to the Treaty to return found objects to the party to the Treaty on whose registry they are carried. The State of registry is required to furnish identifying data if so requested. The third sentence, in providing for the return of space objects, can be regarded as a companion provision to Article V which provides for the assistance and return of astronauts. The return of space vehicles to the State of registry has been considered by the Legal Subcommittee in previous sessions as a part of a treaty that, if adopted, would regulate the assistance and return of astronauts.

Article VIII was taken from Article V of the Soviet draft which virtually repeated Paragraph 7 of the Declaration of Legal Principles. Article 7 of the United States draft was a similar provision but was concerned with control of persons and ownership of objects only on celestial bodies. Also, the United States version did not contain a provision for the return of objects. However, the United States delegate readily acceded to the Soviet version, applicable to both outer space and celestial bodies, subject to a few minor drafting changes. The most noticeable change was the substitution of the word "landed" for "delivered to" in the second sentence. Agreement on the final text of Article VIII was reached one week before the close of the Geneva portion of the Session, prior to the agreement on the final text of any other article.

* * *

I. Parties to the Treaty Shall Avoid Harmful Contamination of Outer Space, Celestial Bodies, and the Environment of Earth, and Shall Consult with Other Parties Regarding Potentially Harmful Experiments.

As stated by a leading proponent of the Treaty as an instrument of international cooperation, Article IX is "a provision which is designed to protect outer space and the celestial bodies from contamination and pollution and to protect the legitimate programs of States from undue interference."

Article IX was taken from Article VIII of the Soviet draft and Article 10 of the United States draft. The Soviet version was in turn a reiteration of Paragraph 6 of the Declaration of Legal Principles. Article IX of the Treaty closely follows the text of the Soviet version. However, the Soviet Union agreed to add specific language making the provision applicable to celestial bodies in addition to outer space, and agreed to add the provision of the United States draft prohibiting parties to the Treaty from conducting experiments which might cause adverse changes in the environment of earth.

* * *

The Japanese delegation proposed to add language which would have required parties planning potentially harmful experiments to report such planned experiments to the Secretary-General of the United Nations before undertaking them.

The Soviet delegate, however, disapproved of this suggestion, stating that the essential information would be communicated more quickly to the other parties to the Treaty if the Secretary-General were not utilized as an intermediary. In addition, and more important, he regarded the Japanese suggestion to be in conflict with the position of the Soviet Union that the Secretary-General not play a role in the application of the Treaty by States. Although the Soviet delegate, after much debate, agreed to Article XI, which provides for the reporting of activities in outer space and celestial bodies to the Secretary-General, he drew sharp distinction between the mandatory consultations in advance of the event, under Article IX, and what he regarded as voluntary reporting after the event, under Article XI. In view of the unequivocal refusal of the Soviet delegation to accept any provision requiring mandatory reporting to the Secretary-General, the Japanese proposal was dropped and agreement was reached on the text of Article IX, including the mandatory provisions for consultations on potentially harmful experiments, shortly before the close of the Geneva portion of the Session.

NOTE

As the above indicates, two key issues occupied the minds of the negotiators—the use of space and celestial bodies for military purposes, and the rights of nations to exercise sovereignty over space, celestial bodies, and the resources to be found therein. These issues were reexamined in more detail in the Moon Treaty (discussed in Chapter 4, *infra*). However, the rules set out in the Outer Space Treaty remain important, particularly as the Moon Treaty has not exactly found favor among the spacefaring nations.

SOVEREIGNTY, PROPERTY RIGHTS, AND SPACE RESOURCES

The rules against extension of sovereignty to outer space and celestial bodies resolved a good deal of confusion regarding such matters—prior to the Outer Space Treaty's entering into force, there had been considerable uncertainty regarding the ability of nations to claim sovereignty in space based on arriving at a particular place first, particularly after the Soviet Union planted a flag on the Moon using an unmanned probe. After the Treaty, there remained a number of questions regarding what was meant by the no-sovereignty provisions, a question examined in the following excerpt from an article by Carl Christol. Essentially, the questions involve the classification of particular activities as inclusive (that is, those in which all nations are allowed to take part) or exclusive (those in which nations may exclude others). For pre-Treaty views on this subject, *see* M. McDougal, H. Lasswell & I. Vlasic, Law & Public Order in Space 749–871 (1963).

Christol, Article 2 of the 1967 Principles Treaty Revisited, 9 Annals of Air & Space Law 217 (1984)

With the constantly enlarging prospects for the exploration, use, and especially the exploitation of the space environment (outer space per se, the Moon, and other celestial bodies) and the resources of the environment, it is appropriate to reexamine the meaning of Article 2 of the 1967 Principles Treaty. This article provides that "Outer space, including the Moon and other celestial bodies, is not subject to national appropriation by claim of sovereignty, by means of use or occupation, or by any other means."

During the negotiations attending the drafting of the agreement, and in subsequent State practice, it has become clear that the space environment is perceived in international law as a *res communis*, that is to say, as an area available for inclusive uses, rather than for exclusive uses. However, pending the final drafting of Article 2, some doubts were expressed as to the prohibitory scope of the Article. Thus, in the early 1960's Jenks, on the basis of the language contained in Assembly Resolution 1721 A, which was the forerunner of Article 2, concluded that its prohibitions applied only to the "national appropriation of outer space or celestial bodies." He added: "The legal regime applicable to any of the natural resources which it may prove possible and profitable to exploit remains for consideration at a later stage in the light of fuller knowledge of what is practicable and probable."

An opposing view was put forward by Brooks. He took note of the fact that the draftsmen of the Principles Treaty, after having taken General Assembly Resolution 1721 A into account, had not limited the ban on appropriation only to territorial areas. In his view Article 2 constituted a ban on exclusive national rights to both the area and its resources. In his words: "Had the Space Treaty drafters intended only a territorial ban they would not have included 'means of use' or 'any other means' in amplifying the ban on national appropriation since ... those terms do in fact move beyond mere territorial appropriation." In his view both States and international organizations were to be entitled to make use of the planetary resources as well as the area of outer space.

Following the final revision and adoption of Article 2 in the Principles Treaty its coverage was examined by Lachs. He concluded that the prohibition against national appropriation should be understood as including not only sovereign but also property rights. He submitted that "it should be read as covering both. 'Appropriation' in the wider sense is involved. States are thus barred from establishing proprietary links in regard to the new dimension."

This issue had been considered by the Legal Sub-Committee of the U.N. Committee on the Peaceful Uses of Outer Space (COPUOS) in 1996 when it was drafting the 1967 Principles Treaty. The Belgian representative stated on August 4, 1966, that notice had been taken of "the term 'non-appropriation' advanced by several delegations—apparently without contradiction—as covering both the establishment of sovereignty and the creation of titles to property in private law."

The representative of France accepted this viewpoint on December 17, 1966, when he stated to the First Committee that a basic principle of the 1967 Principles Treaty was that there was a "prohibition of any claim to sovereignty or property rights in space." Lachs also called attention to the reasoning of Ortolan relating to the absence of property rights in the ocean: "La mer n'est pas susceptible de tomber dans la propriete des hommes parce que la mer ne peut etre possedee."

The *res communis* quality of the space environment and its natural resources has, with the increasing maturity of international space law, been reflected in international agreements and international practice. Such agreements, applicable to States and to international intergovernmental organizations, contain formal prohibitions against the assertion of national sovereignty over the space environment. They also negate national and international claims to exclusive property rights over the in-place resources of that environment. Thus, Article 11(3) of the Agreement Governing the Activities of States on the Moon and Other Celestial Bodies, approved unanimously by the UN General Assembly on December 5, 1979, provided that "Neither the surface nor the subsurface of the Moon, nor any part thereof or natural resources in place, shall become property of any State, international intergovernmental organization or non-governmental organization, national organization or non-governmental entity or of any natural person." In keeping with the *res communis* principle, allowance was made for the holding of property rights in natural resources which had been removed from their "in place" position on the surface of or from the subsurface of the Moon or other celestial bodies.

*   *   *

The relevant articles of the Treaty employ different terminology in adopting the *res communis* principle. Article 3 refers to the "activities" of States, which become parties to the agreement, in the exploration and use of the space environment. Article 6 makes reference to the outer space "activities" of non-governmental entities. Both Articles 6 and 13 authorize space "activities" by international organizations. Article 1, on the other hand, does not make specific reference to "activities," but does identify States as having the right to engage in the free and equal exploration and use of the space environment, and as having the right to free access to all areas of celestial bodies.

From these provisions certain conclusions can be drawn. Presumably the additional right of free access to outer space, *per se,* exists, since, if this right were not present, the right of free access to the Moon and to other celestial bodies would be frustrated. It is generally accepted that mention of celestial bodies in the Treaty includes reference to the Moon. It is now considered to be the right of natural and juridical persons other than States, as well as States, to have the right of free and equal access to the space environment, *per se*. Moreover, the rights of such persons are extended to exploration, exploitation, and use. They may also engage, pursuant to Article 1, in scientific investigations, and pursuant to Article 4, in scientific research. These are all operational as distinguished from management activities.

It is, however, a fact that the Principles Treaty makes no explicit reference to the exploration, use, and exploitation of the resources of the environment. The agreement neither expressly authorizes nor prohibits, the exclusive acquisition of the resources of the area. Nonetheless, the general availability of such resources for inclusive exploration, exploitation, and use, by way of space-related "activities," can be supported on several grounds. First, as noted, the *res communis* principle measurably affected the thinking and the conclusions of the negotiators. Second, international practice has gone forward on the basis of the principle. Third, Article 2, through the acceptance of the principle of non-appropriation of the area—thereby rejecting the *res nullius* principle—ordained that the area was not "subject to national appropriation by claim of sovereignty, by means of use or occupation, or by any other means."

Thus, the conclusion may be drawn that States and other natural and juridical persons have the right of free and equal access to space environment, *per se*. Moreover, their rights are also extended to exploration, exploitation, and use. All of this is based on the fundamental proposition that Article 1 authorizes the exploration, exploitation and use of the area and the resources of the area provided such "activities" are carried out, as Article 1 specifies, "for the benefit and in the interests of all countries, irrespective of their degree of economic or scientific development, and shall be the province of all mankind."

* * *

The central issue presented by the foregoing prescriptions and examined here is whether the Principles Treaty in its entirety, as supplemented by subsequent international agreements, and by international practice, prevents juridical persons, other than States—and in particular international intergovernmental organizations—from claiming exclusive operational, as well as management, rights, which are denied to States. Being prevented from claiming sovereignty and exclusive property rights located in the space environment for themselves, it will be argued that States are also prohibited from granting quasi-sovereign and exclusive property rights over such areas and resources to those natural and juridical persons which are subject to national jurisdiction and which are created through international agreements.

It is clear that Article 2 prohibits national claims relating to the area of the space environment, and to the resources of that area, subject to the "not in place" terms of the 1979 Moon Treaty. This raises the question initially whether Article 2 can be construed to prevent the effective assertion by an international intergovernmental organization of exclusive rights—both operational, e.g., exploration, exploitation, and use, and governmental, e.g., prescription of rights and duties—to the area and its resources. The terms of Article 13 address themselves separately to the same question. Affecting the meaning to be accorded to these articles are the provisions of Articles 1 and 6. In short, does the Principles Treaty, particularly on the basis of the foregoing articles, impose the same constraints on international intergovernmental organizations respecting the space environment and its resources as are imposed on the States which are parties to the 1967 agreement?

With respect to Article 2, the inquiry will depend on the meaning to be accorded to the "by any other means" limitation. In assessing that limitation it must be kept in mind that, at the time the Principles Treaty was being drafted, the negotiators were focusing principally on the behavior and activities of the legal entities traditionally able to assert exclusive claims to areas and to resources, namely, States. But, in the negotiating history of Article 2 there is also a respectable view that the "by any other means" clause extends to the possible future claims of international intergovernmental organizations. Here the question is whether the "by any other means" provision denies to the signatories the power to grant to an international organization the power to make claims which States, acting on their own account and on behalf of their separate interests, may not assert. If this thesis can be maintained, such organizations would be subject to the same constraints as were specifically directed in Article 2 against States.

*   *   *

This thesis raises the potential applicability of a number of key legal concepts affecting authority over activities in the area and the resources of the area. The provisions of all of the space law treaties are relevant as are the 1969 Vienna Convention on the Law of Treaties, and the 1973 and 1982 ITU Conventions and accompanying Radio Regulations. Both international law generally, as well as the UN Charter, have relevance. The status and powers of international intergovernmental organizations, the utility of legal analogies, the terms of General Assembly resolutions between 1959 and 1967, the statements of negotiators, the views of commentators, the resolutions and reports of private groups of scholars, and such basic concepts as equity are applicable in achieving valid insights respecting the meaning to be accorded to Article 2. There is also the prospect of conflict between treaties and possibly the need to determine the respective powers of different international intergovernmental organizations. Aside from the critical legal issues there are also fundamental political issues which flow from the major differences between the advanced States and the developing States respecting their capabilities for engaging in the practical exploration, exploitation, and use of the space environment and its resources.

*   *   *

That the negotiators were successful in imposing limitations on purely national claims is not to be doubted. Further, it is clear that the negotiators were not laboring under the assumption that the Principles Treaty was a definitive statement of the emerging international law of outer space. Rather, they acknowledged without exception that they were at the threshold of the law, and that much of the book yet remained to be opened. Thus, from the perspective of scholarly analysis it is clear that excessive claims should not be made as to the meaning to be ascribed to the "by any other means" limitation of Article 2. While this is true, it would also not be appropriate to exclude from Article 2 any interdictory meaning that was considered relevant by the negotiators, and which constituted a meaningful part of the negotiating history of the Article and of the entire Treaty. In particular the terms of Article 2 must be viewed from the perspective of Article 1, which was designed to safeguard the interests of all mankind against exclusive claims and uses from whatever source or direction they might come.

NOTES

1. Christol makes two key points: that the restrictions of Article 2's no-sovereignty provision apply equally to international organizations and to states, and that those restrictions do not bar the exploitation of space resources, but merely the staking of exclusive claims to tracts of celestial bodies or space. This is a sensible reading based on the *res communis* principle: by way of analogy, the fact that the high seas are considered *res communis* does not prevent nations from fishing there, but only from excluding other nations from doing the same. In addition, this interpretation makes economic sense for a variety of reasons discussed in the context of the Moon Treaty in Chapter 4, *infra*.

2. As Christol mentions, some scholars writing in the wake of the Outer Space Treaty's ratification took the position that Article 2's no-sovereignty provisions bar *any* property rights in outer space resources. That position has lost its popularity over time, however, and is no longer held by many scholars. This particular debate has, at any rate, been overshadowed in the 1980s by the debate over language in the Moon Treaty dealing with resources, sovereignty, and the "common heritage of mankind" discussed in Chapter 4. *See generally* Glenn H. Reynolds, International Space Law: Into the Twenty-First Century, 25 Vanderbilt Journal of Transnational Law 225, 229–37 (1992).

ARMS CONTROL PROVISIONS

The Outer Space Treaty contains a number of provisions limiting military activities in outer space. These provisions do not come close to banning all military activity, and there is some dispute concerning exactly what they do prohibit. Nonetheless, they place limits on military activity by prohibiting the emplacement of fortifications or military installations on the moon or other celestial bodies, or the orbiting of nuclear weapons or other weapons of mass destruction, and state generally that the moon and other celestial bodies are to be used exclusively for peaceful purposes. The use of outer space (as opposed to celestial bodies) for military purposes is intentionally subjected to fewer restrictions because ballistic missiles pass through space in flight and neither the United States nor the Soviet Union was willing to abandon its reliance on such missiles at the time the treaty was negotiated.

The following excerpts explore the meaning of these provisions, including what constitutes a nuclear weapon or other "weapon of mass destruction" and whether there is a distinction between "peaceful" and "nonmilitary" uses of outer space. As you read these, you should consider the following: Were the drafters of the Outer Space Treaty wise to use language susceptible of some ambiguity ("peaceful"; "other kinds of weapons of mass destruction") in order to maintain flexibility, or would they have been better off with more precise language of the sort used in the Test Ban Treaty? And, in light of what we know of the history of the negotiations leading up to the Treaty, which interpretations of these terms are more in accord with the Treaty's spirit?

Orr, The Treaty on Outer Space:
An Evaluation of the Arms Control Provisions,
7 Columbia Journal of Transnational Law 259 (1968)

On October 10, 1967, the Treaty on Principles Governing the Activities of States in the Exploration and Use of Outer Space, Including the Moon and Other Celestial Bodies entered into force, and, hopefully, because of it "man's earthly conflicts will not be carried into outer space." The measures intended to restrict these conflicts are the arms control provisions of the Treaty, which President Johnson described as "the most important arms control development since the limited test ban treaty of 1963."

In his Letter of Transmittal to the Senate requesting its advice and consent to ratification, the President portrayed the Treaty as "enlarg[ing] the perimeters of peace by shrinking the arenas of potential conflict." He further saw in it a fundamental principle that "[n]o one may use outer space or celestial bodies to begin a war." Such statements as these could leave an overly optimistic impression of the extent to which military activities will be barred from outer space. While the Treaty surely can be considered "the basic charter for the future conquest and utilization of outer space," it does not guarantee that outer space will be free from the burden of man's conflicts. This conclusion follows from a careful reading of the text of the Treaty, especially the arms control provisions. Recent military developments also raise doubts about the effectiveness of the Treaty in limiting the military use of outer space. This comment will explore some of these developments in relation to the Treaty language.

* * *

The principal arms control provisions—found in Article IV of the Treaty—restrict military activities in two ways. First, the parties agree not to place in orbit around the earth, install on the moon or any other celestial body, or otherwise station in outer space, nuclear or any other weapons of mass destruction.

Second, the parties pledge that the moon and other celestial bodies shall be used exclusively for peaceful purposes and expressly forbid their use for the establishment of military bases, installations or fortifications, testing of any type of weapons, or conducting military maneuvers. However, this Article does permit the use of military personnel for scientific research or for any other peaceful purpose and the use of any equipment or facility necessary for the peaceful exploration of any celestial body.

The first restriction is based on United Nations Resolution 1884 (XVIII) commonly known as the "no bombs in orbit" resolution. This resolution welcomed expressions [of intent] by the United States and the Union of Soviet Socialist Republics "not to station in outer space any nuclear weapons or other kinds of weapons of mass destruction" and called upon all states "to refrain from placing in orbit around the earth any objects carrying nuclear weapons or any other kinds of weapons of mass destruction, installing such weapons on celestial bodies, or stationing such weapons in outer space in any other manner."

* * *

The language of the second restriction resulted from a compromise between similar language found in both the United States and the Soviet draft treaties. Much of the Treaty was taken verbatim from, or at least inspired by, a 1963 United Nations Resolution, entitled "Declaration of Legal Principles Governing the Activities of States in the Exploration and Use of Outer Space" [hereinafter referred to as the Declaration on Legal Principles]. Yet the measures designed to insure that the moon be used only for peaceful purposes were not specifically mentioned in that Declaration.

Additional Treaty provisions intended to assure compliance with the arms control objectives are in Articles I, II and XII. Article I guarantees "free access to all areas of celestial bodies." This follows the principle previously embodied in the Antarctic Treaty of 1959; namely, free access by all parties to installations of other parties.

Also operating against an arms race in space is the provision in Article II forbidding national appropriation of outer space or celestial bodies. Finally, Article XII provides that "[a]ll stations, installations, equipment and space vehicles on the moon and other celestial bodies shall be open to ... other ... Parties ... on a basis of reciprocity." It should be emphasized that the "free access" provisions apply only to the moon and other celestial bodies and not to objects otherwise in outer space, i.e., a satellite in orbit around the earth.

The more general provisions of Articles I and III may also be relevant to an interpretation of the Treaty in the case of a particular space system. These provisions set out some of the basic principles which guided the draftsmen. It is primarily through the careful study of the Treaty language and history in light of actual and possible military space systems that the value of the arms control measures in limiting military activities in space can be determined.

*   *   *

Both the United States and the Soviet Union are using earth satellites for military reconnaissance. Such systems clearly do not fall within the specific arms control provisions of Article IV. Paragraph 1 of that Article is limited to "nuclear weapons or any other kinds of weapons of mass destruction" while the second paragraph applies only to "the moon and other celestial bodies." Under any interpretation of the Article, a reconnaissance satellite could not be a "weapon of mass destruction." It is arguable, however, that such satellites could be proscribed by the provision stipulating that "[t]he ... *use of outer space* ... shall be carried out *for the benefit and in the interest of all countries ...*" (emphasis added). The meaning of this language is not clear as witnessed by the lengthy discussion it provoked in the Foreign Relations Committee hearings on the Treaty.

It was principally Senator Gore [Sr.] who questioned the breadth of this language, particularly as it related to reconnaissance satellites. He was concerned that this provision might be interpreted as prohibiting certain unspecified "uses" of outer space—not an unreasonable concern in light of its plain language. United States Ambassador to the United Nations, Arthur Goldberg, in addressing this point, stated that there was "no prohibition" in the language questioned. In explaining the admittedly broad language, the Ambassador included the following analysis:

> Article I, paragraph 1, is quite general in character. The specific obligations regarding exploration and use of outer space that the Treaty imposes are set forth in succeeding provisions.
>
> Where it was the intention of the Treaty drafters to provide specific legal obligations relating to benefits to be derived from space activity, this was clearly expressed.

The Ambassador was apparently saying that the language in question is too general to embody, or to be intended to embody, specific obligations. If this is so, then one wonders why the language was not placed in the preamble instead of the body.

Additional broad language which might be used to challenge the legality of reconnaissance satellites is found in Article III. There it is stated that "Parties ... shall carry on activities in the ... *use of outer space* ... in the *interest of maintaining international peace* and security..." (emphasis added). The meaning of this provision is likewise unclear but it did not generate any lengthy discussion in the hearings. Many of the same questions raised with reference to the previous broad language are appropriate here.

The characterization presented, at least by the United States, styles satellite reconnaissance as "peace-keeping." It would therefore fall within the mandate of the language in question. Of course the validity of this characterization depends upon the role of reconnaissance in promoting or retarding the tensions which produce war. Admitting that space reconnaissance is a military use of space, the United States argues that its use is defensive which deters potential aggressive action and therefore maintains international peace.

The Soviet attitude toward reconnaissance from space has been quite different, at least prior to the adoption of the Declaration on Legal Principles. The Soviet draft of that Declaration contained a provision branding reconnaissance satellites "incompatible with the objectives of mankind in its conquest of outer space." Such a provision, however, was not included in either the Declaration or the Treaty. This omission speaks strongly for the conclusion that reconnaissance satellites are not prohibited under any intended interpretation of the Treaty.

*   *   *

Aerospace vehicles—vehicles which can function in both sensible atmosphere and the space environment—are an example of potential military systems which present problems of interpretation under the Treaty. One proven example of this combination airplane-spacecraft vehicle is the X–15. During flight at lower altitudes it operates partly on lift generated by passage through the air, but when it reaches top altitude of about 70 miles it depends solely on its rocket engine propulsion system to maintain it in flight.

Another aerospace vehicle—called the "DynaSoar"—was extensively designed by the United States but never actually flown. The project for its development was cancelled by the Department of Defense in December, 1963. A rocket would have lifted the vehicle to an altitude of about 100 miles (in the same way that a present-day manned spacecraft is fired into orbit around the earth) where it would have traveled much like a satellite. However, unlike a satellite, it would have dropped into that part of the atmosphere in which aerodynamic lift can be generated, and would have glided back to earth much like an airplane. In terms of today's aircraft this vehicle would have traveled great distances at high altitudes.

If it is assumed that both of the above vehicles could carry weapons of mass destruction, and laying aside the possibility of their being in orbit, the language most relevant to their status under the Treaty is "station such weapons in outer space in any other manner."

No attempt was made in the body of the Treaty to define "outer space" even though it appears in numerous provisions, including the title. There was little discussion of its meaning prior to the Treaty's adoption, but this does not mean that suggested definitions were unavailable. Numerous proposals have been made by both legal and technical writers although no general agreement can be found on any one definition. These proposals are valuable in revealing the problems facing any attempt at definition.

There was recognition by the United Nations that the problem of determining where air space ends and outer space begins would require its attention. In the General Assembly resolution adopting the Treaty, a study of the definition problem was requested. Responding to this request, the Committee on the Peaceful Uses of Outer Space recently held a number of sessions at which the problem was considered. While a definition has not been agreed upon, these sessions have produced enough discussion to justify analyzing the relevant considerations as judged by the Treaty's draftsmen.

The French were the first to advocate a study of the definition of outer space as it applied to the Treaty, and were the first to present their view of the issues involved. Central to their concern was that the Treaty affirmed renunciation by states of any sovereignty over outer space. Pointing out that states now retain sovereignty over congruent air space, they desired some delineation of where air space ends and outer space begins. In light of aerospace vehicles, this delineation seems even more desirable. Even if a nation's vehicle remained "over" its own territory, it might not be subject to that nation's jurisdiction and might even be in violation of the Treaty.

* * *

Even with an introduction this brief, one realizes the complexity of the problem of defining outer space. It is this complexity, coupled with the need for additional scientific data, that has led a number of countries to urge a cautious approach to the definition problem. Many feel that definition does not require priority attention. The one thing about the definition of outer space that can be said with certainty is that anything in orbit is generally accepted as being in outer space.

In determining how to treat aerospace vehicles under the Treaty, the word "station" and how it affects the interpretation of "such weapons in outer space" in Article IV could be relevant. No information pertinent to this admittedly subtle inquiry was found in the record of the draftsmen's discussions. "Station" seems to imply something more permanent than the passing through outer space which describes the flight of an aerospace vehicle. ... The fact that ICBM's which simply pass through outer space are not considered violations of the Treaty supports an interpretation of "station" implying permanency.

* * *

The weapons prohibited "in orbit around the earth" and "station[ed] ... in outer space" are "nuclear weapons or any other kinds of weapons of mass destruction." Usually given as examples of "other kinds of weapons of mass destruction" are bacteriological and chemical weapons. Conventional weapons are not included. Even the largest of the non-nuclear explosive weapons are not considered weapons of mass destruction. Any weapon developed in the future with the capacity to cause the extent of destruction or loss of human life which nuclear weapons can wreak would also be prohibited.

Even a term seemingly so clear as "nuclear weapon" is subject to conflicting interpretations when read in the context of a particular military system. One long range proposal for a defensive system against missiles includes a satellite using a focused beam of radiation from a nuclear reactor [i.e., an X-Ray laser] as an atomic heat ray to destroy an enemy missile. A similar system was studied by the United States but later abandoned as too expensive and unreliable. With the rapid advance of technology one cannot safely assume that it will not be revived.

A nuclear reactor used as the source of a radiation beam differs from the usual nuclear weapon in that it does not explode. While it is nuclear and a weapon, it is not necessarily therefore a weapon of mass destruction. Article IV could be read as prohibiting only nuclear weapons of mass destruction. Some support is found for this view in the Treaty language "nuclear weapons or any *other* kinds of weapons of mass destruction ..." (emphasis added). It could be argued that the use of "other" implies that nuclear weapons were included only as an example of what the Treaty provision was actually intended to prohibit—weapons of mass destruction. This being true, then the status of a nuclear weapon under the Treaty should be decided on the basis of whether it can cause mass destruction.

In rejecting this argument, the Legal Adviser to the Secretary of State, Leonard C. Meeker, stated that "any nuclear weapon is forbidden in space ... [e]ven a small one is considered ... to be a weapon of mass destruction." His interpretation of the language would read "other" as assimilating nuclear weapons to weapons of mass destruction, and prohibiting both.

NOTE

Mr. Orr's piece provides a good survey of many of the issues as they appeared when the Outer Space Treaty was ratified. In many ways, little has changed—he describes the DynaSoar, which was never built, but the legal problems he describes in connection with the DynaSoar are just as applicable regarding the Space Shuttle or various aerospace plane designs now under consideration. Similarly, he describes the potential employment of space-based nuclear reactors to power X-Ray lasers for antimissile use. Although such designs are considered as impractical now as when he wrote, there has been considerable discussion of the use of X-Ray lasers powered instead by nuclear explosives. Unlike reactor-powered lasers, though, such devices would clearly violate the provisions of both the Test Ban and the Outer Space Treaty since they would involve both the placing of nuclear weapons in orbit and (when used) the detonation of nuclear weapons in orbit—although the Test Ban Treaty forbids such detonations only in peacetime, a condition that would presumably have passed if antimissile systems were in use. Still, the Test Ban Treaty would forbid any in-space tests of such a system, leaving its reliability in doubt. In addition, of course, such a system (whether bomb- or reactor-powered) would face problems with the ABM Treaty, problems discussed in the following chapter.

As discussed earlier, however, some space powers could make use of nuclear explosives for space propulsion without violating any treaty obligations. The Limited Test Ban Treaty applies only to its signatories, a group that does not include a number of emerging space powers. The Test Ban Treaty forbids *any* nuclear explosion, whether peaceful or military, in outer space. The Outer Space Treaty forbids only the placing in orbit of "any objects carrying nuclear weapons or any other kinds of weapons of mass destruction" rather than prohibiting the use or orbiting of nuclear *explosives*. Nuclear explosives used for propulsion would not constitute "weapons" conceptually, since they are not intended to produce harm, and probably would for technical reasons be unsuited for destructive purposes. Thus, the Outer Space Treaty's arms control provisions would probably not bar the use of ORION type nuclear propulsion, at least for peaceful purposes. Users of such systems would, however, remain liable under Article VII for any damage caused by use of such a system, meaning that its use anywhere near the earth would be limited by dangers to other spacecraft and satellites from radiation and electromagnetic pulse.

Gorove, Arms Control Provisions in the Outer Space Treaty: A Scrutinizing Reappraisal, 3 Georgia Journal of International and Comparative Law 114 (1973)

Nuclear and Other Weapons of Mass Destruction

Paragraph one of article IV of the Treaty relates to nuclear weapons and any other kinds of weapons of mass destruction. The initial problem presented by the Treaty is the lack of a definition of what constitutes a "nuclear weapon" or a "weapon of mass destruction." It may be presumed that all arms which utilize atomic energy in accomplishing their intended purpose, irrespective of their size or destructive force, would be regarded as nuclear weapons. At the same time, it may also be assumed that conventional weapons do not come under the category of either nuclear weapons or any other weapons of mass destruction. While there is no indication in the Treaty as to how many people must be affected to constitute a weapon of mass destruction, a group of 20 to 30 people or less probably would not constitute such a mass. If on the other hand, bacteriological and chemical weapons were used, even against a small group, then these weapons would seem to fall under the category of weapons of mass destruction.

Second, the states parties to the Treaty undertake not to *install* nuclear and other weapons of mass destruction on celestial bodies or *station* them in outer space in any other manner. The drafters omitted any reference to the moon in this provision even though in other parts of the Treaty they have fairly consistently referred to the "moon and other celestial bodies." It is by no means clear, however, whether the omission of the word "moon" was intentional, or if the implication is correct that no restriction is placed on the installation of atomic weapons on the moon. One may surmise, however, from the frequently used phrase "moon and other celestial bodies" that the moon is to be regarded as a celestial body under the Treaty. Moreover, it would make little sense to permit installation of weapons of mass destruction on the moon while prohibiting such installation on other celestial bodies, when man's use of the latter looms in the more distant future.

Significant questions with respect to the interpretation of paragraph one of article IV relate to the meaning of the words "install" and "station." At what point does a weapon become installed? Is the mere presence of a weapon on a celestial body prohibited? Furthermore, what constitutes stationing in outer space? Is this identical with orbiting, or does it have a distinct meaning? Any definition of installation of a weapon should require something more than the mere presence of a weapon on a celestial body. On the other hand, station should be interpreted to include the placing of a weapon in a relatively fixed orbit in relation to the underlying celestial body, such that the speed of the orbiting object would coincide with the speed of rotation of the celestial body.

* * *

Use for "Peaceful" Purposes

The second paragraph of article IV states that the moon and other celestial bodies shall be used by the parties exclusively for peaceful purposes. Like paragraph one, this provision obligates only the states parties to the Treaty and is not declaratory of a more general obligation. It should also be noted that this provision makes no reference to outer space. This is not an accidental omission. Both paragraphs one and two of article IV express the underlying policy of prohibiting only certain uses of atomic and other weapons of mass destruction in outer space, yet not completely outlawing their use.

* * *

Another interesting problem that may have some practical relevance to the future application of paragraph two relates to the size of celestial bodies. How large must a celestial body be to be considered such a body? Would a meteorite or asteroid or a small moon of a celestial body constitute such a body under the terms of the Treaty? An example of the potential problems was indicated when not long ago scientists reported that it might become technically feasible for a future space expedition to steal one of the smaller size moons (5–10 miles in diameter) of Mars, to remove it from its Martian orbit and to place it in orbit around the earth, and thus effectively change the solar system. Would the removal of a celestial body from its natural position by human intervention change its characterization as a celestial body under the Treaty? A meteorite which lands on earth by natural forces and without human interference presumably loses its designation as a celestial body under the Treaty. But the same is probably not true with respect to the example of the Martian moon.

Paragraph two contains one of the most controversial provisions in the Outer Space Treaty. The meaning of "peaceful" has given rise to at least two major interpretations. Under one interpretation the word "peaceful" means nonmilitary, while under a second interpretation the term means nonaggressive.

There is a vast difference insofar as the outcome of these two different interpretations is concerned. Under the former interpretation no military activities could be conducted on the moon and other celestial bodies except those which are specifically permissible under the paragraph two language, e.g., the use of military personnel for scientific research. Under the latter interpretation, activities nonaggressive in nature would be permissible, even if they are conducted by the military, with certain exceptions. These exceptions are those specifically forbidden by article IV, e.g., the establishment of military bases, installations and fortifications, the testing of any types of weapons and the conduct of military maneuvers on celestial bodies. Those advocating this second position have referred to the Charter of the United Nations for their meaning of peaceful. The former position is supported by the Statute of the International Atomic Energy Agency which distinguishes peaceful from military uses of atomic energy.

In reality it would appear that the drafters of the Outer Space Treaty have not adopted either of the above interpretations. Two facts support a meaning of peaceful that is distinct from earlier usages. First, certain activities, such as scientific research or the use of any equipment and facility necessary for peaceful exploration are not prohibited, even if undertaken by the military. Second, certain other activities, such as the establishment of military bases, installations and fortifications, the testing of any type of weapons and the conduct of military maneuvers, are forbidden even if these activities are of a nonaggressive nature.

*   *   *

One possible standard is the relation of an activity to national security. Certain activities may not be as critical or significant as others. Therefore, it would be better to identify those activities which constitute minimal threats to national security and permit those regardless of the ultimate purpose for such activities or their conduct by military personnel. In this manner the whole bothersome issue of peaceful versus military or aggressive could be avoided for the most part, although questions of interpretation would still remain. For example, nation states may decide to permit photography of their underlying territories from outer space regardless of the ultimate purpose for the photographs. If this were to be done, the type of problem which might arise would relate only to the interpretation of the word "photography," which would appear to be much more easily identifiable than any ultimate use or hidden purpose.

*   *   *

It may also be of interest to point out that the use of any equipment or facility is permissible under paragraph two so long as such use is necessary for the peaceful exploration of the moon and other celestial bodies. Therefore, it would appear that military equipment or facilities could legitimately be used for such purpose. However, as pointed out, it may be argued that the word peaceful was not meant to imply nonmilitary.

A similar argument may be predicated on the language in paragraph two that allows the use of military personnel for scientific research or for any other peaceful purposes. Thus, scientific research is regarded by the drafters as an activity basically of a peaceful character. This is the connotation that may reasonably be drawn from the use of the phrase "for scientific research or for any other peaceful purposes." It may then be safe to assume that no scientific research is prohibited by the Treaty regardless of whether or not it is conducted by civilian or military personnel. There may be strong doubts about this assumption, but the express language does not place any restriction on the objective of the research. Thus, the object of the research, whether the advancement of science, military defense, or perhaps even outright aggression, would have no bearing on the lawfulness of any research activity under paragraph two. Admittedly, this construction may run contrary to the general spirit and other provisions of the Treaty, i.e., that the exploration and use of outer space be carried out for the benefit and in the interests of all countries, and that the moon and other celestial bodies be used exclusively for peaceful purposes. However, the wording of the provision pertaining to the free use of military personnel for scientific research makes no mention of the moon or other celestial bodies or, for that matter, of outer space. Thus, one may assume that it was meant to apply generally. The drafters of the Treaty have indicated that scientific research should not be curtailed and realistically they have allowed the use of military personnel to further such research. It is reasonable to conclude that regardless of its objective or where it takes place, scientific research is favored by the Treaty terms.

NOTES

1. In his call for more precise definitions of terms, Gorove takes a different position than Orr, who generally seems more comfortable with flexible interpre-

tations. There are arguments both ways: overly specific definitions may be rapidly rendered obsolete by technological or other change, while overly broad definitions may be so vague as to be meaningless. The Outer Space Treaty's reference to "nuclear weapons or any other kinds of weapons of mass destruction" seems a good compromise: it includes what the drafters were most immediately concerned with, the stationing of nuclear bombs in orbit, as well as possible new weapons, unforeseen by the drafters but posing similar threats to global security, that might arrive later. *See generally* Peaceful and Non-Peaceful Uses of Space: Problems of Definition for the Prevention of an Arms Race (B. Jasani ed. 1991); Centre for Research of Air and Space Law, Space Without Weapons (1990); Dana Johnson, The Impact of International Law and Treaty Obligations on United States Military Activities in Space, 3 High Technology Law Journal 33 (1988).

2. Despite the concerns mentioned by both Orr and Gorove, the legality of satellite reconnaissance is no longer a major issue. Partly because the technology for such reconnaissance has become widespread and familiar, and partly because the benefits of such systems in promoting stability and in verifying arms control agreements are widely recognized, few nations now dispute the legality of such activities. The Soviet Union formerly opposed satellite surveillance, but has ceased to do so; in 1972 it signed the SALT I Treaty, May 26, 1972, U.S.-U.S.S.R., 24 U.S.T. 3462 (expired), in which each party undertook not to interfere with the other's "national technical means" of verification, a term encompassing satellite reconnaissance (see Chapter 4). More recently, the United Nations COPUOS has drafted principles on remote sensing that underscore its legality in general. For more on the international legal status of remote sensing, see Chapter 5. There have also been some interesting developments in U.S. domestic law relating to private entities' use of satellite reconnaissance technology. *See* Merges & Reynolds, News Media Satellites and the First Amendment, 3 High Technology Law Journal 1 (1988), and Chapter 8, *infra*.

3. Many issues touched on by the Outer Space Treaty only briefly and in general, such as the treatment of liability or the duty to rescue and return astronauts, are addressed in more detail by later agreements—for example, the Liability Convention or the Rescue and Return Agreement. These "miscellaneous treaties," along with other issues, are discussed in Chapter 5.

4

Development and Defense: Treaties of the 1970s

With the early treaties discussed in Chapter 3, the international community established some basic principles to govern space. In the 1970s, attention was focused on more specific goals. That decade produced two important treaties that will have a significant impact on future activities in space: the Antiballistic Missile (ABM) Treaty of 1972, and the Agreement Governing the Activities of States on the Moon and Other Celestial Bodies of 1979, known as the Moon Treaty.

In this chapter we will keep to the chronological order established in Chapter 3 and consider the ABM Treaty first. Although this Treaty is far less comprehensive in its treatment of space activities, it is more important than the Moon Treaty in at least one respect: its signatories—the United States and the former Soviet Union (now the Commonwealth of Independent States)—are the major space powers, while neither these nations nor any other space power (save France) has yet signed the Moon Treaty. *See* Christol, The Moon Treaty (Current Developments), 79 American Journal of International Law 163 (1985).

In the second part of this chapter, we will explore the reasons for this. As we will see in the excerpts from Rene-Jean Dupuy and Eilene Galloway, both *infra*, the major controversy revolved around the provisions of Article XI, which declared that outer space and celestial bodies are "the common heritage of mankind." At issue was the future development regime that would govern the exploitation of the vast resources of outer space. A definitive review of those resources concluded that the moon alone contained huge amounts of raw materials for making "structural metals, silicon glass, and ceramic products." Staff of Senate Comm. on Commerce, Science and Transportation, 96th Cong., 2d Sess., Agreement Governing the Activities of States on the Moon and Other Celestial Bodies, Part 4 at 415 (1980). Although the meaning of the "common heritage" principle is shrouded in mystery, its origins in the ideologically divisive Law of the Sea Treaty guaranteed that its interpretation in the space context—where so many potentially important natural resources are at stake—would become politicized. While some observers from the developed countries believed the Moon

Treaty would promote development, *see* the excerpt from Finch and Moore, *infra,* the consensus of this group, reflected in the excerpts from Dula and the Georgetown student note by Alan Duane Webber, *infra,* was that the vaguely communitarian "common heritage" principle would put a crimp on pioneering space development activities. In this view, the common heritage principle would lead to a centralized administrative structure requiring firms and governments to share their bounty with all the nations of the earth—thus standing as a major disincentive to high-risk development activities.

Representatives from the underdeveloped countries take a different view of the common heritage principle. As the excerpt from Rao, *infra,* shows, they saw the Moon Treaty as the first step in the essential process of bringing the underdeveloped world into parity with the wealthy nations. The Treaty in this view invites the establishment of an international regime to equitably distribute the proceeds from space resource development, on the theory that such resources belong to all mankind. In this sense, the Treaty is one of the first manifestations of the New International Economic Order, a proposed restructuring of the global economy based generally on principles of sharing and equitable development rather than "neo-colonialist exploitation." This new economic thinking is described in a brief note after the Rao excerpt.

Western legal commentators and economists remain unpersuaded of the merits of the principles underlying the New International Economic Order, however, as the excerpts from Webber and Dula, and the Note on Common Property Resources and Efficient Allocation, all *infra,* demonstrate. They believe instead that the best way to encourage development is to permit pioneering firms and governments to keep their profits. Without the lure of substantial profits—undiminished by the uncertainties of a scheme of international sharing—they argue that space development is too risky to be undertaken by any rational organization. Dula takes perhaps the extreme free-market view; others, notably Webber, and some of the economists cited in the Note, see some merit in an international regime for allocating development rights—so long as the profit-sharing component of the regime is kept separate from the system used to allocate development rights.

So we have some interesting issues awaiting us in this chapter. We turn first to the ABM Treaty, its background, and what it means for space activities.

THE ABM TREATY

The ABM Treaty severely limits the deployment, testing, and use of missile systems designed to intercept incoming strategic ballistic missiles. It is a bilateral treaty between the United States and the Soviet Union that took effect in 1972. Missiles, launchers, and ABM-related radars are prohibited or sharply limited under the Treaty, which applies to sea-, ground-, and space-based ABM systems (see Article V, reproduced below). There is one exception to the general prohibition of Article II: Article III permits each side to maintain one ABM system around its capital and another around a group of Inter-Continental Ballistic Missile (ICBM) silos of its choosing. Article IV also allows the U.S. and the Soviet Union to keep the development and testing operations they had at the time the Treaty was signed.

BACKGROUND

The ABM Treaty grew out of the Strategic Arms Limitation Talks (SALT I), which began in November of 1969. The basic philosophy behind the Treaty was simple. The recently developed ABM systems, with their potential to give one side protection against the other's missiles, might give one nuclear power the impression that it could launch an attack against the other without suffering significant damage itself. This was obviously a frightening scenario; importantly, it was just as dangerous whether or not it was true, so long as one side *believed* it had an advantage. The solution to this problem (and the related threat of a massive "spending race"), it was agreed, was a treaty limiting the deployment of these systems. Thus the ABM Treaty was born.

Only two of the Treaty's sixteen articles relate to space, Articles V and XII. They are set forth below.

Treaty on the Limitation of Anti-Ballistic Missile Systems, May 26, 1972, U.S.-U.S.S.R., 23 U.S.T. 3435

Article V

1. Each Party [i.e., the United States and the Soviet Union] undertakes not to develop, test, or deploy ABM systems or components which are sea-based, air-based, space-based, or mobile land-based.

2. Each Party undertakes not to develop, test, or deploy ABM launchers for launching more than one ABM interceptor missile at a time from each launcher, nor to modify deployed launchers to provide them with such a capability, nor to develop, test, or deploy automatic or semi-automatic or other similar systems for rapid reload of ABM launchers.

* * *

Article XII

1. For the purpose of providing assurance of compliance with the provisions of this Treaty, each Party shall use national technical means of verification at its disposal in a manner consistent with generally recognized principles of international law.

2. Each Party undertakes not to interfere with the national technical means of verification of the other Party operating in accordance with paragraph 1 of this Article.

3. Each Party undertakes not to use deliberate concealment measures which impede verification by national technical means of compliance with the provisions of this Treaty. This obligation shall not require changes in current construction, assembly, conversion or overhaul practices.

NOTE

There are two points worth mentioning about Article V. Paragraph 1 specifically refers to "space-based" ABM systems even though in 1972, when the Treaty was signed, no such systems were operational. Second, Paragraph 2, limiting the capacity of ABM missile launchers to one missile at a time, does not prevent a party from placing more than one non-missile projectile on a launcher. (This was one component in the controversial Reagan Administration "reinterpretation" of the ABM Treaty, discussed in the following section.)

Article XII is significant in that it represents the codification of the "open skies" principle. (The SALT I Agreement, another bilateral treaty adopted in 1971, also prohibited interference with the "national technical means of verification" of the other country; it has since expired. *See* Interim Agreement on Certain Measures with Respect to the Limitation of Strategic Offensive Arms, with Protocol (SALT I), 23 U.S.T. 3462 (effective Oct. 3, 1972; expired).) With this provision, space-based surveillance satellites not only became legal; they became an essential component of the international arms-control regime.

THE ABM "REINTERPRETATION"

From the time the ABM Treaty was signed until 1985, there seemed to be general agreement concerning its meaning. Both the Soviet Union and the United States conducted research into such futuristic alternative technologies as lasers and particle beams (research is not prohibited under the Treaty). At the same time, neither nation went ahead with either testing or deployment of mobile ABM systems or components, since both these activities are banned under Article V.

In 1985, however, the Reagan Administration needed to obtain legal clearance for the testing of "Star Wars"/Strategic Defense Initiative space-based defense components. The SDI concept, immediately dubbed "Star Wars" by the press when it was formally launched in 1983, called for the U.S. to embark on a massive research program to develop defensive systems that would render nuclear weapons (or at least those delivered via ICBMs) obsolete. Such a system, it was thought, could use satellites equipped with lasers or other high-energy beams to destroy incoming missiles, thus ensuring the safety of the United States. In short, the Star Wars proposal resurrected the dream of a "peace shield" over the country—a dream that would seem to have been surrendered in the ABM Treaty of 1972.

The Reagan Administration was not so quick to give up on the dream, however. Under a "broad interpretation" of the ABM Treaty, the Administration, headed by State Department Legal Adviser Abraham D. Sofaer, put forth an alternative interpretation. Just as the in-house counsel of a major corporation is unlikely to disappoint its Chief Executive Officer in the rendering of legal opinions, so the State Department's Legal Adviser did not disappoint the President by declaring his plans contrary to the Treaty. Not surprisingly, the new interpretation would have allowed the government to begin full-scale testing of space-based lasers and other advanced weapons; under the State Department's reading of the ABM Treaty, "Star Wars" could continue on schedule.

The structure of the reinterpretation is somewhat elaborate. Basically it revolves around Agreed Statement D, a controlling interpretive addendum to the Treaty that was agreed to by both parties. It reads as follows:

> In order to insure fulfillment of the obligation not to deploy ABM systems and their components except as provided in Article III of the Treaty [reproduced above], the Parties agree that in the event ABM systems based on other physical principles and including components capable of substituting for ABM interceptor missiles, ABM launchers, or ABM radars are created in the future, specific limitations on such systems and their components would be subject to discussion in accordance with Article XIII and agreement in accordance with Article XIV of the Treaty.

The Reagan Administration reinterpretation places great emphasis on one aspect of Statement D: it is the only provision in the Treaty that *explicitly* refers to technologies that might be developed in the future—"ABM systems based on other physical principles." Sofaer and other Reagan Administration officials drew one simple conclusion from this provision: Only this Statement, which concerns the two ABM system permitted in Article III, applies to technologies that were not in existence when the Treaty was signed. Thus the remainder of the Treaty, under this view, has no bearing on the testing of new ABM technologies. (Note that even Sofaer *et al.* did not argue that ABM systems based on new technologies can be *deployed;* presumably, even they read the language of Statement D as requiring the Parties to confer on new developments prior to deployment.) The upshot: Star Wars/SDI testing does not violate the ABM Treaty.

There are a great many problems with the reinterpretation. Whether one looks to the plain language of the Treaty's text (in its *entirety*), the conduct of the Parties subsequent to signing the Treaty, the negotiating history, or the understandings of the ratifying bodies, it is difficult to escape the conclusion that the proposed reinterpretation of the Reagan Administration was wrong. The broad language of Article V(1) banned "ABM systems or components" as defined in

Article II. Article II defines such systems by their *function* ("a system to counter strategic ballistic missiles") and states that such systems are those "*currently consisting of*" missiles, launchers, and radars (emphasis added). The only exception is set forth in Article III, which allows each side to keep two ABM systems in place. As is clear from its language and the accounts of the treaty negotiators, Statement D was meant to clarify this exception. (Notice that Statement D—the linchpin in the reinterpretation—begins with "In order to insure fulfillment of the obligation not to deploy ABM systems and their components except as provided in Article III of the Treaty. ...")

The reinterpretation thus fails to pass the test of even minimum plausibility. Raymond L. Garthoff, one of the key U.S. officials who negotiated the Treaty, puts it this way:

> In examining the text of a treaty, the most important facts are the effect of the language, intent of the parties, and purpose of the provisions. The interrelation and mutually reinforcing effect of the several provisions in its articles (and related agreed statements expanding on them) are also important. Judge Sofaer [as he prefers to be called] in effect turns the process of interpretation of the text on its head: instead of interpreting the terms of the treaty as a whole, he disaggregates and then reassembles them, often with great violence to the clear meaning of the language. Bending the parts to fit his preferred pattern, he constructs a kind of ABM Treaty Mod II, "Made in the USA," to suit the needs of a policy giving priority to the Reagan administration's SDI [i.e., Star Wars] program, rather than to the intent and purpose of the United States and the Soviet Union when together they concluded the ABM Treaty.

R. Garthoff, Policy Versus the Law: The Reinterpretation of the ABM Treaty 20 (1987).

NOTES

1. Prior to the dramatic reinterpretation of the ABM Treaty, military leaders and the Reagan Administration argued that the Star Wars program, or Strategic Defense Initiative (SDI), was not a violation of the Treaty because it was only in the research stage. As General James A. Abrahamson, Director of the Strategic Defense Initiative Organization, explained in Congressional testimony on the program, "[The ABM] agreement does permit research short of field testing of a prototype ABM system or breadboard model. Our research under the SDI program will be within those limits." Department of Defense Appropriations for 1986: Hearings Before the Subcomm. on Defense Appropriations of the House Comm. on Appropriations, 99th Cong., 1st Sess. 568–69 (1985).

2. Sofaer presented his views on the reinterpretation in an article in the Harvard Law Review. *See* Sofaer, The ABM Treaty and the Strategic Defense Initiative, 99 Harvard Law Review 1972 (1986).

3. Garthoff, in the book quoted from above, has recreated the negotiating history behind the "currently consisting of" language in Article II. Quoting from Memoranda of Conversations made at the time, he concludes:

> I argued that "the Soviet side, as well as the American, recognized that there could be *future* systems, and while the question of constraints on future systems would be settled elsewhere than in Article II, the correct way of indicating a valid connection between components and systems in Article II would be to include the word 'currently.'" Ginevsky [the chief Soviet negotiator] agreed to take up that proposal with his delegation, and the next day brought a new Soviet draft of Article II incorporating the language. ... A fully agreed upon Article II was incorporated into the latest version of the Joint Draft Text of the treaty. ...

R. Garthoff, *supra,* at 44.

4. A 1986 article has rehearsed in detail the Senate hearings leading up to ratification of the Treaty. The author concludes his analysis with the following statement:

> Considering the legislative history as a whole, the Reagan administration's permissive interpretation of the ABM Treaty appears to differ substantially from the consenting Senate of the Treaty. A fair reading of the Senate hearings strongly suggests two conclusions about the meaning of the ABM Treaty: first, when Article III, paragraph 1 of Article V and Agreed Statement D are read together, their import is that the development and testing of "Star Wars" technology in any basing mode other than a fixed, land-based mode is prohibited; and, second, that the deployment of such technology in even the fixed, land-based mode is prohibited under the Treaty.

Kennedy, Treaty Interpretation by the Executive Branch: The ABM Treaty and "Star Wars" Testing and Development, 80 American Journal of International Law 854, 866 (1986). *See also* A. Sherr, A Legal Analysis of the "New Interpretation" of the Anti-Ballistic Missile Treaty (1986); Chayes & Chayes, Testing and Development of "Exotic" Systems Under the ABM Treaty: The Great Reinterpretation Caper, 99 Harvard Law Review 1956 (1986).

5. Many members of Congress were so incensed at the proposed reinterpretation that the Senate threatened to block ratification of another arms control treaty—the Intermediate Nuclear Forces (INF) Treaty of 1988—until the Reagan administration withdrew the ABM reinterpretation. *See* Norman, Showdown Nears on ABM Treaty, 238 Science 147, 149 (1988). In addition, because the ABM reinterpretation goes against the understanding of many Senators who ratified that treaty, some Senators demanded that they be given access to the entire negotiating record of any future treaties, to assure that detailed understandings of all provisions could be embedded in the ratification proceedings, thus undercut-

ting any future reinterpretation maneuvers. *See also* Norman, Senator Blasts Administration's Reinterpretation of ABM Treaty, 234 Science 1489 (1988).

THE MOON TREATY

Agreement on Activities of States on the Moon and Other Celestial Bodies G.A. Res. 34/68, U.N. GAOR, 34th Sess., Supp. No. 46, U.N. Doc. A/34/664 (1979)

The States parties to this Agreement,

Noting the achievements of states in the exploration and use of the moon and other celestial bodies,

Recognizing that the moon, as a natural satellite of the earth, has an important role to play in the exploration of outer space,

Determined to promote on the basis of equality the further development of co-operation among states in the exploration and use of the moon and other celestial bodies,

Desiring to prevent the moon from becoming an area of international conflict,

Bearing in mind the benefits which may be derived from the exploitation of the natural resources of the moon and other celestial bodies,

Recalling the [1967] Treaty on Principles governing the Activities of States in the Exploration and Use of Outer Space, including the Moon and Other Celestial Bodies, the Agreement on the Rescue of Astronauts, the Return of Astronauts and the Return of Objects launched into Outer Space, the Convention on International Liability for Damage caused by Space Objects, and the Convention on Registration of Objects launched into Outer Space,

Taking into account the need to define and develop the provisions of these international instruments in relation to the moon and other celestial bodies, having regard to further progress in the exploration and use of outer space,

Have agreed on the following:

Article 1

(1) The provisions of this Agreement relating to the moon shall also apply to other celestial bodies within the solar system, other than the earth, except in so far as specific legal norms enter into force with respect to any of these celestial bodies.

(2) For the purposes of this Agreement reference to the Moon shall include orbits around or other trajectories to or around it.

(3) This Agreement does not apply to extraterrestrial materials which reach the surface of the earth by natural means.

Article 2

All activities on the moon, including its exploration and use, shall be carried out in accordance with international law, in particular the Charter of the United Nations, and taking into account the Declaration of Principles of International Law concerning Friendly Relations and Co-operation among States in accordance with the charter of the United Nations, adopted by the General Assembly on Oct. 24, 1970, in the interests of maintaining international peace and security and promoting international co-operation and mutual understanding, and with due regard to the corresponding interests of all other states parties.

Article 3

(1) The moon shall be used by all states parties exclusively for peaceful purposes.

(2) Any threat or use of force or any other hostile act or threat of hostile act on the moon is prohibited. It is likewise prohibited to use the moon in order to commit any such act or to engage in any such threat in relation to the earth, the moon, spacecraft, the personnel of spacecraft or man-made space objects.

(3) States parties shall not place in orbit around or other trajectory to or around the moon objects carrying nuclear weapons or any other kinds of weapons of mass destruction or place or use such weapons on or in the moon.

(4) The establishment of military bases, installations and fortifications, the testing of any type of weapons and the conduct of military maneuvers on the moon shall be forbidden. The use of military personnel for scientific research or for any other peaceful purposes shall not be prohibited. The use of any equipment or facility necessary for peaceful exploration and use of the moon shall also not be prohibited.

Article 4

(1) The exploration and use of the moon shall be the province of all mankind and shall be carried out for the benefit and in the interests of all countries, irrespective of their degree of economic or scientific development. Due regard shall be paid to the interests of present and future generations as well as to the need to promote higher standards of living and conditions of economic and social progress and development in accordance with the Charter of the United Nations.

(2) States parties shall be guided by the principle of co-operation and mutual assistance in all their activities concerning the exploration and use of the moon. International co-operation in pursuance of this Agreement should be as wide as possible and may take place on a multilateral basis, on a bilateral basis or through international inter-governmental organizations.

Article 5

(1) States parties shall inform the Secretary-General of the United Nations as well as the public and the international scientific community, to the greatest extent feasible and practicable, of their activities concerned with the exploration and use of the moon. Information on the time, purposes, locations, orbital parameters and duration shall be given in respect of each mission to the moon as soon as possible after launching, while information on the results of each mission, including scientific results, shall be furnished upon completion of the mission. In the case of a mission lasting more than 60 days, information on conduct of the mission, including any scientific results, shall be given periodically at 30-day intervals. For missions lasting more than six months, only significant additions to such information need be reported thereafter.

(2) If a state party becomes aware that another state party plans to operate simultaneously in the same area of or in the same orbit around or trajectory to or around the moon, it shall promptly inform the other state of the timing of and plans for its own operations.

(3) In carrying out activities under this Agreement, states parties shall promptly inform the Secretary-General, as well as the public and the international scientific community, of any phenomena they discover in outer space, including the moon, which could endanger human life or health, as well as of any indication of organic life.

Article 6

(1) There shall be freedom of scientific investigation on the moon by all states parties without discrimination of any kind, on the basis of equality and in accordance with international law.

(2) In carrying out scientific investigations and in furtherance of the provisions of this Agreement, the states parties shall have the right to collect on and remove from the moon samples of its mineral and other substances. Such samples shall remain at the disposal of those states parties which caused them to be collected and may be used by them for scientific purposes. States parties shall have regard to the desirability of making a portion of such samples available to other interested state parties and the international scientific community for scientific investigation. States parties may in the course of scientific investigations also use mineral and other substances of the moon in quantities appropriate for the support of their missions.

(3) States parties agree on the desirability of exchanging scientific and other personnel on expeditions to or installations on the moon to the greatest extent feasible and practicable.

Article 7

(1) In exploring and using the moon, states parties shall take measures to prevent the disruption of the existing balance of its environment whether by intro-

ducing adverse changes in that environment, by its harmful contamination through the introduction of extra-environmental matter or otherwise. States parties shall also take measures to avoid harmfully affecting the environment of the earth through the introduction of extraterrestrial matter or otherwise.

(2) States parties shall inform the Secretary-General of the United Nations of the measures being adopted by them in accordance with Paragraph 1 of this Article and shall also, to the maximum extent feasible, notify him in advance of all placements by them of radio-active materials on the moon and of the purposes of such placements.

(3) States parties shall report to other states parties and to the Secretary-General concerning areas of the moon having special scientific interest in order that, without prejudice to the rights of other states parties, consideration may be given to the designation of such areas as international scientific preserves for which special protective arrangements are to be agreed upon in consultation with the competent bodies of the United Nations.

Article 8

(1) States parties may pursue their activities in the exploration and use of the moon anywhere on or below its surface, subject to the provisions of this Agreement.

(2) For these purposes states parties may, in particular:

(a) Land their space objects on the moon and launch them from the moon;

(b) Place their personnel, space vehicles, equipment, facilities, stations and installations anywhere on or below the surface of the moon.

Personnel, space vehicles, equipment, facilities, stations and installations may move or be moved freely over or below the surface of the moon.

(3) Activities of states parties in accordance with Paragraphs 1 and 2 of this Article shall not interfere with the activities of other states parties on the moon. Where such interference may occur, the states parties concerned shall undertake consultations in accordance with Article 15, Paragraphs 2 and 3 of this Agreement.

Article 9

(1) States parties may establish manned and unmanned stations on the moon. A state party establishing a station shall use only that area which is required for the needs of the station and shall immediately inform the Secretary-General of the United Nations of the location and purposes of that station. Subsequently, at annual intervals that state shall likewise inform the Secretary-General whether the station continues in use and whether its purposes have changed.

(2) Stations shall be installed in such a manner that they do not impede the free access to all areas of the moon by personnel, vehicles and equipment of

other states parties conducting activities on the moon in accordance with the provisions of this Agreement or of Article 1 of the Treaty on Principles governing the Activities of States in the Exploration and Use of Outer Space, including the Moon and Other Celestial Bodies.

Article 10

(1) States parties shall adopt all practicable measures to safeguard the life and health of persons on the moon. For this purpose they shall regard any person on the moon as an astronaut within the meaning of Article V of the Treaty on Principles governing the Activities of States in the Exploration and Use of Outer Space, including the Moon and Other Celestial Bodies and as part of the personnel of a spacecraft within the meaning of the Agreement on the Rescue of Astronauts, the Return of Astronauts and the Return of Objects launched into Outer Space.

(2) States parties shall offer shelter in their stations, installations, vehicles and other facilities to persons in distress on the moon.

Article 11

(1) The moon and its natural resources are the common heritage of mankind, which finds its expression in the provisions of this Agreement, in particular in Paragraph 5 of this Article.

(2) The moon is not subject to national appropriation by any claim of sovereignty, by means of use or occupation, or by any other means.

(3) Neither the surface nor the subsurface of the moon, nor any part thereof or natural resources in place, shall become property of any state, international intergovernmental or non-governmental organization, national organization or non-governmental entity or of any natural person. The placement of personnel, space vehicles, equipment, facilities, stations and installations on or below the surface of the moon, including structures connected with its surface or subsurface, shall not create a right of ownership over the surface or the subsurface of the moon or any areas thereof. The foregoing provisions are without prejudice to the international regime referred to in Paragraph 5 of this Article.

(4) States parties have the right to exploration and use of the moon without discrimination of any kind, on the basis of equality and in accordance with international law and the provisions of this Agreement.

(5) States parties to this Agreement hereby undertake to establish an international regime, including appropriate procedures, to govern the exploitation of the natural resources of the moon as such exploitation is about to become feasible. This provision shall be implemented in accordance with Article 18 of this Agreement.

(6) In order to facilitate the establishment of the international regime referred to in Paragraph 5 of this Article, states parties shall inform the Secretary-General

of the United Nations as well as the public and the international scientific community, to the greatest extent feasible and practicable, of any natural resources they may discover on the moon.

(7) The main purposes of the international regime to be established shall include;

(a) The orderly and safe development of the natural resources of the moon;

(b) The rational management of those resources;

(c) The expansion of opportunities in the use of those resources;

(d) An equitable sharing by all states parties in the benefits derived from those resources, whereby the interests and needs of the developing countries, as well as the efforts of those countries, which have contributed either directly or indirectly to the exploration of the moon, shall be given special consideration.

(8) All the activities with respect to the natural resources of the moon shall be carried out in a manner compatible with the purposes specified in paragraph 7 of this Article and the provisions of Article 6, Paragraph 2, of this Agreement.

Article 12

(1) States parties shall retain jurisdiction and control over their personnel, space vehicles, equipment, facilities, stations and installations on the moon. The ownership of space vehicles, equipment, facilities, stations and installations shall not be affected by their presence on the moon.

(2) Vehicles, installations and equipment or their component parts found in places other than their intended location shall be dealt with in accordance with Article 5 of the Agreement on the Rescue of Astronauts, the Return of Astronauts and the Return of Objects launched into Outer Space.

(3) In the event of an emergency involving a threat to human life, states parties may use the equipment, vehicles, installations, facilities, or supplies of other states parties on the moon. Prompt notification of such use shall be made to the Secretary-General of the United Nations or the state party concerned.

Article 13

A State party which learns of the crash-landing, forced landing or other unintended landing on the moon of a space object, or its component parts, that were not launched by it, shall promptly inform the launching state party and the Secretary-General of the United Nations.

Article 14

(1) States parties to this Agreement shall bear international responsibility for national activities on the moon, whether such activities are carried out by governmental agencies or by non-governmental entities, and for assuring that na-

tional activities are carried out in conformity with the provisions set forth in this Agreement. States parties shall ensure that non-governmental entities under their jurisdiction shall engage in activities on the moon only under the authority and continuing supervision of the appropriate state party.

(2) States parties recognize that detailed arrangements concerning liability for damage caused on the moon, in addition to the provisions of the Treaty on Principles governing the Activities of States in the Exploration and Use of Outer Space, including the Moon and Other Celestial Bodies and the Convention on International Liability for Damage caused by Space Objects, may become necessary as a result of more extensive activities on the moon. Any such arrangements shall be elaborated in accordance with the procedure provided for in Article 18 of this Agreement.

Article 15

(1) Each state party may assure itself that the activities of other states parties in the exploration and use of the moon are compatible with the provisions of this Agreement. To this end, all space vehicles, equipment, facilities, stations and installations on the moon shall be open to other state parties. Such states parties shall give reasonable advance notice of a projected visit, in order that appropriate consultations may be held and that maximum precautions may be taken to assure safety and to avoid interference with normal operations in the facility to be visited. In pursuance of this Article, any state party may act on its own behalf or with the full or partial assistance of any other state party or through appropriate international procedures within the framework of the United Nations and in accordance with the Charter.

(2) A state party which has reason to believe that another state party is not fulfilling the obligations incumbent upon it pursuant to this Agreement or that another state party is interfering with the rights which the former state has under this Agreement may request consultations with that state party. A state party receiving such a request shall enter into such consultations without delay. Any other state party which requests to do so shall be entitled to take part in the consultations. Each state party participating in such consultations shall seek a mutually acceptable resolution of any controversy and shall bear in mind the rights and interests of all state parties. The Secretary-General of the United Nations shall be informed of the results of the consultations and shall transmit the information received to all states parties concerned.

(3) If the consultations do not lead to a mutually acceptable settlement which has due regard for the rights and interests of all states parties, the parties concerned shall take all measures to settle the dispute by other peaceful means of their choice appropriate to the circumstances and the nature of the dispute. If difficulties arise in connection with the opening of consultations, or if consultations do not lead to a mutually acceptable settlement, any state party may seek the as-

sistance of the Secretary-General, without seeking the consent of any other state party concerned, in order to resolve the controversy. A state party which does not maintain diplomatic relations with another state party concerned shall participate in such consultations, as its choice, either itself or through another state party or the Secretary-General as intermediary.

Article 16

With the exception of Articles 17 to 21, references in this Agreement to states shall be deemed to apply to any international inter-governmental organization which conducts space activities if the organization declares its acceptance of the rights and obligations provided for in this Agreement and if a majority of the states members of the organization are states parties to this Agreement and to the [1967] Treaty of Principles governing the Activities of States in the Exploration and Use of Outer Space, including the Moon and Other Celestial Bodies. States members of any such organization which are states parties to this Agreement shall take all appropriate steps to ensure that the organization makes a declaration in accordance with the provisions of this Article.

Article 17

Any state party to this Agreement may propose amendments to the Agreement. Amendments shall enter into force for each state party to the Agreement accepting the amendments upon their acceptance by a majority of the states parties to the Agreement and thereafter for each remaining state party to the Agreement on the date of acceptance by it.

Article 18

Ten years after the entry into force of this Agreement, the question of the review of the Agreement shall be included in the provisional agenda of the General Assembly of the United Nations in order to consider, in the light of past application of the Agreement, whether it requires revision. However, at any time after the Agreement has been in force for five years, the Secretary-General of the United Nations, as depository, shall, at the request of one-third of the states parties to the Agreement and with the concurrence of the majority of the states parties, convene a conference of the states parties to review this agreement. A review conference shall also consider the question of the implementation of the provisions of Article 11, Paragraph 5, on the basis of the principle referred to in Paragraph 1 of that Article and taking into account in particular any relevant technological developments.

Article 19

(1) This Agreement shall be open for signature by all states at United Nations Headquarters in New York.

(2) This Agreement shall be subject to ratification by signatory states. Any state which does not sign this Agreement before its entry into force in accordance with Paragraph 3 of this Article may accede to it at any time. Instruments of ratification or accession shall be deposited with the Secretary-General of the United Nations.

(3) This Agreement shall enter into force on the 30th day following the date of deposit of the fifth instrument of ratification.

(4) For each state depositing its instrument of ratification or accession after the entry into force of this Agreement, it shall enter into force on the 30th day following the date of deposit of any such instrument.

(5) The Secretary-General shall promptly inform all signatory and acceding states of the date of each signature, the date of deposit of each instrument of ratification or accession to this Agreement, the date of its entry into force and other notices.

Article 20

Any state party to this Agreement may give notice of its withdrawal from the Agreement one year after its entry into force by written notification to the Secretary-General of the United Nations. Such withdrawal shall take effect one year from the date of receipt of this notification.

Article 21

The original of this Agreement, of which the Arabic, Chinese, English, French, Russian and Spanish texts are equally authentic, shall be deposited with the Secretary-General of the United Nations, who shall send certified copies thereof to all signatory and acceding states.

Nash, Contemporary Practice of the United States Relating to International Law, 74 American Journal 418, 421–26 of International Law (1980)

Moon Treaty

Senator Frank Church, chairman of the Senate Committee on Foreign Relations, and Senator Jacob K. Javits, ranking minority member of the committee, addressed a joint letter to Secretary of State Cyrus R. Vance on October 30, 1979, in which they expressed concern that several aspects of the (United Nations) Agreement Governing the Activities of States on the Moon and Other Celestial Bodies (Moon Treaty) could prove damaging to the national economic and security interests of the United States.

One source of concern was their view that the law of the sea negotiations had shown that the meaning attached to the concept, "common heritage of mankind," by many countries of the world was contrary to the economic interests of the United States and of other countries with free enterprise/free market economies. Another source of concern was their view that the treaty would result in a "de facto moratorium" on resource-related activities in outer space (through the commitment to negotiate a subsequent resource regime), which would not deter the Soviets from moving forward in resource development under the guise of scientific investigation because they would have "no fear of significant competition from the West, which must rely on its industry to provide commercial initiative."

Secretary Vance, in his replies to Senators Church and Javits on November 28, noted that on November 1, Ambassador Richard W. Petree had placed on record the U.S. interpretation of various treaty provisions, including those of concern to the Senators, during the debate on the resolution of the UN Special Political Committee commending the Moon Treaty and recommending that it be opened for signature. The United States had joined with 27 other countries, including the United Kingdom, the Federal Republic of Germany, France, Belgium, the Netherlands, Italy, Canada, Australia, and Japan, in sponsoring the resolution, which had been adopted by consensus on November 2. (The General Assembly approved the resolution on December 5, 1979.)

The Secretary clarified the legal significance of the U.S. actions to date in connection with the treaty, stating, in part:

> Of course, our cosponsorship of the resolution and joining in consensus approval of the resolution does not entail legal obligations for the United States. Only ratification of the Treaty after the advice and consent of the Senate can impose binding obligations upon the United States. The Administration has not yet turned to questions relating to signature of the Treaty or its submission to the Senate. When we begin to consider such matters, we will give the most careful consideration to concerns which you and others have raised in regard to the Moon Treaty. I would, however, like to address myself to some of your points in a preliminary way.
>
> In regard to the important matter of the exploitation of the natural resources of the moon and other celestial bodies, the Treaty contains no moratorium on exploitation and, in fact, has provisions designed to facilitate and encourage such exploitation. For example, Article XI(3) of the Moon Treaty makes clear that although the 1967 Outer Space Treaty provides that "Outer space, including the moon and other celestial bodies, is not subject to national appropriation by claim of sovereignty, by means of use or occupation, or by any other means," this "non-appropriation" principle applies to the natural resources of celestial bodies only when such resources are "in place." Thus, Article XI(3) would permit ownership to be exercised by States or private entities over those natural resources which have been removed from their

"Place" on or below the surface of the moon or other celestial bodies. (Such removal is permitted by the article contained in the 1967 Outer Space Treaty which states, inter alia, that "Outer space, including the moon and other celestial bodies, shall be free for exploration and use by all States. ...")

We also do not believe that the Treaty would benefit the Soviet Union to the disadvantage of the United States. While the Soviet Union first proposed a Moon Treaty, their draft text contained no detailed provisions concerning exploitation. It was, rather, characterized by the Soviets as a "navigation treaty." It was the United States which in 1972 first proposed detailed provisions concerning exploitation and the common heritage concept. (The 1967 Outer Space Treaty, which the United States has ratified with the Senate's advice and consent, already had provided that outer space was the "common province" of mankind and that "the exploration and use of outer space, including the moon and other celestial bodies, shall be carried out for the benefit and the interests of all countries, irrespective of their degree of economic or scientific development ..." (Article I).) Until July of 1979, the Soviet Union maintained strong opposition to the common heritage concept, and it was essentially because of this opposition that the Treaty was not concluded several years ago. Likewise, the Soviets, as well as the United States, opposed the concept of a moratorium on exploitation of natural resources.

The statement of Ambassador Richard W. Petree, U.S. Deputy Representative to the Security Council, enclosed with the Secretary's letters, summarized important U.S. space activities during the year and U.S. views on issues before the UN Outer Space Committee. In regard to the Moon Treaty, Ambassador Petree stated, in part:

[T]he draft Moon Treaty ... is, in its own right, a meaningful advance in the codification of international law dealing with outer space, containing obligations which are of both immediate and long-term application in regard to such matters as the safeguarding of human life on celestial bodies, the promotion of scientific investigation and the exchange of information relative to and derived from activities on celestial bodies, and the enhancement of opportunities and conditions for evaluation, research and exploitation of the natural resources of celestial bodies. We think it useful to address some of the especially significant provisions contained in the draft Moon Agreement, this "fifth star" in the constellation of outer space treaties.

* * *

The common heritage concept, which was initially suggested by Argentina, but formally proposed by the United States in 1972, is set forth in Article XI, paragraph 1, which makes clear that its meaning for purposes of the Moon Treaty is to be found within the Moon Treaty itself. Likewise, its meaning in the Moon Treaty is without prejudice to its use or meaning in any other treaty. Article XI also makes clear that the parties to the treaty undertake, as the exploitation of the natural resources of the celestial bodies other than the earth is about to become feasible, to enter into negotiations to establish a mutually acceptable international regime to govern the exploitation of those mineral and other substantive resources which may be found on the surface or subsurface of a celestial body. My Government will, when and if negotiations for such regime are called for under Articles XI and XVII, make a good faith effort to see that such negotiations are successfully concluded.

* * *

The draft treaty, as part of the compromise by many delegations, places no moratorium upon the exploitation of the natural resources on celestial bodies by States or their nationals, but does provide that any exploitation of the natural resources of celestial bodies be carried out in a manner compatible with the purposes specified in paragraph 7 of Article XI and the provisions of paragraph 2 of Article VI. We view the purposes set forth in paragraph 7 as providing both a framework and an incentive for exploitation of the natural resources of celestial bodies. They constitute a framework because even exploitation which is undertaken by a State Party to the Treaty or its nationals outside of the context of any such regime, either because the exploitation occurs before a regime is negotiated or because a particular State may not participate in the international regime once it is established, will have to be compatible with those purposes set forth in Article XI, paragraph 7, of the Moon Treaty.

In a letter of November 13, 1979, Senator Richard Stone, also a member of the Senate Committee on Foreign Relations, urged Secretary Vance to reevaluate the U.S. position on the draft moon treaty, which he described as having "extremely dangerous potentialities" because it appeared to decrease "the ability of the United States to advance in yet unexplored fields" and to "greatly inhibit the actions and desires of U.S. corporations in space, negate the notion of free enterprise, and ... place the United States in a position subservient to the Soviet Union."

J. Brian Atwood, Assistant Secretary of State for Congressional Relations, replied to Senator Stone on behalf of the Secretary in a letter of January 2, 1980, as follows:

The provisions of the Moon Treaty must be considered in the context established by the 1967 Treaty on Principles Governing the Activities of States on the Exploration and Use of Outer Space, Including the Moon and Other Celestial Bodies (the "Outer Space Treaty") to which approximately 75 countries, including the United States, are parties. This Treaty received the advice and consent of the Senate without reservations.

* * *

The Moon Treaty places no limitations on the exploitation of celestial natural resources by any government or private entity beyond those already contained in the 1967 Outer Space Treaty except that the "activities with respect to the natural resources of the moon shall be carried out in a manner compatible with the purposes specified in paragraph 7." (See Article XI(8) and the environmental protections contained in Article VII.)

* * *

In regard to the international regime dealt with in Article XI(5) of the Moon Treaty, neither the "common heritage of mankind" concept as embodied in the Moon Treaty nor any other provision of the Treaty compels any specific form of international arrangement for the regulation of the exploitation of moon or other celestial body resources. Neither the Treaty nor the "common heritage" concept entails any specific obligation on States in regard to the establishment of such a regime except the commitment to engage in good faith negotiations to establish a mutually acceptable international regime to govern the exploitation of natural resources on celestial bodies when exploitation of such natural resources is about to become feasible.

The Law of the Sea experience with the common heritage concept, while relevant, would in no way be controlling regarding the negotiations of any such future agreement. Article XI(1) of the Moon Treaty makes clear that the common heritage concept in the Moon Treaty finds its meaning totally within the text of the Moon Treaty itself. A future negotiation for the regime to govern [the] moon or other celestial body resources could, however, benefit from the Law of the Sea experience, just as it could benefit from the experience of such multinational cooperative ventures in outer space as INTELSAT, which organization is evidence that the criteria set forth in Article XI(7) of the Moon Treaty can be met by institutional arrangements quite different from those contemplated in the Law of the Sea negotiations on sea-bed mining.

* * *

We do not believe that the Moon Treaty language would inhibit commercial investment by non-government entities in the exploitation of celestial natural resources or the operation of the free enterprise system in outer space generally. The article of the Moon Treaty most relevant, Article X, makes clear that all States Parties to the Treaty have a significant interest in the possible future exploitation of the natural resources of the moon and other celestial bodies and that their views are to be given serious consideration at any future international conference which may attempt to establish an international regime specifically concerned with exploitation of celestial natural resources. Given the legal context established by the 1967 Outer Space Treaty, such an interest can be neither denied nor ignored.

It is important to note that efforts by some developing countries to have the Treaty provide for a moratorium on the exploitation of the natural resources of celestial bodies except under the auspices of an international regime were rejected. The Treaty contains no moratorium on exploitation and, in fact, has provisions designed to clarify certain important ambiguities in the 1967 Outer Space Treaty and to otherwise facilitate and encourage the exploitation of celestial natural resources. For example, Article XI(3) of the Moon Treaty makes clear that although the 1967 Outer Space Treaty provides that "Outer Space, including the moon and other celestial bodies, is not subject to national appropriation by claim of sovereignty, by means of use or occupation, or by any other means," this "non-appropriation" principle applies to the natural resources of celestial bodies only when such resources are "in place."

NOTE

This excerpt summarizes the position of those who negotiated and helped draft the Moon Treaty. The views of the State Department, which supported the Moon Treaty, are set out more fully in Staff of Senate Comm. on Commerce, Science and Transportation, 96th Cong., 2d Sess., Agreement and Governing the Activities of States on the Moon and Other Celestial Bodies, Part 3 at 316–18, 363–65 (Comm. Print 1980). Unfortunately for them, a host of other space interest groups mounted a storm of protest over the Treaty, culminating in the failure of the Senate to even vote on ratification. *See, e.g., id.* at 318–26, 366–79 (summary of space group L5 Society's Objections to Moon Treaty, and text of L5 Society point-by-point rebuttal of State Department memorandum). The issues that the negotiators thought were resolved in the Treaty's text in fact proved to be the downfall of the agreement, particularly the "common heritage" language in Article XI. In the excerpt that follows, a student Note written at the time the Treaty was being debated points out some of the problems with the Treaty.

Spitz, Note, SPACE LAW—Agreement Governing the Activities of States on the Moon and Other Celestial Bodies, 21 Harvard International Law Journal 579 (1980)

Most of the provisions of the Agreement have already been set forth in previous space accords. The 1967 Treaty on Principles Governing the Activities of States in the Exploration and Use of Outer Space, including the Moon and Other Celestial Bodies, which has seventy-six member states including the United States and the Soviet Union, set forth the principle that the moon and other celestial bodies shall be used exclusively for peaceful purposes.

*   *   *

The significant change in space law which the Agreement makes is the application of the "common heritage" principle to the natural resources of the moon. The [Outer Space] Treaty declared that the moon was not subject to national appropriation and that outer space was the "province of all mankind." However, neither it nor subsequent agreements have addressed the natural resources question. A commitment to "an equitable sharing" by all states in the moon's resources and the establishment of an international regime to achieve that purpose will have a significant effect on the exploitation of the solar system. The common heritage provisions of the Agreement, when viewed with similar themes raised in the Law of the Sea Conference and the discussions on Antarctica, points to a trend growing in acceptance in the international community. If it achieves broad acceptance, the Agreement could have great impact outside the area of space law.

However, a great potential limitation on the effectiveness of the Agreement is that it makes no provision for signatory states to compel the participation of other states. There is also no mechanism to protect the interests of member states against non-participants. Even though the Agreement may be adopted widely enough to have some force as customary international law, it will need the acceptance of those states capable of conducting space operations to be effective.

Though the Agreement should have no trouble winning acceptance by developing states, the support of the two current space powers is more problematic. The Soviet Union in particular opposes international control of the natural resources of space, and from the beginning of the discussion it opposed the application of any part of the Agreement to celestial bodies other than the moon. Soviet ratification of the Agreement, if it occurs at all, will be reluctant. The United States stance on the Agreement is less clear. Since the exploitation of the moon's natural resources has seemed far in the future, the State Department and the National Aeronautics and Space Administration have been supporting the drafting process since its inception. Recently however, the United States seems to have reconsidered its position.

This points up the basic dilemma of the Agreement. Without the common heritage provision, the Agreement is largely a reiteration of previous treaties. With them, it loses its appeal to the two space powers whose support it will probably need. The success of the Agreement may hinge on the willingness of the United States and the Soviet Union to accept the common heritage provisions.

NOTES

1. The author of this Note states that "a great potential limitation on the effectiveness of the Agreement is that it makes no provision for signatory states to compel the participation of other states. There is also no mechanism to protect the interests of member states against non-participants." Was it a mistake for the drafters of the Treaty to assume that the central administrative organization called for in Article 2 would be joined by all countries? What problems could a

single non-joiner cause for those who have joined? Is the "equitable distribution" provision enough of an incentive for developing countries to join?

2. The excerpt from an article by noted space lawyer Art Dula, reproduced *infra,* is an example of the writing that came out of the anti-treaty camp. A similar piece appeared in the magazine of the L5 Society at the time of the Treaty debate. *See* Dula, Free Enterprise and the Proposed Moon Treaty, L5 News, Oct. 1979, at 1. *See also* Christol, The ABA and the Moon Treaty, 9 Journal of Space Law 77 (1981) (describing deliberations behind ABA's formal recommendations on the Treaty).

3. As of this writing, the Soviet Union has yet to sign the Treaty. It has long taken the position that space resources should be freely exploitable by the nations that find and develop them. Did the fact that the U.S. refused to ratify the Treaty make it politically easier for the Soviet Union—which sometimes styles itself the friend of the developing world—to refrain from ratifying it itself? What would be the dynamics of a centralized international agency governing space resources having only one of the two major powers—the U.S. or the Soviet Union—as a member? Would it be economically feasible for one to join and not the other? Also, it is interesting to at least ponder the thought that the Soviet Union, the nation with the greatest practical experience in the area of centralized economic planning and control, may know all too well the pitfalls of such arrangements.

Absent adoption by the major space powers, the Moon Treaty is unlikely to play a major role in the future. Nevertheless, the failure of the major space powers to ratify the Treaty does not mean it is irrelevant. For one thing, as one of the first international documents to embody concepts identified with the New International Economic Order, it reflects important intellectual trends among the developing nations of the world. In addition, it should be recalled that the U.S.-Soviet domination of space capability is by no means a permanent affair; other nations—some of whom have already signed the Moon Treaty—are rapidly developing such a capability, as was shown in Chapter 1. Thus the Moon Treaty is far from a dead letter on the international scene.

Galloway, Issues in Implementing the Agreement Governing the Activities of States on the Moon and Other Celestial Bodies, in Proceedings of the Twenty-Third Colloquium on the Law of Outer Space 19, 20 (1980)

Article I, paragraph 1 of the Moon Agreement text provides that "the provisions of this Agreement relating to the Moon shall also apply to other celestial bodies within the solar system, other than the earth, except in so far as specific legal norms enter into force with respect to any of these celestial bodies." COPUOS related this principle to paragraph 1 of Article 11 which provides that "The moon and its natural resources are the common heritage of mankind, which finds its expression in the provisions of this Agreement, in particular in paragraph 5 of this article." Paragraph 5 of Article 11 provides for the establishment of an international regime when exploitation of the natural resources of the moon and other celestial bodies is "about to become feasible" but states that this provision must be implemented in accordance with article 18 of the Agreement. ... The official COPUOS Understanding is as follows:

> The Committee agreed that by virtue of article I, paragraph 1, the principle contained in article XI, paragraph 1, would also apply to celestial bodies in the solar system other than the Earth and to its natural resources. (Paragraph 62)

This is a significant interpretation regarding natural resources of celestial bodies, and it is part of the negotiating history, but its form—and the fact that this COPUOS understanding (as well as the other understandings) is usually omitted when the Moon Treaty text is distributed—raises the issue of the exact legal status of such an understanding. When the General Assembly voted on the treaty text, specific reference was made to the COPUOS understandings as paragraphs 62, 63, and 65, which could tend to strengthen the status of the understandings; nevertheless, this is an issue which can arise in the future to create problems, and when analysts first read these understandings and realize their importance, they wonder why these points are not included in the treaty text.

The delegates to the 1979 COPUOS session thought it was necessary to clarify article I, paragraph 2 which provides that "For the purposes of this Agreement references to the moon shall include orbits around or other trajectories to or around it." In response, COPUOS recorded this understanding:

> Following a suggestion for clarification of article I, paragraph 2, the committee agreed that the trajectories and orbits mentioned in article I, paragraph 2 do not include trajectories and orbits of space objects in Earth orbits only and trajectories of space objects between the Earth and such orbits. (Paragraph 63)

This means that trajectories to the Moon—and other celestial bodies—and orbits around the Moon are covered by the Agreement, but not covered are earth-orbiting spacecraft and trajectories from the earth to orbits around the earth.

NOTE

The Moon Treaty does not cover earth orbits or trajectories into earth orbit. In 1976, however, there was an attempt to make earth orbits subject to a "common heritage"-like regime. In the Bogota Resolution, a group of developing nations located near the equator on various continents declared that geosynchronous orbits overhead were subject to their sovereignty. The geosynchronous orbit issue is discussed in Chapter 8. Much of the common-resource discussion later in this chapter applies to that resource as well. It is safe to say that the Resolution has not met with widespread international acceptance.

Walsh, Controversial Issues
Under Article XI of the Moon Treaty,
5 Annals of Air & Space Law 489 (1981)

III. National Appropriation and Property Rights

Another issue in Article XI ... is what its provisions regarding national appropriation and property rights entail. Paragraph two of this article provides that "the moon is not subject to national appropriation by any claim of sovereignty, by means of use or occupation, or by any other means." Consistent with this paragraph is the first sentence in paragraph three which states that:

> Neither the surface nor the subsurface of the moon, nor any parts thereof or natural resources in place, shall become property of any State, international, intergovernmental or non-governmental entity or of any natural person.

These two provisions in Article XI appear to greatly limit the extent of an entity's activities on the moon and other celestial bodies, although definitions for appropriation and property are not given. The latter provision regarding property may, in fact, be of greater consequence because it applies not only to States, but to international, intergovernmental and non-governmental entities, and natural persons.

The prohibitions imposed by the two aforesaid provisions appear, however, to be negated by a subsequent provision in the article. A latter part of paragraph three states that:

> The placement of personnel, space vehicles, equipment facilities, stations and installations on or below the surface of the moon, including structures connected with their surface or subsurface, shall not create a right of ownership over the surface or subsurface of the moon or any areas thereof.

Thus, even though national appropriation of the moon is prohibited, and even though the surface and the subsurface of the moon cannot become property of the various listed entities, numerous activities which are usually associated with appropriation and property rights are explicitly allowed.

* * *

IV. Exploitation of Natural Resources

Closely related to the issues regarding the common heritage of mankind, national appropriation and property rights is the issue of the exploitation of natural resources. The specific issue is whether Article XI of the Moon Treaty prohibits or limits the exploitation of natural resources on the moon and other celestial bodies. ...

[I]t is clear that the treaty places no moratorium upon the exploitation of natural resources on the moon and other celestial bodies. ...

NOTES

1. This article draws on some useful Congressional hearings on the Moon Treaty. *See* U.S. International Space Activities: Hearings Before the Subcomm. on Space Science and Applications of the House Comm. on Science and Technology, 96th Cong., 1st sess. (1979).

2. Walsh notes these seemingly paradoxical positions in the Treaty: it prohibits national appropriation of the moon and celestial bodies, and says that the surface and the subsurface of the moon cannot become property of the various listed entities, yet it also explicitly allows numerous activities which are usually associated with appropriation and property rights—e.g., "the placement of personnel, space vehicles, equipment facilities, stations and installations on or below the surface of the moon, including structures connected with their surface or subsurface." Can they be reconciled? Does the right to exploit always imply what we would consider full ownership?

Consider the following quote from a noted space law authority:

> The CHM [Common Heritage of Mankind] principle does not impact upon preferences as to forms and means of economic organization and production. More specifically, the CHM principle cannot reasonably be considered to be in opposition to the free-enterprise system of economic relationships. Both the free-enterprise and socialist states will be able to live very comfortably within the CHM principle. This result is assured by the provision of Article II, par. 7(d) which prescribes that as much special consideration is to be accorded to those countries "which have contributed either directly or indirectly to the exploration of the Moon" as is to be given to the developing countries.

C. Christol, The Modern International Law of Outer Space 288 (1982).

Another attempt to find limitations on the Common Heritage principle in specific provisions of the Treaty was made by another space law commentator:

> The principle that "the ownership of space vehicles, equipment, facilities, stations and installations" shall not be affected by their presence on the Moon (Article

12(1)), suggests that ownership of mineral resources displaced on, or removed from, the Moon may be established under the internal law of the state involved.

J. Fawcett, Outer Space: New Challenges to Law and Policy 14 (1984).

3. Regarding the question in Note 2, consider these examples: (a) mining rights on government land (where the claimant is required to perform minimum developmental activities to maintain her claim); *see, e.g.*, Lindley, A Treatise on the American Law Relating to Mines and Mineral Lands within the Public Land States and Territories (3d ed. 1914); and (b) the law of prescriptive easements, which allows one who repeatedly uses a right of way over another's land to obtain an equitable right to continue such use. *See generally* R. Powell, Real Property § 1026 (P. Rohan ed. 1977). Keep in mind that these are doctrines of Anglo-American law; they might not be persuasive to representatives from the developing world, where legal structures are often considerably different.

4. The example of ships at sea, described in the following excerpt, is also instructive. Note that this topic is also described in the discussion of Article II of the Outer Space Treaty in Chapter 3.

Reynolds & Merges, The Role of Commercial Development in Preventing War in Outer Space, 25 Jurimetrics: Journal of Law, Science & Technology 130, 143–44 (1985).

An obvious corollary to [any] discussion of incentives [for space development] is the necessity that enterprises have some assurance that their efforts to make use of space resources will not be subject to interference by other enterprises or by the military branches of states. Such assurance does not constitute a right to exclusive use of a resource, except in the narrowest sense (i.e., in the same sense that an oceangoing vessel's passage requires the exclusive use of the small patch of ocean which it occupies). Rather, it embodies the very basic right to be left alone. To some extent, of course, that right will be protected by whatever military forces the enterprise can claim protection from (its own, if the enterprise is a governmental one, or its government's, if the enterprise is a private one). Such protection may be enough—it is, after all, about all that is available to enforce the maritime order. [For a discussion of this topic see Reisman, Sanctions and Enforcement, in International Law Essays 381 (M. McDougal and W. M. Reisman eds., 1981).]

ORGANIZATIONAL STRUCTURES FOR CARRYING OUT THE MOON TREATY

In the excerpts that follow, we explore Articles 2 and 18 of the Moon Treaty. These provisions call for an international organization to supervise the exploitation of space resources. How would such an organization be structured? How would it be governed? How broad would its authority be? These are the questions we turn to next.

Although the Moon Treaty itself is unlikely to ever be ratified in the U.S., the issues it raises—especially those concerning possible organizational structures for a space resources agency—are quite worthy of study. This is so for several reasons. First, it is likely to serve as the basis for any future proposed agreements on space; it was, after all, many years in the making, and thus reflects a careful balancing of current international interests. Second, the "common heritage" concept, and especially the new developing-nation economic thinking on which it is based, is not likely to fade any time soon. These are ideas that western policymakers need to become familiar with—whether their goal is to oppose them or merely understand them. And third, as we will see in the Note on Common Property Resources and Efficient Allocation at the end of this chapter, even some western economists believe that an international organization will be required to allocate development rights over space resources. Consequently, it is important to carefully explore the alternative organizational forms a space resource allocation agency might assume. That is the goal of this section; we start with the second part of the Galloway article excerpted above.

Galloway, Issues in Implementing the Agreement Governing the Activities of States on the Moon and Other Celestial Bodies, in Proceedings of the Twenty-Third Colloquium on the Law of Outer Space 22–23 (1980)

5. Appropriate Body to Formulate an International Regime

According to Article 18 of the Moon Agreement, an international regime can be planned by States Parties any time after the treaty has been in force for five years, or as a result of action in ten years by the General Assembly. Under the first option, it is possible for a small group of States Parties to control planning for operations which affect "the common heritage of mankind." Under the second procedure provided in Article 18, it is possible that planning for operations of a technological space system would be assigned to the Legal Subcommittee of COPUOS. In any event, it will be many years before feasibility for exploiting natural resources can be established and thus we have time to consider additional approaches to this problem. The existing model which is apt to be most adaptable is that of INMARSAT which affords a realistic example of how to relate the attainment of general objectives to institutional arrangements. This task should not be regarded as primarily an issue for argument but as an opportunity for sober, objective analysis of the most effective technical means required for the smooth operation of a necessary function.

The method used thus far to formulate space law has been outstandingly successful as compared to the law of the sea. The law of the sea is being negotiated from a composite text which includes every conceivable problem, a method which naturally raises a maximum number of questions and takes much longer to achieve international agreement. In contrast, space law started from the charter 1967 Treaty on Outer Space and as different problems developed new treaties were formulated to meet specific situations. Space law was expanded to cover assistance to astronauts, their return and the return of space objects; liability for damage from space objects; and registration of space objects. Similarly, space law as developed by the International Telecommunication Union (ITU) is tailor-made for space communications. The specific function of space communications is further provided for by INTELSAT and INTERSPUTNIK. Navigation has been improved by using satellites, and INMARSAT takes "into account that a very high proportion of world trade is dependent upon ships" and therefore provides "for the benefit of ships of all nations through the most advanced suitable space technology available, [and] for the most efficient and economic facilities possible consistent with the most efficient and equitable use of the radio spectrum and of satellite orbits."

In addition, space law has been formulated during the past 22 years in numerous bilateral and multilateral agreements on specific programs requiring the use of space technology.

The only conclusion that can be drawn is that extraordinary expertise has been demonstrated in handling specific functions which can be improved by the use of space science and technology and this has brought about a remarkable degree of international cooperation in the peaceful uses of outer space. This same ability can be used in working out viable operational and economic arrangements for the Moon and other celestial bodies, and if we are temporarily overcome by this task, it is only because we are trying to formulate space law many years, perhaps decades, in advance of the actual commitment of resources to the Moon and other celestial bodies.

NOTES

1. Many of the excerpts in this chapter refer to the negotiations concerning the United Nations Law of the Sea Treaty. This was an international agreement drawn up to govern the development of mineral resources in the deep seabed—primarily manganese nodules, given today's technology.

2. The Moon Treaty tries to make law far in advance of the actuality of space resource development. How does this compare with the general approach taken in the Outer Space Treaty of 1967? Is the Moon Treaty more specific in its aims than the OST? Is this perhaps the reason it was more divisive—i.e., unlike in 1967, more than general principles were at stake? Consider also the following differences between the OST negotiations and those surrounding the Moon Treaty: (a)

political developments in the U.N. since 1967, (b) more advanced technologies in the late 1970s as compared to the mid-1960s, and (c) an increase in the number of nations with space capabilities or the potential for developing them.

Christol, Alternative Models for a Future International Space Organization, in Proceedings of the Twenty-Fourth Colloquium on the Law of Outer Space 173, 175–78 (1981)

It is becoming increasingly evident that an optimization of opportunities and benefits may require the establishment of a new body capable of dealing in a practical way with increasingly large-scale and complex operational activities. ...

As a regime emerges for the Moon and its natural resources, attention will have to be given to the characteristics of the mandated organization. In assessing the role and the functions of that future body, including its powers and duties, it may become highly desirable to determine if it, over time, will be augmented by a number of other space-oriented organizations having special and discrete responsibilities. An alternative would be to consider the establishment of a broadly based international space agency or organization having general and wide-ranging rights and duties.

* * *

The Special Issue of Voting

In the creation of international intergovernmental organizations the issue of voting rights has become a central issue. Two basic alternatives have been the bureaucratic model in which each member possesses one vote and the corporate model in which there can be weighted voting based either on the ownership of shares or on the amount of use. Votes may be allocated on the basis of regional interests as well as a very wide combination of other factors.

INTELSAT's voting procedures are particularly instructive. The Assembly, whose functions are more political than technical, makes recommendations to the Board of Governors respecting general policy and long-term objectives. Voting is on a one-State, one-vote basis. INTELSAT's Meeting of Signatories, composed of technicians, also operates on a one-State, one-vote basis. However, the Board of Governors, limited to about 20 representatives of States, operates on a weighted-voting formula. Under the terms of the agreement a signatory possesses an investment share corresponding to its percentage of use of the system when compared with the total amount of the use of the INTELSAT space segment. No State may possess more than 40% of the quota of votes with the United States being restricted to this percentage. INTELSAT has demonstrated that the bureaucratic organizational model can be joined effectively to a corporate organizational model in which ownership of shares or allocation of shares can be dependent on the extent of use with the heavier user being given voting rights in proportion to use. [For more on INTELSAT, see Chapter 6, *infra.*]

INMARSAT also allows for a hybrid voting process. Each of the parties possesses one vote in the Assembly. In the Council, however, 18 of the 22 members hold investment shares, while the remaining four do not have to meet this requirement. No representative may posses on behalf of one signatory more than 25% of the total voting participation in the organization. This is subject to an exception contained in Article 14(3)(b)(iv), which reads: "To the extent that the investment share of the Signatory is in excess of 25% offered for distribution in accordance with the procedure set forth in this paragraph, the voting of the representative of the Signatory may exceed 25 percent."

*   *   *

Another technical organization, the ITU, accords to each of its members a single vote in its periodic world administrative radio conferences.

No single model necessarily fits the needs of a future special or general international space organization. It would be expected that there would be a need for an accommodation of views among the space-resource States and those which are in the process of development.

*   *   *

Parties Subject to the Jurisdiction of a Space Tribunal

*   *   *

Existing international intergovernmental organizations have been granted the judicial power to resolve disputes arising among their members respecting their respective rights and duties pursuant to the terms of their several constitutions. Further, such organizations may, in specified circumstances, initiate legal actions before the tribunal of the institution in order to obtain a clarification of their own rights and duties.

It has already been recognized that international organizations dealing with space-environment activities need a judicial arm. For example, pursuant to the terms of the relevant INTELSAT agreements and annex, an arbitral tribunal can arrive at a binding decision both where member States and INTELSAT, per se, have presented justiciable issues. Where the decision is that rules and regulations of an organ of INTELSAT are invalid, the decision is binding on all of the members as well as the organization. Likewise, the terms of the 1973 ITU Convention made provision for a number of procedures for the resolution of disputes including arbitration. The members are bound by the terms of the decision.

The 1976 INMARSAT Convention also made provision for wide-ranging processes for dispute resolution including both arbitration and reference to the

World Court. These processes contemplate disputes between members and also between members and the organization. If the holding confirms that the organization has exceeded its authority the ruling becomes binding on all the parties to the agreement.

* * *

Under Article 11, paragraph 5 of the Moon Treaty, it would be possible to establish a special dispute-resolving instrumentality to deal with the equitable distribution of Moon benefits. While not all space uses and activities may be equally amenable to dispute-resolving procedures, since contending claimants for equitable shares to the benefits derived from the exploitation of the Moon's natural resources will be seeking to obtain something that has previously been unavailable for distribution, they may be more inclined to support the process than in a situation where they might fear having to give up something already within their possession or control.

* * *

In terms of policy it would be possible to establish a Space Court as was suggested in 1962, or a separate and special International Spatial Tribunal as was suggested in 1976. Alternatively, a space tribunal might form a part of a more complete international organization where it optimally would have the same authority as has been assigned to the International Court of Justice.

* * *

It has been possible to devise in the ITU an international organization capable of dealing with the allocation and sharing of constantly renewing electronic spectra. ... It should be no more difficult to formulate a governing body having the power to distribute on an equitable basis the benefits derived from the disposition of Moon minerals or other Moon resources.

NOTES

1. Christol says that nations may be less inclined to support an allocation scheme in a situation where "they might fear having to give up something already within their possession or control." How does this square with the point made in the introduction to the Outer Space Treaty in Chapter 3, that the OST was drafted before it was known how widespread space capabilities would become, and that the OST was therefore less concerned with national self-interest than it otherwise might be? Again, note the similarities to the Rawlsian "veil of ignorance," and its predecessor, Jean-Jacques Rousseau's "state of nature." *See* J. Rawls, A Theory of Justice 118–92 (1971) (Chapter 3, The Original Position). Note also the limitations of this concept in the space arena; the U.S. and Soviet

Union are obviously closer (at this point) to development of space resources than many other nations. They are thus less analogous to individuals in a hypothetical "original position," since this assumes complete ignorance over what attributes one will have when one leaves the original position.

2. For an assessment of the relationship of organizational structures to the purposes and goals of six international intergovernmental space organizations, four of which engage in communications activities, see the background paper on "Multilateral intergovernmental cooperation in Space Activities," U.N. Doc. A/CONF.101/BP/10, 10 January 1981. The study was made in connection with plans for the Second United Nations Conference on the Exploration and Peaceful Uses of Outer Space.

3. Christol concludes that INTELSAT might be the best model for an organization to govern space resources; it "has demonstrated that the bureaucratic organizational model can be joined effectively to a corporate organizational model in which ownership of shares or allocation of shares can be dependent on the extent of use with the heavier user being given voting rights in proportion to use." Compare this to the assessment of INTELSAT in the excerpt from Allen Duane Webber's article in the Georgetown Law Review, *infra. See also* Fleming et al., State Sovereignty and the Effective Management of a Shared Universal Resource: Observations Drawn from Examining Developments in the International Regulation of Radiocommunication, 10 Annals of Air & Space Law 327 (1985) (most workable systems to allocate rights over shared universal resource such as radio frequencies do not rely on claims of sovereignty, but instead on pragmatic allocation schemes). For more discussion on the optimal design for a central administrative agency, *see* the Note on Common Property Resources and Efficient Allocation at the end of this chapter.

4. The operating agreements for INMARSAT, ARABSAT, INTELSAT and INTERSPUTNIK are reproduced in Senate Committee on Commerce, Space and Transportation, 95th Cong., 2d Sess., Space Law—Selected Basic Documents (Comm. Print 1978). *See also* Chapter 6, *infra,* for more on INTELSAT and the ITU.

Goedhuis, Some Recent Trends in the Interpretation and the Implementation of the Rules of International Space Law, 19 Columbia Journal of Transnational Law 213 (1981)

[S]ome States continue to assert that under the terms of the [Outer] Space Treaty the *whole* of outer space—like the seabed by virtue of the U.N. Resolution adopted on 17th December 1970—has been established as the common heritage of mankind.

Although the discussions in the Law of the Sea Conferences have shown that the import of this term is far from agreed upon, the following basic implications of this concept are generally recognized: first, that the area to which it applies cannot be appropriated; second, that it requires a system of management in which all countries share; third, that it requires an active sharing of benefits from the exploration of the resources between all countries; and fourth, that it requires the dedication of the area to exclusively peaceful purposes.

When one examines the content of the [Outer] Space Treaty, one notices that it satisfies *only one* of the abovementioned requirements. Art. II of the treaty provides that outer space, including the moon and other celestial bodies, is not subject to national appropriation. Whereas this article has prohibited the appropriation of *areas of* outer space it is silent on the appropriation of *resources*. Although a number of commentators have contended that the appropriation of resources by a State would violate the "benefit clause" contained in Art. I(1) [*see, e.g.*, the excerpt from Rao, *infra*], the great majority of States, including the two Space Powers, consider that *de lege lata* the appropriation of the natural resources of outer space, by analogy with the *present* rules underlying the freedom of the seas, merely forms part of the freedom of that space for exploration and use, a freedom which has been confirmed by the Treaty. Nothing has been said in the Treaty about the sharing or management of these resources. [Note: These issues are discussed in the section dealing with the Outer Space Treaty in Chapter 3.]

It should further be noted that the Treaty has not dedicated the use of the *whole* of outer space to exclusively peaceful purposes. The only exception is contained in Art. IV(2) which provides that the moon and other celestial bodies shall be used by all States Parties exclusively for peaceful purposes. ...

On the basis of the above considerations, it seems clear that the contention that the Outer Space Treaty has established the *whole* of outer space as the common heritage of mankind is untenable.

* * *

Despite the fact that a number of States continued even during the last, 22nd, Session of the Committee, to voice their opposition to the adoption of the common heritage concept and stressed the need of a Moratorium, the text of a draft containing both the notion of common heritage and provisions implying the permissibility for States to start their operations on the moon before an international regime has been established, was finally unanimously accepted. As several of the deliberations on the Draft took place behind the scenes, one can only speculate on the reasons which prompted the opponents of these two principles to withdraw their objections. One may not be too wide off the mark if one suggests that the following factors led to the achievement of a consensus.

First, as was mentioned above, a great number of States vigorously criticized the lack of progress in the implementation of the rules of the Space Treaty. There appeared to be a strong feeling of the need to achieve a breakthrough on at least one of the issues which for many years had been discussed.

The second explanation may be sought in the influence of the two most powerful decision-makers in the field of space law, namely the United States and the

Soviet Union, who apparently were in agreement both on the need to complete without further delay the Draft and on the provisions it should contain.

* * *

Among the problems which are likely to arise during the interim period, attention may be given to two of the most important issues. According to Art. IX of the Agreement, States Parties may establish manned and unmanned stations on the moon. What happens when the States which are capable of establishing such stations wish to erect such stations in the same area? Art. XV contains a number of provisions to be applied when disputes between States Parties arise. In paragraph 2 it has been laid down that a State Party which has reason to believe that another State Party is not fulfilling the obligations incumbent upon it pursuant to the Agreement or that another State Party is interfering with the rights which the former State has under the Agreement, may request consultations with that Party. Any other State Party which requires to do so shall be entitled to take part in the consultations. Paragraph 3 provides that if the consultations do not lead to a mutually acceptable settlement which has due regard for the rights and interests of all the States Parties, the parties concerned shall take all measures to settle the disputes by other peaceful means of their choice and appropriate to the circumstances and the nature of the dispute.

Experience in the field of international disputes in general has demonstrated the extent to which the reluctance of States to submit their disputes to adjudication or arbitration is due to the uncertainties regarding the content and the meaning of the legal rules to be applied. The Agreement contains in particular one provision the interpretation of which will give rise to wide and serious divergences. Art. II(1), reproducing a rule contained in Art. IV(2) of the [Outer] Space Treaty, provides that the moon shall be used by all States Parties exclusively for peaceful purposes. Since the conclusion of the Space Treaty, this provision has proved to be one of the most controversial ones laid down in the Treaty. On the meaning of the term "peaceful purposes" two fundamentally different interpretations came to the fore. Under one interpretation the term means *non-military* while under the other the term means *non-aggressive*. In this connection it should be noted that, notwithstanding the fact that more than half of all American and Soviet spacecraft at present orbiting the Earth serve military purposes, both countries describe *all* their space-missions as "peaceful." The unacceptable consequences of interpreting the term "peaceful" as "non-aggressive" have been set forth in an article published in 1968 by the present writer. [*See* Goedhuis, An Evaluation of the Leading Principles of the Treaty On Outer Space of 1967, 15 Netherlands International Law Review 24 (1968), at 24.]

* * *

One example may be given of the dissensions which would result from permitting the use of the moon for "non-aggressive" purposes. In doctrine it has been submitted that since defensive and *deterrent* capabilities serve the cause of peace, it is only when such devices are *intentionally* used for aggressive purposes that they lose their peaceful status. [*See* C. Christol, The International Law of Outer Space 268 (1966).] As all arms have deterrent capabilities, such an interpretation would enable States to claim that the deployment of any arms on the moon—except those carrying nuclear weapons or any other kind of weapons of mass destruction, which under the terms of Art. III(3) of the Agreement have been forbidden—would constitute a use of the moon for peaceful purposes.

* * *

Postscript

I [wish to] make a few observations on the political objections to the Treaty voiced by some members of Congress and leading aerospace companies.

The main object of this opposition was the concept of the moon and its natural resources being declared to be the common heritage of mankind, a concept of which the U.S. delegation in COPUOS was the main architect. It has been asserted that the acceptance of this theory would create "a system of international socialism" and "would foreclose the commercial uses of outer space by American enterprise." The submission that the Treaty would foreclose the commercial uses of outer space by American enterprise is based on a misinterpretation of Art. II of the Treaty, which—as mentioned above—permits the exploitation and use of the natural resources of the moon *before* an international regime governing the exploitation of these resources has been established. It further was noted that the purpose of the insertion in paragraph 3 of Art. II of the words "natural resources in place" (proposed by the American delegation in the COPUOS in 1973), was to allow for the existence of property rights over natural resources when removed from the places on the moon where they were obtained.

By the opponents of the present Moon regime it was further submitted that free enterprise institutions simply cannot make significant investments in space when there is the threat of suit over treaty terms of "ex post facto" appropriation of their investments by a nebulous future international regime. In this context attention should be drawn to paragraph 7 of Art. XI in which under (d) it has been laid down that in the *equitable* sharing by all States Parties in the benefits derived from the natural moon resources special consideration shall be given to the efforts of those countries which have contributed either directly or indirectly to the exploration of the moon. The provision that the sharing of the benefits should be "equitable" does obviously not mean that the sharing should be "equal."

Although, when, at some time in the future, efforts will be made to arrive at the intended international regime, considerable difficulties may arise in assessing the compensation of the efforts of the countries or companies which have been exploiting and using the natural moon resources in the period prior to the establishment of an international regime, there appears to be one crucial factor which should be able to allay the fears expressed regarding the appropriation of investments made. The United States, as one of the two major Space Powers, will have a decisive influence on the terms of the international regime to be established. It can hardly be assumed that the American negotiators would agree to any elimination of the profits earned through the taking of risks by those companies which started the exploitation and use of moon resources.

Although it should of course be admitted that in general disputes in the interpretation of any treaty of highly political content can never be avoided, the question may be asked whether, insofar as the Moon Treaty is concerned, the disputes which have arisen could not have been prevented if the final text of the Treaty had not been rushed through the United Nations in a great hurry before a consensus on the exact meaning and content of the concept of the moon and its natural resources being the common heritage of mankind had been achieved.

NOTES

1. Goedhuis notes that the Moon Treaty had reached somewhat of an impasse during U.N. negotiations. He gives two reasons why it was broken and progress was finally made: (a) the desire of all countries to enact some kind of Treaty expanding on the Outer Space Treaty; and (b) what he calls "the influence of the two most powerful decisionmakers in the field of space law, namely the United States and the Soviet Union, who apparently were in agreement both on the need to complete without further delay the Draft and on the provisions it should contain." Does this suggest that the critics of the Treaty—whose main point is that the U.S. would come out a loser during negotiations to actually set up the administrative organization to govern space resources—might have underestimated the bargaining power of the U.S.? What does this tell you about the legitimacy of the point made by some commentators, that a key problem in the ratification process was the lack of communication between space industry and the diplomatic agencies that negotiated the Treaty? *See, e.g.*, Goldman, Reflections on the Proposed Moon Treaty, Space Law, and the Future, in People in Space: Policy Perspectives for a "Star Wars" Century (J.E. Katz ed. 1986).

2. A number of the preceding excerpts have referred to the United Nations Law of the Sea Treaty; this was the international document that introduced the phrase "common heritage of mankind." Owing to this fact, and to its importance as a precedent-setting agreement, we have included an article by Hufford, *infra*, which describes the Law of the Sea Treaty and its background.

3. In a recent publication by Stephen Gorove, Studies in Space Law: Its Challenges and Prospects (1977), Gorove, discussing the problem arising in the inter-

pretation of the term "peaceful purposes," suggests that "it would be better to identify those activities which constitute minimal threats to national security and permit those regardless of the ultimate purpose for such activities or their conduct by military personnel." *Id.* at 91. Regarding this proposal, the question is whether there is any chance of States agreeing on a definition of what constitutes a minimal threat to their national security.

Dupuy, The Notion of the Common Heritage of Mankind Applied to the Seabed, 8 Annals of Air and Space Law 347 (1983)

The common heritage of mankind concept was solemnly established when it was applied to the deep seabed following presentation of the Pardo Doctrine at the United Nations and its embodiment in the Declaration of Principles by the XXVth General Assembly (1970). ... The introduction of such a notion is intriguing for jurists, since, so far, reference to humanity has appeared only in the broadest sense in so-called humanitarian law, including not only the choice of armed conflicts but also "humanitarian intervention" or "crimes against humanity."

The reference to the notion of heritage has repeatedly raised the question whether humanity or mankind may be considered a "subject" of international law able to be endowed legally with a heritage. It was wondered in which form mankind could be embodied to be the holder of rights, and it was sometimes believed that the United Nations, an organization with a universal vocation, could act on behalf of mankind. Some observers contended that, in a strictly interstate system, the United Nations could not properly claim to represent peoples and individuals, while others responded that governments have this dual role and that, in the absence of a federal structure at the world level, there was no alternative but to consider the United Nations as being able to execute this function.

In the writer's view, this kind of debate is meaningless. Indeed, it neglects one basic question: what is meant by humankind? The answer seems easy: grouping human beings as a whole, mankind embraces all peoples in common ownership of a domain which is rich in resources. The concept of the common heritage thus appears as fundamentally harmonistic; but, in fact, such a view fails to take into account the contradiction and conflicts between States, and was denounced. It was said that the super powers proceeded to a "recovery of all concept." ... From the outset, behind the reassuring veil of the common heritage, clashes occurred at the Third Conference on the Law of the Sea, and they will continue within the organs of the Authority. As soon as a transcendental notion is established, social forces strive to capture it. This is all the more evident in the case of the international seabed, since provision was made that it should be under an Authority endowed with powers which go beyond those of a State. However, the problem arose as to who would control the Authority: the technologically advanced countries, or the developing countries which claim numerical superiority and the democratic legitimacy this confers.

It should be mentioned here that the common heritage regime was defined by States—the legislators of international laws; and, naturally, governments are inclined to make decisions in terms of the immediate benefits to be derived.

It is remarkable that, despite the difficulty in perceiving the overall interests of mankind, States participating in the Conference were able to separate a notion based on a legal philosophy from singularly rich prospects. There will always be a risk of misappropriation or seizure, but the ideological pattern on which the concept rests will remain as a reference model. It is this aspect which the writer wishes to analyze.

To a great extent, it is a result of the efforts of the Third World. The basic philosophy of the concept is not only harmonistic, but also prospective and strategic. The notion of mankind has a twinfold meaning:

—it is interspatial, in that it regroups all contemporaries irrespective of the location of their establishment;

—its scope is intertemporal, because mankind includes not only today's people, but also future generations.

NOTE

The following excerpt, written by D. Brian Hufford, describes the Law of the Sea Treaty from the U.S. perspective.

Hufford, Ideological Rigidity vs. Political Reality: A Critique of Reagan's Policy on the Law of the Sea, 2 Yale Law & Policy Review 127 (1983)

I. An Historical Overview

The Third United Nations Conference on the Law of the Sea [UNCLOS] was convened in 1973. These negotiations received continuous U.S. support throughout the Administrations of Presidents Nixon, Ford and Carter. By 1980, U.S. officials were predicting that a treaty effectively protecting U.S. interests could soon be adopted.

President Reagan's election, however, frustrated these predictions. Fearing that his new Administration would be forced to vote on an unacceptable treaty, President Reagan took the unprecedented step of withdrawing the United States from UNCLOS in March 1981 to allow a thorough review of the Convention. By January 29, 1982 the review had been completed, and the President announced that the U.S. was ready to return to negotiations.

* * *

The proposed changes were so radical they were generally ignored. ... By that time, however, the negotiations were effectively over.

* * *

On April 30, 1982 UNCLOS member nations adopted the Convention by a vote of 130–4, with 17 abstentions. Breaking from the traditional reliance in the Conference on consensus in decision-making, the U.S. asked for a recorded vote. Subsequently, it voted "no," along with Israel, Venezuela and Turkey. When the Convention was opened for signature on December 10, 117 nations signed on the first day—a record number, according to the General Counsel to the U.N., and a level of support unexpected by the Reagan Administration.

* * *

U.S. opposition to the Convention focuses on the regulation and use of the deep seabed beyond national jurisdiction. All activities in this area are to be regulated by the International Sea-Bed Authority (ISA), empowered to grant mining rights to both public and private ventures. An organization called the Enterprise will operate a "parallel system" for exploring and exploiting the ocean resources. Because the seabed is recognized as a "common heritage," all mining operators will be expected to contribute a portion of their revenues to the ISA. This is in addition to revenues expected from the states for resource development beyond 200 miles but within the continental shelf, and thus under national jurisdiction. To ensure international access to ocean resources, the Convention further requires mining contractors to sell to the ISA technology that cannot be obtained on the open market. The regulations for mining the deep seabed beyond national jurisdiction, and the procedures under which the Authority and the Enterprise will operate, are left to be developed by a Preparatory Commission (PrepCom). Although the U.S., despite its opposition to the treaty, is entitled to become involved in the PrepCom negotiations, the Reagan Administration has refused to participate.

NOTES

1. As of December 1993, there were 158 signatories to the Convention and 60 ratifications. The Convention entered into force on November 16, 1994.

2. The U.N. had sponsored two previous conferences on the law of the sea. The first was held in 1958, adopting four treaties: the Convention on the Continental Shelf; the Territorial Sea and Contiguous Zone; the High Seas; and Fishing and Conservation of the Living Resources of the High Seas. The second conference, held in 1960, failed to accomplish its goal of determining the width of the territorial sea. The 1958 treaties can be found in C. Franklin, International Law Studies 1959–1960, The Law of the Sea: Some Recent Developments (Vol. 53, Naval War College Blue Book Series).

3. For a good review of the issues raised by the Law of the Sea Treaty, *see* Dyke & Yuen, "Common Heritage" and "Freedom of the High Seas," Which Governs the Seabed? 19 San Diego Law Review 493, 527 (1982).

4. For the official position on the U.S "revisions" that were ignored by the other Convention members, *see* Presidential Statement on United States Participation in the Third United Nations Conference on the Law of the Sea, 1 Public Papers of Ronald Reagan 92 (Jan. 29, 1982). *See also* Whitaker, Outside the Mainstream, The Atlantic, October, 1982, at 21; Citizens for Ocean Law, U.S. Options on the Law of the Sea: The Preparatory Commission 1 (Dec. 1, 1982).

5. In an interesting article, Wertenbaker, A Reporter at Large: The Law of the Sea, The New Yorker, Aug. 1, 1983, at 42–44, the author points out that ending the negotiations was unnecessary. Although the Conference was coming to a close, the U.S. could have obtained a continuance in the negotiations to delay final consideration of the Convention while Reagan was reviewing his law of the sea policy. The U.S. had done just this in previous presidential transitions. The decision to withdraw was a surprise to most other nations as well as to the U.S. negotiating team.

DEVELOPED WORLD AND THIRD WORLD VIEWS ON SPACE DEVELOPMENT

As several of the excerpts that follow make clear, western economists see the need for property rights to ensure the orderly and efficient development of space resources. But as some of the other excerpts show, many developing country economists stress the need for equitable sharing of space resources and opportunities, to avoid the economic colonization of space along neo-imperialistic lines. This view is intimately tied to Third World perceptions of the economic basis for the developed world's wealth: the large-scale exploitation of natural resources. *See, e.g.*, H. Magdoff, The Age of Imperialism (1969); P. Jalee, The Pillage of the Third World (1965).

The first selection that follows, written by Edward R. Finch, Jr. and Amanda Lee Moore, reflects a minority position in the developed world: that the Moon Treaty is helpful to western interests, because it creates a framework for allocating development rights and settling disputes. As you can see from the excerpt, written by Art Dula, that follows that of Finch and Moore, other western commentators disagree sharply. They view the Moon Treaty—and especially the "common heritage of mankind" principle—as a significant threat to space development.

The Dula excerpt, and the Wihlborg and Wijkman excerpt at the end of this section, argue that space development will occur only if clear user rights are established, and only if those rights are enforceable under a well-defined liability scheme. Without such a system, the argument continues, there is no incentive to develop space, since there is no way to insure that each extra dollar spent in space is going to its most efficient use.

This kind of reasoning, of course, stands in stark contrast to the common heritage principle, with its emphasis on international sharing of resources. Unlike most Western commentators, Finch and Moore avoid discussing the fact that sharing *presumes* the existence of something to share. In the eyes of most developed-world commentators, when it comes to undeveloped space resources, this is of course the key problem: there *is* nothing yet to share or at least nothing much.

From this perspective, the "common heritage" principle is primarily concerned with allocating profits from space development—what might be termed "dividing the pie." (Note, however, that Article XI, paragraph 7 does mention other principles besides equity that must be taken into consideration in developing the moon's resources, including "The *orderly* and safe *development* of the natural resources of the moon," and "[t]he expansion of opportunities in the use of those resources." (emphasis added).) Meanwhile, as shown by the articles from "western" sources reproduced below, the developed world has a different concern: what might be called, to extend the metaphor, collecting the apples that go into the pie. That is, those in the west are concerned primarily with creating incentives to *find and develop* space resources; equitable sharing, in this view, is not a prime concern until the resources have been identified and exploited.

One way to view the conflict between equitable distribution of resources and incentives to develop them in the first place is to see it as a reflection of fundamental cultural differences. For an example of western thinking, consider the discussion in the Wihlborg and Wijkman excerpt, *infra*, concerning the need for clearly defined property rights to allow for efficient space development. For some insight into the Third World perspective on these issues, note the view of property implicit in the Rao excerpt *infra*, which describes an alternative vision of the Common Heritage concept made popular by advocates of the New International Economic Order.

Finch & Moore, The 1979 Moon Treaty Encourages Space Development, in Proceedings of the Twenty-Third Colloquium on the Law of Outer Space 13–15 (1980)

Understandings and Clarifications

The Moon Treaty should be signed by the US President and ratified by the US Senate. However, certain legal understandings, which simply reiterate the US position already stated before various UN bodies, should be included. While clarifying the obligations assumed by the US, these understandings at the same time address pertinent issues raised by critics of the Moon Treaty provisions.

Subject to the approval of the House of Delegates of the ABA, the recently approved report by the Section of International Law of the American Bar Association includes four sample understandings: [Section of International Law, Report to the House of Delegates, American Bar Association, April 1980].

"(a) It is the understanding of the United States that no provision in this Agreement constrains the existing right of governmental or authorized non-governmental entities to explore and use the resources of the moon or other celestial bodies, including the right to develop and exploit these resources for commercial or other purposes. In addition, it is the understanding of the United States that nothing in this Agreement in any way diminishes or alters the right of the United States to determine how it shares the benefits derived from exploitation by or under the authority of the United States of natural resources of the moon or other celestial bodies;

"(b) Natural resources extracted, removed or actually utilized by or under the authority of a State Party to this Agreement are subject to the exclusive control of, and may be considered as the property of, the State Party or other entity responsible for their extraction, removal or utilization;

"(c) The meaning of the term 'common heritage of mankind' is to be based on the provisions of this Agreement, and not on the use or interpretation of that term in any other context. Recognition by the United States that the moon and its natural resources are the common heritage of all mankind constitutes recognition (A) that all States have equal rights to explore and use the moon and its natural resources, and (B) that no State or other entity has an exclusive right of ownership, property or appropriation over the moon, over any area of the surface or subsurface of the moon, or over its natural resources in place. In this context, the United States notes that, in accordance with Articles XII and XV of this Agreement, States Parties retain exclusive jurisdiction and control over their facilities, stations and installations on the moon, and that other States Parties are obligated to avoid interference with normal operations of such facilities;

"(d) Acceptance by the United States of an obligation to undertake in the future good faith negotiation with other States Parties of an international regime to govern exploitation of the natural resources of the moon in no way prejudices the existing right of the United States to exploit or authorize the exploitation of those natural resources. No moratorium on such exploitation is intended or required by this Agreement. The United States recognizes that States Parties to this Agreement are obligated to act in a manner compatible with the provisions of Article VI(2) and the purposes specified in Article XI(7); however, the United States reserves to itself the right and authority to determine the standards for such compatibility unless and until the United States becomes a party to a future resources exploitation regime. In addition, acceptance of the obligation to join in good faith negotiation of such a regime in no way constitutes acceptance of any particular provisions which may be included in such a regime; nor does it constitute an obligation to become a Party to such a regime regardless of its contents."

In effect, these understandings clarify the obligations assumed by the US and emphasize the US position that the Moon Treaty recognizes that once lunar resources have been moved or extracted they may be considered the property of the extractor. Understanding (A) is similar to one attached by the US Senate when ratifying the 1967 Outer Space Treaty. [International Law Section Report, p. 7.] It should clarify as a matter of law the limits of any obligation assumed by the US in sharing benefits, and should legally protect the independence and flexibility of future US negotiators in deciding what, if any, specific obligations should be assumed in any new international resources exploitation regime.

Common Heritage Language

*   *   *

A review of the Moon Treaty's negotiating history supports the view that the term does not [imply] and need not lead to the use in a lunar resources regime of procedures and criteria developed in any other context. There is no generally accepted definition of this term. To quote one space law commentator, the phrase is "purely declaratory ... and open to all interpretations." [Adrian Bueckling, "The Strategy of Semantics and the 'Mankind Provisions' of the Space Treaty," *Journal of Space Law,* 7:21 (Spring 1979).] Conversations with delegates to the Outer Space Committee reinforces [sic] the feeling that the phrase is in essence a continuation of the very general concept from the 1967 Outer Space Treaty of space as the "common province of mankind" with an attempt to move into language more commonly used in international law. In addition, to date, no two delegations have said the term means the same thing at any given time.

*   *   *

Advantage for Space Investment

... It may be stated that there is a clear advantage in the Moon Treaty for research and development for space manufacturing facilities, solar power satellites, and other large-scale manned space activities using lunar and other space natural resources. At the very least, a green light has been given for pilot projects in the ten years recommended before the first review of the Moon Treaty.

The more practical question is the investment of money, time and effort and how to obtain enough of each. The question of investment security to attract money will exist whether or not the US becomes a party to the Moon Treaty. Such investment protection can only come from the US Government. It is not the province of a multilateral treaty, nor could it meaningfully be provided by such. Legislation encouraging exploitation of lunar resources, to be effective, would have to come from the US Congress, the way it has for mineral exploitation in the Law of the Sea.

NOTES

1. Finch and Moore state that no two countries have defined the "common heritage" in the same way. But note also that in arguing in favor of the Treaty, they defend the use of this language as "an attempt to move into [sic] language more commonly used in international law." Is it rational to defend the phrase on both these grounds?

2. Finch and Moore state that failure to ratify "would simply and devastatingly exclude the U.S. from legal entitlement to the benefits and protections included in the Moon Treaty." Are there alternative ways—e.g., a series of bilateral treaties—to achieve the same "benefits and protections"? *Cf.* U.S. Senate Committee on Commerce, Science and Transportation, Agreement Governing the Activities of States on the Moon and Other Celestial Bodies, Part 4, 96th Cong., 2d Sess. (1980), at 465 (stating, in summary of arguments against Moon Treaty, that, *inter alia,* it is "superfluous because the basic freedoms in space are already protected by the Outer Space Treaty," and "[n]o ongoing activities are constrained ... but [it] ... present[s] many possibilities for future constraints").

Dula, Free Enterprise and the Proposed Moon Treaty, 2 Houston Journal of International Law 3 (1979)

The Moon Treaty is vague, lengthy, and complex. Many of its critical terms are not well-defined.

* * *

"Exploitation" vs. "Use" of Natural Resources

One reason consensus was reached during the 1979 COPUOS session was that the Soviet Union accepted a Brazilian formulation of the treaty's "common heritage" language. This language is now in Article XI of the treaty: "The moon and its natural resources are the common heritage of mankind, which finds its expression in the provisions of this agreement and in particular in paragraph 5 of this article."

* * *

The United States, through Neil Hosenball, National Aeronautics and Space Administration's (NASA) General Counsel and chief U.S. representative to COPUOS, made a number of unilateral statements defining the United States' interpretation of several parts of the Moon Treaty. Two of these statements seem intended to contradict the clear language of the treaty regarding exploitation of space natural resources.

* * *

The clear language in Article VI of the Moon Treaty specifically permits scientific "use" of lunar resources. Conversely, equally clear language in Article XI states that as "exploitation" of those resources becomes feasible, negotiations for a new international legal regime must be begun. The U.S. position contradicts this treaty language by stating that the Moon Treaty places "no moratorium on the exploitation of the natural resources of the moon, pending establishment of an international regime."

* * *

In addition to limiting the "use" and "exploitation" of natural resources from space, the Moon Treaty goes to great length to deny any possible legal entity the capacity of owning any part of these resources.

* * *

On April 19, 1973 the U.S. representative to the COPUOS Legal Subcommittee unilaterally contradicted the clear meaning of the words "in place" appearing in an earlier working draft of the Moon Treaty:

> As is apparent from the text, this working paper excludes the concept of a pre-regime moratorium. References to the words "in place" in the first sentence of that paragraph ... make this clear. More particularly, the words "in place" ... are intended to indicate that the prohibition against assertion of property rights would not apply to natural resources once reduced to possession through exploitation either in the pre-regime period or, subject to the rules and procedures that a regime would constitute, following establishment of the regime. [Oversight Hearings on the Activities of the U.N. Committee on the Peaceful Uses of Outer Space: Hearings Before the Subcomm. on Space Science and Applications of the House Comm. on Science and Technology, 96th Cong., 1st Sess. at 90–100 (1979) (statement of Neil Hosenball, at 11).]

* * *

If the United States becomes a party to the Moon Treaty, the opportunities and prospects for private enterprise development of the resources of the Moon and other celestial bodies will be negligible if not non-existent. Specifically, the draft treaty would:

1. Create a moratorium on commercial exploitation of the resources of the [M]oon and other celestial bodies, until a second, much more comprehensive treaty for regulating resource activities is concluded;
2. Establish guiding principles for the negotiation of this second treaty which are completely antithetical to the commercial development of outer space resources by private enterprise; and

3. Thereby give the Soviet or Third World countries tremendous political control over the timing and direction of expanding commercial uses of outer space, as well as the question of whether to permit such uses.

The Administration, particularly the negotiators of this draft treaty, argue that United States public statements to the effect that the treaty does not establish a moratorium negate the implicit moratorium in the treaty. Unfortunately, such a moratorium is now contemplated in the treaty and underscored by the U.S. delegation's statements on the record. However, even if it is conceded that the United States' unilateral statements control the treaty's meaning, the fact remains that no private enterprise, or even a government, is going to invest billions of dollars in developing new commercial applications of space technology if most of the world disputes its legal right to deploy and profit from that technology.

It may be asserted that the guiding principles set out in the treaty for constructing the legal regime to control exploitation of outer space resources are empty phrases to be given later meaning. The Moon Treaty, however, must be considered in the context of international law and practice. These phrases all have a very well-defined meaning and have been exhaustively elaborated in other treaty negotiations. Since the Soviet Union first introduced a draft text on the Moon in 1971, the politics of resource development in areas beyond the territorial borders of nations have changed dramatically. The Law of the Sea Conference has moved to near-completion of a treaty establishing a deep seabed resource regime based on virtually identical guiding principles to those contained in the Moon Treaty. Examples of parallel provisions prove that such resources are the "common heritage of mankind," that their development should be orderly and rationally managed, and that the benefits (both financial and technological) should be equitably distributed.

Regardless of whether the Law of the Sea Treaty ever enters into force, the Third World has now developed a very sophisticated position on the content of an international resource regime that best serves its interests. Many informed observers will support the view that this detailed elaboration of these revolutionary new ideas reflects the international custom, practice, and consensus as to how so-called "common property" resources are to be regulated, managed, and developed.

The Draft Law of the Sea Treaty requires the collectivization of resource development through a global monopoly under the political control of a General Assembly-type body dominated by the Third World. It restricts the rights of states and private enterprise to carry out profit-making activities, by limiting these activities to an initial period during which the necessary technology is fully transferred to the monopoly. Finally, it provides for international regulation of production levels and prices in order to discriminate in favor of developing countries.

* * *

In summary, the Moon Treaty, if adopted as the basis for negotiating a future resource regime for the Moon and other celestial bodies, would borrow meaning from these precedents. There are many other imaginative approaches which would enable the nations of the world to cooperate peacefully in expanding the commercial applications of outer space technology to resource exploration and development. Good examples already exist for commercial utilization of outer space, and there is no reason why the United States should permit outer space resource development to be thrust into a quagmire of political principles derived from the "new international economic order."

In view of the enormous capital and technology requirements contemplated for the future industrialization of outer space, political stability for investments will be absolutely critical. If this treaty is ratified by the United States, however, any commercial application of outer space technology which involves use of Moon or other celestial resources will be subject to the greatest insecurity imaginable. While the spillover effect for other commercial activities in outer space cannot be fully predicted, it may be very significant.

Specific Negative Implications of the Moon Treaty for Free Enterprise

*   *   *

[Another key] issue is the definition of "scientific investigations." To the extent that it excludes research and development activities undertaken by a commercial entity in the hope of future profit, paragraph 2 of Article VI would prohibit such an entity's using resource samples collected from the Moon and other celestial bodies either for research and development or for the support of its missions. Paragraph 8 of Article XI reinforces this apparent prohibition on the conduct of interim resource activities by states and persons who are not pursuing scientific purposes.

It is highly doubtful that the United States Department of State would support authorization of U.S. nationals to engage in the commercial exploitation of Moon resources prior to agreement on a new international regime, even if it is possible to make the legal case that the treaty does not prohibit these activities. State authorization is required under paragraph 1 of Article XIV (as it is under Article VI of the 1967 Treaty on Principles). An affirmative act by the United States to permit commercial development of the Moon's resources by private entities would probably require legislation and would be deemed an interference with the international negotiations by the United States State Department.

Finally, the practical effect of an international commitment to negotiate a new, unknown legal regime covering the Moon and other celestial resources will be to deter industrialists, and probably governments, from spending research and development dollars in related activities during the interim period. The precedent of the U.N. Conference on the Law of the Sea will convince them that Third World demands at the "Moon Conference" are going to be extreme, that existing investments may not be respected under the resulting treaty, and that the industrialized countries may not be very successful in negotiating a system of exploitation that permits commercial or industrial use of the resources under realistic terms and conditions.

* * *

For developing countries, "common heritage" means common ownership of the resources and majority control over their disposition. This translates into insistence that no single country, or entity under its control, has the independent right to use the commonly owned resource. Access to the resources must first be approved by the international community on the basis of one-nation, one-vote. As a result, the developing countries would collectively control who is allowed to exploit and use the resource. The concept of the "common heritage of mankind" does not, in the view of the Third World, recognize that industrialized countries with space technology should have a greater voice in regulating outer space resource development.

Paragraph 7 of Article XI further compounds the future negotiating difficulties of the highly industrialized countries with space technology. First, it establishes the principles of "orderly and safe development" and "rational management" of the Moon and other celestial resources. Most nations of the world interpret these principles as mandating central planning of resource development and international controls over resource uses and/or marketing. In short, these principles are the antitheses of a free market approach to the exploitation and use of resources on the Moon and other celestial bodies. Today, many believe that free market economics in the traditional sense will have only a small role to play in space industrialization. Yet it may be short-sighted to concede in a binding treaty that the political will of the majority of nations, rather than market-oriented forces, should dictate the pace and substance of outer space resource development.

Second, the principle of "expansion of opportunities in the use of those resources" will ultimately evolve into a Third World position that access to the Moon and other celestial resources must be limited for industrialized countries, so that developing countries have a chance to participate. (The Soviet bloc can also use the principle to insist that Western and Soviet activities using the Moon's resources be kept at the same level of intensity.) The clearest evolution of this concept is found in the draft Law of the Sea Treaty which creates an international mining monopoly for half of the deep seabed's mineral resources, based on the argument that developing countries can only expand their opportunities to use the resources on a collective and subsidized basis.

Finally, the principle of "equitable sharing of benefits" could be interpreted to require a system of international taxation of any profits made by commercial resource developers. Since the term "benefits" is not restricted to the financial realm, the principle should dictate mandatory transfer to all countries of the technology used to exploit the resources.

*   *   *

Conclusions

*   *   *

Present space law, including the Moon Treaty, has been forged almost entirely out of high academic ideals in advance of any practical commercial reality. True space law, if it allows free enterprise to operate at all, will evolve to meet the needs of practical commercial ventures. In this author's opinion, practical business space law would, if not preempted, evolve shortly after space-based exploitation of basic resources and energy begins to yield substantial profits. History teaches that the transition between academic and practical legal regimes can be gradual or traumatic, but that such transitions inevitably occur.

Ominously, the world now spends far more for military purposes in space than for academic studies. Apparently the only remaining substantial possibility for free enterprise non-military development of space requires large scale commercial development of basic natural resources, *i.e.*, raw materials and energy from space. Only basic raw materials and energy from space can return a profit commensurate with the capital expense and risk that will be required to start up space industry. Only large scale development of these basic space resources can provide sufficient economies of scale to permit development of space as an industrial frontier by free enterprise capitalism.

Such large capital investments cannot be made by free enterprise without clear legal guidelines that allow commercial operations to exploit space resources for profit. Free enterprise institutions simply cannot make significant investments in space while they are under the threat of lawsuits over the meaning of treaty terms or *ex post facto* appropriation of their investments by a nebulous future international regime.

NOTES

1. Dula makes the point that the Third World countries could challenge the legality of U.S. enterprises initiated prior to the formation of an international space regime. As a practical matter, what form could these challenges take? Keeping in mind the general principles of the 1967 Outer Space Treaty—especially that space is to be used for peaceful purposes—would it be legal for an

international regime to mount a military challenge to unauthorized U.S. enterprises, or the enterprises of any country? *See also* Moon Treaty, Article 3. Without the threat of *military* action to back up any policing effort, how much of a disincentive to development is the possibility of hostile reaction by a future space regime?

2. Dula mentions that a space development regime could unilaterally expropriate non-authorized facilities and resources. One justification for this move could be that development whose benefits were not shared was in violation of Article 11(8) of the Moon Treaty, which requires that "*[a]ll* the activities with respect to the natural resources of the moon shall be carried out in a manner compatible with" the specific provisions of Article 11, i.e., an international regime, designed to facilitate an "equitable sharing," etc. Note in this regard that one way the U.S. government could mitigate the uncertainty associated with possible expropriation would be to establish a political risk insurance pool for space activities, similar to the Overseas Private Investment Corporation (OPIC), which provides political risk insurance for U.S. companies involved in overseas activities.

3. Throughout this article, Dula uses "the Soviet Bloc" and "the Third World" as interchangeable terms. Keep this in mind when reading the excerpt from Rao, *supra,* on Third World views of the Common Heritage Concept. Especially in light of the fact that the Soviet Union has joined the U.S. in refusing to sign the Moon Treaty, do you think Dula's categorizations are accurate? Also, bear in mind that the Soviet Union joined the U.S. in resisting the introduction of Common Heritage language into the Law of the Sea Treaty.

4. For an article that suggests an even more "libertarian" view of space, and condemns all space treaties that give states, but not individuals, rights in space, see Wassenbergh, The Unfreedom Under Outer Space Law, 10 Air Law 161 (1985). *But cf.* J. Fawcett, Outer Space: New Challenges to Law and Policy 121 (1984) ("... perhaps no human activity has ever been so basically international").

Webber, Extraterrestrial Law on the Final Frontier: A Regime to Govern the Development of Celestial Body Resources, 71 Georgetown Law Journal 1427 (1983)

In 1969, when two United States astronauts landed on the Moon, Neil Armstrong proclaimed their success to be "one giant leap for mankind." Ten years later, the United Nations Committee on the Peaceful Uses of Outer Space (COPUOS) also took one giant leap for mankind—backwards. The committee reached an agreement, commonly known as the "Moon Treaty," which will, if given effect, significantly inhibit commercial exploitation of natural resources on celestial bodies.

*   *   *

The Moon Treaty Does Not Eliminate the Problems of Colonialism

Prior to the establishment of the regime required by article XI paragraph 5, the Moon Treaty would permit a period of colonialism. During this period, each nation would be left free to follow its own interpretation of the treaty's provisions, and ... these interpretations differ widely. Nations would interpret the provisions in their own interest instead of for mankind's benefit. Differing interpretations would increase the likelihood of conflict.

The problems of colonialism would also surface during the negotiations to establish the regime. The treaty expressly states that nations will perform the task of establishing the regime. Negotiations would be conducted under one-nation, one-vote procedures. This would pit conflicting national interests against each other. The developing nations would have the votes to push through a regime similar to the Sea Bed Authority. The space powers, however, which by then would have invested large amounts of capital and technology in development, could refuse to abide by such an agreement, claiming that it deviated from their longstanding interpretation of the provisions of the Moon Treaty. Unless the developing countries agreed to the interpretation of the space powers, the space powers would be likely to proceed with development unencumbered by the regime. The Moon Treaty, therefore, does little to abate the problems of colonialism.

* * *

The United Nations Is an Inappropriate Body for Celestial Body Resource Development

Although the United Nations, through its committee structure, has contributed a great deal to the development of space law, it is not the appropriate organization to control the development of extraterrestrial resources. The United Nations is institutionally weak and incapable of enforcing any mandate. A slow and cumbersome body, it cannot respond effectively to conflicts among nations. In addition, because the United Nations deals with a wide range of activities, it would be unable to govern resource development on celestial bodies independent of terrestrial concerns. The involvement of terrestrial conflicts in celestial body decision-making would interject extraneous issues into the process, and burden and delay any decisions that were made. As a result, the United Nations could not provide the investment security necessary to foster the development of celestial body resources. ...

INTELSAT Does Not Offer an Adequate Model

A regime modeled after INTELSAT ... would have serious flaws. Such a regime would engage in resource exploitation itself, create a monopoly, and freeze out independent public and private initiatives. These actions would violate the principle of free use. If an organization modeled after INTELSAT has any role in the development of outer space, it should be as a participant within a legal regime, not as a governing body.

In addition, the political conditions that led to INTELSAT's successful establishment have ceased to exist today. The organization's operational decisions are made by a committee in which each signatory's voting power is determined by its investment in and utilization of INTELSAT. Developed countries would not be able to gain similar control over a lunar regime under existing political conditions. INTELSAT was formed before the challenges by developing countries to the existing distribution of international economic power became an important influence in world politics.

Another reason that INTELSAT's success would not be transferable to a lunar regime is that INTELSAT provides telecommunication services, the value of which lies in their widespread availability. Nation-states have a mutual interest in the expansion of international communications. One country can not fully enjoy the benefits of the organization unless a significant number of other nations also participate. [Note: These benefits from broad participation, known as "network externalities," are a key feature of the telecommunications world. *See* Chapter 6, *infra,* for more on how such considerations shaped the structure of INTELSAT.] This is not true for celestial bodies, where the benefits can be profitably monopolized by one nation.

Finally, INTELSAT uses resources that, when the organization was created, were virtually limitless and did not threaten the natural resource markets dominated by the developing countries. In contrast, activities on the Moon will produce a vast supply of natural resources that potentially will compete with the resources of developing countries in terrestrial markets. The developing countries, therefore, would be threatened by a regime, dominated by the developed countries, that could diminish the value of their vital exports.

The Antarctica Treaty Does Not Offer an Adequate Model

The treaty to ensure the peaceful scientific exploration of Antarctica has been mentioned as a model for a celestial body regime. The Antarctica agreement, however, does not provide for an authority governing exploration and development, but only for a conference mechanism to permit consultations between signatories.

*   *   *

A Proposed Regime for Exploitation of Celestial Body Resources

... In order to consider the interests of mankind as a whole, as well as mankind's responsibility to reserve celestial bodies, a new type of regime is required. Mankind should establish an extraterrestrial regime for the sole purpose of controlling celestial body ... development.

* * *

The regime should concentrate on facilitating the development of celestial body resources for the benefit of all mankind. In determining whether a particular resource should be extracted, the regime should consider economic benefits to mankind from exploitation, preservation of future rights of access to the body's resources, and protection of the environment of the celestial body. First, without the exploitation of resources, mankind will receive no benefits from celestial bodies. Second, the maintenance of free access is important in assuring lesser-developed countries that they will be able to use celestial body resources when they acquire the capability. Finally, mankind cannot rely solely on profit-motivated entities to protect the environment of celestial bodies.

The regime should institute a licensing system to ensure the benefit of mankind, future access, and environmental protection. An entity wishing to develop resources or use the surface of a celestial body in any way should be required to submit its proposal to the regime and the regime should have the authority to grant or deny the request. If the proposal met previously established criteria, the regime would issue a license. The license would cover only an area sufficient to allow an adequate return on investment, and would be subject, upon proof of adherence to established criteria, to renewal or revocation. The license would not confer any permanent property rights over the area. Only the resources exploited by the licensed entity would come under its exclusive control.

The primary goal of the licensing procedure should be to limit the domination of investing entities to an area that they can profitably exploit over a limited period of time, in a manner consistent with the benefit of mankind principle. For example, the regime could license a mining company to utilize a one square mile area over the course of one year, and simultaneously grant provisional options over adjacent square mile plots for the next ten years. So long as the entity's activities were consistent with the conditions of the license, the regime would renew it each year, so that the entity would always have rights to mine resources ten years into the future. This would provide the security necessary to induce investment without giving the investing entity control over a large land mass. Such a system would prevent foreclosure of a large area from newcomers.

The Regime Should Have the Power to Tax Entities Utilizing Celestial Body Resources

The taxation of resource exploitation would be the regime's primary source of income. The regime should use the revenue to meet its administrative costs, conduct public research to improve the quality of human life on celestial bodies, learn more about the environment of celestial bodies, and discover information that might prove useful on earth. Information acquired by the regime would be available to all.

* * *

The Regime Should Not Attempt to Redistribute Wealth Among Nations or Organizations

The only purpose of the regime should be to develop extraterrestrial resources for the benefit of mankind in accordance with the free access and environmental protection principles, not to redistribute wealth.

* * *

Participating Developers Should Be Given Greater Input than Nonparticipants

Entities that participate in the development of celestial body resources have a greater interest in the effective operation of the regime than the rest of mankind, and consequently should have a greater input into the decisionmaking process than nonparticipants.

NOTES

1. Webber criticizes the role of the U.N. in the space development regime envisioned by the Moon Treaty, stating that U.N. involvement "would interject extraneous issues [i.e., "terrestrial concerns"] into the process" of making decisions. But what alternative international body could possibly eliminate the inclusion of "terrestrial concerns" in its decision-making? Even with voting weighted in favor of nations active in space, an international organization could be expected to reflect political and ideological tensions. Even INTELSAT, the international communications satellite consortium, has seen its share of political wrangling; a recent example is the controversy over U.S. establishment of a private communications satellite industry outside the auspices of INTELSAT. *See, e.g.*, 1 Meredith et al., American Enterprise, the Law, and the Commercial Use of Space 22–24 (1986). This topic is discussed at length in Chapter 6, *infra*, as are the circumstances leading to INTELSAT's creation.

2. Webber states that "INTELSAT uses resources that, when the organization was created, were virtually limitless." This is somewhat misleading. The formation of INTELSAT can more accurately be described as an effort to centralize resources to create a facility that would be difficult for each nation to duplicate.

See Sandler & Schulze, *The Economics of Outer Space,* 21 National Resources Journal 371 (1981). *See generally* Edelson, *Global Satellite Communications,* 236 Scientific American 58 (1977). Thus, it was the pooling of capital for creating what might be described as a "natural monopoly," rather than a lack of competition over communication frequencies, that led to the establishment of INTELSAT. For a detailed description of the negotiations leading up to the formation of INTELSAT, *see* Colino, International Telecommunication Satellite Organization (INTELSAT), in 1 Manual on Space Law 363–99 (Jasentuliyana and Lee eds., 1979).

3. Webber reaches an interesting conclusion by employing the logic of self interest often used by developing nation economists to describe the behavior of the U.S.: "activities on the Moon will produce a vast supply of natural resources that potentially will compete with the resources of developing countries in terrestrial markets." Thus the Note implies that a Third World–dominated space regime might act to *restrict* the output of space-derived resources to protect domestic markets for the same or complementary resources. Note that several considerations might mitigate this brand of protectionism: (1) the fact that the majority of the Third World countries each produces only a handful of natural-resource commodities, which makes it less likely they would have a unified economic interest in excluding or restricting any particular resource; and (2) the Moon Treaty itself states in Article 11(7) that one of the principles to be implemented by a space regime is "the expansion of opportunities in the use of [space] resources," which presumably would not be served by a restrictive self-interested policy of limited development. Nonetheless, Mr. Webber's point is well-taken.

Rao, Common Heritage of Mankind and the Moon Treaty, 21 Indian Journal of International Law 275 (1981)

The Agreement Governing the Activities of States on the Moon and Other Celestial Bodies, 1979, is largely addressed to regulate "exploration and use" of the Moon and other celestial bodies.

* * *

A point for consideration is whether it is permissible for a State Party to exploit, and thereby expropriate, the resources of the Moon, pending the establishment of an international regime. This issue assumes some significance in view of the fact that the developing countries did not insist on a provision for a moratorium on the exploitation of the natural resources of the Moon, pending the establishment of such an international regime like they did in the case of sea-bed resources.

* * *

[I]t appears that the absence of a moratorium clause in the Agreement amounts to licensing unilateral exploitation of the resources of the Moon, pending the establishment of an international regime and that the reference in Article 11(8) to Article 6(2) does not place any limit on the extent of commercial exploitation of natural resources of the Moon. These ideas come out clearly despite the contrived attempt to conform to Article 6(2). ... [This became] all the more clear when the U.S. Representative approvingly referred, albeit impliedly, to the views bluntly presented earlier by the U.S. Representative to the Legal Sub-Committee of the UNCOPUOS on April 19, 1973:

> The United States is not prepared to accept an *express* or *implied* prohibition on possible natural resources before the international conference meets and agrees on appropriate machinery and procedures [and] a treaty containing them take[s] effect.

That there is no express prohibition against a Member State exploiting the resources is apparent. The U.S. Representative, however, rightly anticipated one implied limitation (and there are many more) in Article 11(3) and then sought to explain it away in the following manner:

> (T)he words "in place" in the first sentence of paragraph 2 are intended to indicate that the prohibition against assertion of property rights would not apply to natural resources once reduced to possession through exploitation either in the pre-regime period or following the establishment of the regime.

The views expressed by the U.S. Representatives lead to two propositions: one, there is no limitation on exploitation of the Moon's resources within the meaning of Article 6(2); and two, a Member State may not claim property rights on the natural resources of the Moon, but once the resources are collected or excavated, a Member State can hold possession of [them] and expropriate [them]. The tenability of these positions may briefly be examined.

Article 11(8) of the Agreement subjects all "activities with respect to the natural resources of the Moon" to article 6(2) (one such activity doubtless being the exploitation of natural resources of the Moon). Article 6(2) ... states:

> In carrying out scientific investigations ... the States shall have the right to *collect on* and *remove from* the Moon samples of its mineral resources and other substances of the Moon in *quantities appropriate* for the support of their mission.

The main ingredients of the provision are: (1) the collection and removal of resources from the Moon are for samples to conduct scientific investigations; (2) the use of *appropriate quantities* of [the] Moon's resources is *permitted* only for scientific investigations; (3) the quantities so contemplated for the use in the latter category [are] *limited* to scientific investigation only; and (4) the expression "mission" is qualified by scientific investigations. ...

The collection or removal or use of the resources of the Moon in all events is consequently confined to scientific investigations, and not beyond. How the U.S. Representative could read such expansive meaning into the provision, encompassing unlimited exploitation, even extending to commercial utilization, is indeed difficult to understand.

* * *

There is one more weighty reason as to why the resources of the Moon shall not be exploited for any reason other than for the common benefit of mankind. Article 11(6) of the Agreement ordains that once any such scientific investigations lead to discovery of any natural resources on the Moon, it shall be the duty of States Parties to inform the UN Secretary-General and the public and international scientific community to facilitate the establishment of the international regime. This provision is to be read with Article 11(5) under which the parties "hereby undertake" to establish an international regime to govern the exploitation of the natural resources of the Moon when such exploitation "is about to become feasible." The combined reading of the two provisions leads to the inevitable conclusion that on discovery of any resources in the Moon by any State Party or a group of States Parties ... the conventional obligation to establish an international regime under Article 11(5) to govern the exploitation comes into operation soon thereafter. Explicit in this commitment—"hereby undertake"—is to agree for an agreement on the establishment of an international regime with the stipulated objective conditions.

NOTES

1. Notice that Rao's interpretation of the "scientific investigation" provision of the Treaty (Article 6(2)) is quite at odds with the official interpretation discussed in the first excerpt in this section. The issue boils down to this: in the absence of a *general* standard of conduct regarding how much material States can remove from the Moon, should the *specific* standard for scientific removal be read as (i) a general standard in disguise, or by implication, or (ii) a specific case with no bearing on the general case (i.e., of non-scientific removals), which suggests recourse to the general principles, including free use of the Moon and other celestial bodies (see Article 4(1), paragraph 1), that would tend to permit appropriation. Rao clearly buys argument (i); the preceding author, Webber, espouses (ii).

2. Rao's article can be read as an application of some new ideas in developing country economic theory, generally referred to as the New International Eco-

nomic Order. The following Note is a brief summary of some of the substance of these ideas.

A NOTE ON THE NEW INTERNATIONAL ECONOMIC ORDER

The New International Economic Order is a loose grouping of economic ideas made popular by a number of Third World economists. As formulated by the United Nations General Assembly, the New International Economic Order is intended, among other things, to "correct inequalities and redress existing injustices ... eliminate the widening gap between the developed and developing countries ... [and to give] preferential non-reciprocal treatment for developing countries, wherever feasible, in all fields of international economic co-operation whenever possible ..." Declaration on the Establishment of a New International Economic Order, May 1, 1974, G.A. Res. 3201, 6 (Special) U.N. GAOR Supp. (No. 1) at 3–5, U.N. Doc. A19559 (1974), reprinted in 13 I.L.M. 715, 716, 718 (1974). Scholars are in general agreement regarding the primary economic objectives of the proponents of the order: "[I]ncreasing LDCs' [Less Developed Countries'] control over their economic destiny; accelerating the LDC's growth rate; tripling the share of global industrial production conducted in the LDCs by the year 2000; and narrowing the gap in per capita income between the developed countries [and the LDCs]." Kreinin & Finger, A Critical Survey of the New International Economic Order, 10 Journal of World Trade Law 493, 493 (1976). *See also* Gamble & Frankowska, International Law's Response to the New International Economic Order: An Overview, 9 Boston College International & Comparative Law Review 257, 259 (1986).

The New International Economic Order has been described a number of ways. Some western observers see it primarily as a manifestation of the new Third World coalition in international law, which finds its expression primarily through the United Nations. *See, e.g.*, E. McWhinney, United Nations Law Making 22 (1984) (describing the new era of "Third World–led" international law). From this perspective, the new order is said to reflect a "pluralistic" and "inclusive" set of norms growing out of shared aspects of Third World cultures. *Id.* at 234. The emergence of the new order thus represents the beginning of a "transition in the world community, from an old system of world public order to a new one." *Id.* at 3.

But proponents of the new order make it clear that they have in mind something more than a Third World–oriented system for resolving international disputes. They seek nothing less than a fundamental restructuring of the norms of international relations. One prominent spokesman for the new order, who writes in a style characteristic of many of its proponents, reflects this questioning of current norms in a passage describing the new order's view of the causes of underdevelopment:

> Walt Rostow's theory [see his The Take-off into Self-Sustained Growth, 66 Econ. J. 25 (1956) and The Stages of Economic Growth (1961)] is well known. According to him, the Third World, which came late to industrialization, has already had the opportunity and will have the capacity to catch up with the countries whose development started earlier. Rostow, ignoring the phenomena of domination and imperialism, reduced underdevelopment to a mere question of backwardness. This soothing belief in an automatic international redistribution of means and incomes in accordance with some sort of natural law is completely unrealistic, since it takes no account of the balance of power. The present international situation is characterized by an intensification of conflict and a widening of the differences in power between states, leading to balkanization rather than redistribution.

M. Bedjaoui, Towards a New International Economic Order 66–67 (1979). In light of the very rapid growth of many Third World nations since Bedjaoui wrote this, is his argument that inequalities are inherently self-sustaining especially credible?

As the McWhinney book, *supra,* makes clear, the new international economic theorists rely heavily on the United Nations as a platform from which to make their case. In fact, it seems likely that without the U.N., which allows so many small, underdeveloped countries to come together, there would have been no New Order movement. It is therefore a valid question whether the new alignment of power envisioned by these theorists is possible outside the bounds of a U.N.-administered system. If not, given the largely voluntary nature of the U.N., one must wonder whether the developed world will tolerate a fundamental U.N.-led restructuring of the international order. *Cf.* M. Benko, W. de Graaff & G. Reijnen, Space Law in the United Nations (1985). But even if this is a difficult prospect to envision, the effect of new order rhetoric on the domestic political scenes should not be underestimated.

NOTES

1. Later in the book quoted from above, Bedjaoui states that, since the developed nations of the world dominate the Treaty-making process, the Common Heritage concept "carries with it obvious dangers in that it could be applied in one direction only and be 'co-opted' by great powers to their exclusive advantage." M. Bedjaoui, *supra,* at 224. Recall that this is precisely the same fear voiced by American critics of the Common Heritage language in the Moon Treaty. Was it a major flaw of the Treaty drafters that they used language so flexible it gives rise to fears of adverse interpretation by both major groups of countries to the Treaty? Could a Treaty using less flexible language have ever been ratified by both groups? Can't opponents of a Treaty always imagine extremely adverse interpretations?

2. Bedjaoui's view of technology, which he also sets forth in the same book, is instructive of some of the basic precepts behind the New International Economic Order. "Technology," he states, "is the archetypal common heritage of mankind. ..." M. Bedjaoui, *supra,* at 231. As such, it should be shared more readily by the "haves." Here we see the extreme concern with *distributional* issues—i.e., sharing—that characterizes so much of this new economic thinking. Without doubt there are strong equitable and even moral reasons for western countries to share technology. The problem is that an administrative structure that *forces* sharing entails a consequence that few would find palatable: there would inevitably be less to share.

In terms of western neoclassical economics, this is explained by appeal to a number of models. These attempt to capture the need for governmental intervention if technological innovation is to take place. Typically, the argument runs as follows: In the absence of government intervention, and assuming that a firm would find it impossible to keep new technologies secret, any firm that invests in research aimed at reducing costs or producing a new product will lose out to its rivals. The rivals will simply copy the new technology and achieve the same cost reduction or new product as the innovating firm. The difference, assuming that the costs of copying are substantially lower than the costs of research and perfecting the innovation, is that the rivals do not have to bear the costs of innovating. Thus, the innovating firm will find itself forced to price its output at levels that do not recoup its investment.

As a consequence, of course, neoclassical economic theory dictates that no firm will undertake research aimed at innovating. That is where government policy comes into play—to cure this instance of "market failure."

Government policy to encourage innovation can take many forms. For the most part, two instruments are used to achieve this goal: direct government funding of research (mostly basic research), and intellectual property protection (chiefly patents) for firms that create new products or cost-reducing processes. Intellectual property rights, by creating temporary monopolies over specific new technologies, provide the incentive required to encourage private firms to undertake costly research and development. For a good general review of these issues, see F.M. Scherer, Industrial Market Structure and Economic Performance (2d ed. 1980). For a discussion of other benefits of the patent system, see Kitch, The Nature and Function of the Patent System, 20 Journal of Law & Economics 266 (1977). In general, "diffusion of information" is one of the secondary benefits often associated with the patent system; it is furthered both by the limited duration of the patent grant (20 years in the U.S.) and by the requirement that each patent be published, with fully enabling details, upon issuance. *See* 35 U.S.C. §§ 100, 112 (1988).

It is important to note, however, that in contrast to the New International Economic Order envisioned by Bedjaoui and like-minded authors, the American patent system does not mandate the *direct* sharing of technology. Diffusion is expected to occur through the expiration of patents as well as the normal competitive process. Thus the *primary* goal of the patent system is to give an incentive to *create* new technologies; diffusion, or the sharing of benefits, is envisioned as an ancillary goal that will necessarily follow when firms take advantage of the incentive posed by patents.

A NOTE ON COMMON PROPERTY RESOURCES AND EFFICIENT ALLOCATION

Bedjaoui emphasizes the notion of common property resources, comparing space resources with technology (see Note 2 above) and even oxygen, which he correctly notes is "produced" in great quantities in the Congo and Amazon River basins, and used by all people on the planet. M. Bedjaoui, *supra*, at 235. Once again, his discussion reveals interesting assumptions behind the brand of developmental economics he espouses.

Western economists would have difficulty accepting the comparisons made by Bedjaoui. In the case of technology, the reasons are clear, as discussed in Note 2; at most, western economists view technology as essentially a "private good" with some "public goods" aspects. *See, e.g.*, Nelson, The Role of Knowledge in R&D Efficiency, 97 Quarterly Journal of Economics 453, 467 (1982). With respect to oxygen, it appears to be a classic example of what western economists would call a "public good"—that is, a good that (i) can be consumed by many without reducing the benefits to any user, and (ii) cannot be kept from potential users by any control or containment procedure. Other classic examples of public goods include sunsets and military protection. *See, e.g.*, R. Carnes & T. Sandler, The Theory of Externalities, Public Goods, and Club Goods 6 (1986).

Space resources are different. They have neither of the characteristics of public goods, nondivisibility (or non-exhaustibility) and nonexcludability. If one firm or nation strip mines one acre of lunar soil, no other firm or nation could follow on the same acre; the benefits would all go to the first firm. Likewise, it would not be impractical for a firm or a nation to build a fence or otherwise "stake a claim" to effectively exclude others from the area it wished to exploit.

Thus the comparisons Bedjaoui makes between oxygen and space resources do not work under conventional Western ideas about public goods. One point he raises, however, can be reconciled with traditional neoclassical analysis, and also finds expression in some provisions of the Moon Treaty: this is his allusion to the effect on Third World countries of developed nation consumption of oxygen and other environmental resources, an example of the economic concept of *externalities*.

In general, an activity that generates costs or benefits to firms or individuals not performing the activity is said to produce externalities. In some sense, the governments of Brazil and Zaire, by not cutting down all of the vast rain forests in their countries, are providing benefits to all the people on earth, since these rain forests produce a good portion of the oxygen in our atmosphere. (Of course, at the time of this writing at least, Third World countries *are* cutting down rain forests at a horrific rate, with consequences that may well turn out to be disastrous.) At the same time, Bedjaoui makes the point that the developed nations of the world, by burning hydrocarbon fuels, produce pollution, which damages the environment for everyone—an example of a negative externality.

The Moon Treaty makes an effort to minimize this form of negative externality in Article 7, which requires signatories to take measures to minimize the harmful impacts of their activities on the moon's environment.

Problems with a Common Resource Regime

Aside from the externalities problem identified above—which can be addressed as easily through a minimal regulatory scheme as through a common resource regime—there are a number of problems with the international development regime envisioned by Bedjaoui and reflected in certain provisions of the Moon Treaty. First, as we have discussed, it is not clear that space resources are the type of good commonly treated in the West under a centralized administrative regime; that is, they do not appear to be a classic public good. Second, as a result of the expense of exploiting these resources, the existence of a centralized, bureaucratic regime might well reduce or eliminate the incentives that would be required to entice private firms into space enterprises. That is, the excessive focus on distributional issues reflected in the Rao and Bedjaoui excerpts overlooks the fact that as of yet there are no benefits to distribute. Third, as a practical matter, a space development regime would be different from INTELSAT as regards the nature of the good they regulate. Because of the efficiencies of scale involved, INTELSAT's market is (or at least was, until recently) a natural monopoly; competing satellite communications systems did not make economic sense. The partners were thus forced by the nature of the market and the technology into banding together. (See Chapter 6, *infra,* for more on this topic.) This is not the case with space resources; there is no inherent reason why nations need band together to form a cooperative venture. Thus the centralized structure would have to be legislated *despite* the economic characteristics of the enterprise, not *because* of them.

On the other hand, economic theory also suggests that there might be some problems with a completely laissez-faire regime. If the most easy-to-exploit resources are located in a relatively small area on the moon, for instance, a substantial theoretical literature suggests that firms and nations will overutilize this area. *See, e.g.,* P. Dasgupta & G. Heal, Economic Theory and Exhaustible Resources (1979); R. Hardin, The Tragedy of the Commons, 162 Science 1243 (1968). *But cf.* Rose, The Comedy of the Commons: Custom, Commerce, and Inherently Public Property, 53 University of Chicago Law Review 711 (1986) (applying concept of "inherently public property" to describe modern land-use law, making some areas nonappropriable by private entities). It was to forestall such "land grabs" that the U.S. government instituted a "claiming" system for mineral deposits on federal lands in the nineteenth century. *See* I. C. Lindley, A Treatise on the American Law Relating to Mines and Mineral Lands Within the Public Land States and Territories 761–95 (3d ed. 1914). As a thought experiment, consider how such a claiming system might be structured for space. A helpful article, applying allocative economic principles to the problem of satellite frequency assignments, and suggesting the adoption of an auction system for frequency and satellite location resources, is Wihlborg & Wijkman, Outer Space Resources in Efficient and Equitable Use: New Frontiers for Old Principles, 24 Journal of Law & Economics 23 (1981); a portion of this article is reproduced *infra*.

The article just mentioned contains a very useful proposal regarding the reconciliation of efficiency and distributional considerations. Under the proposed scheme, all property rights over frequencies and satellite location would initially belong to a centralized agency. The agency would then auction off the rights to specific frequencies and locations, distributing the proceeds from the auction as it saw fit—e.g., by some "fairness" principle among members. As a second thought experiment, consider how this auction system might work in the context of space development. First, only those resources that are relatively easy to develop would be included in the centralized agency. Second, the agency would have to have some enforcement mechanism to punish non-members for transgressing on the agency's property rights. Third, the right to develop a particular resource would be time-limited, so that future bidders would have an opportunity to gain access to the same resource. Such a scheme would insure that the resources went to the highest bidder, and that no group of early bidders could monopolize resources long after the initial bidding. Such a regime would also solve the "tragedy of the commons" problem alluded to above.

In addition, since the bidding scheme would be independent of the system for allocating profits, it would in no way constrain the centralized agency from allocating its profits to assist less developed countries in achieving space capabilities or simply in developing their economic systems in general.

Do you think such a system would be compatible with the principles and provisions of the Moon Treaty? What position would you have to take on the two key interpretive issues in the Treaty—the meaning of "in place" resources and the "common heritage of mankind"—in order to espouse such a system? How would it square with the arguments and ideology associated with the New International Economic Order?

Wihlborg & Wijkman, Outer Space Resources in Efficient and Equitable Use: New Frontiers for Old Principles, 24 Journal of Law & Economics 23 (1981)

Space is the common property of mankind. Traditionally, access to common property resources such as the oceans has been open and free. This is appropriate for resources that are plentiful. At first glance, space appears to be not only abundant but infinite. However, future demand for space resources may soon make them scarce in the sense that an allocation mechanism will be needed for their efficient utilization. Satellites already perform traditional and new services using outer space resources, and plans for industrial ventures in space are under way. Space activities compete with more earthly activities for use of the scarce electromagnetic spectrum.

This paper demonstrates how the general principles of efficient markets easily can be extended to space resources. In fact, the market mechanism is particularly well suited to achieving efficient use of these resources given the difficulty for a central authority to obtain the necessary information. The paper is inspired by two seminal articles by R.H. Coase on the organization of economic activity. Our application is one of many possibilities: the same reasoning could be applied to other property resources.

*   *   *

II. Properties of Efficient Markets for Space Resources

This section argues that markets allocate rights to use orbit-spectrum resources more efficiently than do the nonmarket mechanisms currently in use. It considers three aspects of efficiency. First, efficiency means that a resource is allocated so that the marginal unit cannot be reallocated to another user without lowering value added. Second, an efficient system moves towards a new efficient allocation in the above sense after any disturbance such as an increase in demand or a reduction in production costs. These two aspects of efficiency will be denoted as *partial* efficiency in the markets for space resources. Third, and more general, an efficient system provides incentives for investment or research in new activities when they are expected to produce higher value added than do current activities.

As an economic resource, space consists of orbital positions and frequency bands. Efficiency requires that these can be combined freely. Currently they are sold as a unit with fixed coefficients. This is like assigning a radio station on earth a specific piece of real estate for a transmitter together with a frequency. Separate markets in frequency bands and orbit positions make it possible for all users of space locations and frequencies to trade the two separable economic resources until a Pareto-optimal situation is reached. In such a situation no user can change location and frequency without paying more than the potential gains generated by the new combination. Note, however, that in order for the markets for the resources to function efficiently, it must be possible to purchase a unit of one of the resources conditional on obtaining a certain unit of the other resource. Not only are the resources in general complementary but specific units of the two resources may be complementary.

[T]he markets for space resources should have the following properties: (a) complete allocation regime, (b) divisible and marketable user rights, (c) long contract periods, (d) well-defined liability rules.

* * *

A. Complete Allocation Regime

An allocation regime can be efficient only if it includes all resources that substitute for, or complement, each other. Thus, marketable user rights to resources in space must be defined to encompass substitutable modes of producing particular goods and services. For instance, long-distance communications can be transmitted by submarine cable, wire, and wireless as well as by satellite. Since real estate on earth is a well-priced and marketed resource, efficiency requires that scarce orbital positions, too, be priced in competitive markets. This allows a firm to compare the true costs of alternative locations for a relay station. If orbital slots remain free though scarce, too many resources will be invested in the building and launching of satellites.

* * *

[In addition,] the close substitutability between different parts of the [electromagnetic] spectrum necessitates that marketable user rights be defined for the entire spectrum—along the ground as well as in space—for the market system to be efficient.

B. Divisible and Marketable User Rights

The trade-offs facing users of the electromagnetic spectrum are more complicated than a simple choice between ground and space frequencies. Many trade-offs exist with respect to strength of signal, size of antennae, weight of satellites, precision in direction of the signal, and precision in the use of frequencies. Trade-offs occur between different geostationary orbits and other orbits and between the choice of orbit and all of the above aspects of frequency use. The length of time a frequency is used can also be traded off against location aspects and the different aspects of frequency use. The number of combinations among all these variables is immense.

* * *

C. Long Contract Periods

User rights may be purchased for either a limited or an indefinite period of time. While both formally are cases of leasing, a lease for an indefinite period of time in effect conveys a title of ownership to the lessee. How does the length of the contract period affect the efficiency of the market system? We show here that efficiency always prevails with indefinite user rights, while inefficiencies can be caused by time-limited user rights if the duration of the lease is shorter than the economic life span of the satellites. More specifically, it is the time-limit combined with costs for transforming the satellite to use by other firms and costs for transferring the satellite to other orbit-slots and/or frequencies that cause inefficiency.

* * *

Partial efficiency in the markets for space resources also prevails in cases involving *factor-specific equipment* with time-limited as well as indefinite user rights. Efficiency with respect to investment and research incentives presumes indefinite rights, however. To show this, consider how efficiency is achieved in the two cases after a technological change. For an *indefinite* user right the new firm must now bid a price that covers the present value of the incumbent's expected rent on the orbit slot and the frequency *plus* compensation to him for capital loss on the equipment. This is efficient because capital destruction should not occur unless new capital is so much more productive that the *increase* in value added covers the expected remaining value added on the old equipment. An identical situation will result with time-limited user rights. It is not sufficient for the new firm simply to bid more for the lease than the current holder pays, because the incumbent will be willing to increase his bid up to the point when he can no longer cover variable costs. The old factor-specific equipment therefore will not be taken out of service until it produces a negative value added at the bid-up price on the user rights. In this situation, the *increase* in value added on the new equipment covers the value added that will no longer be produced with the equipment that is taken out of service.

* * *

D. Well-Defined Liability Rules

The previous sections assumed that use of the spectrum is precise with respect to frequency and area affected, and that location of satellites in space is exact. These assumptions, however, are seldom valid. Users of the spectrum interfere with each other and space objects can collide. Thus social and private costs in the uses of the two resources can diverge.

A common regulatory response to such external effects is either to forbid the interference of one activity with others or to put specific technical limits on the external effects. The latter is particularly common in the use of common property resources. Well-known examples are quantitative regulations for air pollution by cars and factories or limits to the amount of waste products discharged in waters. Economists have often argued against specific technological constraints and instead have suggested the taxation of polluting activities. The advantage of this method is that those polluters whose costs of decreasing their pollution are lowest will do so first. The desired level of pollution is thus obtained at least cost.

Coase has argued [in The Problem of Social Cost, 3 Journal of Law & Economics 1 (1960)] that the so-called Pigovian approach [named after Arthur Pigou, 1877–1959, a noted English economist] is often inefficient. It may cost less for the activity harmed by pollution to reallocate or to protect itself than for the polluter to reallocate or decrease its emissions. Furthermore, Coase argued, an efficient allocation of resources could come about via market-induced negotiations without any intervention from regulatory agencies. Which system of reducing external effects is more efficient depends on information, transactions, negotiations, and enforcement costs—that is, on systems costs. ...

We contend that most external effects in the uses of space resource can be reduced to efficient levels by market-induced negotiations once liability rules are defined and enforced. This is superior to a system of Pigovian taxes because most interferences in the uses of space resources occur between very few parties at adjoining frequencies or orbit slots. The external effects are then relatively "individualized" so that the costs of finding negotiating parties become relatively low for space resources. The Pigovian solution is superior on the other hand when external effects are "generalized," and many parties are affected by a particular activity so that the costs of starting and conducting negotiations are relatively high.

* * *

It follows from Coase's argument that an optimal degree of interference and collision risk can be brought about, whether or not a liability rule is defined, if no costs are involved in identifying potential sources of interference for uses of adjoining resources, in setting up negotiations, in conducting negotiations, and in enforcing an agreement. The definition of a liability rule will determine who bears the costs of adjusting to interferences; it will not affect the level of interference.

The optimal degree of interference would be reached even when current holders and new entrants interfere with one another. All parties would gain by negotiating mutual improvements in equipment until the costs of improvements exceed the gains. The assumptions under which this market solution would be reached are very restrictive, however. For instance, the users of adjoining frequencies and locations are assumed to know the degree of interference that will be caused by the new entrant. When this information is lacking, a liability rule is necessary or newcomers could benefit by installing low-quality, interfering equipment that is very expensive to modify once it is in use. Measures to decrease interference are likely to be much cheaper if they are implemented before the space objects are installed. Current users of adjoining frequencies and locations must pay a higher price, therefore, to reduce interference to an optimal level (as defined in the case with perfect information). If instead the new entrant were liable for damages caused by his satellite, he would be induced to start negotiations when the costs of modifying the equipment are at a minimum.

* * *

Choice of Management Regime: Efficiency and Equity Considerations

Is there any need for an international orbit and frequency authority, and, if so, what roles should such an authority have? This section concludes that an authority can contribute little to achieving *efficiency* once the institutional framework for complete markets exist. However, well-functioning international markets may require international trade and legal conventions. The main task of an international space resource authority is instead to achieve *equity* in the distribution of rents among nations. We suggest, therefore, creating an international condominium to auction the electromagnetic spectrum and the orbits and to distribute the resulting revenues.

The current regime has been called a squatters'-rights regime because ownership is distributed on a first-come, first-served basis. This is a misnomer in one important respect. Once a squatter's claim is secured, his property rights are complete and he can sell his farm to more efficient, more eager farmers or subdivide it for development. This was the case on the American frontier during the 1800s. While it is true that a user of orbit slots or the frequency spectrum is a squatter in the sense of claiming resources not used by anyone else, his claim and use of these resources do not grant him the right to sell all or part of them. His property rights are therefore circumscribed in an important respect which distinguishes the current regime from a true squatter's regime. Currently there are restrictions on the intranational transfer of user rights as well on their international trading. For example, the Federal Communications Commission must approve users of the electromagnetic spectrum in the United States.

A true squatters'-rights regime may be less efficient than auctioning user rights even when the conditions for efficient markets are fulfilled. One reason is that transfer costs between different orbits and frequencies may prevent a latecomer in space from obtaining an optimal position or frequency, since the resources cannot be claimed without physical presence. The complementary nature of orbit slots and frequencies emphasizes this inefficiency of the squatters'-rights regimes because a potential user of space resources cannot claim parts of the two resources simultaneously. An auctioning system could be designed in such a way that this complementarity could be recognized, however. ... However, the major difference between a squatters'-rights regime and a resource auction is related to the problem of equity rather than efficiency. We shall return to this issue below. ...

Thus, there is an important role for international conventions similar to those of the General Agreement on Tariffs and Trade (GATT). The optimal tariff argument suggests that one country could gain by restricting trade in its shares of the space resources if these were imperfect substitutes for the shares of other countries and possessed a comparative advantage in producing specific services demanded by other nations. Therefore, in an initial distribution of property rights no single country or small group of countries should be given a monopoly on specific space resources that it can exploit by imposing an optimal tariff.

Some nations may also wish to allocate all or parts of their resources in a spectrum for military purposes or for other services that are supplied by government authorities. The frequency spectrum can provide public goods, such as emergency communications and military services, which are nonmarketable, but this should not free the respective government authority from the market test of the willingness to pay for the use of a scarce resource. ...

Inevitable interferences in the use of spectrum and orbit resources suggest the need for an international legal convention, because liability rules must be defined and enforced. Such a convention would not be necessary if enough national laws were directly applicable to the use of space resources. Lacking these, international interference requires an international legal framework that is accepted and enforced by all nations. Specification of such a legal framework would not be unique. Parallels exist in international law, such as the liability rules regulating collision at sea. Liability rules could either be accepted internationally and enforced by courts in individual nations, or the international authority could serve as a court for cases involving damages in the use of the frequency spectrum and the physical space resource. ...

The major task of an international authority for managing space resources will be to distribute rents. When a nonreproducible resource becomes scarce, it generates rents. Discussion of the normative questions of who should enjoy these rents and how the desired distribution can be achieved has often been confused since space has traditionally been considered an international common property resource to which access is open and free. Property rights to the resource consequently have usually not been precisely defined and their rents have seldom appeared explicitly. The importance of rents is nevertheless illustrated by the struggle over property rights at the World Administrative Radio Conference (WARC-79) proceedings.

Allocating user rights through a regime of squatters' rights would resemble the acquisition of titles to gold and land during the westward push of the American frontier. Space would be a new frontier and firms and nations would rush to claim the most valuable orbit slots and frequencies. The best-equipped firms in the most technologically advanced nations could quickly claim valuable space property, and little of the rents would remain for other nations. Such a regime is unacceptable to most countries.

The current regime regulating access to the electromagnetic spectrum and orbits is similar to that traditionally used for commons. Governments apply for user rights to the International Telecommunications Union which grants such rights on a first-come, first-served basis for an unlimited time period. The applicant is in effect granted rents for the period of use. If entry were not regulated by this nonmarket method, rents would be dissipated through congestion and interference.

Some developing countries have proposed either that user rights be reserved for future use by countries that have no current use for them or that the electromagnetic spectrum and the satellite orbit be subdivided and title to its parts distributed among countries in an equitable manner. These two procedures are equivalent in terms of equity when user rights are accorded in perpetuity. However, unless markets for resale or subleasing of space resources are also allowed, greater equity is achieved at the expense of less efficiency since scarce resources will be hoarded for future use.

The auction method for allocating user rights as a way to ensure efficiency in resource use is consistent with any distribution of rents. The equity aspect of managing orbits and frequencies could therefore be separated from efficiency aspects.

NOTES

1. The authors suggest that an international authority is only necessary from an efficiency standpoint when so many activities are affected by some particular activity that liability rules and/or bargaining over property rights are not sufficient to reduce interference to an optimal level, that is, when there are excessive transaction costs. Is outer space sufficiently large to avoid the need for a centralized agency to achieve efficiency? Would it be wise to plan now for the day when interference between rival space developers is more likely? On the need to regulate communication via space satellite, *see* R. White & H. White, Jr., The Law and Regulation of International Space Communication 5–8 (1988); *see also* Chapter 6, *infra*. Note that the 1988 Space WARC (World Administrative Radio Conference), concluded as this book was in press, adopted a new regime for allocating geosynchronous orbital slots. This regime is discussed in Chapter 6.

2. The authors also note that equity, if not efficiency, requires an international "condominium" or central agency. Is it too early to worry about equity in space development? Is "fair development" an important enough principle to cause us to sacrifice "early development"? These are questions that will not die with the Moon Treaty; they are likely to be with us for a long time.

3. On these topics generally, *see* Coase, The Federal Communications Commission, 2 Journal of Law & Economics 1 (1959) and Coase, The Problem of

Social Cost, 3 Journal of Law & Economics 1 (1960). Together with William Meckling and Jora Minasian, Coase wrote Problems in Radio Frequency Allocation (Rand Corp. 1963). Although this manuscript remained unpublished, the coauthors later published two important contributions. *See* William H. Meckling, Management of the Frequency Spectrum, 1968 Washington University Law Quarterly 26 (1968); and Jora R. Minasian, Property Rights in Radiation: An Alternative Approach to Radio Frequency Allocation, 18 Journal of Law & Economics 221 (1975). *See also* A.S. DeVany *et al.*, A Property System for Market Allocation of the Electromagnetic Spectrum: A Legal-Economic-Engineering Study, 21 Stanford Law Review 1499 (1969).

COMMON PROPERTY AND THE COLLECTIVE ACTION PROBLEM

Proposals to fairly and efficiently allocate space resources, such as those under discussion here, have the virtue of coordinating rights allocation (and hence development more generally) through a centralized agency. Centralization solves a number of problems, most notably the transaction costs of locating rights owners and finding out about the rules of ownership and transfer. (This advantage obviously is a major motivating force behind the proposals discussed in this section.) But these proposals ignore a tough question: how to rouse the various nations (and fractious forces within them) into organizing themselves into a unified group. In other words, these proposals *assume* an international organization to administer space rights, and proceed directly to a discussion of how best to structure the organization.

A large and important literature has extensively documented the difficulties involved in organizing any large group to cooperate. This is known as the *collective action problem*—a problem which, if you stop and think about it, is ubiquitous in social and economic life. To take one simple example, consider legislation that benefits only one small group (say, sheep farmers whose sheep produce a certain rare type of wool) at a high cost to taxpayers in general. It is easy for the sheep farmers to identify each other, and thus to form a lobbying group, and thence for this group to know its goal clearly (maximizing the subsidy and/or import tariff for this type of wool). On the other hand, taxpayers in general each suffer only a slight economic harm due to the special wool-protecting legislation backed by the small lobby. As a consequence, although it is rational for them to oppose the legislation in principle (because it is not cost-justified), they almost surely will not. It is simply not worth the cost of organizing and fighting the special legislation. The taxpayers, in other words, are likely to be unable to overcome the collective action problem facing them. *See* Mancur Olson, The Logic of Collective Action: Public Goods and the Theory of Groups (2d ed. 1971). The same process has already been documented in the brief history of the U.S. space program. *See* Howard McCurdy, The Space Station Decision: Incremental Politics and Technological Choice (1990); Robert Smith, The Space Telescope: A Study of NASA, Science, Technology & Politics (1989).

Quite clearly, the same sort of problem may confront those who try to organize an outer space resource allocation organization. As attempts at multilateral coordination have shown from time immemorial, it is difficult to get diverse nations together to agree on basic principles and procedures. This is especially true where there is a great deal of uncertainty over the future value of the activity being organized; it is natural for the various parties to negotiations such as these to try to influence the structure to be agreed upon in a manner that reflects both their current and anticipated interests. *See* Douglass North, Institutions, Institutional Change and Economic Growth (1990) (pointing out that institutional change always brings an opportunity for specific groups to capture more economic rents, and thus that some beneficial change does not take place because other groups know this and fear it). *See also* Edwin W. Paxson III, Sharing the Benefits of Outer Space Exploration: Space Law and Economic Development, 14 Mich. J. Int'l L. 487, 509–13 (1993) (arguing the improbability of establishing various types of international regimes for space development).

Indeed, clear examples of multilateral attempts at coordinated development that end in impasses abound today. *See, e.g.*, Barbara Ellen Heim, Exploring the Last Frontiers for Mineral Resources: A Comparison of International Law Regarding the Deep Seabed, Outer Space, and Antarctica, 23 Vand. J. Transnat'l L. 819 (1990). Heim points out that three areas which have potential as sources of mineral deposits (Antarctica, outer space, and the deep seabed) share two common problems which have frustrated agreement between industrialized countries and less developed countries (LDCs): (1) a definition of the common heritage principle; and (2) a workable management regime.

Although the author suggests the adversaries compromise and find a solution quickly, there is little real hope they will do so, as her own research shows. (She points out, for instance, that the proposed Antarctic Mineral Convention, which gave strong voice to the "common heritage" principle, would have created more problems than it solved: it gave developing countries ultimate control over developed country activities, even though in the early years at least it is the latter group which will bear the risks of mineral development.)

Heim argues that a regime should be structured that both the numerous developing countries and the wealthy, technologically advanced countries would ratify under a one-nation, one-vote system. Preferably, she says, this system would provide immediate gains and control of development to the countries or entities that take the initial risks and would provide the developing countries with a future opportunity to take part in either the development or conservation of the areas. *Id.* at 846. Yet she gives no indication of any recent precedent indicating that such a scheme would have any chance of being created.

In fact, recent evidence indicates that countries are only too willing to take advantage of existing institutions to further selfish goals. A recent article provides one relevant example from the space field. Jonathan Ira Ezor, in an article entitled Costs Overhead: Tonga's Claiming of Sixteen Geostationary Orbital Sites and the Implications for U.S. Space Policy, 24 Law & Pol'y Int'l Bus. 915 (1993), describes how the nation of Tonga successfully acquired six valuable orbital slots through the ITU allocation process, over the objection of INTELSAT. The author says that Tonga's actions will affect the satellite telecommunications market and pricing structure and may even influence who the players are in the satellite area. This incident should serve as a wake-up call to the U.S. in particular, the author concludes, which has up until now not monitored the allocation process as carefully as it should have.

Even if a centralized institution could be created, rational economic agents can be expected to spend significant sums of money to influence the rights-allocation process. The general outline of such expenditures, as well as the payoffs from them, are only too familiar to students of administrative agencies responsible for doling out economically valuable rights. To take one simple example, consider the vast sums expended to influence the awarding of defense contracts, or government computer processing services contracts. It is wise where possible to avoid these expenditures and instead encourage activities that are more directly productive.

Thus even though one must acknowledge that there might be significant advantages in convening a centralized agency to administer rights to outer space resources, it may be practically impossible to achieve consensus on the specific form such an agency will take. And it may turn out to be wasteful to encourage the expenditure of resources on the rights allocation process, given that total expenditures for all space-related activities are of course limited.

Even assuming this is so, an interesting question arises whether something short of a centralized administrative agency might emerge (or be agreed upon) to perform some of the same functions. Institutions of social control, after all, run the gamut from such large formalized agencies through more local authority, common law rules that emerge from isolated disputes over time, and even to informal (strictly speaking, non-legal) norms of acceptable and unacceptable conduct. *See, e.g.*, Robert Ellickson, Order Without Law (1991). With the large caveat that any discussion of such intermediate rules is necessarily speculative, it might be useful to explore a few possibilities.

First is the possibility that something less than full international agreement might join together not all potential spacefaring nations, but at least all (or most of) the important ones. Something like a "European Economic Community" for space, for example, might be feasible. Then, once such an institution were up and running, other countries would join. This would certainly be so if membership in the institution were seen as conferring significant benefits, e.g., if the stability and predictability in the definition and exchange of property rights were seen as desirable. Then new members would "opt in" to avail themselves of these benefits, and the institution would, over time, establish itself as the standard. The alternative, of course, competing groups, some in the system and others outside it, either as non-affiliates or members of a rival group, is conceivable; but the possibility for conflict under these circumstances would certainly be present. Indeed, it is not hard to imagine a war under this scenario; it certainly matches to some extent the conditions that created conflicts among rival European powers in the then-newly exploited North American colonies in the seventeenth and eighteenth centuries.

A second possibility is that some purely national law will emerge as a standard, or at least as a model for other countries to follow. In other legal areas national leaders have effectively established patterns that have been followed by other countries; commercial law in the U.S. (much in evidence in the United Nations Convention on the International Sale of Goods) and patent law in Great Britain come to mind. Other countries could adopt the basic framework worked out in the pioneer country, or private entities could specifically "opt into" coverage under this country's laws, e.g., by choice of law provisions in private contracts. This scenario is obviously more likely when a single country dominates the industry; experience shows that the legal framework often follows from this fact. The effect would be somewhat similar to the limited-membership group just described, with a jurisdictionally limited legal regime emerging as the de facto international standard.

A third possibility is that the space industry will settle on a set of non-formal rules or norms that govern their activities. This is the case in some industries, such as diamond selling, where disputes are very rarely referred to formal legal institutions such as courts, but are instead resolved by respected industry members according to well-understood and agreed-upon norms. *See, e.g.*, Sally Falk Moore, Law and Social Change: The Semi-Autonomous Social Field as an Appropriate Subject of Study, 7 Law & Soc'y Rev. 719 (1973); Lisa Bernstein, Opting Out of the Legal System: Extralegal Contractual Relations in the Diamond Industry, 21 J. Leg. Stud. 115 (1992). It should be noted, however, that arrangements such as these are usually stable only in small, close-knit societies, where nonlegal sanctions such as negative gossip or reduced standing in a common religious or ethnic community are effective disincentives against rulebreaking. *See* Landa, A Theory of the Ethnically Homogeneous Middleman Group: An Institutional Alternative to Contract Law, 10 J. Leg. Stud. 349 (1981); Allen & Lueck, The "Back Forty" on a Handshake: Specific Assets, Reputation, and the Structure of Farmland Contracts, 8 J. L. Econ. & Org. Beh. 366 (1992); Glenn C. Stevenson, Common Property Regimes: A General Theory and Land Use Applications (1991); Daniel Bromley, ed., Making the Commons Work (1992); Elinor Ostrom, Governing the Commons (1991); Ellickson, *supra*. The parallels between these societies and the "society" of international space commerce being limited, it is not clear how far shared norms can be expected to carry the industry toward stable legal relations.

An interesting argument along these lines is put forward in Lawrence D. Roberts, The Law of the Commons: A Framework for the Efficient and Equitable Use of the Lagrange Points, 6 Conn. J. Int'l L. 151 (1990). Roberts argues that the unique "gravity-neutral" areas around the Moon and Earth known as the Lagrange Points could be governed by what he calls the "traditional Law of the Commons," which maximizes efficiency and equity without incurring substantial transaction costs. According to Roberts, three main features of this law as applied to this valuable space resource are: (1) sovereignty is invested in no specific user, but all users are entitled not only to freedom of access but also freedom of use regulated within a strict code of conduct, *Id.* at 166; (2) rights are granted only to those entities which exploit the resource, *Id.* at 167; and (3) because several of these points tend to draw objects toward their centers, the danger of collision is high, either placing competing orbital facilities in physical contact or pre-agreed, binding arbitration might be necessary as the community grows large, *Id.* at 169–70.

Alternatives to Centralized Rights Allocation

Of course, the legal forum that applies rules is really only as effective as the content of the rules themselves. Thus we must return to a discussion of which property rules make sense in the space context. The centralized agencies that are most often discussed envision a structure that allocates pre-existing rights on some basis, e.g., by auction. There are obviously a variety of alternatives. One alternative among many that can be imagined will be discussed. It envisions an administrative structure to facilitate trading in and other exchanges of rights, the ownership of which are determined outside the exchange system, according to a simple rule, such as first possession. It would also involve a regime to resolve disputes among multiple claimants.

Discussion of this alternative begins with the notion that it is difficult, and perhaps foolhardy, to specify the precise content of property rights before the economic activity they will cover has matured. Consider a famous article on the emergence of property rights in beaver hunting territories among native inhabitants on Labrador in the eighteenth century. The author argues that before property rights emerged it was too expensive (i.e., not worthwhile) to get everyone to agree voluntarily on the optimal beaver harvest, and then to enforce the agreement by policing the harvesting ground or the place where pelts are traded. This was not a problem until western traders in effect increased the value of beaver pelts by paying more for them, for sale in the European fur market. At this point the lack of coordination among the native inhabitants becomes too costly to continue. The problem is solved by giving a single individual exclusive control over some specific portion of the hunting ground. Under private ownership, it is the owner who suffers due to overharvesting; since she knows this, and (critically) since *she alone* controls the harvest rate, she will adjust that rate so as to harvest only the optimal number of beavers. That is, she will make her plot self-sustaining, if possible. The key is that she cannot foist off the negative consequences from her decisions onto the community at large; she must "internalize" these externalities and hence take account of them in her decision-making. The point is generalized in the article as follows:

> [W]hat converts a harmful or beneficial effect [e.g., the effect of harvesting one more beaver] into an externality is that the cost of bringing the effect to bear on the decisions of one or more of the interacting persons is too high to make it worthwhile.
>
> Internalizing such effects refers to a process, usually *a change in property rights*, that enables these effects to bear (in greater degree) on all interacting persons. A primary function of property rights is that of guiding incentives to achieve a greater internalization of externalities.

Demsetz, Toward a Theory of Property Rights, in Ownership, Control and the Firm: The Organization of Economic Activity: Vol 1 (1988) (emphasis added).

A similar statement can be found in Yoram Barzel, Economic Analysis of Property Rights (Cambridge Univ. Press, 1989), at p. 65:

> People choose to exercise rights when they believe the gains from such actions will exceed their costs. Conversely, people fail to exercise rights when the gains from owning properties are deemed insufficient, thus placing (or leaving) such properties in the public domain. What is found in the public domain, therefore, is what people have *chosen* not to claim. As conditions change, however, something that has been considered not worthwhile to own may be newly perceived as worthwhile; conversely, what was at first owned may be placed in the public domain.

The famous Coase theorem makes a related point. It states that, given some initial assignment of property rights, those rights will be traded until they reach the hands of the highest-valuing user, regardless of who holds the rights in the first place (assuming low transaction costs). This is of course most famous as applied to legal rules; at least in its "strong" form, it implies a thought that chills many a lawyer and judge—viz., that legal rules are irrelevant, at least in terms of their impact on overall output. *See* R. Cooter, The Coase Theorem, in The New Palgrave (1987). *See also* Robert Ellickson, Property in Land, 102 Yale Law Journal 1315, 1337–1341 (1993) (noting that assignment of private land plots greatly increased agricultural productivity in the earliest colonies).

Applying these theoretical points to the design of a regime for space entails taking care not to foreclose greater specification of rights in the future. While from the point of view of the "strong" form of the Coase theorem the initial allocation of rights does not matter, in practice it surely will. Transaction costs are likely to be high, at least where rights holders are widely dispersed and the value of rights is subject to a great deal of uncertainty. If, for instance, space minerals are discovered that were not known at the time rights were initially allocated, it may be practically difficult for a company well-positioned to take advantage of the new mineral to locate and bargain with all rights holders whose permission must be obtained to take advantage of the new mineral. The system of property rights must be designed with this sort of future contingency in mind. Yet it must also be uniform enough to create settled expectations. *See* Ellickson, *supra*, at 1362 ("A group that is willing to recognize private property in land must decide what standard bundle of rights to confer on a meritorious occupier of a part of its territory.") For present purposes, it is important to keep in mind that the initial allocation of rights will be subject to subsequent refinements, and, as a consequence, subsequent transactions, and to design it accordingly.

This emphasis on future flexibility does not preclude any of the models of rights allocation mentioned so far. Certainly the international rights "condominium" could be founded with the principle of future flexibility in mind. On the other hand, if flexibility is the most important attribute of the system, it must be conceded that a centralized administration is not the *only* system that will work. And if there are costs to such a system—for example, as argued above, the costs of activities designed to influence the allocation and content of rights (i.e., "rent seeking" costs)—then alternatives that provide the same flexibility without these costs must be explored. We turn to this task in the following section.

Modified First Possession and "Deed Registry" As an Alternative

Economic theory in general does not look favorably upon a rule of first possession, at least in the terrestrial context. Most economists who have considered the question agree that "squatting," as well as the various forms of "homesteading" that were used to settle the American West in the nineteenth century, probably encouraged people to enter the land earlier than they would have under a system of competitive bidding. Aside from the assumptions inherent in the economic models used (e.g., the usual one regarding complete information concerning future activities on and therefore value of the land), this consensus view makes a realistic point: the race to possess free (or nearly free) land can be expected to pull resources out of other productive uses at a faster rate than seems optimal. Indeed, an important and interesting branch of economics has consistently concluded that goods whose prices are regulated will come to be rationed by a combination of price and non-price "expenditures," e.g., waiting in line, that are always less efficient than allocation by price alone. *See* Yoram Barzel, The Economic Analysis of Property Rights (1989). Importantly, what empirical evidence there is on the topic seems to support this view: the failure rate among farms started on cheap (i.e., "underpriced") homestead lands appears to have been significantly higher than it was on other farms. *See, e.g.*, R. Taylor Dennen,

Some Efficiency Effects of Nineteenth-Century Federal Land Policy: A Dynamic Analysis, 51 Ag. Hist. 718, 734 (1977). *See also* Terry L. Anderson & Peter J. Hill, The Race for Property Rights, 33 J. L. & Econ. 177 (1990); David D. Haddock, First Possession Versus Optimal Timing: Limiting the Dissipation of Economic Value, 64 Wash. U. L.Q. 775 (1986). Other historical sources support the same point:

> [I]nnumerable tumults must have arisen, and the good order of the world been continually broken and disturbed, while a variety of persons were striving [to see] who should get the first occupation of the same thing, or disputing which of them had actually gained it. [2 William Blackstone, Commentaries *4]

In the face of all this theory—which is explicitly applied to space by Wihlbog and Wijkman in this chapter—how can anyone oppose a centralized rights-allocation authority to auction space rights? In a sense, the answer is no one. But this ignores an important point. As mentioned earlier, the forces that will be called upon to form this authority go beyond—and in many ways, can be expected to be inconsistent with—the forces of reason in support of efficient space development. To be blunt, politics will enter. And when this happens, the efficient auction mechanism could be transformed into a hideous bureaucratic monster. To some extent, the point is that an approximation to the ideal solution may be worse than another solution entirely—a classic case of the "theory of the second best," artfully described by Professor Leff:

> [I]n complex processes ... a move in the right direction is not necessarily the right move. To pick a simple example, if I am on a desert island, subsisting solely on coconuts and oysters and beginning to hate it a lot, and across the bay from me there is another island, lush and fertile, I do not improve my position in life by swimming half way across.

Arthur A. Leff, Economic Analysis of Law: Some Realism About Nominalism, 60 University of Virginia Law Review 451, 456 (1974).

Thus, although considerable centralized authority is necessary to the efficient auction schemes mentioned here, it should be recognized that strong centralized authority could be far from efficient if used for more than rights auctions. The fall of the Soviet Union and many Eastern European governments is the only evidence that need be cited here.

At the same time, history also teaches that pure anarchy has its costs as well. Indeed, an intriguing analysis of the emergence of informal (or, perhaps better, quasi-formal) property rights among gold miners in the lawless (i.e., "stateless") gold mining country of California in the 1850s recapitulates a story that must be common in pre-history: the gold miners discovered that it was cheaper to respect certain rights than to fend off usurpers. In a lawless regime, in other words, they found that too much effort was devoted to physical defense of a claim, leaving too little time and effort to actually develop it. They thus formulated a classic instance of the Hobbesian bargain where power was ceded to some "authority" for definition and protection of rights, resulting in more stable claims and therefore more efficient economic production. *See* John Umbeck, A Theory of Property Rights with Application to the California Gold Rush (1981). It is hoped that explorers and developers of space resources will not have to recapitulate this experience yet again. Yet if they fail to institute some minimalist state in the early days of space industry, they surely will.

What is needed, then, is arguably a simple rule for allocating space property rights, together with something akin to the semi-centralized, fairly minimal system of deed registries that flourishes in many countries. This system has the benefit of simplicity, ease of administration, yet sufficient coordination to make property transactions feasible. Both parts of this "minimalist proposal" will be explored in the sections that follow: the first-possession rule of title acquisition, and the deed-registry system for claims.

Why First Possession?

As indicated above, first possession is often a poor way to allocate property. However, three factors make it attractive in the space context.

First, it is simple; it requires very little government involvement. Aside from a method of recording claims, and some threat or sanction to deter stronger second-comers from displacing rightful first possessors (discussed below), very little in the way of governmental authority is needed. *See* Richard Epstein, Possession as the Root of Title, 13 Georgia Law Review 1221 (1979).

Second, its very defect from the point of view of theory—too-rapid development—may be a needed countermeasure when people are (inefficiently) risk averse and when non-economic goals are also served by development. Given the state of weapons of mass destruction and environmental threats on earth, it is not too ridiculous to assert that encouraging space development might be a good insurance policy for the species. If special incentives are needed to serve this valuable goal, incentives which might be viewed as excessive from the limited perspective of maximizing current expected net profit, then they may well be justified in light of the importance of the goal.

Finally, the "rent dissipation" from frontier land development served no useful purpose; it was pure economic waste. In space, however, inefficient races to claim and develop space resources will come with a very significant spillover benefit: the development of more rapid and more diverse space exploration vehicles. This is a very important difference from the land development analogies, where racing depletes fixed resources in the context of static technologies. In much the same way that society encourages technical progress through what might be described as "racing for patents," on the belief that the spillovers to society exceed the costs of racing, it should consider encouraging a race into ever deeper space. *Cf.* Robert P. Merges & Richard R. Nelson, On the Complex Economics of Patent Scope, 90 Columbia Law Review 806 (1990) (criticizing economists' patent race models along these lines).

An important scholar of property rights has written that "Individual ownership does, however, generate some new transaction costs, mainly those arising from the proliferation of boundaries and ownership entities." Robert Ellickson, Property in Land, 102 Yale Law Journal 1315, 1329 (1993). For this reason, private ownership, at least where population growth begins to cause some degree of crowding, entails the creation of a system for proving title claims and keeping them straight—a deed registry. *See, e.g.*, George L. Haskins, The Beginning of the Recording System in Massachusetts, 21 Boston University Law Review 281 (1941) (discussing earliest colonial recording systems). Note, however, that Ellickson, in the article just cited, does provide an interesting prediction applicable to the space context:

> The efficiency thesis predicts that innovations in technologies for marking, defending, and proving boundaries lead to more parcelization because they reduce the transaction costs of private property regimes. According to this view, for example, Glidden's invention of barbed wire in 1874 should have stimulated more subdivision of rangeland in the American West. And this indeed appears to have occurred.

Ellickson, *supra*, at 1330. According to this hypothesis, which is simply that legal rules maximize overall efficiency in close-knit societies, property boundaries in space are important enough that we can expect innovations in the technology of marking, defining, and perhaps recording them, so that over time the task of keeping track of claims becomes cheaper and easier.

Potential Pitfalls of First Possession, and Some Modest Suggestions on How to Avoid Them

At the outset, we must clarify precisely what interest we intend to be perfected via possession; that is, what *content* we will assign to the "bundle of rights" obtained by first possession. In western legal systems, the variety of property rights is amazing, but one basic distinction can be used to separate rights into two broad classes. This is the distinction between the usufruct, a right to continued use for a limited time, and the fee, a more permanent interest that can be traded, devised, etc. For some purposes the usufruct may prove to be valuable in the space environment. But generally, we have in mind a fee interest, more specifically a right akin to the fee simple of Anglo-American law. This has the advantage of predictability (given the thousand-plus year history of these interests) and flexibility which, as mentioned earlier, is a key advantage given our current lack of knowledge about the full range of resources that may be encountered in space. Thus we work with the fee interest.

Second, we need to clarify what we mean by "possession." This is important for more than definitional reasons. It is quite clear that one important problem ignored in our discussion up to now is the problem of overclaiming. If possession is defined too loosely (e.g., the apocryphal "I claim this continent for Spain"), then the first visitors or inhabitants in a given area of space would have almost limitless rights. But a narrow definition could cause other problems. For example, if a certain mineral is distributed unevenly in various extraterrestrial rock formations, it may be difficult to predict how wide an area must be claimed to ensure a viable mining operation. Limiting the definition of possession unduly must necessarily create uncertainty under these circumstances.

The solution to the problem will come in two parts, one theoretical and the other empirical. The theoretical part entails placing some "reasonable" limits on the geographic scope of claims. This is the rationale behind a number of provisions in other regimes where property rights are defined. Patent law, with its explicit attention to claim scope, comes most readily to mind. Indeed, the theoretical rationale for the tradeoff between adequate property rights to spur investment and excessive property rights that concentrate an inefficient degree of control in a single pair of hands (and hence slow down those who follow) has been described at length. *See* Robert P. Merges & Richard R. Nelson, On the Complex Economics of Patent Scope, 90 Columbia Law Review 806 (1990). But other property regimes have arrived at similar schemes. The law of gold mining, for example, limits the size of individual claims; requires claims to be recorded and surveyed; requires them to be perfected by some minimum investment of time and/or labor; and causes them to be forfeit for failure to perform any of these requirements. *See* Comment, The General Mining Law and the Doctrine of *Pedis Possessio:* The Case for Congressional Action, 49 U. Chi. L. Rev. 1026 (1982). In his study on the evolution of property rights among prospectors during the California Gold Rush, John Umbeck observes that even the earliest contracts establishing such rights included limitations on claim size and minimum working requirements. John Umbeck, A Theory of Property Rights With Application to the California Gold Rush 91–96 (1981). (Query: why should we be worried about granting rights that are "too broad"; if a third party is in a better position to exploit the rights than the original right holder, won't the two strike a deal? Does the worry stem from the costs involved in striking and enforcing these deals?) So the theoretical point is straightforward: rights must be limited to prevent overclaiming. The costs of paying off extortionate claim holders would add too much to an already uncertain enterprise.

So much for the theoretical point. The empirical point is simpler to make, but harder to carry out: the "reasonable" scope of rights will have to be arrived at over time. It may vary from one region or type of resource to another; it may be subject to refinement and revision over time. But it will have to be decided not upon the premises of theory, but rather the accretion of experience.

Finally, note that some technology for indicating possession and marking the boundaries of claims will be necessary. *See* Ellickson, *supra*. Ideally, whatever devices are used for this purpose would be coordinated with the "deed registry" on earth, so that the positions of boundaries could be confirmed remotely, from the registry office. Given the advent of (terrestrial) global positioning technology, it is realistic to anticipate such a technology. It certainly would have the benefit of reducing the cost of establishing and enforcing claims, which should make it an attractive technology to develop. Like the development of barbed wire on the American frontier, such demarcation technologies can have significant overall benefits. Indeed, this is important enough that the U.S. government might consider investing funds in research to develop such a technology at the outset of space development activities. The payoff would surely be very large.

Setting Aside Preserved Areas

For the most part the preceding discussion has quietly trumpeted the virtues of private property. It has pushed aside the concerns of those who back the application of the common heritage principle to space development. We will not dwell on the reasons again, as they are detailed throughout this chapter, and indeed throughout the book. We must admit of one troubling aspect to our analysis, however. Although in theory when developing nations have attained the economic wherewithal to exploit space resources they will bid on them, and granting rights to these nations before this time would be inefficient, there are reasons to believe that some system of "development preserves" would make sense, perhaps totalling 10 percent of the area capable of development. For one thing, there is an argument akin to "intergenerational equity" to be made for giving developing countries some opportunity to exploit near-earth resources well after the initial development period by advanced nations has passed. For another, it makes good political sense: it will surely give developing countries a greater stake in the space development, and perhaps even bring them more readily into an international regime to recognize property rights in the first place. For arguments along these lines, see Edwin W. Paxson III, Sharing the Benefits of Outer Space Exploration: Space Law and Economic Development, 14 Mich. J. Int'l L. 487 (1993). Paxson argues that a regime to use lunar mining, involving transferable credits based on a nation's population and allowing Moon mining for finite periods, would benefit developing countries and therefore merits investigation.

In addition to development preserves, there should be environmental research and conservation preserves. It should not be necessary at this point to defend such an idea. Perhaps 10 to 15 percent of the area capable of being developed ought to be preserved for this purpose. If preserves are built in to the development scheme from the beginning, many of the problems of terrestrial environmental preservation can be avoided. If it turns out over some suitably long period of time that there is little of interest in the preserved areas, then they can be auctioned off or given to developing countries.

Preserves will be established and maintained by the same "recording authority" that keeps title records, arranges transfers, and the like. One possible way to enforce the boundaries of preserves would be to give a bounty to any party who discovers encroachment on preserve lands—e.g., in the form of a grant of title over some moderately large claim. This would create an incentive for enforcement without the need for the enforcing authority to have an extensive presence in the area. The basic point, however, is that preserved space for future development and pure conservation should be built into the space property regime from the beginning, to avoid the cost and political difficulties of creating such preserves after property becomes valuable. Of course, if possession plus adherence to some minimum formalities are recognized as the international standard for securing a claim, all spacefaring nations must agree to recognize preserves and abide by their boundaries. In the beginning this should not be too difficult practically, since the number of spacefaring nations will be small. Over time, a simple mechanism may come to be used to ensure multilateral recognition of preserves—e.g., a rule that claims will not be enforced if made by a national of a country that does not recognize the legitimacy of preserves, or that has permitted incursions into them by claimants.

5

Other Treaties, Agreements, and Issues

The preceding two chapters dealt with the overarching treaties governing activity in outer space. This chapter deals with a number of remaining treaties and issues that—although not necessarily of lesser importance—involve matters of less general application. Some, like the Liability Convention or the Rescue and Return Agreement, implement portions of the treaties described previously; others simply involve more specific topics. We will deal with the most important remaining space agreements at some length, and will at least touch on many other issues. We will also attempt to illustrate the ways in which different space agreements may interact in the context of a real-world fact situation.

THE LIABILITY CONVENTION

One major space law agreement that has seen dramatic application is the Convention on International Liability for Damage Caused by Space Objects of 1972, 24 U.S.T. 2389, T.I.A.S. 7762. That treaty provides detailed rules that flesh out the general liability provisions contained in the Outer Space Treaty of 1967 (*see* Chapter 3, *supra*). The Liability Convention is applicable to both military and civilian space activities of its signatory nations; it provides for absolute liability by launching states for damage caused by their space objects on the surface of the earth or to aircraft in flight (Article II), and liability based on fault where the damage is to space objects of another launching state elsewhere than on the surface of the earth (Article III). The launching state may, however, be exonerated where the injury is caused by the gross negligence or malice of a third party—for example, a terrorist bomb that causes a Space Shuttle explosion. The Convention also provides for joint and several liability where more than one launching state's space object, or space objects belonging to more than one launching state, are involved.

The Liability Convention has been applied in the real world amid rather dramatic circumstances: the crash in Canada of a Soviet satellite powered by a nuclear reactor. The following article by Alexander Cohen describes the satellite's crash and the legal and political response thereto. Cohen's article, part of a symposium on international incidents as a source of international law, shows how concrete events can shed considerable light on how different groups interpret international law.

Cohen, Cosmos 954 and the International Law of Satellite Accidents, 10 Yale Journal of International Law 78 (1984)

I. Problem

Falling satellites are an unavoidable hazard of space exploration: at the current level of technology, a certain number of satellites will inevitably fall out of orbit. Nevertheless, the traditional sources of international law provide little help in determining what norms would govern a situation in which a falling satellite causes injury. The 1978 crash of the U.S.S.R.'s Cosmos 954 satellite has shed some light on the normative expectations of states concerning satellite accidents.

From the events leading up to and following the crash of Cosmos 954, four governing norms emerged: (1) A state that becomes aware that one of its satellites will crash has the duty to forewarn a state that is in danger; (2) The state whose satellite has crashed in the territory of another state has the duty to provide that state with information (regarding the specifications of that satellite) to enable the endangered state to assess the dangers and act to counter them; (3) Special rules govern the duty to clean up the remains of a state's satellite that has crashed in another state's territory; and (4) The state whose satellite has crashed has the duty to compensate a state injured as a result of the crash.

II. Facts

The U.S.S.R. launched the nuclear-powered Cosmos 954 naval surveillance satellite on September 18, 1977. In late November or early December 1977, Cosmos 954's orbit became erratic. The U.S. soon calculated that the satellite would fall on or about January 23, 1978, although it was not known where it would land. In response, the U.S. initiated a series of secret meetings with the U.S.S.R. in mid-January 1978, during which the U.S.S.R. provided the U.S. with information about Cosmos 954's reactor. The U.S. also warned its NATO and Organization for Economic Cooperation and Development (OECD) partners that Cosmos 954 was expected to fall, and offered to help clean up any radioactive contamination that might result.

Cosmos 954 crashed to earth on January 24, 1978:

> [T]he satellite entered the earth's atmosphere intruding into Canadian air space at about 11:53 A.M. Greenwich Mean Time to the north of the Queen Charlotte Islands

> on the west coast of Canada. On re-entry and disintegration, debris from the satellite was deposited on Canadian territory, including portions of the Northwest Territories, Alberta, and Saskatchewan.

U.S. President Carter notified Canadian Prime Minister Trudeau within fifteen minutes of the accident, and repeated the U.S. proposal of assistance. Trudeau accepted Carter's offer.

Some hours later, Canada asked the U.S.S.R. to provide information about the specifications of the Cosmos 954. The U.S.S.R. responded that day by offering to help clean up Cosmos 954's remains. In contrast to its reaction to the earlier U.S. proposal, Canada declined the Soviet offer.

The joint U.S.-Canadian cleanup operation that resulted from this exchange, dubbed "Operation Morning Light," cost Canada nearly C$14 million, while the U.S. spent some U.S.$2–2.5 million. Canada billed the U.S.S.R. for C$6 million of its outlay on January 23, 1979, but did not seek reimbursement for the U.S. expenditure. The U.S.S.R. paid C$3 million to Canada on April 2, 1981, "in full and final settlement of all matters connected with the disintegration of the Soviet satellite 'Cosmos 954' in January 1978."

III. Conflicting Claims

Canada and the U.S.S.R. asserted different versions of the facts of the accident. First, the U.S.S.R. blamed the fall of Cosmos 954 on a mid-space collision. Academician L. I. Sedov explained that:

> On Jan. 6, 1978, for reasons that as yet remain unclear, sudden depressurization of the satellite took place outside the visibility zone of our facilities for tracking space objects. Judging from the fact that the depressurization process was very rapid, it can be assumed that the satellite collided in flight with some other body of natural or artificial origin. As a result the satellite's onboard systems went out of commission, it lost orientation, and began an uncontrollable descent.

Canada, in contrast, blamed the fall of the satellite on a faulty motor. "The U.S.S.R. admitted that Cosmos 954 had failed, and that it was not possible to lift the satellite into a much higher orbit, as had been planned in case of an emergency, because of failure of a rocket system."

Second, the U.S.S.R. claimed that Cosmos 954 had been completely destroyed during reentry. The official Soviet news agency (TASS) stated that, "in the afternoon of Jan. 24, 1978, the Kosmos-954 satellite entered the dense layers of the atmosphere over Northern Canada and ceased to exist." Notwithstanding this claim, Canada found charred pieces of the satellite that had returned to the ground.

Finally, the U.S.S.R. declared that the remains of Cosmos 954, if any, posed a minimal radiation hazard. According to Sedov, "[i]t was emphasized [to the

Canadian government] that if individual fragments of the satellite did reach the earth's surface, only limited local pollution might occur, and only in the immediate area of the fall, and that this would require the application of ordinary decontamination measures." Canada, in contrast, found that "all but two of the fragments recovered were radioactive. Some fragments located proved to be of lethal radioactivity."

IV. Conflicting Conceptions of Lawfulness

The Cosmos 954 incident suggests that elites in Canada and the U.S.S.R. held divergent expectations of how states that are involved in satellite accidents should behave. These expectations concerned the substantive content of four governing norms: the duty to forewarn, the duty to provide information, the duty to clean up, and the duty to compensate for injury.

A. The Duty to Forewarn

It appears from the record that Canadian elites expected the Soviet Union to warn Canada as soon as the U.S.S.R. had discovered that Cosmos 954 might conceivably land in Canada:

> In the course of the day January 24, 1978, an official of the Department of External Affairs expressed to the Ambassador of the Union of Soviet Socialist Republics the surprise of the Government of Canada that the Government of the Union of Soviet Socialist Republics had failed to give notice of the possible re-entry of the satellite into the earth's atmosphere in the region of Canada, and, subsequently, of the imminent re-entry of the satellite.

Elites in Canada thus seemed to believe that the U.S.S.R. was obligated to forewarn all potentially endangered states of the hazards posed by its falling satellite, no matter how remote the possibility of injury.

Soviet elites viewed the norm differently. They claimed that the U.S.S.R. had an obligation to warn only the United States of the impending crash of Cosmos 954:

> Calculations made on the basis of [Cosmos 954's] last orbits within the visibility range of our tracking facilities showed that if, because of the satellite's emergency condition, individual parts of the satellite were not fully consumed in the atmosphere and reached the earth's surface, they might fall into the open sea in the region of the Aleutian Islands. In this connection, the appropriate information was given to the U.S. government.

Two possible conceptions of the duty to forewarn may explain this assertion. First, Soviet elites may have interpreted the norm as a requirement that the

U.S.S.R. warn the state in whose territory the satellite was most likely to crash. Alternatively, the U.S.S.R. may have agreed with Canada that the duty to forewarn required the notification of all potentially endangered states. Elites in the U.S.S.R. may not have believed, however, that they were required to notify these states directly if they were part of a political and military alliance hostile to the U.S.S.R. Rather, Soviet elites may have believed that the U.S.S.R. could discharge its duty under the norm by notifying the leading state in the hostile alliance—in this case, the U.S.—which would relay the warning to the other members of that alliance.

B. The Duty to Provide Information

Consistent with their position regarding the duty to forewarn, Canada's elites believed that the U.S.S.R. was under an obligation to disclose information. Canada repeatedly questioned the U.S.S.R. about Cosmos 954's specifications, and expressed frustration at the U.S.S.R.'s refusal to answer their inquiries:

> In this regard, Canada has requested the assistance of the Soviet authorities in furnishing information about the nature and characteristics of the nuclear core contained in the satellite. These requests have been conveyed on several occasions. ... The Canadian authorities regret that they have not to date received answers to these questions.

Elites in Canada also expected that this information be publicly disclosed. Indeed, "Canada decided to publish the documents establishing the claim together with texts of its diplomatic exchanges with the Soviet Union on the matter. In so doing, the Canadian government departed from normal practice regarding the confidentiality of diplomatic communications."

Under the Soviet interpretation, however, the duty to provide information imposed a more limited burden. According to this interpretation, the U.S.S.R. was required to provide only the minimum degree of information that Canada needed to conduct a cleanup. In addition, the Soviet Union reserved the right to determine what that minimum included:

> In connection with the request made by the Canadian side for information regarding the power unit which was on board the Cosmos-954 satellite, the Embassy would remind that the necessary information about the satellite was already made available which, in the opinion of the Soviet side, is sufficient to organize and carry out effective search for possible consequences of its cessation to exist over Canadian territory.

The statements made in Pravda show that the U.S.S.R. also believed that any information it provided should be transmitted secretly. The Soviets chided

Canada for the highly public manner in which Canada had handled the Cosmos 954 incident; they were particularly displeased at the fact that Canada did not notify them officially of its findings concerning the wreckage for two weeks, a considerable time after such information was released to the press. Indeed, the U.S.S.R. charged that Canada was using requests for information as a pretext for intelligence gathering. "The Soviet side finds it also necessary to note that some of the questions put by the Canadian side obviously relate to information which is outside the scope of the amount [sic] necessary to secure the health and safety of persons and the environment."

C. The Duty to Clean Up

In the Soviet view, the cleanup should be undertaken jointly by the injured state and the state that had launched the satellite. As the Soviet representative to the Scientific and Technical Sub-Committee of the UN Committee on the Peaceful Uses of Outer Space stated soon after the crash of Cosmos 954, "[i]f a satellite or any spacecraft, when it goes out of control should cause damage to another State, then the launching State is duty-bound to compensate for this damage: it is duty-bound to participate in the search and recovery of the debris of the satellite. ..." Indeed, the U.S.S.R. repeatedly expressed frustration at Canada's refusal to allow it to participate in the cleanup.

Under the Canadian version of this norm, the injured state is entitled to choose which country or countries will carry out the cleanup. Accordingly, Canada turned down the U.S.S.R.'s offer of assistance but permitted its American ally to participate in the operation.

D. The Duty to Compensate for Injury

Canada evidently considered there to be a norm requiring the U.S.S.R. to make full payment for the cost of repairing the injury caused by its satellite. Although Canada eventually demanded only C$6 million in damages out of an expenditure of C$14 million, it clearly based its claim on the total cost of cleaning up the radioactive debris. Canadian elites also believed that the U.S. would help pay for the cleanup. If one conceives of the unreimbursed U.S. expenditure on the cleanup of US$2–2.5 million as a form of payment to Canada, the U.S. "paid" Canada C$2.5–3.125 million as a result of the crash of Cosmos 954. Canada never offered to repay the U.S. for its outlay on the cleanup, nor did it press the U.S.S.R. to do so.

Actions by Soviet elites showed partial disagreement with this interpretation. Unlike Canada, the U.S.S.R. viewed the duty to compensate for injury as an obligation to reimburse only the incremental costs that the injured state incurred in repairing the injury. Thus the Soviet officials who negotiated the U.S.S.R.'s payment to Canada "made it very clear that they wouldn't pay [Canadian] fixed costs." At the same time, the U.S.S.R.'s elites seemed to concur in the Canadian view that the U.S. should not be reimbursed for its role in the cleanup. The U.S.S.R., therefore, did not offer to reimburse the U.S. expenditure. Indeed, the Soviet refusal to pay Canada's "fixed costs" tends to suggest that the U.S.S.R. would have rejected a claim for U.S. cleanup expenditures.

V. International Appraisal

The conflicting expectations of elites in Canada and the U.S.S.R. were never appraised in a formal judicial setting. Nevertheless, their claims of what constitutes proper action by states that are involved in a satellite accident did receive widespread informal evaluation by a broad range of state and media elites. From the standpoint of norm creation, the crucial appraisals were those of elites in the United States.

The legal conceptions expressed by U.S. elites were much closer to those of Soviet than to those of Canadian elites. The United States assumed the burden of notifying its NATO and OECD partners, apparently without the U.S.S.R. having asked it to do so. Furthermore, the U.S. government never joined in Canada's public criticism of the U.S.S.R. for having failed to notify Canada of the impending crash of Cosmos 954. From this it would appear that the U.S. shared the Soviet view that the launching state was under a duty to forewarn only the leading state of a hostile alliance, and was not responsible for warning each of its political adversaries individually.

The United States also appeared to agree with the U.S.S.R. on the issue of how to interpret the second norm, the duty to provide information. U.S. elites interpreted this norm as an obligation to provide only that information needed to conduct the cleanup. Unlike Canada, the U.S. chose to question the U.S.S.R. about the specifications of Cosmos 954 in secret, and evidently expected only minimal compliance with American requests for information:

> [M]any American specialists were skeptical that the Soviet Union would provide any information about its out-of-control space satellite, when national security advisor Zbigniew Brzezinski, on Jan. 12, first raised the issue with Soviet Ambassador Anatoly F. Dobrynin. "Frankly, I thought they were likely to tell us to go to hell," said one administration specialist.

Again, the United States seemed to take the same view as the Soviets of the duty to compensate for injury. The U.S. never joined Canada in criticizing the U.S.S.R.'s payment to Canada as too small, apparently conceiving of the norm as imposing an obligation to reimburse the injured state only for the incremental cost of repairing the injury. Since the U.S. did not ask reimbursement for its share of the cleanup expenses from either Canada or the U.S.S.R., it would seem that the U.S. elites agreed with both countries that the U.S. was obliged to pay Canada under the norm.

While concurring generally in the Soviet formulations of the first three norms, the United States rejected the Soviet interpretation of the fourth, concerning the duty to clean up. There is no indication that the U.S. ever expected Canada to permit the U.S.S.R. to play any part in the cleanup operation. Nevertheless, the apparent difference in legal conceptions obscures the possibility that the two superpowers were motivated by similar concerns. It is not unreasonable to suppose, as did some Canadian observers, that each was anxious to participate in the cleanup chiefly to gather intelligence, or to prevent the other from doing so. The U.S. eagerness to examine what was left of Cosmos 954 was surely matched by Soviet desires to deny the U.S. just such an opportunity. It would therefore seem misleading to characterize the U.S. appraisal as an affirmation of free choice for the injured state. Rather, it appears to be an assertion of the right of the injured state to invite only its political allies to participate in the cleanup.

VI. Outcome

The norms established by the Cosmos 954 incident provide that the major satellite launching nations—the U.S. and the U.S.S.R.—notify each other of hazardous events due to satellite failure, relay information to facilitate damage control, assist their political allies in cleanup operations, and share the cost of compensating the state injured by a falling satellite, regardless of whose satellite caused the injury and regardless of fault.

The critical norm is that of joint compensation. This norm would appear to provide compensation only for the incremental costs of cleanup associated with the accident. It may also be limited in application to surveillance satellites.

Although it is possible that the payments made by the U.S. and the U.S.S.R. were *ex gratia* and, hence, devoid of normative content, at least the size of the Soviet payment tends to argue otherwise; in the context of negotiations with the U.S.S.R., a fifty percent settlement is apparently quite high. Indeed, that the U.S.S.R. paid anything is striking in light of the fact that it was not obligated to pay under the 1972 Liability Convention. That the U.S. paid its share without being at fault lends further support to the existence of this norm.

VII. Writer's Appraisal

The Cosmos 954 incident illustrates the paradox of satellite utilization: satellites simultaneously protect and endanger the international community. Reconnaissance satellites play a crucial role in maintaining the stability of the U.S.-U.S.S.R. nuclear balance. At the same time, nuclear-powered satellites present clear hazards, as the Cosmos 954 incident demonstrated.

One response to this problem would be to prohibit the use of those satellites that are most hazardous. At the time of the Cosmos 954 incident, President Carter suggested a ban on nuclear-powered satellites: "If we cannot evolve those fail-safe methods, then I think there ought to be a total prohibition against [nuclear-powered] earth-orbiting satellites. I would favor at this moment an agreement with the Soviets to prohibit earth-orbiting satellites with atomic radiation material in them."

A ban on nuclear-powered satellites does not seem a realistic solution. In the first place, the U.S. and the U.S.S.R. are unlikely to consent to a prohibition, because certain satellites must carry an on-board nuclear power source in order to perform their missions. Indeed, Canada's attempt, in the wake of the Cosmos 954 incident, to impose a new regime on the use of nuclear power sources in space through the United Nations Committee on the Peaceful Uses of Outer Space, has made little progress. In addition, the costs of such a ban might well outweigh its benefits in that restrictions on nuclear-powered satellites could conceivably destabilize the nuclear balance.

The norm of joint compensation that appears to emerge from the Cosmos 954 incident is a better answer to the paradox of satellite utilization. The states with the greatest investment in satellites are exposed to the greatest potential of liability, but that liability is limited, and is not such as to discourage satellite use. This norm takes into account the probability that some satellites will inevitably fall, by requiring payment regardless of fault.

The outcome of the Cosmos 954 incident may well have had a positive effect on world order. The U.S. and the U.S.S.R. apparently recognized that it was in their mutual interest to cooperate rather than to turn the incident into a propaganda battle. The U.S. and the U.S.S.R. thus demonstrated their ability to take joint steps to deal with the dangerous items over which they exercise control. Their cooperation helps to increase the security of the two states and the world. While a price is paid for this security by the unlucky victims in such third states as Canada, the norm established by the incident provides at least for the payment of substantial reparations.

The use of nuclear-powered satellites will continue to threaten the earth with falling debris. The Cosmos 954 incident offers hope that cooperative measures can be taken to offset the damages that result, and to enhance global security in the satellite age.

NOTES

1. Although good practice calls for satellites carrying nuclear materials to be boosted into long-duration orbits at the end of their useful lives, accidents like the Cosmos 954 crash are likely to happen from time to time. In this context a

strict liability regime makes sense. The operators of most satellites are likely to be either wealthy nations able to afford the cleanup cost out of pocket or (though there are currently no civilian applications for nuclear-powered satellites) corporations able to insure against loss. And, of course, the Outer Space Treaty of 1967 imposes ultimate liability for launches by non-governmental or intergovernmental organizations on the launching state or states. Since the countries involved tend to fly many satellites, a strict liability regime allows "spreading" of the total liability over a number of satellites. *See generally* G. Calabresi, The Cost of Accidents 39 *et seq.* (1970). Imposition of fault-based liability only as between space objects also makes sense from a "spreading" standpoint.

2. Note the magnitude of the costs involved in the Cosmos 954 cleanup, which by the standards of most earthbound disasters were relatively minuscule. Although the Liability Convention is important, misconceptions as to the magnitude of harm likely to result from satellite crashes are common. The Cosmos 954 crash, which involved a nuclear powered craft, nonetheless resulted in rather minor damages, something that should be borne in mind in the context of discussions concerning liability limits and insurance. While enormous damages are possible in some circumstances (for example, a loaded Titan, launched from Cape Canaveral, that crashes into the Vehicle Assembly Building while two Space Shuttles are being prepared for launch—with possible damages in excess of $5 billion), most scenarios for such large sums involve launch accidents. Even in this setting, most risks are not great by earthly standards. A March, 1988 internal study by the Office of Commercial Space Transportation (see Chapter 8) concluded that the total chemical energy of three typical launch vehicles approximated that of a wide-body airliner. *See* Congress Moves Toward Subsidizing ELVs, Aerospace America, August, 1988, at 8. Launches are included within the Convention's coverage, but most launch accidents will take place within the launching state's own territory and involve its own nationals, a situation in which the Convention does not apply.

3. The Liability Convention is a detailed treatment of the 1967 Outer Space Treaty's liability provisions. Given the limited magnitude of damages likely to be covered by the Convention (compared to, say, the Chernobyl accident or to many other accidents that take place more frequently), such attention is surprising in some ways. Perhaps it reflects lawyers' fascination with liability issues, but it may also reflect a view by the non-spacefaring countries that space travel is an ultrahazardous activity for which the space powers (at the time of the Convention, limited to large and wealthy countries) should be held strictly to account—hence the different treatment of damages on earth as opposed to damage to other space objects. This view may change as more and more nations traditionally regarded as "third world" opinion leaders (such as India and Brazil) become active space powers themselves. If, as a result of this broader participation, space activity comes to be viewed as an economic mainstay of all nations rather than as a special activity only of the wealthy we may see a shift to limitations on

liability such as exist in the maritime or aeronautical industries. For more on these and related liability issues in a private law context *see* Chapter 8, *infra*.

4. The Liability Convention makes no provision for punitive damages, indirect or consequential damages, or "moral damages," and discussions regarding these issues at the time of the Convention's drafting reached no conclusion. International law draws no clear distinction between "direct" and "indirect" harm as many nations' municipal law systems do. The United States did remark at the time that moral damage claims (that is, claims for insults to a nation's dignity or sovereignty) might be valid under some circumstances, a position supported by Hungary as well. There was no provision for punitive damages because the Convention provides for unlimited liability for actual damages, which was considered enough to provide adequate incentive for states to avoid unnecessary risks. For more on these and other topics relating to liability for space activity *see* Christol, International Liability for Damage Caused by Space Objects, 74 American Journal of International Law 346 (1980).

5. Article XI provides that a claimant state may present its claim under the Convention to the launching state without exhausting its local remedies under the law of the launching state. The claimant state is also given the option, however, of electing to proceed under the launching state's own judicial or administrative procedures instead of the Convention; however, claims presented in such fora cannot simultaneously be made under the Convention. Where claims made under the Convention are disputed, there are provisions for arbitration (Article XIV).

6. The Liability Convention provides for strict liability in the case of harm to victims on earth, but for fault-based liability in the case of harm to other spacecraft. This is similar to the regime governing aircraft, where there is strict liability for injury to persons and property on the ground and fault-based liability with regard to other aircraft. *See* Restatement (Second) of Torts, Section 520A. This is entirely reasonable as an incentive for risk-minimizing activities. Persons on the ground can do little to protect themselves from crashing satellites, after all, and the low likelihood that any particular person or locality will be struck further dilutes any incentive to do so. Those who launch spacecraft, on the other hand, have considerable ability to reduce the chance that they will crash to the ground and harm individuals, and the certain knowledge that if they are allowed to crash in populated areas someone will be hurt. As among spacecraft operators, on the other hand, avoidance of injury is a mutual matter: the number of spacecraft is not that large, and all parties have the ability to avoid collision with one another.

The problem of space debris, discussed later in this chapter, may create considerable difficulty under the Liability Convention: since space debris (made up of fragments from defunct satellites, spent boosters, and space weapons tests) is a growing threat, but since it may be difficult to tell after a collision which nation's craft created the particular particle of debris causing damage, liability may be difficult to assign. Aside from this problem of proof, in order to recover the complaining party would have to show that (1) the accused party was negligent in either creating the debris or in failing to warn of its presence; and (2) that its own actions were not the primary cause of the injury. Given the difficulty of proving the origin of a particular piece of debris, a more workable solution might be for the space nations to contribute toward damage awards based on the proportion of space debris that each has caused, much as has been done in some pharmaceutical cases. *See, e.g.*, Sindell v. Abbott Laboratories, 26 Cal. 3d 588, 612, 607 P.2d 924, 937, *cert. denied*, 449 U.S. 912 (1980) (defendant's liability based on market share in offending product). For political reasons it is unlikely that such a compensation scheme would be agreed to, however, although it would have a valuable incentive effect as it would discourage nations from contributing to the amount of space debris in orbit.

7. Cohen speaks of "joint compensation" by the United States and the Soviet Union. This is an incorrect characterization, however. Although both the United States and the Soviet Union made payments to Canada, the payments were for differing purposes. The Soviet Union's payments were compensation under the Liability Convention; the U.S. payments and assistance were in exchange for access to intelligence data concerning Cosmos 954, an important military satellite. *See* W. Burrows, Deep Black (1986).

8. As a formal matter, the procedures of the Liability Convention were never invoked over the Cosmos 954 crash, as the matter was settled rather smoothly. Canada's claim appears at 18 International Legal Materials 899 (1979); the settlement protocol appears at 20 International Legal Materials 689 (1981). Obviously, however, the Convention was very important as governing law.

SPACE REMOTE SENSING

Use of satellites for earth observation is not a new idea: in 1946 a secret Douglas Aircraft/RAND Corporation report for the U.S. Army recommended making use of captured German rocket technology to launch reconnaissance satellites that could observe the Soviet Union and other potentially hostile nations. Douglas Aircraft Co. Inc. Report No. SM11827, Preliminary Design of an Experimental World-Circling Spaceship (May 2, 1946). By the early 1950s, even though the United States was years away from launching any kind of satellite, plans were already underway for orbital reconnaissance (see Chapter 1). *See also* P. Stares, the Militarization of Space: U.S. Policy 1945–84 (1985); W. Burrows, Deep Black: Space Espionage and National Security (1986). Civilian remote sensing did not get under way for some time afterwards, but by the 1970s it was already becoming a reality. On civilian remote sensing generally, *see* T. Lillesand & R. Kiefan, Remote Sensing and Image Interpretation (1987); R.M. Hord, Remote Sensing: Methods and Applications (1986).

Although such activities held the promise of more accurate maps, better crop and resource management, discovery of new deposits of mineral wealth, and more effective environmental monitoring, they also raised concerns on the part of two classes of nations: less developed countries who feared that corporations and developed nations would have unfair bargaining advantages regarding resources if they possessed such information, and totalitarian or authoritarian countries who regarded such sensing as an intrusion on their jealously guarded sovereignty. These fears led to considerable discussion in the United Nations and COPUOS, with results discussed in the articles below, which also provide some information regarding the technology behind and uses of remote sensing.

Logsdon & Monk, Remote Sensing from Space: A Continuing Legal and Policy Issue, 8 Annals of Air & Space Law 409 (1983)

3. International and Foreign Policy Issues

The capability to make useful observations of all parts of the earth's land surface from orbit, using a U.S.-developed and operated satellite system, has provided a foreign policy opportunity for the United States. It has also created international demands that the United States, along with other potential operators of earth observation systems, be governed by a series of existing and emerging international obligations and principles related to remote sensing from space. These opportunities and obligations define an essential part of the context within which various scenarios related to a permanent U.S. remote sensing venture must be evaluated.

Current U.S. government policy with respect to the international aspects of remote sensing dates back to Richard Nixon's 1969 pledge before the U.N. General Assembly that "this program will be dedicated to producing information not only for the U.S. but also for the U.N. community." In the years following this statement, the United States has put forth, and strongly defended against criticism, a policy of open and nondiscriminatory access on the part of all countries and their citizens to the product of the LANDSAT system. The United States has taken positive steps to implement Nixon's 1969 statement and its open access policy, ranging from permitting other countries direct access to LANDSAT spacecraft through their own ground stations to providing technical assistance to countries wishing to use LANDSAT information. Any attempts to reverse the policy—to change the expectations or to modify the patterns of use that have evolved over the past decade—will be certain to create international tension.

The current state of international thinking on remote sensing at the governmental level is perhaps best reflected in the report of the 1982 United Nations Unispace Conference. This report noted that although remote sensing is still in a "preoperational" stage, "it is only a matter of time—and a short time—before this very important application attains a completely operational status." Given this reality, the report recommended that "agreement should be reached on principles governing satellite remote sensing. Work to this effect ... should be continued as a matter of priority, aimed at speedy agreement on such principles." In addition to a framework of general principles, concern was expressed that:

> Satellite operators should give assurance about continuity of data flows and provide indications about estimated lifetime [of] preoperational and operational systems in order to help all countries, in particular the developing countries. Compatibility of various systems and data formats is another important aspect. ...
>
> Since remote sensing can collect data from all countries, it is therefore possible to use shared or internationally owned remote sensing satellites. ...
>
> It is suggested that a study be undertaken to assess the need for and the viability of a worldwide remote sensing system. Such a study could consider various ways of providing remote sensing data—including regional, bilateral, multilateral, and international arrangements—with the users bearing therefore the development, production, launching and operation costs of the satellites. Assuming that any one of these systems could provide assurance of continuity of data formats, avoid forced obsolescence of equipment, and enable the development and use of standardized data analysis software, the study should in particular indicate the comparative cost of such systems to the users vis-à-vis systems currently in operation and/or under development.

A persistent issue in international discussions is "a possible situation in which data are not available to the sensed State but are available for commercial and other forms of exploitation by another country." At the conference

> Some delegations expressed serious concern regarding the dissemination of data collected by remote sensing satellites. While several developed and developing countries felt that such information should be freely available to an interested State, most delegations felt that the consent of the sensed State should be required before data could be released to a third State, organization, or third party. Some developing nations felt that the consent of the second State must be obtained before sensing, even if the information was not to be disseminated beyond the concerned States; some felt that in no case should the information be available to any State other than the sensor and sensed States. Most representatives expressing an opinion on the point agreed that priority in access to data must be accorded the sensed State.

The central points made by potential foreign users of land remote sensing products are:

The need for continuity in operation and overall system characteristics.

The need for guaranteed access at an acceptable price with provisions to avoid intrusions on national sovereignty.

The United States has attempted to deal with these pressures from the international community in ways that maximize the following U.S. policy objectives:

Maintaining U.S. leadership in space technology.

Assisting the economic and social developments of the developing countries.

Promoting international cooperation as a means of achieving common objectives as an example of the benefits of harmonious relationships among nations.

Ensuring U.S. ability to use space technology for its own national objectives, including operation of earth observation systems by both civil and national security agencies.

Enhancing the development of the U.S. economy by fostering new industries, new employment opportunities and new markets for U.S. firms.

In seeking to achieve these objectives the U.S. government has entered into a series of legal and political obligations. These include:

The provision of the Outer Space Treaty of 1967 that requires "States party to the Treaty" to "bear international responsibility for national activities in outer space, whether such activities are carried on by governmental agencies or by nongovernmental entities," such nongovernmental activities "require authorization and continuing supervision by the appropriate State party to the Treaty."

A series of agreements negotiated with other governments to permit their access, under mutually agreeable terms, to the output of U.S. remote sensing satellites using foreign-owned and operated ground stations.

Through U.S. advocacy of the policy of open nondiscriminatory access in U.N. forums and otherwise, a fairly explicit obligation not to create either formal or informal (such as unaffordable prices or continuing changes in technical format or the system output) barriers to any country, organization or individual who wants to use the system, with all users receiving nondiscriminatory treatment.

Through negotiations in the International Telecommunications Union, agreement not to use the frequencies allocated for communicating remote sensing data streams to ground stations for any other purposes.

Given this melange of concerns, objectives and obligations, international issues suggested included:

a. Future International Negotiations

Over coming years, as remote sensing capabilities evolve, there are sure to be continuing international negotiations. These will take place in the United Nations, other permanent multilateral organizations, ad hoc ... multilateral groups, or on a bilateral basis. Participation in these negotiations may vary, depending on the framework adopted for U.S. remote sensing activities. If a private sector option is selected, what international role, if any, will the private sector operator want the U.S. government to play? What role will U.S. government agencies believe is required to protect U.S. public interests?

b. Evolution of International Principles to Govern Remote Sensing

The interests of a commercial operator might sometimes conflict with the long standing U.S. policy in this area; one way of increasing the value of remote sensing products is to limit their dissemination. Another is by providing priority access to some users. The U.S. Department of Commerce Land Remote Sensing Advisory Committee recommended that there be a government requirement "that the operator, whether it be the government and/or the private sector, subscribe to the open sky policy—meaning that anyone, anywhere, in any country can purchase the data at equitable prices." The current government policy, as enunciated in President Reagan's space policy statement of July 4, 1982, is to "support the public, nondiscriminatory direct readout of data from federal civil systems to foreign ground stations and the provision of data to foreign users under specified conditions." The policy is silent on requirements for nongovernment systems.

One way to restrict access to remote sensing data is to adopt policies that are explicitly discriminatory. Another means is to price certain data (such as "quick looks") in ways that exclude some potentially interested users. This possibility has been noted by the international community; for example, a Romanian spokesman told COPUOS in the spring of 1983 of his concern about "the relatively new question of considering satellite remote sensing activities as operational, on a purely commercial basis, with the immediate consequence of augmenting by several times the costs of remote sensing products. Under these conditions, effective access to the data is practically possible only for developed countries."

How will considerations of cost recovery and commercial profit interact with an open access policy as an operational system evolves? Will system products be provided to poorer countries on a subsidized basis? What are the interactions among U.S. policy objectives vis-à-vis developing countries, the economic viability of an operational system and the general concern of avoiding tension? Although poorer countries may in the long-term have the prospect of receiving the most benefits from remote sensing, who will make the investments required for them to be effective users, and thus expand the market for the system? In the short run, would more expensive products from a private commercial system drive away non-U.S. users?

c. Meaning of U.S. Leadership in Space Technology

Current U.S. policy is to "maintain United States space leadership," particularly in "critical aspects of space, applications, and technology"; in these areas, the objective is "preeminence." The meaning of this policy with respect to remote sensing technology is unclear. Given the emerging foreign competition in the field, how will the U.S. government respond: by a continued program of R&D in the remote sensing area, keyed to staying ahead of competing systems; by reliance on the private sector to develop a superior system for the United States, without continuing government R&D subsidies; by providing subsidies or incentives beyond R&D to a commercial operator in order to help it best foreign competition and thus bring the benefits of a growing remote sensing industry (sales of equipment, training of non-U.S. personnel, consulting services, etc.) to the U.S. economy? Or is civil remote sensing not a "critical" area, and thus not one that requires U.S. leadership? What would be the costs in terms of more general foreign policy or economic objectives of a non-U.S. system dominating the world market for remote sensing? This could happen if no commercial system is established and the U.S. government withdraws from remote sensing activity after LANDSAT-5 reaches the end of its lifetime, or if the U.S. commercial venture is unsuccessful.

* * *

4. U.S. National Security Issues

It is a matter of public record that the United States uses earth observation satellites as one means of gathering intelligence information with respect to other areas of the world; these satellites are assets of extremely high value to U.S. national security interests. The capabilities of these satellites have also been extensively discussed, and in most parameters, they clearly exceed those available for civilian use. However, it is also reasonable to suggest that some information with intelligence significance can be extracted from existing civilian land observation satellites and that present national security systems may not duplicate all capabilities available in civilian satellites (for example, coverage in particular spectral bands). Thus, there are unavoidable national security aspects to the routine operation of a civilian land remote sensing system. In times of international tensions or crises, these aspects become more pronounced; the U.S. government will want to ensure that its national security agencies will be able to obtain immediate control over all earth observation systems.

Just as earth observation systems have both civilian and national security applications, the technologies on which they are based have "dual use" characteristics. Capabilities developed initially for national security purposes have potential relevance to civilian uses, and the technologies involved in sensors, data processing, image interpretation, etc., are sensitive in terms of export control regulations.

Given these realities, resulting national security issues include:

a. "Open Skies" Precedent and Ability to Carry Out National Security Observations

One not quite incidental fallout from the U.S. policy of open, non-discriminatory access to the products of civil earth observation systems is the creation of a climate in which all U.S. observation satellites can function without drawing protests from the countries of the world. Any modification of an open access policy, particularly by a private operator seeking competitive advantage or increased economic returns, could change this situation. For example, in the wake of the recent Administration announcement of its intent to transfer ownership and operation of civilian earth observation satellites to the private sector, one Canadian official indicated that his government was "very concerned," saying "we have a satellite looking down at our country and we don't call it a spy satellite because we have nondiscriminatory access to it. But if we were charged 100 times as much by some company, then we might have to begin to wonder about this."

b. Tradeoffs Between National Security Interests and Economic Competitiveness Concerns

Under continued government ownership and operation of the land remote sensing satellite system, past patterns of coordination between national security agencies and civilian agencies such as NASA and NOAA would likely persist. Some civilian sector objectives differ from those of the intelligence community, as illustrated by the conservative position adopted by national security agencies toward making advanced sensor capabilities available for civil sector use. On the whole, however, the relationship between the two sectors of the government has worked well. The potential for the transfer of the system out of government control does create serious questions regarding the extent of government supervision necessary and possible. National security-related areas for which a possible regulatory regime might engage itself include: spectral resolution, center frequency and tunable range; spatial resolution; geographic coverage; timeliness of data availability; tasking procedures and controls; and data dissemination policies.

The kind of quiet coordination that is possible within the government would be much more difficult to maintain in a relationship with a private sector entity. In the instance of private sector operation of the system, it becomes very important to recognize the need to temper national security considerations when designing an appropriate regulatory regime. Due regard must be given to the international market in which the private entity is operating, so that regulatory practices do not seriously erode the system's competitive position. A private operator may find, for example, that improved sensor characteristics may be required in order to keep itself economically solvent.

From the national security point of view, those sensor characteristics may present problems either in terms of revealing sensitive U.S. technological capabilities or in terms of providing images of the United States or other countries from which intelligence information could be extracted. If sensor capabilities were to be improved, then the intelligence community might want to involve itself in the process of determining appropriateness of data for dissemination. [NOTE: Precisely this issue has since arisen in the United States concerning civilian systems—*see* Chapter 8, *infra.*]

Reaching a balance between considerations of national security on one hand, and the need to develop a high performance, economically competitive system on the other, will continue to be a very difficult and complicated issue as land remote sensing satellite technology develops. Further aggravating this balance is the fact that U.S. national security interests and controls are in a large part derived from a different set of motivations and values than the potential security controls that might be applied to the French, European, or Japanese systems. Thus there is unlikely to be easy agreement among operators of remote sensing systems over what are acceptable limits on system performance from a national security perspective.

c. Export Control Regulations and Land Remote Sensing

There is heightened concern in recent years that U.S.-developed technology is being acquired by its adversaries and used as a major basis for their military capabilities. There is also recognition that the export of products and services based on advanced technology is a major source of positive U.S. balance-of-trade. Creating an operational U.S. land observation system aimed at dominating the international market brings with it an export control issue: will the United States aggressively seek to supply all elements required for other countries to participate in such a system, e.g., ground stations, computing capabilities and image interpretation capabilities, or will concern over the export of sensitive dual-use technologies limit the ability of the United States to capitalize fully on such a market opportunity?

National security concerns such as those embodied in the last two issues discussed above, in the context of a privately operated system, must be addressed within the framework of whatever regulatory regime is created to oversee such a system.

NOTES

1. Since Logsdon & Monk's article, the remote sensing industry has experienced considerable growth, with new entries from France (SPOT Image) and the

Soviet Union (Soyuz Karta). In addition, a number of American media interests, spurred by the use of SPOT and LANDSAT images of the Chernobyl accident and scenes from the Iran/Iraq war, have discussed the possibility of a "Media-Sat"—that is a civilian satellite with resolution approaching that of military reconnaissance satellites. This has created considerable debate within the United States already (*see* Chapter 8, *infra*); if such a satellite is actually launched (which is unlikely until the late 1990s), it is likely to promote protests from a number of countries, although it appears that such a system would be legal under the new principles on remote sensing. *See* George Paul Sloup, MediaSat, Gray Reconnaissance, and the New United Nations Principles on Remote Sensing, paper presented at the 38th Congress of the International Aeronautical Federation, Brighton, U.K., October 10, 1987. *See also* Merges & Reynolds, News Media Satellites and the First Amendment, 3 High Technology Law Journal 1 (1988); Reynolds, The First Amendment and Satellite Newsgathering, The Air & Space Lawyer, Fall, 1987, at 3 *et seq.*

2. The U.S. law governing the operation of civilian remote sensing systems is the Land Remote Sensing Commercialization Act of 1984, Pub. L. 98-365, 98 Stat. 451, codified at 15 U.S.C. §§ 4201 *et seq.* and scattered sections of 49 U.S.C., implemented by regulations at 15 CFR 960 *et seq.* The law was repealed in 1992 and replaced by the Land Remote Sensing Policy Act of 1992, Pub. L. 102-555, 106 Stat. 4171, codified at 15 U.S.C. 5601 *et seq.* (1993). In keeping with the U.S. policies described above, it requires the operator to make all data available to parties on equal terms. While this may be good from an international relations standpoint, it might (as Logsdon & Monk suggest) make it difficult for a commercial operator to succeed in the marketplace. For more on these topics, *see* Chapter 8, *infra*. *See also* Joanne Gabrynowicz, Bringing Space Policy into the Information Age, Space Policy, May, 1992, at 167.

3. In January of 1987 the United Nations Committee on the Peaceful Uses of Outer Space adopted new principles on remote sensing. The following excerpt from a paper by Professor DeSaussure explains why this latest round in the continuing debate over the legal status of remote sensing has not done much to settle matters.

Hamilton DeSaussure, Remote Sensing: The Interaction of Domestic and International Law. Paper presented at the 38th Congress of the International Astronautical Federation, Brighton, U.K., October 10–17, 1987

On January 22 of this year the General Assembly adopted principles relating to remote sensing of the Earth from space. The Principles had been drafted within and approved by the U.N. Committee on Peaceful Uses of Outer Space (COPUOS). The road to consensus within COPUOS had been a long and tortuous one.

The legal and political problems raised by remote sensing activity were first examined at the First U.N. Conference on the Peaceful Uses of Outer Space in Vienna in 1968. Argentina was the first nation, in June 1970, to submit a formal draft to govern remote sensing. A Working Group was then established with the Legal Subcommittee of COPUOS to work out rules which would be acceptable to the COPUOS members. From the outset there was disagreement on fundamental principles pertaining to international law and state sovereignty. One major dispute related to the question of prior consent. Argentina, Brazil, and other Latin American countries believed that the states whose resources were the subject of remote sensing had a proprietary right to the data about their wealth derived from this new technique. Their position was that certain U.N. resolutions providing that states have permanent sovereignty over their own natural wealth and resources were declaratory of international law, and that information about these physical assets was included in the concept of sovereignty. Therefore, the prior consent of the surveyed state was necessary so as not to intrude upon sovereign rights. ... From the outset, the United States has rejected any notion that international law requires the operator of a remote sensing system to secure approval of the sensed states. The United States opposed the Argentine/Brazil draft on the basis it was inconsistent with the provisions of the Outer Space Treaty which provide that outer space shall be free for exploration and use by all States without discrimination. A second major dispute revolved around the right to have access and to disseminate the data retrieved by remote sensing. The position of Latin American states, following their view on sovereign rights, would accord a priority of access to the retrieved data to the target state. In addition the target state would have the final decision as to distribution to third parties. Again the United States and other industrial nations were in opposition to any limitations on the open dissemination of the acquired data. In the view of the United States, this would conflict with the principle of free use. It would also be contrary to the Universal Declaration of Human Rights which provides for the freedom to receive and impart information regardless of frontiers. Certain compromises between the opposing views were attempted within the Working Group. One in particular was a joint proposal of the Soviet and French delegates to divide into two classes data retrieved through remote sensing. On the one hand, data acquired with a spatial resolution of more than fifty meters would be classified as global and subject to an open sensing and dissemination regime. Data retrieved through the use of finer sensors, resolving objects of less than fifty meters, would be classified as local. Local data would be subject to the control of the sensed state which would decide on any distribution. Consensus on this compromise could not be achieved in the face of the strong objections of the United States to any curtailment of the open dissemination of basic data. Other debated issues included the matter of defining the scope of remote sensing, whether human activity was to be covered, any limitations on the spectral resolution, and the role of the United Nations in supervising and regulating a remote sensing regime.

After debating these and other questions for seventeen years, consensus was reached within the Working Group in April 1986. The draft principles were approved by the full committee in June 1986 and were adopted by the General Assembly, as noted above, in January 1987. It is unfortunate the Resolution does not represent substantial progress in the development of a remote sensing legal order. This is not because of any lack of hard work by the COPUOS membership. The maximum level of agreement was achieved in a forum where consensus on all issues is required. Rather, failure to reach substantive agreement on crucial issues was the result of conflicting views on sovereignty, proprietary rights, freedom of information, and privacy. As the membership of COPUOS expanded and the increased value of the derived information became apparent, agreement on many of the ideological disputes became impossible. The result is a set of U.N. principles which are little more than a reaffirmation of those ideals incorporated into the major space treaties.

Perhaps the U.N. Principles have been left deliberately general and nonspecific in order that the states having control over remote sensing systems will have a large degree of flexibility in developing the rule of law. It is the proprietor states whose practices will largely shape the remote sensing regime of the future. The United States was the first nation to pronounce an open-skies policy for remote sensing activity. It is now taking the lead in setting forth a specific framework for the private enterprise operations. The United States launched the first remote sensing satellite in 1960. Since then the United States has launched five earth resource satellites, known as Landsats, with a sixth scheduled for delivery to a private company. ... The United States is not alone in commercializing remote sensing. Sales from the French SPOT system of remote sensing are expected to exceed ten million dollars. According to the New York Times, the Soviet Government is also "seeking big profits" from commercial remote sensing ventures.

The Act went into effect July 17, 1984. The Secretary of Commerce was delegated responsibility for the Landsat system, including the orbit, operation and disposition of Landsats 1, 2, 3, 4 and 5. The Secretary was also made responsible for providing data to foreign ground stations pursuant to agreements between the United States and nations operating those stations. The Act provided for the licensing of private remote-sensing space systems under regulations to be promulgated. The National Oceanic and Atmospheric Administration (NOAA) was delegated the responsibility for drafting procedures for licensing private operators. In March 1986, NOAA published proposed rules and invited public comment. On July 10, 1987 the rules were made final and published. Many of the legal issues which had been debated within COPUOS while drafting the U.N. Principles, are covered in the Act and implementing rules (hereinafter called the Regulations). [For more on U.S. laws and regulations governing remote sensing, *see* Chapter 8.]

Since none of the multilateral space treaties cover remote sensing as a distinct regime, it is left to the practice of states to define the law in this area. The U.N.

Resolution on Remote Sensing is simply too weak. Even if it were not, one state after another has declared that U.N. resolutions do not constitute binding obligations upon states.

* * *

Ever since the launch of Sputnik I in 1957, the development of customary rules has been fast moving. Technological advances, and the rapid expansion of state participation in space activity, demand certainty in the rules of space use. The centuries through which maritime law had time to develop is a luxury which cannot be afforded in outer space. It is left to states which pioneer the field of remote sensing to develop the law. By clearly placing civilian remote sensing in the private sector, the United States is the first state to establish a role for the private entrepreneur in this field. Commercial activity will expand into many areas of space exploration and use. The United States remote sensing legislation is a confirmation of that fact. In deciding the effect of domestic legislation on the development of maritime law, United States Supreme Court Justice Strong wrote more than a century ago that "many of the usages which prevail (in international law as to maritime navigation) ... and which have the force of law, doubtless originated in the positive prescriptions of some single state ... but which when generally accepted became of universal obligation." The birth of the United States Land Remote Sensing Act and its regulatory implementation, reflect the "positive prescriptions of a single state" which lay the cornerstone for a complete remote sensing regime enveloping both the public and the private operator.

[The principles themselves follow.]

Principles Relating to Remote Sensing of the Earth from Space

Principle I

For the purposes of these principles with respect to remote sensing activities:

(a) The term "remote sensing" means the sensing of the Earth's surface from space by making use of the properties of electromagnetic waves emitted, reflected or diffracted by the sensed objects, for the purpose of improving natural resources management, land use and the protection of the environment;

(b) The term "primary data" means the raw data that are acquired by remote sensors borne by the space object and that are transmitted or delivered to the ground from space by telemetry in the form of electromagnetic signals, by photographic film, magnetic tape or any other means;

(c) The term "processed data" means the products resulting from the processing of the primary data, needed to make such data usable;

(d) The term "analysed information" means the information resulting from the interpretation of processed data, inputs of data and knowledge from other sources;

(e) The term "remote sensing activities" means the operation of remote sensing space systems, primary data collection and storage stations, and activities in processing, interpreting and disseminating the processed data.

Principle II

Remote sensing activities shall be carried out for the benefit and in the interests of all countries, irrespective of their degree of economic, social or scientific and technological development, and taking into particular consideration the needs of the developing countries.

Principle III

Remote sensing activities shall be conducted in accordance with international law, including the Charter of the United Nations, the [1967] Treaty on Principles Governing the Activities of States in the Exploration and Use of Outer Space, including the Moon and other Celestial Bodies, and the relevant instruments of the International Telecommunications Union.

Principle IV

Remote sensing activities shall be conducted in accordance with the principles contained in article I of the Treaty on Principles Governing the Activities of States in the Exploration and Use of Outer Space, including the Moon and other Celestial Bodies, which, in particular provides that the exploration and use of outer space shall be carried out for the benefit and in the interests of all countries, irrespective of their degree of economic or scientific development, and stipulates the principle of freedom of exploration and use of outer space on the basis of equality. These activities shall be conducted on the basis of respect for the principle of full and permanent sovereignty of all States and peoples over their own wealth and natural resources, with due regard to the rights and interests, in accordance with international law, of other States and entities under their jurisdiction. Such activities shall not be conducted in a manner detrimental to the legitimate rights and interests of the sensed State.

Principle V

States carrying out remote sensing activities shall promote international cooperation in these activities. To this end, they shall make available to other States opportunities for participation therein. Such participation shall be based in each case on equitable and mutually acceptable terms.

Principle VI

In order to maximize the availability of benefits from remote sensing activities, States are encouraged, through agreements or other arrangements, to provide for the establishment and operation of data collecting and storage stations and processing and interpretation facilities, in particular within the framework of regional agreements or arrangements wherever feasible.

Principle VII

States participating in remote sensing activities shall make available technical assistance to other interested States on mutually agreed terms.

Principle VIII

The United Nations and the relevant agencies within the United Nations system shall promote international co-operation, including technical assistance and co-ordination in the area of remote sensing.

Principle IX

In accordance with article IV of the Convention on Registration of Objects Launched into Outer Space and article XI of the Treaty on Principles Governing the Activities of States in the Exploration and Use of Outer Space, including the Moon and Other Celestial Bodies, a State carrying out a programme of remote sensing shall inform the Secretary-General of the United Nations. It shall, moreover, make available any other relevant information to the greatest extent feasible and practicable to any other State, particularly any developing country that is affected by the programme, at its request.

Principle X

Remote sensing shall promote the protection of the Earth's natural environment. To this end, States participating in remote sensing activities that have identified information in their possession that is capable of averting any phenomenon harmful to the Earth's natural environment shall disclose such information to States concerned.

Principle XI

Remote sensing shall promote the protection of mankind from natural disasters. To this end, States participating in remote sensing activities that have identified processed data and analysed information in their possession that may be useful to States affected by natural disasters, or likely to be affected by impending natural disasters, shall transmit such data and information to States concerned as promptly as possible.

Principle XII

As soon as the primary data and the processed data concerning the territory under its jurisdiction are produced, the sensed State shall have access to them on a non-discriminatory basis and on reasonable cost terms. The sensed State shall also have access to the available analysed information concerning the territory under its jurisdiction in the possession of any State participating in remote sensing activities on the same basis and terms, taking particularly into account the needs and interests of the developing countries.

Principle XIII

To promote and intensify international co-operation, especially with regard to the needs of developing countries, a State carrying out remote sensing of the Earth from space shall, upon request, enter into consultations with a State whose territory is sensed in order to make available opportunities for participation and enhance the mutual benefits to be derived therefrom.

Principle XIV

In compliance with article VI of the Treaty on Principles Governing the Activities of States in the Exploration and Use of Outer Space, including the Moon and Other Celestial Bodies, States operating remote sensing satellites shall bear international responsibility for their activities and assure that such activities are conducted in accordance with these principles and the norms of international law, irrespective of whether such activities are carried out by governmental or non-governmental entities or through international organizations to which such States are parties. This principle is without prejudice to the applicability of the norms of international law on State responsibility for remote sensing activities.

Principle XV

Any dispute resulting from the application of these principles shall be resolved through the established procedures for the peaceful settlement of disputes.

RESCUE AND RETURN OF ASTRONAUTS

The Agreement on the Rescue of Astronauts, the Return of Astronauts, and Objects Launched into Outer Space of 1968, 19 U.S.T. 7570, T.I.A.S. 6599, expands upon the language in Article V of the Outer Space Treaty, which declares that astronauts are to be regarded as "Envoys of Mankind" and to be rendered "all possible assistance." (*See* Chapter 3.) The Agreement calls for a state in which a spacecraft crashes or a state operating in space that is in a position to assist astronauts in distress to conduct rescue operations (if it is a manned craft) and to speedily return both astronauts and hardware to the launching state.

The Agreement focuses (largely because of technological constraints at the time of its drafting) on earth-based events, though its language applies to space rescues as well. It leaves many questions unanswered, however: What if a rescued astronaut wishes to defect to the rescuing country? The Agreement's language is mandatory and does not admit of any exceptions based on the wishes of the astronauts involved, although other international law (such as the United Nations Charter and the Universal Declaration of Human Rights) at least seems to suggest otherwise. Some states signing the agreement reserved the right to grant political asylum to an astronaut. *See* U.N. Doc. A/AC.105/C.2/SR.87, 2 February 1968 pp. 10 *et seq.* (this position taken by Australia and France). The United States rejects this position, as do most nations, on the ground that requests for asylum may be coerced—particularly when the requestor is the victim of a recent space accident and may not be in full possession of his or her faculties. *See* U.N. Doc. A/AC.105/C.2/SR.86, 9 February 1968, at 8; U.S. Congress, Committee on Foreign Relations, Hearings on the Treaty on Outer Space, 90th Cong., 1st Sess. 1967 at 27. Other questions: How should rescue expenses be treated? Is the launching state obligated to reimburse the rescuing state? What if a rescue attempt is bungled—will the rescuing state be liable, or does some sort of Good Samaritan principle apply? Should there be such a principle, since rescue is mandatory? In light of these questions, it may be time for an update of the Agreement in order to avoid confusion or ill will. This has been suggested by Nathan Goldman. Goldman, Transition or Confusion in the Law of Outer Space, in International Space Policy: Legal, Economic and Strategic Options for the Twentieth Century and Beyond 157, 162 (D. Papp & J. McIntyre eds. 1987).

REGISTRATION OF SPACECRAFT

The Convention on the Registration of Objects Launched into Outer Space of 1976, 28 U.S.T. 695, T.I.A.S. 7762, provides that each signatory shall maintain a registry of all objects that it launches into earth orbit or beyond. The launching state shall also provide to the Secretary-General of the United Nations information concerning each object on its registry, including: the name of the launching state or states, a designation or number, the location of the launch, the object's basic orbital parameters (including nodal period, inclination, apogee, and perigee), and the general function of the object. Nations are also to provide the Secretary-General with information regarding objects on their registry that have ceased to be in orbit.

Where an object is launched by more than one nation, the nations involved are to determine which of them shall register the object. This is not simply an administrative matter, since the state on whose registry the object is carried retains full jurisdiction and control over the object under Article 8 of the Outer Space Treaty of 1967—although Article 7 of the Space Treaty and Article I of the Liability Convention of 1972 do not assign responsibility on the basis of registry but on the basis of who is responsible for the launching of the spacecraft, and Article IV of the Liability Convention allows for joint and several liability in the case of multiple launching states. This leaves open the possibility of one nation having jurisdiction over an object (a matter of considerable significance with regard to manned craft, *see* U.S. Congress Office of Technology Assessment, Space Stations and the Law: Selected Legal Issues—Background Paper (1986); Reynolds, Book Review, 27 Jurimetrics: Journal of Law, Science & Technology 431, 434–35 (1987)) while another bears international responsibility therefor. Although such matters are easily resolvable through negotiation, lawyers involved in such matters (for example drafting memoranda of understanding regarding joint missions or space stations) should bear such matters in mind. Typically, launch services contracts specify that the space object launched will be placed on the registry of a particular nation and provide that the launching entity will ensure that that is done. For more on this topic, *see* Chapter 8.

SPACE ENVIRONMENTAL MATTERS

Because the space environment is infinite in size, the very concept of worrying about maintaining the space environment seems absurd to many, particularly as (at the time of this writing) no life is known to exist beyond the Earth's biosphere. Yet in fact the outer space environment has already been the subject of considerable pollution, and some space environmental problems demand immediate attention if they are not to create serious problems here on earth.

Space pollution dates back to the dawn of the space age. In 1962 a series of very high altitude nuclear tests, code named Fishbowl, led to the creation of an artificial radiation belt around the earth that damaged a number of satellites and interfered with scientific experiments. At around the same time, Project West Ford, a misguided communications experiment, established a ring of copper dipole antennas around the earth; these were supposed to serve a primitive relay function by reflecting radio signals back to the surface. Radio astronomers raised a furor regarding these antennas, which threatened their observations. Because of negative public reaction, neither experiment has been repeated. For more on these and other issues *see* Gorove, Pollution and Outer Space: A Legal Analysis and Appraisal, 5 New York University Journal of International Law & Politics 53 (1972).

Another space environmental issue is the question of contamination, both "forward" and "back." "Forward contamination" occurs when, for example, microorganisms from earth are carried to other planets or celestial bodies. Such contamination could conceivably have disastrous effects: for example, if earth-based organisms were able to survive on the surface of Mars they could institute drastic and unplanned changes in its climate, as well as greatly complicating efforts by scientists to determine whether Mars supports life of its own. In order to prevent this from happening, space probes are sterilized prior to launch, a practice originated very early in the space age. *See* Horowitz, Sharp & Davies, Planetary Contamination I: The Problem and the Agreements, 155 Science 1501 (1967); Murray, Davies & Eckman, Planetary Contamination II: Soviet and U.S. Practices and Policies, 155 Science 1505 (1967); Sagan, Leventhal & Lederberg, Contamination of Mars, 159 Science 1191 (1968).

"Back contamination" involves the contamination of earth by foreign microorganisms (or conceivably other substances not necessarily "alive" by terrestrial standards but still capable of causing problems). Such contamination is unlikely for two reasons: first, there is (as of this writing) no evidence that life exists outside earth's biosphere, and second, any life that could live, say, on Mars or the Jovian moons would probably be poorly adapted to earth and hence not much of a threat. Still, earth history is full of cases in which whole peoples were decimated by the introduction of diseases to which they had no previous exposure, and science fiction is full of accounts of such horrors being brought to earth from space. In response to such fears, astronauts returning from the Moon were quarantined (along with their samples) in the Lunar Receiving Laboratory until scientists and physicians were certain that no contamination had occurred. *See* McClane, *et al.*, Lunar Receiving Laboratory, 155 Science 525 (1967). Such precautions, in the case of future manned or unmanned missions, are required by the Outer Space Treaty, as discussed in Chapter 3, *supra. See also* Darlene Cupser, International Law and Policy of Extraterrestrial Planetary Protection, 33 Jurimetrics: Journal of Law, Science and Technology 315 (1993). Existing U.S. regulations designed to protect against extraterrestrial contamination are discussed in Chapter 8, *infra.* They do not, however, address other more immediately pressing space environmental problems.

The most pressing such problem is the matter of earth orbital pollution, or space debris. As was mentioned earlier in this chapter in the context of liability issues, space near the earth is becoming filled with an increasing quantity of debris from spent boosters, defunct satellites, and the aftermath of space weapons tests. Since such debris travels at enormous speed (approximately 18,000 miles per hour in most cases), even small fragments can do enormous damage. Worse yet, collisions between space debris and other space objects create still more fragments, which themselves threaten to do damage.

At some point this process can become self-sustaining, a chain reaction known as the "Kessler effect" because the pioneering analysis was done by Donald Kessler. *See* Kessler & Cour-Palais, Collision Frequency of Artificial Satellites: The Creation of a Debris Belt, 83 Journal of Geophysical Research 2637

(1978). At present, it is impossible to tell how close we are to the creation of a self-sustaining debris belt, but it does appear that the artificial debris flux in near earth orbits exceeds the natural meteorite flux—meaning that already a spacecraft in those orbits is more likely to collide with a piece of space junk than with a natural meteorite. *See* Kessler, Earth Orbital Pollution, in Beyond Spaceship Earth: Environmental Ethics and the Solar System, 47, 48–49 (E. Hargrove ed. 1986); David Enrico Reibel, Prevention of Orbital Debris (paper presented at 38th annual congress of the International Astronautics Federation, Brighton, U.K., October 10, 1987). As of this writing, there is evidence that orbital debris is not merely a menace to navigation in space, but may in fact be working substantial changes in the near-earth space environment. *See, e.g.*, Konradi, Effect of the Orbital Debris Environment on the High-Energy Van Allen Proton Belt, 242 Science 1283 (1988). On space pollution issues generally, *see* Restatement (Third) of Foreign Relations Law § 601 (1987), esp. at note 6. The following excerpt describes the problems created by orbital debris and some accompanying legal issues.

U.S. Congress, Office of Technology Assessment, Orbiting Debris: A Space Environmental Problem (1990)

Introduction

Debris, left in a multitude of orbits about Earth as the result of the exploration and use of the space environment, poses a growing hazard to future space operations. Unless nations reduce the amount of orbital debris they produce each year, future space activities could suffer loss of capability, loss of income, and even loss of life as a result of collisions between spacecraft and debris.

Because of their concerns about the safety of spaceflight, the Senate Committee on Commerce, Science, and Transportation, and the House Committee on Science, Space, and Technology requested an assessment of the future hazard from orbital debris, and an examination of strategies for reducing that threat. This background paper derives primarily from a workshop on orbital debris held at OTA on September 25, 1989. In preparing this paper, OTA also received assistance from other contributors. OTA gathered information from many other sources, including the 1989 U.S. Report on Orbital Debris prepared by the Interagency Group (Space), the 1988 European Space Agency (ESA) Report Space Debris, and a workshop convened jointly by OTA and the U.S. Space Foundation in April 1989.

Since the launch of Sputnik 1 by the Soviet Union in 1957, nations and organizations involved in the exploration and exploitation of space have completed over 3200 launches, which have placed more than 3800 payloads into orbit around the Earth. About 6500 artificial objects orbiting Earth, weighing about 2 million kilograms in sum, are now cataloged by the Space Surveillance Network

(SSN), operated by the U.S. Space Command (USSPACECOM). However, only 6 percent of the cataloged objects in Earth orbit are functional satellites, the rest fall into the category of "orbital" or "space" debris. Moreover, analysts believe that the total orbital debris population is much greater, because orbital debris includes a wide variety of artificial objects, which range in size from a millimeter or smaller to the full bulk of a deactivated satellite or spent rocket stage.

Orbital debris travels in the full range of orbits used by Earth-orbiting satellites. Unlike natural meteoroids, which pass through near-Earth space in a matter of a few minutes as the Earth sweeps through space, orbital debris, depending on its altitude, may continue to orbit Earth for periods as long as centuries. It moves in many different orbits and directions, at velocities ranging from 4 kilometers per second to over 7 kilometers per second, and constitutes a potential hazard to working spacecraft. In the near-vacuum of outer space, no forces act to slow debris down. Even very small objects, if they have high velocities relative to the objects they hit, may do considerable damage. For example, in 1983, a tiny titanium oxide paint chip, estimated to have been about 0.2 millimeter in diameter, collided with the Shuttle orbiter *Challenger* at very high velocity and damaged a window. Although the damage posed no immediate danger, the window was weakened beyond the allowable safety limits for reflight and was replaced before the orbiter's next launch.

Cataloged objects, some weighing up to several tons, reenter the atmosphere at a rate of two to three per day. Over the past 30 years, some 14,000 trackable objects have fallen to Earth. The largest have attracted worldwide attention. Although the risk to individuals is extremely small, the probability of striking populated areas [is] still finite. For example: 1) the U.S.S.R. Kosmos 954, which contained a nuclear power source, reentered the atmosphere over northwest Canada in 1978, scattering debris over an area the size of Austria; 2) a Japanese ship was hit in 1969 by pieces of space debris that were assumed to be of Soviet origin, injuring five sailors; 3) in October of 1987, a 7-foot strip of metal from a Soviet rocket landed in Lakeport, California, causing no damage; 4) portions of Skylab came down over Australia in 1979. The biggest piece of Skylab that reached the ground weighed over 1000 pounds.

This background paper treats the issue of artificial debris in space, its causes, and the potential for reducing the hazards that it poses to space activities and the outer space environment. Yet orbital debris is part of a larger problem of pollution in space that includes radio-frequency interference and interference to scientific observations in all parts of the spectrum. For example, emissions at radio frequencies often interfere with radio astronomy observations. For several years, gamma-ray astronomy data have been corrupted by Soviet intelligence satellites that are powered by unshielded nuclear reactors. The indirect emissions from these satellites spread along the Earth's magnetic field and are virtually impossible for other satellites to escape. The Japanese Ginga satellite, launched in 1987 to study gamma-ray bursters, has been triggered so often by the Soviet reactors that over 40 percent of its available observing time has been spent transmitting unintelligible "data." All of these problem areas will require attention and positive steps to guarantee access to space by all countries in the future.

* * *

Legal Implications

Domestic and international law regulating space activities began to develop in the late 1950s and early 1960s. Yet only recently have managers of space systems recognized that the hazards of space debris might require some sort of regulatory regime. Earlier law, including the international treaties and agreements on space, failed to address orbital debris explicitly. Any domestic and international legal regimes for debris should address the generation of debris, its removal from orbit, the question of jurisdiction and control over space debris, detection and identification of space debris, international responsibility for space debris, and possible remedies for damage caused by debris. This section explores the legal implications of orbital debris and suggests areas where new international agreements may eventually be needed.

The Definition of Orbital Debris

One of the impediments to developing new laws to address the problems posed by space debris is the lack of an adequate definition of space debris. Existing national laws and international space treaties and agreements contain neither a definition nor a description of orbital debris. While orbital debris may be divided into four classes for descriptive purposes, legal experts disagree whether the legal scope of orbital debris includes all technical classes.

The seriousness of the debris problem for space operations, the possible confusion over the literal meaning of "debris," and the need to define the scope of debris all suggest the need for a legal term of art. Such a term would provide a starting point for discussing the legal issues arising from the orbital debris problem.

An explicit definition of orbital debris might not be necessary, however, if that term were subsumed under an existing space law treaty definition. Although the term "contamination," found in Article IX of the Outer Space Treaty, might be thought to serve this purpose, it refers only to harmful microbiological organisms of terrestrial origin, which might be accidentally released in the aftermath of a collision or explosion in outer space. The term "space object" is more promising. The Liability Convention provides that "space object" includes a spacecraft, the launch vehicle, and the component parts of both. The Registration Convention also contains this description. However, existing international law does not define space object.

During the debates over the terms of the Liability Convention, negotiators could not agree on a description for "space object," nor was the question of whether orbital debris is included in "space object" specifically addressed. Negotiators were primarily concerned with which artificial objects should be considered "space objects," not with the effects of those objects following their active lives. During these debates, legal experts put forward two definitions of "space object." The narrow definition included the object itself and its component parts, as well as the means of delivery and its component parts. Although some delegates offered a much broader definition, which would have included articles on board the space object and articles detached, thrown or launched from the space object, the narrower interpretation was adopted. Consequently, it is unclear which classes of space debris, if any, are included implicitly in "space object." Consider, for example, inactive payloads. The Liability Convention is silent on whether a payload must be active to qualify as a "space object" capable of causing damage. If inactive payloads are included, then they are space debris, with liability for compensation attaching to the launching state.

Orbital debris may also be considered a "space object" if it falls under the term "component parts." Yet what exactly constitutes "component parts" is not settled. According to the description of space object in the Liability Convention, all operational debris except litter appears to be "component parts," although jurists do not agree on this point. Whether all fragmentation debris and microparticulate matter are included is even more problematic, even if the broader interpretation of "space object" is invoked. This fuzziness is unfortunate because fragmentation debris represents about half of the orbital debris population.

Summarizing, the only classes of orbital debris included in current treaty law, with any degree of certainty, are operational debris, to the exclusion of inactive payloads, fragmentation debris, microparticulate matter, and litter. The degree of difficulty already manifest in attempting to obtain international agreement on the definition of debris clearly suggests that early voluntary national action to limit and reduce debris may be far more effective than attempting to obtain any international agreement on debris reduction procedures in the near term.

Jurisdiction and Control

Who has jurisdiction and control over space debris? If remedial action is to be included in any regulatory scheme for orbital debris, consideration should be given to the issue of who is authorized to remove orbital debris. Article VIII of the Outer Space Treaty provides that the State of registry of "an object launched into outer space" has the right to make and enforce domestic law in relation to that object and "any personnel thereof," and that ownership of a space object is not affected by its presence in outer space. Two legal issues raised by this provision are whether orbital debris falls within the scope of Article VIII and the extent to which jurisdiction and control over space objects is permanent.

Legal analysts agree that both active and inactive payloads fall under Article VIII. They do not agree, however, on an appropriate method for distinguishing active payloads from inactive ones. Although a test of "effective physical control" has been proposed, successfully applying this test is hampered by several obstacles. First, legal opinion favors the view that jurisdiction and control of a State over its space objects is permanent. Moreover, because ownership of a space object also is permanent, regardless of its use and condition, and because the owner retains the rights of possession, use, and disposal, states or other legal entities would require the consent of the State of registration in order to interfere in any way with that space object.

Applying a doctrine of permanency to debris objects appears to impede attempts to minimize the quantity of orbital debris as it only accounts for inactive payloads, and it applies only to identifiable space objects. There may be two possible exceptions to this doctrine, however: the analogy to abandonment, and sentence 1 of Article IX of the Outer Space Treaty.

In maritime law, abandonment arises where no personnel remain on board a vessel and there is no intent to return and reactivate it. Then the vessel becomes a derelict subject to salvage. It is not yet clear, however, whether the hazard posed by orbital debris is sufficient justification for its removal without the consent of the State of registration. Sentence 1 of Article IX of the Outer Space Treaty provides in part that State parties to the Treaty have obligations to cooperate, to provide mutual assistance, and to have due regard for the corresponding interests of other State parties. Although some have suggested that these legal obligations fetter the absolute nature of jurisdiction and control and ownership, application of sentence 1 may be limited. First, some have argued that corresponding interests exclude threats posed by orbital debris. Second, the Outer Space Treaty provides for competing interests among states, but does not lay down any rules for designating priority among these interests, which include a right to hazard-free space navigation as well as a right to leave an inactive payload in orbit.

Suggestions providing for timely removal of hazardous space objects, without consent of the State of registration, are limited in their effectiveness. They refer at best to inactive payloads and other identifiable space objects, and offer no preventive measures, but only compensation after the fact. Given the inchoate nature of the law regarding orbital debris, a rigorous analysis of analogous provisions in other legal regimes would probably be quite useful.

Detection and Identification

To remove orbital debris from outer space and to hold States accountable for damage caused by their orbital debris entails a method of identifying the State responsible for the debris. Identification of space objects is addressed in the Registration Convention.

Identification of space objects involves two phases: detection of the object and identification of its State of registry. The Registration Convention contains no provisions for detection and does little to establish a system that would identify the States of registry of space objects that do not appear in the registration lists. Consequently, this treaty is of little use in identifying orbital debris, especially in its untrackable manifestations. Without proper identification, the Liability Convention cannot be invoked because the State of registry cannot be ascertained. Another possible weakness of this treaty is the absence of a provision for compulsory markings, although markings must be registered if they are used. Therefore, what would be the most obvious and convenient method for identifying space objects is voluntary. Large components could be identified relatively easily. Very small components and microparticulate debris cannot readily be marked.

Liability for Damage Caused in Outer Space

The Liability Convention sets out a legal regime to provide compensation for damage caused in outer space by space objects. In outer space, liability is based on fault. It is significant to note that negotiations for the Liability Convention did not consider the question of the risks posed by orbital debris. As a result, the negotiators did not address several liability issues of extreme importance related to damages caused by orbital debris. These issues include the meaning of "damage" and the reasonableness of a fault-based liability regime for damage caused in outer space by orbital debris.

Experts generally agree that damage to the outer space environment per se is not within the scope of the Liability Convention. Consequently, launching States cannot be held liable for the mere presence of orbital debris in outer space. In this regard, microparticulate matter and very small pieces of fragmentation debris are of particular concern because launching States have no legal incentive to avoid generating these types of orbital debris, although they have enormous operational incentives to do so. It would be possible to amend the Liability Convention so as to include damage to the outer space environment per se, based on the fact that outer space is a global commons. Yet, even if accepted, resolution of three significant legal issues beyond the scope of space law would still remain: legal standing for claimant States (who is going to speak for mankind?), assessment of damages, and the nature of the liability.

The principle of fault-based liability is a further impediment to compensation for damage caused in outer space by orbital debris. Application of the fault-based outer space liability regime of the Liability Convention to orbital debris is doubtful because the Convention "appears to be primarily concerned with a possible collision between [active] space objects." Even if damage caused by orbital debris were within the scope of this regime, several other important legal issues, such as proof of negligence, and contributory negligence, among others, would remain unresolved.

Article III of the Liability Convention does not specify whether the damage caused must be reasonably foreseeable, that is, whether the damage caused by orbital debris is of a kind that specialists in the field would expect to occur. It has been argued that, as a result of the impossibility of foreseeing all the different situations that could lead to damage in outer space, only two factors need to be established—the damage, and a cause-and-effect relationship between the damage and the incident giving rise to the damage.

The terms of the Liability Convention place restrictions on who may seek compensation for damage caused in outer space by orbital debris. For example, compensation is unavailable for any damage resulting from a collision between two space objects, each owned by a different private entity, if both entities are under the jurisdiction of the same launching State. The same result would follow if one of the space objects were a piece of identifiable orbital debris. Nor is compensation available under the convention to injured parties who are either nationals of a launching State or foreign nationals participating in any phase of a space activity. This restriction extends to nationals of all States participating in any one launch activity, and to nationals of all States entering into joint ventures with any State participating in any launch activity. Additionally, certain provisions of NASA launch agreements that allocate risk among the participating parties further limit eligible claimants by arranging reciprocal cross-waivers of claims among participants.

One serious shortcoming of the decision to base damage in outer space on fault has been that the rationale for fault-based liability must be applied to damage caused in outer space by orbital debris. This rationale, ostensibly based on the equality of States in undertaking space activities, makes three fundamental assumptions: States participating in space activities accept the risks involved; States are free to conduct any space activity as long as fault-based damage does not result; and absolute liability for damage to space objects in outer space would lead to absurdities and inequities.

Although the fault rationale may well be justified in the event of collisions between two active, and therefore controlled, satellites, its application seems unreasonable where damage in outer space is caused by orbital debris. In this situation, application of the rationale for absolute liability may be more appropriate. First, space flight and space activities may be considered ultrahazardous or abnormally dangerous activities for which "responsibility [should be] imputed to the person or entity making the initial decision to engage in the activity which exposes others to risks where possibly no amount of foresight or feasible protective measures may avert injuries." Therefore, in cases where orbital debris causes damage, those who create the risk should bear the cost of not only compensating for damage done to persons and property in outer space, but also protecting the space environment itself. Second, absolute liability is considered necessary when it is unlikely that fault can be established. In the outer space context, and particularly when orbital debris is being considered, problems of establishing the proof of fault necessary for satisfying the courts are magnified. The problems encountered with making the case under existing or even strengthened liability provisions make it essential to concentrate on establishing a preventive set of measures and enforcement mechanisms.

6

Space Communications

The importance of outer space to communications law stems from the use of satellites (almost exclusively in geosynchronous orbit) as relays for communications from one point on the earth to another, a use first proposed by Arthur C. Clarke in his famous *Wireless World* article of October 1945. By the late 1950s communications satellite experiments were underway, although many believed that such satellites were unlikely to enter commercial use for decades at the very least. (For an interesting view of critics' fears that did not come true *see* A. Haley, Space Law and Government 190–212 (1963).) Those critics were proven spectacularly wrong: the first successful geosynchronous communications satellite was the NASA Syncom satellite of 1963, and the first commercial communications satellite in geosynchronous orbit was the Early Bird, launched in 1965. Within a very short time, the satellite communications industry became a global reality. For a time it appeared that that industry would be a near monopoly of the international communications satellite consortium, INTELSAT, but the forces of competition have caused satellite communications, at both the domestic and international levels, to become a business with many participants.

Like all other businesses, satellite communications is subject to regulation. The communications satellite industry is regulated at both the domestic and international level: at the international level there are two types of governance, the frequency and orbital slot assignments undertaken by the International Telecommunications Union (ITU) and its International Frequency Registration Board (IFRB), and the global requirements imposed by the INTELSAT agreement. At the domestic American level, regulation is by the Federal Communications Commission, which enforces its own rules and which has a number of responsibilities relating to the ITU and INTELSAT.

Although the distinction between international and domestic affairs is blurring in many areas, it is vanishing fastest in the area of communications regulation. For that reason, this chapter addresses both international and domestic regulation of international space communications. Following is a short description of the international regulatory mechanisms governing space communications (drawn in large part from R. White & H. White, The Law and Regulation of International

Space Communication (1988)), after which is a short discussion of domestic regulation. Then are excerpts from some government documents that provide considerable perspective on the nature of the regulatory process and the kinds of problems that come up.

SPACE AND INTERNATIONAL TELECOMMUNICATIONS

The principal body governing international communications in general is the International Telecommunication Union, a specialized agency of the United Nations which was originally formed as the International Telegraph Union in 1865 to coordinate the developing world telegraph network. The ITU has expanded its responsibilities over time to take account of the rapidly changing technologies of communications, and now governs communications via radio and cable, whether for broadcast or message service. Satellite communications, of course, are entirely by radio at present (though laser communications are a distinct possibility in the future) and hence are regulated as radio services.

The ITU's concern with regulation of radio service goes back many years. In the early days of radio communications, the lack of any frequency assignment mechanism led to substantial problems with interference, especially at sea and among the many and crowded nations of Europe. After some decades of wrangling over the problem, regulation of frequency use to avoid harmful interference was taken over by the ITU, with many technical aspects administered by its International Frequency Registration Board (which coordinates frequency use) and the International Consultative Committee on Radio (in French, the master language of the ITU, the *Comite Consultatif International des Radiocommunications* and hence abbreviated as CCIR). Following is a short description of the ITU's current composition.

Structure of the ITU

The constitutive document of the International Telecommunication Union is the International Telecommunication Convention. That document, as amended from time to time, sets out the purposes and structure of the Union. The ITU's goals include:

> to maintain and extend international cooperation between all Members of the Union for the improvement and rational use of telecommunications of all kinds, as well as to promote and to offer technical assistance to developing countries in the field of telecommunications;
>
> to promote the development of technical facilities and their most efficient operation; [and]
>
> to harmonize the actions of nations in the attainment of those ends.

In serving those ends, the Union's primary function is to regulate the world's international telecommunications so as to ensure an efficient and far-reaching global telecommunications system. In so doing, the Union is to:

> effect allocation of the radio frequency spectrum and registration of radio frequency assignments in order to avoid harmful interference between radio stations of different countries [and]
>
> coordinate efforts to eliminate harmful interference between radio stations of different countries and to improve the use made of the radio frequency spectrum.

International Telecommunication Convention, Nairobi, 1982, Article 4. In addition, the ITU is charged with the responsibility to foster international cooperation in assisting the developing countries with the development of their networks, with harmonizing the development of telecommunications facilities, with helping its members to organize international services so as to maintain rates at levels as low as possible consistent with an efficient international service, to promote efficient emergency communications services, and to undertake studies, adopt resolutions, formulate recommendations and opinions and collect and publish information concerning telecommunications matters. *Id.* These provisions, like others contained in the Convention, are binding on the Union and its members, although individual countries may note reservations to any particular part of the Convention with which they disagree, at the price of being unable to enforce that part of the Convention against other nations.

The Convention may be (and is) updated and amended by the Plenipotentiary Conference of the Union. The Plenipotentiary Conference meets regularly (normally, every five years) and is the primary law-making body of the Union. Aside from the Convention itself, Plenipotentiary Conferences promulgate Resolutions (usually directing other bodies of the ITU to take particular actions), Recommendations (regarding actions that should be taken by member countries or the United Nations), and Opinions (which preserve the views and legal interpretations of the delegates to the Conference at which they are adopted, thus providing a sort of "legislative history").

In between Plenipotentiary Conferences, the Administrative Council of the Union meets once a year to address matters that cannot wait for attention from the full membership of the Union or that are too routine for such attention. The ITU also possesses a General Secretariat responsible for its day-to-day operations and for preparing for Plenipotentiary and Administrative meetings.

Also, from time to time, Administrative Conferences may be called to deal with special topics. These Administrative Conferences may be regional or they may be global. Space matters are addressed in Space World Administrative Radio Conferences (or Space WARCs) or, occasionally, in Space Regional Conferences, or Space RARCs. Three geographic regions are able to call regional conferences: Region 1, which consists of Europe, Africa, the Middle East, the states of the former Soviet Union, and Mongolia; Region 2, consisting of the Americas, the Caribbean, and Greenland; and Region 3, consisting of Asia and the Pacific exclusive of Hawaii. World Administrative Conferences can make partial or complete revisions of the ITU Radio Regulations, while regional conferences may deal only with regional matters.

The ITU promulgates Radio Regulations which are binding on all members of the Union, although states can make reservations to particular parts of the Regulation subject to the principle that their domestic uses of frequencies may not cause harmful interference outside their borders. The Radio Regulations set out frequency allocations for different nations and for different services (*e.g.*, satellite direct broadcasting, satellite mobile communications, fixed satellite service, etc.). Interpretation of the Radio Regulations in case of dispute is entrusted to the International Frequency Registration Board (IFRB), which also maintains the Master International Frequency Register into which information concerning national assignments of frequencies is entered, and which provides technical assistance and promulgates technical standards and procedures. The IFRB is also responsible for recording the positions assigned by countries to geostationary satellites and for providing assistance in selecting those positions.

The International Radio Consultative Committee (CCIR) exists to provide technical advice on the setting of international standards. Although the CCIR standards are not binding on members, they are generally accepted in practice and incorporated into the Radio Regulations. For an up-to-date account of the ITU structure and prospects *see* Audrey Allison, Meeting the Challenges of Change: The Reform of the International Telecommunication Union, 45 Federal Communications Law Journal 491 (1993).

INTELSAT

Shortly after it became apparent that satellite communications were to have real utility, negotiations began to create an international agency that would provide international satellite communications services. The result was INTELSAT, an international consortium providing satellite communications among nations.

INTELSAT's structure and operation are governed by the Multilateral International Telecommunications Satellite Agreement of 1973, 23 U.S.T. 3813, TIAS 7532. At the time that that agreement was arrived at, INTELSAT had been operating for several years already, under an interim arrangement in which the U.S. participant in INTELSAT, the Communications Satellite Corporation (COMSAT), provided management and technical services. After the agreement, these services were gradually taken over by INTELSAT. INTELSAT had 112 member countries by the end of 1987, with membership continuing to grow slowly. Those countries are all part owners of INTELSAT, with their ownership share varying according to their use of INTELSAT facilities. INTELSAT's structure reflects its overall philosophy in favor of participation. It is governed by a Board of Governors, an Assembly of Parties, a Meeting of Signatories, and an Executive Organ. The Assembly of Parties consists of all member countries and meets biannually to decide issues of long-term importance. The Meeting of Signatories is made up of designated representatives of member countries; those representatives are telecommunications providers such as COMSAT from the United States. The Board of Governors meets four times a year to make executive decisions, while the Executive Organ, headed by a Director General, oversees the day-to-day operations of INTELSAT. INTELSAT is headquartered in the United States, in Washington, D.C. For more on the organization and operation of INTELSAT, *see* R. White & H. White, The Law and Regulation of International Space Communication 216–221; M. Kinsley, Outer Space and Inner Sanctums (1976). *See* Chapter 4 for economic analysis applicable to the establishment of INTELSAT as an efficient way to make use of shared orbit and spectrum resources.

The interesting legal and policy questions relating to INTELSAT grow out of two issues: its pricing structure and the requirement in Article XIV(d) of the Agreement requiring that parties establishing separate systems consult with INTELSAT to ensure technical compatibility and to avoid significant economic harm. Both issues have become items of considerable controversy over recent years.

The pricing policy is one of global averaging. Members of INTELSAT share revenues and adjust their investment amounts in proportion to their use of the system, as mentioned above. Under this system, therefore, the price that members pay for an INTELSAT circuit is approximately equal to the globally averaged cost of circuits throughout the INTELSAT system. Because the fixed costs of providing service are high and the marginal costs low, economies of scale are very significant. This results in a subsidy for thinly used routes (such as the Pacific and the Indian Ocean) and a "tax" on service over the heavily used routes such as those between the United States and northern Europe.

Although this subsidy was deliberate, in order to help move less-developed countries into the global village, it leads to considerable inefficiencies. On thin routes, the subsidy means that the network will be used more often than it would if prices were equal to costs, while on heavily used routes the tax means that there will be less traffic than if prices were equal to costs. Of course, such an outcome was precisely the goal of the subsidy scheme when INTELSAT was organized, but as the more advanced nations find themselves increasingly struggling for economic competitiveness with the LDCs (and particularly those in the Pacific and Indian Ocean regions), whose costs in many areas are already lower, they increasingly seem to resent that subsidy, particularly given the increasing importance of telecommunications services in the growing information economy. For an excellent analysis of this topic *see* Kwerel & Pitsch, FCC Regulation of International Telecommunications Satellites and Cables, in 2 American Enterprise, the Law, and the Commercial Use of Space 119 (P. Mink ed. 1986);

Federal Communications Commission, Office of Plans & Policy, Promoting Competition Between International Telecommunication Cables and Satellites (OPP Working Paper No. 19, January, 1986); U.S. Congress Office of Technology Assessment, International Cooperation and Competition in Civilian Space Activities at Ch. 6 (1985). Similar issues have arisen in the U.S. domestic arena as a result of the breakup of AT&T. *See generally* Kahn, The Road to More Intelligent Telephone Pricing, 1 Yale Journal on Regulation 339 (1984).

Of course, as the LDC economies grow (something that, at this writing, appears likely to continue), so too will use of the parts of the INTELSAT network serving them, meaning that the problem may well solve itself within a decade or two. The question is whether the more advanced countries will be willing to continue the subsidy until things even out, given the level of economic competition that appears to be growing. The United States, at least, appears somewhat hostile to the subsidy, as the discussion of U.S. satellite policies later in this chapter shows. In addition, as Kwerel & Pitsch point out, maintaining the subsidy will be difficult for other reasons. The growth of fiber optic cable systems—which are not subject to restriction under the INTELSAT Agreement—will provide considerable competition for satellite services and will as a result force prices toward costs.

For the time being, however, the subsidy remains, and the Agreement requires that member nations take steps in the satellite field to avoid "significant economic harm" to INTELSAT. The following discussion outlines the way in which the United States has attempted to balance its general position in favor of free markets and against subsidies with the responsibilities growing out of its role in INTELSAT.

U.S. REGULATION OF SPACE COMMUNICATIONS

The United States regulates space communications involving its territory and nationals under a framework of both domestic and international law. The following excerpt provides an overview of that system.

Office of Commercial Space Policy, U.S. Department of Commerce, Space Commerce: An Industry Assessment 38–40 (1988)

The cornerstone of U.S. telecommunications law is the Communications Act of 1934 as amended [47 U.S.C. 151 (1982)]. It establishes the Federal Communications Commission (FCC) as the regulatory and licensing authority for non-Federal Government uses of the radio-frequency spectrum. Against this backdrop, the 1962 Communications Satellite Act (Satellite Act) [47 U.S.C. 701 (1982)] provides for the establishment of a global, commercial communications satellite system (now known as INTELSAT) and provides for the establishment of a private corporation, Comsat, as the sole U.S. participant and investor in the system. The Satellite Act requires Comsat to provide non-discriminatory access to the system for all authorized users [47 U.S.C. 731 (1982)]. Importantly, the Satellite Act states that it is not intended to preclude the establishment of communications satellites separate from INTELSAT that are determined to be in the national interest or required to meet unique governmental needs.

Three separate policies have been established to ensure that U.S. domestic and international satellite telecommunications activities are consistent with U.S. law and international agreements: (1) the U.S. Domestic Satellite Policy, which is intended to ensure a robust domestic satellite marketplace, (2) the Transborder Policy that applies to domestic systems used to provide incidental international services to neighboring countries, and (3) the U.S. Separate Systems Policy for satellite systems intended specifically to provide international public telecommunications services separate from INTELSAT. U.S. obligations under the INTELSAT Agreement were a major consideration in the creation of each of these policies.

In the early 1970s, the FCC adopted a policy of "open entry" for qualified domestic communications satellite systems (domsats) [35 FCC2d 86 (1970), *recon. granted in part,* 38 FCC2d 844 (1972)]. This policy, which is still in effect, is based on the concept that licensing all applicants meeting the FCC's established technical, legal and financial fitness requirements for obtaining a license will encourage the development of new technologies and services at lower costs to the public. These requirements have been tightened over the years as the number of domsats has increased and the orbit/spectrum resource has become more congested. The FCC has stated that if the number of domsat applications ever exceeds the orbital positions and spectrum available, it might have to resort to administrative selection procedures, such as comparative hearings, auctions or lotteries [48 Fed. Reg. 40,233 (Sept. 6, 1983)].

Use of U.S. domestic satellites for transborder services is governed by the U.S. Transborder Policy. The Transborder Policy was established by the Executive branch and the FCC to balance the efficiencies of using U.S. domestic satellites to provide service to neighboring countries within the footprint of the satellite, with the U.S. desire to avoid causing significant economic harm to INTELSAT. The Transborder Policy, established in 1981, requires: (1) a showing by the applicant that INTELSAT could not practically or economically provide the same services as the requested domestic satellite, and (2) consultation with INTELSAT pursuant to Article XIV(d) of the INTELSAT Agreement, prior to initiation of service [88 FCC2d 258 (1981)]. The FCC's transborder decisions to date have been limited almost exclusively to the authorization of video and private line voice and data services.

In 1984, the President determined that U.S. international satellite systems separate from INTELSAT (separate systems) are in the national interest. This determination was made in accordance with the 1962 Satellite Act and was accompanied by the conditions that (1) such systems may provide services only through the sale or long-term lease of space segment capacity for communications not interconnected with the public-switched network, and (2) at least one foreign authority must authorize use of each separate system and participate in consultations with the United States under the INTELSAT Agreement, to ensure technical compatibility with the INTELSAT system and avoid causing it significant economic harm. In 1985, the FCC used this determination and the conditions as the basis for its decision to license qualified applicants [101 FCC2d 290 (1985), *recon. granted in part,* FCC 86–144 (April 17, 1986), *further recon. denied,* 1 FCC Rcd. 439 (1986)].

The Transborder Policy has always been distinguished from the U.S. policy on separate international systems, because it only concerns U.S. domsats used to provide incidental services to nearby countries. The Separate Systems Policy, on the other hand, concerns satellites that are specifically intended to provide international services, and are considered a greater threat to INTELSAT's economic well-being. Unlike the separate systems policy, the Transborder Policy does not expressly prohibit interconnection with the public switched network, nor does it require the sale or long term lease of transponder capacity as a precondition to use. These differences, coupled with the recognition that INTELSAT has developed into a robust and highly profitable global communications satellite system, has prompted the Administration to initiate a comprehensive review of U.S. international satellite policy. This process is underway.

NOTE

For a thorough survey of U.S. regulatory affairs, *see* Pamela Meredith & Franceska Schroeder, Privately Owned Commercial Telecommunication Satellites: Licensing and Regulation by the Federal Communications Commission, 27 California Western Law Review 107 (1991). *See also* Michael Straubel, Telecommunication Satellites and Market Forces: How Should the Geostationary Orbit be Regulated by the FCC? 17 North Carolina Journal of International Law and Commercial Regulation 205 (1992). The United States' decision regarding separate satellite systems was arrived at only after extensive study and considerable dissension. The following excerpt from an internal paper prepared by the Senior Interagency Group on International Communication and Information Policy explains the rationale behind the decision in considerable detail. A number of experts—not to mention those at COMSAT and INTELSAT—dispute its conclusions. For a good summary of their views *see* Sarreals, International Telecommunications Satellite Services: The Spirit of Cooperation versus the Battle for Competition, 26 Jurimetrics: Journal of Law, Science & Technology 267 (1986).

Senior Interagency Group on International Communication and Information Policy, A White Paper on New International Satellite Systems, February, 1985

Since 1983, several U.S. firms have filed applications with the Federal Communications Commission (FCC) to establish international communications satellite systems in addition to the global system owned by the International Telecommunications Satellite Organization (INTELSAT). Orion Satellite Corporation, International Satellite, Inc. (ISI), and Cygnus Corporation propose new transatlantic communications systems, and RCA American Communications, Inc. (RCA) has applied to use capacity on a U.S. domestic satellite to provide international service. Pan American Satellite Corporation (PanAmSat) proposes to establish a system which would serve Latin America. In addition to existing and planned regional satellite systems independent of INTELSAT, other transoceanic satellite systems are under consideration abroad. Approved and proposed transatlantic submarine cable communications facilities, many of which are actually or potentially competitive with INTELSAT, are pending as well.

Focus of Report

The filing of U.S.-based satellite system applications with the FCC prompted action by the Executive branch, which has special responsibilities in this field under the Communications Satellite Act of 1962, as amended (47 U.S.C. 701 et seq.), including the responsibility to determine whether additional U.S. international satellite systems are "required in the national interest." The Senior Interagency Group on International Communication and Information Policy (SIG) reviewed U.S. international satellite policy to determine whether, and under what conditions, authorizing satellite systems and services in addition to INTELSAT would be: (a) consistent with prevailing U.S. law, practice, and international treaty obligations; (b) compatible with sound foreign policy and telecommunications policy goals; and, (c) in the U.S. national interest.

The Executive agencies represented on the SIG undertook a study and reached a unanimous position in favor of new entry, subject to certain limitations. A recommendation subsequently was made to the President by the Secretaries of State and Commerce. The President determined on November 28, 1984, that international satellite systems separate from INTELSAT were required in the U.S. national interest, subject to certain conditions. Specific criteria relating to the President's determination were then forwarded to the FCC by the Secretaries of Commerce and State jointly. *See* Appendixes A and B.

This report provides background information regarding the President's determination, and it also provides information on important regulatory and other parallel measures which are desirable to ensure that the Executive branch's fundamental policy goal—an efficient and responsive international communications environment—is achieved. The discussion here focuses on the major communications and information policy issues raised by the applications before the FCC. It addresses commercial, trade, and legal matters, and also examines major U.S. foreign policy interests and concerns.

* * *

I. The International Communications Marketplace Today

* * *

There are two principal international transmission modes: submarine cables and communications satellite facilities. The submarine cables which provide U.S. international service are owned collectively by AT&T, the IRCs [International Record Carriers], and their foreign correspondents. Seven transatlantic cables now terminate in the United States and an eighth, 38,000-circuit, fiber optic cable has been approved by the FCC. U.S. international satellite circuits are provided by Comsat, which has functioned as a "carrier's carrier" and holds a 23 percent interest in INTELSAT, the 109-nation organization that owns and manages the global satellite system. Comsat's investment share is adjusted annually to reflect U.S. use of the INTELSAT system.

* * *

U.S. Policy Goals

The international communications and information policy goals of the United States are the following:

- To enhance the free flow of information and ideas among nations;
- To promote harmonious international relations and contribute to world peace and understanding through communications;
- To promote, in cooperation with other nations, the development of efficient, innovative, and cost-effective international communications services responsive to the needs of users and supportive of the expanding requirements of commerce and trade;
- To ensure the continued technological and economic strength and leadership of the United States in the communications, information, and aerospace fields;
- To expand U.S. private sector investment and involvement in civil space and related activities;
- To promote expanded international trade and to ensure opportunities to U.S. firms to participate in such trade;

- To promote the continuing evolution of an international configuration of communications services that can meet the needs of all nations of the world, with attention toward providing such services to developing nations;
- To ensure efficient utilization of the geostationary orbit and the electromagnetic radio frequency spectrum;
- To promote competition and reliance on market mechanisms, as feasible, and to foster cost-based pricing, quality service, and more efficient use of resources; and,
- To ensure the needs of national defense, security, and emergency preparedness are satisfactorily met.

* * *

The INTELSAT system and the number of facilities which access INTELSAT's satellites have expanded rapidly. INTELSAT's 15 satellites today serve 173 countries, territories, and possessions directly or indirectly, and the organization leases satellite capacity to 26 nations for domestic services. Nineteen new earth stations and 39 new international communications antennas were added in 1982 alone. As of November 1984, there were 198 INTELSAT earth station sites and 293 international antennas in 157 countries, dependencies, and areas of other special sovereignty.

INTELSAT now handles about two-thirds of the world's transoceanic telecommunications traffic and most international television transmissions. Demand for full-time voice, record, and data services for INTELSAT grew by 18 percent in 1982; these services accounted for about 86 percent of the total satellite utilization revenue received by INTELSAT that year. The most recently published INTELSAT annual report states that INTELSAT expects continued strong growth of 15 percent annually on an expanded base of conventional international traffic over the 1988–2000 time period.

* * *

With the growth of the INTELSAT system, circuit charges have steadily declined. The annual charge for a 1965 INTELSAT I "Early Bird" half-circuit, for example, was $32,000, while the 1982–83 charge for an equivalent, though technically superior, half-circuit was $4,680. There is disagreement, however, over whether the substantial INTELSAT charge reductions over the past decades have been fully reflected in the prices which Comsat has charged U.S. international carriers or the prices which those carriers have charged their customers. At present, end-user prices for many international satellite services both here and abroad typically are between two to ten times INTELSAT's charges. U.S. international communications costs, moreover, often are very substantially above those for comparable domestic service.

INTELSAT has continued to grow and to prosper in an increasingly competitive international communications environment. Since 1981, the FCC has sanctioned certain international communications services using U.S. domestic satellite systems. At present, U.S. and Canadian satellites are used to provide certain services throughout North America and the Caribbean. Additional proposals for such transborder satellite service will be the object of consultations with INTELSAT. INTELSAT recently accelerated its plans and now offers a number of international communications services aimed particularly at meeting specialized and sophisticated business community needs.

Significance to Industry and Government

International communications services constitute an essential component of international trade today. Efficient and effective international communications are necessary to international finance, to facilitate the production and shipment of goods, and to manage U.S. off-shore operations, assets, and investments. International communications are also critical to the continued development of U.S. trade in services, which exceeded $40 billion in 1982. International communications, moreover, play a central role in facilitating the further economic development of less developed nations, thus permitting these countries to participate more fully in the world economy and contributing to peace, stability, and greater understanding.

Space communications is a major part of the aerospace industry, one of the world economy's most important "high-tech" or "sunrise" sectors, and an area where the excellence of U.S. manufacturing techniques and high technologies is reflected in the preeminence of the U.S. aerospace industry. U.S. aerospace trade is forecast to accelerate in 1985 as both exports and imports reach record highs. Aerospace exports should climb to a projected $18.9 billion, while imports will rise to $5.0 billion. The resultant trade surplus of $13.9 billion will be more than 30 percent above the level recorded in 1984. Total U.S. aerospace employment will rise an estimated 4 percent in 1985 to 739,000, with an estimated gain of 7 percent in the number of production workers.

Existing Policies and Objectives

* * *

The established foreign and domestic policies of the U.S. Government in this area seek to further the basic goals which are outlined above. These policies include:

- Adhering to the requirements and provisions of the Communications Act of 1934, as amended (47 U.S.C. 151 et seq.) and the 1962 Satellite Act, as amended (47 U.S.C. 701 et seq.);

- Complying with the terms of the INTELSAT Agreement (TIAS 7532) and all the privileges and obligations the Agreement provides its Parties and Signatories;
- Supporting INTELSAT as "a single global commercial telecommunications satellite system as part of an improved global telecommunications network" (Preamble, INTELSAT Agreement), and as a key element providing all countries of the world access to global communications services;
- Concurring in the development, separate from INTELSAT, of customized, regional, and transborder satellite services where technical or economic consultation, or both, is accomplished as required under the terms of the INTELSAT Agreement and such systems are consistent with the Agreement;
- Pursuing a nondiscriminatory satellite launch policy;
- Adopting domestic communications policies which emphasize reduced Government regulation, wherever feasible, and increased reliance on market forces in the provision of communications and information services;
- Advocating and adopting international communications policies which stress reliance on free enterprise, competition, and free trade, wherever feasible, with full recognition that provision of international communications and information services involves joint undertakings among sovereign nations requiring mutually acceptable agreements to accommodate differing national policies;
- Supporting and fostering the development of a diversity of international communications technologies and modes, including fixed, mobile, and broadcast satellite, microwave, terrestrial and undersea cable, and optical fiber;
- Supporting and undertaking bilateral consultations and agreements, as well as multilateral deliberations in appropriate international forums, to ensure order and cooperation in the evolution of international communications and information services.

*   *   *

II. Institutional Limits on Competition

The United States since the early 1970s consistently has sought to reduce outmoded communications regulation and to eliminate unnecessary barriers to competition chiefly domestically, but internationally as well. Important changes and regulatory reforms have been accomplished. All recognize, however, that achieving a regulation-free international communications environment is not foreseeable at this time. There will remain significant U.S. limitations on competition in international communications as well as limits imposed by communications administrations abroad. Understanding some of these limits on potential competition is important to addressing the issues presented by the satellite applications pending before the FCC and reinforces our assessment that these applications imply continued evolutionary development, not radical or disruptive change.

Regulatory Constraints

There are, to begin with, a number of statutory requirements and limitations which bear on the level and intensity of potential competition in the international communications field. To enter the international communications satellite business, U.S. firms require FCC permission under title III of the 1934 Communications Act, provisions of title II of that Act (for would-be common carrier entrants), as well as provisions of the 1962 Satellite Act. The FCC is required by law to make an affirmative "public interest" finding prior to issuing construction permits and licenses to use the radio frequency spectrum. Considerable regulatory review of proposed systems typically is entailed. It is also relevant in this regard to note that given spectrum use limitations and international procedures governing the use of the geostationary orbital resource, there are significant technical constraints on possible entry into international satellite communications. [*See generally* Orbital Locations, 54 P. & F. Radio Reg. 2d 550 (1983); Orbital Spacing, 54 P. & F. Radio Reg. 2d 577 (1983); Robinson, Regulating International Airwaves: the 1979 WARC, 21 Virginia Journal of International Law 1, 44 (1980).]

Entrants proposing to operate on a common carrier basis are subject to many provisions of title II of the 1934 Communications Act (e.g., 47 U.S.C. 214). Under title II, the FCC must generally find that the public interest, convenience, and necessity will be furthered by approving an additional international common carrier facility. Existing common carriers, moreover, must generally receive permission to make use of new facilities. As with other regulatory agencies, the FCC is required to weigh competitive factors when it functions as a "gatekeeper" with respect to common carrier communications. Under present law, however, the FCC may not legally authorize new common carrier systems simply to foster competition. It must instead make affirmative public interest findings that competition, for example, will spur technological progress, increase efficiency, and more rapidly expand customer choice.

Executive Responsibilities

In addition to the limitations on entry and competition contained in titles II and III of the Communications Act, section 102(d) of the Satellite Act recognizes the foreign policy, trade, and national security aspects of international satellite communications and provides that the President is responsible to determine whether additional international satellite systems are required to meet unique governmental needs or are otherwise required in the national interest.

The term "national interest" is not defined in the Satellite Act, but it encompasses considerations broader than those implicit in the FCC's regulatory "public interest" standard, a standard which the courts have ruled is not limitless. [*See* NAACP v. Federal Power Commission, 425 U.S. 662, 669 (1976); National Organization for Women v. FCC, 555 F.2d 1002, 1017 (D.C. Cir. 1977).] "National interest" is within the mandate of the Executive branch and includes such factors as general competition policy, whether entry will advance technological progress and innovation, promote U.S. international trade in goods and services, expand the international communications options available to the U.S. business community, and further overall U.S. spectrum management goals. Foreign policy and national security considerations are also important aspects of the national interest, and matters which are the Constitutional responsibilities of the Executive branch. The FCC in the past has generally deferred to Executive branch views on policies which are not directly within its regulatory purview. In sum, the "national interest" standard in the 1962 Satellite Act should be read as according the Executive branch responsibility to determine the compatibility of proposed international satellite systems with the broad range of U.S. programs and policies affected by such enterprises.

International Obligations

In addition to the limitations on competition implicit in the 1934 Communications Act and the special "national interest" criterion in the 1962 Satellite Act, U.S. international obligations are relevant. Certain responsibilities under Article XIV of the INTELSAT Agreement are also discussed in the Memorandum of the Legal Adviser of the Department of State which was transmitted to the FCC in 1984 and which is set forth as Appendix B to this report.

The INTELSAT Agreement entered into force for the United States on February 12, 1973. While the INTELSAT Agreement implicitly acknowledges that nations party to the Agreement retain the sovereign right to establish satellite telecommunications facilities separate from the INTELSAT system, the Agreement establishes: (1) a generalized obligation of the parties to act in a manner consistent with and in furtherance of the principles stated in the Preamble and other provisions of the Agreement (Article XIV(a)); and (2) a consultation process to be undertaken before a nation or its designated operating entity (a "Signatory") establishes, acquires, or utilizes separate, non-INTELSAT space segment facilities to meet its telecommunications requirements (Article XIV).

Article XIV(d) of the INTELSAT Agreement addresses the consultation obligation with regard to international public telecommunications services. In substance, it provides that a nation member or its Signatory shall furnish all relevant information to INTELSAT and shall consult with INTELSAT: (1) to ensure technical compatibility of the contemplated satellite facilities with the use of the radio frequency spectrum and the geostationary orbital space by the existing or planned INTELSAT satellites; and (2) to avoid significant economic harm to the global system of INTELSAT. At the conclusion of the consultation process, the INTELSAT Assembly of Parties (the principal organ of INTELSAT, composed of the representatives of all member nations) makes findings in the form of recommendations on the subjects of the consultation and further regarding the assurance that the proposed satellite facility will not prejudice the establishment of direct telecommunications links through the INTELSAT space segment among all the participants in the proposed system.

* * *

III. Foreign Policy Considerations Regarding International Satellites

Addressing the issues raised by the proposed establishment of U.S. international satellite systems separate from INTELSAT requires consideration of U.S. foreign policy objectives. These objectives have been considered within the Executive branch and do not constitute an appropriate matter for independent determination by a regulatory agency. Here, however, the major foreign policy matters that were weighed are generally discussed to further understanding of the President's determination.

In his September 1983 letter to Chairman Charles H. Percy of the Senate Committee on Foreign Relations, Secretary of State George P. Shultz reiterated the basic foreign policy objectives of the United States in international communications, and they are similar to those enumerated in detail above: "To promote an environment in which ideas and information can flow freely among nations, to support the advancement of international commerce through the efficient and innovative use of communications resources, and to expand information access and communications capabilities of developing countries."

The 1962 Satellite Act reflects these objectives and others which have been furthered through our participation in developing and supporting the INTELSAT system. INTELSAT's manifest success has:

- Provided a dramatic example of U.S. leadership in the peaceful use of space in the interest of all countries;
- Contributed to meeting evolving U.S. commercial needs for efficient international communications services;
- Provided developing countries with improved communications at reasonable and affordable rates;
- Confined the Soviet INTERSPUTNIK system to a relatively small portion of the world;

- Supplied developing countries with access to the geostationary orbit and satellite radio frequencies; and,
- Provided benefits to U.S. companies through open international procurement for the international system's space communications equipment and services.

Permitting U.S. international satellite systems separate from INTELSAT, however, could:

- Bring new diversity and flexibility to international communications;
- Create or expand markets in new areas, such as customized, data, and video services;
- Provide incentives for INTELSAT and its Signatories to be more efficient and innovative; and,
- Permit outside financial sources to undertake high-risk, speculative ventures, thereby enabling INTELSAT to concentrate its resources on further extending basic services through prudent financial management.

* * *

Access to the Geostationary Orbit

How all nations can enjoy "equitable access" to the geostationary satellite orbit and to the associated radio spectrum is a major concern within the International Telecommunication Union (ITU). The results of the ITU's consideration of this issue at the upcoming World Administrative Radio Conference on the Use of the Geostationary Satellite Orbit and the Planning of the Space Services Utilizing It (Space WARC) in August 1985 and June 1988 [are] important to the United States and many other countries. INTELSAT's role in meeting developing countries' communications needs could make it a critical, if indirect, participant in the resolution of this issue on terms acceptable to ITU member nations. [*See* Chapter 4, *supra*, for a discussion of economic rationales for INTELSAT's role. The outcome of the 1988 Space WARC is discussed in this chapter, *infra*.]

For more than a decade, some developing countries have sought a guaranteed share of the geostationary orbit and the radio spectrum allocated to space services. They maintain that unconstrained growth of commercial satellite communications systems could exhaust the geostationary orbit and the frequencies currently available. Fearful of losing their share of what they understand to be limited global resources, developing countries in 1983 inscribed "equitable access" provisions into the ITU Convention. By the 1979 WARC, they were determined to write new rules for the use of the geostationary orbit and associated radio spectrum and obtained a commitment for the two-part Space WARC in the 1980s.

The availability of INTELSAT has not eliminated developing country demands for equitable access to the geostationary orbit and related spectrum. Nevertheless, its existence offers an alternative to the implementation of costly national satellite systems. So long as low-cost and technically attractive service is available through an international organization which accommodates the sovereignty interests of each country, there is added hope that developing countries may meet some of their needs through INTELSAT.

The proliferation of communications satellite systems already in progress, moreover, will heighten the importance of INTELSAT's role in frequency conservation. Increasing demand for the radio spectrum is hastening the development and implementation of innovative technologies which expand the capacity of the geostationary orbit resource and permit greater efficiency through multiple uses of the same frequency. Large-scale space platforms and other techniques have the potential to increase frequency usage efficiency by perhaps 50- to 100-fold; INTELSAT's multinational consolidation of demand—domestic, regional, and transoceanic—will thus have particular attraction. With these considerations in mind, the United States lent strong support at the October 1982 INTELSAT Assembly of Parties to the principle of domestic service using INTELSAT facilities, despite European opposition.

An indication of the developing countries' growing stake in INTELSAT can be found in INTELSAT's evolution toward playing a larger role in the provision of domestic satellite service. In 1974, Algeria proposed to lease INTELSAT capacity for enhancement of its domestic telecommunications network. Today, some 26 countries use INTELSAT to provide domestic service. INTELSAT has responded to this demand by committing itself to include planned domestic capacity, as opposed to relying solely on preemptible, spare capacity, in future generations of satellites. It has also developed higher power satellites that are compatible with the small earth stations that have proved most economical for domestic service.

* * *

U.S. Role in INTELSAT

The U.S. role in INTELSAT continues to be strong, although it has changed over the past 20 years. The U.S. investment share has decreased from 61 to 23 percent; hence the U.S. weighted vote in the Board of Governors has decreased to the current 23 percent. An international secretariat of some 600 INTELSAT staff now manages the system rather than Comsat. A U.S. citizen was recently elected Director General of INTELSAT. INTELSAT no longer purchases almost all of its equipment from U.S. manufacturers, although the United States still supplies about 70 percent of INTELSAT's purchases. The United States is the host country for the INTELSAT headquarters.

The United States has been and should continue to be a strong leader and contributor to the INTELSAT system. Changing technology, competitive economics, and diversifying user needs, however, have created a new international telecommunications environment. There is a manifest trend toward coexistent, separate national and regional satellite systems. This does not obviate the continued need for a global system providing an essential core for public-switched international communications. The 1962 Satellite Act and the INTELSAT Agreement both specifically anticipated communications satellite systems outside INTELSAT, and provided the flexibility to allow for and to respond to such systems.

* * *

INTELSAT faces growing competition from new fiber optic cables, which may constitute a more significant challenge to it than separate satellite systems. The transatlantic cable (TAT-8) planned for 1988 by AT&T and the IRCs, Teleglobe Canada, and European telecommunications administrations will have a capacity equivalent to about 38,000 telephone circuits, as previously noted, and nearly quadruple the current submarine cable capacity across the North Atlantic. This fiber optic cable, moreover, will have technical capabilities, including the ability to transmit high-quality video signals, which existing submarine cables lack.

A "status quo approach" often has short-term appeal and merit from a foreign policy standpoint. Change inherently creates pockets of concern in the complex environment of international relations. By its very nature, however, telecommunications is uniquely amenable to change. The issues associated with international telecommunications cannot and will not stand still. They are driven by technology—and technology, in turn, is driven by continuing innovation and evolution.

U.S. policy leaders 20 years ago could not easily have envisioned the exponential expansion of communications horizons through new technology which has subsequently occurred. They did, however, anticipate the need for flexibility to develop the then-uncharted telecommunications frontier.

NOTES

1. The U.S. policy on separate systems is dependent on a number of use restrictions in order to be effective, primarily the requirement that separate satellite circuits not be connected to the public switched network. This presents two problems, one potential, the other unavoidable. The potential problem lies in the FCC's legal authority to enforce such restrictions. The history of telecommunications regulation over recent years has been made up primarily of the demise of such restrictions. *See* Hush-A-Phone Corp. v. United States, 238 F.2d 266 (D.C. Cir. 1956); Use of the Carterfone Device, 13 FCC2d 420 (1968); MCI Telecommunications Corp. v. FCC, 561 F.2d 365 (D.C. Cir. 1977), *cert. denied,* 434 U.S. 1040 (1978)

(usually known as *Execunet I*); MCI Telecommunications Corp. v. FCC, 580 F.2d 590 (D.C. Cir.), *cert. denied*, 439 U.S. 980 (1978) (*Execunet II*). *See generally* Comment, Competition in the Telephone Equipment Industry, 86 Yale Law Journal 538 (1977). On the other hand, these restrictions are likely to be on firmer ground than those based simply on a desire to shape domestic markets. That is because the Communications Act, in Section 301, prohibits any radio transmission except in accordance with the Communications Act and applicable regulations, while Section 303(r) of the Act authorizes the FCC to prescribe such restrictions and conditions as may be necessary to carry out the Act or to effectuate U.S. obligations under treaties or conventions relating to radio or wire communications. Since the INTELSAT Agreement clearly qualifies as a "treaty or convention" it may be possible to sustain the use restrictions imposed on separate systems.

The unavoidable problem is technology. Given the complex structure of modern networks, both public and private, virtually any system above the tin-can-and-string level is likely to connect with the public network at some point and policing such interconnections has proven virtually impossible. *See* P. Huber, The Geodesic Network: 1987 Report on Competition in the Telephone Industry (1987) at Chs. 2, 16. The FCC has had little luck in dealing with the problem of "leaky PBXs," in which private networks allow callers to place "local" calls in distant cities without paying long distance access charges, *see* MTS and WATS Market Structure, Second Supplemental Notice of Inquiry and Proposed Rulemaking, 77 FCC2d 224, 241 (1980); In the Matter of Amendment of Part 69, 2 FCC Rcd. 7441 (1987). Separate satellite operations are likely to pose similar problems. Whether the leakage that exists will be sufficient to pose a significant risk of economic harm to INTELSAT is unclear—certainly such risk will not materialize until separate satellite systems have been around for many years.

2. The White Paper mentions the problem of geosynchronous orbital slot allocation. The problem is that satellites may not be placed too close together without harmful interference. The appropriate spacing interval has dropped over the years as technology has improved, from five degrees to only two at the time of this writing. Further reductions are likely over time, increasing the number of satellites that can be accommodated. Nonetheless, many less developed countries fear that they may be left behind and that by the time they are ready to launch their own satellites there will be no room for them. A variety of measures have been suggested to deal with this; the economic theory involved is discussed in Chapter 4 in the more general context of common resource allocation.

The 1985 Space WARC proposed principles to deal with this problem, including a guarantee of access and a guarantee that resources would be allocated on an equitable basis. The details of administration were left to be worked out in the 1988 Space WARC.

After this book first went to press, the 1988 Space WARC reached a conclusion that, though less elegant than many academic proposals, achieved the sort of pragmatic solution for which the ITU has traditionally been known. The plan is marked by (1) guaranteed orbital slots for developing nations and (2) recognized access rights for current satellite operators for at least 20 years. The 937 delegates, representing 120 nations, voted to establish 480 national slots for nations that so far have not filed applications for domestic systems in the fixed satellite service. Nations are not guaranteed specific slots, but are guaranteed access within a suitable segment of the geosynchronous arc. Most countries, including the United States, were very pleased with the outcome: Theodore Brophy, chair of the U.S. Space WARC delegation, pronounced it a "major breakthrough." *See* Space WARC Guarantees Rights of Existing and Planned Satellite Systems, Communications Daily, October 11, 1988 at 1. For the full text of the agreement, *see* International Telecommunications Union, ORB-88 Final Acts (1988).

3. In actually implementing the recommendations set out in the White Paper, the FCC made some significant alterations and clarifications. First, it adopted a one-year lease requirement in place of the five-year requirement recommended. It also clarified that although the separate systems could not provide any switched services (such as ordinary Message Telephone Service (MTS), telex, telegrams, and high-speed switched data) they could provide all nonswitched services, including video and private line service. Under no circumstances, however, are the systems allowed to interconnect to the switched network, even on a store-and-forward basis. And the Commission promised to strictly enforce these restrictions and to monitor international telecommunications to ensure that they are not being violated. Establishment of Satellite Systems Providing International Communications, 101 FCC2d 1046 (1985). Nonetheless, the interconnection requirement will be very difficult to enforce and some "cheating"—whether deliberate or accidental—is inevitable. At this time, the FCC is in the process of eliminating the limitations on separate satellite systems, though many restrictions still remain. *See* Permissible Services of U.S. Licensed International Telecommunications Satellite Systems Separate from the International Telecommunications Satellite Organization, 7 FCC Rcd. 2313 (April 13, 1992).

4. As a signatory to the INTELSAT Agreement, the United States was forced to consider whether its separate satellites decision implicated concerns covered by the INTELSAT accord and whether as a result consultation with INTELSAT was mandated. The following legal opinion from the State Department's Legal Adviser, reproduced in its entirety except for the summary, explains the U.S. view of the subject.

Department of State
The Legal Adviser
Washington, D.C. 20520

MEMORANDUM OF LAW

The Orion Satellite Corporation and International Satellite, Inc. Applications for International Satellite Communication Facilities

Background and Question Presented

The Orion Satellite Corporation (Orion) and International Satellite, Inc. have applied to the FCC for authority to provide privately owned international satellite communications facilities to customers on a commercial basis. Orion argues that its system, which would sell or lease transponders to major business users on both sides of the Atlantic, is subject to coordination with INTELSAT only for technical compatibility with the INTELSAT system. The essence of its argument is that it does not propose common carrier services and only such services are "public international telecommunications services" which require coordination with INTELSAT for avoidance of significant economic harm as well. Although International Satellite, Inc. (ISI) argues that its system will not cause significant economic harm to INTELSAT, it does not explicitly concede that its system is subject to coordination under Article XIV(d) of the INTELSAT Agreement.

These applications present the following threshold legal question under the INTELSAT Agreement of 1971, TIAS 7532:

> Do the Orion and ISI proposals involve the use of non-INTELSAT space segment facilities for international "public telecommunications services" within the meaning of Article XIV(d), requiring coordination with INTELSAT for both technical compatibility *and* the avoidance of significant economic harm, or do they propose "specialized telecommunications services" under Article XIV(e) which require coordination for only technical compatibility?

*　*　*

Analysis

1. ***Authorization of a space segment to provide public international telecommunications services requires technical and economic harm coordination with INTELSAT.***

Under the definitive INTELSAT arrangements, the United States has an obligation, set out in the Agreement's preamble and made operative by Article XIV, to help maintain a single global commercial international telecommunications system as part of an improved global telecommunications network. The obligations extend to what is defined in the Agreement as the "space segment" of INTELSAT. This includes the satellites and related facilities and equipment which are required to support the operation of the satellites.

While available for other purposes, the INTELSAT Agreement contemplates use of the INTELSAT space segment essentially for international public telecommunications. It expressly permits parties to use non-INTELSAT space segment facilities to provide public domestic services [Article XIV(c)] or specialized services [Article XIV(e)] after coordination with INTELSAT solely for technical compatibility. The use of non-INTELSAT space segment for international public telecommunications services [Article XIV(d)] is contemplated after consultation with INTELSAT to ensure technical compatibility and to determine that the services will not cause significant economic harm to the INTELSAT system. Article XIV(g) totally excepts non-INTELSAT space segment facilities used solely for national security purposes. The XIV(d) and (e) provisions are the crux of the issue.

The coordination requirements of Article XIV are a key element of the general obligation of INTELSAT members to help maintain INTELSAT as a single global telecommunications network. The INTELSAT Agreement negotiating history shows that Article XIV was a compromise between the desire of certain European countries, led by France, that the Agreement allow for possible "regional" satellite systems, and the desire of the United States that other international satellite systems be precluded. France, in fact, proposed that INTELSAT be only a federation of regional systems. Several definitions of what would constitute a regional system were put forward, but none was adopted in the final text. It appears that the negotiators felt that the economic harm test incorporated in Article XIV(d) for international public telecommunication services made a definition unnecessary.

2. *"Public telecommunications services" are not limited to "common carrier services."*

The INTELSAT Agreement, Article I(k), defines public telecommunications services as follows:

> "Public telecommunication services" means fixed or mobile public telecommunication services which can be provided by satellite and which are available for use by the public, such as telephony, telegraphy, telex, facsimile, data transmission, transmission of radio and television programs between approved earth stations having access to the INTELSAT space segment for further transmission to the public, and leased circuits for any of these purposes; but excluding those mobile services of a type not provided under the Interim Agreement and the Special Agreement prior to the opening for signature of this Agreement, which are provided through mobile stations operating directly to a satellite which is designed, in whole or in part, to provide services relating to the safety or flight control of aircraft or to aviation or maritime radio navigation.

The applicable rules of international law governing the interpretation of international agreements do not sustain the view that the term "public telecommunications services" means only services analogous to those considered "common carrier" in United States telecommunications law. In interpreting an international agreement, the general rule is that the terms of the agreement will be given their ordinary meaning in the context of the entire agreement and in light of its object and purpose, unless it can be established that the parties intended a special meaning to attach. The rules call for taking into account as well, *inter alia,* any subsequent practice in the application of the treaty. Secondary sources of interpretation can be resorted to in order to confirm the resulting interpretation or to resolve ambiguities. These secondary sources include the agreement's preparatory work and the circumstances of its conclusion. The purpose of all the rules is to establish the agreed intent of the parties, as reflected in the text. (See the Vienna Convention on the Law of Treaties, Articles 31 and 32, which the United States accepts as a generally accurate statement of the applicable international law on the interpretation of international agreements.)

Applying these rules, we note first that, while it was certainly contemplated that access in the United States to the INTELSAT space segment would be made through common carriers, there is nothing in the text of the INTELSAT Agreement which links or limits the concept of "available to the public" in the definition of "public telecommunications services" to the concept of common carriage, which is essentially a United States domestic regulatory concept. Nor is there anything in the text which links or limits that concept to the analogous term "public correspondence," used in the ITU Radio Regulations, where it is defined as: "any telecommunication which the offices and stations must, by reasons of their being at the disposal of the public, accept for transmission." Radio Regulations, Chapter I, Article 1, Section 5.1.

The text of the INTELSAT definition appears to be largely self-contained and susceptible of a reasonable meaning in context without resorting to the special meaning given the term in the regulatory framework of one of the participants or in a different agreement which defines an analogous term for a different object and purpose. Article I(k) defines "public international telecommunications services" by reference to types of services, e.g., telephony and telegraphy, which were services to which the public had access at the time of the INTELSAT negotiations. It appears to use the phrase "available for use by the public" to make clear that new telecommunications services which satellites could provide would fall under the INTELSAT mandate as they came into public use. This construction of the phrase "available for use by the public" appears to be in accord with INTELSAT's practice in interpreting the concept of public telecommunications services over the years.

The definition itself appears to contemplate expressly that such services will be considered "public" even when offered via the leasing of a circuit by INTELSAT through one of its members. There is no requirement that the lease be only to a common carrier rather than an entity or small group of entities for their own communications needs.

The strongest argument for the interpretation put forth by Orion is that the concept "public telecommunications" and the analogous term "public correspondence" were in use at the time of the INTELSAT negotiations in both the U.S. domestic telecommunications field and in the ITU Radio Regulations, a broad multilateral telecommunications instrument with which all the participants in the INTELSAT negotiations were familiar. In both those settings it denoted, *inter alia*, availability to the public at large, not just selected customers, a key element of common carriage. However, that fact does not appear to be sufficient to establish legally that the parties to the INTELSAT Agreement intended to so link and limit it, in light of a number of factors:

First, there are many different definitions of "public."

Second, within the telecommunications authorities and administrations of most of the participants in the INTELSAT negotiations, provision of circuits dedicated to the user's own communications are considered part of the public network, and wholly "private" systems are not a feature.

Third, the practice of the parties in the application of the INTELSAT Agreement includes the authorization of circuits dedicated to direct use by an end user, not merely circuits for use by a carrier offering telecommunications services to the public at large.

Fourth, it has not been U.S. practice under the INTELSAT Agreement to equate "public" with "common carrier." The FCC has held entities purchasing transponders not to be common carriers, yet the services they provided have been coordinated with INTELSAT as domestic public telecommunications services under Article XIV(c).

Fifth, the concept of common carriage, as it existed in the United States at the time of the INTELSAT Agreement, is itself shifting as formerly regulated services are deregulated and new services come on stream in a deregulatory climate. For example, in the *Computer II* decision, the FCC decided to forbear from regulating computer processing type services which, nevertheless, are services offered to the public and are not "private" services.

Finally, the theory that "public international telecommunications services" under the INTELSAT Agreement do not include the provision of a space segment on a commercial basis to users who own or lease individual transponders on the satellite would allow any INTELSAT member to authorize the establishment of such a space segment *even if it were to do significant economic harm* to INTELSAT. This would appear to run counter to the object and purpose of the Agreement, the maintenance of a "single global commercial satellite telecommunications system," to provide the space segment required for expanded "international public telecommunications services of high quality and reliability to be available ... to all areas of the world." [Preamble, Article III and Article XIV(a).]

The Orion application cites INTELSAT's non-discrimination provision as an indication that "public telecommunications service" under INTELSAT means carrier service. However, the "non-discrimination" clause cited by Orion, which occurs in the Preamble to the INTELSAT Agreement, clearly refers to the requirement of the Agreement that services be available on a non-discriminatory basis to the nations, large and small, developed and developing, who are members of INTELSAT. This is consistent with the non-discrimination policy in the

Communications Satellite Act. It does not refer to a requirement that INTELSAT be restricted to services made available to all members of the potential user public in participating states on a non-discriminatory basis.

3. *Although a private non-commercial space segment might not require economic harm coordination with INTELSAT, the proposals are not for such service.*

There is no indication that the development of purely private space telecommunications systems was considered by the negotiators of the INTELSAT Agreement or that such limited satellite systems would, in any event, be likely to cause significant economic harm. Nevertheless, from the INTELSAT Agreement's Article 1(k) reference to leased circuits and the overall object and purpose of INTELSAT as a single "commercial" telecommunication system, one might logically infer that the INTELSAT Agreement does not require economic harm coordination for a privately-owned satellite system in which all the capacity is dedicated to the communications needs of its owner. However, the proposals do not involve a privately owned satellite for exclusive owner use.

While not necessarily dispositive of the INTELSAT interpretation issue, neither Orion nor ISI proposes a genuinely private facility even in U.S. regulatory terms. The FCC's regulations on private radio systems are found in 47 CFR Part 90. The services most analogous to those proposed to be provided by Orion and ISI are found in Subpart D, Industrial Radio Services. These are services which have been established by companies to satisfy their own communications needs. For example, a pipeline transmission company has been permitted to establish a private communications system to serve itself along its right of way. The Commission's regulations (Subpart M) permit companies operating these private systems to provide services to others, or permit any person to provide private services to any person eligible for licensing under Subpart D. However, the Subpart M regulations permit the arrangements only on a "not-for-profit, cost-shared basis." Both Orion and ISI intend to sell or lease satellite transponders, and to maintain satellite control centers and furnish telemetry, tracking, and control functions for a profit. Neither Orion nor ISI will therefore be a private system as those systems are defined in the FCC regulations.

4. *The proposals are not for the type of services which the "specialized services" category, requiring no economic harm coordination, was intended to include.*

The INTELSAT Agreement, Article I(1), defines "specialized telecommunications services" as:

> telecommunications services which can be provided by satellite, other than those defined in paragraph (k) of this Article ["public telecommunications services"], including, but not limited to, radio navigation services, broadcasting satellite services

for reception by the general public, space research services, meteorological services, and earth resources services.

While the category of "specialized services" might be a catch-all to assure that any service which is not a public service would, nevertheless, be technically coordinated with INTELSAT under Article XI(e), the drafters had certain kinds of exceptions in mind for its principal content. The negotiating history of the INTELSAT Agreement gives clear guidance that "specialized" as opposed to "public" services were intended to comprise principally those services, excluding generalized telecommunications, under the direct control of governments as a matter of special national policy (such as direct broadcasting) or services provided by governmental or intergovernmental entities incident to their functions. The negotiators intended to permit members and intergovernmental organizations full freedom to provide such services outside of and without regard to the economic well-being of INTELSAT. Numerous references in the negotiating history indicate that, before INTELSAT undertakes specialized services, it should consult with the U.N. specialized agencies already involved in providing such services, such as the International Civil Aviation Organization (ICAO) or the International Maritime Consultative Organization (IMCO).

The data and TV services that Orion and ISI propose to offer are not specialized services within the sense of that term as used in the INTELSAT Agreement.

Conclusion

While the issue is not free from doubt, the proposals would appear to contemplate providing public international telecommunications and require coordination with INTELSAT both to avoid economic harm and for technical compatibility.

NOTES

1. The U.S. separate systems are not the only systems outside of INTELSAT. There has been consultation with INTELSAT regarding other systems, such as the European system EUTELSAT, the Indonesian Palapa system, the Arabsat consortium, Algeria's use of the Soviet Intersputnik system, and the use of U.S. domestic satellites to connect the United States with Canada, Mexico, and Bermuda. A complete survey of the ever-changing array of new satellite consortia is beyond the scope of this book; for more information on these *see* R. White & H. White, The Law and Regulation of International Space Communication (1988). Although these systems vary, the issues they raise are generally the same as those explained above—competition for scarce spectrum, economic harm to existing systems, and national sovereignty.

2. Having decided to license separate satellite systems, the United States faced greater difficulties in implementing its decision. The domestic telecommunications of virtually all nations other than the United States fall under the supervision of Postal Telephone and Telegraph authorities, or PTTs. These organizations, as monopolists, tend to be hostile to competition, and since they are usually regulators as well as providers they are able to do much to obstruct the entry of new providers into their markets. They do this not because of concern about economic harm to INTELSAT, but because they fear competition with their lucrative participation in the international cable business, and because they fear that U.S. deregulation, if too successful, might spill over into their own markets. For a discussion of many of these issues *see* Rein *et al.*, Implementation of a U.S. "Free Entry" Initiative for Transatlantic Satellite Facilities: Problems, Pitfalls, and Possibilities, 18 George Washington Journal of International Law and Economics 459 (1985); Godwin, The Proposed Orion and ISI Transatlantic Satellite Systems: A Challenge to the Status Quo, 24 Jurimetrics: Journal of Law, Science & Technology 297 (1984).

The PTTs' position is probably untenable over the long run, given the growing importance of flexible and inexpensive telecommunications services to international competitiveness—efforts, for example, to maintain jobs within the telecommunications establishments of particular nations will be superseded by concern for maintaining the competitiveness of the economies of those nations as a whole. That is because the importance of information industries to the overall economy of a nation far exceeds their value in terms of the jobs and national income that they create directly on their own. *Cf.* Bresnahan, Measuring the Spillovers from Technical Advance: Mainframe Computers in Financial Services, 76 American Economic Review 742 (1986) (estimating that consumer benefits from computers used in financial services far outweigh benefits to computer companies); T. Howell *et al.*, The Microelectronics Race (1988). Thus, obstructionist telecommunications regulation intended to keep out foreign competition will be seen as the equivalent of destroying roads and harbors in order to reduce imports of foreign television sets—effective in a narrow sense, perhaps, but suicidal from a broader perspective. All nations can be expected to learn this lesson sooner or later—although pressures for protection of domestic telecommunications jobs are likely to be substantial in many cases. For more on these issues *see* Glenn H. Reynolds, United States Telecommunications Trade Policy: Critique and Suggestions, 58 Tennessee Law Review 573 (1991); Glenn H. Reynolds, Speaking With Forked Tongues: Mercantilism, Telecommunications Regulation and International Trade, 21 Law & Policy in International Business 119 (1990).

DIRECT SATELLITE BROADCASTING

Broadcasting in general has the capability of transcending national boundaries, something that naturally concerns those who desire to maintain control over the dissemination of information within their domains. Satellites, however, offer the possibility of broadcasting to many nations at once in a way that no other technology does. Although shortwave radio may travel around the world, the signals that television depends on are limited by line of sight. From a satellite, however, an enormous portion of the earth is within view, so that three satellites in geosynchronous orbit can blanket the entire planet. Given that television is generally seen as a more powerful medium than other broadcast services, the possibility of Direct Broadcast Satellite (DBS) television has created considerable concern among those governments who see it as their right to control the kinds of information that their citizens may receive.

As a result, DBS has been on the agenda of the Legal Subcommittee of the Committee on the Peaceful Uses of Outer Space since 1968—and, indeed, was discussed in COPUOS as early as 1964. Such discussions, though often heated, have achieved little. Generally, the Soviet Union, together with many other authoritarian regimes, has championed principles demanding that no broadcasts be made to any state without its prior consent. Western nations, and particularly the United States, have on the other hand favored a far more open approach. The United States in particular has taken the position that such broadcasting should be limited only to the extent necessary to ensure that copyright and trademark laws are observed and to avoid harmful interference with other broadcast signals.

Not surprisingly, given the political makeup of the globe, the United States' position is distinctly in the minority. Nonetheless (and probably fortunately), the consensus procedure within COPUOS has meant that no principle could be agreed to. However, the United Nations General Assembly and the United Nations Educational, Scientific and Cultural Organization (UNESCO) have adopted positions (which do not have binding force) that reject the United States approach in favor of a more restrictive one.

Arguments in favor of such a position are often couched in terms that avoid politics and stress the need for "cultural sovereignty" or a "New International Information Order." (For an interesting and thorough discussion of these issues from a Third World perspective, *see* Addis, International Propaganda and the Developing Countries, 21 Vanderbilt Journal of Transnational Law 491 (1988). While we do not mean to minimize cultural concerns, and we recognize that most international news organizations *do* possess a generally Western orientation, the fact is that politics form the real motivation for most governments' hostility to DBS. Most governments in the world are decidedly authoritarian, and even many governments that *are* generally democratic have a tendency to try to control the nature and amount of information to which their citizens have access. The Soviet Union's history is well known, but even the United States—unquestionably the world's leading champion of open access to information—has had a somewhat checkered record in that regard. *See generally* L. Powe, American Broadcasting and the First Amendment (1987) on this topic. Wherever their employ, the instinct of bureaucrats and politicians is to protect their jobs and promote their interests by using the power of the state to silence their enemies and proclaim their own views. In some countries they are restrained in this tendency by domestic laws or political ideologies; in others they have free rein.

The existing international law (or its aspirational equivalent) is quite clear, though. Article 19 of the Universal Declaration of Human Rights, which has been assented to (if not necessarily followed) by virtually every nation in the world, provides that:

> Everyone has the right to freedom of opinion and expression; this right includes freedom to hold opinions without interference and to seek, receive and impart information and ideas through any media and regardless of frontiers.

Nations should not be permitted to depart from this principle in the DBS context simply because a novel technology is involved. Although governments often attempt to control new communication technologies to a degree that would not be tolerated with regard to those that are more established, if history teaches anything it is that governments are not to be trusted, *under any circumstances*, with control of their citizens' right to receive and impart ideas. Such control is almost inevitably abused, and the results of such abuse are consistently worse than the consequences of freedom—at least from the viewpoint of the governed.

Fortunately, however, the rapid dissemination of technology and the continued progress in the field of electronics that have marked this century will make control of satellite broadcasting less and less feasible. Already, at the time of this writing, satellite dishes capable of receiving programs from communications satellites not intended for broadcasting at all are widespread, both within the United States and throughout the Third World. Given time, the size and cost of such facilities (already well within the limits of individuals and small organizations) will likely become small enough that even concerted government efforts to stamp them out will be fruitless—and the widespread presence of video recorders, even within East Bloc countries, already ensures that any program received can be widely circulated. As satellites specifically designed for broadcast purposes grow common, reception will become easier and censorship even more difficult. Furthermore, the growth of two-way satellite technologies will undoubtedly allow the spread of inexpensive portable uplink equipment, meaning that incriminating evidence of (say) a massacre of civilians in a remote region can be sent to the world within minutes regardless of efforts by the regime in power to prevent it.

This is as it should be. As the Universal Declaration of Human Rights recognizes, free exchange of ideas is a basic human right. The explosion of information technologies in the late 20th century has made it steadily easier to realize that right, and the importance of those technologies to national economic competitiveness has meant that nations cannot for long resist their spread without paying a fearsome price. While the technologies of space communication will not in themselves make tyranny impossible, they will make its task far more difficult, and ensure that its actions do not escape notice and censure in the world community. The benefits from this will far exceed the costs.

Although the DBS debate has generated far more heat than light, it does offer a fascinating (if not especially encouraging) view of how the international system responds to new technologies. For more on this topic, including good histories of the debate, *see* R. White & H. White, The Law and Regulation of International Space Communication (1988), especially at Chapter 9, E. van Bogaert, Aspects of Space Law 223 *et seq.* (1986), and Paul, Images from Abroad: Making Direct Broadcasting by Satellites Safe for Sovereignty, 9 Hastings International & Comparative Law Review 329 (1986).

7

Space-Related International Trade Issues

Throughout the 1980s, space industries began to take on a more commercial tone. With the entry of the European Arianespace as a quasi-private commercial entity, competition for satellite-launching business began in earnest. At first, such competition was between NASA's Space Shuttle and Ariane, but after the 1986 *Challenger* tragedy that competition became more widespread. Pursuant to the Commercial Space Launch Act of 1984 Pub. L. 98-575, 98 Stat. 3055 (codified at 49 U.S.C. § 2601 *et seq.*), as amended in 1988, the U.S. government had already begun the process of establishing a private sector commercial launch industry. The enormous disruption created by the *Challenger* accident and by unfortunately timed problems with other launch systems accelerated this process, and focused attention on the importance of a diverse and robust U.S. launch capacity. Meanwhile, the Soviet Union (later, the Russian Federation) and the People's Republic of China began aggressively marketing launch services on their own launch vehicles, while new entrants, including Japan, Brazil, and India appeared on the horizon.

Similarly, growing competition was developing in the payload sector. European satellite manufacturers, having gained experience with the early *Symphonie* communications satellite in the mid-1970s, became more and more involved in the satellite construction field, while a French concern, Spot Image, entered the private remote-sensing field in competition with the United States' EOSAT. India began building and launching its own remote sensing and communications satellites, Brazil began moving toward entry into that area, and Japanese executives were heard talking excitedly about the prospects for Japanese "hegemony" in satellite telecommunications, to the discomfiture of their commercial rivals in other nations. Despite calls for the development of "rules of the road" for international trade in space goods and services, the stage at this writing is obviously set for a series of trade disputes in the area, disputes for which existing international trade law is clearly inadequate, whether embodied in international agreements or U.S. municipal law.

Because at this writing we are only now on the verge of such disputes, this chapter will not attempt a microscopic dissection of existing international trade law, such as it is, nor will it attempt to foresee all of the possible disputes in the offing. Instead, it will examine the reasons why such disputes are likely to occur, will discuss the forces that will tend to shape them, and will suggest some things that might be done to reduce the magnitude of the problem and to safeguard U.S. national interests. In addition, this chapter discusses the impact of U.S. and international technology controls on space industries and activities.

ECONOMICS OF SPACE INDUSTRIES

Although the term "space industries" encompasses a wide variety of enterprises, from launch services to microgravity manufacturing to telecommunications, such industries have, in broad, some important elements in common. First, they tend to be at or near the cutting edge of technological development. Second, they tend to be characterized by substantial economies of scale. Third, they tend to be of considerable importance to both "upstream" industries (that is, suppliers) and "downstream" industries (that is, customers)—for example, the telecommunications satellite industry is a consumer of many high technology products, as well as a key input for long distance telephone companies and television networks. And fourth, space industries are often of "dual use" character, having both civilian and military applications which are largely inseparable—for example, the technologies involved in entering the civilian launch industry are little different from those needed to construct ballistic missiles capable of carrying nuclear warheads, a fact not overlooked by the Indian and Brazilian governments, or their neighbors.

Aside from their military implications, space industries are strategic in an economic sense as well, for the reasons listed above. Nations involved in marketing space goods and services do so for the opportunity to gain economies of scale, to move up the learning curve, to drive development of key technologies, and to gain hard currency and international prestige. Although these are all legitimate and even desirable goals, they do pose problems from an international trade standpoint, since they may be better served by national strategies involving pricing below cost ("dumping") and unfair government subsidies than by strategies based solely on commercial competitiveness. Dumping and subsidization are generally considered unfair practices in international trade; however, they are often engaged in by nations (particularly mercantilistic or non-market economies) for strategic reasons. Such behavior is likely in a number of space-related areas, particularly the launch services field, and is hence likely to lead to disputes. For more on these economic issues *see* Reynolds & Merges, Toward an Industrial Policy for Outer Space: Problems and Prospects of the Commercial Launch Industry, 29 Jurimetrics: Journal of Law, Science & Technology 7 (1988).

To provide a bit of the flavor of such disputes, and to allow a bit of perspective on the discussion to follow, we reproduce here excerpts from one recent international dispute over international trade in the launch services field. Following those excerpts is a discussion of how U.S. law and existing international trade agreements apply to trade in space-related goods and services, and some observations for the future.

The Transpace Section 301 Petition

As the move toward commercialization of the launch services market began to get underway, several companies were organized to enter that market. Unfortunately for these entities, market prospects were difficult: NASA shuttle launches were still subsidized, and NASA's only active competitor, the European consortium Arianespace, was meeting NASA's prices in an effort to attract business. Since NASA was backed by the U.S. treasury, and Arianespace by the scarcely less formidable resources of the major European countries, it was difficult for entities that had to make a profit to compete. One of the new companies, Transpace Carriers, Inc., thus filed a so-called "Section 301 petition" with the United States Trade Representative. The following discussion will make clear why Transpace chose that approach, after which are excerpts from both the petition and the Presidential determination stemming from it.

Reynolds & Merges, Toward an Industrial Policy for Outer Space: Problems and Prospects of the Commercial Launch Industry, 29 Jurimetrics: Journal of Law, Science & Technology 7 (1988)

Because of the likely importance of price in this market, new foreign competitors can be expected to price aggressively, and even to dump, in order to obtain market share and scale economies. Existing U.S. trade laws, however, are not admirably suited to the problem of unfair trade in launch services. The antidumping law, Section 731 of the Tariff Act of 1930 as amended [19 U.S.C. § 1673(1) (1988)], focuses on "a class or kind of foreign merchandise" that "is being, or is likely to be, sold in the United States at less than its fair value." Launch services almost certainly would not be found to be "merchandise" for the purpose of this provision, nor is it likely to be found that a foreign launch provider, by contracting with a U.S. customer, has "sold" anything "in the United States." Similarly, U.S. countervailing duty law [19 U.S.C. § 1671 (1988)] provides for imposition of a duty in response to "a subsidy with respect to the manufacture, production, or exportation of a class or kind of merchandise imported or sold (or likely to be sold) for importation, into the United States." Both laws also apply an injury test, although in the case of the countervailing duty law the injury requirement is omitted as to countries not party to the GATT subsidies code. Because these laws were designed to deal with traditional trade in goods, they are poorly suited to dealing with predatory pricing in the launch services field.

Somewhat more success might be expected under Section 301 of the Trade Act of 1974 as amended [19 U.S.C. § 2411 (1988)]. Among other things, Section 301 allows the President to "take all appropriate and feasible action within his power" in response to any foreign practice that "is unjustifiable, unreasonable, or discriminatory and burdens or restricts United States commerce." Unlike the antidumping and countervailing duty laws, Section 301 explicitly applies to services as well as merchandise, and grants the President sweeping power to respond via duties, restrictions on foreign services, and actions in trade sectors other than the one in dispute. Thus (for example) predatory pricing in Chinese launch services might be penalized via a ban on imports of Chinese textiles or agricultural products.

Despite the power and flexibility of Section 301, however, there is surprisingly little enthusiasm among space and international trade lawyers for its application to launch services. This is because in 1985 the United States refused to take action against the European Space Agency in response to the petition by Transpace Carriers, a U.S. launch company. Despite this refusal to act, however, Section 301 may profitably be applied to the future, given the changes in the industry, in U.S. practice, and in the degree and nature of foreign competition. However, trade legislation specifically aimed at launch services *would* be beneficial, not least as a signal to foreign providers that the United States takes the matter seriously.

Another possible solution, which we endorse, would be to pursue multilateral trade talks regarding launch services with all other spacefaring nations. Some such talks have been going on informally already; these could be expanded into a full-scale trade agreement governing launch services, or perhaps incorporated into the current round of negotiations under the General Agreement on Tariffs and Trade. Such talks are certainly worth pursuing and such an agreement, if well-drafted, would be worth concluding. In general, though, the effectiveness of such agreements in preventing unfair trade practices has not been stellar; at best they prevent the most egregious abuses, at worst they simply introduce market distortions that ultimately harm the competitiveness of domestic industries. To survive in the long run, U.S. launch services industries need to be better than their foreign competitors, which means that the launch technology they employ must be more efficient and at least as reliable.

Before the Office of the United States Trade Representative Chairwoman, Section 301 Committee; Petition Seeking Presidential Action Under Section 301 of the Trade Act of 1974 as Amended (19 U.S.C. § 2411, *et seq.*) by Transpace Carriers, Inc. Against the Governments of Belgium, Denmark, France, Germany, Ireland, Italy, the Netherlands, Sweden, Spain, Switzerland and the United Kingdom and Their Space-Related Instrumentalities

This petition is filed on behalf of the civil expendable launch vehicle services industry, by Transpace Carriers, Inc. ("TCI") pursuant to § 301 *et seq.* of the Trade Act of 1974, as amended, 19 U.S.C. § 2411, *et seq.* (Supp. III 1979) (hereinafter "the Act") and 15 C.F.R. § 2006.0(b) (1982). This petition contains all information reasonably available to petitioner.

The subject of the petition are acts, policies and practices undertaken by the Member States of the European Space Agency ("ESA"), *i.e.*, Belgium, Denmark, France, Germany, Italy, Ireland, the Netherlands, Spain, Sweden, Switzerland and the United Kingdom, and their space-related instrumentalities, that are unjustifiable, unreasonable or discriminatory and that burden or restrict United States commerce in trade in services within the meaning of section 301(a)(2)(B) of the Act. Specifically, the above-referenced governments and their instrumentalities, particularly the French national space agency, Centre National d'Etudes Spatiale ("CNES"), are subsidizing the activities of a French company, Arianespace, S.A., which is in direct competition with petitioner in the provision of civil expendable launch vehicle services to customers in the United States and third countries.

The specific subsidy practices of which petitioner complains, include:

—The two-tiered pricing of launch services offered by Arianespace. Member States of ESA have agreed to pay 25% to 33% per "launch" more than is charged to the export market for the same services.

—The provision of launch and range facilities and services and/or personnel at no charge, or unreasonably low cost, to Arianespace by the French national space agency, CNES. The cost of launch and range facilities and services represents approximately one-third of the total cost of a launch.

—The provision of CNES administrative, management and/or technical personnel to Arianespace either at no charge or at rates that are unreasonably low.

—The subsidization of mission insurance rates which Arianespace customers would otherwise pay.

As a beneficiary of such subsidy practices, Arianespace has been able to offer launch services to United States companies and third country customers at rates which are substantially less than those charged to Member States of ESA and substantially below those prices that Arianespace would be able to charge in the absence of subsidization. This unfair competitive advantage has resulted in lost sales to petitioner and price suppression, if not depression, of bid prices. Furthermore, it poses a serious threat to the establishment of a United States commercial launch services industry.

Petitioner therefore requests, pursuant to section 301(a) of the Act, that the President take all appropriate and feasible action within his power to obtain the elimination of such acts, policies or practices that are unjustifiable, unreasonable or discriminatory and that burden or restrict this important new service industry, and to take such other action as is sanctioned by section 301(b) of the Act.

In particular, petitioner requests the President to seek the immediate discontinuance of the two-tiered pricing policy for Arianespace launches observed by the

Member States of ESA, the elimination of the cost-free or below-cost support in facilities, services and personnel provided by the French national space agency, CNES, and the subsidization of mission insurance rates, such that all outstanding and future Arianespace bids for launch services reflect actual costs plus a reasonable profit for each launch. Pending the elimination of such acts, policies and practices, the President is requested to retaliate by prohibiting Arianespace U.S.A. from advertising and marketing its services in the United States and by imposing economic sanctions against the goods and services of the Member States of ESA.

NOTE

Under Section 301, action is not mandatory. The United States Trade Representative, whose office is part of the Executive Office of the President, investigates and makes a recommendation to the President, who determines whether or not to act. Although time limits vary depending on the allegations involved, the President must in no case take longer than 12 months to respond. The President's determination, along with the reasons behind it, is then published in the Federal Register. Because the language of Section 301 is permissive, not mandatory, the President may be swayed by political considerations unrelated to trade issues. (Legislation under consideration at the time of this writing would reduce the amount of discretion under Section 301 and would shift the decision from the President to the United States Trade Representative. These changes are unlikely to have major impact in the space context.) Many have criticized Section 301 on this ground, and on the basis that it does not clearly define the conduct to which the President is permitted to respond. *See, e.g.*, Hansen, Defining Unreasonableness in International Trade: Section 301 of the Trade Act of 1974, 96 Yale Law Journal 1122 (1987). There is no right to appeal from a determination not to act, but petitioners may withdraw their petition in order to avoid a negative determination. Although negative determinations do not have a binding precedential effect, they represent a distinct burden on further efforts by the petitioner and thus are to be avoided where possible.

In the case of the Transpace petition, the result was a negative determination: the President found that the practices complained of were not sufficiently different from those of NASA at the time. A major influence on this decision was the absence of any viable domestic commercial launch industry: although Transpace and others were attempting to obtain business, none had signed a launch contract and many doubted whether they could succeed on a commercial basis. (Of course, given the need to compete with NASA and Arianespace at artificially low prices, this may well have been true.) It is unlikely that this negative determination would be a bar to a future proceeding if circumstances justified, however: there is now a substantial and growing U.S. launch industry, and NASA is no longer competing for commercial launch contracts. Certainly Transpace's experience is no reason for international trade and space lawyers to despair of *ever* using Section 301 in response to unfair foreign practices in the space field, despite the negative determination excerpted next.

Determination Under Section 301 of the Trade Act of 1974, 50 Fed. Reg. 29631 (July 22, 1985)

Pursuant to Section 301(a) of the Trade Act of 1974, as amended (19 U.S.C. 2411(a)), I have determined that the practices of the Member States of the European Space Agency (ESA) and their instrumentalities with respect to the commercial satellite launching services of Arianespace, S.A. are not unreasonable and a burden or restriction on U.S. Commerce. While Arianespace does not operate under purely commercial conditions, this is in large measure a result of the history of the launch services industry, which is marked by almost exclusive government involvement. I have determined that these conditions do not require affirmative U.S. action at this time. But because of my decision to commercialize expendable launch services in the United States, and our policies with respect to manned launch services such as the Shuttle (STS), it may become appropriate for the United States to approach other interested nations to reach an international understanding on guidelines for commercial satellite launch services at some point in the future.

Reasons for Determination

Based on a petition filed by Transpace Carriers, Inc. (TCI), the United States Trade Representative (USTR) initiated an investigation on July 9, 1984, of the European Space Agency's policies with respect to Arianespace S.A. Arianespace is a privately owned company, incorporated under the laws of France for the purpose of launching satellites. Arianespace's shareholders include the French national space agency, and aerospace companies and banks incorporated in the ESA Member States.

The Petitioner alleged that 1) Arianespace uses a two tier pricing policy whereby Arianespace charges a higher price to ESA Member States than to foreign customers; 2) the French national space agency (CNES) subsidizes launch and range facilities, and services and personnel provided to Arianespace; 3) the French national space agency subsidizes the administrative and technical personnel it provides to Arianespace; and 4) Arianespace's mission insurance rates are subsidized. In addition to these allegations, the U.S. also investigated three other areas: government inducements to purchasers of Arianespace's services; direct and indirect government assistance to Arianespace; and, Arianespace's costs and pricing policies.

Our findings with respect to these allegations are set forth below. Many of the factual allegations were not supported by evidence on the record. While other allegations were substantiated, the practices were not sufficiently different from U.S. practice in this field to be considered unreasonable under Section 301.

* * *

Since there are no international standards of reasonableness for launch services, we have compared ESA practices to United States practice, and to reasonable commercial practices. The ESA practices are not sufficiently different from those of the U.S. to be actionable under Section 301. This determination is not an endorsement of ESA practices. Our policies in this area are now undergoing revision, and in the future we may wish to reexamine ESA's practices and their effect on U.S.G. launch services. At that time it may be in our mutual interest to engage in international discussions aimed at establishing appropriate guidelines for the commercial launch industry.

The determination shall be published in the Federal Register.

RONALD REAGAN

THE WHITE HOUSE
Washington, July 17, 1985

NOTES

1. At the time of this writing, there are informal talks going on between the United States, the Europeans, and various other governments regarding the establishment of "rules of the road" for trade in launch services. The goal is to determine what conduct should be regarded as fair and unfair in promoting a nation's launch business. This is made more important by the complete absence of any international agreement covering launch services. This absence may be remedied during the upcoming round of negotiations over the General Agreement on Tariffs and Trade (GATT)'s coverage of service industries, although prospects at this writing do not appear especially hopeful.

2. The Transpace petition involved subsidies that (although they may have been real) were difficult to quantify and hard to separate from activities that any responsible government could be expected to engage in—such as safety inspections, assistance in planning launch ranges, etc. And the prices charged by Ariane were not dramatically lower than those charged for launches on what was then its only competitor, the Space Shuttle. Future trade disputes are more likely to deal with purely state-operated launch services, such as the Russians and Chinese are beginning to market.

3. International trade lawyers refer to sales of products or services at prices below the seller's cost as "dumping." The following excerpt explains why dumping is considered an unfair practice in international trade, and why nations engage in what, at first glance, may seem like a counterproductive practice: selling goods for less than they cost.

Glenn H. Reynolds & John Ragosta, International Trade in Launch Services: Some Problems and Solutions

Although dumping seems beneficial to consumers in the short run, since they are able to buy at below the seller's cost, it is very harmful to national economies in the long run. Dumping allows the producing country to achieve sales volumes great enough to produce substantial scale economies and dramatic moves up the learning curve, giving that country tremendous long-term advantage over competitors. Such moves up the learning curve can produce a near-insurmountable advantage in high technology capital-intensive industries—just as, in a different context, the money spent on air mail subsidies in the 1920s and 1930s allowed the U.S. aircraft industry to "bootstrap" itself into levels of efficiency that produced 50 years of American predominance in aviation.

And where dumping targets a particular "bottleneck" sector, it can allow other, more profitable sectors to flourish, often to the extent that revenue from those sectors offsets the cost of the dumping. For example, Japanese dumping of computer memory chips has allowed them to virtually eliminate the U.S. industry in that area; now it appears that they are manipulating supplies and prices of those chips to disadvantage U.S. competitors in high value-added sectors that depend on memory chips, such as whole computers, disk drives, and custom chips. While the United States is now, after the fact, working diligently to respond to Japanese chip-dumping, Japan has leveraged its advantage into other markets, gained in violation of international trade rules, that it could effectively control for years.

In the same way, one might imagine the Japanese exploiting a similar position in the launch services area to disadvantage U.S. satellite manufacturers, remote-sensing operators, etc. There is certainly no question that the Japanese hope to compete in the payload sector as well as in the launch services arena—in fact, Teruo Masuda, a senior section officer of C. Itoh's information systems and technology department, was recently quoted as saying "We have to have hegemony in satellite telecommunications," a goal that in light of recent Japanese successes should send shivers up the spines of U.S. satellite manufacturers. A decisive advantage in the launch services area, however achieved, could substantially help Japan in achieving such control.

NOTE

The above excerpt embodies new economic thinking about international trade. Classical and neoclassical economists maintain that nations cannot be harmed by dumping or subsidization on the part of competitors. Many economists are now arguing that this may not be the case, at least with regard to key "strategic industries." For a good survey of such thinking, *see* Strategic Trade Policy and the New International Economics (P. Krugman, ed., 1986); R. Gilpin, The Political Economy of International Relations 215–230 (1987); Tyson, Ask the Right Tough Questions About America's Strategic Industries, Harvard Business Review, November-December, 1988, p. 103. For applications of this thinking to the commercial space field *see* Reynolds, International Trade Conflict in High Technology Sectors, The Japanese Satellite Example 12 U.C.L.A. Pac. Bas. L.J. 295 (1994); Reynolds & Merges, Toward an Industrial Policy for Outer Space: Problems and Prospects of the Commercial Launch Industry, 29 Jurimetrics: Journal of Law, Science & Technology 7 (1988). The following excerpt explores some of the problems that have developed so far.

Congressional Research Service, Commercial Space Launch Services: The U.S. Competitive Position 56–67 (1991)

U.S./European "Rules of the Road" Negotiations

The extent to which Arianespace is or is not subsidized by the French government (or other European governments) has been a matter of contention since the company assumed operations of Ariane. There are no specific international guidelines that govern launch competition. It is generally guided by implicit guidelines known as "rules of the road" based on free and fair trading practices. Up to the present, the considerable government involvement in developing launch vehicles and associated infrastructure in all countries with space launch capabilities has meant that the relationship between customer launch charges and real costs is not easy to establish. For example, most civilian rockets were derived from military missiles and a considerable proportion of the expenditures in building the prototype and developing early models was covered by defense budgets.

In general, launch prices are based on an estimation of a cluster of basic factors such as the period of time necessary to write off the initial investment, the projected number of flights during this period, which depends on demand expectations, and the projected cost and desired rate of return on the investment. However, in the space business, not all fixed costs are recouped due to the specific nature of this activity and the involvement of governments in the establishment of space capabilities. For example, since the U.S. space shuttle is considered a national resource which is maintained for public purposes, R&D spending and in general non-recurring costs were not included in the cost base for the pricing of the shuttle launching service in the early 1980s when the shuttle services were being offered commercially.

It is generally acknowledged that most launch services are subsidized either directly or indirectly. This affects the pricing of services in the short- and long-term. Pricing policies are affected by the amount of subsidization that has occurred in past development and the amount of current subsidies that may allow the launch firm to offer its services at a lower price. Future price competitions will be dependent upon the amount of subsidization that takes place. Without future subsidizations, costs (and hence prices) per flight may decrease if progress is made in increasing launch efficiencies. Growth in satellite demand would also increase launch demand and could reduce the price per launch. Alternatively, prices may increase if subsidies are phased out because companies may have to make up the difference with higher prices. Competition between the world's launching firms may depend highly upon countries' subsidization policies. It may be difficult to develop agreements that would create a level playing field.

Transpace Carrier Unfair Pricing Allegations

The issue concerning subsidized pricing of commercial launches was formally raised in 1984 by Transpace Carriers, Inc., a U.S. company then attempting to market launch services on the Delta ELV.

In 1984, Transpace initiated a complaint against Arianespace with the Office of the U.S. Trade Representative (USTR) for unfair trade practices under Section 301(a) of the Trade Act of 1974. The petition was filed on behalf of the civil expendable launch services industry. The complaint alleged that the member countries of ESA, particularly France, were subsidizing the activities of Arianespace which was in direct competition with Transpace in selling launch services. The specific subsidy practices that Transpace complained about included:

- The two tiered pricing of launch services offered by Arianespace, where Member states of ESA agreed to pay 25 percent to 33 percent per launch more than is charged to the export market for the same services;
- The provision of launch and range facilities and services and/or personnel at no charge, or unreasonably low cost, to Arianespace by the French national space agency, CNES (the cost of launch and range facilities as services represents approximately one-third of the total cost of a launch);
- The provision of CNES administrative, management and/or technical personnel to Arianespace either at no charge or at rates that are unreasonably low; and
- The subsidization of mission insurance rates which Arianespace customers would otherwise pay.

Transpace stated that as a result of these subsidies, Arianespace had been able to offer launch services to U.S. companies and third country customers at rates which were substantially less than those charged to member states of ESA and substantially below those prices that Arianespace would be able to charge in the absence of subsidization. Transpace concluded that such subsidies posed a serious threat to the establishment of a U.S. commercial launch services industry.

USTR investigated, but ultimately dismissed the complaint because the European government backing of Arianespace was found to be no greater than U.S. Government backing of the commercial launches on the U.S. space shuttle. (As discussed elsewhere in this report, commercial launches are no longer offered on the space shuttle unless the cargo requires the unique capabilities of the shuttle or overriding foreign policy concerns exist.)

U.S./European Negotiations

The Transpace Carriers case raised the question of what "rules of the road" to follow in pricing launch services. Both sides agreed to discussions, but little progress was made in the late 1980s. In 1988 and 1989 when the U.S. was negotiating with China over its entry into the launch services market (see below), some Europeans expressed displeasure that the U.S. Government was moving ahead more quickly with China than with them. The Bush Administration's commercial space launch policy released in September 1990 stated that the U.S. Government would enter into negotiations to achieve an agreement with ESA, ESA member states, and others as appropriate, which defines principles of free and fair trade. On September 24, 1990, talks commenced between the USTR and ESA on establishing such rules of the road and looking at how the United States and Europe should respond to the entry of countries with non-market economies (NMEs, specifically the Soviet Union and China) into the launch services business.

The first actual negotiating session was held on February 26–27, 1991, where the two groups offered "framework" documents setting out their respective positions. Two working groups were then created to try to meld the position papers. The working groups do not have the authority to negotiate; they are simply developing documents that set forth both positions and indicate areas of agreement and disagreement. The first is dealing with "common principles" on pricing; the second deals with the NME issue. The working groups have met regularly since February. The Departments of Commerce, Defense, State and Transportation and USTR are represented on the first working group; all but DOD are on the second. The individuals representing DOC, DOS, DOT and USTR are the same for both groups.

A negotiating session was scheduled for April 29–30, 1991, but the decision was made to have the working groups meet again at that time instead. Another negotiating session was planned for July 10–12, 1991, but it also was postponed until the fall. The working groups continue to meet. Both sides anticipate that negotiations will continue through 1991. The U.S. expects that the final agreement would be signed not only by ESA, but by individual member countries of ESA that are involved in the Ariane launch vehicle and/or have satellites.

Scope of Discussions

A fundamental issue between the two sides is the scope of the agreement to be negotiated. According to USTR, ESA wants to limit the discussion to issues involving government support for launch service providers, such as research and development funding, use of launch facilities, insurance, etc., while the U.S. wants to broaden the scope to include "market behavior/trade" issues such as government "inducements" to customers (such as a European government offering rocket engine technology to a customer if the customer chooses an Ariane launch), as well as unfair business practices (such as bribes). The U.S. also wants a general statement on the principles of pricing. ESA's chief negotiator and director of administration, George van Reeth, asserts that ESA does not have the power to negotiate a comprehensive trade agreement and the U.S. is complicating the talks by insisting on its position.

European Access to the U.S. Government Satellite Market

Another controversial topic is whether Arianespace should be able to bid for launches of U.S. Government satellites. Officially this issue is not a subject of the negotiations, but is often raised nonetheless.

Current U.S. policy requires U.S. Government satellites to be launched on U.S. launch vehicles. Arianespace wants that restriction lifted. Charles Bigot, Arianespace's Chairman and Chief Executive Officer, noted in a 1990 interview that although Arianespace has 50–55 percent of "the market" for satellite launches, that market does not include U.S. Government satellites and therefore Arianespace actually launches only 15 percent of the total number of satellites placed in orbit. "We are not complaining, but our American competitors have access to the American government market and we do not have this access. So we say the rules are not the same for everybody and we ask that they be changed."

U.S. observers counter that although France and other European governments apparently do not have written policies requiring the use of Ariane for their government satellites, a de facto policy exists nonetheless. Steven Dorfman, a corporate vice president for satellite manufacturer Hughes Aircraft, Inc., extends the criticism to satellites. He asserts that European governments (and China) will not purchase American-made satellites and that if Europe wants to sell launch services in the U.S., they should be prepared to procure launch services and satellites on a free-market basis. Others note that the Europeans do not purchase U.S. launch vehicle components, either—all Ariane parts are made by European companies.

The issue of whether or not U.S. Government satellites could be launched on foreign launch vehicles became controversial during deliberations on the FY 1992 NASA authorization bill that passed the House on May 2, 1991 (H.R. 1988). Some Members wanted to permit foreign launches of certain NASA environmental satellites (part of the Mission to Planet Earth program) because the U.S. could not launch mid-sized satellites into polar orbits. Such launches take place from Vandenberg Air Force Base, CA, and there is no launch pad there for the new Atlas launch vehicle (Atlas IIAS) required for "medium" sized spacecraft. Rather than being forced into building either much larger satellites that would take advantage of the Titan's substantial lift capability or smaller satellites sized to fit on Delta, the Members recommended flexibility on the issue of using foreign launch capabilities. Other Members, however, were concerned about the effect this might have on the U.S. commercial launch industry and on the trade talks with ESA. Ultimately, Representative Torricelli succeeded in amending the NASA authorization bill so it states that existing U.S. policy should be maintained, a waiver from the President should be required for any exemption to the policy, and exemptions only should be granted if the U.S. does not have the needed launch capability, U.S. companies would not be harmed by the waiver, and program benefits would accrue. Representative Torricelli recommended that a launch pad be built at Vandenberg for the new Atlas launch vehicle to remedy the problem, and suggested that the Department of Defense "contribute" to paying for its construction. DOD subsequently announced plans to request funding to refurbish a launch pad at Vandenberg so it can support Atlas IIAS launches.

*   *   *

Controversy Over the Arabsat Agreement

In March 1990, Arianespace charged that CGWIC had reached agreement to launch the Arabsat 1-C satellite for the Arabsat Consortium for a price below fair market prices in contradiction to the agreement China signed with the U.S. Chinese officials confirmed that their price was $25 million, approximately half of what would be normally charged by Arianespace or a U.S. company, although they asserted that they had no choice because Arianespace lowered its offer to $34.35 million. The Arabsat satellite was built by a European company (Aerospatiale), but a U.S. company (Space Systems/Loral—formerly Ford Aerospace) was a major subcontractor and approximately 60 percent of the components are American-made. Thus, Arianespace appealed to the French and U.S. Governments to deny an export license for the satellite.

Trade talks between the United States and China were already scheduled for July 1990 and according to press reports, the U.S. raised this issue. U.S. delegation leader Donald Phillips, from USTR, was quoted as saying that the Chinese "presented information and their own rationale" for their actions, and that the issue is "still under review." The White House commercial space launch policy issued a month later said only that, "[t]here also must be an effective means of enforcing international agreements related to space launch goods and services." The National Space Society (NSS), a grass-roots space advocacy group, filed a draft petition under Section 301 of the 1974 Trade Act demanding that the agreement with China be enforced, although a formal petition was never filed. Since the U.S. has decided not to approve export licenses for other reasons (discussed above), NSS is not pursuing the issue at this time.

On February 20, 1991, the Senate passed S.320, the Omnibus Export Amendments Act of 1991, which contains language (section 126) prohibiting export of U.S.-made satellites to China for launch unless the President certifies that China is adhering to the launch services agreement it signed with the U.S. in 1989. The language is identical to that contained in H.R.4643, the Export Facilitation Act, which passed Congress in 1990, but was vetoed by the President. (The language in H.R.4643 was in an amendment sponsored by Representative Solomon during House consideration of the bill on June 10, 1990. During the debate, Representative Solomon said that he did not intend to affect the AUSSAT export licenses.) House action on S.320 is pending.

Regarding the Arabsat contract, Chen Shouchun, vice president of CGWIC asserted that Arianespace, not China, charges unfair prices. For example, he noted that it took only 18 months to develop the Long March 2E booster (the newest version), compared to the 3–4 years it would have taken in the West. Therefore, CGWIC can charge lower prices that nevertheless accurately reflect its costs. He also stated that Ariane has had more failures than Chinese launch vehicles and those costs must be borne by customers. From his point of view, China was abiding by the terms of the U.S.-China agreement. Lin Huabao, deputy chief of engineering at the Chinese Academy of Space Technology (attached to the Ministry of Aerospace Industry), went further in stating that the U.S.-China agreement itself is unfair. "China is a sovereign country. There should not be any limits imposed by outside governments like this. For a sovereign nation, this is not a good thing."

This particular issue became moot in the spring of 1991 when the Arabsat consortium terminated the contract with CGWIC and subsequently signed with Arianespace for the launch. The Arabsat Consortium has not revealed what led to the change in plans, nor have any of the parties revealed Arianespace's price. One media report asserted that the change was due "at least in part to Arabsat's realization that the infrastructure/support required to launch on Long March would be more complicated and expensive than originally anticipated." A Chinese space official, Zhang Jianye, asserts that "Aerospatiale acted in a very unfriendly and unfair way," delaying action to apply for an export license, and substantially inflating the charges it would assess the Arabsat Consortium for launch support services. Zhang alleges that Aerospatiale would have charged four or five times as much as Hughes charged for supporting the Asiasat launch in 1990.

An Aerospatiale representative countered that the company had made an "exhaustive study" of how much support would be needed to assure a successful launch and determined its charges accordingly.

At about the same time, the Indonesian government selected an American company, McDonnell Douglas, over CGWIC and Arianespace for launch of a Palapa communications satellite. The issue garnered much interest because CGWIC had indicated willingness to accept goods (such as oil) in lieu of cash to pay part of the price. Western reports indicated that some of the Indonesian government's rationale in choosing McDonnell Douglas was uncertainty about whether the U.S. would issue an export license if CGWIC were selected. China's Zhang argues that the U.S. Government pressured the Indonesians not to choose a Chinese launch vehicle; a Department of State official responded that the Indonesians asked for the Department's advice and were given no recommendation, but "all the hoops" through which the export license request would have to go were explained.

EXPORT CONTROLS AND TRADE IN SPACE-RELATED GOODS AND SERVICES

The earlier part of this chapter deals with space-related international trade issues from the perspective of ensuring that U.S. industry enjoys possible opportunities to sell its goods and services abroad, an avowed goal of the U.S. government. Set against this U.S. policy, however, are numerous laws and regulations designed to restrict the availability of the same goods and services. These laws and regulations, collectively known as "export controls," are intended to protect U.S. national security and to promote U.S. foreign policy interests by preventing the export of U.S. goods, services, and technical information to specified countries, or to permit such exports only under strict controls. In general, U.S. export controls focus on controlling products, services, and data from U.S. high technology industries, including U.S. space and space-related industries, that could contribute significantly to the military potential of U.S. adversaries. In order to protect such items from diversion, some form of license is generally required to export or reexport them to almost any destination in the world (Canada is a special exception), including the United States' closest allies. (The authors gratefully acknowledge the extensive assistance of H. Jack McCall, Hunton & Williams, and James Schoettler, Dewey Ballantine, with this section.)

Existing U.S. export controls fall into two broad categories: national security controls, which relate to transfers of goods or technical data to designated "controlled countries" (for example, the People's Republic of China), and foreign policy controls, which are parallel controls implemented to fulfill specific goals of U.S. foreign policy (for example, and of particular note here, chemical, biological, nuclear and missile nonproliferation). *See* Berlack and Hunt, Overview of U.S. Export Controls, in Coping with U.S. Export Controls 13–26 (E. Berlack & C. Hunt eds. 1991).

Obviously, U.S. export controls offer considerable potential for conflict with another important policy, that of promoting U.S. trade, either by denying to U.S. companies access to potential markets or, more typically, by imposing burdensome licensing requirements that impede the ability of U.S. companies to make sales in already established markets. *See, e.g.*, Committee on Science, Engineering & Public Policy, Balancing the National Interest: U.S. National Security Export Controls and Global Economic Competition (1987) (finding that overcomplex and overinclusive export control regulations impede domestic innovation and harm ability of U.S. firms to compete in international markets). As the United States attempts to adapt its Cold War–based export control framework to a post–Cold War world, efforts are being made to simplify and streamline the control environment.

Whether the objective of simplified licensing will be achieved is difficult to predict, however, as the strictness with which the United States applies export controls is more a function of U.S. policy requirements than of the legal infrastructure upon which export controls are based. In addition, the overlapping regulatory jurisdictions, the web of institutional loyalties, and the spectrum of regulation in this area of law are such as to confound the legal practitioner and delay, frustrate and possibly thwart various commercial transactions. With over a dozen federal agencies and departments having a role to play in export licensing decisions, affecting as many as 81,000 individual licensing cases yearly (*see* Committee on Science, Engineering, and Public Policy, Finding Common Ground: U.S. Export Controls in a Changed Global Environment 80, 94–103 (1991)) delays in obtaining export licenses should simply be considered a cost of doing business.

A strong, general impetus for action to strengthen export controls was provided in the mid-1980s by Japanese and Swedish sales to the Soviet Union of sophisticated equipment useful in modernizing the Soviet submarine fleet, resulting in the so-called "Toshiba-Kongsberg scandal." *See* Wrubel, The Toshiba-Kongsberg Incident: Shortcomings of CoCom and Recommendations for Increased Effectiveness of Export Controls, 4 American University Journal of International Law and Policy 241 (1989). It took Iraqi use of improved SCUD missiles against Iran, Israel, and Saudi Arabia (not to mention U.S. troops) in spite of existing export controls governing missile technology to bring the issue of missile nonproliferation to the attention of policymakers.

Yet tensions and crosscurrents remain. At the time of this writing, the U.S. Government seems to be contemplating additional reforms in the export control area in order to boost U.S. exports and simplify the regulatory maze. *See, e.g.*, Iannotta, Administration to Relax Rocket Export Rules, Space News, August 16–22, 1993 at 1. Nonetheless, the prospect for substantial reform (as opposed to mere loosening) of U.S. export licensing procedures and rules seems poor at this writing.

On the other hand, export controls may themselves be used in service of the goals of promoting U.S. trade—for example, restrictions on the export of U.S. satellite technology may be used to frustrate foreign dumping of launch services by depriving the offending foreign country of payloads. Using export controls in this fashion is, however, a two-edged sword. While restrictions on export of U.S. technology may accomplish important goals in the short run, they encourage foreign nations reliant on that technology to work harder to achieve independence, ultimately undermining U.S. leverage and creating new competition in international markets. In addition, to the extent that export controls are seen as a tool for maintaining U.S. economic position rather than as a means of promoting international security, cooperation from allied nations—which is absolutely essential if export controls are to be effective—is likely to diminish markedly.

Maintaining international security is, of course, the primary purpose of export controls, and it is an important purpose in the context of many space goods and services. Many space-related technologies are of considerable military importance: for example, any nation capable of launching satellites (or even sizable suborbital payloads) is capable of delivering nuclear warheads via ballistic missile. At the time of this writing, a number of nations have such a capability or are likely to acquire it in the near future: such nations number not only the traditional space powers but also the European nations, the People's Republic of China, Japan, India, Pakistan, Argentina, Brazil, Israel, and South Africa, with more entrants likely. It is no coincidence that many of these nations possess (or are developing) nuclear weapons technology as well.

U.S. and international efforts to limit the spread of nuclear weapons technology have been a qualified success to date. Although some nations have acquired nuclear capabilities, that number has been smaller than many expected in the 1960s and no nation since World War II has exploded a nuclear weapon in anger. This has been made possible by a system of international controls on nuclear technology that, although far from seamless, has served (in combination with political pressure) to restrict the transfer of such technology considerably.

At the heart of the matter is the dual use conundrum. The United States and other nations have attempted to institute a similar regime (discussed *infra*) with regard to missile and space technologies capable of delivering nuclear warheads, but the prospects for success there are much less. There are two key reasons for this grim scenario. First, the agreement comes much later in the day: many nations have already developed or acquired basic launch technology, making it harder to keep the lid on matters—particularly as that technology is, overall, less difficult than that embodied in nuclear weapons. The German V-2, which was the first liquid fuelled launch vehicle, would easily have sufficed as a nuclear delivery vehicle; the now-infamous SCUD, a postwar Soviet derivative of the V-2, is also adequate for the purpose. Second, the "dual use" character of many space technologies means that they necessarily appear in various commercial incarnations that are virtually impossible to control entirely.

H. Jack McCall, "The Inexorable Advance of Technology"? American and International Efforts to Curb Missile Proliferation 32 Jurimetrics: Journal of Law, Science and Technology 387 (1992)

One of the most pernicious problem areas in assessing export controls and curbing missile proliferation is in monitoring dual-purpose technologies, technologies that present at the same time both legitimate civil and military purposes. Due to their inherent capabilities of being used for both functions, dual-purpose (or dual-use) technologies present a dilemma: how does a nation prevent the transfer of militarily critical missile technologies capable of boosting another nation's military potential, while not impeding scientific, technical or commercial progress? The resulting attempts to formulate unilateral and multilateral answers to this dilemma have generated a wide compendium of statutes and regulatory regimes with frequently overlapping—and, also frequently, competing—jurisdictions and policy goals.

A few examples will illustrate the complexities presented in identifying, monitoring, and tracking such items, as opposed to the relative ease of observing and tracking shipments of completed missiles or military-specific technology.

i. Commercial- and Space-Related Rockets and Boosters

Historically, the nations that have taken the lead in space exploration have done so by utilizing what were essentially military missiles or military booster rockets to loft the first satellites, space probes, and manned space capsules. The Soviet Union launched Sputnik I, its Lunik moon probes, and all its manned capsules using modified intercontinental ballistic missiles. Likewise, America relied on its first ballistic missiles to launch early satellites as well as Mercury and Gemini manned capsules. The Chinese have followed suit, developing their series of satellite boosters from earlier military ballistic missiles.

Japan and Europe entered the space launch field with their own civilian satellite launch boosters, and other commercial enterprises and concerns have entered the field with a host of small sounding rockets, used for atmospheric testing, up to larger boosters capable of putting satellites into orbit. However, as one observer has noted, dual uses are always implicit in even purely civilian, commercial booster designs and sales: "The only essential differences between a [space-launch vehicle] and a ballistic missile are its trajectory and the payload it carries. Suppliers cannot 'denature' space-launch technology and be certain that it will be used only for civilian purposes. Once a nation has the ability to place a satellite in orbit it is, at most, only a few years from being able to launch an intermediate range ballistic missile. ... The differences relate to intentions, not capabilities."

The minimal nature of such differences is amply provided by the experiences of a German company, Orbital Transport und Raketen, A.G. ("OTRAG"). After designing and testing a variety of boosters with varying success, OTRAG marketed itself as "a peaceful commercial alternative to Western and Soviet launch services." After using test facilities in Zaire and Libya—at a time when Libya's highly controversial leader Muammar Quaddafi had already declared his intentions to acquire missile technology—OTRAG was denounced by many Western nations, including the United States, in 1978–81, and ultimately withdrew its operations to Germany and Sweden.

Brazil, too, has adapted its own government-financed rockets, originally conceived as sounding rockets for upper atmospheric research, for military purposes. Its Sonda III sounding rocket, originally intended for atmospheric testing, was converted into a short-range missile. However, its follow-up model—also ostensibly a civilian sounding rocket—has been successfully test-launched and has been touted to foreign customers as the Orbita MB/EE-600, allegedly developed with Libyan assistance. Iraq was also alleged to have contributed financially to another Brazilian missile program, the Avibràs SS-300, under development in 1989.

Israel has launched two satellites into orbit to date using an unusually powerful booster, the Shavit II, in September 1988 and April 1990. Although Israel claimed that the Shavit II is intended purely for peaceful space exploration purposes, various analysts have rejected this description: "[I]t is difficult to imagine that Israel, with its over-stretched defense budget, would develop two completely different sets of boosters for missiles and space-launch purposes, when one set could be used for both missions."

Civilian booster technology is perhaps the most obvious example of uncontrolled dual-purpose technology's latest threat: "Because of the inherent similarities [and also the mixed motivations], even the most genuinely civilian program has military potential ... [and such programs] will be defended by their makers as peaceful space launchers up to the moment they are used to deliver military warheads."

ii. Other Dual-Purpose Technology Transfers

A host of items with civilian uses conceivably can also have military purposes that require monitoring or export controls to limit or halt their transfers. These items run the gamut from components and testers of missile-related final products (end items)—such as high-speed electronic switches, or krytons, useful in civilian centrifuges but also in nuclear warhead triggers; flash X-ray machines; chemicals, such as ammonium perchlorate, useful for rocket propellants and a key component of commercial fertilizers (and, of course, missile engines); gyroscopes; high-speed capacitors, used in everything from cars to high-speed laser research, but also for nuclear device timer triggers—to the end items themselves, such as computer systems; Global Positioning System satellite navigational signals, useful for commercial aircraft (and for cruise missiles) to adjust their accuracy; and even to commercial trucks modified to serve as mobile missile transporters.

In summation, the entire heart of the legal challenges posed by the dual-use dichotomy is best expressed by a quotation from President Kennedy. When asked what was the difference between the Atlas rocket that launched astronaut John Glenn's capsule and the same nuclear-tipped Atlas missiles directed toward the Soviet Union, JFK responded simply: "Attitude."

The modern industrial world is so dependent on precision machining, high-strength and high-temperature alloys, sophisticated avionics, and other technologies that collectively constitute "space launch technologies" that a complete ban on exports would constitute technological and market suicide. Some seepage is thus inevitable. Despite controls, then, the primary barrier to the spread of nuclear missile technology is likely to be political pressure from the more advanced countries. Whether those nations possess the political will and wherewithal to exert that pressure in the face of other (often conflicting) policy goals is unclear.

In the meantime, however, export controls remain in existence, and it is likely that they will be of some use in retarding, if not halting, the spread of nuclear, chemical and biological missile capability. The following section provides a brief overview of existing controls, with emphasis on U.S. mechanisms.

Existing Export Controls

The current U.S. and international export control regime constitutes one of the most confusing and technically demanding areas of law practice. The export of commercial space products, services and technology, for example, is generally controlled under the provisions of the State Department's International Traffic in Arms Regulations, 22 CFR pts. 120–130 (1993). Issued under the authority of Section 38 of the Arms Export Control Act, 22 U.S.C. § 2778, the ITAR governs the licensing of exports and reexports of "defense articles and services," i.e., goods and services that are "inherently military in character" and consequently included on the U.S. Munitions List, 22 CFR 120.3. If an item appears on this list, which is administered by the State Department's Office of Munitions Controls, an exporter must obtain a license from the office before the item can be exported. Besides items generally considered to be weapons or war material, three categories—categories IV, VII, and XV—specifically list launch vehicles, spacecraft, and associated launch equipment as being Munitions List items. *Id.* § 121.11. Not all space-related products fall under the ITAR, however. Certain commodities intended for commercial space applications are exempt from ITAR control and instead fall under the Commerce Department's Export Administration Regulations (EAR), 15 CFR pts. 770–799 (1993). These items are overseen by the Commerce Department's Bureau of Export Administration (BXA). The fact that the purchaser of these commodities may be a military entity is not necessarily relevant to whether a space-related product is considered a "defense article" or a "dual-use" item, 22 C.F.R. 120.3. Similar regulations circumscribe exports that are capable of violating nuclear nonproliferation policies, 15 CFR 778.2–778.6 (1993). Certain nonmilitary communications satellites, formerly listed on the munitions list, have recently been moved to BXA supervision.

Given the overlap between the ITAR and the EAR, it is often difficult to determine precisely which controls are applicable in a given case. Indeed, export control practice requires not only a substantial knowledge of the technology involved, but the necessarily arbitrary practice of classifying technologies and destinations results in an administrative practice of case-by-case evaluation of license applications, with predictably arbitrary and variable results. Worse yet from the perspective of lawyers and their clients, some international export control agreements (for example, the recent multinational agreement on nuclear missile technologies) are actually secret, necessitating the partial secrecy (and/or the considerable ambiguity) of many implementing regulations. *See, e.g.*, Committee on Science, Engineering, and Public Policy, Finding Common Ground: U.S. Export Controls in a Changed Global Environment 134 (1991). Leaving aside the dubious constitutionality of subjecting U.S. citizens to what amount to bodies of secret law, this practice unavoidably adds additional layers of complexity. Furthermore, the enabling legislation for the EAR, the Export Administration Act, 50 U.S.C. App. § 2401 *et seq.*, is expressly exempt from provisions of the Administrative Procedure Act, 5 U.S.C. §§ 551–59, particularly the APA's provisions for judicial review. This exemption has been accused of costing U.S. firms business opportunities abroad even as it denies them basic administrative due process at home. *See generally* Howard Fenton, Reforming the Procedures of the Export Administration Act: A Call for Openness and Administrative Due Process, 27 Texas International Law Journal 1 (1992).

In dealing with these problems, and export controls generally, it is strongly recommended that space lawyers and businesspeople seek experienced and qualified specialist counsel in the export control field; export control lawyers, meanwhile, are urged to consult closely with space counsel and clients, as a complete knowledge of the industry and its overall legal environment is essential to dealing with its export control problems. Because of the intricate and fast-changing nature of the field, this book cannot hope to serve as a detailed guide. The most it can provide is some sense of the outlines and flavor of the field.

The most important point to remember is that export controls affect far more than the average layperson would expect. Almost anyone would expect to run into export control issues when exporting ballistic missiles, or guidance systems for the same. But the prohibitions and restrictions of U.S. export controls are much farther reaching than that. Not only goods, but also technology and information may constitute prohibited exports. Seemingly innocuous items, like communications satellites or computers, may be restricted. And the term "export" encompasses not only the shipment of goods or information from the United States to a point outside the United States, but also other transactions, such as the communication of information to a foreign citizen within the United States, or the "reexport" of information from an approved destination abroad to some other location. Furthermore, penalties are severe, authorities have considerable discretion, and the right to appeal an adverse decision is extremely limited. For a good survey of the structure of export controls, *see* McFadden, Snyder & Schoettler, The Structure of Export Licensing, in The Commerce Department Speaks 379 (D. Riggs ed. 1987).

NOTES

1. From reading the above, it should be obvious that many space-related transactions will require close cooperation with specialist export control counsel. Because of the broad sweep of export controls and the dual-use character of many space technologies, virtually any transborder shipment of space hardware or technical information is likely to raise export control issues. Leaving aside such obvious elements as launch vehicles, many other space technologies—such as satellites, radiation-hardened chips (essential for satellites but with obvious military implications), and telemetry gear—are treated as "munitions" for export purposes, 22 CFR 121.1 (1993) (Category XV). Given the stiff penalties that can result from illegal exports, it is very important that all technology transfers in the space area be scrutinized for export control compliance.

As mentioned above, such transfers need not involve any shipment of goods (or even data) across borders. For example, disclosure of technical data needed to mate a communications satellite to a foreign launch vehicle, even if such disclosure is made within the United States to a representative of the foreign launch provider, and even if the satellite itself is manufactured abroad, could qualify as an "export" of technical data. Leaving aside the question of the treatment of data that are classified and therefore subject to special controls, *see* Department of Defense, Industrial Security Manual for Safeguarding Classified Information (1987), the mere disclosure within the United States of nonclassified data controlled by either the ITAR or the EAR can be subject to export license requirements if the disclosure is made to a foreign national or with the intent or knowledge that the data will be released to a foreign national or taken out of the United States.

A broad definition of the term "export" raises special concerns for companies offering launch services, because the launch of a vehicle could be considered to be an export from the United States. Indeed, prior to the enactment of the Commercial Space Launch Act of 1984, a launch was considered an export subject to ITAR licensing requirements, S. Rep. No. 656, 98th Cong., 2d Sess. 17–18 (1984). Section 21 (b) of the Commercial Space Launch Act, however, specifically provides that the mere launching of a payload or a vehicle cannot, solely by reason of the launch, be considered an export under any export control law, Pub. L. 98-575, § 21 (b), 98 Stat. 3055, 3063 (1984) codified at 49 U.S.C. 2620 (1992). In accordance with this provision, the ITAR now specifically excludes the launch of a payload or vehicle from its definition of an export, but of course the statutory language would preclude the application of any export control regulation in any case.

2. The criminal penalties for violation of the ITAR and EAR are significant. Under the Export Administration Act, each willful violation of the EAR, with knowledge that the export will be used with the benefit of, or that the ultimate destination of the exported goods or technology is, a country to which exports are restricted for national security or foreign policy purposes, may subject the violator to a $250,000 fine, ten years imprisonment or both if an individual or, if a corporation, a fine of one million dollars or up to five times the value of the exported items, whichever is greater, 50 U.S. C. app § 2410 (b). The federal Sentencing Guidelines also designate criminal penalties for such violations, as does the Arms Export Control Act, 22 U.S.C. § 2778. *See generally* United States v. Helmy, 712 F. Supp. 1423 (E.D. Cal. 1989), *aff'd in part* 951 F.2d 933 (9th Cir. 1991), which upheld the constitutionality of the Export Administration Act, the AECA, the ITAR and EAR, and U.S. Sentencing guideline § 2M5.2 setting base offense levels for the export of "sophisticated weaponry." The "sophisticated weaponry" in this case was material for the construction of rocket engine nozzles destined for the infamous Condor II project, a joint Iraqi/Egyptian/Argentine project to construct a ballistic missile similar to the U.S. Pershing II.

3. Iraq's "War of the Cities" against Iranian cities in 1987–88, its 1990 invasion of Kuwait, and the ensuing Gulf War of 1991 drew international attention to the threats posed by rampant missile proliferation in the Third World, especially when accompanied by nuclear or chemical weapons development programs. The use of Iraqi SCUD missiles against predominantly civilian targets, in tandem with barely veiled threats to equip such missiles with chemical or biological warheads brought international condemnation. Revelations that American and German firms had provided the Iraqi government with much necessary equipment, in apparent defiance of the ITAR and EAR, added to the impetus to curb missile, chemical, and nuclear proliferation. *See generally* U.S. House of Rep., Comm. on Govt. Operations, Strengthening the Export Licensing System, H. Rep. No. 102–37, 102d Cong. 1st Sess. (1991).

In March 1991, the Bush Administration and the Bureau of Export Administration promulgated the so-called Enhanced Proliferation Control Initiative (EPCI) in order to prevent the acquisition or further development of biological, chemical and missile warfare technologies by various nations. In support of this initiative, BXA issued three new regulations imposing major "foreign policy controls" on dual use chemicals, equipment and data. *See* 15 CFR 778.7–778.9 (1993). The following excerpt explores the issues created by these regulations.

Glenn Reynolds, New Developments in International Trade, October 1991

This notice represents a heightened effort to use export controls to limit the spread of nonnuclear weapons of mass destruction. The new rule contains three types of restrictions:

- controls on specific commodities and technical data believed to be particularly useful with regard to chemical or biological weapons, or missiles;
- controls on exports and reexports to specific end-users found to be engaged in production, development, etc., of chemical or biological weapons, or missiles;
- controls on many activities—some of which do not involve exports or reexports—by U.S. entities that might contribute to the proliferation of chemical or biological weapons or missiles.

The outlines of these controls are addressed below.

Technology Controls

These controls are aimed at specific products, technical data, and software that are used in the design, development, production, or use of missiles and chemical or biological weapons. An *individual validated license* (IVL) is required for export or reexport of these items to any country in groups QSTVWYZ—*i.e.*, to any country other than Canada. The specific chemicals subject to U.S. foreign policy controls are identified in ECCN 4798B; the specific equipment and materials are identified in ECCNs 5129F, 5132F, 5133F, 5134F, 5135F, 5140F, 5141F, and 5797F. Chemicals under ECCN 4798B require an IVL for export to all destinations except CoCom members, Austria, Iceland, New Zealand, and Switzerland. Equipment and materials require a validated license for export to Country Groups S and Z, and the regions and countries listed in Supplement 5 to part 778 of the EAR.

Limitations on biological weapons, certain viruses, bacteria, fungi and protozoa, identified in ECCNs 4997B and 4998B are even more stringent: exports require an IVL to all destinations except Canada. Equipment and material deemed useful for the production of biological agents are covered under ECCNs 5165F, 5167F, 5170F and 5997F. These items, too, require an IVL for export to Country Groups S and Z, and the regions and countries listed in Supplement No. 5 to EAR Part 778.

Technical data are equally subject to these controls. For example, technical data license GTDR is not available for export, reexport, transfer or release of technical data for the production of chemical precursors under ECCN 4798B, except for exports and reexports to CoCom countries, Austria, Iceland, New Zealand, and Switzerland. An IVL is required instead. Similarly, GTDR is not available for the export, reexport, release or transfer of technical data related to the production of the biological agents subject to these new controls. An IVL is required to export to *all* destinations except Canada. Similar restrictions apply to data related to the materials or equipment subject to these controls. GTDR is also now unavailable for the export, reexport, transfer or release of technical data for facilities to produce the precursors controlled by ECCN 4798B, except to the CoCom countries, Austria, Iceland, New Zealand, or Switzerland. This includes:

- overall plant design
- design, specification or procurement of equipment
- supervision of construction, installation, or operation of complete plant or components thereof;
- training of personnel; or
- consultation on specific problems involving such facilities

End User Controls

The second type of restriction is based on whether the end-user (that is, the foreign purchaser or user of the exported product) is engaged in prohibited activities related to chemical or biological weapons or missiles. For missiles, the new rule requires an IVL to export any commodity, software, or technical data (except for technical data that are eligible for general license GTDA and commodities identified in ECCNs 7599I or 7999I), when the exporter knows or is informed by the Commerce Department that the export or reexport:

1. is destined for a project listed in supplement 6 to EAR Part 778; or
2. will be used in the design, development, production or use of missiles in or by a country where a project listed in Supplement 6 is located, whether or not that use involves a listed project. Note, however, that Supplement 6 is currently still being prepared. [It has since been published.]

For chemical or biological weapons, an IVL is required to export any commodity, software or technical data (again, excluding technical data eligible for general license GTDA and commodities identified in ECCNs 7599I or 7999I), when the exporter knows or is informed by the Commerce Department that it will be used in the design, development, production, stockpiling or use of chemical or biological weapons in or by a country listed in Supplement 5 to part 778. In addition to these controls, an IVL is also required for an export or reexport to an individual, entity or project *anywhere in the world* where Commerce has informed the exporter or reexporter that an IVL is required. Such notice may be either through publication of a change to the EAR, or through notice directly to the exporter or reexporter. Direct notice may be oral or in writing, although oral notice must be followed up with written notice within two days.

Restrictions on U.S. Persons

Beyond the above restrictions, the new rule also imposes controls on the activity of U.S. entities which could aid in the design, development, or use of missiles in or by a country where a project listed in Supplement 6 is located, or of chemical or biological weapons in or by a country listed in Supplement 5. Such assistance need not involve exports of controlled goods or data—it can include anything from financing to supplying paper clips. "U.S. person" is defined in the new rule as including:

- any citizen or permanent resident alien of the U.S.;
- any entity organized under U.S. laws or the law of any political subdivision, territory, etc. of the United States, including the foreign branches of such entities; and
- any person in the United States.

NOTE: *Great care must be exercised in relying on the technical definition of U.S. person to define liability under this regulation.* U.S. authorities are likely to take the position that any participation by any U.S. person in a prohibited activity is sufficient to apply this rule—even if the activity in question is actually carried out by an entity or person not falling within the technical definition of U.S. person. Therefore, even if no U.S. goods or technology are involved, great care must still be exercised before undertaking any dealings with *any* facility, entity, or individual known to be engaged in chemical, biological, or missile weapons activities. This *in terrorem* effect of the regulations is entirely intentional.

These new rules are likely to make a significant difference in the way U.S. companies—particularly those in the chemical, biological, or aerospace and semiconductor fields—do business abroad. In particular, it is absolutely essential that all such companies screen their shipments to ensure that they identify any end users who are engaged in an activity related to the proliferation of these weapons systems. This screening should be incorporated into their Export Control Internal Control Programs, and the companies should take great care to stress to line managers that this process is vitally important. These new rules are the beginning—not the end—of the process of realigning U.S. export control laws to adjust to a new and different world. Sales to third-world countries that would have been winked at (or even, alas, tacitly encouraged) a few years ago are now strictly prohibited, and are likely to generate severe sanctions, bad publicity, and perhaps even criminal prosecution. As the world changes, companies must change with it. Companies that work vigorously to establish good internal controls, and a strong internal culture of export control compliance, will have an advantage as the rules grow in the next decade.

These regulations have been subjected to considerable criticism from a number of commentators. *See, e.g.*, Waite & Goldberg, Responsible Export Controls or "Nets to Catch the Wind?" The Commerce Department's New U.S. Controls on Exports of Chemical Precursors, Equipment and Technical Data Intended to Prevent Development of Chemical and Biological Weapons, 22 California Western International Law Journal 193 (1991–92). Many commentators have suggested that the impact of these regulations might chiefly be to advantage one exporter over another—and particularly to advantage foreign exporters over domestic exporters. Furthermore, the "knows or has reason to know" standard has been attacked as essentially conscripting U.S. manufacturers and suppliers—who may have very little ability to gather intelligence about their customers—as front-line troops in export enforcement. Certainly this approach represents a substantial change from previous policy. *See* 22 CFR Supplement No. 6 to Part 778 (1993), and Sloniewski & DeVaughn, Developments in Export Controls: The Non-Proliferation Initiatives, in The Commerce Department Speaks (1992) at pp. 1027–49 (Wendell Wilkie ed. 1992).

The EPCI regulations supplement additional rules that are designed to limit the spread of usable technology for missiles capable of delivering nuclear weapons, rules known as the Missile Technology Control Regime (MTCR). For more on this topic *see* H. Jack McCall, The Missile Technology Control Regime: An Update, 20 Journal of Space Law 61 (1992); H. Jack McCall, "The Inexorable Advance of Technology"? American and International Efforts to Curb Ballistic Missile Proliferation, 32 Jurimetrics: Journal of Law, Science and Technology 387 (1992); Note, Arms Control: Export Controls on Missile Technology, 29 Harvard International Law Journal 142 (1988).

The MTCR does not ban *all* missiles or rockets capable of carrying nuclear payloads. Rather, recognizing that dual uses are necessarily implicit in many nations' rocketry programs, the MTCR focuses only on those nuclear-capable systems with ranges in excess of 190 miles (300 kilometers) and payloads greater than 1100 pounds (500 kilograms). Nevertheless, many rockets and space launch vehicles fit within these rather broad parameters. The MTCR, in fact, specifically lists as "items of greatest sensitivity" complete rocket systems, including space launch vehicles and sounding rockets, as well as booster stages, reentry vehicles (capsules), and guidance systems. Agreement on Guidelines for the Transfer of Equipment and Technology Related to Missiles, April 16, 1987, 26 International Legal Materials 599–600 (1987). Since 1987 fifteen more nations have entered the MTCR's fold, with many—in particular, the U.K. and Germany—devising their own domestic implementing regulations.

The U.S. regulations implementing the MTCR, which have been incorporated into the EPCI revisions to the EAR, are far reaching. They require a "validated license" for export of equipment and technical data to every country except Canada. Requiring a validated license, rather than a general or special license, means that each shipment must be separately approved. The term "missiles capable of delivering nuclear weapons" is defined as "rocket systems (including ballistic missile systems, space launch vehicles, and sounding rockets) and unmanned air vehicle systems (including cruise missile systems, target drones and reconnaissance drones) capable of delivering at least 500 kilograms (kg) payload to a range of at least 300 kilometers." 15 CFR § 778.7 (a) (1993).

Since a validated license is required, exports will be reviewed on a case-by-case basis. This will prove to be a complex and time-consuming affair, since the regulations cover 26 commodity classifications (including aircraft electronics, radiation and temperature hardened computer chips, vibration test equipment, and analog-to-digital converters), many of which have important civilian applications, 15 CFR Supplement No. 1 to part 799.1 (1993).

It is unclear how successful these controls will be in curbing the spread of nuclear missile technology. Although modern nuclear missiles certainly depend on components of the sort described in the regulations, the power of nuclear weapons allows missile designers substantial leeway in terms of accuracy and means that even relatively primitive vehicles (such as the German V-2 of World War II) or extremely small vehicles (such as cruise missiles or private aircraft) can deliver nuclear weapons. Thus, although the regulations may make it more difficult to construct nuclear missiles, they by no means make it impossible. The same general principles apply to missile delivery of chemical weapons, the "poor man's atomic bomb." For more on these themes, see generally Aaron Karp, The Commercialization of Space Technology and the Spread of Ballistic Missiles, in International Space Policy: Legal, Economic and Strategic Options for the Twentieth Century and Beyond 179–91 (D. Papp & J. McIntyre eds., 1987); Dyslin, Reform of the Multilateral Export Control Mechanism for the Twenty-First Century: Redefining "the Enemy" and "War," 10 Boston University International Law Journal 1, 22–31 (1992).

As the Dyslin article notes, the existing export control framework was designed for a Cold War environment, and was primarily intended to keep critical technologies out of the hands of the Soviet Union and its allies. As the Cold War wound down, and after the breakup of the Soviet Union, the challenge became greater. Today's problem lies in keeping such technologies out of the hands of rogue states and terrorist groups. Given the more modest goals of such entities, and their greater number and variety, this is likely to be difficult to achieve—and even more difficult to achieve without sacrificing civil liberties or commercial markets.

8

The Law of Private Commercial Activities in Outer Space

Although many of the topics in prior chapters contain material that touches on non-public activities in space, most of the discussion has centered on public law issues. For instance, private entities play a major role in the space satellite communications industry, but our discussion in Chapter 6 focused primarily on the governance structure and international dimensions of such quasi-public bodies as INTELSAT and the ITU. Likewise, Chapter 7, on space-related trade issues, emphasized the applicability (or lack thereof) of the international legal regime established by the General Agreement on Tariffs and Trade (GATT), as well as trade disputes arising under the trade laws of the United States.

In this chapter, we turn our attention to issues of private law that are of importance to commercial activities in space. We are concerned here not with the large-scale legal regimes that govern the interactions between States in space, but rather with the law that governs the smaller-scale interactions between private parties' space activities. (Actually, as you will see, the fact that national governments still dominate most sectors of the space "industry" means that one of the private parties to a space-related transaction may be a State; but the legal issues involved—contracts, torts, and the like—are still *private*, bilateral legal issues.)

Thus in this chapter we address the following topics:

- Jurisdiction: Which country's law applies to private space activities?
- Tort law: How are private parties, as opposed to governments, to be compensated for damage suffered as a result of accidents in outer space?
- Contracts: What special problems are presented by private agreements concerning space activities—primarily commercial launch contracts?
- Intellectual Property: How are inventions made in space protected under U.S. patent law?
- Administrative law: How are private commercial space activities regulated by the U.S. government?

We turn now to the first of these topics, jurisdiction.

JURISDICTION

The following excerpt is from an Office of Technology Assessment (OTA) study of the legal aspects of space stations. It concisely summarizes the major jurisdictional issues raised by space activities.

Office of Technology Assessment, Space Stations and the Law: Selected Legal Issues 25–32 (1986)

Jurisdiction over Space Station Activities

This section examines the concept of jurisdiction and explains how it might be applied to private and government-owned space stations.

A. The Concept of Jurisdiction

Jurisdiction is a legal concept used to describe a state's right to take action—e.g., to prescribe and enforce rules of law—with respect to a particular person, thing, or event. In its inception, the principle of jurisdiction was primarily territorial, deriving from the belief that the power of a nation to act within its own borders was "necessarily exclusive and absolute ... susceptible of no limitation not imposed by itself." [Comments of Chief Justice Marshall in Schooner Exchange v. McFaddon, 11 U.S. (7 Cranch) 116, 136 (1812).] But the actions of nations have rarely been limited to their territory. As a result of international trade and travel, and military and political cooperation and competition, the concept of jurisdiction had to expand to comprehend the myriad interactions of states. [The following paragraph is from a footnote in the original.]

Although there are many jurisdictional rationales, all require that there be some genuine link between the state and the persons, property, or events over which jurisdiction is claimed. States have traditionally sought to assert jurisdiction on certain bases or principles. As usually identified, these include:

1. *The Territorial Principle*—A state may exercise jurisdiction with respect to an act occurring in whole or in part in its territory.
2. *The Nationality Principle*—A state may exercise jurisdiction with respect to its own national, wherever he may be.
3. *The Protective Principle*—A state may exercise jurisdiction with respect to certain types of acts wherever, and by whomever, committed where the conduct substantially affects certain vital state interests, such as its security, its property, or the integrity of its governmental process.
4. *The Universality Principle*—A state may exercise jurisdiction with respect to certain specific universally condemned crimes, principally piracy, wher-

ever and by whomever committed, without regard to the connection of the conduct with that state.

5. *The Passive Personality Principle*—A state may exercise jurisdiction with respect to any act committed outside its territory by a foreigner which substantially affects the person or property of a citizen.

(S. Houston Lay, Howard J. Taubenfeld, The Law Relating to Activities of Man in Space, The University of Chicago Press, 1970).

Jurisdiction must be exercised some*where*, with respect to some*thing or person*. [J]urisdiction cannot be applied to the high seas or to outer space [except insofar as a nation may exercise jurisdiction and control over a ship *on* the high seas or a space object *in* outer space] because these areas are considered *res communis* under international law and therefore are not "places" that can be appropriated by claim of sovereignty. However, the 1967 Outer Space Treaty declares that a nation may exercise jurisdiction and control over objects in space, much as a nation may exercise jurisdiction over a ship at sea. Objects in space and ships at sea are treated (with some important limitations) as if they were part of the territory of the country on whose registry they are entered and whose flag they fly. [The legal fiction that ships on the high sea and space objects in orbit are like "floating islands" has not been universally accepted. The U.S. Supreme Court, in Cunard S.S. v. Mellon Co. 262 U.S. 100, 123 (1923), referred to the floating island theory as "a figure of speech, a metaphor."]

B. Extent of National Jurisdiction

International law recognizes a nation's jurisdiction over its citizens, its territory, territorial waters and airspace, and those ships and aircraft which it has registered. Whether nations have, through the exercise of their domestic laws, actually extended their jurisdictions to the full extent allowed by international law is a more complicated question.

With reference to U.S. jurisdiction over space activities, it will be important to distinguish between what the United States is capable of doing and what, through congressionally enacted legislation, it has already done. Absent a specific statement of congressional intent, U.S. courts have been reluctant to give extraterritorial reach to certain domestic laws. For example, in McCulloch v. Sociedad Nacional de Marineros de Honduras [372 U.S. 10 (1963)], the Court was asked to decide whether U.S. labor laws would apply to ships registered in Honduras and owned and operated by the Honduran subsidiary of a U.S. corporation. The Court noted that Congress had the "constitutional power to apply the National Labor Relations Act to the crews working foreign-flag ships, at least while they are in American waters," but decided that the resolution of the case depended on "whether Congress exercised that power." The court held: "to sanction the exercise of local sovereignty in this 'delicate field of international relations there must be present the affirmative intention of the Congress clearly expressed.'... Since neither we nor the parties are able to find any such clear expression, we hold the [National Labor Relations] Board was without jurisdiction. ..."

Similarly, in United States v. Cordova [89 F. Supp. 298 (E.D.N.Y. 1950)], the Court was asked to decide whether an assault committed in a U.S. flag airplane flying over the high seas was within the admiralty and maritime jurisdiction as described in the then current U.S. Criminal Code (18 U.S.C.A. Sec. 451). [At the time, 18 U.S.C.A. Sec. 451 stated that the admiralty and maritime jurisdiction of the United States extended to "American vessels on [the] high seas."] Although the Court noted that "Congress could, under its police power, have extended federal criminal jurisdiction to acts committed on board an airplane owned by an American national...," the applicable legislation (18 U.S.C.A. § 451) spoke only of "vessels" on the "high seas." The Court then concluded that "'vessel' ... evokes in the common mind a picture of a ship, not of a plane," and that no case or legal principle would "justify the extension of the words 'high seas' to the air space over them." [Cordova involved the interpretation of a criminal statute; therefore, under U.S. law, the statute was strictly construed. Not all statutes are strictly construed. For example, the Death on the High Seas Act [41 Stat. 537] (46 U.S.C. § 761), which provides a remedy for wrongful death occurring "on" the high seas, has been interpreted by several Federal courts to apply to tortious conduct "over" as well as "on" the high seas. *See* D'Aleman v. Pan American World Airways, 259 F.2d 493 [(2d Cir. 1958)].]

The U.S. statute defining the "special maritime and territorial jurisdiction of the United States" for criminal jurisdiction has since been modified to resolve the problem presented in United States v. Cordova and to try to anticipate those problems which might arise in future space activities. [18 U.S.C.A. Sec. 7.] Currently, this special jurisdiction includes:

1. ... any vessel belonging in whole or in part to the United States, or any citizen thereof, or to any corporation created by or under the laws of the United States. ...

5. Any aircraft belonging in whole or in part to the United States, or any citizen thereof, or to any corporation created by or under the laws of the United States, ... while such aircraft is in flight over the high seas, or over any other waters within the admiralty and maritime jurisdiction of the United States. ...

6. *Any vehicle used or designed for flight or navigation in space and on the registry of the United States pursuant to the [1967 Outer Space Treaty] ... and the [Registration Convention] ... while that vehicle is in flight ...* [emphasis added]

7. Any place outside the jurisdiction of any nation with respect to an offense by or against a national of the United States.

Given the restrictive interpretation of the U.S. jurisdiction presented in the McCulloch and Cordova cases, it is possible to imagine further problems even under the revised Criminal Code. For example, is a large, manned space vehicle "used or designed for flight or navigation in space"? If so, then paragraph 6 of the Criminal Code (above) would include a space station within the "special maritime and territorial jurisdiction" of the United States. However, since space stations have attributes which differ from those of space transportation vehicles—e.g., their size, complexity, multinational nature, duration in orbit, etc.—[the code provisions] might be more applicable to shuttle-type vehicles. If space stations did not meet the requirements of paragraph 6, they still might be included under the general provisions of paragraph 7.

In the future, it is entirely possible that some space stations will be privately owned. It is also possible that space stations owned in whole or in part by U.S. nationals or corporations will be registered in other countries. A state is generally considered to have jurisdiction to prescribe (though not necessarily enforce) rules of law regarding the conduct of its nationals wherever that conduct occurs. [Restatement (Third) of Foreign Relations Law of the United States, § 402 (1986).] The extension of U.S. law to privately owned space stations that were registered in other countries would be complicated by the fact that the law of the state of registry might conflict with that of the United States. This could cause problems since the United States, under article VI of the Outer Space Treaty, would remain responsible for the acts of its nationals in space.

Finally, should the United States have the right to exercise its jurisdiction in a particular instance, it would still be necessary to decide how to share power between the Federal government and the individual States. This generally means deciding: 1) whether the grant of jurisdiction in a particular case is exclusively limited to Federal courts or is shared with the state courts, and 2) whether the individual States would be allowed to pass laws in this area. [Some laws may have to be exclusive (e.g., registration laws and laws pertaining to the spaceworthiness of spacecraft); other laws might be amenable to concurrent State/Federal jurisdiction (e.g., criminal and tort law pertaining to individuals on board).] The Judiciary Act of 1789 granted Federal courts exclusive jurisdiction over *in rem* (action against the vessel) admiralty questions. However, *in personam* (action against the owner of the vessel) maritime cases can be brought in State courts. [Maritime causes of action brought *in personam* in State courts must rely on maritime law and not the common law of the State of the forum. (*See* Garret v. Moore McCormack Co., 317 U.S. 239 (1942).) Justice Black, writing in Hossidt v. United Fruit Co., 365 U.S. 731 (1961), noted that "Article VI of the Constitution carries with it the implication that wherever a maritime interest is involved, no matter how slight or marginal, it must displace a local interest, no matter how pressing and significant." The supremacy and uniformity doctrines that prevail in maritime law could be applied to law in outer space.] Similar grants or restrictions of the jurisdiction of Federal and State courts may be necessary for cases involving space activities. In addition, Congress may choose to limit the ability of States to pass laws in certain areas while allowing State courts to apply Federal law. For example, the Federal Aviation Act [49 U.S.C. § 40101, *et seq.*] limits the right of States to legislate with respect to commercial air travel; however, State courts share with Federal courts the ability to interpret the Federal Aviation Act. The "Commercial Space Launch Act" [49 U.S.C. § 70101 *et seq.*], establishes a Federal licensing mechanism but notes that the "authority of States to regulate space launch activities within their jurisdictions, or that affect their jurisdictions, is unaffected by this Act. ..."

To summarize, the issue of jurisdiction is fundamental to the application of U.S. laws to space activities. The fact that international law would allow an extension of U.S. jurisdiction in a particular instance does not mean that such an extension has occurred. Laws meant to regulate U.S. domestic activities may not apply to U.S. space activities (just as the U.S. criminal laws did not apply to the Cordova case) unless Congress has clearly established its intention to so extend these laws. Should international law allow an extension of U.S. jurisdiction and should Congress establish its intention to take advantage of such an extension, it would still be necessary to decide whether Federal laws would preempt State laws with respect to space activities, and whether jurisdiction was shared by both Federal and State courts.

C. Jurisdictional Alternatives for Governments.

A space station could have at least four different types of legal status, making it either:

1. *a national space station* under the jurisdiction and control of a single nation; [Space stations owned by private sector entities and registered under the laws of a single state would also fall in this category. A space station that was owned by a U.S. national but registered in another country would fall in this category but would raise a more complicated set of legal issues.]
2. *a multinational space station* under the joint jurisdiction and control of several nations;
3. *a multinational space station* the individual modules of which are under the independent jurisdiction and control of separate nations; or
4. *an international space station* under the jurisdiction and control of an international governmental organization similar to INTELSAT.

Under each of these options, the rights and liabilities of the U.S. Government and its citizens could be substantially different:

1) *U.S. Jurisdiction and Control.* To avoid the controversy and complexity of cooperative international ownership and operation, the United States may wish to retain complete control over the space station. Assuming the space station is owned and registered solely by the United States under the terms of the 1976 Registration Convention, its legal status would be similar to that of a ship or air-

plane flying the U.S. flag. As discussed above, ships [Restatement (Third) of Foreign Relations Law of the United States, § 501 (1986)] and aircraft [1944 Convention on International Civil Aviation, 61 Stat. 1180; T.I.A.S. 1591] have the nationality of the state in which they are registered. The United States would have the sole power to make and enforce rules of law regarding the operation of such a space station as long as such rules did not violate international law. Presumably, the United States would coordinate many of these rules with the foreign participants in the space station.

As discussed above, Congress could apply U.S. laws to the activities aboard a U.S. space station, but in the absence of clear congressional intent such laws might not be independently applied by the courts.

2) *Joint Jurisdiction and Control.* Nations considering investing a substantial portion of their financial, technical, and human resources in the space station may wish to jointly own and register it through some type of international joint venture. Under current international law, joint *registration* (as distinguished from ownership) of space objects is not provided for. Article VIII of the 1967 Outer Space Treaty establishes the principle that "A State ... on whose registry an object launched into space is carried shall retain jurisdiction and control over such object." [1967 Outer Space Treaty, Article VIII.] The 1976 Registration Convention maintains that where two or more states may be considered "launching states" [defined in Article I of the Registration Convention as: (i) A State which launches or procures the launching of a space object; (ii) A State from whose territory or facility a space object is launched], "they shall jointly determine which one of them shall register the object ... bearing in mind the provisions of article VIII." [The Registration Convention, Article II.] Under the Registration Convention then, participants in a joint space endeavor must choose which one shall be the registering state. Nonetheless, the Registration Convention also states that such a joint determination is to be without prejudice "to appropriate agreements concluded ... among the launching States on jurisdiction and control over the space object and over any personnel thereof." [*Id.*]

Therefore, nations wishing to jointly own and jointly exercise jurisdiction and control over a space station can follow the Registration Convention's suggestion to engage in an agreement separate from the actual registration.

It is not clear now—and may not be clear until a body of case authority is available—just how "appropriate agreements" would modify the "jurisdiction and control" granted by article VIII of the Outer Space Treaty. The Registration Convention is patterned after maritime law. The 1958 Convention on the High Seas states that a ship may only sail under one flag and, save in exceptional circumstances provided for by treaty, the flag state has exclusive jurisdiction on the high seas. [13 U.S.T. 2312; T.I.A.S. 5200.] Article 71 of the 1958 Convention states:

1. Ships shall sail under the flag of one State only and, save in exceptional cases expressly provided for in international treaties, or in these articles, shall be subject to its exclusive jurisdiction on the high seas. ...

2. A ship which sails under the flag of two or more States, using them according to convenience, may not claim any of the nationalities in question with respect to any other State, and may be assimilated to a ship without nationality.

Article 92 of the 1982 United Nations Convention on the Law of the Sea contains language almost identical to the language of the 1958 Convention. [The United States is not a party to the 1982 Convention.] Both maritime law and space law hold that registration implies jurisdiction. Similarly, both bodies of law allow this presumption of jurisdiction to be rebutted by specific agreements between the concerned parties. Although this practice has not been extensively used in maritime law it could be used for the space station.

3) *Jurisdiction and Control over Independent Modules.* It is possible that nations may wish to join together to form a space station, yet retain control over their individual contributions. A space station could conceivably be composed of different modules, each owned, registered, and under the jurisdiction and control of separate countries. Common elements of the station such as power modules might be owned separately and shared through specific agreement (option one, above) or jointly owned (option two, above).

In such an environment, each module would be under the jurisdiction and control of the country that owned, operated, and registered it. The problems with registering the common elements of such a station would be similar to those encountered in option two.

4) *Jurisdiction and Control by an International Organization.* Assuming nations would wish to avoid some of the problems caused by concurrent national jurisdictions, it is possible that an international organization similar to INTELSAT could be formed to own, operate, and register the space station. Since such an organization would not be able to develop a completely independent body of law to regulate space activities, it would still be necessary to decide which national laws or combinations of national laws would apply to the organization.

Such an organization could have quasi-legislative powers (subject, of course, to the concurrence of the member states) similar to those held by INTELSAT. Such powers would allow the organization to make normal operational, management, and safety decisions without the need to renegotiate separate agreements among the member states.

NOTES

1. The OTA Report notes that the "floating island" theory of jurisdiction has not been universally accepted, citing Cunard S.S. Co. v. Mellon, 262 U.S. 100, 123 (1923). In that case, however, the Supreme Court went on to say that

> The jurisdiction which [the "floating island" theory] is intended to describe arises out of the nationality of the ship, as established by her domicile, registry and use of

> the flag, and partakes more of the characteristics of personal than of territorial sovereignty. [Cites omitted.] It is chiefly applicable to ships on the high seas, where there is no territorial sovereign; and as respects ships in foreign territorial waters it has little application beyond what is affirmatively or tacitly permitted by the local sovereign.

Id.

The Registration Convention (discussed in Chapter 3), in conjunction with the Outer Space Treaty, provides for jurisdiction-by-registry for "space objects" in much the same way ships are required to be registered under the international law of the sea. *See* H. Meyers, The Nationality of Ships (1967); M. McDougal & W. Burke, The Public Order of the Oceans (1962). *See also* Chapter 2 (discussing maritime analogies generally). And, given that the Outer Space Treaty prohibits declarations of sovereignty over territory in space, national jurisdiction in space is highly analogous to the personal jurisdiction found by the Court in the Cunard S.S. case. That is, assertions of jurisdiction are based not on declarations of territorial sovereignty but instead on the nationality of the persons (or, in this case, spacecraft) involved, and the nation of registry has jurisdiction under the Registration Convention.

2. The OTA Report refers to the principle of single state registration enunciated in both the Outer Space Treaty and the Convention on the High Seas. *See* Geneva Convention on the High Seas, Article 5, April 29, 1958, 13 U.S.T. 2312, T.I.A.S. No. 5200 (entered into force on September 30, 1962). *See also* Restatement (Third) of Foreign Relations § 501 (1986). On jurisdiction over aircraft, *see* The Convention on International Civil Aviation of December 7, 1944, 61 Stat. 1180. The Report also refers to the fact that both the Outer Space Treaty and the Convention on the High Seas appear to allow states and private parties who jointly operate a space or sea-faring vessel to stipulate which country shall have jurisdiction over the endeavor. In this connection, consider the following passage, taken from one of the most detailed studies ever made of jurisdiction in outer space:

> [N]o hard and fast rules as to who the state of registration should be, would suffice. In fact, the framework must be flexible so as to admit of optional arrangements for registration between the parties concerned *inter se*. ... For the sake of peace, order, and good government in outer space, a rebuttable presumption and legal obligation should be created to the effect that the State from whose territory the space object was launched ... shall register the object and give adequate notification thereof. ...

I. Csabafi, The Concept of State Jurisdiction in International Space Law 22 (1971). *See also id.* at 18 (Soviets recommended a flexible, consensual registration regime in connection with the 1967 Outer Space Treaty). On the problems that will have to be faced when modules from different countries are assembled in space to form a "new" composite craft or vessel, *see* Glazer, Domicile and Industry in Outer Space, 17 Columbia Journal of Translational Law 67, 73–74 (1978) (discussing how composite spacecraft such as international space labs would be treated in light of Outer Space Treaty's references to "space objects").

3. In certain circumstances, primarily when a "flagless" and thus stateless ship is involved in criminal activities on the high seas, a state may exercise jurisdiction outside its territory over people who are not nationals of that state. *See* Rivard v. United States, 375 F.2d 882 (5th Cir.), *cert. denied,* 389 U.S. 884 (1967); Rocha v. United States, 288 F.2d 545 (9th Cir.), *cert. denied,* 366 U.S. 948 (1961); 6 M. Whiteman, Digest of International Law 278 (1968). *See generally* Landau, Extraterritorial Penal Jurisdiction and Extradition, 29 International & Comparative Law Quarterly 274 (1980); Restatement (Third) of Foreign Relations Law of the United States §§ 522 (1965). Presumably, the same principle would apply to criminal activities in space, including the fanciful situation of "space pirates" preying on lawful space stations or settlements. For a critique of recent developments in this theory of jurisdiction, *see* Roos, Comment, Stateless Vessels and the High Seas Narcotics Trade: United States Courts Deviate from International Principles of Jurisdiction, 9 Maritime Lawyer 273 (1984).

4. For a well-argued plea for the formation of an international convention to address legal issues concerning the governance of permanent manned space colonies, *see* Vereshchetin, Legal Status of International Space Crews, 3 Annals of Air and Space Law 545 (1978). *Cf.* G. Robinson & H. White, Jr., Envoys of Mankind: A Declaration of First Principles for the Governance of Space Societies (1986) (discussed in Chapter 9).

5. Even if an international treaty on jurisdiction were established—whether it governed temporary or permanent activities—the U.S. Congress would be free to override its terms by statute. *See* Lobel, The Limits of Constitutional Power: Conflicts Between Foreign Policy and International Law, 71 Virginia Law Review 1071, 1072 (1985) (describing current law and proposing that certain trends away from the current law toward making international law binding are to be encouraged and furthered). *See also* Casenote, Congressional Power to Abrogate the Domestic Effect of a United Nations Treaty Commitment: Diggs v. Shultz (D.C. Cir. 1972), 13 Columbia Journal of Transnational Law 155 (1974) (describing case where plaintiffs claimed that the United States was violating specific treaty commitments by resuming trade with Rhodesia in violation of a U.N. Security Council resolution; the Court dismissed action in part because Congress can override treaty obligations by enacting a subsequent clearly inconsistent statute); Note, Security Council Resolutions in United States Courts, 50 Indiana Law Journal 83 (1974). The theory behind this rule is that Congress is free to abrogate treaty obligations since it has plenary power over domestic affairs, and that the U.S. should be subject to punishment in the international sphere by whatever enforcement mechanisms operate there. *See* Lobel, *supra,* at 1073. The same reasoning has been applied by some commentators who argue

that the President is free to abrogate international obligations, e.g., by Executive Order. *See* L. Henkin, Foreign Affairs and the Constitution 221–22 (1972).

6. The OTA Report refers to a number of occasions when U.S. Courts have declined to extend U.S. jurisdiction to non-territorial events or objects in the absence of clear Congressional authorization. Courts have also been reluctant to consider a treaty an operative component of U.S. law unless (1) Congress has passed clear implementing legislation or (2) the treaty on its face provides clear standards and other guidance on how it is being implemented—i.e., it is "self-executing." *See, e.g.*, Foster v. Neilson, 27 U.S. (2 Pet.) 253 (1829), Man Hing Ivory & Imports v. Deukmejian, 702 F.2d 760 (9th Cir. 1983); 14 G. Hackworth, Digest of International Law § 29 (1943) (discussing history of doctrine). Some commentators have argued that the phrasing of certain provisions of the Outer Space Treaty renders it non-self-executing. *See* S. Gorove, Studies in Space Law: Its Challenges and Prospects 145 (1977); Menter, Jurisdiction Over Man-Made Orbital Satellites, 2 Journal of Space Law 19, 22 (1974) (noting that Article VI of the Treaty states that "[t]he activities of non-governmental entities in outer space shall require authorization and continuing supervision by the appropriate State Party to the Treaty," and that this could be interpreted as requiring implementing legislation). On the other hand, Congress has exercised jurisdiction over U.S. registered space objects through such statutes as the Federal Criminal Code (discussed in the OTA Report excerpt), the Communications Satellite Act of 1962 (47 U.S.C. §§ 701–744 (1964)), and the National Aeronautics and Space Act of 1958 (42 U.S.C. §§ 2451–2484 (1995)). Also, the act of registering a space object and reporting it to the United Nations could be viewed as sufficient implementing action under Article VIII of the Outer Space Treaty (re: jurisdiction); by analogy, the very act of attributing national character to an ocean-going vessel by registering it in a particular country is said to authorize the state of registry to exercise jurisdiction over it. *See* M. McDougal, Foreword to B. Boczek, Flags of Convenience at xii (1962); *see also* H. Meyers, The Nationality of Ships (1967). In any event, for practical reasons it is generally conceded that the U.S. does have jurisdiction over "space objects" listed on its registry. *See, e.g.*, Cunningham, Space Commerce and Secured Financing—New Frontiers for the U.C.C., 40 Business Lawyer 803, 816 (1985). *But cf.* DeSaussure & Haanappel, A Unified Multinational Approach to the Application of Tort and Contract Principles to Outer Space, 6 Syracuse Journal of International Law & Commerce 1, 4 (1978) (arguing that jurisdictional provision of Outer Space Treaty is of only limited effect without implementing legislation in common law countries).

7. There is usually a choice of law provision in a contract for commercial space activities, such as the ones excerpted later in this chapter. Note that some courts look with disfavor on contracts that attempt to divest them of jurisdiction. For example, a French citizen has a statutory right to resort to the French judicial system even if she was damaged on foreign soil or by a foreigner. The French Civil Code, Article 14, provides:

> An alien, even one not residing in France, may be summoned before the French courts for the fulfillment of obligations contracted by him in France; he may be brought before the French courts for obligations contracted by him in a foreign country toward French persons.

Fr. C. Civ. Article 14, *reprinted in* H. DeVries, N. Galston, & R. Loening, Materials for the French Legal System 2 (2d ed. 1977). Note that under French law, "obligations" refers to tortious as well as contractual obligations.

8. For an interesting discussion of these issues, *see* Helen Shin, Note, "Oh, I have slipped the surly bonds of earth": Multinational Space Stations and Choice of Law, 78 California Law Review 1375, 1375 (1990), which includes the following hypothetical:

> An American biologist is conducting an experiment aboard an orbiting multinational space station built by the United States, Canada, Japan, and the European Space Agency. The biologist is passing through the Canadian module, where a French astrophysicist is repairing an instrument panel. The astrophysicist carelessly pushes aside a wrench, which floats away and injures the biologist. Which state's choice of law rules—and institutions—determine which state's substantive laws will apply to the issues of the astrophysicist's liability and the American's ability to recover damages?

The author argues that maritime choice of law rules for torts occurring onboard vessels at sea is the best model for deciding which state's laws govern the problem. She also states that arbitration rather than full-scale litigation is the preferred forum for deciding the issue. *Id.*, at 1378. She goes on to list the three traditional factors from maritime choice of law that should influence choice of law determinations: the registry state of the space vessel in which the incident takes place; the nationality of the plaintiff; and the nationality of the defendant. *Id. See also* Mary McCord, Note, Responding to the Space Station Agreement: The Extension of U.S. Law into Space, 77 Georgetown Law Journal 1933 (1989) (arguing for use of a "minimum contacts test ... to determine the reasonableness of the U.S. exercise of jurisdiction over non-U.S. nationals in or on non-U.S. elements [of a space station]").

9. For a discussion of allocation of jurisdiction by international agreement, *see* David C. Stewart, Resolution of Legal Issues Confronting the International Space Station Project: A Step Forward in the Development of Space Law, 29 Va. J. Int'l L. 745 (1989).

Smith v. United States
113 S.Ct. 1178 (1993)

Chief Justice REHNQUIST delivered the opinion of the Court.

This case presents the question whether the Federal Tort Claims Act (FTCA), 28 U.S.C. §§ 1346(b), 1402(b), 2401(b), 2671–2680 (1988 ed. and Supp. II), applies to tortious acts or omissions occurring in Antarctica, a sovereignless region without civil tort law of its own. We hold that it does not.

[From footnote 1: Without indigenous human population and containing roughly one-tenth of the world's land mass, Antarctica is best described as "an entire continent of disputed territory." F. Auburn, Antarctic Law and Politics 1 (1982). Seven nations—Argentina, Australia, Chile, France, New Zealand, Norway, and the United Kingdom—presently assert formal claims to pie-shaped portions of the continent that total about 85 percent of its expanse. Boczek, The Soviet Union and the Antarctic Regime, 78 Am.J.Int'l L. 834, 840 (1984); Hayton, The Antarctic Settlement of 1959, 54 Am.J.Int'l L. 349 (1960). The United States does not recognize other nations' claims and does not itself assert a sovereign interest in Antarctica, although it maintains a basis for such a claim. Lissitzyn, The American Position on Outer Space and Antarctica, 53 Am.J.Int'l L. 126, 128 (1959). In any event, these sovereign claims have all been suspended by the terms of the Antarctic Treaty, concluded in 1959. Antarctic Treaty, Dec. 1, 1959 [1961] 12 U.S.T. 794, T.I.A.S. No. 4780. Article 4 of the Treaty states that no claim may be enforced, expanded, or compromised while the Treaty is in force, *Id.*, Article IV, 12 U.S.T., at 796, thus essentially freezing nations' sovereign claims as of the date of the Treaty's execution.]

Petitioner Sandra Jean Smith is the widow of John Emmett Smith and the duly appointed representative of his estate. At the time of his death, Smith worked as a carpenter at McMurdo Station on Ross Island, Antarctica, for a construction company under contract to the National Science Foundation, an agency of the United States. Smith and two companions one day took a recreational hike to Castle Rock, located several miles outside of McMurdo Station. On their return, they departed from the marked route to walk across a snow field in the direction of Scott Base, a New Zealand outpost not far from McMurdo Station. After stopping for a snack, one of the three men took a step and suddenly dropped from sight. Smith followed, and he, too, disappeared. Both men had fallen into a crevasse. Despite search and rescue efforts, Smith died from exposure and internal injuries suffered as a result of the fall.

Petitioner filed this wrongful death action against the United States under the FTCA in the District Court for the District of Oregon, the district where she resides. Petitioner alleged that the United States was negligent in failing to provide adequate warning of the dangers posed by crevasses in areas beyond the marked paths. It is undisputed that petitioner's claim is based exclusively on acts or omissions occurring in Antarctica. Upon the motion of the United States, the District Court dismissed petitioner's complaint for lack of subject-matter jurisdiction, 702 F.Supp. 1480 (1989), holding that her claim was barred by 28 U.S.C. § 2680 (k), the foreign-country exception. Section 2680(k) precludes the exercise of jurisdiction over "[a]ny claim arising in a foreign country."

The Court of Appeals affirmed, 953 F.2d 1116 (CA9 1991). It noted that the term "foreign country" admits of multiple interpretations, and thus looked to the language and structure of the FTCA as a whole to determine whether Antarctica is a "foreign country" within the meaning of the statute. Adopting the analysis and conclusion of then-Judge Scalia, see Beattie v. United States, 244 U.S.App.D.C. 70, 85–109, 756 F.2d 91, 106–130 (1984) (Scalia, J., dissenting), the Court of Appeals ruled that the FTCA does not apply to claims arising in Antarctica. To hold otherwise, the Court of Appeals stated, would render two other provisions of the FTCA, 28 U.S.C. §§ 1402(b), 1346(b), nonsensical. The Court of Appeals held, in the alternative, that petitioner's suit would be barred even if Antarctica were not a "foreign country" for purposes of the FTCA. Because the FTCA was a limited relinquishment of the common-law immunity of the United States, the Court of Appeals concluded that the absence of any clear congressional intent to subject the United States to liability for claims arising in Antarctica precluded petitioner's suit. We granted certiorari to resolve a conflict between two Courts of Appeals, 504 U.S.——, 112 S.Ct. 2963, 119 L.Ed.2d 585 (1992), and now affirm.

Petitioner argues that the scope of the foreign-country exception turns on whether the United States has recognized the legitimacy of another nation's sovereign claim over the foreign land. Otherwise, she contends, the land is not a "country" for purposes of the FTCA. Petitioner points out that the United States does not recognize the validity of other nations' claims to portions of Antarctica. She asserts, moreover, that this construction of the term "foreign country" is most consistent with the purpose underlying the foreign-country exception. According to petitioner, Congress enacted the foreign-country exception in order to insulate the United States from tort liability imposed pursuant to foreign law. Because Antarctica has no law of its own, petitioner claims that conventional choice-of-law rules control and require the application of Oregon law, the law of her domicile. Thus, petitioner concludes, the rationale for the foreign-country exception would not be compromised by the exercise of jurisdiction here, since the United States would not be subject to liability under the law of a foreign nation.

Petitioner's argument for governmental liability here faces significant obstacles in addition to the foreign-country exception, but we turn first to the language of that proviso. It states that the FTCA's waiver of sovereign immunity does not apply to "[a]ny claim arising in a foreign country." 28 U.S.C. § 2680(k). Though the FTCA offers no definition of "country," the commonsense meaning of the term undermines petitioner's attempt to equate it with "sovereign state." The first dictionary definition of "country" is simply "[a] region or tract of land." Webster's New International Dictionary 609 (2d ed. 1945). To be sure, this is not the only possible interpretation of the term, and it is therefore appropriate to examine other parts of the statute before making a final determination. But the ordinary meaning of the language itself, we think, includes Antarctica, even though it has no recognized government.

Our construction of the term "foreign country" draws support from the language of § 1346(b), "[t]he principal provision of the Federal Tort Claims Act."

Richards v. United States, 369 U.S. 1, 6, 82 S.Ct. 585, 589, 7 L.Ed.2d 492 (1962). That section waives the sovereign immunity of the United States for certain torts committed by federal employees "under circumstances where the United States, if a private person, would be liable to the claimant in accordance with the law of the place where the act or omission occurred." 28 U.S.C. § 1346(b) (emphasis added). We have construed § 1346(b) in determining what law should apply in actions brought under the FTCA. See Richards, supra. But by its terms the section is more than a choice-of-law provision: it delineates the scope of the United States' waiver of sovereign immunity. If Antarctica were not a "foreign country," and for that reason included within the FTCA's coverage, § 1346(b) would instruct courts to look to the law of a place that has no law in order to determine the liability of the United States—surely a bizarre result. Of course, if it were quite clear from the balance of the statute that governmental liability was intended for torts committed in Antarctica, then the failure of § 1346(b) to specify any governing law might be treated as a statutory gap that the courts could fill by decisional law. But coupled with what seems to us the most natural interpretation of the foreign-country exception, this portion of § 1346(b) reinforces the conclusion that Antarctica is excluded from the coverage of the FTCA.

Section 1346(b) is not, however, the only FTCA provision that contradicts petitioner's interpretation of the foreign-country exception. The statute's venue provision, § 1402(b), provides that claims under the FTCA may be brought "only in the judicial district where the plaintiff resides or wherein the act or omission complained of occurred." Because no federal judicial district encompasses Antarctica, petitioner's interpretation of the FTCA would lead to yet another anomalous result: the FTCA would establish jurisdiction for all tort claims against the United States arising in Antarctica, but no venue would exist unless the claimant happened to reside in the United States. As we observed in Brunette Machine Works, Ltd. v. Kockum Industries, Inc., 406 U.S. 706, 710, n. 8, 92 S.Ct. 1936, 1939, n. 8, 32 L.Ed.2d 428 (1972), "Congress does not in general intend to create venue gaps, which take away with one hand what Congress has given by way of jurisdictional grant with the other." Thus, in construing the FTCA, it is "reasonable to prefer the construction that avoids leaving such a gap," ibid., especially when that construction comports with the usual meaning of a disputed term.

Our decisions interpreting the FTCA contain varying statements as to how it should be construed. See, e.g., United States v. Yellow Cab Co., 340 U.S. 543, 547, 71 S.Ct. 399, 403, 95 L.Ed. 523 (1951); Dalehite v. United States, 346 U.S. 15, 31, 73 S.Ct. 956, 965, 97 L.Ed. 1427 (1953); United States v. Orleans, 425 U.S. 807, 813, 96 S.Ct. 1971, 1975, 48 L.Ed.2d 390 (1976); Kosak v. United States, 465 U.S. 848, 853, n. 9, 104 S.Ct. 1519, 1523 n. 9, 79 L.Ed.2d 860 (1984). See also United States v. Nordic Village, Inc.,—— U.S.——, ——, 112 S.Ct. 1011, ——, 117 L.Ed.2d 181 (1992). A recent statement of this sort, and the one to which we now adhere, is found in United States v. Kubrick, 444 U.S. 111, 117–118, 100 S.Ct. 352, 357, 62 L.Ed.2d 259 (1979): "We should also have in mind that the Act waives the immunity of the United States and that ... we should not take it upon ourselves to extend the waiver beyond that which Congress intended. [Citations omitted.] Neither, however, should we assume the authority to narrow the waiver that Congress intended." Reading the foreign-country exception to the FTCA to exclude torts committed in Antarctica accords with this canon of construction.

Lastly, the presumption against extraterritorial application of United States statutes requires that any lingering doubt regarding the reach of the FTCA be resolved against its encompassing torts committed in Antarctica. It is a longstanding principle of American law "that legislation of Congress, unless a contrary intent appears, is meant to apply only within the territorial jurisdiction of the United States." EEOC v. Arabian American Oil Co., 499 U.S.——, ——, 111 S.Ct. 1227, 1230, 113 L.Ed.2d 274 (1991) (quoting Foley Bros., Inc. v. Filardo, 336 U.S. 281, 285, 69 S.Ct. 575, 577, 93 L.Ed. 680 (1949)). In applying this principle, "[w]e assume that Congress legislates against the backdrop of the presumption against extraterritoriality." Arabian American Oil Co., *supra*, 499 U.S., at ——, 111 S.Ct. at 1230; accord, *e.g*., Argentine Republic v. Amerada Hess Shipping Corp., 488 U.S. 428, 440, 109 S.Ct. 683, 691, 102 L.Ed.2d 818 (1989) ("When it desires to do so, Congress knows how to place the high seas within the jurisdictional reach of a statute"). The applicability of the presumption is not defeated here just because the FTCA specifically addresses the issue of extraterritorial application in the foreign-country exception. To the contrary, as we stated in United States v. Spelar, 338 U.S. 217, 222, 70 S.Ct. 10, 13, 94 L.Ed. 3 (1949), "[t]hat presumption, far from being overcome here, is doubly fortified by the language of this statute and the legislative purpose underlying it." Petitioner does not assert, nor could she, that there is clear evidence of congressional intent to apply the FTCA to claims arising in Antarctica. [From Footnote 5: Petitioner instead argues that the presumption against extraterritoriality applies only if it serves to avoid "'unintended clashes between our laws and those of other nations which could result in international discord.'" Brief for Petitioner 16 (quoting EEOC v. Arabian American Oil Co., 499 U.S. ——, ——, 111 S.Ct. 1227, 1230, 113 L.Ed.2d 274 (1991)). But the presumption is rooted in a number of considerations, not the least of which is the common-sense notion that Congress generally legislates with domestic concerns in mind.]

For all of these reasons, we hold that the FTCA's waiver of sovereign immunity does not apply to tort claims arising in Antarctica. Some of these reasons are based on the language and structure of the statute itself; others are based on presumptions as to extraterritorial application of Acts of Congress and as to waivers of sovereign immunity. We think these norms of statutory construction have quite likely led us to the same conclusion that the 79th Congress would have reached had it expressly considered the question we now decide: it would not have included a desolate and extraordinarily dangerous land such as Antarctica within the scope of the FTCA. The judgment of the Court of Appeals is therefore Affirmed.

Equal Employment Opportunity Commission v. Arabian American Oil Company, 499 U.S. 244 (1991)

Chief Justice REHNQUIST delivered the opinion of the Court.

These cases present the issue whether Title VII applies extraterritorially to regulate the employment practices of United States employers who employ United States citizens abroad. The United States Court of Appeals for the Fifth Circuit held that it does not, and we agree with that conclusion.

Petitioner Boureslan is a naturalized United States citizen who was born in Lebanon. The respondents are two Delaware corporations, Arabian American Oil Company (Aramco), and its subsidiary, Aramco Service Company (ASC). Aramco's principal place of business is Dhahran, Saudi Arabia, and it is licensed to do business in Texas. ASC's principal place of business is Houston, Texas.

In 1979, Boureslan was hired by ASC as a cost engineer in Houston. A year later he was transferred, at his request, to work for Aramco in Saudi Arabia. Boureslan remained with Aramco in Saudi Arabia until he was discharged in 1984. After filing a charge of discrimination with the Equal Employment Opportunity Commission (EEOC), he instituted this suit in the United States District Court for the Southern District of Texas against Aramco and ASC. He sought relief under both state law and Title VII of the Civil Rights Act of 1964, 78 Stat. 243, as amended, 42 U.S.C. §§ 2000a–2000h–6, on the ground that he was harassed and ultimately discharged by respondents on account of his race, religion, and national origin.

Respondents filed a motion for summary judgment on the ground that the District Court lacked subject matter jurisdiction over Boureslan's claim because the protections of Title VII do not extend to United States citizens employed abroad by American employers. The District Court agreed, and dismissed Boureslan's Title VII claim; it also dismissed his state-law claims for lack of pendent jurisdiction, and entered final judgment in favor of respondents. A panel for the Fifth Circuit affirmed. After vacating the panel's decision and rehearing the case en banc, the court affirmed the District Court's dismissal of Boureslan's complaint. Both Boureslan and the EEOC petitioned for certiorari. We granted both petitions for certiorari to resolve this important issue of statutory interpretation.

Both parties concede, as they must, that Congress has the authority to enforce its laws beyond the territorial boundaries of the United States. Cf. Foley Bros., Inc. v. Filardo, 336 U.S. 281, 284–285, 69 S.Ct. 575, 577, 93 L.Ed. 680 (1949); Benz v. Compania Naviera Hidalgo, S.A., 353 U.S. 138, 147, 77 S.Ct. 699, 704, 1 L.Ed.2d 709 (1957). Whether Congress has in fact exercised that authority in this case is a matter of statutory construction. It is our task to determine whether Congress intended the protections of Title VII to apply to United States citizens employed by American employers outside of the United States.

It is a long-standing principle of American law "that legislation of Congress, unless a contrary intent appears, is meant to apply only within the territorial jurisdiction of the United States." Foley Bros., 336 U.S., at 285, 69 S.Ct., at 577. This "canon of construction ... is a valid approach whereby unexpressed congressional intent may be ascertained." *Id.* It serves to protect against unintended clashes between our laws and those of other nations which could result in international discord. See McCulloch v. Sociedad Nacional de Marineros de Honduras, 372 U.S. 10, 20–22, 83 S.Ct. 671, 677–678, 9 L.Ed.2d 547 (1963).

In applying this rule of construction, we look to see whether "language in the [relevant act] gives any indication of a congressional purpose to extend its coverage beyond places over which the United States has sovereignty or has some measure of legislative control." Foley Bros., *supra,* 336 U.S., at 285, 69 S.Ct., at 577. We assume that Congress legislates against the backdrop of the presumption against extraterritoriality. Therefore, unless there is "the affirmative intention of the Congress clearly expressed," Benz, *supra,* 353 U.S., at 147, 77 S.Ct., at 704, we must presume it "is primarily concerned with domestic conditions." Foley Bros., *supra,* 336 U.S., at 285, 69 S.Ct., at 577.

Boureslan and the EEOC contend that the language of Title VII evinces a clearly expressed intent on behalf of Congress to legislate extraterritorially. They rely principally on two provisions of the statute. First, petitioners argue that the statute's definitions of the jurisdictional terms "employer" and "commerce" are sufficiently broad to include U.S. firms that employ American citizens overseas. Second, they maintain that the statute's "alien exemption" clause, 42 U.S.C. § 2000e–1, necessarily implies that Congress intended to protect American citizens from employment discrimination abroad. Petitioners also contend that we should defer to the EEOC's consistently held position that Title VII applies abroad. We conclude that petitioners' evidence, while not totally lacking in probative value, falls short of demonstrating the affirmative congressional intent required to extend the protections of the Title VII beyond our territorial borders.

Title VII prohibits various discriminatory employment practices based on an individual's race, color, religion, sex, or national origin. See §§ 2000e-2, 2000e-3. An employer is subject to Title VII if it has employed 15 or more employees for a specified period and is "engaged in an industry affecting commerce." An industry affecting commerce is "any activity, business, or industry in commerce or in which a labor dispute would hinder or obstruct commerce or the free flow of commerce and includes any activity or industry 'affecting commerce' within the meaning of the Labor-Management Reporting and Disclosure Act of 1959 [(LMRDA)] [29 U.S.C. § 401 *et seq.*]." § 2000e(h). "Commerce," in turn, is defined as "trade, traffic, commerce, transportation, transmission, or communication among the several States; or between a State and any place outside thereof; or within the District of Columbia, or a possession of the United States; or between points in the same State but through a point outside thereof." § 2000e(g).

Petitioners argue that by its plain language, Title VII's "broad jurisdictional language" reveals Congress's intent to extend the statute's protections to employment discrimination anywhere in the world by a U.S. employer who affects trade "between a State and any place outside thereof." More precisely, they assert that since Title VII defines "States" to include States, the District of Columbia, and specified territories, the clause "between a State and any place outside thereof" must be referring to areas beyond the territorial limit of the United States. Reply Brief for Petitioner 3.

Respondents offer several alternative explanations for the statute's expansive language. They contend that the "or between a State and any place outside thereof" clause "provide[s] the jurisdictional nexus required to regulate commerce that is not wholly within a single state, presumably as it affects both interstate and foreign commerce" but not to "regulate conduct exclusively within a foreign country." Brief for Respondents 21, n. 14. They also argue that since the definitions of the terms "employer," "commerce," and "industry affecting commerce," make no mention of "commerce with foreign nations," Congress cannot be said to have intended that the statute apply overseas. In support of this argument, petitioners point to Title II of the Civil Rights Act of 1964, governing public accommodation, which specifically defines commerce as it applies to foreign nations. Finally, respondents argue that while language present in the first bill considered by the House of Representatives contained the terms "foreign commerce" and "foreign nations," those terms were deleted by the Senate before the Civil Rights Act of 1964 was passed. They conclude that these deletions "[are] inconsistent with the notion of a clearly expressed congressional intent to apply Title VII extraterritorially." Brief for Respondents 7.

We need not choose between these competing interpretations as we would be required to do in the absence of the presumption against extraterritorial application discussed above. Each is plausible, but no more persuasive than that. The language relied upon by petitioners—and it is they who must make the affirmative showing—is ambiguous, and does not speak directly to the question presented here. The intent of Congress as to the extraterritorial application of this statute must be deduced by inference from boilerplate language which can be found in any number of congressional acts, none of which have ever been held to apply overseas. [Citations omitted.]

Petitioners' reliance on Title VII's jurisdictional provisions also finds no support in our case law; we have repeatedly held that even statutes that contain broad language in their definitions of "commerce" that expressly refer to "foreign commerce," do not apply abroad.

* * *

The EEOC places great weight on ... [the] "broad jurisdictional grant in the Lanham Act" that this Court held applied extraterritorially in Steele v. Bulova Watch Co., 344 U.S. 280, 286, 73 S.Ct. 252, 256, 97 L.Ed. 319 (1952). Brief for Petitioner in No. 89–1838, p. 12. In Steele, we addressed whether the Lanham Act, designed to prevent deceptive and misleading use of trademarks, applied to acts of a U.S. citizen consummated in Mexico. The Act defined commerce as "all commerce which may lawfully be regulated by Congress." 15 U.S.C. § 1127. The stated intent of the statute was "to regulate commerce within the control of Congress by making actionable the deceptive and misleading use of marks in such commerce." *Id.* While recognizing that "the legislation of Congress will not extend beyond the boundaries of the United States unless a contrary legislative intent appears," the Court concluded that in light of the fact that the allegedly unlawful conduct had some effects within the United States, coupled with the Act's "broad jurisdictional grant" and its "sweeping reach into 'all commerce which may lawfully be regulated by Congress,'" the statute was properly interpreted as applying abroad. Steele, *supra,* 344 U.S., at 285, 287, 73 S.Ct., at 255, 256.

The EEOC's attempt to analogize this case to Steele is unpersuasive. The Lanham Act by terms applies to "all commerce which may lawfully be regulated by Congress." The Constitution gives Congress the power "[t]o regulate Commerce with foreign Nations, and among the several States, and with the Indian Tribes." U.S. Const., Art. I, § 8, cl. 3. Since the Act expressly stated that it applied to the extent of Congress's power over commerce, the Court in Steele concluded that Congress intended that the statute apply abroad. By contrast, Title VII's more limited, boilerplate "commerce" language does not support such an expansive construction of congressional intent. Moreover, unlike the language in the Lanham Act, Title VII's definition of "commerce" was derived expressly from the LMRDA, a statute that this Court had held, prior to the enactment of Title VII, did not apply abroad. McCulloch, *supra,* 372 U.S., at 15, 83 S.Ct., at 674.

*   *   *

Congress [also] failed to provide any mechanisms for overseas enforcement of Title VII. For instance, the statute's venue provisions, § 2000e-5 (f) (3), are ill-suited for extraterritorial application as they provide for venue only in a judicial district in the state where certain matters related to the employer occurred or were located. And the limited investigative authority provided for the EEOC, permitting the Commission only to issue subpoenas for witnesses and documents from "anyplace in the United States or any Territory or possession thereof," § 2000e-9, suggests that Congress did not intend for the statute to apply abroad.

It is also reasonable to conclude that had Congress intended Title VII to apply overseas, it would have addressed the subject of conflicts with foreign laws and procedures. In amending the Age Discrimination in Employment Act of 1967, 81 Stat. 602, as amended, 29 U.S.C. § 621 *et seq.* (ADEA), to apply abroad, Congress specifically addressed potential conflicts with foreign law by providing that it is not unlawful for an employer to take any action prohibited by the ADEA "where such practices involve an employee in a workplace in a foreign country, and compliance with [the ADEA] would cause such employer ... to violate the laws of the country in which such workplace is located." 29 U.S.C. § 623 (f) (1). Title VII, by contrast, fails to address conflicts with the laws of other nations.

* * *

Our conclusion today is buttressed by the fact that "[w]hen it desires to do so, Congress knows how to place the high seas within the jurisdictional reach of a statute." Argentine Republic v. Amerada Hess Shipping Corp., 488 U.S. 428, 440, 109 S.Ct. 683, 691, 102 L.Ed.2d 818 (1989). Congress's awareness of the need to make a clear statement that a statute applies overseas is amply demonstrated by the numerous occasions on which it has expressly legislated the extraterritorial application of a statute. *See, e.g.*, the Export Administration Act of 1979, 50 U.S.C. App. §§ 2401–2420 (1982, and Supp. III ed.) (defining "United States person" to include "any domestic concern (including any permanent domestic establishment of any foreign concern) and any foreign subsidiary or affiliate (including any permanent foreign establishment) of any domestic concern which is controlled in fact by such domestic concern") § 2415 (2); Coast Guard Act, 14 U.S.C. § 89(a) (Coast Guard searches and seizures upon the high seas); 18 U.S.C. § 7 (Criminal code extends to high seas); 19 U.S.C. § 1701 (Customs enforcement on the high seas); Comprehensive Anti-Apartheid Act of 1986, 22 U.S.C. §§ 5001–5116 (1982 ed. Supp. V) (definition of national of the United States as "a natural person who is a citizen of the United States ...") § 5001 (5) (A); the Logan Act, 18 U.S.C. § 953 (applying act to "[a]ny citizen ... wherever he may be ..."). Indeed, after several courts had held that the ADEA did not apply overseas, Congress amended § 11 (f) to provide, "[t]he term 'employee' includes any individual who is a citizen of the United States employed by an employer in a workplace in a foreign country." 29 U.S.C. § 630 (f). Congress also amended § 4 (g) (1), which states, "[i]f an employer controls a corporation whose place of incorporation is in a foreign country, any practice by such corporation prohibited under this section shall be presumed to be such practice by such employer." 29 U.S.C. § 623 (h) (1). The expressed purpose of these changes was to "mak[e] provisions of the Act apply to citizens of the United States employed in foreign countries by United States corporations or their subsidiaries." S. Rep. No. 98-467, p. 2 (1984), U.S. Code Cong. & Admin. News 1984, pp. 2974, 2975. Congress, should it wish to do so, may similarly amend Title VII and in doing so will be able to calibrate its provisions in a way that we cannot.

Petitioners have failed to present sufficient affirmative evidence that Congress intended Title VII to apply abroad. Accordingly, the judgment of the Court of Appeals is Affirmed.

NOTES

1. What implications do these decisions have for assertion of federal U.S. jurisdiction over outer space activities? What guidelines and specific language would you suggest if called upon to advise Congress on the drafting of a bill to provide for federal jurisdiction over space activities? Consider at least the following issues: (1) venue; (2) enforcement procedures; (3) conflict with foreign legal systems; and (3) definitions of persons and acts over which the bill will assert jurisdiction.

2. With respect to the *Smith* case, how similar is the physical and legal environment of Antarctica to outer space? What specific drafting issues must Congress confront in asserting jurisdiction over space activities in light of *Smith* and these similarities?

TORT LAW

At the outset, one should be careful to distinguish private tort law from the kind of internationally established liability adopted in the 1972 Liability Convention (discussed in Chapter 5). The latter type of liability attaches to *states* by virtue of the language of the Convention; it was designed to provide a means of settling liability claims between rival states. The claims of the Canadian government against the Soviet Union for cleanup costs associated with the crash of the Soviet Cosmos 954 Satellite (described in detail in the excerpt from Cohen in Chapter 5), for instance, are the type of claims dealt with in the Liability Convention. In addition, the Outer Space Treaty and the Liability Convention provide for state-level liability for damage caused by space objects of one state to another state or its natural or juridical persons, Outer Space Treaty, Article VII. Under these treaties, the launching state is liable for damage caused by any launches from its territory—from the government itself, corporations, or even individuals. The treaties establish that the launching state is absolutely liable for damage on Earth or in the air between Earth and outer space. (See Chapter 1 for a discussion of the end of airspace and the beginning of outer space.) But when the damage is "caused elsewhere than on the surface of the Earth to a space object of one launching state or to persons or property on board such a space object by a space object of another launching State," liability will result only if the damage is due to the fault of the "defendant" launching State or persons for whom it is responsible, Liability Convention, Article III. *See generally* G. Zukhov & Y. Kolosov, International Space Law 106 (B. Belitzky trans. 1984) (Soviet view).

In the excerpt that follows, taken from the same OTA Report excerpted earlier in this chapter, the law governing private activities after launch is discussed:

Office of Technology Assessment, Space Stations and the Law: Legal Issues 44–50 (1986)

A. Applicable Law

As people begin to live and work in space, incidents of damage caused by intentional actions or negligence are certain to occur. Individuals seeking compensation for damage to property or personal injury may look either to international space law or to the tort laws of their own or other nations. Unfortunately, none of these courses of action is without difficulty. Current international space laws are little more than agreed fundamental principles, and no efficient mechanisms exist for applying these principles to specific cases. National tort laws, on the other hand, are well developed but vary drastically from country to country. In the United States, certain elements of tort law are not even consistently applied among the different States. Furthermore, some States have recently enacted legislation that limits the recovery of certain types of damages in tort suits.

1) International Law

... Article VI of the Outer Space Treaty provides that states party to the treaty bear "international responsibility for national activities in outer space," and that the activities of "nongovernmental entities" (i.e., individuals, corporations, etc.) "shall require authorization and continuing supervision by the appropriate State Party to the Treaty." Article VII of the Outer Space Treaty declares that a launching state is "internationally liable for damage to another State Party to the Treaty or to its natural or juridical persons. ..." The 1973 Liability Convention restates and expands on the principles established in article VII of the Outer Space Treaty and provides specific procedures for making and settling claims.

Although the Outer Space Treaty and the Liability Convention establish several key principles—e.g., absolute liability for damage on Earth or in the air, and liability of the launching state for either government or private sector activities—both treaties leave a great many questions unanswered. Three important problems raised by the current international space liability regime are:

Uncertain applicability to activities aboard space stations. There is considerable doubt as to whether the Liability Convention could ever be applied to injury or damage caused by persons participating in space station activities. Article VII states that the Convention does not apply to either the "nationals of [the] launching state" or "foreign nationals ... participating in the operation of that space object. ..." This [OTA Study] previously examined four different ways to own, operate, and register a space station. No matter which of these was chosen, it is likely that the participants would either be "nationals of [the] launching state" or "foreign nations ... participating in the operation of that space object. ..." Therefore, the Liability Convention would not apply. For example, under article VII of the Liability Convention, if a U.S. astronaut were killed by the negligence of either another U.S. astronaut or a foreign astronaut, the family of the U.S. astronaut could not file a claim for damages under the Liability Convention because the United States was the "launching state."

Lack of attention to damage caused by, and the liability of, individuals. [*See* DeSaussure and Haanappel, A Unified Multinational Approach to the Application of Tort and Contract Principles to Outer Space, 6 Syracuse Journal of International Law and Commerce 1 (1978).] Both the Outer Space Treaty and the Liability Convention focus on damage caused by space objects rather than on damage caused by individuals in space. This is understandable because the primary concern of the drafters was probably to offer some degree of protection from falling or colliding space objects. The crash of the radioactive Soviet satellite, Cosmos 954, in Canada was an example of the kind of injury best suited to the protections of the international treaties.

On a space station, however, individual personal injury actions resulting from intentional actions or negligence are likely to predominate. A good example of the Liability Convention's lack of attention to the role of individuals in space can be seen in its application of the doctrines of "strict" and "fault" liability. According to the terms of the treaty, a launching state whose space objects cause damage on the surface of the Earth or to aircraft in flight is strictly liable for the damage caused. States whose space objects cause damage to other objects in space are liable only after fault has been established. However, no such division between strict liability and fault liability is made with respect to individual conduct.

It is generally held, at least in common law countries, that strict liability applies to certain abnormally dangerous conditions and activities. [DeSaussure and Haanappel, *supra.*] Since, at present, most space activities might be regarded as "abnormally dangerous," one might argue that "fault" should play a diminished role in space. [It might be argued that eliminating the necessity to prove fault and thereby forcing all actors in space to cope with a strict liability scheme would be socially desirable for many of the same reasons that strict liability is used on Earth; that is, to make those engaged in dangerous activities liable for the consequences of such activities.] However, such a requirement could diminish the pursuit of commercial space opportunities by placing a heavier liability burden on these activities. On the other hand, one could also argue that all persons on the space station are to some degree engaged in an "abnormally dangerous" activity and that this is quite different from the situation on Earth where the injured party might not be a participant in the activity in question. [The following paragraph was in a footnote in the original.]

Maritime law offers some interesting insights into the question of liability for injury to individuals on board a space station. Under maritime law, the shipowner must furnish a vessel that is seaworthy in all respects. (*see* Mitchell v. Trawler Racer, Inc., 362 U.S. 539 [1960].) The shipowner's duty is nondelegable and the fact that the shipowner used "due diligence" to make the vessel seaworthy is no defense if a member of the ship's crew is injured by some defect. What constitutes a defect has been broadly construed, and so has the question of who is a seaman for the purpose of bringing an unseaworthiness action.

The concept of "seaworthiness"—or in this case, "spaceworthiness"—may eventually be a useful addition to space law, as it could serve to protect space workers and transfer the risk of liability to the spacecraft owner, who presumably, is in a better position to assess the risks of a particular activity.

With respect to liability as *between* spacefarers, the concept of fault may be more useful. How fault would be determined and what defenses would be permitted (e.g. contributory negligence, fellow servant rule, assumption of risk) are some of the most challenging questions that are likely to accompany the development of a tort law for space.

No efficient mechanism for resolving disputes between individuals. Serious questions exist as to whether current international laws could be applied to assist individuals. The 1967 Outer Space Treaty and the Liability Convention establish no cause of action, no courts, no rules of procedure, and no method of enforcing even agreed resolutions. Lacking such mechanisms, claimants are forced to rely on the diplomatic procedures commonly used between nations.

Article VIII of the Liability Convention requires that the state—not the injured person—present the claim to the "launching state"—not the person who caused the injury. Because nations and not individuals are involved, under article IX, claims for compensation must be presented "through diplomatic channels." If the two states in question do not have diplomatic relations then the claimant may present its claim through another state or through the Secretary General of the United Nations. Assuming that a claim has been filed and diplomatic negotiations have failed for a year, then article XIV authorizes the parties to set up a "Claims Commission" composed of three members (the two parties and an agreed chairman).

2) National Tort Laws

Perhaps in anticipation of the problems mentioned above, the drafters of the Liability Convention stated in article XI that: "Nothing in this Convention shall prevent a State, or the natural or juridical persons it might represent, from pursuing a claim in the courts ... of a launching state." Indeed, given the vague nature of the Liability Convention as compared with the well-defined state of domestic law, it would be unlikely that any individual would ever use it to obtain compensation for injury. [*See,* e.g., March, 7 Hastings International Dispute Resolution in Space, and Comparative Law Review 211 (1983).]

Having acknowledged this, it is then necessary to inquire which domestic laws would be applicable to a given case. Whenever individual relationships transcend the boundaries of one jurisdiction, conflicts arise concerning the applicable substantive law, the jurisdiction of national courts, and enforcement of foreign judgments. For example, every nation has its own methods for choosing the law applicable in a specific case. The most common of these are:

The *lex loci delecti,* that is, the law of the place where the offense occurred. Outer space, being *res communis* and, therefore, not subject to national law, has no clear "law of the place." Whether or not the *lex loci delecti* rule can be applied to the space station will depend on how nations agree to exercise jurisdiction and control over the space station.

The *lex fori,* that is, the law of the forum where the case is brought. This approach could be used on the space station, but again, would depend on how questions of jurisdiction and control are resolved.

The law of the state having the greatest interest. This rule—probably the prevailing U.S. standard—looks to which state's contacts with the incident are the most substantial and applies the relevant laws of that state. Because of its flexibility, this rule could have the greatest applicability to space station activities.

An important alternative (at least in contract, if not in tort cases) would be for the parties to stipulate both the applicable national law, and the applicable forum. This practice is frequently followed in multinational business contracts. This approach has two major defects. First, such stipulations would constrain only those who signed them. As space stations become larger, employing greater numbers of people, it may be impossible to anticipate and draw up contracts to cover all the interpersonal relationships that could develop. Second, some courts look with disfavor on contracts that attempt to divest them of jurisdiction. [See the introduction to this chapter.]

Given the current level of space activity, another solution to the problem of liability might be to negotiate interparty waivers of liability. The limitation of such agreements is that they only cover signatories. Interparty waivers of liability were used in the 1973 Spacelab Agreement [Space Laboratory: Cooperative Program, 24 U.S.T. 2049; TIAS 7722], the 1985 Memorandum of Understanding (MOU) regarding Phase B of the space station negotiations [*See* "Memorandum of Understanding Between the National Aeronautics and Space Administration and the European Space Agency for the Conduct of Parallel Detailed Definition and Preliminary Design Studies (Phase B) Leading Toward Further Cooperation in The Development, Operation and Utilization of a Permanently Manned Space Station," June 3, 1985], and are regularly used in shuttle launch agreements.

Article 11(A) of the Spacelab Agreement, for example, provides that the United States "shall have full responsibility for damage to its nationals ... [resulting from] ... this agreement." The ESA nations accept a similar "responsibility" under this article. In other words, the United States would not sue ESA for damage to U.S. nationals or property and vice versa. However, article 11(C) acknowledges that in the event injury is caused to persons not party to the agreement, "... such damage shall be the responsibility of ... [the United States or ESA] depending on where the responsibility falls under applicable law." The

1985 space station MOU between NASA and ESA extends the interparty waiver of liability to the Phase B contractors and subcontractors; however, third parties are still not covered under the agreement.

B. Future Developments

Current international space law will continue to be an effective means for allocating responsibility and liability for incidents which occur between nations. For example, should a space object of one nation fall on the territory of another nation or should one nation's space object collide with a space object of another nation, the principles found in the 1967 Outer Space Treaty, the Registration Convention, and Liability Convention will, when combined with serious diplomatic efforts, be sufficient to resolve these problems. As space activities increase and technologies grow more complex, some refinement of these principles will probably be necessary; nonetheless, the existing framework is workable *when applied to national activities.*

Unfortunately, the legal regime for redressing individual grievances resulting from space activities is not nearly so well established. As discussed above, international space law, with its heavy reliance on diplomacy, is too unwieldy for most tort actions between individuals, and negotiated interparty waivers of liability do not address the problem of third-party plaintiffs.

National tort laws, although well defined, differ considerably and no consensus exists on when to apply the law of one or another nation. The actions necessary to resolve this problem vary with time:

Short-term solutions (shuttle activities). Because the shuttle carries multiple and often multinational payloads, NASA has had to develop policies regarding both liability between mission participants (interparty liability) and liability with respect to parties unrelated to the mission (third-party liability). [*See* Brown, Commercial Law and Liability Issues of the Space Transport System, 23 Air Force Law Review 424 (1982–83) discussed in the notes at the end of this excerpt.] With respect to interparty liability, the standard shuttle launch agreement contains a mutual covenant not to sue similar to the one found in the Spacelab Agreement.

To cover the possibility of third-party suits, NASA also requires shuttle payload owners to purchase insurance to protect against damage to property and injury to persons unrelated to the space activities. This third-party insurance would, for example, be used to compensate individuals on Earth for damage they sustained as a result of de-orbiting space debris.

The liability procedures currently used by NASA are sufficient while the U.S. Government operates the shuttle, the shuttle crews are small and well-disciplined, and commercial insurance is available. As space activities become more complex and numerous, existing procedures will have to be reexamined.

Medium-term solutions (government space stations). Liability issues on the first generation of government-owned space stations could be handled by using the methods similar to those NASA now employs on the shuttle. The space station owner and operator, whether it be one nation or a consortium of nations, could require all other nations to waive their right to sue each other and require all participants to self-insure or purchase commercial insurance for third-party claims.

As space stations grow in size and complexity and become staffed by civilian employees, it will probably be necessary to develop more flexible rules for compensating individuals injured in space. A logical next step might be to negotiate international agreements similar to the NATO Status of Forces Agreements that would designate which nation's laws would apply in which situations. As mentioned above, it is not clear whether all national courts would feel constrained to respect these contracts.

Long-term solutions (private space stations and beyond). Eventually, space travel will be quite common and individuals may visit neighboring space stations much as we now visit neighboring countries. A rule could develop which places on the space traveler the burden to know the law of the place visited; that law would govern all civil and criminal actions resulting from the traveler's visit. Alternatively, nations may strive to achieve international uniformity in the application of "conflicts rules." The 1955 "Hague Convention on the Law Applicable to the Sale of Corporeal Movable Objects" and the 1973 "Hague Convention on the Law Applicable to Products Liability" are examples of such attempts. In the 1973 Products Liability Convention, nations agreed to apply the law of the habitual residence of the victim, or subsidiarily, the law of the place where the damage has occurred. Similar international agreements for applying Earth law to space activities may be necessary. Finally, nations may attempt to create a uniform substantive tort law system for activities in outer space. [International aviation law conventions such as Warsaw (49 Stat. 3000; T.I.A.S. 876; U.N.T.S. 11) and Rome (310 U.N.T.S. 181) might serve as models.]

NOTE ON LIABILITY: APPROACHES AND STANDARDS

A number of theories have been advanced regarding the open legal questions concerning private party liability identified by the OTA Report. The consensus seems to be that space activities should give rise to absolute liability (i.e., liability without fault) where they are the proximate cause of personal or property damage on earth or in earth airspace. *See, e.g.*, A. Haley, Space Law & Government 237–40 (1963); Haanappel, Product Liability in Space Law, 2 Houston Journal of International Law 55 (1979). What these proposals do, in effect, is to import the principles of international liability developed in the major treaties into the private law of torts. Thus the same principles that apply to accidents between space objects of two nations would be made to apply to accidents between individuals or between individuals and a single national. Extending the analogy further would require one to advocate a fault-based liability regime for accidents occurring in space, in keeping with the treatment of space mishaps in the Outer Space Treaty and Liability Convention. For more on these nation-to-nation liability issues, see Chapter 5.

The strict liability principle for space launches is based on the notion that these are "ultrahazardous activities," that is, activities which "necessarily involve a risk of serious harm to the person, land or chattels of others which cannot be eliminated by the exercise of utmost care" and which are "not a matter of common usage." Restatement of Torts § 520 (1977), Restatement (Second) of Torts §§ 519, 520 (1977). In the book cited above, noted early space lawyer Andrew Haley made the point that early in the history of aviation courts held that airflight, and even balloon flights, were ultrahazardous, but that a negligence standard for airflight conduct had since become the dominant rule. A. Haley, *supra,* at 238–39. This rule was stated in the Uniform Aeronautics Act, a codification of the negligence standard adopted by twenty-four states. *See* Prentiss v. National Air Lines, Inc., 112 F. Supp. 306, 308 (D.N.J. 1953). *See also* Boyd v. White, 128 Cal. App. 2d 641, 651, 276 P.2d 92, 99–100 (1954) (expressing the general view that an airplane is not an inherently dangerous instrument when handled by a competent pilot). *But see* Restatement (Second) of Torts § 520A (1977) (maintaining strict liability standard despite authority to the contrary). From his review of the historical record, Haley concluded that,

> the operator of a rocket range or service in the years to come can expect that his activities will be viewed by the courts as being ultrahazardous and that, at least until such operations become commonplace, he can expect to be held liable for damage caused by an errant rocket although he is free from negligence. As technology advances and rockets become less of a novelty, it is probable that the rule will be changed and that, as in the case of aircraft, liability will be based solely on fault.

Id. at 239–40 (footnotes omitted). *But cf.* Deem, Liability of Private Space Transportation Companies to Their Customers, 51 Insurance Counsel Journal 340, 350–51 (1984) (collecting cases where testing of high performance aircraft and rocket motors gave rise to strict liability for property damage on the ground, *e.g.*, from noise and vibrations stemming from supersonic flight). Note that Haley was writing in the era prior to the Outer Space Treaty of 1967 (discussed in Chapter 3) and the Liability Convention of 1972 (discussed in Chapter 5). Note also that the liability standard for the operation of aircraft has become less important in light of the growth of strict product liability for defective products, including airplanes and related equipment. *See, e.g.*, Herndon v. Seven Bar Flying Service, Inc., 716 F.2d 1322 (10th Cir. 1983); Nesselrode v. Executive Beechcraft, Inc., 707 S.W.2d 371 (Mo. 1986); D. Barry, Choice of Law Problems in General Aviation Accident Cases: Liability and Damages, in General Aviation Accident Litigation 65 (Practicing Law Institute 1986) (PLI Litigation and Administrative Practice Course Handbook Series Litigation No. 312). *See generally* Priest, The Current Insurance Crisis and Modern Tort Law, 96 Yale Law Journal 1521 (1987) (discussing drastic increases in insurance premiums necessitated by rapidly escalating damage awards in tort cases, including those based on strict liability); Brody, When Products Turn Into Liabilities, Fortune, March 24, 1986, at 18; Wall Street Journal, January 21, 1986, at 31, col. 5. *Cf.* Dillingham & Oldham, Developments and Trends in Aviation Insurance, 21 Tort Insurance Law Journal 44 (1985).

Nevertheless, negligence of one type or another is often asserted as an alternative basis of liability in aircraft accident cases. *See, e.g.*, Brooks v. United States, 695 F.2d 984 (5th Cir. 1983); *In re* Air Crash Disaster Near Chicago Ill., 500 F. Supp. 1044 (N.D. Ill. 1980), *aff'd in part and rev'd in part,* 644 F.2d 594 (7th Cir. 1981), *cert. denied,* 454 U.S. 878 (1981). *Cf.* Product Liability in Air and Space Transportation (K. Bockstiegel ed. 1978). In fact, the standard of care differs from state to state in the United States. *See* P. Foss & R. Adams, Pre-Trial Strategy in American Air Disaster Litigation, 14 Transportation Law Journal 327 (1986) (describing different standards of care and attempts by counsel to bring cases in more "favorable" states).

Although the amount of damages a private firm may have to pay is unlimited, several factors—some in place, others only possibilities—have the potential to limit damages. First among these is the regulations establishing the amount of insurance a firm must carry to legally launch a private payload into space. Although many launch service companies have substantial assets (*e.g.*, Martin Marietta, McDonnell Douglas, or General Dynamics), some are small "start-ups" for whom the insurance coverage is for all practical purposes a ceiling on liability. Note, however, that there is some reason to believe that a court would "pierce the corporate veil" if it found that a launch company was too thinly capitalized given the risk inherent in its activities. This is one reason why there is so much interest in limiting liability in the launch industry.

The second factor that may limit damage awards is the possibility of legislation to place explicit limits on damages that may be collected in the event of a space launch disaster. This would be analogous to the Price-Anderson Act of 1957, Pub. L. No. 85–256, § 4, 71 Stat. 576 (1957), *as amended by* Act of September 29, 1965, Pub. L. No. 89–210, § 1, 79 Stat. 855 (1965) *and* Act of December 31, 1975, Pub. L. No. 94–197, §§ 2–14, 89 Stat. 1111 (1975) (codified at 42 U.S.C. § 2210 (1995)). The Price-Anderson Act limits the liability of nuclear energy companies in the event of a disaster. The Act has been criticized, however, as an unfair subsidy of a dangerous industry—a criticism not likely to be as effective against the space industry. *See* Brauer, The Price-Anderson Act: A Constitutional Meltdown of Tort Liability, 8 Hastings Constitutional Law Quarterly 731 (1981).

Some commentators have called for a Price-Anderson Act for outer space activities. *See* A. Dula, Management of Interparty and Third-Party Liability for Routine Space Shuttle Operations, in Space Shuttle and the Law 93 (U. Miss. L. Center, Monograph Series No. 3, 1980). *See also* Bosco, The United States Government as Defendant—One Example of the Need for a Uniform Liability Regime to Govern Outer Space and Space-Related Activities, 15 Pepperdine Law Review 581 (1988) (pointing out widely divergent damages that would be paid to third party claimants from different states in suits against the government for a space-related disaster, and calling for unified tort claims regime for space-related accidents). In his paper Dula also calls for (1) *mandatory* cross-waivers of liability among all parties to commercial space contracts; (2) amendment of the NASA Authorization Act to permit NASA to indemnify users of the space shuttle against the risk of loss of satellites and other payloads; and (3) a budget for on-the-spot settlement of claims against NASA for property damage on earth due to launch operations. The second of these proposals was adopted by NASA; Section 2458b of the NASA Act now reads as follows:

42 U.S.C. § 2458b. Insurance and Indemnification

(a) Authorization

The Administration is authorized on such terms and to the extent it may deem appropriate to provide liability insurance for any user of a space vehicle to compensate all or a portion of claims by third parties for death, bodily injury, or loss of or damage to property resulting from activities carried on in connection with the launch, operations or recovery of the space vehicle. Appropriations available to the Administration may be used to acquire such insurance, but such appropriations shall be reimbursed to the maximum extent practicable by the users under reimbursement policies established pursuant to section 2473(c) of this title.

(b) Indemnification

Under such regulations in conformity with this section as the Administrator shall prescribe taking into account the availability, cost and terms of liability insurance, any agreement between the Administration and a user of a space vehicle may provide that the United States will indemnify the user against claims (including reasonable expenses of litigation or settlement) by third parties for death, bodily injury, or loss of or damage to property resulting from activities carried on in connection with the launch, operations or recovery of the space vehicle, but only to the extent that such claims are not compensated by liability insurance of the user, provided that such indemnification may be limited to claims resulting from other than the actual negligence or willful misconduct of the user.

Pub. L. 85–568, title III § 308, 93 Stat. 348; Pub. L. 96–48, § 6(b)(2), Aug. 8, 1979.

New legislation, discussed in the notes accompanying the 1984 Commercial Space Launch Act, *infra,* has been passed to provide additional limits on liability. Unfortunately, it was passed after this book went to press, so it is not excerpted here. The notes, *infra,* provide a clear outline of the liability limits' operation, however, and the policy issues analyzed here remain just as relevant as before. The Office of Commercial Space Transportation, which is the central federal agency responsible for regulating the commercial space launch industry, has expressed its intention to exercise flexibility in its review of launching companies' insurance arrangements, which review is authorized by Executive Order 12465, Feb. 24, 1984, and the Commercial Space Launch Act, codified at 49 U.S.C. § 70101 (1995). This is in keeping with a number of comments the Office received in response to an Advanced Notice of Proposed Rulemaking on the topic of minimum insurance requirements for commercial space launches. *See* 50 Fed. Reg. 19280–01, May 7, 1985.

LIABILITY FOR DAMAGE TO CARGO

So far, we have been focusing on the various theories that have been invoked to establish liability for personal injury and property damage arising from aircraft accidents. But what legal standards apply in the event that cargo *on board* an aircraft is damaged?

In the case of aircraft, goods damaged on international flights are covered by the Warsaw Convention, which limits liability to $9.07 per pound or a maximum of $75,000. *See* Reukema, No New Deal on Liability Limits for International Flights, 18 International Lawyer 983 (1984) (describing Supreme Court case refusing to abrogate liability limits of Warsaw Convention); Note, Torts—Liability Limitation Under the Warsaw Convention, 50 Journal of Air Law & Commerce 155 (1984).

As for cargoes in space, no binding rules have yet emerged, but firms and governments have begun to follow certain practices that may eventually be codified. For the most part, the standard procedure is that both parties to a space launch agreement agree to hold each other harmless for damage that may occur. *See* the Launch Services Agreement excerpted later in this chapter. *See also* Brown, Commercial Law and Liability Issues of the Space Transport System, 23 Air Force Law Review 425, 431 (1982–1983). *Cf.* Deem, Comment, Liability of Private Space Transportation Companies to Their Customers, 1983 Brigham Young University Law Review 755 (1983). Of course, this waiver has no effect on the claims of third parties. *See* Wolcott, Some Aspects of Third Party Liability in Space Shuttle Operations, 13 Akron Law Review 613, 615 (1980). One commentator has explained the rationale behind this "no-fault, no-subrogation, interparty waiver of liability," as it is called, in the following terms:

> Although insurance coverage becomes more readily available in increasingly favorable terms with the passage of time [in a developing industry], there is some concern about the ability of the insurance industry to underwrite such enormous risk potential. Since the covenants also protect a user from another user, the participation of small users is fostered by eliminating the necessity for a user of a $50,000 package to take out a liability policy to cover damage done by his package to the rest of the users' packages and the [spacecraft] itself in an amount which could exceed nine figures. Finally, such a policy serves to simplify risk allocation among NASA and all users. It is important to note that the cross-waiver provision resulted from lengthy negotiations and discussions with representatives of the insurance industry and prospective users.

Brown, *supra,* 23 Air Force Law Review, at 431.

By waiving liability, these agreements skirt a number of issues that may arise in the future. One is the status of commercial launch vehicles. Under standard commercial law analysis, a transporter of goods is either a "common carrier" or a private carrier. The distinction is well described in the article by Deem, *supra:*

> A common carrier has been defined as "one who, by virtue of his calling, undertakes, for compensation, to transport personal property from one place to another for all who may choose to employ him, and everyone who undertakes to carry for compensation all persons indifferently, is as to liability, to be deemed a common carrier." Because it is held to a standard of care higher than that for ordinary negligence,
>
> > the common carrier is regarded as a practical insurer of the goods against all losses of whatever kind with the exception of (1) those arising from what is known as an act of God, and (2) those caused by the public enemy; to which modern times have added (3) those arising from the act of the public authority, (4) those arising from the act of the shipper, and (5) those arising from the inherent nature of the goods.
>
> A private carrier or contract carrier, as opposed to a common carrier, does not undertake to carry for all persons indiscriminately but only for those with whom he wishes to contract.
>
> > Subject to statutory restrictions, state or federal, concerning performance of a transportation service none of which are applicable here, a person has the right to engage in the business of a private carrier. He asserts that right when, seeking all potential business as avidly as any other businessman desirous of a profit, it is yet his practice to treat each individual shipment on a separate basis and accept or reject it as wished and on terms and at rates satisfactory to him at the time.
>
> [Home Ins. Co. v. Riddell, 252 F.2d 1, 4 (5th Cir. 1958).] [Importantly,] a private or contract carrier is held to the traditional standard of due care.
>
> During the early years of the space transportation era, it is doubtful that a space carrier would be considered a common carrier. Space carriers are not likely to hold themselves out to the public to transport goods into space for all persons. ... This

> practice of contracting each shipment on a separate basis is one factor indicating that a transportation company is a private carrier rather than a common carrier. Additionally, space carriers are more likely to be considered private carriers because they will tend to serve a unique limited class of persons, satellite users, rather than the public at large. ... Presumably, absent contrary state or federal regulation, space carriers could remain private carriers even in a well-developed space transportation industry [with substantial volume] if they contracted separately for each carriage and did not hold themselves out to the public to transport goods or persons into space indiscriminately.

51 Insurance Counsel Journal 340, 355.

THE *CHALLENGER* DISASTER

Because of the mutual waivers of liability for damage to goods that proliferate in space launch agreements, many observers were surprised to learn that the victims of the Space Shuttle *Challenger* disaster had not signed any waivers at all. As a consequence, the estates of these victims were free to pursue claims against both NASA and the government contractors responsible for the defective rocket engine seal that led to the disaster. *See generally* M. McConnell, Major Malfunction (1987). All these claims have now been settled. But they may prove instructive for future space-related suits (which we hope never arise).

While it would be impossible to review all the intricacies of these actions for recovery on behalf of the *Challenger* victims' estates, several points are worth noting.

First, there were three classes of people aboard the *Challenger:* (1) military personnel, (2) NASA personnel, and (3) one civilian. Because the Federal Employees Claim Act (FECA) applies exclusively to federal employees operating within the scope of their duties, it was the only source of recovery available to the first two classes of claimants against the government. And the Act makes it clear that no recovery can be had by military personnel killed in the line of duty. *See* Feres v. United States, 340 U.S. 135, 146 (1950); *cf.* Myers Comment, The *Feres* Doctrine: Has it Created Remediless Wrongs for Relatives of Servicemen? 44 University of Pittsburgh Law Review 929 (1983) (criticizing *Feres* doctrine). The lone civilian on board the Shuttle (Christa McAuliffe) was not covered by this provision, however, and her estate did reach a settlement with the government.

As for the other two claimants in the case, they pursued claims solely against the government contractors in the case, primarily Morton Thiokol. Because Thiokol appeared to be negligent in its decision to recommend launch of the Shuttle on that fateful, cold morning in January, and because the rocket seals were defective in the first place, all three claimants had strong cases under both negligence and strict product liability theories. Personal Conversation with Ronald D. Krist, attorney for several victims' estates, July 26, 1988.

It is difficult to predict what effect the reportedly large settlement in the case will have on future insurance practices and/or space activities in general. One effect, however, is likely to be far greater care in deciding whether launch conditions are safe. Waivers of liability may also be introduced at some point.

CONTRACTS RELATING TO OUTER SPACE

Although a host of contracts could be described as "space-related," including those between NASA and its subcontractors or between those subcontractors and their suppliers, we will consider here only those contracts that directly relate to launch services. This is one of the few major areas of truly space-related commerce where enough contracts have been negotiated and signed to allow any room for generalizing about principles, trends, etc. Thus, although we will briefly discuss such agreements as space insurance contracts and NASA Joint Endeavor Agreements, our primary focus will be on launch service contracts.

With NASA now out of the commercial launch business for the most part, most launch agreements are now between a private company desiring to have a payload (usually a satellite) put into orbit and a private launch services company. Keep in mind, however, that these are not the only parties with an interest in the agreement. The purchase of launch services, for example, is quite often financed by banks; these banks may actually be providing the early payments to the launch services company, with the purchaser to repay the banks out of revenue generated by the satellite. In addition, the government is directly involved as well: at present, it still has a monopoly on launch sites.

Launch agreements reflect the involvement of these additional parties in a variety of ways. Since banks may be making early payments, they are especially interested in the payment schedule (i.e., the percentage of the contract price due at each stage of preparation for the launch), as well as the provisions governing liquidated damages for early termination, re-flight schedulings in the event of a mishap, etc. The government, for its part, shows up in the agreements in a standard provision reminding the parties that it has priority in the use of the launch sites.

Launch service contracts are fairly elaborate in their coverage of issues, though actually quite short relative to other commercial agreements for transactions of similar value ($100–200 million). This is due primarily to the fact that the commercial space launch community is so small, and to the shared belief in the community that the high uncertainties of space activities, rather than one's negotiating partner, are the true adversaries. In any event, the typical launch agreement includes provisions on (1) allocation of the risks of loss, (2) safety and accident prevention, (3) payment schedules, (4) performance criteria, (5) rescheduling arrangements in the event of delay, and (6) miscellaneous matters, such as termination and dispute settlement procedures, nondisclosure covenants, and choice of law. In addition, the agreement may include detailed appendices describing (1) the payload, and (2) if the payload is a satellite (as is usually the case), the exact orbit it is to be placed into.

Commercial Launch Services Contracts Between Martin Marietta Corporation, P.O. Box 179, Denver, Colorado, 80201, and International Telecommunications Satellite Organization "INTELSAT," 3400 International Drive, N.W., Washington, D.C., 20008-3098, Contract for Commercial Launch Services

THIS CONTRACT is entered into this tenth day of August, 1987, by and between MARTIN MARIETTA CORPORATION, a Maryland corporation, with offices in Denver, Colorado, hereinafter called "Martin Marietta," and the International Telecommunications Satellite Organization (hereinafter referred to as "INTELSAT"), an international organization established by the Agreement Relating to the International Telecommunications Satellite Organization INTELSAT and the Operating Agreement relating thereto, done at Washington, D.C., 20 August 1971. This Contract shall constitute the understanding of the Parties and stipulate the respective rights, responsibilities and liabilities understood and accepted by both Parties regarding the provision of Launch Services to INTELSAT by Martin Marietta.

Article 1—*Definitions*

Unless the context shall otherwise require, capitalized terms used herein shall have the following meanings:

1.1 *Adjustment in Price or Terms*—An increase or decrease in the price(s) included in this Contract, the allowance of a reasonable increase or decrease in specified performance time, and any other adjustment of the provisions of this Contract and authorized by an appropriate amendment to this Contract.

1.2 *Best Efforts*—Diligently working in a good and workman-like manner as a reasonable, prudent manufacturer of launch vehicles and provider of Launch Services.

1.3 *Launch or Launching*—The intentional ignition of the Titan III solid rocket motors.

1.4 *Launch Day*—A calendar day during the Launch Slot set for the Launch during which the Launch may take place within the Launch Window.

1.5 *Launch Opportunity*—The availability to INTELSAT of a Payload position on a Titan III within a Launch Period which shall include such considerations as: (1) adequate time to perform the mission analysis and implementation of the Titan III/Payload interfaces; (2) then existing commitments for Launch Services to others.

1.6 *Launch Period*—A period of consecutive months during which a Launch may take place as set forth herein.

1.7 *Launch Services*—Those activities including performance of mission analysis, furnishing the Titan III Launch Vehicle and Launch crew and arranging for the launch complex and range services necessary to Launch the Titan III with INTELSAT's Payload as specified in Exhibit A, Launch Services for INTELSAT.

1.8 *Launch Slot*—A period of a minimum of 30 calendar days within the Launch Period during which a Launch may occur.

1.9 *Launch Time*—The instant that the ignition of the Titan III solid rocket motors is scheduled to take place within the Launch Window defined in hours, minutes and seconds in Greenwich Mean Time (GMT).

1.10 *Launch Window*—The time period(s) within the Launch Day established from requirements defined in Exhibit B, Interface Control Document when the Launch may occur.

1.11 *Party or Parties*—INTELSAT or Martin Marietta or both according to the usage.

1.12 *Payload*—All property to be flown aboard the Titan III which is provided by INTELSAT, its contracts or subcontractors.

1.13 *Payload Mission*—The mission of the Payload after separation from the Titan III.

1.14 *Reflight*—A priority Launch, without charge to INTELSAT subject to the Best Efforts of Martin Marietta, arising from failure of the Titan III Mission to achieve its mission objectives causing the Payload not to achieve a geo-synchronous transfer orbit.

1.15 *Replacement Launch*—A priority Launch, paid by INTELSAT, subject to the Best Efforts of Martin Marietta, arising from failure of the Titan III or the Payload to achieve its mission objectives for any reason.

1.16 *Shared Launch*—A Launch on one Titan III of two Payloads one of which is the Payload supplied by INTELSAT.

1.17 *Third Party*—Any person or entity, including the United States Government or any agency, department, or instrumentality thereof, which is not a Party to this Contract.

1.18 *Titan III*—The Titan Launch Vehicle, excluding the Payload, utilized to furnish Commercial Launch Services.

1.19 *Titan III Mission*—The mission assigned to the Titan III as specified in Exhibit B, Interface Control Document.

Article 2—*Services to be Provided*

Martin Marietta, in consideration for payment made by INTELSAT under this Contract, shall in accordance with the terms and conditions contained herein, make its Best Efforts to furnish Launch Services for the purpose of delivering INTELSAT's Payload into orbit from Cape Canaveral Air Force Station (CCAFS), Cape Canaveral, Florida, in accordance with the following:

2.1 Launch Services in accordance with "Launch Services for INTELSAT", date 21 May 1987, attached and incorporated by reference into this Contract as Exhibit "A."

2.2 Physical, Functional, Mission and Operational interface requirements in accordance with the "Titan III to INTELSAT VI Interface Control Document (ICD)", dated 21 May 1987, attached and incorporated by reference into this Contract as Exhibit "B".

2.3 Responsibilities of INTELSAT in accordance with "INTELSAT's Responsibilities", date 21 May 1987, attached and incorporated by reference into this Contract as Exhibit "C".

*   *   *

Article 4—*Schedule for Delivery of Payload*

INTELSAT shall furnish, at its expense, to Martin Marietta at the location and in accordance with the schedule set forth in Exhibit C, INTELSAT's Responsibilities, each Payload to be Launched, which shall meet the requirements of Exhibit B, Interface Control Document, for integration and assembly into the Titan III. INTELSAT shall deliver the Payload checked out and ready for integration onto the Titan III.

Article 5—*Completion of Launch Services*

Martin Marietta shall be deemed to have completed the Launch Services for each Launch under this Contract upon the intentional ignition of the Titan III solid rocket motors, except for delivery of post-launch data identified in Exhibit A, Launch Services for INTELSAT.

Article 6—*Best Efforts Replacement Launch*

6.1 INTELSAT may request a Replacement Launch in the event that following any Launch under this Contract, the Titan III Mission or the Payload Mission has not been accomplished for any reason.

6.2 The request of INTELSAT for a Replacement Launch must be in writing and received by Martin Marietta no later than ninety (90) days after Launch. The request shall indicate the Launch Period desired for the Replacement Launch.

6.3 Martin Marietta shall make its Best Efforts to provide a Replacement Launch within twelve (12) months from the receipt of INTELSAT's request and shall inform INTELSAT after receipt of the request if a Launch Opportunity exists within the requested Launch Period. If a Launch Opportunity does not exist for the Launch Period requested by INTELSAT, then the Parties will negotiate in good faith for a mutually acceptable Launch Period subject to then existing Launch Services commitments to others.

6.4 The replacement Payload shall be designed, built, tested and integrated with the Titan III in accordance with the requirements of Exhibit B, Interface Control Document and Exhibit C, INTELSAT's Responsibilities.

6.5 INTELSAT shall pay Martin Marietta the same price for the Replacement Launch as paid for the Launch being replaced subject to escalation in accordance with ARTICLE 11, ECONOMIC PRICE ADJUSTMENT. Additional charges shall be paid by INTELSAT for any Titan III or other equipment modifications that may be required, increased charges that may be imposed by the Government and any charge for rearranging the Launch schedule which Martin Marietta may incur on account of providing INTELSAT a priority Replacement Launch. Payment for Replacement Launch Services shall be made by INTELSAT in accordance with the Payment Due Date schedule for Firm Launches set forth in ARTICLE 8, PAYMENT FOR LAUNCH SERVICES. The first payment for Replacement Launch Services shall be made by INTELSAT at the time of written agreement of the Parties for Martin Marietta to provide Replacement Launch Services. Such first payment shall include all cumulative sums necessary to make the payments current, including escalation, depending on where the Replacement Launch schedule falls within the payment schedule set forth in ARTICLE 8. Payments shall be made by INTELSAT in accordance with ARTICLE 10, TERMS OF PAYMENT.

6.6 The Replacement Launch shall be provided in accordance with the terms and conditions of this contract.

6.7 The remedies set forth in this ARTICLE 6 shall be the sole and exclusive remedies of the Buyer from Martin Marietta in the event the Titan III mission fails for any reason.

Article 7—*Prices for Launch Services*

7.1 Firm Launch Services—INTELSAT shall pay to Martin Marietta, for the firm Launch Services performed under this Contract, the total price of $219,960,000.00 (U.S. Dollars), allocated as follows:

Titan III Launch Services No. 1 $111,530,000.00

Titan III Launch Services No. 2 $108,430,000.00

The above prices include the price of all standard, non-standard and optional Launch Services specified in Exhibit A except as otherwise expressly stated therein.

Article 8—*Payment for Launch Services*

8.1 *Firm Launches*—INTELSAT shall pay the price due under this Contract to Martin Marietta with respect to each firm Titan III to be Launched in accordance with the following schedule:

Payment Due Date	*% Price Due*
At contract effective date	5.0%
33 Mo. prior to Scheduled Launch	5.0%
30 Mo. prior to Scheduled Launch	5.0%
27 Mo. prior to Scheduled Launch	7.5%
24 Mo. prior to Scheduled Launch	7.5%
21 Mo. prior to Scheduled Launch	7.5%
18 Mo. prior to Scheduled Launch	10.0%
15 Mo. prior to Scheduled Launch	10.0%
12 Mo. prior to Scheduled Launch	10.0%
9 Mo. prior to Scheduled Launch	10.0%
6 Mo. prior to Scheduled Launch	10.0%
3 Mo. prior to Scheduled Launch	7.5%
2 Mo. prior to Scheduled Launch	5.0%

8.2 *Launch Option*—Note: If INTELSAT elects to purchase a Launch Services Option during the course of this Contract then the following payment provision shall apply:

If the Launch Services Option contained in ARTICLE 9, LAUNCH SERVICES OPTION, is exercised by the INTELSAT, INTELSAT shall pay the price due under this Contract to Martin Marietta for the option Titan III to be Launched in accordance with the following schedule.

Payment Due Date	*% Price Due*
At exercise of the option	5.0%
33 Mo. prior to Scheduled Launch	5.0%
30 Mo. prior to Scheduled Launch	5.0%
27 Mo. prior to Scheduled Launch	7.5%
24 Mo. prior to Scheduled Launch	7.5%
21 Mo. prior to Scheduled Launch	7.5%
18 Mo. prior to Scheduled Launch	10.0%
15 Mo. prior to Scheduled Launch	10.0%
12 Mo. prior to Scheduled Launch	10.0%
9 Mo. prior to Scheduled Launch	10.0%
6 Mo. prior to Scheduled Launch	10.0%
3 Mo. prior to Scheduled Launch	7.5%
2 Mo. prior to Scheduled Launch	5.0%

*   *   *

Article 16—*Right To Destruct Titan III and Payload*

INTELSAT acknowledges that the U.S. Government shall have the absolute right to intentionally destroy the Titan III and the Payload following the ignition of the Titan III solid rocket motors for range safety purposes including protection of persons and property. In such event, INTELSAT agrees not to assert any claim against Martin Marietta, or its subcontractors, the U.S. Government or its contractors or employees based upon injury to or death of persons and loss of INTELSAT's property resulting from such destruction and for damages incurred resulting from U.S. Government safety actions.

Article 17—*Allocation of Certain Risks*

17.1 *General*—The following risks, arising out of or incident to the Launch Services to be provided by Martin Marietta and its subcontractors at every tier under this Contract are allocated between INTELSAT and Martin Marietta as set forth in this ARTICLE 17, notwithstanding any other provision of this Contract.

17.2 *Third Party Liability*

17.2.1 Martin Marietta shall procure and maintain Third Party liability insurance to protect Martin Marietta and INTELSAT against injury, death and property damage caused to Third Parties, arising out of or resulting from Launch Services provided under this Contract at CCAFS or Kennedy Space Center (KSC) and/or after Launch, and/or arising out of or resulting from the Payload while situated at CCAFS or KSC and/or after Launch, including but not limited to work performed on or relating to the Payload under this contract. Such insurance shall be in an amount of U.S. $100 million, combined single limit, or as prescribed by any regulation, directive or order of any United States government agency having authority to regulate commercial launch vehicle transportation, provided that, if such amount is not commercially available at a reasonable premium in light of prevailing standards in the industry as determined by Martin Marietta, using its reasonable judgment, such insurance shall be in any lesser amount commercially available at a reasonable premium, and acceptable to the government agency referred to in this sentence. Insurance provided pursuant to this paragraph 17.2.1 shall commence upon the arrival of the Payload and INTELSAT's personnel incident to the Payload Launch campaign at CCAFS or KSC, and shall continue for a term of ninety (90) days after the actual date of launch. Further, Martin Marietta shall, either directly or through the U.S. Government, indemnify and hold INTELSAT harmless from any and all loss, damage, liability or expense resulting from property damage and bodily harm caused to Third Parties to the extent not covered by said insurance, which damage or harm arises out of or in connection with (i) Launch Services furnished under this Contract and/or (ii) any Payload, provided that the occurrence giving rise to such damage or harm is during the period commencing on the day of the Launch and ending 36 months after the actual date of Launch. Martin Marietta shall at its sole expense defend any claims, action, suits and proceedings, whether in law equity, brought against INTELSAT on account of such damage or harm, and shall pay expenses, including attorney's fees, and satisfy all judgments as may be incurred by or rendered against INTELSAT in connection therewith, provided Martin Marietta is given prompt notice of any such claim, action, suit or proceeding and provided Martin Marietta is given, at Martin Marietta's written request and sole expense, such assistance and information as may be reasonably provided by INTELSAT.

17.2.2 The insurance obtained by Martin Marietta pursuant to paragraph 17.2.1 of this ARTICLE 17 shall name INTELSAT and may name the U.S. Government, and agents, employees, contractors and subcontractors of the U.S. Government, as additional insureds and shall contain a waiver of subrogation rights in favor of any such additional insureds. Martin Marietta shall, at its own expense, submit for INTELSAT's review and approval within 90 days prior to the first day of the Launch Slot a certificate of insurance evidencing the coverage and liability limits required above. The insurance required by paragraph 17.2.1 shall expressly provide that all of the provisions thereof except the limits of liability, shall operate in the same manner as if there were a separate policy with and covering each insured.

17.3 *Release of U.S. Government*—INTELSAT and Martin Marietta hereby waive any cause of action in tort against the U.S. Government, its agents, employees, contractors and subcontractors, to the extent required by the U.S. Government, and agree to furnish appropriate waivers and releases as may later be required to implement this paragraph 17.3, in connection with the use of U.S. Government launch facilities, equipment or required launch support services under this Contract and hereby indemnify and hold harmless the U.S. Government from such claims to the extent of insurance coverage purchased under paragraph 17.2 above. Except for said indemnity, each Party shall incorporate a similar provision containing the substance of this paragraph 17.3 into contracts with all customers, associated contractors, and subcontractors who participate in activities at CCAFS and/or KSC.

17.4 *Worker's Compensation and Employer's Liability Insurance*—Each party shall comply with applicable worker's compensation and occupational disease statutes and shall procure and maintain insurance policies with limits of liability and coverages required in accordance with such statutes. Employer's liability coverage in the minimum amount of $100,000 shall be required except in states with exclusive or monopolistic funds which do not permit the writing of worker's compensation by private carriers.

17.5 *Inter-Party Waiver for Damages Caused to the Persons, Goods, or Property of the Parties*

17.5.1 Martin Marietta and INTELSAT agree that, with respect to injury to or death of persons involved in, or damage to property used in connection with, Launch Services to be furnished under this Contract, neither Party will make any claim against the other or against the contractors, subcontractors, officers, directors, agents, servants and employees of the other, or any of them, or against any other Titan III launch services buyers, and each Party shall bear its own risk of loss with respect to injury to or death of its own employees or damage to its own property howsoever caused.

17.5.2 INTELSAT and Martin Marietta shall each be responsible for such insurance as they deem necessary to protect their respective property. Any insurance carried in accordance with this paragraph 17.5.2 and any policy taken out in substitution or replacement for any such policy shall provide that the insurers shall waive any rights of subrogation against Martin Marietta, INTELSAT, and the U.S. Government, as the case may be, and their contractors and subcontractors at every tier. Each party shall arrange to have an appropriate certificate issued to the other evidencing any waiver of subrogation required pursuant to this subparagraph 17.5.2.

17.5.3 INTELSAT shall require its contractors and subcontractors to agree to make no claims against Martin Marietta, the contractors and subcontractors of Martin Marietta, the officers, directors, agents, servants and employees of Martin Marietta, or any of them, or against any other Titan III launch services buyers, with respect to injury to or death of INTELSAT's contractors' or subcontractors' employees involved in, or damage to INTELSAT's contractors' or subcontractors' property used in connection with, Launch Services to be furnished under this Contract; further, INTELSAT shall require persons or entities to which INTELSAT has, prior to the completion of the furnishing by Martin Marietta of Launch Services for a particular Payload, sold or leased portions of or services on that Payload, to agree not to make claims for damage arising out of the performance of this Contract against Martin Marietta, the contractors and subcontractors of Martin Marietta, the officers, directors, agents, servants and employees of Martin Marietta, or any of them, or against any other Titan III launch services buyers.

17.5.4 Martin Marietta shall require its contractors, subcontractors and other Titan III launch services buyers to agree to make no claims against INTELSAT, the contractors and subcontractors of INTELSAT, the Signatory members, officers, directors, agents, servants and employees of INTELSAT, or any of them, with respect to injury to or death of such other buyers', or Martin Marietta's contractors' or subcontractors', employees involved in, or damage to such other buyers' or Martin Marietta's contractors' or subcontractors' property used in connection with, Launch Services to be furnished under this Contract.

17.5.5 Nothing in subparagraphs 17.5.3 and 17.5.4 shall be construed as limiting the rights of Martin Marietta regarding its own contractors and subcontractors or the rights of INTELSAT regarding its own contractors and subcontractors.

17.6 *Limitation of Liability*—Martin Marietta's liability to INTELSAT and to persons claiming by or through INTELSAT, whether or not arising under contract, or in negligence, strict liability, or under any other theory of tort or liability, shall not include any loss or use or loss of profit or revenue or any other indirect, special, incidental or consequential damages. In no event shall Martin Marietta's liability to INTELSAT for any claim arising out of a particular Launch Services exceed the price for that Titan III Launch Services to be paid by INTELSAT as provided in ARTICLE 7, PRICES FOR LAUNCH SERVICES, of this Contract, without any Economic Price Adjustments, provided however that nothing in this paragraph shall affect any right of INTELSAT to a Replacement Launch, a Reflight or a Cash Refund under ARTICLE 6, if purchased by INTELSAT, or obligation of Martin Marietta to INTELSAT under subparagraph 17.2.1. MARTIN MARIETTA HAS NOT MADE NOR DOES MAKE ANY REPRESENTATION OR WARRANTY, WHETHER WRITTEN OR ORAL, EXPRESSED OR IMPLIED, INCLUDING, BUT NOT LIMITED TO ANY WARRANTY OF DESIGN, OPERATION, CONDITION, QUALITY, SUITABILITY OR MERCHANTABILITY OR OF FITNESS FOR USE OR FOR A PARTICULAR PURPOSE, ABSENCE OF LATENT OR OTHER DEFECTS WHETHER OR NOT DISCOVERABLE, OR EXCEPT AS OTHERWISE PROVIDED IN ARTICLE 6, REFLIGHT/CASH REFUND GUARANTEE IF PURCHASED BY INTELSAT, ANY OTHER WARRANTY WHATSOEVER, EXPRESS OR IMPLIED, WITH RESPECT TO THE TITAN III OR ASSOCIATED EQUIPMENT.

17.7 *Infringement of Intellectual Property Rights of Third Parties*

17.7.1 Martin Marietta indemnifies and holds INTELSAT harmless with respect to any damage, claim or cost resulting from an infringement or claim for infringement of the patent rights or any other intellectual property rights of a Third Party which may arise from INTELSAT's use of Martin Marietta's Launch Services, including, but not limited to, the use of any and all products, processes, articles of manufacture, supporting equipment, and facilities.

17.7.2 INTELSAT indemnifies and holds Martin Marietta harmless with respect to any damage, claim or cost resulting from an infringement or claim for infringement of the patent rights or any other intellectual property rights of a Third Party which may arise from the design or manufacture of INTELSAT's Payload.

17.7.3 The rights to indemnification provided hereunder shall be subject to the observance of the following conditions:

a. The Party seeking indemnification shall promptly advise the other Party of the filing of any suit, or of any written or oral claim alleging an infringement of the third party's rights, upon receipt thereof; and shall provide the indemnitor at its request with copies of all relevant documentation.

b. The Party seeking indemnification shall not make any admission nor shall it reach a compromise or settlement without the prior written approval of the other Party which approval shall not be unreasonably withheld or delayed.

17.7.4 The Party required to hold the other harmless shall assist and shall have the right to assume, when not contrary to the governing rules of procedure, the defense of any claim or suit and/or settlement thereof, and shall pay all reasonable litigation and administrative costs and expenses incurred in connection with the defense of any such suit, shall satisfy and judgements rendered by a court of competent jurisdiction in such suits, and shall make all settlement payments.

* * *

Article 21—*Applicable Law*

This Contract shall be governed by, subject to and construed according to the laws of the State of Maryland, United States of America. Each Party agrees to comply with all applicable local, state, federal and foreign laws and shall indemnify and hold the other harmless from any damage a Party incurs from the other Party not being in compliance with such laws.

Article 22—*Export Requirements*

22.1 This Contract is subject to all United States laws and regulations relating to exports and to all administrative acts of the U.S. Government pursuant to such laws and regulations.

22.2 The parties to this Contract agree that the obligations contained in this Contract shall not affect the performance of any obligations created by prior contracts or subcontracts which the parties may have individually or collectively with the U.S. Government.

22.3 The technical data subject to U.S. export regulations and laws and furnished under this Contract to INTELSAT shall not be retransferred except in compliance with applicable U.S. law.

22.4 INTELSAT indemnifies and holds Martin Marietta harmless for all claims, demands, damages, costs, fines [,] penalties, attorneys' fees and all other expenses arising from failure of INTELSAT to comply with this ARTICLE 22.

*   *   *

Article 29—*Permits and Approvals*

29.1 Each Party agrees to support the other in obtaining any required permits, licenses and/or approvals.

29.2 Martin Marietta shall undertake to register the Titan III with the appropriate launching state or states as required by the Convention on Registration of Objects Launched into Outer Space of 1974 [28:1 U.S.T. 695 (1976–77)]. INTELSAT and Martin Marietta shall cooperate with the appropriate launching state or states in providing all information required by such state or states for state registration and registration in the register of space objects maintained by the Secretary-General of the United Nations pursuant to the Convention on Registration of Objects Launched into Outer Space.

Martin Marietta Corporation v. International Telecommunications Satellite Organization, 991 F.2d 94 (4th Cir. 1993)

ERVIN, Chief Judge:

Martin Marietta agreed to launch a satellite for the International Telecommunications Satellite Organization (INTELSAT), but the satellite ended up in a useless orbit. Martin Marietta then sought a declaratory judgment that it owed INTELSAT nothing under the agreement between the parties, and INTELSAT counterclaimed for negligence, negligent misrepresentation, gross negligence, and breach of contract. Martin Marietta moved to dismiss INTELSAT's counterclaims for failure to state a claim upon which relief may be granted, under Federal Rule of Civil Procedure 12 (b) (6), and the district court granted the motion as to all of INTELSAT's claims. Finding that INTELSAT has stated two claims upon which relief may be granted, breach of contract and gross negligence, we affirm in part, reverse in part, and remand.

I

Martin Marietta and INTELSAT reached an agreement under which Martin Marietta would launch two satellites for INTELSAT. The relevant provisions of the parties' contract follow. In Article 2, Martin Marietta contracted to "make its Best Efforts to furnish Launch Services for the purpose of delivering INTELSAT's payload into orbit." In Article 1.2, the parties defined "Best Efforts" as "[d]iligently working in a good and workman-like manner as a reasonable, prudent manufacturer of launch vehicles and provider of Launch Services." Article 6 was entitled "Best Efforts Replacement Launch." Article 6.1 stated, "INTELSAT may request a Replacement Launch in the event that following any Launch under this Contract, the Titan III Mission or the Payload Mission has not been accomplished for any reason." In Article 6.7, the parties stated that a replacement launch "shall be the sole and exclusive remed[y] of the Buyer from Martin Marietta in the event the Titan III mission fails for any reason." Article 17 was entitled "Allocation of Certain Risks." In Article 17.1, the parties agreed that: The following risks, arising out of or incident to the Launch Services to be provided by Martin Marietta and its subcontractors at every tier under this Contract are allocated between INTELSAT and Martin Marietta as set forth in this ARTICLE 17, notwithstanding any other provision of this Contract. Article 17.5.1 provided: Martin Marietta and INTELSAT agree that, with respect to injury to or death of persons involved in, or damage to property used in connection with, Launch Services to be furnished under this Contract, neither Party will make any claim against the other ... , and each Party shall bear its own risk of loss with respect to injury to or death of its own employees or damage to its own property howsoever caused. Article 17.6, entitled "Limitation of Liability," stated: Martin Marietta's liability to INTELSAT ... whether or not arising under contract, or in negligence, strict liability, or under any other theory of tort or liability, shall not include any loss of use or loss of profit or revenue or any other indirect, special, incidental or consequential damages. In no event shall Martin Marietta's liability to INTELSAT for any claim arising out of a particular Launch Services exceed the price for that Titan III Launch Services to be paid by INTELSAT ... , provided however that nothing in this paragraph shall affect any right of INTELSAT to a Replacement Launch ... under Article 6. Finally, Article 21 specified that the contract was to be governed by Maryland law.

The first launch was unsuccessful. The satellite failed to separate from the launch vehicle when it was supposed to, due to Martin Marietta's wiring mistake. Eventually, INTELSAT separated the satellite from the launch vehicle, but the process of doing so (which involved separating the satellite from its booster rocket) made it impossible for the satellite to attain its proper orbit. The satellite is the one that the National Aeronatics and Space Administration (funded by INTELSAT) recently rescued. The second launch the parties contracted for, which involved another satellite, was successful.

After INTELSAT threatened to sue over the first launch, Martin Marietta filed a declaratory judgment action in the District of Maryland, seeking a declaration that it owed INTELSAT nothing under their contract. INTELSAT counterclaimed for breach of contract, negligence, gross negligence, and negligent misrepresentation. INTELSAT sought $400 million in damages for the lost value of the launch services, the lost use of the satellite, lost profit, damage to the satellite, and the cost of rescuing the satellite. Martin Marietta then made a 12(b) (6) motion to dismiss the counterclaims. The district court granted the motion to dismiss the tort claims in April 1991, in an opinion published in edited form in May 1991, Martin Marietta Corp. v. INTELSAT, 763 F.Supp. 1327 (D.Md.1991), and granted the motion to dismiss the breach of contract claim in November 1991, in an unpublished opinion.

As to INTELSAT's negligence and negligent misrepresentation claims, the district court held that INTELSAT had not shown a tort duty of due care distinct from the duties the contract between the parties created. As for gross negligence, the district court held that the Commercial Space Launch Act Amendments of 1988 established a federal policy that overrode Maryland's common law rule that parties ordinarily cannot waive liability for gross negligence. Later, in ruling on the breach of contract claim, the district court held that the parties' contract clearly and unambiguously barred a breach of contract action. Citing Article 6.7 of the contract, the court reasoned that INTELSAT's sole remedy for a "mission failure" was a replacement launch and that the satellite's failure to separate from the rocket at the proper time constituted a "mission failure." The court also quoted Article 17.6 (the Limitation of Liability section) and stated that "[h]ere, again, the contract unambiguously bars any contract claim beyond that permitted in Article 6." J.A. at 656.

II

We first consider the breach of contract claim, bearing in mind that "a complaint should not be dismissed for failure to state a claim unless it appears beyond doubt that the plaintiff can prove no set of facts in support of his claim which would entitle him to relief." Conley v. Gibson, 355 U.S. 41, 45–46, 78 S.Ct. 99, 101–102, 2 L.Ed.2d 80 (1957). In considering a motion to dismiss, the claims must be construed in the light most favorable to the non-moving party and its allegations taken as true. Jenkins v. McKeithen, 395 U.S. 411, 421–22, 89 S.Ct. 1843, 1848–49, 23 L.Ed.2d 404 (1969). Most importantly, dismissals for failure to state a claim are reviewed de novo on appeal. Revene v. Charles County Comm'rs, 882 F.2d 870, 872 (4th Cir.1989). INTELSAT's theory is that Martin Marietta breached its obligation to use its "best efforts," a duty established in Article 2 of the contract and defined in Article 1. The district court found that the contract clearly and unambiguously barred that claim. As the district court noted, the construction of ambiguous contract provisions is a factual determination that precludes dismissal on a motion for failure to state a claim. Wolman v. Tose, 467 F.2d 29, 34 (4th Cir.1972).

After our required de novo review, we find that the contract is not free from ambiguity and that the district court erred in granting Martin Marietta's motion to dismiss.

While, as a matter of common sense, it seems reasonable to label what happened as a "mission failure," INTELSAT argues that its claim is not for mission failure, but for failure of separation of the Titan III payload and booster. With the parties' contract and Interface Control Document silent on this point, the district court erred in accepting Martin Marietta's construction of the contract.

The district court found that the "Limitation of Liability" provision in Article 17 unambiguously barred any contract claim other than the replacement launch remedy in Article 6. INTELSAT claims that the contract is ambiguous because Article 6.7 states that a replacement launch is INTELSAT's "sole and exclusive" remedy, while the Article 17 "Limitation of Liability" provision puts a damages cap on claims "arising under contract, or in negligence, strict liability, or under any other theory of tort or liability." INTELSAT argues that an Article 6 replacement launch could not be an exclusive remedy when Article 17 recognized the possibility of other claims, especially when Article 17 stated that it would govern the allocation of risks between the parties "notwithstanding any other provision of this Contract." At the very least, INTELSAT contends, the two articles together create an ambiguity precluding dismissal.

Martin Marietta argues that the statement in the Article 17 "Limitation of Liability" provision that it did not affect INTELSAT's right to an Article 6 replacement launch shows that the two provisions are independent, and that the exclusive remedy language in Article 6 controls. On the other hand, INTELSAT argues based on the same provisions that a replacement launch and a breach of contract claim are not mutually exclusive, and that Article 17 controls. We disagree with the district court's conclusion that the interplay of the two provisions is unambiguous. Martin Marietta certainly could have included clearer language, if it intended at the time of contracting to limit INTELSAT's remedy in the way it now argues.

Alternatively, Martin Marietta offers an explanation of this apparent ambiguity. Martin Marietta argues that the Article 6 replacement launch remedy is the exclusive remedy when there have been post-launch damages, because Article 6 only applies "following any launch." See Art. 6.1. Under Martin Marietta's construction, the Article 17 "Limitation of Liability" provision applies to pre-launch damages such as "efficient breach" (a refusal by Martin Marietta to go forward). However, while Martin Marietta's interpretation plausibly harmonizes the two articles, the contract is far from crystal clear and never refers to "pre-launch" or "post-launch" damages or otherwise mandates Martin Marietta's interpretation.

In light of these ambiguities, it does not appear beyond doubt that INTELSAT can prove no set of facts constituting breach of Martin Marietta's contractual duty to use its "best efforts," and we must therefore reverse the district court's dismissal of INTELSAT's breach of contract claim. *See* Conley, 355 U.S. at 45–46, 78 S.Ct. at 101–102.

III

A.

As to INTELSAT's negligence and negligent misrepresentation claims, we agree with the district court's analysis of Maryland law and reasons for dismissal: Equally sophisticated parties who have the opportunity to allocate risks to third party insurance or among one another should be held to only those duties specified by the agreed upon contractual terms and not to general tort duties imposed by state law. ... Consistent with the Court's discussion of whether tort duties are applicable in contractual relationships, Maryland law holds that a claim for negligent misrepresentation is improper when, as here, the only relationship between the parties is contractual, both parties are equally sophisticated, and the contract does not create an express duty of due care in making representations. The case before the Court does not present circumstances in which the law creates a tort duty of due care independent from the parties' contractual relationship. Such tort duties of care with respect to representations are imposed by courts to protect a peculiarly vulnerable party. In particular, such duties are imposed in the context of a patient's or client's dealings with a professional in whom one places a great degree of personal trust and confidence—such as a physician, an attorney, an architect or a public accountant. No such relationship of special trust exists here. Nor is INTELSAT an unsophisticated consumer, unfamiliar with the subject matter of the contract, who relied on the representations of someone holding himself or herself out as possessing special expertise. 763 F.Supp. at 1332–33 (citations omitted). We therefore affirm the dismissal of INTELSAT's negligence claim on the basis of the district court's reasoning.

INTELSAT's negligent misrepresentation argument raises two points worth further discussion. First, INTELSAT relies on Maryland-Nat'l Capital Park and Planning Comm'n v. Washington Nat'l Arena, 282 Md. 588, 386 A.2d 1216 (1978). There, in upholding a noncontestability clause in a lease, the court held that "unless clearly prohibited by statute, contractual limitations on judicial remedies will be enforced, absent a positive showing of fraud, misrepresentation, overreaching, or other unconscionable conduct on the part of the party seeking enforcement." *Id.* at 1231. INTELSAT argues that the Arena court intended "misrepresentation" to include negligent misrepresentations, but we must disagree, because negligent misrepresentations do not rise to the level of "fraud," "overreaching," or "unconscionable conduct."

Second, INTELSAT argues that the Article 6 "Replacement Launch" provision should not apply because INTELSAT only approved the fated launch, which triggered Article 6, in reliance on Martin Marietta's post-contract misrepresentations. INTELSAT reasons that an exclusion of remedy provision is invalid when one party's misrepresentations induced the other to take an action that caused the provision to take effect. However, Maryland law will enforce exclusion of remedy provisions unless one party's misrepresentations have induced the other party to enter into the contract in the first place. *Id.*

The two Maryland cases INTELSAT cites do not support its theory that post-contract misrepresentations may also invalidate contractual limitations on remedies. First, because Weisman v. Connors, 312 Md. 428, 540 A.2d 783, 792 (1988), only involved pre-contractual misrepresentations, we do not believe that case fairly supports INTELSAT's theory. Next, INTELSAT quotes from a footnote in Martens Chevrolet, Inc. v. Seney, 292 Md. 328, 439 A.2d 534, 539 n. 7 (1982): Appellees have also argued that even if negligent misrepresentation is a viable tort action in this State, it can never be applied to statements made in connection with consummation of an arm's length transaction, as was involved in the present case. We find nothing in Virginia Dare or its progeny to support such a sweeping assertion and we reject it. The statement in Martens Chevrolet only refers to the "consummation" of an arm's length transaction. Here, INTELSAT is relying on negligent misrepresentations made after the parties signed a contract. The same footnote in Martens Chevrolet also quoted a New York Court of Appeals statement: A party to a contract cannot, by misrepresentation of material fact, induce the other party to the contract to enter into it to his damage, and then protect himself from the legal effect of such misrepresentation by inserting in the contract a clause to the effect that he is not to be held liable for the misrepresentation which induced the other party to enter into the contract. *Id.* (quoting Jackson v. State, 241 N.Y. 563, 150 N.E. 556 (1925)). That court also referred to "enter[ing] into" a contract, while INTELSAT's theory rests on statements made after the parties reached their contract. Therefore, the cases INTELSAT relies on are inapposite, and we have not found any authority that is more helpful. Because INTELSAT's negligent misrepresentation arguments are without support, and in view of Maryland law on tort duties arising out of contractual relationships, we affirm the district court's dismissal of this claim.

B.

Finally, we consider INTELSAT's gross negligence claim. Initially, Martin Marietta questions whether Maryland law invalidates contractual waivers of liability in cases of gross negligence where the parties are of equal bargaining power. INTELSAT relies on two decisions by the Maryland Court of Special Appeals: State Highway Admin. v. Greiner Eng'g Sciences, 83 Md.App. 621, 577 A.2d 363 (Md.Ct.Spec.App.), cert. denied, 321 Md. 163, 582 A.2d 499 (1990); and Boucher v. Riner, 68 Md.App. 539, 514 A.2d 485 (Md.Ct.Spec.App.1986). In Greiner, the court held that an unambiguous no-damage-for-delay clause was enforceable. Then the Court noted:

This is not to say that unambiguous no-damage-for-delay clauses will be enforced in every case. The better reasoned approach does not enforce the exculpatory clause where there is "intentional wrongdoing or gross negligence," "fraud or misrepresentation," on the part of the agency asserting the clause. No such wrongdoings were alleged in this case.

Greiner, 577 A.2d at 372 (citations omitted). The earlier case, Boucher, involved a customer who sued the inaptly named "Parachutes Are Fun, Inc." after he parachuted into power lines. Boucher argued that the exculpatory agreement he signed did not shield Parachutes Are Fun from liability for gross negligence. The court agreed, holding that "[a] waiver of a right to sue, such as the one executed between Boucher and Parachutes, is ineffective to shift the risk of a party's own willful, wanton, reckless, or gross conduct." Boucher, 514 A.2d at 488. Boucher is a further indication that, under Maryland law, a party to a contract cannot waive liability for gross negligence.

Martin Marietta tries to distinguish Boucher in two ways. First, Martin Marietta argues that Boucher involved parties of unequal bargaining power. Boucher signed a standard preprinted form containing an exculpatory clause, while Martin Marietta and INTELSAT negotiated a complex agreement. In response, we note that the language in Boucher is broad and not limited to parties of unequal bargaining power, and that the facts and the court's language in Greiner also undercut Martin Marietta's argument. Second, Martin Marietta argues that Boucher established a very high standard for gross negligence (wanton or reckless disregard) that the plaintiff failed to satisfy on facts more egregious than the facts in this case. However, there is no doubt that INTELSAT sufficiently alleged gross negligence so as to survive a 12(b) (6) motion. *See* Transcript of Oral Argument at 99, J.A. at 524. Whether INTELSAT convinces a jury that Martin Marietta was grossly negligent, or even survives summary judgment, is another question.

Although recognizing Boucher to be the law of Maryland, the district court held that Congressional intent, as reflected in the 1988 Amendments to the Commercial Space Launch Act ("CSLA"), 49 U.S.C.App. §§ 2601–2623, required the court to interpret the parties' contract to preclude claims of gross negligence. 763 F.Supp. at 1333–34. We find absolutely no support for the court's conclusion that the CSLA 1988 Amendments overrode Boucher, because the parties' contract was signed in 1987, more than one year before Congress passed the Amendments. Even if the CSLA Amendments could apply retroactively, neither the language of the Amendments nor their legislative history reflects a Congressional intent to protect parties from liability for their own gross negligence. Accordingly, we hold that the district court erred in dismissing INTELSAT's gross negligence claim.

As we have upheld the dismissal of INTELSAT's negligence and negligent misrepresentation claims, but overturned the dismissal of INTELSAT's breach of contract and gross negligence claims, the judgment of the district court is hereby

AFFIRMED IN PART, REVERSED IN PART, AND REMANDED.

From the District Court Opinion, 763 F.Supp. 1327, 1333–1334 (D. Md. 1991)

Conceding that it is precluded by the contractual waivers in Article 17 from pursuing claims based on ordinary negligence for property damage, lost profits and incidentals, INTELSAT argues that public policy invalidates such waivers as they apply to gross negligence. It is true that courts normally find public policy to prohibit enforcement of contractual waivers of liability in cases of gross negligence. See Boucher v. Riner, 68 Md.App. 539, 543, 514 A.2d 485, 487 (1986) (holding that contractual waivers cannot shift risk of a party's own willful, wanton, reckless or gross conduct). However, the Court finds that in the special context of this case, public policy strongly favors enforcement of waivers of all tort claims, including those for gross negligence.

This case presents that rare instance in which Congress has actually pronounced public policy via legislation, here by requiring the parties to agree to contractual waivers under which each party assumes its own risk of loss. As noted above, prior to the 1988 Amendments to the 1984 Commercial Space Launch Act, the unwillingness of insurance companies to cover the huge liability risks incurred by private launch service providers seriously threatened the U.S. commercial space launch industry. In a successful effort to revive the industry, Congress passed legislation designed to eliminate the need for insurance, the primary roadblock to industry expansion, by requiring parties to waive their rights of recovery and assume the risk of their own loss.

The legislative history of the Amendments indicates that Congress intended the mandatory waivers to bar recovery in all instances, including cases where parties were grossly negligent. The Senate Report accompanying the 1988 Amendments states that Congress intended the mandatory waiver requirement "(1) to limit the total universe of claims that might arise as a result of a launch; and (2) to eliminate the necessity for all of these parties to obtain property and casualty insurance to protect against these claims." S.Rep. No. 593, 100th Cong., 2nd Sess. 14 (1988), U.S. Code Cong. & Admin.News 1988, pp. 5525, 5538.

If this Court were to invalidate the subject tort claim waivers as they apply to gross negligence, it would substantially undermine the protections Congress intended for commercial space launchers. Plaintiffs would be able to sue for damages on every imperfect space launch, simply by claiming under a gross negligence theory rather than an ordinary negligence theory. The resulting costs of litigation, as well as the potential exposure, would require launch providers to obtain expensive insurance, if available, or alternatively to self insure and "bet the farm" on every space launch. This is precisely the situation Congress sought to avoid.

As mankind ventures forth from the home planet, great hazards, known and as yet unknown, will confront us. Now, and perhaps for as long as the human race seeks to go where it has not gone before, there shall be missions which cannot be "safe" as that term is used in the context of terrestrial activities. Those who seek to explore, and to exploit, outer space must do so charged with acceptance of the unknown, and perhaps unknowable, perils to be faced in that vast and potentially hostile environment.

The public policy of this country, as stated by Congress, requires that those using the service of a licensed space launch provider do so at their own risk. Accordingly, in order to carry out the Congressional intent behind the 1988 Amendments, the Court interprets the waivers in Article 17 of the contract to preclude liability for gross, as well as ordinary, negligence.

For the foregoing reasons, this Court concludes that INTELSAT may not recover on its tort claims.

NOTES

1. In light of the Fourth Circuit opinion reprinted above, what additional language would you include in the inter-party waiver provision of a future launch contract? Is there anything in the Fourth Circuit opinion that would indicate a potential problem with enforcing a waiver of liability for gross negligence? If so, does the District Court's policy argument—essentially, that Congress intended to reduce tort liability as a way of encouraging space exploration—provide a good rationale for permitting contractual waivers of gross negligence in launch contracts? Note that a widely accepted historical account of the development of tort law in nineteenth century America describes a legal regime that indirectly fostered economic development by refusing to impose tort liability in many cases. *See* Morton J. Horwitz, The Transformation of American Law 1780–1860 (1977), at 85–101. Does this history shed light on what Congress was trying to do in the Commercial Space Launch Act? How much do you think increased tort liability woud increase the costs and risks of space exploration? *See* Guy De-

Maertelaere, INTELSAT II: The Erratic Orbit of the Fourth Circuit (draft, on file with authors), which argues that the court in *Martin Marietta* set a dangerous precedent because it failed to consider the parties' intent and misinterpreted Congressional intent on the issue of whether gross negligence claims invalidate contractual waivers of liability. The author concludes that, if followed, this case will frustrate the very purpose of the 1988 amendments to develop and protect the launch services industry. *Id.* at 23–24.

2. Assume the same facts as in the preceding case, except that the contract is signed in 1993, so that the 1988 Commercial Space Launch Act Amendments definitely apply to the transaction. What effect would the Act have on the Agreement, given that (1) the Act mandates cross-waivers of liability; and (2) the parties did not include such waivers in their Agreement. Does the law imply them? Is there any remedy available to either or both of the parties due to the failure to include these waivers? If no such remedy exists, how meaningful is the law's requirement?

3. What evidence would you introduce on remand to show the presence or absence of gross negligence?

4. In tort law, the term "negligence" is generally defined by reference to "reasonable" conduct. Popular touchstones include custom within the industry, standards set by regulators or by statute, or the "Learned Hand" risk/benefit formula. How should such standards be applied in the context of space launches?

5. In light of the fast-changing nature of the space launch industry, should courts be more or less tolerant of poorly drafted contracts? Should courts be more or less willing to supplement vague or incomplete statements with judicially created rules or presumptions? *See generally* Tanja L. Masson-Zwaan, The Martin Marietta Case: Or How to Safeguard Private Commercial Space Activities, 18 Air & Space L. 16 (1993) (arguing that *Martin Marietta* illustrates why efforts at the international level to reach agreement on an objective international standard for the settlement of disputes regarding space activities, and especially the establishment of an international arbitration tribunal, must be continued and reinforced).

6. In general, under the Uniform Commercial Code enacted in every state in the U.S., courts will enforce contract clauses limiting buyer's recovery for breach of warranty to a particular exclusive remedy outlined in the agreement—often an obligation to repair or replacement of a defective product sold under contract. *See, e.g.*, Mostek Corp. v. Chemetron Corp., 40 U.C.C. Rep. Serv. 840, 642 S.W.2d 20 (Tex. App. 1982) (interpreting section 2–719 of the Uniform Commercial Code as enacted in Texas).

One limitation that applies in these cases is that exclusive remedy clauses will be unenforceable if they are "unconscionable." In general, terms are unconscionable only if they bring about surprise results (called "procedural unconscionability") or are oppressive (called "substantive unconscionability"). *See* U.C.C. section 2–302; Henningsen v. Bloomfield Motors; Sierra Diesel Injection

Service, Inc. v. Burroughs Corp., Inc., 8 U.C.C. Rep. Serv. 2d 617, 874 F2d 653 (9th Cir. 1989) (contractual exclusions of warranties are generally disfavored and standardized form contracts are construed against drafter, and are subject to general obligation of good faith and of not imposing unconscionable terms upon party).

Another limitation is supplied by the language of U.C.C. section 2–719, which provides that an exclusive remedy provision will be unenforceable when the remedy "fails of its essential purpose." Generally this has been construed to mean that the agreed-upon exclusive remedy fails to meet a minimum level of consumer expectation, such as where a "lemon" automobile is repeatedly repaired but continues to break down regularly. Unlike the law of unconscionability (which measures "fairness" as of the date of formation), this section is intended to deal with circumstances that arise after contract formation that were not contemplated when the contract was formed. *See, e.g.*, Riley v. Ford Motor Co., 422 F.2d 670, 8 U.C.C. Rep. Serv. 1175 (5th Cir. 1971) (14 defects in new automobile; exclusive remedy failed of essential purpose). Significantly for space-related contracts, this principle has been applied in cases where, unlike *Riley* and its ilk, both parties to the contract are sophisticated business entities. *See* Phillips Petroleum Co., Norway v. Bucyrus-Erie Co., 1 U.C.C. Rep. Serv. 2d 667, 388 N.W.2d 584 (1986) (where buyer had incurred substantial damages as a result of the use of defective adapters in buyer's North Sea off-shore drilling platforms, seller's contractual disclaimer provision limiting damages to replacement of the defective parts F.O.B. seller's place of business failed of its essential purpose—to make the injured party whole—under 2-719(2), and thus buyer was permitted to resort to the remedies provided in the U.C.C.). *See generally* James J. White and Robert S. Summers, Uniform Commercial Code § 12-10 (3rd ed. 1988).

7. In a related line of cases, courts have established that contract provisions excluding or limiting consequential damages for breach—an example of which can be found in section 17.6 of the Martin Marietta/INTELSAT agreement excerpted above—are usually enforceable. For a good discussion, *see* Jones v. Asgrow Seed Co., 13 U.C.C. Rep. Serv. 2d 1032, 749 F. Supp. 836 (N.D. Ohio 1990) (Clause denying seller's liability for consequential damages for loss due to sale of defective seed found to be neither procedurally nor substantively unconscionable). Note, however, that some opaque language in the U.C.C. has caused consternation under a specific set of circumstances. In particular, when a contract contains both an "exclusive remedy" provision *and* an exclusion (or, presumably, limitation) of consequential damages for breach, courts have split over whether a failure of the exclusive remedy (as in cases such as *Riley, supra*) necessarily also renders the limitation on consequential damages provision unenforceable. *See, e.g., Riley, supra* (yes; contractual limitation on damages goes out with exclusive remedy that fails); American Elec. Power Co. v. Westinghouse Elec. Corp., 418 F. Supp. 435, 19 U.C.C. Rep. Serv. 1009 (S.D.N.Y. 1976) (no;

court upholds limitation on liability clause despite failure of repair and replace remedy).

Hughes Communications Galaxy, Inc. v.
The United States, (Fed. Cir. 1993)

Before Rich, Mayer and Lourie, Circuit Judges.
Mayer, J.

Hughes Communications Galaxy, Inc., appeals the judgment of the United States Court of Federal Claims, 26 Cl. Ct. 123 (1992), which held it could not recover damages under its contract with the National Aeronautics and Space Administration (NASA) when NASA's failure to launch Hughes' satellites was the result of the President's decision to stop launches of commercial satellites. We reverse and remand.

Background

On December 5, 1985, Hughes Communications entered into a contract with the United States, represented by NASA, in which NASA agreed to use its "best efforts" to launch ten of Hughes' commercial satellites through its Space Shuttle program. At that time, NASA operated a fleet of four manned shuttles. The United States government was then promoting commercial use of its shuttle fleet by private industry to offset the costs of its space program. To further this goal, NASA actively marketed its shuttles as launch vehicles for commercial payloads to both domestic and foreign users.

The contract executed between Hughes and NASA was, as the Claims Court recognized, unique. Labeled a Launch Services Agreement (LSA), the contract provided at the outset that "[a]11 Launch and Associated Services to be furnished by NASA to the Customer under this Agreement shall be so furnished by NASA using its best efforts." Art. I. [Unless otherwise indicated, citations to Article numbers refer to the Articles and subsections contained in the LSA. The contract is divided into four Parts. Part I is comprised solely of Article I and contains the "Customer unique Provisions" for all or part of the ten Hughes spacecraft. Parts II and III both contain Articles II through VII. Part II pertains to Hughes' spacecraft HC-9 and HC-10. Part III pertains to Hughes, spacecraft HC-11 through HC-18. Where there is no relevant difference between the Articles of these Parts, the Articles will be cited without reference to a particular Part. Part IV contains Articles VIII through XXI which apply to all ten spacecraft.] The contract included a cut-off date of September 30, 1994, at which time NASA's obligations under the contract would expire, whether or not Hughes' spacecraft had been launched. [Article II, Par. 3 provided: NASA's obligation to provide Shuttle Launch and Associated Services to the Customer under this Agreement shall remain in force through September 30, 1994 (unless mutually extended by NASA and the Customer) or until all the obligations and responsibilities of the parties herein have been fulfilled, whichever occurs first.] The LSA also granted both parties termination rights. Hughes was given the right to terminate the contract at virtually any time, provided it pay NASA any costs actually incurred by NASA at the time of termination. Art. VII, P 2. NASA's right to terminate was somewhat more limited, and included the right to terminate "upon a determination in writing that NASA is required to Terminate such services for Reasons Beyond NASA's Control." Art. VII, P 1.a. (iv).

Article I of the contract designated a "Planned Launch Date" for each of Hughes' spacecraft. [Article XX, P 21 of the contract defined "Planned Launch Date" as "the date, which initially defines the beginning of the interval during which launch is to occur, agreed to by the parties at the time of execution of the Agreement, at the time the Customer exercises a launch option given in this Agreement or at the time a Payload launch is rescheduled to occur greater than one year thereafter."] Three of Hughes' spacecraft were designated as "Scheduled Launches" while the remaining seven were designated as "Standby Launches." Art. I, P 1.a. Standby Launches were subject to more uncertain launch dates, "with each launch to nominally occur within one year following its respective Planned Launch Date." Art. IV, P 1.b. (2). The "Firm Launch Date and Shuttle flight assignment for the Payload will be selected solely by NASA." Id. Scheduled Launches, however, were to be "implemented as set forth in Subparagraph 1.a. "Art. IV, P 1.b. (1). Subparagraph 1.a. of Article IV provided that for launches which are not Standby Launches, the Planned Launch Date would mark the beginning of a ninety-day launch period. About one year before this Planned Launch Date, NASA was to assign the payload to a shuttle and establish a Firm Launch Date by coordinating with Hughes and other customers scheduled to share the same shuttle launch. Despite these provisions, Article IV allowed both Hughes and NASA considerable flexibility in the actual launch date of the satellites by permitting both parties to delay or postpone a scheduled launch. Art. IV, PP 2–5.

In addition, Article XV, entitled "Services Consistent with United States' Obligations, Law and Published Policy" provided that, "NASA shall provide Launch and Associated Services under this Agreement to the extent consistent with the United States' obligations (including any intergovernmental memorandum of understanding entered into by NASA and the Customer), United States' Law and United States' published policy." Article IV also addressed NASA's obligation to provide launch services, and provided in relevant part, "With respect to launch priority and scheduling, NASA will provide Launch and Associated Services in accordance with the United States policy governing launch assistance approved by the President of the United States on August 6, 1982. Consistent with this policy, NASA will generally treat all comparable payloads on the same basis." The referenced policy was issued by President Reagan on August 6, 1982, and was entitled "Space Assistance and Cooperation Policy." It provided: With respect to the priority and scheduling for launching foreign payloads at U.S. launch sites, such launchings will be dealt with on the same basis as U.S. launchings. Each launching will be treated in terms of its own requirements and as an individual case. Once a payload is scheduled for launch, the launching agency will use its best effort to meet the scheduling commitments. Should events arise which require rescheduling, the U.S. will consult with all affected users in an attempt to meet the needs of users in an equitable manner.

NASA compiled a list of all scheduled payloads to be launched, including Hughes', into a "manifest." The manifest listed commercial payloads in order of their Planned or Firm Launch Dates, and indicated which payloads were to be launched on which shuttle. Hughes' spacecraft were assigned specific slots on this manifest. However, on January 28, 1986, the Shuttle Challenger exploded shortly after takeoff from the Kennedy Space Center at Cape Canaveral, Florida. None of Hughes' spacecraft had been launched at this point, less than two months after Hughes and NASA executed the LSA.

As a consequence of the Challenger tragedy, NASA's shuttle fleet was reduced to three craft. Also, NASA immediately initiated an investigation to determine the cause of the accident. Ultimately, following extensive evaluation of space policy by various governmental entities, the President issued an order on August 15, 1986, in which he announced that NASA would no longer be in the business of launching commercial spacecraft. However, the government was left with the question of how best to handle the remaining 44 commercial payloads it had contracted to launch.

In response to this problem, the government grouped the remaining payloads into four categories—"Shuttle Unique," "National Security and Foreign Policy," "Costly to Retrofit," and the "Remainder." The "Shuttle Unique" category included payloads which could not be launched using an expendable launch vehicle (ELV) but require a manned vehicle launch. The "National Security and Foreign Policy" category included those payloads which were designated as having national security or foreign policy implications. The third category referred to payloads which could be launched by an ELV, but with considerable additional expense. Three of Hughes' satellites fell into this category, while the other seven were included in the "Remainder" category.

Based on these categories and the President's revised policy, NASA announced a new manifest for its shuttle fleet. This manifest included only those payloads which fell into the "Shuttle Unique" and "National Security and Foreign Policy" categories. Accordingly, on October 30, 1986, NASA issued a letter to Hughes informing it that the new manifest did not include Hughes' spacecraft. The letter also stated:

> It appears almost certain you will not be provided launch services either prior to or after your current contract expires. At the very least, it can be said with absolute certainty that your payloads will be delayed far in excess of the nine-month period de-

scribed in Article VII, sub-paragraph 2.b. of Parts II and III of your Launch Services Agreement (LSA). Thus, should you wish to terminate your LSA prior to expiration, Article VII provides you may do so based on these delays. Upon termination, your payments to NASA will be refunded in accordance with the terms of the LSA.

Hughes filed suit in the United States Claims Court claiming that NASA breached the LSA and that Hughes' contract rights were taken in violation of the Fifth Amendment. On cross motions for summary judgment, the court granted the government's motion and held that Hughes could not recover under either of its claims.

With regard to the first claim, the Claims Court held that there was no breach of the LSA. Initially, the court determined that in spite of its "unusual features," the LSA was a binding contract because the government was obligated to use its best efforts to launch Hughes' spacecraft. 26 Cl.Ct. at 134. The court declined to determine whether or not the combined effect of the government's actions operated to invoke the contract's termination clause. *Id.* at 136. Instead, the Claims Court determined that the new manifest, and the exclusion of Hughes' spacecraft, were the result of a valid sovereign act—a policy decision issued by the President with proper authority. The court reasoned that Article XV of the contract incorporated the sovereign act defense by its terms and that the LSA was therefore explicitly made subject to changes in policy. *Id.* at 140. The claims Court concluded that because the reorganization of the manifest was in compliance with the new policy announced by the President, the government did not breach the LSA.

The Claims Court also determined that the Fifth Amendment did not provide any basis for compensating Hughes. Recognizing that Hughes must have an identifiable property interest in order to establish a Fifth Amendment taking, the court determined that Article XV's incorporation of all future policy changes precluded Hughes from establishing any "'distinct investment-backed expectation' that its slot on the Shuttle manifest would be unaffected by subsequent sovereign acts." *Id.* at 145. Hughes now appeals.

Discussion

Contract interpretation is a matter of law which we review *de novo*. Blake Constr. Co. v. United States, 987 F.2d 743, 746 (Fed. Cir. 1993). We hold that the Claims Court erred in its conclusion that Hughes' right to have its spacecraft launched under the LSA was subject to all policy changes issued after August 6, 1982. Instead, Article IV of the LSA unambiguously required the government to schedule launch services according to "the United States policy governing launch assistance approved by the President of the United States on August 6, 1982." Art. IV P 1.a.

We disagree with the conclusion that Article XV, and not Article IV, is the more specific provision of the contract. Article XV limits NASA's obligation to provide Launch and Associated Services "to the extent consistent with United States' obligations ... , United States' Law and United States' published policy." Article IV, on the other hand, states that NASA "will provide Launch and Associated Services in accordance with the United States policy governing launch assistance approved by the President of the United States on August 6, 1982."

By identifying and incorporating an existing, specific and dated item of presidential policy, Article IV is manifestly more specific than Article XV, which subordinates the contract only to unspecified United States obligations, law and published policy. "Where specific and general terms in a contract are in conflict, those which relate to a particular matter control over the more general language." Hills Materials Co. v. Rice, 982 F.2d 514, 517 (Fed. Cir.1992). To the extent that Articles IV and XV are in conflict, Article IV's specific reference to the policy issued by the President on August 6, 1982, controls. [Because we conclude that the contract shifts responsibility to the government for changes in policy which conflict with the provisions of Article IV, we offer no opinion about the presidential actions as they might pertain to the sovereign act doctrine.]

This interpretation of the contract does not render Article XV redundant or superfluous. By its reference to all obligations, law and policy, Article XV has broader scope than Article IV, which only limits launch priority and scheduling to comply with the August 6, 1982, policy. There could be changes in the United States' obligations, laws or policy which are not superseded by Article IV's more narrow language and would still apply to the contract. A contract should be interpreted in such a way that all parts make sense. United States v. Johnson Controls, Inc., 713 F.2d 1541, 1555 (Fed. Cir.1983). Article IV's reference to the August 6, 1982, policy would be superfluous and meaningless if launch priority and scheduling remained subject to any subsequent change in policy.

We also believe the government's reiteration that Article XV embodies the sovereign act defense contributes nothing in aid of interpreting the contract. Under the sovereign act doctrine, the United States as contractor will not be held responsible for the acts of the United States as sovereign. Atlas Corp. v. United States, 895 F.2d 745, 754 (Fed. Cir.1990) (citing Horowitz v. United States, 267 U.S. 458, 461 (1925)). The sovereign act defense is an inherent element of every contract to which the government is a party, whether or not explicitly stated.

Finally, we address the government's invocation of the principle that it retains the authority to act as sovereign unless it surrenders this right in "unmistakable terms." Bowen v. Public Agencies Opposed to Social Security Entrapment, 477 U.S. 41, 52 (1986) (citing Merrion v. Jicarilla Tribe, 455 U.S. 130, 147 (1982)). Under our interpretation of the contract, we have no trouble concluding that Article IV obligates the government to provide launch priority and scheduling in accordance with the August 6, 1982, policy in language which more than satisfies the "unmistakable terms" requirement.

We do not share the concern that our reading of Article IV "would have the effect of allowing NASA to contract away Congressional and Presidential power to set space policy for the entire term of the LSA, twelve years." 26 Cl.Ct. at 139. In the cases relied on for this proposition, the plaintiffs sought literally to enjoin the exercise of sovereign power. It was in this context that the "unmistakable terms" standard was developed. *See* Public Agencies, 477 U.S. 41 (the state of California and other parties sought to enjoin Congress from enforcing an amended provision of the Social Security Act of 1935, 42 U.S.C. § 301 *et seq.*); Jicarilla Apache Tribe, 455 U.S. 130 (Oil and gas companies who, entered into long term leases to extract and produce oil and gas from tribal land sought to enjoin the tribe from acting as sovereign by imposing a severance tax on oil and gas removed from the land.); *see also* Transohio Sav. Bank v. Director, OTS, 967 F.2d 598 (D.C.Cir.1992). (Thrifts challenged Congress' authority to revise capital accounting rules issued by government agencies for thrifts with forbearance agreements.) These cases also required the reviewing court to determine whether Congress, by enacting the legislation which authorized the government to enter into the contracts in question, waived in "unmistakable terms" its right to exercise certain sovereign powers.

In contrast, the present case simply involves the question of how liability for certain contingencies was allocated by the contract. In its contractual capacity, the government executes countless agreements with private entities to receive and provide services, goods and supplies. These contracts routinely include provisions shifting financial responsibility to the government for events which might occur in the future. [For instance, Federal Acquisition Regulation (FAR) 52-222-43 requires government entities entering into certain fixed price service contracts to include a price adjustment clause specifying that the government will compensate service contractors for increases in wages and fringe benefits resulting from compliance with Department of Labor wage and fringe benefits determinations. In Hills Materials Co. v. Rice, 982 F.2d 514 (Fed. Cir.1992), we held that pursuant to FAR 52.236-7, the Air Force contractually accepted financial responsibility for changes in certain OSHA regulations. "While [the contractor's] compliance with subsequent changes would not be excused, it could entail additional compensation." *Id.* at 516.] That some of these events may be triggered by sovereign government action does not render the relevant contractual provisions any less binding than those which contemplate third party acts, inclement weather and other force majeure. The policy approved by the President on August 6, 1982, remained controlling "[w]ith respect to launch priority and scheduling" as provided in Article IV. Our conclusion does not prevent the President or Congress from implementing space policy, but does require NASA, absent the successful assertion of another defense in this case, to bear the cost of changes in launch priority and scheduling resulting from the revised policy.

Conclusion

Accordingly, the judgment of the Court of Federal Claims is reversed, and the case is remanded for further proceedings consistent with this opinion.

REVERSED AND REMANDED.

NOTES

1. A key element in the preceding opinion is the distinction between the government's right to act (embodied in the "sovereign act" defense) and its ability to accept (via contract) liability for financial losses caused by its actions. What if the costs of compensating an injured party are so high that sovereign actions are effectively limited? Are some sovereign actions—for example, responses to acts of war—so fundamental that contractual obligations such as those described in the preceding case should be deemed unenforceable? On the general problems faced by private companies wishing to sign launch agreements with the government, *see* Ralph L. Kissick, Commercial Space Launch Contracts: Disputes and Remedies, 4 J.L. & Tech. 31 (1989). Kissick argues that these agreements differ significantly from standard government contracts because they involve a reversal of roles: the government is the supplier of a service, and the private company is the buyer. In addition, Kissick notes that the two agencies that are involved (NASA & the Air Force) use different agreements, adding to the confusion. He advocates not only use of a uniform agreement by the government, but also strict attention to detail by private contractors, given that traditional government contract rules (e.g., the Federal Acquisition Regulations, or FARs) do not apply.

2. One constant complaint of space entrepreneurs has been that the U.S. government is an unreliable partner. Since in this early stage of space industrialization government is often either a supplier of services not available elsewhere (for example, shuttle launches or spaceport facilities) or a major customer, this unreliability may be a major brake on the progress of space commercialization. The following excerpt explores this phenomenon, and some potential remedies.

Impact of Start Agreements and Other Industry Incentives on Commercial Space Markets: Hearings Before the Subcommittee on Space, Comm. on Science, Space & Tech., U.S. House of Representatives, 102d Cong., 1st. Sess., July 31, 1991 at 61, Testimony of Prof. Glenn H. Reynolds

C. Government Unreliability and Unpredictability

Government unreliability and unpredictability can come in two forms: in the form of regulatory shifts that destroy settled expectations, and in the form of unreliability and unpredictability in ventures where the government is important as a customer or partner. ... Government contracts to purchase particular goods or services over a period of years may be an essential part of a company's business plan, but such contracts may be terminated at any time when Congress refuses to appropriate enough money. ... Run-of-the-mill government contractors, in a cost-plus environment, can survive such shifts. Commercial enterprises cannot—or, if they adapt so that they can, will become less viable as commercial enterprises.

The existing procurement environment hurts companies in several ways. First, they cannot deal with the government on the same kinds of terms and conditions applicable to their commercial customers. [To provide a simple example, if a commercial company approaches NASA or NOAA and says "we have a better way to address your problem," and convinces the responsible officers that its approach really is better, current law and practice will likely require that the new approach be put out for bids—both undermining the company's intellectual property, and reducing incentives for such companies to approach the government in the first place. This is not how things are done in the private sector.] Second, if they adapt to the unique environment of government contracting, they are likely to become less competitive in the commercial arena—letting a program "slip" a year is typical in a cost-plus environment, but often lethal in a commercial one. Third, they cannot trust the government officials with whom they deal, because those officials cannot make promises without the risk—indeed the likelihood—that Congress will change the rules.

These are problems that are endemic to the government procurement system, which is based on an enormous unwillingness to grant government contracting officials the kind of discretion commonly granted to procurement personnel in the private sector. This has the salutary effect of limiting corruption, but produces enormous costs in the return. [*See generally* S. Kelman, Procurement and Public Management: The Fear of Discretion and the Quality of Government Performance (1990).] Reforming the entire government procurement system would be a colossal task, but many people have urged that the government experiment with streamlined systems in particular areas (*see, e.g.,* Jerry Mashaw, The Fear of Discretion in Government Procurement, 8 Yale Journal on Regulation 511, 519 (1991)], and the commercial space area—given its enormous importance, the existing national commitment to its flourishing, and its relatively small size compared to other sectors like health and defense—seems like a good place to start.

Ideally, such reforms would involve the government acting exactly like a commercial customer. After all, we want our commercial space enterprises to be well adapted to competitive markets. But, often, the government will be among their first and largest customers. Thus, if commercial space companies are to become well-adapted to serving commercial customers, the government must mimic customers in its dealing with them. This might require significant changes in existing procurement laws and practices (or at least exceptions to them), but such changes would certainly be worthwhile.

NOTES

1. At this writing, the beginnings of such reform efforts are becoming visible. The Launch Services Purchase Act of 1990 [CITE] ordered NASA to purchase launch services from commercial providers, rather than purchasing vehicles and launching them itself. And a launch voucher demonstration program, initiated by language in 1992's NASA authorization act, will create a market-like system in which space researchers will receive vouchers good for a flight on anyone's rocket, rather than a free ride on select NASA vehicles. Such efforts are merely the beginning of serious procurement reform, however.

2. What concerns should dominate in an effort to promote commercial space industries? How should the welfare of space industries be balanced against other social concerns, such as national security, government efficiency, equal opportunity or affirmative action in contracting, political control of government spending, and so on? Is it possible to formulate general principles of law that would address these issues, or is specific legislative attention required?

3. For insights into recent commercialization policy, *see* Glenn H. Reynolds, The Omnibus Space Commercialization Act of 1993, 20 Rutgers Computer & Technology Law Journal 501 (1994).

SAMPLE LAUNCH AGREEMENT

Based on Agreement Between the United States of America Represented by the National Aeronautics and Space Administration and Satellite Business Systems for Launch and Associated Services, Launch Agreement No. 1009–001, Effective Date: June 17, 1980

Preamble

This Agreement is entered into between the United States of America represented by the National Aeronautics and Space Administration (hereinafter called "NASA") and Satellite Business Systems, a general partnership (hereinafter called the "User"), and sets forth the terms and conditions under which NASA will furnish Launch and Associated Services to the User for the launching of SBS telecommunication spacecraft (hereinafter called the "Spacecraft") into earth orbits.

*   *   *

Article II—Description of Services to Be Provided by NASA

1. Definition of Launch and Associated Services

[In addition to the basic launch, NASA agrees to provide services which will consist of:]

*   *   *

d. [P]roviding, at no additional cost to the User, one reflight of the Shuttle (hereinafter called "Shuttle Reflight Launch") for each Payload launch provided [under this Agreement], and for each Shuttle Reflight Launch prior to which the User has paid to NASA an additional Reflight Premium ... in accordance with ... this Agreement, if the events described in both Subparagraphs 1.d.(1) and 1.d.(3) below or in both Subparagraphs 1.d.(2) and 1.d.(3) below occur. ...

(1) through no defect of the Payload or fault of the User, the User's contractors or subcontractors or the upper stage contractor (i) Payload operations do not result in the Deployment of the Payload, if the Payload is intended to be Deployed, (ii) Payload operations do not commence, if the Payload is not intended to be Deployed, or (iii) the Payload is Jettisoned after liftoff of the Shuttle and (iv) such launch, if itself a Shuttle Reflight Launch, is covered by an additional reflight premium paid by the User to NASA as defined above.

(2) the Payload is Deployed and the Deployment deviates from the specifications defined in the Payload Integration Plan ... , unless NASA conducted the Deployment without actual knowledge prior to Deployment, based solely on United States Government instrumentation and data, that the ensuing Deployment would deviate from the specifications, or unless NASA received such knowledge at a time when Deployment activities could not be safely halted.

(3) the particular Payload is returned to the launch site and provided to NASA in a flightworthy condition or another substantially identical Payload is provided by the User. ...

*   *   *

Article V—Allocation of Certain Risks

1. General

a. To the extent that a risk of Damage, as defined below, is not dealt with expressly in this Agreement, the United States Federal Law shall govern the allocation of such risk between the User and the United States Government.

2. Third Party Liability

a. The User shall obtain, at no cost to NASA, insurance protecting the User, the United States Government and, to the extent the United States Government is liable to reimburse them for costs they incur for Liability, the United States Government's contractors and subcontractors from any third party Liability for Damage arising out of the performance of this Agreement.

b. The User shall obtain, at no cost to NASA, insurance protecting the User, the United States Government and, to the extent the United States Government is liable to reimburse them for costs they incur for Liability, the United States Government's contractors and subcontractors from any third party Liability for any Damage resulting from a deployable Payload element following Deployment.

c. The insurance policy may take into account the agreement by NASA, the User and other identified persons, in Paragraph 3. below, not to make a claim for Damage under the conditions described therein. The policy may exclude from coverage the Liability of an insured to his own employee.

d. The amount of insurance and the terms and conditions of such insurance to be purchased pursuant to this Paragraph 2. shall be agreed to by the User and NASA in view of the insurance available in the world market at a reasonable premium. Notwithstanding such agreement by NASA, the User shall have the responsibility to meet the requirements in Subparagraphs 2.a. and 2.b. above. Such insurance shall not be required in an amount in excess of 500 million dollars (U.S.).

3. Damage to Persons or Property Involved in STS Operations

a. To simplify the allocation of risks among NASA and all users of the Space Transportation System and to make the use of the Space Transportation System feasible for the use and exploration of outer space by all potential users, the parties agree to a no-fault, no-subrogation inter-party waiver of liability under which each party agrees to be responsible for any Damage which it sustains as a result of Damage to its own property and employees involved in [Space Shuttle] Operations during such operations, which Damage is caused by NASA, the User or other users involved in STS Operations during such operations, whether such Damage arises through negligence or otherwise. Thus, if NASA's property, while involved in [Space Shuttle] Operations, is damaged by the User or another user, NASA agrees to be responsible for that Damage and agrees not to bring a claim against or sue any user. Similarly, if any user's property, while involved in these Operations, is damaged by NASA or another user, the user whose property is damaged agrees to be responsible for that Damage and agrees not to bring a claim against or sue NASA or another user. It is the intent of the parties that this inter-party waiver of Liability be construed broadly to achieve the intended objectives.

b. NASA obligates itself to require all users of the Space Transportation system and third parties as described in Subparagraphs 3.1., 3.b., and 3.c. above to agree to an identical waiver of Liability as described therein.

NOTES

1. Of critical importance in this Agreement is precisely what NASA agrees to. In Article I, NASA, like the private carrier in the agreement excerpted earlier, agrees to provide a launch, or a "Shuttle Reflight" in the event that certain contingencies occur. These are, (1) "Through no defect of the Payload or Fault of the User," the Payload is not "Deployed" or doesn't work, or (2) "the Deployment deviates from specifications." In any event, even if (1) or (2) occurs, NASA is not obligated to try again unless the Payload, or a replacement, is returned to the launch site prior to a reflight. In other words, NASA bears the risk of an improper deployment, so long as it is not the User's fault.

But what if something goes wrong prior to deployment, or after deployment but prior to positioning of the satellite in an operational orbit? (This latter possibility is quite important since satellites typically require an additional boost to place them in useful orbits, which are higher than the Space Shuttle's highest operational orbit.) In these events, the basic message of the Agreement to the user is: you're out of luck.

In the first place, the Agreement gives NASA the right to suspend and postpone a launch for a variety of reasons; since neither party is liable for the other's consequential damages under Article V, the risk of loss due to any delay falls on the user of launch services. *See* Footer, Legal Issues and Answers for Commercial Users of the Space Shuttle, 13 Transportation Law Journal 87 (1983). Secondly, NASA retains the right to "jettison" the user's payload if, in its sole discretion, it concludes that this must be done for reasons of safety or mission success. (However, if a NASA review later concludes that NASA's decision to jettison was unwarranted, the user is entitled to a new launch—but not, one should note, to compensation for the jettisoned item.) Third, "deployment" is so defined that NASA is required to provide a reflight only if it is responsible for the faulty deployment, which includes the caveat that NASA is *not* liable if it conducted the deployment without knowledge that it would be faulty, such knowledge to be "based solely on United States Government instrumentation and data." Thus, NASA has to *knowingly* bungle the deployment to be liable.

Finally, as noted above, NASA's responsibility ends with the successful deployment of the satellite. But that is not equivalent to a working satellite; it has to be in a proper orbit normally much higher than the Shuttle's. Therefore, NASA also does not bear the risk of a faulty "upper stage" in the satellite's final booster mechanism. As Footer notes, "[a] guarantee for the higher orbit would require an additional cost to be sustained by the user [in the form of] an additional fee for 'optional' services or by an additional premium for insurance." *Id.*

2. Another critical element of the Agreement concerns NASA's requirement that the user obtain insurance. As we mentioned earlier in this chapter, Congress in 1979 gave NASA the right to limit the required insurance to reasonable amounts, and to indemnify launch users who could not obtain the appropriate amounts of insurance. Nonetheless, in the Agreement excerpted above, NASA required launch users to provide $500 million worth of insurance for third-party losses. *See* Article V, Section 2(d). Interestingly, this is precisely the figure that many in the insurance industry reportedly identified as the maximum amount of insurance that would be available in the world market per user, per shuttle mission. *See* Footer, Legal Issues, *supra. But see* P. Blassel, Space Projects and the Coverage of Associated Risks, 10 The Geneva Papers on Risk & Insurance 51, 78 (1985) (reporting that one U.S. insurance broker, with NASA's assistance, had set up a syndicate offering up to $1 billion of coverage for all users of a given shuttle flight). *See generally* Margo, Some Aspects of Insuring Satellites, 1979 Insurance Law Journal 555 (1979). On space insurance issues as of the time of this writing, *see* 100th Cong. 2d. Sess. S. Print No. 100–112, Insurance and the U.S. Commercial Space Launch Industry (July, 1988). *See also* Ritorto and Mitchell, Telecommunications Satellite Insurance, 18 Air & Space Law 136 (1993).

3. A problem of interest, though largely theoretical in application so far, is how one would go about perfecting a security interest in a satellite or other space object—e.g., research facilities in orbit. The problem is that the property is not in any state, so the rules governing the perfection of security interests under the U.C.C. are difficult to apply. For a thorough article that suggests a number of important considerations, *see* Cunningham, Space Commerce and Secured Financing—New Frontiers for the U.C.C., 40 Business Lawyer 803 (1985).

4. Another species of space contract of importance in commerce is an expendable launch vehicle commercialization agreement. This is an agreement between a private company and a government launch facility—for example, the Eastern or Western Space and Missile Centers of the U.S. Air Force, at Cape Canaveral and Vandenberg Air Force Bases, respectively. Under the Commercial Space Launch Act of 1984, Pub. L. 98–575, 98 Stat. 3055, codified at 49 U.S.C. § 70101 *et seq.* (1995), government agencies connected with space are directed to make their facilities available to private companies and to assist in any way the development of the private industry. (In addition, the 1984 Act established a centralized "one-stop" agency for regulatory approval for the private space launch industry, codifying Executive Order 12465, which created the Office of Commercial Space Transportation within the Department of Transportation; this is discussed in the final section of this chapter.) In general, these commercialization agreements make the government's launch facilities available to private

companies essentially "at government cost." The idea behind the legislation was that the government should make its resources available to private sector entrepreneurs to spur the growth of this important young industry. As might be expected, the government requires fairly elaborate waivers of liability. But on the whole, the space launch industry has applauded this government program.

A similar species of agreement is the NASA Joint Endeavor Agreement (JEA). Under these agreements, which have been used primarily to foster the materials processing in space industry, NASA agrees to underwrite a certain portion of the costs of pre-launch and launch services. The basic goal is to foster the development of the materials processing industry, to help "grow" a major customer that will help keep NASA's shuttle and non-shuttle flights fully booked in the future. Some agreements actually involve an explicit "fly-now-pay-later" arrangement.

INTELLECTUAL PROPERTY

One of the most important problems facing efforts to commercialize outer space in the 1980s was uncertainty regarding the patentability of inventions made, used, sold, or reduced to practice in outer space. After considerable effort, this problem has been largely addressed through legislation adding a new section to the patent law devoted to the protection of inventions in outer space. The path of this legislation was long and tortured; its history is recounted at length in Dan L. Burk, Application of United States Patent Law to Commercial Activities in Outer Space, 6 Santa Clara Computer & High Technology Law Journal 295 (1991). The following excerpt provides some sense of the reasons why the legislation was passed.

P.L. 101–580, Inventions in Outer Space, Senate Report No. 101–266, 1990 U.S.C.C.A.N. 4058, April 19, 1990

III. Discussion Commercialization of Space

On July 24, 1984, the Reagan administration announced a national policy to encourage commercial use of outer space. Subsequent to this announcement, it has been policy of the Government to promote private sector investment in outer space projects. The approach taken to accomplish this goal has been to foster a regulatory atmosphere conducive to commercialization of space. Private research initiatives have been encouraged aboard U.S. spacecraft, including the space shuttle and the planned multinational space station. It is believed that such research, conducted in the microgravity of outer space, will uncover many innovative products and processes beneficial to high technology industries. For example, recent experiments aboard the space shuttle indicate that crystallization of biological molecules proceeds more efficiently in the microgravity of outer space. Such biological crystals allow enhanced x-ray diffraction studies of protein structure, and are expected to benefit the biotechnology industry by facilitating design of genetically engineered proteins. The microgravity crystallization process may also become important in purification of pharmaceutical products. This crystallization is accomplished by a proprietary process that should be proper subject matter for a U.S. patent claim. S. 459 is calculated to clarify the law with respect to such innovations, and thus offer an incentive to their development and disclosure. As one commentator has observed, "just as on Earth, patents can serve as an important stimulus to industrial progress in outer space."

Extraterritorial Application of the Patent Laws

Article I, section 8, clause 8 of the U.S. Constitution empowers Congress to promote the development of science and the useful arts by granting a limited monopoly to inventors. Such patents offer an economic incentive to foster creativity, and are granted in return for disclosure of the invention. To qualify for a patent under title 35 of the U.S. Code, the invention must be novel, useful, and non-obvious. In other words, the invention must be the first of its kind, it must be functional, and it must be a significant advancement over the prior art. Once an inventor is granted a valid U.S. patent, he may exclude anyone from the manufacture, use, or sale of the patented invention for a period of seventeen years. It is beneficial for the United States that this incentive be available to spur industry and innovation in outer space. However, the current state of the patent law is ambiguous with respect to jurisdiction over activities in outer space. This ambiguity stems from the patent law's territorial application. 35 U.S.C. 100(c) provides that for purposes of the patent law: The terms "United States" and "this country" mean the United States of America, its territories and possessions. Although this language was intended to be descriptive rather than limiting, the U.S. Supreme Court has stated that "our patent system makes no claim to extraterritorial effect." However, some caselaw supports the proposition that the decks of U.S.-flag vessels may be treated as U.S. territory for jurisdictional purposes in patent infringement proceedings. A court held in the case of Gardiner v. Howe, that patent law jurisdiction extended to the deck of a U.S.-flag vessel on the high seas. Similarly, in Marconi Wireless Telephone Co. v. United States, jurisdiction of U.S. patent law was extended to activities on the grounds of the American Legation at Peking. Some commentators have suggested that the holdings of these cases could be extended by analogy to activities aboard U.S.-flag spacecraft. Others have cautioned that more recent decisions appear to have retreated from territorial rationale found in previous holdings. For example, the U.S. Court of Claims in Decca Ltd. v. United States cautioned against application of this territorial principle to orbiting satellite technology. Noting that the law has changed since Gardiner, the Decca court stated in dicta: In view of the foregoing, we think a decision founded on the fiction that for purposes of the Patent Laws, United States ships and planes wherever found are United States territory, would be founded on water. The Gardiner rationale was again disapproved of by the Court of Claims in a subsequent case, Ocean Science & Engineering v. U.S. The court suggested the need for a clear signal from Congress on the matter: Of course, the constitutional power of Congress to make our patent laws applicable to processes carried out on U.S. flag ships and planes at sea is not challenged; the question is whether Congress has done so in view of the Supreme Court's view of strict construction. Perhaps the patent bar will note the possible loophole in the coverage of the U.S. patent laws and will invite the attention of Congress to it. Meanwhile, it is well to adjudicate cases on other grounds when possible, as we do in this case. In addition, numerous decisions in other areas of the law have declined to uphold this rationale with regard to United States flag ships and aircraft. For example, in Air Line Stewards and Stewardesses Association v. Northwest Airlines, the court declined to apply the Railway Labor Act to U.S.-flag Aircraft operating outside the United States, stating that: [w]e have in mind the rule that unless there is an explicit and unequivocal showing of contrary intent, Acts of Congress are to be given an interpretation which is domestic in nature. Consequently, the proposition that U.S. patent law may be applied to activities aboard U.S. spacecraft, simply because spacecraft are analogous to ocean vessels, is uncertain at best. Some clarification from Congress is needed. Without such a clarification, protection for outer space innovations may be found lacking. This situation could be detrimental to inventors in at least three instances where U.S. patent law does not recognize extraterritorial activity. First, U.S. inventors may have difficulty establishing priority of invention if the activities determining conception of the invention, reduction to practice, and diligence took place in outer space. Second, activities in outer space relevant to the prior art of a patent application could not be raised in an interference proceeding. Finally, the holder of a valid U.S. patent would be unable to enjoin or collect damages for infringing activities conducted in outer space. Uncertainty as to the application of the patent law in these areas may chill prospects for commercial investment in outer space research and manufacturing.

THE EFFECT OF INTERNATIONAL TREATIES

The United States is signatory to international treaties governing the exploration of outer space. These international obligations further obscure the applicability of the territorial principle to patent law in outer space. For example, article I of the Treaty on Principles Governing the Activities of States in the Exploration and Use of Space, Including the Moon and Other Celestial Bodies (Outer Space Treaty) encourages international cooperation in assuring scientific freedom in outer space. Article II prohibits any nation from claiming sovereignty over areas of outer space. Article XI of the treaty requires that states report the nature, conduct, and results of space explorations to the Secretary General of the United Nations, who will in turn disseminate the information. One commentator has suggested that these treaty provisions could be read together to preclude patent protection based on territoriality. Other analyses of these international agreements reach a different conclusion. Article I of the Outer Space Treaty provides that space is free for exploration and use by all states, yet under article VIII, states retain jurisdiction and control over objects launched into outer space, and over personnel aboard such objects. Article VIII also specifies that ownership of objects do not change merely because they are launched into outer space. Moreover, under article VII, states are liable for the damages caused by objects or personnel under their jurisdiction and control. These provisions support the proposition that outer space is available for use by all, but that property rights, both tangible and intangible may be protected. S. 459 should clearly demonstrate congressional intent with respect to the patent law as applied to activities in outer space. S. 459 is intended to extend the protection of U.S. patent law to applicable activities conducted in outer space. It is anticipated that this clarification of the intellectual property law will significantly encourage scientific discovery and innovation in outer space.

The above excerpt identifies the problems that the "Patents in Space" legislation was intended to solve (a much lengthier discussion appears in Glenn H. Reynolds, Legislative Comment: The Patents in Space Act, 3 Harvard Journal of Law and Technology 13 (1990)). The new section of the federal patent law created to deal with these problems appears below. Does it solve all patent related problems regarding space inventions?

United States Code 35 U.S.C. 105, Inventions in Outer Space

(a) Any invention made, used or sold in outer space on a space object or component thereof under the jurisdiction or control of the United States shall be considered to be made, used or sold within the United States for the purposes of this title, except with respect to any space object or component thereof that is specifically identified and otherwise provided for by an international agreement to which the United States is a party, or with respect to any space object or component thereof that is carried on the registry of a foreign state in accordance with the Convention on Registration of Objects Launched into Outer Space.

(b) Any invention made, used or sold in outer space on a space object or component thereof that is carried on the registry of a foreign state in accordance with the Convention on Registration of Objects Launched into Outer Space, shall be considered to be made, used or sold within the United States for the purposes of this title if specifically so agreed in an international agreement between the United States and the state of registry.

The following excerpt, from hearings held on the Patents in Space legislation in 1989, illustrates both the purpose of the legislation, and some unsolved problems.

Patents in Space, Wednesday, October 4, 1989

Hearings Before the House of Representatives,
Subcommittee on Courts, Intellectual Property, and the
Administration of Justice, Committee on the Judiciary

Mr. KASTENMEIER. In your view, either of your views, would this proposed law cover activities that would take place on a celestial body, the moon, Mars, et cetera, not on a space vehicle of any particular country or combination of countries?

Mr. KEMPF. I have some thoughts on that.

Mr. KASTENMEIER. Yes, Mr. Kempf?

Mr. KEMPF. I believe that it does, with one proviso, and that is the articles that are placed on this celestial body are launched from the earth. Article VIII of the Outer Space Treaty, which this is keyed to, does—if I can find it—yes, here it is. It does encompass an object while in outer space or on a celestial body, but the article to which it refers is an article launched from the United States, it should make no difference whether it continues in motion in outer space or whether it lands on a celestial body.

I think this legislation would cover it.

Mr. KASTENMEIER. Well, let's say the year 2100, we are talking about really a space colony in which earth people have sort of colonized a place in space, not talking about vehicles any longer, would it still apply?

Mr. KEMPF. My interpretation is if the materials from which the colony is assembled are based on materials and objects and the like that have been launched up there from outer space, it would apply.

*　　*　　*

Mr. HUGHES. Thank you, Mr. Chairman.

I appreciate, first of all, the panel coming in to testify. I wonder if you can tell me how you would interpret the term "made in outer space on a space object," with respect to whether they are under the jurisdiction or control of the United States. Does that mean it would have to be made on the space object to be covered by this law?

Let me give you a hypothetical. Suppose it was made outside a space object, say by somebody in space not on the object. Would that be covered, in your judgment? Anybody?

Mr. KEMPF. If the individual were outside the space object but not attached to any other equipment or hardware or conveyance, I am not sure that it does. I really don't know, but assuming that the individual who is outside a given space object also has some sort of support equipment that carries him outside, that is a conveyance, or that he arrives on, that support equipment is a space object that would be under the jurisdiction or control of the United States.

As long as he is on that, a person on that object is under our jurisdiction or control, as registered by us. I would assume that whatever he is attached to is piece of our territory for those purposes. If he is out there solely by himself—

Mr. HUGHES. Do you see a problem then if he is out by himself? Let's say there is no connection, not connected by cable, not connected by anything, he is basically free-standing outside the space object. Covered?

Mr. KEMPF. If he is totally free-standing, I guess I do not know, but—

Mr. HUGHES. I guess we better try to find out.

Mr. KASTENMEIER. Would the gentleman yield, because I asked a somewhat similar question about the space colony on a celestial object, and you indicated that you thought that would be covered, but this is a much—the nexus to the space vehicle here is much closer than the space colony, which might be more or less free-standing.

Mr. KEMPF. Let me answer it in this sense. The term "made" in the patent law essentially refers to either conception or first actual reduction to practice. Conception is a mental thing, and under patent law generally it doesn't make any difference what territory in which you have your conception.

It would only apply to filing a patent application. Reduction of practice requires practice of the invention in a practical physical environment, which one assumes requires an object to be associated with your reduction of practice within a facility or on a vehicle. Even your space suit or any tether that may be associated with the individual's extraterrestrial or extravehicular activities is an object. As long as there is some tangible object which the individual is associated with, that object is a piece of the U.S. territory under this provision.

Mr. KRECZKO. If I could, sir, I would like to associate with that comment and note that one of the changes that has been made in this bill from prior bills dealing with this subject is that rather than using the term space vehicle, it uses the term space object.

Space object is taken from the Outer Space Treaty and Registration Convention, and it was intended to have the broadest possible meaning, and I think unless you are talking about somebody in outer space that had absolutely no equipment within him, even though unattached from the space vehicle, the issue really would be covered.

Mr. HUGHES. Well, I suppose at the very least, we should define what we mean by a space object, because we seem to condition coverage and its jurisdiction on use, made, used, sold in outer space on a space object.

I would think reasonable minds might differ on just what we mean, because we say specifically in outer space on a space object or component thereof, and I would think a strict interpretation of that would mean that if it were not made, used or sold in outer space on that space object, it wouldn't be covered.

At least it certainly invites challenge, I would think.

Mr. KEMPF. Unless an individual is in outer space without clothes or without any other nexus to a space vehicle or without any life support equipment, I think that he is covered because even an extravehicular suit, life support equipment, oxygen supplying equipment and whatever environmental protection he has around him is a space object in the most generic sense of the way it is being interpreted, and in all probability, that space object associated with a U.S. launch vehicle, for example, would be registered, and that object and all components thereof are considered a piece of the U.S. territory for patent law purposes, and that individual can be interpreted as being on that object.

Mr. HUGHES. Where is the term space object defined?

Mr. KRECZKO. Its origin is in article I of the Registration Convention, and it is not defined. Instead, it provides for purposes of this convention the term space object includes component parts of a space object, as well as its launch vehicle and parts thereof. The reason that the phrase object was chosen, and the reason that it was not defined was a desire to avoid any limiting to the concept, and instead, the most generic term possible was chosen, objects.

Terms like vehicle were not—were considered and not adopted, so while I think it should be clear from this exchange and perhaps in the legislative history that we intend a very broad meaning. My concern with an actual definition would be that we be careful not to exclude things.

Mr. HUGHES. Let me ask—

Mr. KEMPF. I would like to follow up on that just a little bit. I did check a dictionary definition of object, recognizing that the Registration Convention did not define it, and the dictionary definition, although I don't have the exact quotes in front of me, but basically, a dictionary definition of object refers to it as any tangible, physical thing, and that is about as broad as one can get for an object, so lacking any limiting legal or statutory definitions of an object, I would always go back to a dictionary definition, which I think would be satisfactory.

* * *

Mr. REYNOLDS. Thank you.

To avoid going over the ground that has already been covered, I will try and provide just a very short summary of my prepared testimony, which I understand will be included in the record. After that, I would like to offer my thoughts on a couple of questions that came up earlier with regard to the definition of a space object and also with regard to the treatment of activities on a lunar base and then answer any other questions that you may have.

Mr. KASTENMEIER. Fine.

Mr. REYNOLDS. First, this bill will make significant and I believe worthwhile changes in U.S. patent law that can be expected over the long term to encourage businesses to invest in space manufacturing and research. This bill will ensure that such research receives protection under U.S. patent law and that it is not subjected to the burdens that U.S. patent law places on inventors whose work is performed outside the United States.

For example, it will ensure that reduction to practice on board a U.S. spacecraft is treated as reduction to practice within the United States and not as reduction to practice abroad. It will also protect against infringement that takes place on U.S. spacecraft and will extend the coverage of the Inventions Secrecy Act of inventions made on U.S. spacecraft.

Second, the bill represents an improvement, I believe, over some of the previous versions of this bill. It explicitly takes account of the character of the multinational space station which will have, as I understand it, habitable modules under the registries of the United States, Europe, and Japan, as well as considerable Canadian participation in infrastructure elements.

It also clears up some other ambiguities in the previous bill, such as the definition of a "space station," which are mentioned in my prepared testimony. Most importantly, I would like to stress that although some have argued otherwise, I believe that this bill is probably necessary if U.S. patent protection is to be extended to U.S. spacecraft and to the U.S. components onboard the space station.

After surveying the case law, I am of the opinion that it is unlikely that a U.S. court would interpret the current patent laws, whose jurisdiction is framed explicitly in territorial terms, to apply to U.S. spacecraft in outer space.

Certainly that has not been the pattern in analogous cases, and although Congress undoubtedly has the power to extend U.S. patent laws to cover U.S. spacecraft I think the courts, in light of the way they have treated these issues in the past, are unlikely to find that it has, in fact, done so in the absence of an explicit declaration to that effect.

With regard to the questions that came up earlier in terms of the definition of a space object, I would like to note that the Registration Convention provides that all objects launched into space must be registered through the Registration Convention, and to my mind that suggests that where you have something that has been launched into space, and the example we had, I believe, was an astronaut on extravehicular activity outside of a spacecraft, it must be covered by some registry. Where an object has been launched into space and has been registered, all components of that object should be considered exactly that, components of that space object, unless they have been given a separate and independent registry for purposes of the registration convention. Therefore, an astronaut doing EVA would be regarded as a component of the space object in which he or she was launched for these purposes. Note that the bill specifically uses the language "space object or component thereof," which I believe is more than sufficient to cover such circumstances in the unlikely event that they come up.

Mr. KASTENMEIER. You are saying that the term "component" can include a human being?

Mr. REYNOLDS. I think for these purposes, yes. If you wish to be more technical, you can tie it to the fact that the astronaut, if he or she planned to stay alive to do any sort of inventive activity outside the spacecraft, would certainly be wearing a space suit and/or rocket backpack and so on, and if you wanted to hang it on that you could, but I don't really think it is necessary, and I think it is something of an academic point at best.

Now, you can imagine circumstances where an object launched within another might be given an independent existence. For example, under the President's plan for Mars missions, I understand the intent is to assemble the Mars spacecraft at the space station. Obviously, before it departed, you would want to give that spacecraft an independent registry under the Registration Convention, and it would then become a space object in its own right and not a component of the space station. I really can't imagine a circumstance in which the definition of a space object in light of the way it is framed in the Registration Convention and in this bill is likely to create any real problems.

The lunar base issue, on the other hand, is a little less clear, and I would like to note in passing that the President has called for the construction of a lunar base sometime in the first decade of the next century, so that the issue is likely to arise at some point.

The 1967 Outer Space Treaty, in article 8, does provide for ownership of objects on the moon or other celestial bodies, but it is worth noting that the language that provides that ownership of space objects and components is not affected by their presence on celestial bodies comes directly after the language which says that jurisdiction and control extend to all spacecraft and space objects.

That being the case, it is not at all clear that jurisdiction and control extend, for example, to structures built on a celestial body. The 1979 Moon Treaty, which this country rightly, I believe, refused to ratify, did in one of its not-so-objectionable portions, address this issue by specifically providing that jurisdiction and control would extend to structures erected on the moon or other celestial bodies.

It is not at all clear whether that is true under current law. Again, I believe Congress would have the power to extend patent protection to those circumstances, at least so far as U.S. nationals were involved, but I am not quite as sanguine as Mr. Kempf was that the mere fact that some components of a lunar base were launched from earth would be sufficient in and of itself to support that jurisdiction. Though I can easily imagine making arguments before a court to the effect that existing law, particularly if this bill is adopted, should be read as extending patent jurisdiction to those circumstances, it is certainly not a question that is beyond debate.

Mr. KASTENMEIER. Yes. I agree with you. The clear reading doesn't really apply to celestial bodies. These are not objects. I don't think these are space objects within the meaning of this bill.

I may be wrong, but it seems to me that the presence of incidental equipment in the area does not confer patent jurisdiction. Normally the type of jurisdiction certainly that we confer here on a "space object," means something like a space craft or module or something of that sort. It seems to me that is quite different.

Mr. REYNOLDS. Exactly.

Mr. KASTENMEIER. But in terms of Mr. Hughes' hypothetical, I think we are in agreement that the bill would apply to an individual, such as an astronaut, whether or not he is tethered to the spaceship, as long as he is in the surrounding area of a space object with whom he was launched. I would think that the bill would certainly be intended to be covered by this.

Mr. REYNOLDS. I think that is right. That issue is more likely to come up in the context of a free-flying experiment package that might be isolated by a few hundred meters from the space station or space shuttle in order to protect it from vibration or electrical interference or something like that, and it seems to me that there would be no need to register that as a separate space object when it is sent out for a few days, and is intended to be retrieved.

NOTES

1. In light of the colloquy above, do you believe that companies considering investments in space-based microgravity experiments will be deterred by uncertainty regarding their intellectual property rights? What about investors interested in processes that would take place on the Moon? Is the uncertainty surrounding some space issues any greater than that found in other legal areas?

2. The space patents legislation was the product of years of work, involving numerous different versions and two sets of hearings. At the first hearing, there was some question as to whether the legislation was necessary, as some commentators had argued that U.S. patent law "followed the flag" into outer space even in the absence of explicit Congressional action. *See, e.g.*, Robert Kempf, Reduction to Practice of Space Inventions, 50 Journal of the Patent Office Society 105 (1968). And the extension of such jurisdiction was certainly justified on policy grounds. As patent expert Donald Chisum pointed out in his testimony in 1985, the limitation on extraterritorial patent jurisdiction was established largely in order to avoid conflicts with other sovereigns. This is not an issue in the context of inventive activity that takes place on board a U.S. spacecraft. Furthermore, denying patent protection to activities in outer space would create incentives counter to the express national purpose of fostering the commercial development of outer space, by discouraging research. *See* U.S. Congress, Patents in Space, Hearings Before the Subcommittee on Courts, Civil Liberties, and the Administration of Justice, Comm. on the Judiciary, 99th Cong., 2d Sess., June 13, 1985, at 18 (testimony of Professor Donald Chisum).

Unfortunately, a close reading of the case authority in the field did not support the notion that courts would extend U.S. patent law to cover processes in outer space. The reason is that U.S. patent jurisdiction is defined in territorial terms, *see* 35 U.S.C. 100(c). But the jurisdiction that the United States enjoys over spacecraft under its registry is (as we have already seen in our jurisdictional discussion) based on the *nationality* (sometimes called the personality) principle. The judicial extension of patent jurisdiction to U.S. spacecraft would thus run afoul of two important judicial rules: that statutes based on one jurisdictional principle will not be extended based on another, and that courts will normally not infer that Congress intended a statute to apply extraterritorially, but instead will require an explicit statement of Congressional intent. *See* Patents in Space: Hearings Before the Subcommittee on Courts, Intellectual Property, and the Administration of Justice, Comm. on the Judiciary, 101st Cong. 1st Sess. 36–81 (1989) (testimony of Professor Glenn H. Reynolds); Glenn H. Reynolds, Legislative Comment: The Patents in Space Act, 3 Harv. J. L. & Tech. 13 (1990).

Subsequent case law has tended to reinforce this point, as the Supreme Court has refused to extend federal statutes extraterritorially in analogous situations. For example, in EEOC v. ARAMCO, 111 S.Ct. 1227,——US——(1991), the Supreme Court refused to apply Title VII of the 1964 Civil Rights Act to a U.S. employer's overseas operation. Unlike the patent law, which expressly couches its jurisdiction in territorial terms, Title VII extends broad jurisdiction over foreign commerce, which led petitioners in ARAMCO to argue that extraterritorial jurisdiction should be inferred. The Supreme Court rejected this argument, relying on the presumption that legislation is intended to apply only within the territory of the United States unless Congress specifically states otherwise. In the space context, such a ruling might be distinguished on the basis of concern over conflicts with the laws of another sovereign, but the Supreme Court later refused to extend the Federal Tort Claims Act to Antarctica, which it described as "a sovereignless region without civil tort law of its own," a characterization that clearly applies to outer space as well. Smith v. United States, 113 S.Ct. 1178,——US——(1993). Once again, the Court relied on the presumption that Congress will explicitly say so when it intends legislation to apply extraterritorially, quoting Argentine Republic v. Amerada Hess, 488 U.S. 428, 440 (1989) to the effect that "[w]hen it desires to do so, Congress knows how to place the high seas within the jurisdictional reach of a statute." Justice Stevens' dissent specifically noted that this ruling would have precedential value for outer space, and perhaps lead to legal confusion:

> Antarctica is just one of three vast sovereignless places where the negligence of federal agents may cause death or physical injury. The negligence that is alleged in this case will surely have its parallels in outer space as our astronauts continue their explorations of ungoverned regions far beyond the jurisdictional boundaries that were familiar to the Congress that enacted the Federal Tort Claims Act (FTCA) in 1946. Moreover, our jurisprudence relating to negligence of federal agents on the sovereignless high seas points unerringly to the correct disposition of this case. Unfortunately, the Court has ignored that jurisprudence in its parsimonious construction of the FTCA's "sweeping" waiver of sovereign immunity.

Id. at 113 S. Ct. 1183, 1184. So although the Supreme Court may have left the question of FTCA application to outer space somewhat confused, it has certainly underscored the notion that it is unwise to take the application of nonspecific federal law to outer space activities for granted. Until this issue is dealt with, lawyers and space entrepreneurs should exercise caution.

3. Several aspects of the legislation under discussion may be superseded by developments currently brewing in the international patent arena. First, the emphasis on national jurisdictions has begun to break down with the advent of interna-

tional patent filing treaties (such as the Patent Cooperation Treaty) and multi-jurisdictional patent systems (such as the European Patent Convention). To the extent the Patents in Space Act was directed specifically at ensuring the application of U.S. patent law (as opposed to the law of another jurisdiction), these efforts at "international harmonization" may dilute the comparative advantage of U.S. law over that of other jurisdictions. Secondly, the importance of "domestic treatment" for the reduction to practice and conception requirements of U.S. patent law may be diminished in the near future as well. In general, these two requirements are important only because they are integral to the U.S. system that gives priority as between two rival inventors to the "first to invent." Virtually every other patent system in the world awards priority to the "first to file" a patent application; under this system, conception and reduction to practice are irrelevant. There is a strong and growing movement in the U.S. in favor of switching to a "first to file" system. One implication of such a switch is that it would eliminate the discriminatory impact of § 104 of the patent code, which allows only domestic conception and reduction to practice evidence to establish priority of invention. Foreign inventors have long complained that the effect of this section was to make only the filing date of foreign inventors available in priority disputes—which means that the "first to invent" system is in effect limited in its full impact to U.S.-based inventors. If first to file is adopted in the U.S., § 104 would become irrelevant and U.S.-based inventors would no longer have an advantage in priority disputes. Accordingly, one aspect of § 105—allowing evidence of space-based conception and reduction to practice in priority contests—would become outmoded. *See generally* Robert P. Merges, Patent Law and Policy: Cases and Materials (1992), at Chapter 4. Even so, of course, the § 105 still makes sense, because it makes clear that space activities are governed by U.S. patent law.

The lesson of the Patents in Space Act experience is mixed. On the one hand, after considerable effort, patent protection has been extended to activities in outer space, an important achievement. On the other hand, there are many more legal areas in need of similar attention: in the intellectual property arena, trade secret protection is still quite uncertain where space-based processes are concerned; in other areas, such as occupational safety, tort law, property law, and so on, things are even more unsettled. The precedent of the space patents legislation suggests that attempting to solve these questions through legislation will be slow, costly, and difficult. The excerpt from an article by Dan Burk later in this chapter explores these issues.

PROTECTING TRADE SECRETS IN SPACE

Reynolds, Book Review, 27 Jurimetrics: Journal of Law, Science & Technology 431 (1987) (Reviewing Office of Technology Assessment, Space Stations and the Law (1986))

Intellectual Property

The background paper next addresses the protection of intellectual property in outer space. Unfortunately, however, the authors' concept of intellectual property seems limited to patent law, which is the only subject discussed. While the patent discussion is interesting and provocative, there are other aspects of intellectual property that present problems just as interesting, and at least as thorny, as those discussed with regard to patents. For example, in most people's minds the commercial activity to which the space station has the most to contribute is manufacturing. While patents obviously are involved in manufacturing processes, it is unavoidably true that most improvements to manufacturing processes—including those of great value—are incremental in nature and hence often not patentable.

Those improvements are instead protected under trade secret law, and by precautions against disclosure. But trade secret law is state law, not federal law, and it is far from clear which (if any) state's trade secret law would apply to a U.S. space station. The regime that would govern a multinational space station in which different modules fall under the jurisdiction of different nations boggles the mind, especially when manufacturing processes might be carried out in more than one module, and when rights of access among modules would be guaranteed to all occupants of the station. Since the station will be small, and occupants will unavoidably have many opportunities to learn about secret processes carried out on board, some sort of contractual scheme seems necessary if those processes are to be protected. It would have been helpful if the OTA had addressed such issues.

It certainly would have helped me, anyway, since I confess to being stumped. I *do* have a suggestion as to what could be done with a U.S. station, or perhaps with regard to the parts of the station governed by the United States. With regard to those circumstances, Congress could [federalize and] extend the Uniform Trade Secrets Act to govern manufacturing processes in outer space, or provide that a particular state's law (say, that of the state from which the station is launched) would govern. This would provide some protection to secret manufacturing processes employed or developed abroad a U.S. station, but I'm not sure that much can be done to protect such secrets in the context of a multinational station. This may encourage companies involved in manufacturing processes to make use of free-flying packages whose secret components are sealed in black boxes, so that those servicing them from the station will be unable to gain access to any secret information. I don't know whether this will place a substantial burden on experiments in space manufacturing or not; much will depend on the nature of the processes experimented with.

Burk, Protection of Trade Secrets in Outer

Space Activity: A Study in Federal Preemption,
23 Seton Hall Law Review 560 (1993)

4. Trade Secret Protection

Enactment of the Patents in Space Act has constituted a major step toward resolving questions of intellectual property protection for outer space activity. Even though the patent question has been clarified, there still remains a large gap in the range of available intellectual property protection. Inventions and discoveries that are ineligible for patents are often protected through another form of intellectual property: trade secrets. The question of trade secret protection for outer space activity has yet to be addressed by Congress, but the need for such protection is clear.

a. Actual v. Trade Secrecy

Much of the incentive for investment in outer space development stems from the possibility that microgravity experiments will yield knowledge that may be applied to produce commercially valuable products. The new manufacturing techniques developed in outer space may be applied on Earth, or eventually in orbital manufacturing facilities. One commentator has pointed out that many valuable industrial processes are ineligible for patent protection and so are protected under the law of trade secrets; consequently, the availability of trade secret protection for outer space activity may be more important than the availability of patent protection.

The necessity of trade secret protection for outer space activity becomes all the more striking when the impossibility of actual secrecy aboard the space station is considered. One possible way for investors to reap the benefits of valuable, but unpatentable, outer space discoveries would be to keep the discoveries a secret. For such a scheme to work, absolute secrecy would be required; absolute secrecy, however, is most likely not feasible in the cramped quarters of the space station. Far more likely is the prospect that all those working aboard the space station, as well as their consultants and colleagues on Earth, will be aware of any new data or techniques arising from research aboard the station.

A possible alternative to actual secrecy might be some private agreement. Participants in outer space ventures might resort to a contractual arrangement designed to preserve the secrecy of valuable discoveries or processes; this approach is used for mining platforms in international waters. A contractual solution is of limited value, however, because it will only cover the situations that the parties anticipate. In addition, a contractual solution cannot bind those who are not parties to it. The Outer Space Treaty provides that nations shall have the right to inspect space objects. Some commentators have suggested that this provision could prove troublesome for outer space investors hoping to maintain confidentiality of their discoveries. Additionally, such inspectors might not be covered under a private contractual arrangement.

Far preferable to actual secrecy or contractual agreements would be the existence of a body of law that could cover unanticipated situations and that would protect investors who could not maintain actual secrecy. Trade secrecy is a form of legal protection that only requires the inventor to take reasonable steps to maintain confidentiality; if that confidentiality is breached, the trade secret holder may have the right to damages. Trade secrecy also exists as a well-developed area of law able to cover virtually any factual circumstance. Thus, the operation of trade secret law may be critical to protect unpatentable but valuable discoveries stemming from outer space research or similarly unpatentable manufacturing processes employed in outer space.

Trade secret law, however, is not federal law, but state law. Ideally, Congress would take the necessary action to provide for trade secret protection aboard United States spacecraft. It has been suggested that this protection might be achieved by enacting a version of the Uniform Trade Secrets Act as federal law, or by simply designating the trade secret law of some state as controlling for outer space activity. Unfortunately, considering Congress's procrastination in passing the relatively minor amendments needed to extend United States patent law to outer space activity, the prospects for congressional consideration of another form of intellectual property protection seem dim.

b. State Jurisdiction

In the absence of any federal law addressing trade secrets in space, participants in outer space ventures might attempt to protect their discoveries under state trade secret law. The interaction of state and federal laws in outer space has received little attention, but legal mechanisms appear to exist for individual states to assert jurisdiction over outer space activity.

Under the principles of jurisdiction outlined by the Supreme Court, states may assert jurisdiction over out-of-state entities if those entities have had certain minimum contacts with the forum state, which has statutorily authorized the exercise of such jurisdiction. In some instances, the defendant's presence in the forum state may be sufficient for jurisdiction to lie; in other instances, a pattern of commercial or juridical conduct relating to the forum will invoke jurisdiction. In addition to the defendant's activities relating to the forum state, the availability of an alternative forum and the inconvenience to the defendant of litigating far from his usual place of residence may also be considered in determining jurisdiction. These principles may extend state jurisdiction not only to United States citizens and corporations, but also to foreign nationals and corporations.

Certain states, such as Texas, have statutorily authorized the very broad exercise of their courts' extraterritorial jurisdiction. Commentators on the developing law of outer space have suggested that the Texas "long arm" jurisdictional statute might permit Texas courts to exercise jurisdiction over persons committing acts in outer space, based upon such person's contact with "mission control" at the Johnson Space Center in Houston. Presumably, Florida or California would have even better claims to assert jurisdiction over persons or entities regularly using NASA launch facilities at Cape Canaveral or landing facilities at Edwards Air Force Base. Numerous other states might have the requisite "minimum contacts" with foreign corporations involved in outer space research or manufacturing that also did business within the given state. Finally, it is very likely that under the doctrine of pendant jurisdiction, federal courts empowered to hear patent infringement cases arising in outer space could also hear related trade secret claims.

Once a court concluded that it in fact had authority to hear a trade secret claim arising from outer space activity, a determination would be required as to which jurisdiction's substantive law should be applied. Some recent commentators have considered the problem of such choice of law decisions for outer space activity, but these analyses have assumed that a choice of law could be made between nations.

Where the United States is concerned, however, no federal or monolithic body of trade secret law exists. Thus, choice of law determination would be greatly complicated by the need to choose between the trade secret laws of fifty peculiar jurisdictions.

* * *

Initially, the answer to the conundrum posed here might seem to be congressional action to fill in those substantive legal areas, such as trade secrecy, that seem devoid of rules for outer space activity. Legislative action may not be the best solution, however, and cannot be the whole solution. It is not realistic to expect Congress to attend to all the many areas of law that might apply to outer space activity. Congress is not likely to lend that much attention to a single area unless some crisis demands such a focus. Even were Congress to devote the time necessary to enacting a comprehensive space code, it probably could not anticipate all the situations that may arise in such a developing area of human endeavor. The question of how and whether to fill those gaps with available state law would remain. This result will be true whether Congress enacts a comprehensive outer space code or simply addresses a few selected areas: The preemption question would remain. In fact, new federal legislation is just as likely to generate preemption questions as to resolve them.

a. Express Language

It might be argued that Congress could forestall these questions by explicitly indicating whether or not state law was to be permitted to operate in a given area of outer space law. But, as suggested above, such explicit statutory language is no more than one factor to be considered in preemption analysis. This concept is aptly illustrated by the difficulty courts have encountered in determining the scope of express language in current federal intellectual property statutes.

Thus, explicit statutory language in and of itself is unlikely to remove the uncertainty surrounding the potential operation of state law in outer space. This realization does not mean that congressional attention to outer space law is not needed and would not go some distance toward resolving the problem. The existence of federal statutes in a given area of outer space law would at least remove one of the major considerations favoring the operation of state law: the development of a "legal vacuum" that neither state nor federal law could touch. Additionally, explicit statutory language as to preemption would at least serve as an indicator or starting point for judicial analysis.

b. Federal Common Law

Ultimately, however, it is the courts that will consider each new question of outer space law and weigh whether state law is to be allowed to function. Interpretation is, of course, the role of the courts, and takes place wherever a legislative enactment is applied. This role, however, becomes particularly important in the type of situation examined here, i.e., where critical statutory gaps need to be filled. Beginning with whatever can be determined about legislative intent, courts extrapolate from the text of a statute, attempting to reach an optimal balance of social interests.

In some instances, the material with which a court must work is quite sparse; for example, in the area of antitrust, a statute that is a few words long has been parlayed into a rich body of case law. The corpus of federal preemption doctrine examined here has in fact been compared to antitrust law, where balancing is employed to resolve some questions and key indicators determine the outcome of others. Of course, unlike antitrust law, preemption is generally a matter of constitutional interpretation, rather than statutory adjudication. Still, concern that the court performing this expanded interpretive function might be overstepping the bounds of its authority is generally unwarranted; "judicial intervention in this sphere [of preemption analysis] is less problematic than in other constitutional realms" because of the possibility of corrective congressional revision.

Consequently, even in the absence of express language regarding federal preemption, judicial review should serve adequately to determine whether in a given instance the application of state law to outer space activity is in the best interests of the nation. Curiously enough, federal courts are also well positioned to resolve the more serious deficiency of substantive law that generates the need for state law to be applied, i.e., the lack of a federal space code. Although the Supreme Court has held that "[t]here is no federal general common law," federal courts clearly have power to create common law in specific areas where uniquely federal interests are at stake. These uniquely federal interests include international relations such as those involved in outer space activity. Thus, the same concerns that favor barring state law from operating in outer space also sanction allowing federal courts to fill the resulting legal "vacuum." A federal common law approach to outer space law also offers the advantage of flexibility in a rapidly changing and expanding area. Those practicing in the area of outer space law have suggested that the only thing worse than no substantive law for outer space would be a code enacted too quickly, before problems and legal standards that might be unique to the outer space environment become apparent. Rather than turning its attention to a comprehensive—or even piecemeal—outer space code, Congress might do better to vest explicitly the federal courts with authority to hear matters of outer space law.

A FEDERAL COMMON LAW FOR OUTER SPACE?

Burk's suggestion that many space-related legal issues might be addressed by the creation of a special body of federal common law has been made before. *See, e.g.*, Glenn H. Reynolds, Space Law in the 1990s: An Agenda for Research, 31 Jurimetrics: Journal of Law, Science and Technology 1 (1990); Elizabeth A. Pucciarelli, The Case for a Federal Common Law of Space, 33 New York Law School Law Review 509 (1988); Glenn H. Reynolds, Space Stations and the Law, 27 Jurimetrics: Journal of Law, Science and Technology 431 (1987). The advantage of such an approach is that it allows law to develop flexibly, and in step with the development of an industry. The disadvantage is that it does not create the sort of *ex ante* certainty that is often necessary to promote investment. It might be best to pursue a two-pronged approach, addressing a small number of especially important issues through legislation, while simultaneously granting general jurisdiction over space-related activities to the federal courts, analogous to admiralty jurisdiction.

Impact of Start Agreements and Other Industry Incentives On Commercial Space Markets: Hearing Before the Subcommittee on Space, Committee on Science, Space and Technology, U.S. House of Representatives, 102d Cong. 1st Sess., July 31, 1991 at 66–69, Testimony of Professor Glenn H. Reynolds

One concrete action that Congress could take in this regard would be to clarify the legal environment for space activity. Some aspects of space activity are covered by federal law now, of course, under the 1984 launch act, as amended, the

1984 remote sensing act as amended, and so on. But much important law applicable to space activity is state law, not federal law: the laws governing security interests, or torts, or trade secrets, for example. Yet often it is unclear what state law—or even *which* state's law—would apply. And much space activity has, at least potentially, important political ramifications that argue against the application of state law, or decisions by state courts.

Creating a New Legal Jurisdiction

A recent Office of Technology Assessment study voiced two key legal concerns: (1) the need for an evolutionary system that would allow space law to develop as needed without the rigidity of some sort of all-encompassing a priori Space Code; and (2) the need for space activity to be free from conflicting, inconsistent (and possibly parochial) state law so as to minimize legal uncertainty and reduce litigation.

These needs have been met before in the context of a special industry, the maritime industry, by the creation of a special jurisdiction, the Admiralty jurisdiction granted to federal courts over maritime matters. And while I certainly would not recommend simply transplanting the existing maritime law into the space context, I believe that Congress should seriously consider doing something similar.

Why did we create a special federal jurisdiction over maritime matters? Essentially, in response to the same kinds of factors I have set out with regard to space. The shipping industry, and maritime commerce generally, were seen as being particularly important to the nation. The success of these industries was seen as depending, in part, on the existence of stable yet flexible law at a national level, free from inconsistent and possibly self-serving state laws. It was thought that a special federal jurisdiction would allow the federal courts to address these concerns in the context of a national forum, so that practical law, attuned to the real needs and practices of the industry, could develop as required without either the balkanizing effect of multiple state laws or the need for each provision to survive the vagaries of the legislative process. In addition, by placing maritime cases (which often have important international implications) in federal courts, this jurisdictional grant was also thought likely to promote smoother international relations, since the decisions of federal courts were likely to receive greater respect from foreign nations than were those of state courts.

Since these concerns exist in the space context, and since the Admiralty approach is generally regarded as having been successful, we should think about doing something similar in the space context. Although this is not the proper place to set forth a detailed proposal, I believe that Congress should look into the matter further. A reasonable approach would be to vest jurisdiction in the District Court for the District of Columbia (where many space suits have been filed already), with appeal to the District of Columbia Circuit, whose considerable expertise in technology-related administrative law cases would ensure competence in understanding space cases as well. Such a jurisdictional grant should be accompanied by language providing general guidance for the courts in this area.

NOTES

1. For discussion and history of the admiralty jurisdiction and why it was created, *see* Charles Black, Admiralty Jurisdiction: Critique and Suggestions, 50 Columbia Law Review 259 (1950); Putnam, How the Federal Courts Were Given Admiralty Jurisdiction, 10 Cornell Law Quarterly 460 (1925); Frank, Historical Basis of the Federal Judicial System, 13 Law & Contemporary Problems 3 (1948).

2. What sort of "general guidance" should Congress provide to courts in this area? The admiralty courts could draw on centuries (some historians say millennia) of custom and code, dating back to the Rules of Oleron and the Rhodian Law. What similar experience base would federal courts have to draw on when deciding space cases? Is that important?

3. When should state law govern space activity, and when should it be preempted by federal law? What rules should determine which state's law should apply, when several states have a credible nexus with particular state activity? What kind of contacts should be more important? Imagine (as is not at all implausible) a satellite or space station built in one state, launched in a second, controlled from a third by a corporation that has its headquarters and place of incorporation in a fourth, all governed by contracts signed in a fifth. What law should govern in such circumstances? In a litigation context, should the litigation's subject matter make a difference? How should such problems be addressed?

4. What structural concerns should govern Congress's approach to creating a new federal jurisdictional grant? On the one hand, there are several arguments for vesting jurisdiction in a single federal district court: it would concentrate the caseload (likely to remain fairly small for several years) into a single court, allowing a unified body of law to develop more quickly; it would simplify otherwise complex venue problems; and it would promote the development of expertise by a particular group of judges. On the other hand, it would narrow the range of individuals involved, and perhaps limit the range of ideas introduced into the law. Would generalist judges be competent to decide the technical questions that would be likely to come up in space cases? Could this problem be addressed by making the appellate court the Court of Appeals for the Federal Circuit—which has expertise in high technology issues through its work in government contract

and patent cases—or would a generalist court like the Court of Appeals for the District of Columbia Circuit provide a broader perspective? Note that generalist judges have generally done a good job in deciding admiralty cases, but that Congress has more frequently created specialized courts (like the Court of International Trade and the Bankruptcy Courts) in recent years.

ADMINISTRATIVE LAW: REGULATION AND DEREGULATION OF SPACE ACTIVITIES

In this final section we consider a number of conceptually related yet distinct legal problems raised by space activities—those relating to government regulation.

The chief legislative initiative on space regulation was the Commercial Space Launch Act of 1984, Pub. L. 98-575, 98 Stat. 3055, codified at 49 U.S.C., §§ 2601 *et seq*. For the most part, the Commercial Space Launch Act attempts to support the private launch industry by (1) streamlining the regulatory approval process governing space activities, and (2) admonishing all branches of the government to support the industry in whatever ways possible. The following excerpt is from the Act:

Commercial Space Launch Act of 1984, 49 U.S.C. §§ 70101 *et seq.*

§ 70101. Congressional Findings

The Congress finds and declares that—

* * *

(6) providing launch services by the private sector is consistent with the national security interests and foreign policy interests of the United States and would be facilitated by stable, minimal, and appropriate regulatory guidelines that are fairly and expeditiously applied;

(7) the United States should encourage private sector launches and associated services and, only to the extent necessary, regulate such launches and services in order to ensure compliance with international obligations of the United States and to protect the public health and safety, safety of property, and national security interests and foreign policy interests of the United States.

* * *

§ 70102. Definitions

In this chapter—

* * *

(3) "launch" means to place or try to place a launch vehicle and any payload—

(A) in a suborbital trajectory;

(B) in Earth orbit in outer space; or

(C) otherwise in outer space.

(4) "launch property" means an item built for, or used in, the launch preparation or launch of a launch vehicle.

(5) "launch services" means—

(A) activities involved in the preparation of a launch vehicle and payload for launch; and

(B) the conduct of a launch.

(6) "launch site" means the location on Earth from which a launch takes place (as defined in a license the Secretary issues or transfers under this chapter) and necessary facilities.

(7) "launch vehicle" means—

(A) a vehicle built to operate in, or place a payload in, outer space; and

(B) a suborbital rocket.

(8) "payload" means an object that a person undertakes to place in outer space by means of a launch vehicle, including components of the vehicle specifically designed or adapted for that object.

* * *

(11) "third party" means a person except—

(A) the United States Government or the Government's contractors or subcontractors involved in launch services;

(B) a licensee or transferee under this chapter;

(C) a licensee's or transferee's contractors, subcontractors, or customers involved in launch services; or

(D) the customer's contractors or subcontractors involved in launch services.

* * *

§ 70104. Restrictions on Launches and Operations

(a) *License requirement.*—A license issued or transferred under this chapter is required for the following:

(1) for a person to launch a launch vehicle or to operate a launch site in the United States.

(2) for a citizen of the United States ... to launch a launch vehicle or to operate a launch site outside the United States.

(3) for a citizen of the United States ... to launch a launch vehicle or to operate a launch site outside the United States and outside the territory of a foreign country unless there is an agreement between the United States Government and the government of the foreign country providing that the government of the foreign country has jurisdiction over the launch or operation.

(4) for a citizen of the United States ... to launch a launch vehicle or to operate a launch site in the territory of a foreign country if there is an agreement between the United States Government and the government of the foreign country providing that the United States Government has jurisdiction over the launch or operation.

(b) *Compliance with payload requirements.*—The holder of a launch license under this chapter may launch a payload only if the payload complies with all requirements of the laws of the United States related to launching a payload.

(c) *Preventing launches.*—The Secretary of Transportation shall establish whether all required licenses, authorizations, and permits required for a payload have been obtained. If no license, authorization, or permit is required, the Secretary may prevent the launch if the Secretary decides the launch would jeopardize the public health and safety, safety of property, or national security or foreign policy interest of the United States.

§ 70105. License Applications and Requirements

(a) *Applications.*—A person may apply to the Secretary of Transportation for a license or transfer of a license under this chapter in the form and way the Secretary prescribes. Consistent with the public health and safety, safety of property, and national security and foreign policy interests of the United States, the Secretary, not later than 180 days after receiving an application, shall issue or transfer a license if the Secretary decides in writing that the applicant complies, and will continue to comply, with this chapter and regulations prescribed under this chapter. The Secretary shall inform the applicant of any pending issue and action required to resolve the issue if the Secretary has not made a decision not later than 120 days after receiving an application.

(b) *Requirements.*—

(1) Except as provided in this subsection, all requirements of the laws of the United States applicable to the launch of a launch vehicle or the operation of a launch site are requirements for a license under this chapter.

(2) The Secretary may prescribe—

(A) any term necessary to ensure compliance with this chapter, including on-site verification that a launch or operation complies with representations stated in the application;

(B) an additional requirement necessary to protect the public health and safety, safety of property, national security interests, and foreign policy interests of the United States ...

(3) The Secretary may waive a requirement for an individual applicant if the Secretary decides that the waiver is in the public interest and will not jeopardize the public health and safety, safety of property, and national security and foreign policy interests of the United States.

* * *

§ 70109. Preemption of Scheduled Launches

(a) *General.*—With the cooperation of the Secretary of Defense and the Administrator of the National Aeronautics and Space Administration, the Secretary of Transportation shall act to ensure that a launch of a payload is not preempted from access to a United States Government launch site or launch property, except for imperative national need, when a launch date commitment from the Government has been obtained for a launch licensed under this chapter. A licensee or transferee preempted from access to a launch site or launch property does not have to pay the Government any amount for launch services attributable only to the scheduled launch prevented by the preemption.

* * *

§ 70110. Administrative Hearings and Judicial Review

(a) *Administrative hearings.*—The Secretary of Transportation shall provide an opportunity for a hearing on the record to—

(1) an applicant under this chapter, for a decision of the Secretary under section 70105(a) of this title to issue or transfer a license with terms or deny the issuance or transfer of a license;

(2) an owner or operator of a payload under this chapter, for a decision of the Secretary under section 70104(c) of this title to prevent the launch of the payload; and

(3) a licensee under this chapter, for a decision of the Secretary under—

(A) section 70107 (b) or (c) of this title to modify, suspend, or revoke a license; or

(B) section 70108(a) of this title to prohibit, suspend, or end a launch or operation of a launch site licensed by the Secretary.

(b) *Judicial review.*—A final action of the Secretary under this chapter is subject to judicial review as provided in chapter 7 of title 5.

§ 70111. Acquiring United States Government Property and Services

(a) *General requirements and considerations.*—

(1) The Secretary of Transportation shall facilitate and encourage the acquisition by the private sector and State governments of—

(A) launch property of the United States Government that is excess or otherwise is not needed for public use; and

(B) launch services, including utilities, of the Government otherwise not needed for public use.

(2) In acting under paragraph (1) of this subsection, the Secretary shall consider the commercial availability on reasonable terms of substantially equivalent launch property or launch services from a domestic source.

*   *   *

§ 70112. Liability Insurance and Financial Responsibility Requirements

(a) *General requirements.*—

(1) When a license is issued or transferred under this chapter, the licensee or transferee shall obtain liability insurance or demonstrate financial responsibility in amounts to compensate for the maximum probable loss from claims by—

(A) a third party for death, bodily injury, or property damage or loss resulting from an activity carried out under the license; and

(B) the United States Government against a person for damage or loss to Government property resulting from an activity carried out under the license.

(2) The Secretary of Transportation shall determine the amounts required under paragraph (1) (A) and (B) of this subsection, after consulting with the Administrator of the National Aeronautics and Space Administration, the Secretary of the Air Force, and the heads of other appropriate executive agencies.

(3) For the total claims related to one launch, a licensee or transferee is not required to obtain insurance or demonstrate financial responsibility of more than—

(A) (i) $500,000,000 under paragraph (1) (A) of this subsection; or

(ii) $100,000,000 under paragraph (1) (B) of this subsection; or

(B) the maximum liability insurance available on the world market at reasonable cost if the amount is less than the applicable amount in clause (A) of this paragraph.

(4) An insurance policy or demonstration of financial responsibility under this subsection shall protect the following, to the extent of their potential liability for involvement in launch services, at no cost to the Government:

(A) the Government.

(B) executive agencies and personnel, contractors, and subcontractors of the Government.

(C) contractors, subcontractors, and customers of the licensee or transferee.

(D) contractors and subcontractors of the customer.

(b) *Reciprocal waiver of claims.*—

(1) A license issued or transferred under this chapter shall contain a provision requiring the licensee or transferee to make a reciprocal waiver of claims with its contractors, subcontractors, and customers, and contractors and subcontractors of the customers, involved in launch services under which each party to the waiver agrees to be responsible for property damage or loss it sustains, or for personal injury to, death of, or property damage or loss sustained by its own employees resulting from an activity carried out under the license.

(2) The Secretary of Transportation shall make, for the Government, executive agencies of the Government involved in launch services, and contractors and subcontractors involved in launch services, a reciprocal waiver of claims with the licensee or transferee, contractors, subcontractors, and customers of the licensee or transferee, and contractors and subcontractors of the customers, involved in launch services under which each party to the waiver agrees to be responsible for property damage or loss it sustains, or for personal injury to, death of, or property damage or loss sustained by its own employees resulting from an activity carried out under the license. The waiver applies only to the extent that claims are more than the amount of insurance or demonstration of financial responsibility required under subsection (a) (1) (B) of this section. After consulting with the Administrator and the Secretary of the Air Force, the Secretary of Transportation may waive, for the Government and a department, agency, and instrumentality of the Government, the right to recover damages for damage or loss to Government property to the extent insurance is not available because of a policy exclusion the Secretary of Transportation decides is usual for the type of insurance involved.

(c) *Determination of maximum probable losses.*—The Secretary of Transportation shall determine the maximum probable losses under subsection (a) (1) (A) and (B) of this section associated with an activity under a license not later than 90 days after a licensee or transferee requires a determination and submits all information the Secretary requires. The Secretary shall amend the determination as warranted by new information.

*   *   *

(e) *Launches involving Government facilities and personnel.*—The Secretary of Transportation shall establish requirements consistent with this chapter for proof of financial responsibility and other assurances necessary to protect the Government and its executive agencies and personnel from liability, death, bodily injury, or property damage or loss as a result of a launch or operation of a launch site involving a facility or personnel of the Government. The Secretary may not relieve the Government of liability under this subsection for death, bodily injury, or property damage or loss resulting from the willful misconduct of the Government or its agents.

* * *

§ 70113. Paying Claims Exceeding Liability Insurance and Financial Responsibility Requirements

(a) *General requirements.—*

(1) To the extent provided in advance in an appropriation law or to the extent additional legislative authority is enacted providing for paying claims in a compensation plan submitted under subsection (d) of this section, the Secretary of Transportation shall provide for the payment by the United States Government of a successful claim (including reasonable litigation or settlement expenses) of a third party against a licensee or transferee under this chapter, a contractor, subcontractor, or customer of the licensee or transferee, or a contractor or subcontractor of a customer, resulting from an activity carried out under the license issued or transferred under this chapter for death, bodily injury, or property damage or loss resulting from an activity carried out under the license. However, claims may be paid under this section only to the extent the total amount of successful claims related to one launch—

(A) is more than the amount of insurance or demonstration of financial responsibility required under section 70112 (a) (1) (A) of this title; and

(B) is not more than $1,500,000,000 (plus additional amounts necessary to reflect inflation occurring after January 1, 1989) above that insurance or financial responsibility amount.

(2) The Secretary may not provide for paying a part of a claim for which death, bodily injury, or property damage or loss results from willful misconduct by the licensee or transferee. To the extent insurance required under section 70112(a) (1) (A) of this title is not available to cover a successful third party liability claim because of an insurance policy exclusion the Secretary decides is usual for the type of insurance involved, the Secretary may provide for paying the excluded claims without regard to the limitation contained in section 70112(a) (1).

* * *

(d) *Surveys, reports, and compensation plans.—*

(1) If as a result of an activity carried out under a license issued or transferred under this chapter the total of claims related to one launch is likely to be more

than the amount of required insurance or demonstration of financial responsibility, the Secretary shall—

(A) survey the causes and extent of damage; and

(B) submit expeditiously to Congress a report on the results of the survey.

(2) Not later than 90 days after a court determination indicates that the liability for the total of claims related to one launch may be more than the required amount of insurance or demonstration of financial responsibility, the President, on the recommendation of the Secretary, shall submit to Congress a compensation plan that—

(A) outlines the total dollar value of the claims;

(B) recommends sources of amounts to pay for the claims;

(C) includes legislative language required to carry out the plan if additional legislative authority is required; and

(D) for a single event or incident, may not be for more than $1,500,000,000.

* * *

(e) *Congressional resolutions.*—

(1) In this subsection, "resolution"—

(A) means a joint resolution of Congress the matter after the resolving clause of which is as follows: "That the Congress approves the compensation plan numbered__ submitted to the Congress on __ , 19__.", with the blank spaces being filled appropriately; but

(B) does not include a resolution that includes more than one compensation plan.

(2) The Senate shall consider under this subsection a compensation plan requiring additional appropriations or legislative authority not later than 60 calendar days of continuous session of Congress after the date on which the plan is submitted to Congress.

(3) A resolution introduced in the Senate shall be referred immediately to a committee by the President of the Senate. All resolutions related to the same plan shall be referred to the same committee.

(4) (A) If the committee of the Senate to which a resolution has been referred does not report the resolution within 20 calendar days after it is referred, a motion is in order to discharge the committee from further consideration of the resolution or to discharge the committee from further consideration of the plan.

(B) A motion to discharge may be made only by an individual favoring the resolution. ...

(f) *Application.*—This section applies to a license issued or transferred under this chapter for which the Secretary receives a complete and valid application not later than December 31, 1999.

* * *

§ 70115. Enforcement and Penalty

(a) *Prohibitions.*—A person may not violate this chapter, a regulation prescribed under this chapter, or any term of a license issued or transferred under this chapter.

* * *

(c) *Civil penalty.*—(1) After notice and an opportunity for a hearing on the record, a person the Secretary finds to have violated subsection (a) of this section is liable to the United States Government for a civil penalty of not more than $100,000. A separate violation occurs for each day the violation continues.

* * *

§ 2616. Enforcement Authority

* * *

(b) Power to Investigate, Inspect or Seize

In carrying out this section, the Secretary may—

(1) make investigations and inquiries, and administer to or take from any person an oath, affirmation, or affidavit, concerning any matter relating to enforcement of this chapter; and (2) pursuant to any lawful process—

(A) enter at any reasonable time any launch site, production facility, or assembly site of a launch vehicle, or any site where a payload is integrated with a launch vehicle, for the purpose of inspecting any object which is subject to this chapter and any records or reports required by the Secretary to be made or kept under this chapter; and

(b) seize any such object, record, or report where there is probable cause to believe that such object, record, or report was used, is being used, or is likely to be used in violation of this chapter.

NOTES

1. For general commentary on this Act, *see* Note, The Commercial Space Launch Act: America's Response to the Moon Treaty? 10 Fordham International Law Journal 763 (1987).

2. In response to their experience in the first few years of commercial space activities, launch service companies led a movement to amend the Commercial Space Launch Act in two crucial respects: First, they attempted to have the insur-

ance provision (§ 2615) amended to explicitly limit the amount of insurance required. The proposed change, embodied in H.R. 4399 and S.2395, the Commercial Space Launch Act Amendments of 1988, 100th Cong., 2d Sess., required that damage to *government property* be insured for no more than $100 million or "the maximum ... available on the world market at a reasonable cost, whichever is less." H.R. 4399, § 4(a); S. 2395 § 16(a)(1)(B)(ii). The proposed amendments also limited insurance for damages to *third parties* to $500 million or the maximum available at a reasonable cost, again, "whichever is less." H.R. 4399 § 4(b); S.2395 § 16(a)(1)(A)(ii).

For the legislative history of recent amendments, *see* Pub.L. 100–657, Nov. 15, 1988, 102 Stat. 3900; Pub.L. 101–611, Nov. 16, 1990, 104 Stat. 3203; *see also* 1990 U.S. Code Cong. and Adm. News, p. 4540.

Code of Federal Regulations, Title 14—Aeronautics And Space

Chapter III—Office of Commercial Space Transportation
Department of Transportation (Parts 400–499) Subchapter B—
Procedure Part 404—Regulations and Licensing
Requirements Subpart B—Rulemaking

§ 404.11 General.

(a) Unless the Director finds, for good cause, that notice is impractical, unnecessary, or contrary to the public interest, a notice of proposed rulemaking is issued and interested persons are invited to participate in proceedings related to each substantive rule proposed.

(b) Unless the Director determines that notice and comment is necessary or desirable, interpretive rules, general statements of policy, and rules relating to organization, procedure, or practice are issued as final rules without notice or other proceedings.

(c) In the Director's discretion, interested persons may be invited to participate in the rulemaking proceedings described in § 404.19 of this Subpart.

*   *   *

§ 411.1 General.

The Office of Commercial Space Transportation may issue and transfer licenses authorizing launches, the operation of launch sites, or both.

*   *   *

§ 411.3 Review Procedures.

(a) The evaluation of license requests for unmanned launches involves two reviews, Safety Review and Mission Review, designed to address in the most effective and least burdensome manner the two general areas of Federal concern: (1) the efficacy of the proposed safety operations to support safe preparation and launch of a launch vehicle and any payload; and (2) significant issues affecting United States national security interests, foreign policy interests, or international obligations which might be associated with the proposed launch. These reviews may be conducted independently of each other and in whichever order, sequential or concurrent, is more appropriate to the needs of the applicant.

(b) Requests for licenses authorizing the operation of a launch site are reviewed on the basis of the applicant's capability to operate a facility where safety operations are conducted on a continuing basis as support for the launching of a specified class of launch vehicles.

* * *

§ 411.5 Safety Approval.

(a) Applicants proposing to conduct all of their own safety operations at a private launch site must demonstrate that they possess the resources needed for safe preparation and launch of a launch vehicle and any payload to be carried by such vehicle. In these circumstances, a comprehensive review of the applicant's proposed safety operations must be performed in order to determine whether safety approval can be granted.

(b) If an applicant proposes to launch from a Federal range, as the Act encourages, it is the Office's view that reliance on safety-related launch property and services found at these ranges is an appropriate means of assuring that the applicant's launch activities can be conducted safely. As a general matter, a commercial launch site operated under the authority of a license issued by the Office should also be capable of providing such an assurance of safety. If an applicant proposes to contract for the services of a Federal range or a private launch site operated under the authority of a license issued by the Office, safety approval will ordinarily be given once the applicant has been accepted by a range or site capable of handling the launch activity proposed. All launch licenses issued under these circumstances shall be conditioned by the requirements that the applicant:

(1) Comply with all specified safety requirements and procedures of the range or launch site in question and

(2) Inform the Office of and obtain approval for any planned or proposed deviations from or alternatives to such requirements or procedures.

* * *

§ 411.7 Mission Approval.

(a) General. Mission approval is granted unless some element of the proposed launch poses a threat to U.S. national security or foreign policy interests, constitutes a hazard to public health and safety or safety of property, or is inconsistent with international obligations of the United States. The Office shall work with applicants to correct or eliminate any defect in a proposal which impedes granting mission approval.

(b) Payloads. A proposal to launch any foreign payload or a payload not covered by existing FCC or NOAA regulation must be reviewed in consultation with other appropriate Federal agencies in order to determine that the launch of such payload will not jeopardize public health and safety, safety or property, or any national security or foreign policy interest of the United States. The Office, when requested to do so, shall provide payload operators or owners with this determination in advance of a launch license request or request for mission approval. Subsequent reviews of payloads within the same category shall be considered on a routine basis and shall focus on new or distinctive elements of the specific payload to be launched.

* * *

§ 411.9 Information Requirements.

The Office shall make available current compilations of the basic information an applicant is required to submit in order to initiate an appropriate review of any proposed commercial launch activity subject to the Office's authority. These information requirements are not intended to be all-inclusive and the submission of the required information does not, in itself, demonstrate the qualifications of an applicant. The nature of individual proposals may require the submission of additional information.

* * *

Subchapter C—Licensing Part 413—Applications

§ 413.3 Pre-application Consultation.

Applicants are encouraged to consult with the Office of Commercial Space Transportation at the earliest possible planning stages.

Such consultation may reveal potential problems with a proposal and allow changes to be made when they are less likely to result in significant delay or costs to the applicant.

* * *

§ 413.5 Application.

(a) Form. Applications shall be in writing and filed in duplicate with the Office of Commercial Space Transportation, S-50, 400 Seventh Street, SW., Washington, DC 20590. Attention: Applications Review Branch.

(b) Types. Applications to the Office may request issuance or transfer of a license authorizing a launch or the operation of a launch site. Applications may also be made, separately and in advance of a license application, requesting an approval or determination that must be secured before a license can be issued or transferred.

(c) Signature. Applications shall be signed as follows:

(1) For a corporation: By an officer authorized to act for the corporation in licensing matters.

(2) For a partnership or a sole proprietorship: By a general partner or proprietor, respectively; or

(3) For an association or other entity: By a principal executive officer.

(d) Payment with application. An application for a license authorizing the conduct of commercial space activities must be accompanied by a license application fee of two thousand, five hundred dollars ($2,500.00).

(1) The license application fee shall be payable upon submission of the application and shall be non-refundable.

(2) The license application fee shall be paid by certified check or wire transfer made payable to the Department of Transportation, Office of Commercial Space Transportation.

(3) Any license issued pursuant to § 413.13 which authorizes activities that continue beyond twelve (12) months may be administratively renewed annually upon payment of a two thousand five hundred dollar ($2,500.00) license fee, payable on or before the anniversary date of the license issued pursuant to § 413.13.

[Added: 56 Fed. Reg. 41068, Aug. 19, 1991]

* * *

§ 413.7 Confidentiality.

(a) Information or data submitted to the Office may be designated as confidential by the person or agency furnishing such data or information.

(b) A request that information or data be treated confidentially should be made in writing at the time the information is submitted and should state the period of time for which confidential treatment is desired.

(c) A request for confidential treatment will be associated with previously submitted information to the extent that it is practicable in light of prior distribution of such information.

(d) Information requested to be treated confidentially must be clearly marked with an identifying legend such as "Proprietary Information" or "Confidential Treatment Requested." Where this marking proves impracticable, a cover sheet containing the identifying legend must be securely attached to the compilation of information for which confidential treatment is requested.

(e) Pursuant to section 9(c) of the Act, information for which confidential treatment has been requested, as provided above, or information that qualifies for exemption under section 552(b) (4) of Title 5, United States Code, will not be disclosed unless the Director determines that the withholding of such data or information is contrary to the public or national interest.

§ 413.9 Review of Applications.

(a) Each application shall contain the information prescribed by the Office in order to initiate an appropriate review of the proposed launch activity. This information can be obtained by writing to the Office of Commercial Space Transportation, S-50, 400 Seventh Street SW., Washington, DC 20590, or by calling (202) 366-5770.

(b) The Office determines whether an application is substantially complete and, if so, accepts the application for review.

(c) Applications found by the Office to be incomplete or so speculative as to make review inappropriate will be returned to the applicant with a statement of the reasons therefor.

(d) Once an application is accepted, the Office initiates an appropriate review in light of the specific action requested in the application. Pursuant to section 20 of the Act, the Office shall consult with the Department of Defense on all matters affecting national security and with the Department of State on all matters affecting foreign policy, including the issuance or transfer of each license.

(e) The Office makes a determination on an application as expeditiously as possible but, in the case of a license application, not later than 180 days after receipt of such application. If the Office has not made a determination within 120 days after receipt of such application, the Office informs the applicant of any pending issues and of actions required to resolve such issues.

§ 413.11 Modifications.

Applications may be modified, supplemented, or corrected by the applicant at any time prior to issuance of the Office's decision.

*   *   *

§ 413.13 Issuance of License.

The Office issues or transfers a license authorizing the conduct of commercial space launch activities by the applicant if the Office determines, after review, that the applicant has, and will continue to have, the ability to comply with all requirements for a license, including the ability to conduct safe launch or launch site operations.

*   *   *

§ 413.15 Terms and Conditions of License.

(a) Each license issued or transferred under this section shall specify the activities authorized by the license, the name of each person responsible under the license for the conduct of such activities, the period of time for which the license is valid, and such other terms and conditions as may be required to protect public safety, the safety of property, and national security and foreign policy interests of the United States.

(b) All licenses shall specify, as a condition of such license, that the licensee maintain an effective on-site means for verifying that the licensed launch activity conforms to representations made in the license application.

*   *   *

§ 413.17 Certain Rights not Conferred by License.

No license shall confer any proprietary, property, or exclusive right in the use of any airspace, Federal launch facility, or Federal launch support facility. Issuance of a license does not affect the authority of the Federal Communications Commission under the Communications Act of 1934 (47 U.S.C. 151 *et seq.*) or the authority of the Secretary of Commerce under the Land Remote-Sensing Commercialization Act of 1984 (15 U.S.C. 4201 *et seq.*).

*   *   *

Subchapter C—Licensing Part 415—Launch Licenses

§ 415.3 When a Launch License is Required.

(a) The launch of a launch vehicle from U.S. territory by any person, or from outside U.S. territory by any individual or any corporation, partnership, joint venture, association of other entity organized or existing under the laws of the United States or any state, must be authorized by a license issued under this part.

(b) The launch of a launch vehicle by a foreign corporation or other entity controlled by a United States citizen, as defined in section 401.5 of this Chapter, at any place which is both outside the United States and outside of the territory of any foreign nation when there is no agreement in force between the United States and a foreign nation which provides that such foreign nation shall exercise jurisdiction over such launch, must be authorized by a license issued under this part.

(c) The launch of a launch vehicle by any foreign corporation or other entity described in paragraph (b) of this section from the territory of a foreign nation, when there is in force an agreement between the United States and such foreign nation concerning the exercise of jurisdiction by the United States over such launch, must be authorized by a license issued under this part.

*   *   *

§ 415.5 Approvals Required for a License.

A license authorizing an unmanned launch is issued or transferred after the Office grants an applicant both mission and safety approvals. These approvals may be requested separately and in advance of a license request, as provided in §§ 415.15 and 415.23 of this subpart.

*   *   *

§ 415.9 Standard Conditions.

All launch licenses shall contain those conditions which the Office determines to be necessary and appropriate to protect public health and safety, the safety of property, and national security and foreign policy interests of the United States. Failure to comply with any license condition may be cause for revocation of the license or the initiation of other enforcement actions by the Office. Standard conditions in licenses include requirements for the licensee to do the following:

(a) Secure at least the minimum amount of third-party liability insurance specified by the Department;

(b) Adhere strictly to specified range safety regulations and procedures;

(c) Comply with requirements concerning pre-launch record keeping and notifications, including those pertaining to Federal airspace restrictions and military tracking operations; and

(d) Comply with Federal inspection, verification and enforcement requirements.

(e) Provide, no later than 30 days after launch, full payment of the launch fee by certified check or wire transfer made payable to the Department of Transportation, Office of Commercial Space Transportation.

[Added: 56 Fed. Reg. 41068, Aug. 19, 1991]

*   *   *

§ 415.10 Registration of Space Objects.

(a) In accordance with Article IV of the 1975 Convention on Registration of Objects Launched Into Outer Space, each licensee is responsible for registering all objects placed in space in the course of conducting activities authorized by its license, except for objects owned by a foreign entity. Registration of objects owned by a foreign entity is the responsibility of that foreign entity.

(b) Each licensee shall, within 30 days after launch, submit to the Office the following information concerning any vehicle or other object it has launched into outer space:

1. The international designator of the space object(s);
2. Date and location of launch;
3. Basic programmed orbital parameters, including:
   a. Nodal period,
   b. Inclination,
   c. Apogee;
4. General function of the space object.

*   *   *

§ 415.23 When to Request Mission Approval.

An application for mission approval, may be made as part of a launch license request or, in the alternative, in advance of a launch license request. Application for a determination on a payload not regulated by the FCC or NOAA may be made as part of or in advance of any other request.

THE LAND REMOTE SENSING

COMMERCIALIZATION ACT

Besides the Commercial Space Launch Act and ensuing OCST regulations, there is another piece of legislation which, with its accompanying regulations, affects one big segment of the commercial space business: the Land Remote Sensing Commercialization Act of 1984, Pub. L. 98-365, 98 Stat. 452, codified at 15 U.S.C. §§ 5601 *et.seq.* (1995). The basic aim of this legislation was to (1) "privatize" the marketing and sale of remote sensing data gathered by U.S.-owned Landsat Satellites, and (2) provide launch licensing procedures for private-sector enterprises that wish to enter the remote sensing business.

Remote sensing is a general term used to describe satellite-based systems that take precise images of the earth's surface for use in such applications as weather prediction and tracking, natural resource location and inventory (e.g., timber and oil and gas deposits), environmental monitoring, and general observation (e.g., by the news media, following natural disaster or international conflict stories). *See* Reynolds, Satellite Newsgathering and the First Amendment, The Air & Space Lawyer, Fall, 1987 at 1; Joyner & Miller, Selling Satellites: The Commercialization of LANDSAT, 26 Harvard International Law Journal 63 (1985); Diederiks-Vershoor, Current Issues in Remote Sensing, 1984 Michigan Year Book of International Legal Studies 305 (1984).

The following excerpt is a condensation of the Commercialization Act.

United States Code, Annotated Title 15— Commerce and Trade

Chapter 82—Land Remote Sensing Policy

§ 5601. Findings

The Congress finds and declares the following:

(1) The continuous collection and utilization of land remote sensing data from space are of major benefit in studying and understanding human impacts on the global environment, in managing the Earth's natural resources, in carrying out national security functions, and in planning and conducting many other activities of scientific, economic, and social importance.

(2) The Federal Government's Landsat system established the United States as the world leader in land remote sensing technology.

(3) The national interest of the United States lies in maintaining international leadership in satellite land remote sensing and in broadly promoting the beneficial use of remote sensing data.

(4) The cost of Landsat data has impeded the use of such data for scientific purposes, such as for global environmental change research, as well as for other public sector applications.

(5) Given the importance of the Landsat program to the United States, urgent actions, including expedited procurement procedures, are required to ensure data continuity.

(6) Full commercialization of the Landsat program cannot be achieved within the foreseeable future, and thus should not serve as the near-term goal of national policy on land remote sensing; however, commercialization of land remote sensing should remain a long-term goal of United States policy.

(7) Despite the success and importance of the Landsat system, funding and organizational uncertainties over the past several years have placed its future in doubt and have jeopardized United States leadership in land remote sensing.

(8) Recognizing the importance of the Landsat program in helping to meet national and commercial objectives, the President approved, on February 11, 1992, a National Space Policy Directive which was developed by the National Space Council and commits the United States to ensuring the continuity of Landsat coverage into the 21st century.

(9) Because Landsat data are particularly important for national security purposes and global environmental change research, management responsibilities for the program should be transferred from the Department of Commerce to an integrated program management involving the Department of Defense and the National Aeronautics and Space Administration.

(10) Regardless of management responsibilities for the Landsat program, the Nation's broad civilian, national security, commercial, and foreign policy interests in remote sensing will best be served by ensuring that Landsat remains an unclassified program that operates according to the principles of open skies and nondiscriminatory access.

(11) Technological advances aimed at reducing the size and weight of satellite systems hold the potential for dramatic reductions in the cost, and substantial improvements in the capabilities, of future land remote sensing systems, but such technological advances have not been demonstrated for land remote sensing and therefore cannot be relied upon as the sole means of achieving data continuity for the Landsat program.

(12) A technology demonstration program involving advanced remote sensing technologies could serve a vital role in determining the design of a follow-on spacecraft to Landsat 7, while also helping to determine whether such a spacecraft should be funded by the United States Government, by the private sector, or by an international consortium.

(13) To maximize the value of the Landsat program to the American public, unenhanced Landsat 4 through 6 data should be made available, at a minimum, to United States Government agencies, to global environmental change researchers, and to other researchers who are financially supported by the United States Government, at the cost of fulfilling user requests, and unenhanced Land-

sat 7 data should be made available to all users at the cost of fulfilling user requests.

(14) To stimulate development of the commercial market for unenhanced data and value-added services, the United States Government should adopt a data policy for Landsat 7 which allows competition within the private sector for distribution of unenhanced data and value-added services.

(15) Development of the remote sensing market and the provision of commercial value-added services based on remote sensing data should remain exclusively the function of the private sector.

(16) It is in the best interest of the United States to maintain a permanent, comprehensive Government archive of global Landsat and other land remote sensing data for long-term monitoring and study of the changing global environment.

§ 5602. Definitions

In this chapter, the following definitions apply:

(1) The term "Administrator" means the Administrator of the National Aeronautics and Space Administration.

(2) The term "cost of fulfilling user requests" means the incremental costs associated with providing product generation, reproduction, and distribution of unenhanced data in response to user requests and shall not include any acquisition, amortization, or depreciation of capital assets originally paid for by the United States Government or other costs not specifically attributable to fulfilling user requests.

(3) The term "data continuity" means the continued acquisition and availability of unenhanced data which are, from the point of view of the user—

(A) sufficiently consistent (in terms of acquisition geometry, coverage characteristics, and spectral characteristics) with previous Landsat data to allow comparisons for global and regional change detection and characterization; and

(B) compatible with such data and with methods used to receive and process such data.

(4) The term "data preprocessing" may include—

(A) rectification of system and sensor distortions in land remote sensing data as it is received directly from the satellite in preparation for delivery to a user;

(B) registration of such data with respect to features of the Earth; and

(C) calibration of spectral response with respect to such data, but does not include conclusions, manipulations, or calculations derived from such data, or a combination of such data with other data.

(5) The term "land remote sensing" means the collection of data which can be processed into imagery of surface features of the Earth from an unclassified satellite or satellites, other than an operational United States Government weather satellite.

(6) The term "Landsat Program Management" means the integrated program management structure—

(A) established by, and responsible to, the Administrator and the Secretary of Defense pursuant to section 5611 (a) of this title; and

(B) consisting of appropriate officers and employees of the National Aeronautics and Space Administration, the Department of Defense, and any other United States Government agencies the President designates as responsible for the Landsat program.

(7) The term "Landsat system" means Landsats 1, 2, 3, 4, 5, and 6, and any follow-on land remote sensing system operated and owned by the United States Government, along with any related ground equipment, systems, and facilities owned by the United States Government.

(8) The term "Landsat 6 contractor" means the private sector entity which was awarded the contract for spacecraft construction, operations, and data marketing rights for the Landsat 6 spacecraft.

(9) The term "Landsat 7" means the follow-on satellite to Landsat 6.

(10) The term "National Satellite Land Remote Sensing Data Archive" means the archive established by the Secretary of the Interior pursuant to the archival responsibilities defined in section 5652 of this title.

(11) The term "noncommercial purposes" refers to those activities undertaken by individuals or entities on the condition, upon receipt of unenhanced data, that—

(A) such data shall not be used in connection with any bid for a commercial contract, development of a commercial product, or any other non-United States Government activity that is expected, or has the potential, to be profitmaking;

(B) the results of such activities are disclosed in a timely and complete fashion in the open technical literature or other method of public release, except when such disclosure by the United States Government or its contractors would adversely affect the national security or foreign policy of the United States or violate a provision of law or regulation; and

(C) such data shall not be distributed in competition with unenhanced data provided by the Landsat 6 contractor.

(12) The term "Secretary" means the Secretary of Commerce.

(13) The term "unenhanced data" means land remote sensing signals or imagery products that are unprocessed or subject only to data preprocessing.

(14) The term "United States Government and its affiliated users" means—

(A) United States Government agencies;

(B) researchers involved with the United States Global Change Research Program and its international counterpart programs; and

(C) other researchers and international entities that have signed with the United States Government a cooperative agreement involving the use of Landsat data for non-commercial purposes.

* * *

§ 5611. Landsat Program Management

(a) Establishment

The Administrator and the Secretary of Defense shall be responsible for management of the Landsat program. Such responsibility shall be carried out by establishing an integrated program management structure for the Landsat system.

* * *

§ 5612. Procurement of Landsat 7

(a) Contract negotiations

The Landsat Program Management shall, subject to appropriations and only under the existing contract authority of the United States Government agencies that compose the Landsat Program Management, expeditiously contract with a United States private sector entity for the development and delivery of Landsat 7.

(b) Development and delivery consideration

In negotiating a contract under this section for the development and delivery of Landsat 7, the Landsat Program Management shall—

(1) seek, as a fundamental objective, to have Landsat 7 operational by the expected end of the design life of Landsat 6;

(2) seek to ensure data continuity by the development and delivery of a satellite which is, at a minimum, functionally equivalent to the Landsat 6 satellite; and

(3) seek to incorporate in Landsat 7 any performance improvements required to meet United States Government needs that would not jeopardize data continuity.

(c) Notification of cost and schedule changes

The Landsat Program Management shall promptly notify the Congress of any significant deviations from the expected cost, delivery date, and launch date of Landsat 7, that are specified by the Landsat Program Management upon award of the contract under this section.

(d) United States private sector entities

The Landsat Program Management shall, for purposes of this chapter, define the term "United States private sector entities", taking into account the location of operations, assets, personnel, and other such factors.

§ 5613. Data Policy for Landsat 4 Through 6

(a) Contract negotiations

Within 30 days after October 28, 1992, the Landsat Program Management shall enter into negotiations with the Landsat 6 contractor to formalize an arrangement with respect to pricing, distribution, acquisition, archiving, and availability of unenhanced data for which the Landsat 6 contractor has responsibility under its contract. Such arrangement shall provide for a phased transition to a data policy consistent with the Landsat 7 data policy (developed pursuant to section 5615 of this title) by the date of initial operation of Landsat 7. Conditions of the phased arrangement should require that the Landsat 6 contractor adopt provisions so that by the final phase of the transition period—

(1) such unenhanced data shall be provided, at a minimum, to the United States Government and its affiliated users at the cost of fulfilling user requests, on the condition that such unenhanced data are used solely for noncommercial purposes;

(2) instructional data sets, selected from the Landsat data archives, will be made available to educational institutions exclusively for noncommercial, educational purposes at the cost of fulfilling user requests;

(3) Landsat data users are able to acquire unenhanced data contained in the collective archives of foreign ground stations as easily and affordably as practicable;

(4) adequate data necessary to meet the needs of global environmental change researchers and national security users are acquired;

(5) the United States Government and its affiliated users shall not be prohibited from reproduction or dissemination of unenhanced data to other agencies of the United States Government and other affiliated users, on the condition that such unenhanced data are used solely for noncommercial purposes;

(6) nonprofit, public interest entities receive vouchers, data grants, or other such means of providing them with unenhanced data at the cost of fulfilling user requests, on the condition that such unenhanced data are used solely for noncommercial purposes.

(7) a viable role for the private sector in the promotion and development of the commercial market for value added and other services using unenhanced data from the Landsat system is preserved; and

(8) unenhanced data from the Landsat system are provided to the National Satellite Land Remote Sensing Data Archive at no more than the cost of fulfilling user requests.

(b) Failure to reach agreement

If negotiations under subsection (a) of this section have not, by September 30, 1993, resulted in an agreement that the Landsat Program Management determines generally achieves the goals stated in subsection (b) (1) through (8) of this section, the Administrator and the Secretary of Defense shall, within 30 days after the date of such determination, jointly certify and report such determination to the Congress. The report shall include a review of options and projected costs for achieving such goals, and shall include recommendations for achieving such goals. The options reviewed shall include—

(1) retaining the existing or modified contract with the Landsat 6 contractor;

(2) the termination of existing contracts for the exclusive right to market unenhanced Landsat data; and

(3) the establishment of an alternative private sector mechanism for the marketing and commercial distribution of such data.

* * *

§ 5615. Data Policy for Landsat 7

(a) Landsat 7 data policy

The Landsat Program Management, in consultation with other appropriate United States Government agencies, shall develop a data policy for Landsat 7 which should—

(1) ensure that unenhanced data are available to all users at the cost of fulfilling user requests;

(2) ensure timely and dependable delivery of unenhanced data to the full spectrum of civilian, national security, commercial, and foreign users and the National Satellite Land Remote Sensing Data Archive;

(3) ensure that the United States retains ownership of all unenhanced data generated by Landsat 7;

(4) support the development of the commercial market for remote sensing data;

(5) ensure that the provision of commercial value-added services based on remote sensing data remains exclusively the function of the private sector; and

(6) to the extent possible, ensure that the data distribution system for Landsat 7 is compatible with the Earth Observing System Data and Information System.

(b) Additional Landsat 7 data policy

In addition, the data policy for Landsat 7 may provide for—

(1) United States private sector entities to operate ground receiving stations in the United States for Landsat 7 data;

(2) other means for direct access by private sector entities to unenhanced data from Landsat 7; and

(3) the United States Government to charge a per image fee, license fee, or other such fee to entities operating ground receiving stations or distributing Landsat 7 data.

* * *

§ 5621. General Licensing Authority

(a) Licensing authority of Secretary

(1) In consultation with other appropriate United States Government agencies, the Secretary is authorized to license private sector parties to operate private remote sensing space systems for such period as the Secretary may specify and in accordance with the provisions of this subchapter.

(2) In the case of a private space system that is used for remote sensing and other purposes, the authority of the Secretary under this subchapter shall be limited only to the remote sensing operations of such space system.

(b) Compliance with the law, regulations, international obligations, and national security

No license shall be granted by the Secretary unless the Secretary determines in writing that the applicant will comply with the requirements of this chapter, any regulations issued pursuant to this chapter, and any applicable international obligations and national security concerns of the United States.

(c) Deadline for action on application

The Secretary shall review any application and make a determination thereon within 120 days of the receipt of such application. If final action has not occurred within such time, the Secretary shall inform the applicant of any pending issues and of actions required to resolve them.

(d) Improper basis for denial

The Secretary shall not deny such license in order to protect any existing licensee from competition.

(e) Requirement to provide unenhanced data

(1) The Secretary, in consultation with other appropriate United States Government agencies and pursuant to paragraph (2), shall designate in a license issued pursuant to this subchapter any unenhanced data required to be provided by the licensee under section 5622 (b) (3) of this title.

(2) The Secretary shall make a designation under paragraph (1) after determining that—

(A) such data are generated by a system for which all or a substantial part of the development, fabrication, launch, or operations costs have been or will be directly funded by the United States Government; or

(B) it is in the interest of the United States to require such data to be provided by the licensee consistent with section 5622 (b) (3) of this title, after considering the impact on the licensee and the importance of promoting widespread access to remote sensing data from United States and foreign systems.

(3) A designation made by the Secretary under paragraph (1) shall not be inconsistent with any contract or other arrangement entered into between a United States Government agency and the licensee.

§ 5622. Conditions for Operation

(a) License required for operation

No person who is subject to the jurisdiction or control of the United States may, directly or through any subsidiary or affiliate, operate any private remote sensing space system without a license pursuant to section 5621 of this title.

(b) Licensing requirements

Any license issued pursuant to this subchapter shall specify that the licensee shall comply with all of the requirements of this chapter and shall—

(1) operate the system in such manner as to preserve the national security of the United States and to observe the international obligations of the United States in accordance with section 5656 of this title;

(2) make available to the government of any country (including the United States) unenhanced data collected by the system concerning the territory under the jurisdiction of such government as soon as such data are available and on reasonable terms and conditions;

(3) make unenhanced data designated by the Secretary in the license pursuant to section 5621 (e) of this title available in accordance with section 5651 of this title;

(4) upon termination of operations under the license, make disposition of any satellites in space in a manner satisfactory to the President;

(5) furnish the Secretary with complete orbit and data collection characteristics of the system, and inform the Secretary immediately of any deviation; and

(6) notify the Secretary of any agreement the licensee intends to enter with a foreign nation, entity, or consortium involving foreign nations or entities.

(c) Additional licensing requirements for Landsat 6 contractor

In addition to the requirements of paragraph (b) of this section, any license issued pursuant to this subchapter to the Landsat 6 contractor shall specify that the Landsat 6 contractor shall—

(1) notify the Secretary of any value added activities (as defined by the Secretary by regulation) that will be conducted by the Landsat 6 contractor or by a subsidiary or affiliate; and

(2) if such activities are to be conducted, provide the Secretary with a plan for compliance with section 5651 of this title.

§ 5623. Administrative Authority of the Secretary

(a) Functions

In order to carry out the responsibilities specified in this subchapter, the Secretary may—

(1) grant, condition, or transfer licenses under this chapter;

(2) seek an order of injunction or similar judicial determination from a United States District Court with personal jurisdiction over the licensee to terminate, modify, or suspend licenses under this subchapter and to terminate licensed operations on an immediate basis, if the Secretary determines that the licensee has substantially failed to comply with any provisions of this chapter, with any

terms, conditions, or restrictions of such license, or with any international obligations or national security concerns of the United States;

(3) provide penalties for noncompliance with the requirements of licenses or regulations issued under this subchapter, including civil penalties not to exceed $10,000 (each day of operation in violation of such licenses or regulations constituting a separate violation);

(4) compromise, modify, or remit any such civil penalty;

(5) issue subpoenas for any materials, documents, or records, or for the attendance and testimony of witnesses for the purpose of conducting a hearing under this section;

(6) seize any object, record, or report pursuant to a warrant from a magistrate based on a showing of probable cause to believe that such object, record, or report was used, is being used, or is likely to be used in violation of this chapter or the requirements of a license or regulation issued thereunder; and

(7) make investigations and inquiries and administer to or take from any person an oath, affirmation, or affidavit concerning any matter relating to the enforcement of this chapter.

(b) Review of agency action

Any applicant or licensee who makes a timely request for review of an adverse action pursuant to subsection (a) (1), (a) (3), (a) (5), or (a) (6) of this section shall be entitled to adjudication by the Secretary on the record after an opportunity for any agency hearing with respect to such adverse action. Any final action by the Secretary under this subsection shall be subject to judicial review under chapter 7 of Title 5.

§ 5624. Regulatory Authority of the Secretary

The Secretary may issue regulations to carry out this subchapter. Such regulations shall be promulgated only after public notice and comment in accordance with the provisions of section 553 of Title 5.

§ 5625. Agency Activities

(a) License application and issuance

A private sector party may apply for a license to operate a private remote sensing space system which utilizes, on a space-available basis, a civilian United States Government satellite or vehicle as a platform for such system. The Secretary, pursuant to this subchapter, may license such system if it meets all conditions of this subchapter and—

(1) the system operator agrees to reimburse the Government in a timely manner for all related costs incurred with respect to such utilization, including a reasonable and proportionate share of fixed, platform, data transmission, and launch costs; and

(2) such utilization would not interfere with or otherwise compromise intended civilian Government missions, as determined by the agency responsible for such civilian platform.

* * *

§ 5631. Continued Federal Research and Development

(a) Roles of NASA and Department of Defense

(1) The Administrator and the Secretary of Defense are directed to continue and to enhance programs of remote sensing research and development.

(2) The Administrator is authorized and encouraged to—

(A) conduct experimental space remote sensing programs (including applications demonstration programs and basic research at universities);

(B) develop remote sensing technologies and techniques, including those needed for monitoring the Earth and its environment; and

(C) conduct such research and development in cooperation with other United States Government agencies and with public and private research entities (including private industry, universities, non-profit organizations, State and local governments, foreign governments, and international organizations) and to enter into arrangements (including joint ventures) which will foster such cooperation.

(b) Roles of Department of Agriculture and Department of Interior

(1) In order to enhance the ability of the United States to manage and utilize its renewable and nonrenewable resources, the Secretary of Agriculture and the Secretary of the Interior are authorized and encouraged to conduct programs of research and development in the applications of remote sensing using funds appropriated for such purposes.

(2) Such programs may include basic research at universities, demonstrations of applications, and cooperative activities involving other Government agencies, private sector parties, and foreign and international organizations.

(c) Role of other Federal agencies

Other United States Government agencies are authorized and encouraged to conduct research and development on the use of remote sensing in the fulfillment of their authorized missions, using funds appropriated for such purposes.

§ 5632. Availability of Federally Gathered Unenhanced Data

(a) General rule

All unenhanced land remote sensing data gathered and owned by the United States Government, including unenhanced data gathered under the technology demonstration program carried out pursuant to section 5633 of this title, shall be made available to users in a timely fashion.

(b) Protection for commercial data distributor

The President shall seek to ensure that unenhanced data gathered under the technology demonstration program carried out pursuant to section 5633 of this title shall, to the extent practicable, be made available on terms that would not adversely effect the commercial market for unenhanced data gathered by the Landsat 6 spacecraft.

* * *

§ 5651. Nondiscriminatory Data Availability

(a) General rule

Except as provided in subsection (b) of this section, any unenhanced data generated by the Landsat system or any other land remote sensing system funded and owned by the United States Government shall be made available to all users without preference, bias, or any other special arrangement (except on the basis of national security concerns pursuant to section 5656 of this title) regarding delivery, format, pricing, or technical considerations which would favor one customer or class of customers over another.

(b) Exceptions

Unenhanced data generated by the Landsat system or any other land remote sensing system funded and owned by the United States Government may be made available to the United States Government and its affiliated users at reduced prices, in accordance with this chapter, on the condition that such unenhanced data are used solely for noncommercial purposes.

§ 5652. Archiving of Data

(a) Public interest

It is in the public interest for the United States Government to—

(1) maintain an archive of land remote sensing data for historical, scientific, and technical purposes, including long-term global environmental monitoring;

(2) control the content and scope of the archive; and

(3) assure the quality, integrity, and continuity of the archive.

(b) Archiving practices

The Secretary of the Interior, in consultation with the Landsat Program Management, shall provide for long-term storage, maintenance, and upgrading of a basic, global, land remote sensing data set (hereinafter referred to as the "basic data set") and shall follow reasonable archival practices to assure proper storage and preservation of the basic data set and timely access for parties requesting data.

(c) Determination of content of basic data set

In determining the initial content of, or in upgrading, the basic data set, the Secretary of Interior shall—

(1) use as a baseline the data archived on October 28, 1992;

(2) take into account future technical and scientific developments and needs, paying particular attention to the anticipated data requirements of global environmental change research;

(3) consult with and seek the advice of users and producers of remote sensing data and data products;

(4) consider the need for data which may be duplicative in terms of geographical coverage but which differ in terms of season, spectral bands, resolution, or other relevant factors;

(5) include, as the Secretary of the Interior considers appropriate, unenhanced data generated either by the Landsat system, pursuant to subchapter I of this chapter, or by licensees under subchapter II of this chapter;

(6) include, as the Secretary of the Interior considers appropriate, data collected by foreign ground stations or by foreign remote sensing space systems; and

(7) ensure that the content of the archive is developed in accordance with section 5656 of this title.

(d) Public domain

After the expiration of any exclusive right to sell, or after relinquishment of such right, the data provided to the National Satellite Land Remote Sensing Data Archive shall be in the public domain and shall be made available to requesting parties by the Secretary of the Interior at the cost of fulfilling user requests.

§ 5653. Nonreproduction

Unenhanced data distributed by any licensee under subchapter II of this chapter may be sold on the condition that such data will not be reproduced or disseminated by the purchaser for commercial purposes.

* * *

§ 5658. Enforcement

(a) In general

In order to ensure that unenhanced data from the Landsat system received solely for noncommercial purposes are not used for any commercial purpose, the Secretary (in collaboration with private sector entities responsible for the marketing and distribution of unenhanced data generated by the Landsat system) shall develop and implement a system for enforcing this prohibition, in the event that unenhanced data from the Landsat system are made available for noncommercial purposes at a different price than such data are made available for other purposes.

(b) Authority of Secretary

Subject to subsection (d) of this section, the Secretary may impose any of the enforcement mechanisms described in subsection (c) of this section against a person who—

(1) receives unenhanced data from the Landsat system under this chapter solely for noncommercial purposes (and at a different price than the price at which such data are made available for other purposes); and

(2) uses such data for other than noncommercial purposes.

(c) Enforcement mechanisms

Enforcement mechanisms referred to in subsection (b) of this section may include civil penalties of not more than $10,000 (per day per violation), denial of further unenhanced data purchasing privileges, and any other penalties or restrictions the Secretary considers necessary to ensure, to the greatest extent practicable, that unenhanced data provided for noncommercial purposes are not used to unfairly compete in the commercial market against private sector entities not eligible for data at the cost of fulfilling user requests.

(d) Procedures and regulations

The Secretary shall issue any regulations necessary to carry out this section and shall establish standards and procedures governing the imposition of enforcement mechanisms under subsection (b) of this section. The standards and procedures shall include a procedure for potentially aggrieved parties to file formal protests with the Secretary alleging instances where such unenhanced data has been, or is being, used for commercial purposes in violation of the terms of receipt of such data. The Secretary shall promptly act to investigate any such protest, and shall report annually to the Congress on instances of such violations.

*   *   *

§ 5671. Prohibition

Neither the President nor any other official of the Government shall make any effort to lease, sell, or transfer to the private sector, or commercialize, any portion of the weather satellite systems operated by the Department of Commerce or any successor agency.

§ 5672. Future Considerations

Regardless of any change in circumstances subsequent to the enactment of this Act, even if such change makes it appear to be in the national interest to commercialize weather satellites, neither the President nor any official shall take any action prohibited by section 5671 of this title unless this subchapter has first been repealed.

NOTE

Section 5623, which provides that the licensing authority may "seek an order of injunction or similar judicial determination from a United States District Court ... if the Secretary determines that the licensee has substantially failed to comply with any ... national security concerns of the United States," changed pre-existing law, which allowed national security concerns to enter into licensing decisions *ex ante,* which some argued was a violation of the first amendment's near-prohibition on prior restraints of publication. *See* Glenn H. Reynolds and Robert P. Merges, News Media Satellites and the First Amendment, 3 High Technology Law Journal 1 (1988).

REMOTE SENSING REGULATIONS

Under the terms of the Act, the Secretary of Commerce delegated his authority to make regulations to the National Oceanic and Atmospheric Administration (NOAA), an arm of the Department of Commerce. The following is an excerpt from NOAA's regulations on remote sensing business licensing:

Civilian Remote Sensing Licensing Regulations [from 15 C.F.R. §§ 960.9 *et seq.* (1988)]

§ 960.9 Review Procedures

(a) The Administrator shall immediately forward a copy of any application or a summary thereof to the Department of Defense, the Department of State, and any other Federal agencies determined to have a substantial interest in the proposed activity, such as the National Aeronautics and Space Administration, and the Department of Transportation. ...

* * *

(e) Within sixty days of receipt of a complete application, each Federal agency consulted under paragraph (a) of this section shall recommend approval or disapproval of the application in writing.

(1) If the Secretary of Defense or the Secretary of State determines that an application may not be approved without modifications or conditions consistent with national security concerns or international obligations, the determination shall clearly state why the modifications or conditions are necessary to accomplish the intended purpose.

(2) If any other agency recommends disapproval, it shall state why it believes the application does not comply with any law or regulation within its area of responsibility and how it believes the application may be amended or the license conditioned to comply with the law or regulation in question.

§ 960.10 Timely Approval or Denial of Application and Issuance of License

* * *

(b) If the Administrator denies the application, he or she shall provide the applicant with a concise statement in writing of the reasons therefor.

* * *

§ 960.11 Criteria for Approval or Denial

Before approving an application and issuing a license or an amendment to a license, the Administrator shall find in writing that:

(a) The licensee will operate the system in a manner consistent with national security and the international obligations of the U.S.;

(b) The licensee will make available unenhanced data to all potential users on a nondiscriminatory basis. ...

In making the findings required by paragraph (a) of this section, the Administrator shall be entitled to rely upon the written recommendations of the Departments of Defense and State described in § 960.9(e).

CRITICISMS OF REMOTE SENSING REGULATIONS

A number of commentators have criticized the breadth of NOAA's discretion under these regulations, and its ability to deny permission to launch a private system or use it if it threatens "national security." These commentators have argued that this amounts to a prior restraint under established First Amendment principles. The following excerpt captures the flavor of these criticisms:

Merges & Reynolds, News Media Satellites and the First Amendment: A Case Study in the Treatment of New Technologies, 3 High Technology Law Journal 1 (1988)

Although military planners might well prefer to exclude news media satellites and reporters from reporting many topics, and might have their jobs made appreciably easier by that exclusion, they may do so only when the interests involved are of sufficient immediacy and importance to pass muster under the first amendment. The fact that the information in question is being gathered via a novel technology is irrelevant: the first amendment was not drafted in contemplation of many new technologies, from telephones to offset printing presses to personal computers. Nor is it sufficient to assert, as some have done, that we live in a perpetually dangerous world and cannot afford to limit the discretion of national security officials by imposing first amendment restrictions on their actions. The choice between taking every conceivable action to promote "national security" ends, and balancing those ends against the importance of preserving essential freedoms, has already been made.

In a way, the advent of civilian imaging technology brings the history of space surveillance full circle. In the earliest days of enthusiasm for space, satellites were one of the benefits identified by early visionaries—private citizens—who encountered more than a little difficulty in selling their ideas to governments. But now that the technology has matured to the point that private interests might be able to afford it, the U.S. government has begun drawing a line around space and declaring it off limits, or at least subject to a level of regulation that would not be tolerated on earth.

And there is irony here on another level as well. The U.S. has long championed an "Open Skies" approach to space reconnaissance; this was in fact an important element shaping early U.S. space policy. While this approach has been taken to mean that space overflight should be open to spacecraft from all countries, satellite technology has now become routine enough to put space within the reach of entities other than countries—private firms, for example, including the media. As a consequence, for the first time the U.S. is being forced to decide just how open it really wants the skies to be.

In that sense, this is just another in a long line of problems posed by new information technologies from the time movable type was invented to the present. The instinct of governments confronted by new technologies is generally to bring them under control (or at least try to do so), especially when those technologies are closely related to matters of power and politics. That instinct is generally wrong, though, at least in nations, like ours, with a tradition of free expression. The proper course is to remain faithful to that tradition, even in the context of new technologies.

Fortunately, the first amendment is flexible enough to accommodate new situations without sacrificing important interests. In this instance, an approach consistent with the first amendment would be to identify subjects and occasions for which media satellite imaging would be inappropriate—troop ship departures and secret military installations, for example—and to prohibit publication of such images, rather than threatening to place a blanket ban on media access to satellite technology.

NOTE

The debate over the "Mediasat" regulations, as they have been called, is only the first of many that will take place as the governmental monopoly over space technologies erodes. As costs drop and capabilities rise, private organizations—such as news organizations, arms control groups, and human rights and environmental advocates—will begin to make greater and greater use of space technologies. This trend is likely to cause considerable consternation within and among various world governments, but it is unlikely that they will be able to do much about it. For more on remote sensing in an international context *see* Chapter 5.

9

Some Issues of the Future

Most of this book has addressed issues of space law that are either of current application or that are likely to be applied in the near future—satellite broadcasting, or patents for space inventions, for example. This chapter, however, deals with issues of space law that are likely to have less immediate application, though in the case of at least one—the governance of space societies—a surprisingly large amount of work has already been devoted to the problem. Not only is the issue extensively treated in the two seminal works of space law, Andrew Haley's *Space Law and Government* (1963) and Myres McDougal, Harold Lasswell, and Ivan Vlasic's *Law and Public Order in Space* (1963), but it has also been the subject of considerable attention in later years.

GOVERNANCE OF SPACE SOCIETIES

Space Settlements and the Law: Address of Justice William J. Brennan, Jr., American Law Institute Annual Dinner, May 21, 1987

Always with us are changes and developments in the law, new terrain to be explored, understood, grappled with, fought for and constantly reassessed and applied under fire. So I thought it would not be inappropriate tonight, in this year of the Bicentennial of the Constitution, if I said something of an important new emerging area of the law that is knocking at the door and demanding our attention. I refer to space law. I confidently predict that we'll soon have to grapple with the question: what law should govern, not only the relationship between earth (particularly the United States) and space societies but, perhaps more importantly, what law should govern within space societies themselves and among space inhabitants who will people space communities. ...

A worrisome concern these days is the Earth's population explosion. The New York Times recently stated in an editorial: "In July 1986 the world's population, which didn't top a billion until 1850, passed the 5 billion mark. The Population Institute warned that the 5 billion may be 10 billion by 2028." Perhaps the development of space communities may be at least a partial answer to these worries. If then, we accept, as I am persuaded we must, that space colonization is inevitable, and that we should therefore prepare for it, what are just some of the legal problems we should be thinking about? ... Here are some: since Earth is part of space and in space and is part of the Cosmos, space societies can't sever their ties with Earth. Is Earth then to determine the shape or nature of governance in space? If so, isn't space then just a new continent, as was our own when the Mayflower landed, to be explored as was our own by several nations—the Spanish, the French, the Portuguese, the English? Should any law then be made for a space society in advance of actual settlement? ... What is the best historical model—the Mayflower Compact, the Articles of Incorporation of the British East India Company or whatever? ... If the United States creates a society populated by U.S. citizens, what federal law should govern that society. ... [d]oes the constitution follow the flag so that its protections are available to every resident of the space settlement?

* * *

Indeed, the American Law Institute itself co-sponsored in November 1981 the International Conference that debated issues on Doing Business in Outer Space: Legal Issues and Practical Problems. Moreover, Congress has extended federal criminal laws to punish criminal conduct on the Moon or other celestial bodies and in space craft outside the Earth's atmosphere. Indeed, a few district court and state court decisions have extended American domestic law to the solution of outer space problems. And doubtless, too, many lawyers here tonight have already had occasion to counsel clients on space law. But I suggest that the actual establishment of space settlements will confront the profession with enormous new responsibilities that we ought to prepare for as thoroughly as we can. For it is accepted by all of us, I am sure, that the United States must be, and must become unequivocally committed to space exploration and exploitation and the settlement of space by Americans. Our very survival requires no less. We have to keep in mind that Russians, Japanese, Europeans, and South Americans also have asserted interests in outer space.

The Smithsonian Institution Press recently published a lengthy and erudite treatment of this topic, G. Robinson & H. White, Envoys of Mankind: A Declaration of First Principles for the Governance of Space Societies (1986), and followed it up with a series of conferences cosponsored with Boston University's Center for Democracy. Many individuals, including such luminaries as Justice Brennan, Professor A.E. Dick Howard, and journalist Walter Cronkite, participated in this process, which culminated in a draft declaration of principles. The following excerpt discusses some issues behind both the book and the conference.

Ragosta & Reynolds, In Search of Governing Principles, 28 Jurimetrics: Journal of Law, Science & Technology 473 (1988)

In fact, the central point of *Envoys of Mankind* is that space is a different environment from any that we have known before, and that laws governing the behavior of people, and societies, in space must take those differences into account. This point is more subtle than it seems—as the authors note, different environments do not simply present legal problems of their own (as, for example, the dry climate of the American West led to new doctrines of riparian law); they also change the very nature of the societies and human beings to whom the laws apply.

* * *

There is considerable evidence already, in the nonspace context, that Robinson and White are right to take seriously the impact of new environments on human behavior and governance. Experience with Antarctic bases and other isolated environments where significant numbers of people must work together demonstrates that traditional methods of organization—particularly hierarchical structures modelled on established military systems—simply do not work well in such circumstances:

> A winter base in Antarctica is a unique world, where the cook often has greater prestige than the officer-in-charge and the radio operator can have more influence than an established scientist. The traditional hierarchical structure of the military, and of government as a whole, breaks down. ... This was a controversial and embarrassing realization for the Navy. Flexible authority and sharing of tasks among everyone are vital. ... This can run against the grain of highly specialized scientists and career military officers. The absence of women was also a factor. Navy traditions excluded females from the continent, and this increased tensions.
>
> Some lessons have been learned. With great reluctance, the Navy eventually allowed women on the continent. ... A more flexible organizational structure is tolerated, and private enterprise is now providing some services and personnel. ... The Antarctican experience reminds us that the dangers of mutiny or psychosis in a space station or colony are as real as the threat of meteors or solar flares.

[Lawler, Lessons from the Past: Toward a Long-Term Space Policy, in Lunar Bases and Space Activities of the Twenty-First Century 757, 762–63 (W.W. Mendell ed. 1985).]

Likewise, the experience of many earthbound colonial efforts demonstrates the problems created by attempts to graft old or poorly thought out social systems on new environments. One such example is in the early years of Australia, where the transition from a penal colony to full fledged settlement was fraught with difficulties stemming from excessive meddling by distant authorities and by local military authorities' lack of skill in building up a civilian economy. Many others abound.

For more on how space environments may differ and on what their unique characteristics may be, *see* Rambaut, The Social and Physical Environment of Space Stations and Colonies, in Beyond Spaceship Earth: Environmental Ethics and the Solar System 263 (E. Hargrove ed. 1986). This excellent book, published by the Sierra Club, contains essays on a wide variety of issues relating to space exploration, the environment, and human society. *See also* Crosby, Life (with all its problems) in Space, in Interstellar Migration and the Human Experience 210 (B.R. Finney & E.M. Jones eds. 1985).

Robinson and White set out at the end of their book a draft treaty relating to the governance of space societies. This effort aroused sufficient interest that the Smithsonian Institution, in cooperation with the Center for Democracy at Boston University, organized a symposium on the topic, which made a further effort at the task. The symposium's final effort is reproduced below; Ragosta & Reynolds, *supra*, analyzes a slightly earlier draft.

Declaration of First Principles for the Governance of Outer Space Societies

Preamble

On the occasion of the Bicentennial of the Constitution of the United States of America and in commemoration and furtherance of its values we, the undersigned petitioners,

Bearing witness to the exploration and inevitable settlement of outer space;

Recognizing the universal longing for life, liberty, equality, peace and security;

Placing our trust in societies that guarantee their members full protection of law, due process and equal protection under the law;

Reaffirming our faith in fundamental freedoms;

Mindful, as were our nation's founders, of the self-evident truth that we are endowed by our Creator with certain inalienable rights;

Recognizing the responsibility of a government to protect the rights of the governed to exist and to evolve;

Do assert and declare in this petition the intrinsic value of a set of First Principles for the Governance of Outer Space Societies and, at the beginning of this third century of nationhood under our Constitution, resolutely urge all people of the United States of America to acknowledge, accept and apply such First Principles as hereinafter set forth.

Article I

A. The rule of law and the fundamental values embodied in the United States Constitution shall apply to all individuals living in outer space societies under United States jurisdiction.

B. Appropriate constraints upon and limitations of authority shall be defined so as to protect the personal freedom of each individual, such as the right to reasonable privacy, freedom from self-incrimination, freedom from unreasonable intrusion, search and seizure, and freedom from cruel and unusual punishment.

C. Toward this end, the imperatives of community safety and individual survival within the unique environment of outer space shall be guaranteed in harmony with the exercise of such fundamental individual rights as freedom of speech, religion, association, assembly, contract, travel to, in and from outer space, media and communications, as well as the rights of petition, informed consent and private ownership of property.

D. The principles set forth here should not be construed to exclude any other such rights possessed by individuals.

Article II

A. Authority in space societies, exercised under principles of representative government appropriate to the circumstances and degree of community development, shall reflect the will of the people of those societies.

B. All petitions to the United States Government from outer space societies under its jurisdiction shall be accepted and receive prompt consideration.

C. The United States shall provide for an orderly and peaceful transition to self-governance by outer space societies under its jurisdiction at such time as their inhabitants shall manifest clearly a belief that such a transition is both necessary and appropriate.

D. In response to aggression, threats of aggression, or hostile action, outer space societies may provide for their common defense and for the maintenance of essential public order.

E. Outer space societies shall assume all rights and obligations set forth in treaties and international agreements, relevant to the activities of such societies, to which the United States is a party and which further freedom, peace and security.

F. The advancement of science and technology shall be encouraged in outer space societies for the benefit of all humanity.

G. Outer space societies shall protect from abuse the environment and natural resources of Earth and space.

The Declaration is easy to critique, though such an effort could just as easily be unfair to its drafters: it is difficult to draft principles for the governance of societies that do not yet exist, and whose outlines are only hazily apparent at this stage in history. These difficulties do not make the effort worthless, but rather dictate the form in which it should be undertaken. Here, however, the Declaration has problems: it is an unwieldy mixture of the general and the specific. Where it is specific, it is often counterproductive: the statement that "fundamental values" embodied in the Constitution should apply to space societies under U.S. jurisdiction might be read as meaning that non-fundamental values would not apply. As discussed in Chapter 8, *supra,* the U.S. Constitution probably applies to all activities in outer space under U.S. jurisdiction, although the Supreme Court has muddied the waters on this issue of late. There is little to be gained, however, by adding to this confusion.

The Declaration also contains language that seems disturbingly similar to the "saving clauses" in many other nations' bills of rights. The United States Constitution does not provide that the guarantees of individual liberty are to be balanced against the good of the community; courts do this, of course, in extraordinary circumstances, but with some reluctance and usually with bad results. *See, e.g.,* Korematsu v. United States, 323 U.S. 214 (1944) (upholding internment of Japanese-Americans during World War II); Aleinikoff, Constitutional Law in the Age of Balancing, 96 Yale Law Journal 943 (1987) (warning against dangers in balancing approach where important rights are at stake); Leff, The Leff Dictionary of Law: A Fragment, 94 Yale Law Journal 1855, 2123–24 (1985) (definition of balancing warns of "the extreme dangers of too facile a use of 'balancing' in a system of justice"). Such balancing, where engaged in, should be done with as much reluctance as possible; the language chosen in the Declaration, calling for the balancing of "community safety and individual survival within the unique environment of outer space" to be "guaranteed in harmony with the exercise of ... fundamental rights" is a trap. Although it may have been meant otherwise by the drafters, it is an invitation to engage in unnecessary balancing, balancing that is likely to be at the expense of those the Declaration is meant to protect. It is true that the outer space environment is a unique one, but no more so than many other environments in which human beings operate.

Where the Declaration is not specific, it is often so general as to be meaningless, or at least unclear. For example, Article IIA says that authority in outer space societies should reflect the will of the people of those societies. But virtually *all* wielders of authority claim that they do so in the name of, and reflecting the will of, the people. And the Declaration's treatment of self-government is unclear as well: it does not make clear whether the transition to self-government means one of complete independence as a new sovereign nation, or simply the inclusion of the space society as a self-governing but not sovereign entity such as Puerto Rico or (speaking practically, regardless of states' rights rhetoric) any one of the United States.

Here a bit more specificity would have been nice. If space societies are to become fully independent, then some measure such as Article 73 of the United Nations Charter, which provides for the gradual independence of Trust Territories, might be a good model. In fact, since the 1967 Outer Space Treaty extends the principles of international law and the U.N. Charter to outer space, Article 73 appears already to apply to space societies: it simply states that members of the U.N. who "have or assume responsibility for the administration of territories whose peoples have not yet attained a full measure of self-government" are to promote self-government and respect fundamental human rights for the inhabitants thereof. Although Article 73 was written with Trust Territories and territories formerly administered under Mandates from the old League of Nations in mind, its language does not exclude application to space societies as well. If, on the other hand, "self-governance" simply means ending a colonial or territorial status while remaining a part of the United States, then the model by which Western territories were admitted to the Union might be a better one. The Declaration's drafters would have been better off clarifying their intent and drawing upon one or the other of these models.

This is not to criticize the Declaration unduly. The effort was a worthwhile one, and helps set the stage for further effort along these lines, with plenty of time left to iron out the kinks before the problem becomes pressing. For an alternative version that answers many (though not all) of the above criticisms *see* Ragosta & Reynolds, In Search of Governing Principles, 28 Jurimetrics: Journal of Law, Science & Technology 473 (1988). Like the United States Constitution, the draft set out therein pays more attention to restrictions on government activity than to affirmative statements of rights. Consider this, however: In space societies, individuals will be far more dependent upon their governments for the basic necessities of life than they are on earth. In such a context, are affirmative statements of rights—to food and air, for example—more appropriate than they are on earth? Or are earth inhabitants actually almost as dependent, making the lack of such rights a defect, rather than a virtue in the U.S. Constitution? For an expression of this view, *see* Black, Further Reflections on the Constitutional Justice of Livelihood, 86 Columbia Law Review 1103 (1986).

The following excerpt, from another recent speech by Justice Brennan, discusses and compares various recent efforts in this field:

Remarks of William J. Brennan, Jr., Associate Justice, Supreme Court of the United States, at Bicentennial Conference of Judges of United States Courts of Appeals October 26, 1988

Let me return now to the Declaration of First Principles that the Smithsonian Conference produced last year. That Declaration was not the only effort in its field. Another, entitled a proposed "Treaty Governing Social Order of Long-Duration or Permanent Inhabitants of Near and Deep Space" (which I shall refer to as the Convention to distinguish it from the Declaration), was advanced in a book "Envoys of Mankind" by George S. Robinson and Harold M. White, Jr. Both the Convention and the Declaration have come under sharp criticism in a review of "Envoys of Mankind" by John A. Ragosta and Glenn H. Reynolds, lawyers practicing in Washington, D.C. [Ragosta & Reynolds, In Search of Governing Principles, 28 Jurimetrics: Journal of Law, Science & Technology 473 (1988).] The criticism of the Declaration may be more serious. While concluding that the Declaration has much to recommend it because it focuses directly on affirmative statements of fundamental and political rights, the review comments:

"The Declaration appropriately guarantees civil and political freedoms that should govern all actions in space of earth and space inhabitants. Such principles can guide analysis of legal issues that arise in whatever context and provide guidance for a discussion of rules for governance of space societies. Unfortunately, the Declaration has a fatal flaw. The Declaration is written solely from the perspective of the United States, failing ... to understand the critical role that the political relations of all Earth nations will have on space inhabitants. ... We do not believe that the Soviet Union, France, China, or any other spacefaring nation will look with favor on principles formulated in such a manner. It is simply not productive to seek to establish principles for laws and government in space that will certainly be perceived by the world's leader in space habitation (the Soviet Union, alas, not the United States) as either irrelevant or insulting."

Having decided that both the Convention and the Declaration were flawed, Messrs. Ragosta and Reynolds offered their own version of a "Declaration of Rights and Principles for the Governance of Space Societies." Their guidelines emphasized focus on the space inhabitants, not an attempt to defuse or resolve all the possible conflicts of Earth nations in space. Accordingly, their focus was on man's exploration and ultimate inhabitation of space, not simply one nation's space activities, and in that respect avoided unnecessary historic, political and cultural ties to one nation. They believe that the Declaration cannot itself be a system of laws and governance but should stop with fostering such a system. Finally, they too would have the Declaration recognize that there are fundamental principles that should apply to governance of any human society.

It's very obvious that neither the Convention nor the two Declarations come even close to being the last word on the subject. As the reviewers observed, "All of the work done to date constitutes little more than a preface to the task of working out a scheme of governance for space societies." But whether permanent human presence in outer space is likely in the near term, or likely only in the distant future, apparently [space societies] are going to be a reality with which we must deal.

And the study of space societies may have a big dividend for Earth. As Walter McDougall has noted, the great age of earth exploration stimulated a burst of inquiry into the laws governing nations and led to our modern system of international law. In the same way, inquiry into the rules that should govern societies in space is likely to provide fresh insights into the governance of societies here on Earth, a field in which, to judge by current events, there is certainly room for progress. This is particularly true because many of the most salient characteristics of space societies, such as strong dependence on sophisticated technology, problems with maintaining environmental quality, the need for people to work together smoothly under stress in close quarters, and the dependence of inhabitants on their society for basic necessities such as food, water, air, and communications, are in many ways simply exaggerations of characteristics already present (and growing) in Earth societies. By studying the problems of space societies we gain a window into not just their future, but our own.

I won't see the day when a code of laws for space communities will become an urgent necessity. Perhaps few of you may see that day. But we can be glad that responsible quarters are beginning to give thought to the law and space communities. For, to repeat President Reagan's admonition, "America must lead the effort to colonize space, because in the next century leadership on Earth will come to the nation that shows the greatest leadership in space."

NOTES

1. Space governance (like the other issues discussed in this chapter) is likely to seem remote and of no immediate concern to many. It is possible, of course, that it is a problem that will never arise at all—over the next few decades, only a modest degree of mismanagement of the world's economy, resources, and political environment will be necessary in order to ensure that human beings will lack the ability to live in outer space, or even to reach it at all, for many years afterward if not forever. On the other hand, if such problems are avoided, the human species (given its expansionist nature) will almost inevitably reach the point at which space societies of some sort become a reality. At that point, they will likely draw on the works of scholars in previous centuries, just as the American colonists drew on the works of political theorists ranging from Aristotle to Locke in formulating their system of government.

There are already rudimentary principles of space governance. *See, e.g.*, 14 C.F.R. §1214.702 (granting Space Shuttle commander legal authority to maintain order and discipline in flight); 18 U.S.C.A. § 451 (West supp. 1988) (extending U.S. criminal jurisdiction to outer space for some purposes). For more on existing U.S. "black letter" law applying to in-space activity *see* Chapter 8, *supra*, and U.S. Congress Office of Technology Assessment, Space Stations and the Law: Selected Legal Issues (1986); *see also* Reynolds, Book Review, 27 Jurimetrics: Journal of Law, Science & Technology 431 (1987) (reviewing OTA space stations paper); Kanowitz, American Labor Law and the United States Space Shuttle, 34 Hastings Law Journal 715 (1983); Robbins, The Extension of

United States Criminal Jurisdiction to Outer Space, 23 Santa Clara Law Review 627 (1983). As experience develops and new problems are encountered, those principles will grow by accretion, and it is even possible that self-governing space societies will be arrived at by a process so gradual that it will hardly be noticed. New legislation, passed after this book went to press, ensures that space governance issues will continue to receive study. Language added to the 1988 NASA Authorization Act requires NASA to report regularly to Congress on the prospects for human settlement in space and on various topics pertaining to such space settlements, including "sociological and legal issues." S. 2209 (100th Cong. 2d Sess.), Pub. L. 100–685, 102 Stat. 4083 (1988).

2. In many ways, as Justice Brennan notes, the problems of space societies are likely to be simply exaggerated versions of those faced by earth societies. In a space society, each member will have the potential to severely disrupt the environment, perhaps threatening all others—just as on earth, terrorists, or incompetents, have similar abilities now: witness the accidents at Bhopal, Chernobyl, and elsewhere. In a space society, each member will be dependent on her society for food, air, communications, housing, and all of the other requirements of life—just as on earth, virtually the entire population is coming to depend on the transportation and communications networks for the delivery of everything from food to medicine to crucial weather information. And, in a space society, it will be a great challenge to balance this interdependence between society and individuals in a way that preserves individual freedoms that we think important—just as on earth, striking that balance is a challenge that many governments and peoples find almost insuperable. For an unhopeful view of space civilizations' ability to meet this challenge, *see* William Wu, Taking Liberties in Space, Ad Astra, Nov. 1991, at 36. Wu argues that a space colony would be the ultimate "company town," with civil liberties suffering accordingly. Fortunately, however, if they are to flourish space societies—like societies on earth—will find themselves more and more dependent on their members' creativity and best efforts, providing an incentive to find that balance. Because of this relationship between space societies and earthbound ones, study of the governance of space societies is likely to have profound uses on as well as off the planet. By examining ways in which people may live in space in the distant future, we may come up with answers—or at least questions—that are of help in determining the way people will live on earth in the next century.

CONTACT WITH EXTRATERRESTRIALS

If governance of space societies may seem a remote issue to some, then possible contact with extraterrestrial beings may seem remoter still, and with some reason. After all, human history has already seen several space stations, but (leaving aside various never-confirmed reports) no contact at all with beings not of this earth. Nonetheless, the possibility has (perhaps for that very reason) intrigued many fine minds. The issue is surveyed exhaustively in A. Haley, Space Law and Government ch. 12 (1963) and M. McDougal, H. Lasswell & I. Vlasic, Law & Public Order in Space ch. 9 (1963), as well as E. Fasan, Relations with Alien Intelligences (1970). Since there has been no gain in experience and no law made since those volumes were published, we refer the reader to them for detailed treatment, providing only a short summary of the issues here.

The first question with regard to extraterrestrial life is whether it exists at all. At the time of this writing, opinions on the subject vary among experts, but those opinions are of limited worth because they are based on so little evidence. What evidence exists is largely negative. Since 1960 scientists have been listening on various radio frequencies, but without detecting any signal that appears connected with intelligent life. In addition, the earth's own man-made radio signals have been steadily expanding out into the galaxy, offering the possibility that alien beings' first indication that there is life on earth might come from their reception of *Gilligan's Island* episodes. Whether those aliens would conclude, on that basis, that earth life is intelligent is a matter of opinion. For whatever reason, however, there has been no response. On the search for intelligent life and its implications as of the time of this writing *see* Easterbrook, Are We Alone? The Atlantic Monthly, August, 1988, at 25.

The negative results achieved to date do not rule out encounters with extraterrestrial life, of course. Efforts so far have merely scratched the surface, the Universe being a rather large place and the number of radio frequencies virtually limitless. And there is always the possibility that we are simply going about it all wrong. It may be that alien beings, once encountered, will consider efforts at communicating via radio odd, if not downright bizarre. Perhaps some fluke in mankind's technological evolution has caused us to overlook a method of interstellar communication that other species rely on, leaving us in the position of an FM radio owner in a town where all the stations are AM—or, perhaps more accurately, of a primitive tribesman climbing to the top of a microwave relay tower to look for smoke signals.

What is certain is that any contact with extraterrestrial life will have a major impact on earth cultures. Earth societies are only now beginning to encompass fully the idea that inhabitants of other nations might be as human as they; it is unclear whether humankind is ready to extend similar consideration to beings with whom we share no genes. And, depending on differences in biology and culture, it may be difficult to determine whether what we have encountered is alive at all, or whether it is intelligent: witness the ongoing debate over just how intelligent dolphins (hardly different from us, on any kind of a cosmic biological scale) really are.

Assuming, however, that we are in no doubt as to these threshold matters, encounters with extraterrestrial life will involve either contact with intelligent beings or contact with "lower" life forms possessing no intelligence, or intelligence on the order of domestic animals (though we stress that such determinations may be quite difficult to make). In the case of the latter, legal questions will essentially be those of environmental law and cruelty to animals: how to avoid harming the habitats of exotic life while taking advantage of opportunities to study, or perhaps farm or otherwise exploit, that life without cruelty. *See generally* Callicott, Moral Considerability and Extraterrestrial Life, in Beyond Spaceship Earth: Environmental Ethics and the Solar System 227 (E. Hargrove ed. 1986).

If we encounter intelligent beings, on the other hand, a number of questions arise. First, the entire environment for relations will be determined by questions of power: are we dealing with beings to whom we are measurably superior in science, technology and military might? To which we are measurably (or perhaps immeasurably) inferior? Or roughly equivalent? Yet again, we note that in practice determining which is the case may be extraordinarily difficult: by any measure of military might Cortez and Pizarro were in a far inferior position to the Aztec and Inca societies that they conquered and destroyed, but by chance their strengths were precisely those needed to exploit their victims' cultural weaknesses.

If contact is made with beings substantially inferior to us in power, we must decide which of many human models we will follow. Will we become ruthless exploiters like the Spanish Conquistadores? Will we attempt to incorporate the aliens into our own civilization via a mechanism like that of Article 73 of the UN Charter, which provides for trust territories? Or will we establish rules designed to minimize interference with alien societies? Note that the Outer Space Treaty of 1967 expressly acknowledges that general international law, including the United Nations Charter, is applicable to activities in outer space. This means that the nonaggression principle contained in Article 2(4) of the charter (along with the rest of international law) is applicable to activities in outer space and, at least arguably, with regard to alien societies.

These are the most remote issues of this rather remote topic. In order to contact intelligent beings of less development than our own, we must go to them, which is likely to be difficult since there is no evidence of any life in our solar system beyond the earth's biosphere (though the possibility of such life continues to exist, based on present knowledge). Beings of greater development than our own—or perhaps even those whose development is roughly equivalent to our own except for a degree of superiority in space transportation—may instead come to us. How we shall deal with them poses fewer moral dilemmas, but greater practical difficulties.

Such beings may be friendly or hostile. Some writers on the topic fear that the latter is more likely. As Gregg Easterbrook says:

> The most disquieting aspect of natural selection as observed on Earth is that it channels intellect to predators. Most bright animals are carnivores: stalking requires tactics, pattern recognition, and, for social animals, coordinated action, all incubators of brainpower. Though the martial heritage of mankind has been exaggerated in

> popular fiction (there's no proof, for example, that our Cro Magnon ancestors waged war against the vanished Neanderthals), it's reasonably certain that the forebears of modern *Homo Sapiens* were hunters, and it's definite that man has been savage during the historical era. This isn't much of a testimonial to "intelligence" [as a civilizing influence].

Easterbrook, *supra,* at 37. On the other hand, even if such beings were friendly (at least by their own rights) we might be well to be concerned, as we might not appreciate any favors they chose to do us. And it is entirely possible, if they are alien enough, that the terms friendly or hostile might mean little as applied to them.

In this context, Haley proposes a principle of "Metalaw" that constitutes a revised Golden Rule: "Do unto others as they would have you do unto them." As Haley says, "To treat others as we would desire to be treated might well mean their destruction." A. Haley, Space Law and Government 395 (1963). Obviously there are limits to such a principle, which appear when the interests of the others begin to collide with our own (science fiction fans might call this the "Klingon Corollary"). And there is, naturally, no guarantee that other civilizations would adopt the same view.

As always, McDougal, Lasswell & Vlasic are more concerned with matters of power than Haley. They outline a number of possible scenarios in which aliens quarantine the earth (as too violent), or in which groups on earth conspire with aliens (or even with dissident groups within alien societies) in various sorts of power-bloc games, or in which even an inferior earth attempts to use balance of power diplomacy (setting rival alien groups against one another) to maintain its independence. It is to be hoped that such eventualities remain as remote as they now seem; if they become concrete, it might be worthwhile to examine the ways in which earth societies have dealt with more powerful foreign rivals, either by absorbing conquerors (as the Chinese and Indians have done) or by absorbing selective aspects of foreign culture (especially technology) while retaining their own essential character (as the Japanese have done).

Even where superior alien beings are demonstrably friendly by our own standards of judgment, their impact on our society may be enormous and not always positive. The realization that other intelligent beings exist would undoubtedly create considerable consternation within many religions, for example. It would also have major secular effects: note how important an effect was created simply by the Apollo photographs of earth from a distance, showing our planet not as the vast expanse we were used to imagining but as a small fragile ball in an enormous universe, its atmosphere so thin as to be barely visible. The result was a tremendous growth in environmental consciousness that has not reached its end yet. *See* Hartmann, Space Exploration and Environmental Issues, 6 Environmental Ethics 227 (1984) on this impact of the space program. Although the impact of learning that we are not alone in the Universe is difficult to estimate, it would likely be greater still. As Easterbrook says:

> A stock assumption is that the first question we would send to an extraterrestrial radio operator would be something like "How do you build a 10,000 megajoule charged particle beam?" Consider the ramifications if instead the question were "Have you seen God?" Many religions expound variations on what Christians call the kingdom of God—the idea that human travails and celestial sufferance of evil are a transitory state of affairs, to be replaced by perfect justice when God manifests Himself and takes active control of events. ... So if any long-lived alien race we might contact testifies that it has walked the cosmos for thousands of millennia without encountering God or obtaining divine grace, a lot of air would rush out of the faiths we Earthlings practice. If, on the other hand, the aliens have met the absolute and will tell us the specifics, human society will shake to its foundations.

Easterbrook, *supra,* at 38. *Cf.* Cobb, Theology and Space, in Beyond Spaceship Earth: Environmental Ethics and the Solar System 291 (E. Hargrove ed. 1986).

Of course, religious believers on earth might reply that God exists only for us, not for those unwashed heathens from Tau Ceti—and aliens who claim to have seen God may have entirely different ideas about what that means, or may be lying, either because they think that is what we want to hear or in order to take advantage of the opportunity to make human society "shake to its foundations."

If the beings encountered are themselves (by humans' own reckoning) markedly superior, the problems created may be more dramatic yet. Though earth cultures vary in their assessment of their own superiority or inferiority in relation to other cultures, there is general consensus that humankind represents the top of the heap not only in terms of sophistication or technological development, but from a standpoint of moral worth. Were we to encounter creatures who seemed to us (as occasionally appears in science fiction films) almost angelic, would we be inspired to emulate them, or would we despair of attaining their perfection and give up trying? And how would it affect our assessment of our own interests? Robert Nozick has argued in favor of a sliding scale of worth, beginning with inanimate matter and continuing onward through plants, animals, and ultimately humans. But he admits of the possibility of alien beings who are (or at least seem to be) superior to humans, and suggests that this would pose unusual problems for moral philosophy, problems for which it is unprepared:

> Some theological views hold that God is permitted to sacrifice people for his own purposes. We also might imagine people encountering beings from another planet who traverse in their childhood whatever "stages" of moral development our developmental psychologists can identify. These beings claim that they all continue on through fourteen further sequential stages, each being necessary to enter the next one. However, they cannot explain to us (primitive as we are) the content and modes of reasoning of these later stages. These beings claim that we may be sacrificed for their well being, or at least in order to preserve their higher capacities. They say that they see the truth of this now that they are in their moral maturity, though they didn't as children at what is our highest level of moral development.

R. Nozick, Anarchy, State & Utopia 46–47 (1974). Nozick concludes that currently popular moral frameworks offer no answer in these circumstances. *See also* R. Nozick, Philosophical Explanations 417 (1981) and Tooley, Would ETIs [ExtraTerrestrial Intelligences] Be Persons? in Extraterrestrial Intelligence: The First Encounter (J. Christian ed. 1976). It seems unlikely that many would be persuaded by this argument, but if humans *were* to be convinced that aliens were morally superior (say, by aliens who demonstrated their goodness but who refrained from spoiling their image with arguments that they may morally sacrifice us to serve their own interests) the impact could be enormous and devastating, much like (but worse than) the dispiriting effect of European conquest on many less advanced peoples. (For an illustration of this impact *see* C. Turnbull, The Lonely African (1962).) On the other hand, human beings might be inspired by the aliens' example, as a sign that it is possible to do better than we have done historically.

By our discussion of the moral implications of contact with superior beings we do not mean to suggest that there are no significant moral issues associated with meeting beings who (again, by our own estimation, which may well differ from that of the beings we meet) are inferior to or on a par with us. However, existing moral frameworks governing our treatment of animals or our treatment of other human beings address similar issues. With regard to relations with superior beings, the only framework that we have that even begins to address the topic is religion. Various religions treat the matter differently, sometimes portraying humans as clever tricksters who can (and who are heroic when they do) deceive supernatural entities with powers greater than their own, and sometimes demanding strict obedience to the slightest whim of those entities. But religions, by their nature, tend to be specific with regard to *which* superior beings they describe; they do not set out general rules for dealing with such beings and they generally involve beings who are not merely superior, but supernaturally so.

Although it may be that any sufficiently advanced technology will *seem* supernatural, it is unlikely to be so, and few are likely to believe that it is. Indeed, given the number of alien-contact movies that have been made to date and their impact on the popular consciousness, it is more likely that angels visiting the earth would be greeted as extraterrestrials than that extraterrestrials visiting the earth would be greeted as angels. Nonetheless, contact with beings who appeared vastly superior to us would have a dramatic, and perhaps crushing, impact on human society, and cushioning that impact, or channelling it in productive ways, would be a major task for governments and opinion leaders worldwide.

On a narrower scale, the introduction of alien customs, technologies, goods, and ideas would also be likely to have a disruptive impact on earth life. Authorities would be faced with difficult problems as to how they could smooth and ease those disruptions while allowing the necessary accommodations with individual and academic freedom and with the general principles of an open world society. A variety of legal problems, some picayune and some interesting, would also arise. For example, most murder laws forbid only the killing of a human being. Thus, the killing of even an intelligent and cultured extraterrestrial, however human-seeming in behavior or (even) appearance, would probably be legally indistinguishable from killing someone's dog—or perhaps subject to even less control, as many states specifically forbid dog-killing by unauthorized persons. On another front, existing regulations requiring quarantine of anyone contacting extraterrestrial matter (discussed at the end of Chapter 8) would come into play, as dramatized in the movie *E.T.* Given the excitement attendant upon contact with alien beings, however, most such legal questions are likely to be pushed to the side at least at first, and we do not consider them worth addressing at any length here.

Finally, at the extreme end of the remoteness continuum lies a favorite idea of science fiction writers: the possibility of incorporating the earth or parts of it into some sort of overarching organization, whether called a "United Federation of Planets" or whatever. McDougal, Lasswell & Vlasic discuss this issue at some length, but seem to treat it as a purely diplomatic issue when in fact (although the diplomatic problems would be far more apparent) there would be legal difficulties as well. The United Nations Charter makes no provision for UN membership in other organizations, meaning that any treaty bringing the earth into a larger organization would have to be negotiated piecemeal to encompass the hundreds of different sovereign entities on the planet, a task sure to prove difficult and divisive. Alternatively, the United Nations Charter could be amended (with the consent of its member governments) to allow it to represent all nations and to enter into appropriate agreements. Getting agreement on such a task might be marginally easier, and somewhat less divisive.

From the standpoint of United States law, even a treaty making the United States a member of such an organization would be open to later abrogation by legislative efforts. *See* L. Tribe, American Constitutional Law 225–26 (2d ed. 1988) and sources cited therein. As a result, only a constitutional amendment could place the United States into an organic relation with a greater body. In the current political climate such an amendment could never be obtained with regard to membership in a purely earth-centered organization, raising doubts as to how voters would view membership in any sort of interstellar organization—indeed, U.S. membership in the United Nations, which entails no loss of sovereignty, is controversial enough at times. Fortunately, this issue is unlikely to arise in the near future, so any detailed speculation regarding current laws and political attitudes is likely to prove pointless.

Reynolds, International Space Law: Into the Twenty-First Century, 25 Vanderbilt Journal of Transnational Law 225 (1992)

Although the likelihood of this sort of event is quite literally incalculable, the potential consequences are significant enough that a bit of preventive lawyering may be in order. The world community, in drawing back from the nuclear brink (something that itself seemed wildly unlikely just a few years ago), has already taken one major step toward rendering itself better able to deal with alien contact. A logical next step would be for lawyers, scientists, and other interested parties to begin thinking about how such a contact would be managed if it should occur.

And, in fact, that very thing is beginning to happen. A recent publication, *First Contact: The Search for Extraterrestrial Intelligence*, [Ben Bova & Byron Preiss eds. 1990] has brought together a number of such parties (including one lawyer) to address just this problem. The book is highly recommended to those interested in the subject. Furthermore, a number of scientists involved in searching for extraterrestrial intelligence have drafted a declaration of principles governing such detection. The text of that declaration follows:

Declaration of Principles Concerning Activities Following the Detection of Extraterrestrial Intelligence

We, the institutions and individuals participating in the search for extraterrestrial intelligence,

Recognizing that the search for extraterrestrial intelligence is an integral part of space exploration and is being undertaken for peaceful purposes and for the common interest of mankind,

Inspired by the profound significance for mankind of detecting evidence of extraterrestrial intelligence, even though the probability of detection may be low,

Recalling the Treaty on Principles Governing the Activities of States in the Exploration and Use of Outer Space, Including the Moon and Other Celestial Bodies, which commits states as parties to that treaty "to inform the Secretary General of the United Nations as well as the public and the international scientific community, to the greatest extent feasible and practicable, of the nature, conduct, locations and results" of their space exploration activities (Article XI),

Recognizing that any initial detection may be incomplete or ambiguous and thus require careful examination as well as confirmation, and that it is essential to maintain the highest standards of scientific responsibility and credibility,

Agree to observe the following principles for disseminating information about the detection of extraterrestrial intelligence:

1. Any individual, public or private research institution, or governmental agency that believes it has detected a signal from or other evidence of extraterrestrial intelligence (the discoverer) should seek to verify that the most plausible explanation for the evidence is the existence of extraterrestrial intelligence rather than some other natural phenomenon or anthropogenic phenomenon before making any public announcement. If the evidence cannot be confirmed as indicating the existence of extraterrestrial intelligence, the discoverer may disseminate the information as appropriate to the discovery of any unknown phenomenon.

2. Prior to making a public announcement that evidence of extraterrestrial intelligence has been detected, the discoverer should promptly inform all other observers or research organizations that are parties to this declaration, so that those other parties may seek to confirm the discovery by independent observations at other sites and so that a network can be established to enable continuous monitoring of the signal or phenomenon. Parties to this declaration should not make any public announcement of this information until it is determined whether this information is or is not credible evidence of the existence of extraterrestrial intelligence. The discoverer should inform his/her or its relevant national authorities.
3. After concluding that the discovery appears to be credible evidence of extraterrestrial intelligence, and after informing other parties to this declaration, the discoverer should inform observers throughout the world through the Central Bureau for Astronomical Telegrams of the International Astronomical Union, and should inform the Secretary General of the United Nations in accordance with Article XI of the Treaty on Principles Governing the Activities of States in the Exploration and Use of Outer Space, Including the Moon and Other Celestial Bodies. Because of their demonstrated interest in and expertise concerning the question of the existence of extraterrestrial intelligence, the discoverer should simultaneously inform the following international institutions of the discovery and should provide them with all pertinent data and recorded information concerning the evidence: the International Telecommunication Union, the Committee on Space Research of the International Council of Scientific Unions, the International Astronautical Federation, the International Academy of Astronautics, the International Institute of Space Law and Commission 51 of the International Astronomical Union.
4. A confirmed detection of extraterrestrial intelligence should be made available to the international scientific community through publications, meetings, conferences and other appropriate means.
5. All data necessary for confirmation of detection should be made available to the international scientific community through publications, meetings, conferences and other appropriate means.
6. The discovery should be confirmed and monitored and any data bearing on the evidence of extraterrestrial intelligence should be recorded and stored permanently to the greatest extent feasible and practicable, in a form that will make it available for further analysis and interpretation. These recordings should be made available to the international institutions listed above and to members of the scientific community for further objective analysis and interpretation.
7. If the evidence of detection is in the form of electromagnetic signals, the parties to this declaration should seek international agreement to protect the appropriate frequencies by exercising the extraordinary procedures established

within the World Administrative Radio Council of the International Telecommunication Union.

8. No response to a signal or other evidence of extraterrestrial intelligence should be sent until appropriate international consultations have taken place. The procedures for such consultations will be the subject of a separate agreement, declaration or arrangement.
9. The SETI Committee of the International Academy of Astronautics, in coordination with Commission 51 of the International Astronomical Union, will conduct a continuing review of procedures for the detection of extraterrestrial intelligence and the subsequent handling of the data. Should credible evidence of extraterrestrial intelligence be discovered, an international committee of scientists and other experts should be established to serve as a focal point for continuing analysis of all observational evidence collected in the aftermath of the discovery, and also to provide advice on the release of information to the public. This committee should be constituted from representatives of each of the international institutions listed above and such other members as the committee may deem necessary. To facilitate the convocation of such a committee at some unknown time in the future, the SETI Committee of the International Academy of Astronautics should initiate and maintain a current list of willing representatives from each of the international institutions listed above, as well as other individuals with relevant skills, and should make that list continuously available through the Secretariat of the International Academy of Astronautics. The International Academy of Astronautics will act as the Depositary for this declaration and will annually provide a current list of parties to all the parties to this declaration.

* * *

The first point to be made about the Declaration set out above is that it is not a set of binding legal principles: it is an agreement among scientists, not among nations—though of course it does not necessarily lose importance, or likelihood of being followed, because of that. Agreements among scientific researchers have a strong history of being followed, and this one is likely to be looked to should the event materialize. Another interesting point is that the agreement, though it appears to contemplate the receipt of extraterrestrial radio signals as the most likely mode of contact, is not limited to such occasions. Paragraph 1 refers to detection of "a signal from *or other evidence of* extraterrestrial intelligence" (emphasis added), a phrase that clearly reaches any situation in which extraterrestrial intelligence is discovered, from radio signals to discovery of artifacts, to outright visits.

Once discovery has been made and confirmed, the next question is what do we do? That is, if we receive alien communications, do we answer? Humans have already attempted communication with alien species on a few occasions: through the gold plaques and recorded messages placed on board space probes whose trajectories will ultimately take them into interstellar space, and through messages beamed from radio telescopes to distant stars. This last effort, originated by Frank Drake in 1974, drew considerable criticism regarding the right of a small group of scientists to quite literally speak for all humanity when the consequences might be incalculable.

One might argue that such criticisms must be unfounded: interstellar distances are so vast, after all, that hostile efforts between stars must be prohibitively expensive, and besides, any alien species that might receive them would be so advanced as to be benign and harmless. The trouble with such arguments is that there is no particular evidence to support them. As to technology, the fact that *we* cannot currently cross interstellar distances is hardly a guarantee that others may not be able to—we are, after all, only a few decades past being unable to cross the distance between the Earth and its Moon. Anyone who has been at the game of space travel at all has probably been at it longer than us. And even we could, with technology readily extrapolatable from the present, send small packages across interstellar distances. If we were paranoid enough, those packages could contain destructive nanodevices, or viruses, or other weapons that might be lethal even in small quantities. I do not believe that humanity is, or is likely to be, that paranoid, but it might not be wise to assume that other species would not be.

This kind of thinking, at any rate, will govern at least one kind of decision: the decision whether to respond should we receive a message from extraterrestrials, especially if the distance is not so great that any reply will take thousands of years. As has been noted earlier, the mere existence of extraterrestrials would be a fact of profound social significance, even if we can't carry on anything resembling a conversation. But there is more to the question of whether to reply or not than social or philosophical questions.

Reynolds, International Space Law: Into the Twenty-First Century, 25 Vanderbilt Journal of Transnational Law 225 (1992)

[T]he scientists in the field have considered this as well, developing a set of proposed rules to govern contact with extraterrestrials once they have been discovered:

Proposed Protocol for the Sending of Communications to Extraterrestrial Intelligence

The Signatories agree that communications with extraterrestrial intelligence will be guided by the following principles:

1. Communications with extraterrestrial intelligence will be undertaken on behalf of all mankind, rather than specific nations, groups, or individuals.
2. Nations, organizations, and individuals will not unilaterally send communications to extraterrestrial intelligence until appropriate international consultations have taken place.
3. The Signatories will not cooperate with attempts to communicate with extraterrestrial intelligence which do not conform to the principles in this protocol.
4. An international group including representation from all interested nations will be formed to deal with the question of whether such a communication should be sent and, if so, what its content should be.
5. If a decision is made to develop a communication to extraterrestrial intelligence on behalf of mankind, the following principles will be observed:
   a. Respect for the value of life and intelligence.
   b. Respect for the value of diversity, including respect for different customs, habits, languages, creeds and religions, approaches to social organization, and styles of life.
   c. Respect for the territory and property of others.
   d. Recognition of the will to live.
   e. Recognition of the need for living space.
   f. Fair play, justice, mercy.
   g. Reciprocity and quid pro quo.
   h. Nonviolation of others.
   i. Truthfulness and non-deception.
   j. Peaceful and friendly welcome.
   k. Cooperation.
   l. Respect for knowledge, curiosity, and learning.
6. The drafters of a communication to extraterrestrial intelligence will consider detailed information about mankind to be a commodity of high value which will not be transmitted without due attention to human security and well-being, and to reciprocity.
7. In the event that extraterrestrials appear to pose a threat to human health, well-being, or peace, no nation shall act without consulting the Security Council of the United Nations.

Though less ambitious than some of the scholarly writings mentioned earlier, the proposed rules do recognize some important points. First, contact with alien intelligences would represent an event so important that a decent respect for the wellbeing of humanity would forbid any individual or single nation from going ahead without proper consultation. Second, that dealings with extraterrestrial beings would set such an important precedent that they should be conducted in a manner that is straightforward, honest, and considerate. Third, that the stakes would be so high that we should be cautious in revealing too much until we are very sure about the consequences. And finally, that nations should make responses to any threats a global matter, not an individual one. In the unlikely but horrific circumstances of an encounter with hostile aliens, we would want all humanity united from the beginning.

One fascinating aspect of the draft proposal—and, indeed, all thinking about contact with extraterrestrials—is the way in which our vision of such contact, taking place as it does against a blank slate, is in large part a product of our own hopes, fears, and predispositions. Between the lines in both of the scientists' documents above is a sense that they would most likely be communicating with their opposite numbers—aliens, perhaps, but alien *scientists*. On the other hand, a healthy dose of caution remains, perhaps because scientists themselves know, from long and sometimes bitter experience, that while doing their jobs they are often doing the bidding of others less scrupulous. Our vision of intelligent aliens has wavered back and forth over the years—sometimes, reflecting Cold War paranoia, they are viewed as malevolent invaders, either wielding weapons of fearsome destructiveness or weaving deceptions of astonishing subtlety, or both. Other times they are pictured as noble teachers, far better than we poor humans, come to save us from ourselves and bring us enlightenment. In reality, of course, neither is likely to be true. The one thing I feel fairly confident in predicting is that if we encounter intelligent extraterrestrials, we will be surprised no matter how much we have thought about the subject.

Surprise is likely, and panic is certainly not out of the question. One of the greatest challenges for lawyers and policymakers in the event of alien contact will be to ensure that all concerned (at least on the human side of things) keep their heads. Whether it allows the formulation of policies that prove useful in the event or not, thinking about contact with extraterrestrials in advance will at the very least provide a highly worthwhile inoculation against "contact shock" at the time. That alone is probably enough to justify the entire venture. For though the likelihood of such contact taking place is impossible to calculate, the magnitude of its importance would be enormous, and the time for reflection might be short. Against this eventuality, a small investment in forethought seems wise.

10

Conclusion

The Earth is the cradle of the mind, but one cannot remain in the cradle forever.
—Konstantin Tsiolkovsky

In the introduction to his excellent history of the space age, ... *the Heavens and the Earth: A Political History of the Space Age* (1985), Walter McDougall compares humankind's emergence into outer space to the emergence of the first lungfish from the oceans. Though dramatic, this comparison is not overdrawn. The emergence of humanity into spaces beyond the earth represents a real qualitative change in human existence. Over the next centuries, if affairs on earth are not too badly mismanaged, humanity will spread to a variety of locations outside the earth, carrying with it parts of earth's biosphere as it goes. Some writers, indeed, have suggested that this is humanity's real role: if one believes, as adherents of the so-called *Gaia* hypothesis do, that life on earth can in many respects be viewed as one meta-organism, then humanity's role may in large part be that of meta-gamete, carrying the seeds of life to new environments where it could not have evolved, and which it could not have reached, in other ways.

Whether one accepts this description or regards it as so much science fiction, there can be no question that the expansion of humanity into outer space will be a drama and a challenge for which there is no real counterpart in recorded history. The great age of earth exploration is the closest analog, but although European discoverers played a vital role in uniting the globe into one network of commerce and communication, they "discovered" mostly places that were already inhabited by human beings, although in their rather ethnocentric view the discoverers did not always recognize that fact. By contrast, in exploring space explorers really do go "where no man has gone before," to use the stirring (if a trifle sexist) language of one popular television program.

Some of the consequences of this expansion will be beyond the purview of space law; they will instead constitute basic changes in the way we view ourselves and our world. To a degree this has already taken place: the Apollo photographs of the earth as seen from the moon have had dramatic and lasting effects on earth-based views of politics and the environment. Writing prophetically (as usual) in 1959, Arthur C. Clarke described this effect:

> We all know the narrow, limited type of mind which is interested in nothing beyond its town or village, and bases its judgments on these parochial standards. We are slowly—perhaps too slowly—evolving from that mentality toward a world outlook. Few things will do more to accelerate that evolution than the conquest of space. It is not easy to see how the more extreme forms of nationalism can long survive when men begin to see the Earth in its true perspective as a single small globe among the stars.

[A. Clarke, The Challenge of the Spaceship 7–8 (1959).] In addition, the adventure involved in meeting the challenges of expanding into space is likely to energize all of earth society. The following excerpt discusses how this might happen.

Reynolds, Structuring Development in Outer Space: Problems of How and Why, 19 Law & Policy in International Business 433 (1987)

I think that we should also look at the more immediate effects of space development on those of us left behind. ... Everyone shares in the excitement of a frontier's opening, and its dynamism filters back into everyday life. Many historians believe that the dynamism and vigor of the East Coast business community during the mid- and late nineteenth century resulted from the psychological effect of the western frontier. [For the most widely known of such arguments, *see* F.J. Turner, The Frontier in American History 1–38, 290–311 (1920).] In the same way, it may be that much of the dynamism and vigor of U.S. society in the 1960s was a product of the excitement generated by the moon program, and that much of the malaise and pessimism of the 1970s grew out of the U.S. retreat from outer space in that decade.

These examples are far from the only ones available. Perhaps the most striking example of the opening of a new frontier energizing a whole society is that of Europe at the opening of the Age of Discovery. In his classic biography, Samuel Eliot Morison describes the impact of Columbus' discovery on a continent sunk in despair and stagnation:

> At the end of the year 1492 most men in Western Europe felt exceedingly gloomy about the future. Christian civilization appeared to be shrinking in area and dividing into hostile units as its sphere contracted. For over a century there had been no important advance in natural science, and registration in the universities dwindled as the instruction they offered became increasingly jejune and lifeless. Institutions were decaying, well-meaning people were growing cynical or desperate, and many intelligent men, for want of something better to do, were endeavoring to escape the present through studying the pagan past. ...
>
> Yet, even as the chroniclers of Nuremberg were correcting their proofs from Koberger's press, a Spanish caravel named *Niña* scudded before a winter gale into

> Lisbon, with news of a discovery that was to give old Europe another chance. In a few years we find the mental picture completely changed. Strong monarchs are stamping out privy conspiracy and rebellion; the Church, purged and chastened by the Protestant Reformation, puts her house in order; new ideas flare up throughout Italy, France, Germany and the northern nations; faith in God revives and the human spirit is renewed. The change is complete and astounding. "A new envisagement of the world has begun, and men are no longer sighing after the imaginary golden age that lay in the distant past, but speculating as to the golden age that might possibly lie in the oncoming future."
>
> Christopher Columbus belonged to an age that was past, yet he became the sign and symbol of this new age of hope, glory and accomplishment. His medieval faith impelled him to a modern solution: expansion.

[S. Morison, Admiral of the Ocean Sea: A Life of Christopher Columbus 3 (1979).] Perhaps a major worldwide commitment to outer space projects would unleash the same sort of energy on a global scale, ushering in a new period of growth and optimism that would benefit everyone, but especially the poorer countries that suffer most from any worldwide economic downturn. And it might be that the challenge and excitement of expanding into outer space would divert energy and attention away from warlike activity by providing a peaceful outlet for feelings of national pride and the need to overcome obstacles.

Physicist Freeman Dyson has argued along these lines in his book *Weapons and Hope*. In looking for ways to overcome the seemingly intractable problems posed by nuclear weapons and superpower conflict, he notes that President Kennedy pursued the moon program with the specific intent of providing an outlet for the frustrations created by the conflict with the Soviet Union:

> Apollo was to be what William James had called for long ago, a moral equivalent of war. The idea was to escape from the stuckness of Soviet-American political quarrels by beating the Russians in a bloodless technological competition instead of by beating them in battle. The idea was a good one, and up to a point it worked. It stopped working when the symbolic battle of Apollo was displaced from the focus of public attention by the real battle of Vietnam. Unfortunately, nobody since 1961 has repeated Kennedy's tactic of deliberately committing a country to a daring non-military enterprise as a substitute for the excitements of war. It is a tactic which we could profitably use again.

[F. Dyson, Weapons and Hope 219 (1984).] It certainly seems worth trying. Outer space is not cheap, but compared to what the world spends on defense it is practically free. Those who are willing to spend hundreds of billions of dollars on tanks, guns, and missiles in the hope that they will deter a nuclear war ought to be willing to spend tens of billions on outer space in the hope that it will prevent the superpowers from reaching the point where deterrence takes on immediate significance.

Though the Cold War appears to have receded, the concerns outlined in the preceding excerpt remain valid. A humanity that looks outward is likely to be far more constructive in its behavior than one that perceives life as a zero-sum game. Of course, for expansion into space to have these sorts of effects it must be carried out on a global scale. If it remains the enterprise of only a few nations, then it may not be seen as a project of humanity as a whole. During the pioneering stage this has not been true: the Outer Space Treaty describes astronauts as "envoys of mankind," and that is for the most part the way they have been perceived. As Apollo 11 astronaut Michael Collins recounts in his excellent history of the space program,

> Travelling around the world several months after the flight, I was continually impressed by the fact that no matter where we were, the reaction was the same and, to me, unexpected. Never did I hear, "Well, you Americans finally did it." Always it was "we," we human beings drawn together for one fleeting moment watching two of us walk that alien surface.

M. Collins, Liftoff 161 (1988). Settlers are different from explorers, though, and they will be perceived differently. If the nations of the world are to continue to see space as a domain for humanity and not an enclave of a favored few, some way of broadening participation will have to be found. It may be that the spread of technology to the Third World will be enough; certainly that spread has occurred far faster than anyone (especially Third World economists) thought possible, and already Third World opinion leaders like China, India and Brazil have credible space programs. If such is not enough, then some other way of promoting meaningful participation (which means more than a simple rake-off of any profits that happen to emerge) must be found. For more on this *see* Reynolds & Merges, The Role of Commercial Development in Preventing War in Outer Space, 25 Jurimetrics: Journal of Law, Science & Technology 130 (1985). Whatever is done, space lawyers will play a crucial role, whether as advocates for clients or as policymakers, a role almost as common to those in the legal profession.

In general, though, the kinds of considerations discussed above will not directly affect space lawyers, although they may very well shape the environment in which they operate. They do, however, explain in part why considerations of space law will have greater importance than just that inhering in the particular issues they involve at any given time. As they deal with particular issues involving, say, rights in space resources or regulation of commercial space launch companies, space lawyers should bear in mind that bad law in those areas can create considerable obstacles to the overall goal of humanity's expansion into space, while good law could do much to promote that goal. As Chapter 1 describes, for example, the British Explosives Act effectively blocked any British work on rocketry in the 1930s, a time when Americans, Germans and Russians were making great strides; by contrast, new legal structures in the United States in the 1980s appear (at this writing, at least) to be creating an explosion of innovation and entrepreneurial activity. In a different way, a confiscatory regime relating to the development of space resources might drastically scale back the scope of space efforts for decades, while an intelligent one mixing incentives for developers with meaningful channels for less developed country participation might stimulate considerable effort and simultaneously help lift many of the world's poorer nations out of poverty.

In short, good law can make a great difference. The development of specialized law relating to maritime affairs is generally regarded as having encouraged a flourishing shipping industry and promoted widespread global commerce in a way that, more often than not, reduces global tensions rather than increasing them. This development was not accidental, but the result of deliberate government and industry efforts. *See* Black, Admiralty Jurisdiction, Critique and Suggestions, 50 Columbia Law Review 260 (1950); G. Gilmore & C. Black, The Law of Admiralty 958 *et seq*. (2d ed. 1975). *See also* Landes, European Expansion: The History of Innovation and Performance, in The Global Economy: Divergent Perspectives on Economic Change 25 (E. Gondolf, I. Marcus & J. Dougherty eds. 1986) (describing growth of global trading system). The challenge for policymakers and lawyers alike in the space arena will be to duplicate this task. Lawyers who understand this challenge, and try to meet it, will be doing a favor not only to the world at large, but also to their clients as they will, for the most part, then be swimming with the tide instead of against it.

It is our hope that this all too brief volume makes some contribution to that endeavor. Space law, like space flight itself, is a relatively new thing, and just as today's Young Astronaut Corps members are tomorrow's astronauts and engineers, so are today's law students tomorrow's lawyers and policymakers. It will be their task to deal with the challenges posed by the next century in ways that will make our world, and the new worlds yet unconquered, a better place for all humanity.

Credits

The excerpts in this book are taken from the following sources. Permissions to reprint are gratefully acknowledged.

Chapter 1

Walter A. McDougall, ... *The Heavens and the Earth: A Political History of the Space Age* 43, 185 (New York: Basic Books, 1985). Copyright © by Basic Books, Inc. Reprinted by permission of the publisher.

Radford Byerly, Jr., "The Commercial/Industrial Uses of Space," in *Beyond Spaceship Earth: Environmental Ethics and the Solar System,* edited by Eugene C. Hargrove (San Francisco: Sierra Club Books, 1986). Copyright © 1986 by Eugene C. Hargrove. Reprinted with permission of Sierra Club Books.

"Power Stations in the Sky," in *The Illustrated Encyclopedia of Space Technology* 226, Kenneth Gatland, ed. (London: Salamander Books, 1984). Copyright © 1984 by Salamander Books, Ltd.; reprinted with permission.

Chapter 2

Hamilton DeSaussure, "Maritime and Space Law, Comparisons and Contrasts (An Oceanic View of Space Transport)," 9 *Journal of Space Law* 93 (1981). Copyright © by Hamilton DeSaussure; reprinted with permission.

White, *Decision-Making for Space: Law and Politics in Air, Sea and Outer Space* 179 (West Lafayette, Ind.: Purdue Research Foundation, 1971). Copyright © 1971 by Purdue Research Foundation; reprinted with permission.

Nicholas Matte, ed., *Space Activities and Emerging International Law* 161 (Montreal: Institute and Centre of Air and Space Law, McGill University, Montreal, Canada, 1984). Copyright © 1984 by Nicholas Matte; reprinted by permission.

Myres McDougal and Leon Lipson, "Perspective for a Law of Outer Space," 52 *American Journal of International Law* 407 (1958). Copyright © 1985 by American Society of International Law; reprinted with permission of the Society and of the authors.

Chapter 3

Philip Jessup and Howard Taubenfeld, "The United Nations *Ad Hoc* Committee on the Peaceful Uses of Outer Space," 53 *American Journal of International Law* 877 (1959). Copyright © 1959 by American Society of International Law; reprinted with permission.

Nicholas Matte, "The Treaty Banning Nuclear Weapons Tests in the Atmosphere, in Outer Space and Under Water (10 October 1963) and the Peaceful Uses of Outer Space," 9 *Annals of Air and Space Law* 391 (1984). Copyright © 1984 by Institute and Centre of Air and Space Law; reprinted with permission.

Paul G. Dembling and Daniel M. Arons, "The Evolution of the Outer Space Treaty," 33 *Journal of Air Law and Commerce* 419 (1967). Copyright © 1967 by Paul G. Dembling, Daniel M. Arons, and *Journal of Air Law and Commerce;* reprinted with permission.

Carl Q. Christol, "Article 2 of 1967 Principles Treaty Revisited," 9 *Annals of Air and Space Law* 217 (1984). Copyright © 1984 by the Institute and Centre of Air and Space Law; reprinted with permission.

John Orr, "The Treaty on Outer Space: An Evolution of the Arms Control Provisions," 7 *Columbia Journal of Transnational Law* 259 (1968). Copyright © 1968, Columbia Journal of Transnational Law Association, Inc.; reprinted with permission.

Stephen Gorove, "Arms Control Provisions in the Outer Space Treaty: A Scrutinizing Reappraisal," 3 *Georgia Journal of International and Comparative Law* 114 (1973). Copyright © 1973 by *Georgia Journal of International and Comparative Law;* reprinted with permission.

Chapter 4

Marion Nash, "Contemporary Practice of the United States Relating to International Law [Section on Moon Treaty]," 74 *American Journal of International Law* 421 (1980). Copyright © 1980 by American Society of International Law; reprinted with permission.

Stephen A. Spitz, "Space Law—Agreement Governing the Activities of States on the Moon and Other Celestial Bodies," 21 *Harvard International Law Journal* 579 (1980). Copyright © 1980 by *Harvard International Law Journal;* reprinted with permission.

Eilene Galloway, "Issues in Implementing the Agreement Governing the Activities of States on the Moon and Other Celestial Bodies," *Proceedings of the Twenty-Third Colloquium on the Law of Outer Space* 19 (Washington, D.C.: American Institute of Aeronautics and Astronautics, 1980). Copyright © 1980 by Eilene Galloway; reprinted with permission of the author and the Institute.

Walsh, "Controversial Issues Under Article XI of the Moon Treaty," 5 *Annals of Air and Space Law* 489, 1981. Copyright © 1981 by the Institute and Centre of Air and Space Law; reprinted with permission.

Carl Q. Christol, "Alternative Models for a Future International Space Organization," *Proceedings of the Twenty-Fourth Colloquium on the Law of Outer Space* 173 (1981). Copyright © 1981 by Carl Q. Christol, Professor of International Law and Political Science, University of Southern California; reprinted with permission.

Goedhuis, "Some Recent Trends in the Interpretation and the Implementation of the Rules of International Space Law," 19 *Columbia Journal of Transnational Law* 213 (1981). Copyright © 1981 by Columbia Journal of Transnational Law Association, Inc.; reprinted with permission.

Rene-Jean Dupuy, "The Notion of the Common Heritage of Mankind Applied to the Seabed," 8 *Annals of Air and Space Law* 347 (1983). Copyright © 1982 by the Institute and Centre of Air and Space Law; reprinted with permission.

D. Brian Hufford, "Ideological Rigidity vs. Political Reality: A Critique of Reagan's Policy on the Law of the Sea," 2 *Yale Law and Policy Review* 127 (1983). Copyright © 1983 by D. Brian Hufford; reprinted with permission.

Edward R. Finch, Jr., and A. L. Moore, "The 1979 Moon Treaty Encourages Space Development," *Proceedings of the Twenty-Third Colloquium on the Law of Outer Space* 13 (1980). Copyright © 1980 by Edward R. Finch, Jr., and A. L. Moore; reprinted with permission.

Arthur Dula, "Free Enterprise and the Proposed Moon Treaty," 2 *Houston Journal of International Law* 3 (1979). Copyright © 1979 by *Houston Journal of International Law;* reprinted with permission.

Webber, "Extraterrestrial Law on the Final Frontier: A Regime to Govern the Development of Celestial Body Resources," 71 *Georgetown Law Journal* 1426 (1983). Copyright © 1983 by *Georgetown Law Journal;* reprinted with permission.

K. Narayana Rao, "Common Heritage of Mankind and the Moon Treaty," 21 *Indian Journal of International Law* 275 (1981). Copyright © 1981 by Indian Society of International Law; reprinted with permission.

Wihlborg and Wijkman, "Outer Space Resources in Efficient and Equitable Use: New Frontiers for Old Principles," 24 *Journal of Law and Economics* 23 (1981). Copyright © 1981 by University of Chicago Press; reprinted with permission.

Chapter 5

Alexander Cohen, "Cosmos 954 and the International Law of Satellite Accidents," 10 *Yale Journal of International Law* 78 (1984). Copyright © 1984 by *Yale Journal of International Law;* reprinted with permission.

John Logsdon and Tracie Monk, "Remote Sensing from Space: A Continuing Legal and Policy Issue," 8 *Annals of Air and Space Law* 409 (1983). Copyright © by the Institute and Centre of Air and Space Law; reprinted by permission.

Hamilton DeSaussure, "Remote Sensing: The Interaction of Domestic and International Law," Paper presented at the 38th Congress of the International Astronautical Federation (1987). Reprinted by permission.

Chapter 6

Office of Commercial Space Policy, U.S. Department of Commerce, *Space Commerce: An Industry Assessment* (Washington, D.C.: Government Printing Office, 1980).

Chapter 7

W. Clark McFadden II, Jeffrey Snyder, and James A. Schoettler, Jr., "The Structure of Export Licensing," in *The Commerce Department Speaks*, D. Riggs, ed. (Washington, D.C.: Government Printing Office, 1987). Copyright © 1987 by W. Clark McFadden II, Jeffrey Snyder, and James A. Schoettler, Jr.; reprinted with permission.

Chapter 8

Glenn H. Reynolds, Book Review, 27 *Jurimetrics: Journal of Law, Science, and Technology* 431 (1987). Copyright © 1987 by Glenn H. Reynolds; reprinted by permission.

Dan L. Burk, "Protection of Trade Secrets in Outer Space Activity: A Study in Federal Preemption," 23 Seton Hall Law Review 560 (1993).

Robert P. Merges and Glenn H. Reynolds, "News Media Satellites and the First Amendment," 3 *Berkeley High Technology Law Journal* 1 (1988). Copyright © 1989 by Robert P. Merges and Glenn H. Reynolds; reprinted by permission.

Chapter 9

William J. Brennan, Jr., "Space Settlements and the Law," Address to the American Law Institute (May 21, 1987). Copyright © 1987 by Justice William J. Brennan, Jr.; reprinted with permission.

John Ragosta and Glenn H. Reynolds, "In Search of Governing Principles," 28 *Jurimetrics: Journal of Law, Science, and Technology* 473 (1988). Copyright © 1988 by the authors; reprinted with permission.

William J. Brennan, Jr., Remarks at the Bicentennial Conference of Judges of United States Courts of Appeals (October 26, 1988). Copyright © by Justice William J. Brennan, Jr.; reprinted with permission.

Chapter 10

Glenn Reynolds, "Structuring Development in Outer Space: Problems of How and Why," 19 *Law & Policy in International Business* 433 (1987). Copyright © 1987 by Glenn Reynolds; reprinted with permission.

About the Book and Authors

This book examines the international and domestic American legal problems associated with activity in outer space from a strong policy perspective, with particular attention given to problems associated with space commercialization and with military activities in outer space. *Outer Space: Problems of Law and Policy* is indispensable as a casebook, reference, and self-teaching tool for students, practitioners, academics, and members of the aerospace industry.

Glenn H. Reynolds, a graduate of Yale Law School, is professor of law at the University of Tennessee. **Robert P. Merges,** also a graduate of Yale Law School, is professor of law, Boalt Hall School of Law, University of California Berkeley.

Index

Kolibri 360 GmbH
Ferdinand-Jühlke-Straße 7
99095 Erfurt, Deutschland
produktsicherheit@kolibri360.de